This book brings together the work of twenty historians, anthropologists, and literary scholars who have examined the nature of the encounter between Europeans and the other peoples of the world from about 1450 to 1800 – the Early Modern Era. The European vision of others is examined in Part I, with special emphasis on Spain and the Columbian voyages. The seemingly obvious but too often neglected need to recognize that the cross-cultural encounters always had at least two sides forms the central theme of Part II. It shows how other peoples viewed Europeans, with case studies on Persia, the Aztecs, the Kongo, Japan, and South and Southeast Asia. Part III examines the ways in which peoples tried to bridge cultural contacts and challenges. Part IV examines the nature of eighteenth-century encounters in the Pacific, Australia, and America. Here, noted scholars grapple with the questions of how we observe and what cultural observation tells us about ourselves as well as others.

Implicit Understandings is worldwide in scope, but is unified by the central underlying theme that implicit understandings influence every culture's ideas about itself and others. These understandings, however, are changed by experience in a constantly shifting process in which both sides participate. This makes such encounters complex historical events and moments of "discovery."

IMPLICIT UNDERSTANDINGS

Studies in
Comparative Early Modern History

Center for Early Modern History
University of Minnesota

Cambridge University Press

I. Tracy, ed., *The Rise of Merchant Empires: Long Distance Trade in the Early Modern World, 1350–1750* (1990)

II. Tracy, ed., *The Political Economy of Merchant Empires: State Power and World Trade, 1350–1750* (1991)

IMPLICIT UNDERSTANDINGS

OBSERVING, REPORTING, AND REFLECTING ON THE ENCOUNTERS BETWEEN EUROPEANS AND OTHER PEOPLES IN THE EARLY MODERN ERA

Edited by

STUART B. SCHWARTZ
University of Minnesota

CAMBRIDGE
UNIVERSITY PRESS

Published by the Press Syndicate of the University of Cambridge
The Pitt Building, Trumpington Street, Cambridge CB2 1RP
40 West 20th Street, New York, NY 10011-4211, USA
10 Stamford Road, Oakleigh, Melbourne 3166, Australia

First published 1994

Reprinted in 1995, 1996

Library of Congress Cataloging-in-Publication Data

Implicit understandings: observing, reporting, and reflecting on the encounters between Europeans and other peoples in the early modern era/edited by Stuart B. Schwartz.

p. cm. – (Studies in comparative early modern history)

Includes bibliographical references and index.

ISBN 0-521-45240-6. – ISBN 0-521-45880-3 (pbk.)

1. Europe – Relations – Foreign countries. 2. Intercultural communication. 3. Ethnopsychology. 4. Discoveries in geography. I. Schwartz, Stuart B. II. Series.

D217.I6 1994

303.482'4 – dc20 94-10675
CIP

A catalog record for this book is available from the British Library.

ISBN 0-521-45240-6 Hardback
ISBN 0-521-45880-3 Paperback

Transferred to digital printing 2004

Contents

Contributors

Rolena Adorno
Department of Romance Languages and Literatures, Princeton University

Eduardo Aznar Vallejo
Department of History, Universidad de La Laguna, Tenerife

Diane Bell
Henry R. Luce Professor, College of the Holy Cross

James A. Boon
Department of Anthropology, Princeton University

Greg Dening
Professor Emeritus of History (formerly Max Crawford Professor of History), University of Melbourne

John B. Friedman
Department of English, University of Illinois

Mary W. Helms
Department of Anthropology, University of North Carolina at Greensboro

Peter Hulme
Department of Literature, University of Essex

Miguel Angel Ladero Quesada
Department of Medieval History, Universidad Complutense, Madrid

James Lockhart
Department of History, University of California at Los Angeles

Wyatt MacGaffey
Department of Sociology and Anthropology, Haverford College

David Morgan
School of Oriental and African Studies, London University

Willard J. Peterson
Department of East Asian Studies, Princeton University

Seymour Phillips
Department of Medieval History, University College Dublin, National University of Ireland

Anthony Reid
Research School of Pacific and Asian Studies, Australian National University, Canberra

Chandra Richard de Silva
Department of History, Indiana State University

Stuart B. Schwartz
Department of History, University of Minnesota

Ronald P. Toby
Department of History, Department of East Asian Languages and Cultures, University of Illinois, Urbana-Champaign

Ann Waltner
Department of History, Department of East Asian Studies, University of Minnesota

Peter H. Wood
Department of History, Duke University

Figures

Preface

IN the years preceding the Columbian Quincentenary the Center for Early Modern History of the University of Minnesota began to consider an appropriate way to mark that anniversary. Our general aim was to situate the Columbian moment – or "the encounter," as it has become popular to call it – in the more general process of European expansion, and to see it not as a singular and isolated historical event but as representative of a process that had occurred many times before 1492, and increasingly thereafter. Of course, cross-cultural encounters had taken place among many peoples throughout human history, but for reasons of coherence and focus we decided to make Europeans consistently one side of the encounters that we wished to study and compare. We recognized, however, that the history of such encounters was long and varied, that different European peoples had participated, and that there may have been a cumulative effect of encounter experiences so that the attitudes and techniques carried into such meetings by Bougainville and Cook in the eighteenth century were considerably different from those of Columbus and Vasco da Gama in the fifteenth century.

Throughout our planning discussions we emphasized the bilateral nature of the first contacts and the need to understand both sides of the cultural equation. The voices and attitudes of the indigenous peoples of Asia, Africa, Australia, and the Americas needed to be recorded, understood, and appreciated, but also subjected to the same kind of nuanced analysis now increasingly accorded to European sources. The cultural contexts of both Europeans and non-Europeans were not unitary, and called for attention to the differences in perceptions and actions based on class, status, gender, age, and other categories.

In order to define an important set of theoretical and methodological issues and to identify scholars at work on these problems, the Center for Early Modern History invited a number of specialists to join with our faculty and graduate students in the Twin Cities in February 1988. In addition to having the presence of Peter Hulme, J. S. Phillips, and Greg Dening, whose essays appear in this book, we also benefited from the participation of Victoria Bricker (Tulane University) and James Fernandez (University of Chicago) at this stage in our deliberations. A second planning meeting in October, 1988 further defined the central themes to be explored and selected the scholars invited to participate.

In October 1990 the Center for Early Modern History brought together twenty scholars from various disciplines and geographical areas of study who shared a common interest in the problem of intercultural contacts. In addition, approximately 100 other students and scholars also attended the sessions. Papers were circulated in advance and most of the meeting was devoted to discussion and debate of the written presentations in meetings chaired by members of the Center for Early Modern History. These discussions were recorded and transcripts later provided to the authors to help in their revisions. The revised papers, with the addition of the essays by Mary Helms and Wyatt MacGaffey, comprise the book now in your hands.

Some particular debts are owed to individuals. Lucy Simler, as Associate Director of the Center, worked tirelessly on all the arrangements for the meeting and provided the kind of hospitality that made the conference more than an intellectual experience. She collaborated on all stages of the project. Luis González, Allyson Poska, Timothy Coates, Donna Lazarus, and Paula Jorge took on the task of translating papers submitted in languages other than English for distribution to participants. Prof. Antonio Stevens-Arroyo (Brooklyn College) did a similar translation service at the meeting.

University of Minnesota graduate students Jennifer Downs, Abby Sue Fisher, Katherine French, Mary Hedberg, Elisabeth Irving, Edmund Kern, Diane Shaw, Jeffrey Stewart, Linda Wimmer, Paul Wojtalewicz, and Robert Wolff served as session recorders and aided with local arrangements. Todd Macmanus and Allyson Poska were especially helpful in the preparation of the manuscripts for distribution and serving as general coordinators of logistics. Robert Wolff, Kris Lane, and Carlos Aguirre assisted in the preparation of the manuscripts for publication.

Special recognition and thanks are due to Professor Richard Price, who, while Visiting Professor at the University of Minnesota, participated in the planning stages of the conference, provided excellent commentaries at the meeting as an invited participant, and later served as an editorial advisor.

A multi-authored volume whose subject matter spans the globe and whose authors represent a number of disciplines presents more than the usual number of editorial challenges. The reader will note certain inconsistencies in usage and terminology between chapters. For example, one author prefers "Iran," another "Persia." While I have standardized spellings and common usages and a single footnote style has been used throughout, I have consciously not sought to eliminate individual authors' preferences. My goal has been consistency within chapters, not necessarily between them. The reader will also note that the essays are not of consistent length. This too is intentional. Authors were encouraged to take the space they felt necessary, and I hoped to provide in this book a few longer essays that exceeded the bounds usually set in academic journals. Ronald Cohen, who carefully copyedited the manuscript, was particularly helpful with these editorial problems. My thanks also to John Jenson, who prepared the index.

A number of institutions provided financial support to the conference and to the publication of this book. The National Endowment for the Humanities (Grant #RX 21100-89) provided a major proportion of the funding. In addition, support was provided by the Calouste Gulbenkian Foundation (Portugal) and the Commission for the History of the Discoveries (Portugal), The Program for Cultural Cooperation (Spain), the U.S.-Spanish Joint Committee, and the Lilly Foundation. At the University of Minnesota, the Graduate School, the College of Liberal Arts, the Department of History and the James Ford Bell Library all provided support.

The Center for Early Modern History wishes to express its thanks to all of the individuals and institutions mentioned here for making the original conference and this book possible.

Finally, I would like to personally thank all those involved in this project, and especially the authors of the essays in this book, for their collaboration, patience, and goodwill throughout the editorial process. I hope that this book does justice to their contributions.

Introduction

STUART B. SCHWARTZ

In 1550 in Rouen, local merchants interested in securing royal support for the newly developing dyewood trade from Brazil staged a *fête brésilienne* for the visiting royal couple, Henry II and Catherine de Medici. Along the banks of the Seine, Brazilian flora and fauna were set out or imitated and a Tupinamba Indian village was recreated, inhabited by Brazilian natives brought for the occasion and, given the small numbers of Indians available to the local planners, by French mariners, who stripped appropriately naked, spoke the Indian language, hunted, and made war according to the custom of that land. The king and queen, it was said, were duly impressed at this representation of the New World, although royal aid was ultimately not forthcoming.[1] One wonders what the planners of this event had in mind as the essential elements of Tupinamba culture that needed to be selected and projected for their representation of Indian life to be convincing. Their choices contained an understood anthropology and their presentation revealed a kind of implicit ethnography. As such, it demonstrated that the contact between cultures always demands a selective understanding of self and other conditioned by context, goals, and perceptions.

First observers of another culture, the traveler to foreign lands, the historian, and the ethnographer all share the common problem of observing, understanding, and representing. In all these cases there are fundamental epistemological problems as well as a permeable barrier between observer and observed in which it is often difficult (some would say impossible) to separate the two. In practical terms, the study of these cultural encounters has generated a variety of approaches. Some scholars have seen the practice of representation itself as the essential act, to such an extent that the possible adequacy of representation to some reality, its truth or falsity, is, if possible at all, of little concern.[2] In this formulation, such portrayals of another cul-

[1] Ferdinand Denis, ed., *Une fête brésilienne célébrée à Rouen en 1550* (Paris, 1851).
[2] Stephen Greenblatt, *Marvelous Possessions* (Chicago, 1991), 119, argues that "European

ture are important for what they tell us about the observer rather than the observed. Many other historians and anthropologists are less willing to abandon a belief in the ability of the observer to portray, record, or analyze another culture and the actions of its members, however imperfectly, in a manner that allows us to cross that barren but mysterious beach that separates cultures and peoples from each other. As anthropologist Sidney Mintz put it in a heated exchange with literary critics at a 1989 meeting in Erlangen, Germany, he for one was not willing to throw out seventy-five years of anthropological field work or see its residual value only in what it revealed about the discourse and assumptions of the observer. The tension between these alternate understandings of the both the project and the results of cultural observation constitutes an ongoing, unresolved scholarly debate.

It was Greg Dening in his study of the Marquesas Islands who employed the powerful metaphor of islands and beaches as a way of understanding cultural encounters, so that each culture forms an island that must be approached across a beach separating it from all others.

> Beaches are beginnings and endings. They are frontiers and boundaries of islands. For some life forms the division between land and sea is not abrupt, but for human beings beaches divide the world between here and there, us and them, good and bad, familiar and strange . . . Crossing beaches is always dramatic. From land to sea and from sea to land is a long journey and either way the voyager is left a foreigner and an outsider. Look across the beach from the sea, there is what the mind's eye sees, romantic, classic, savage but always uncontrollable. The gestures, the signals, the codes which make the voyager's own world ordered no longer work. He does not see the islander's colors or trees or mountains. He sees his.[3]

In such meetings across cultures, an "implicit ethnography" existed on both sides of the encounter. Members of each society held ideas, often unstated, of themselves and "others" and the things that gave them such identities: language, color, ethnicity, kinship, gender, religion, and so on. These understandings were often implicit in the sense of being unstated or assumed, a kind of common knowledge or common sense that did not have to be articulated or codified but that

contact with the New World natives is continually mediated by representations; indeed contact itself, at least where it does not consist entirely of acts of wounding or killing, is very often contact between representatives bearing representations."

[3] Greg Dening, *Islands and Beaches. Discourse on a Silent Land: Marquesas 1774–1880* (2nd ed., Chicago, 1988), 33–34.

permeated the way in which people thought and acted.[4] In time, encounters might be described and inscribed, but the underlying ideas and understandings that governed the actual encounter were at a level of reflection that is rarely recorded. People represented or "wrote" these ideas in different ways and in genres that often seem to have little overtly to do with the study of other peoples. These concepts or categories, based on previous experience, ideology, and cosmology, could be applied to any new situation and provide a structure of understandings to make the strange into the familiar and the unintelligible into the understood. They dictated the ways in which interactions took place and determined how, for example, Columbus would view the Tainos, or how the Hawaiians might respond to Captain Cook. Each group's sense of its own cultural identity shaped its perception of others, and this in turn was refracted back on self-understanding.

But the process was complicated and unstable. Whatever the previous understandings and expectations, however generalized the common understanding of "others," the contacts themselves caused readjustments and rethinking as each side was forced to reformulate its ideas of self and other in the face of unexpected actions and unimagined possibilities. Thus a dynamic tension between previous understanding and expectations and new observations and experiences was set in motion with each encounter, and modified as the encounters changed over time. Both sides might be convinced that their interpretations of the situation were correct, and sometimes cultural similarities caused more confusion than did differences. But it was the process itself that was crucial. The interplay of these implicit ethnographies, these changing understandings, and their reshaping in the face of each other, over the three centuries of European contact with the rest of the world in the Early Modern era, form the subject of this book.

The theme of cultural encounters, or "implicit ethnographies," raises some of the central questions in the fields of history, literature, and anthropology: perceptions of self and others, epistemology, and the dynamic nature of cross-cultural contact. All these disciplines (and others) have been concerned with the way in which the process of perceiving others reveals self-perception, and for some how what one says about another culture is more interesting as self-projection than

[4] The essays in Mary Douglas, *Implicit Meanings* (London, 1975) and Clifford Geertz, *Local Knowledge* (New York, 1983) both deal with the assumed and unstated aspects of cultural definition.

as a reliable description of the "other."[5] Differences will be noted in this book between those who focus on how the texts reveal the structure of European thought, those who seek to understand the categories of analysis used in the encounters, and those who are most interested in what the texts reveal about the observed and how interactions changed over time. The imposed insularity and tribalization of modern academic disciplines has sometimes led to a narrow conceptualization of problems that are in fact shared, but in the essays presented here the differences of focus do not overshadow the commonality of goal. Moreover, the variety of approach is to be welcomed, for we need not assume that there is an interdisciplinary perspective that is more valid than the insights that the several disciplines provide.

Clearly the problem of cultural encounters and implicit ethnographies could be studied in any number of locales and historical periods, and in no way need be limited to contacts involving Europeans. However, the peculiarities of the Early Modern Era merit special attention. The encounters discussed in these essays took place along with and as part of the expansion of Europe and the creation of its political and economic hegemony over much of the globe from the late fifteenth through eighteenth centuries. That long-term process provides a focus and a unity to the development of concepts of alterity among Europeans and other peoples and with the post-encounter processes of cultural adaptation and response.

In the years between the voyages of Columbus and Captain Cook, the peoples of the world, for better or worse, were brought into contact in a continuous way that lay the foundations for the modern world. The term "Early Modern Era" has usually been applied only to Europe between the Renaissance and the late eighteenth century, but it also seems useful for describing a stage of global history marked by the intensification of interactions that left few parts of the world and few peoples untouched.

Over the course of nearly three hundred years, the business of perceiving and judging other peoples and other customs went through many transformations in many parts of the world. And to some extent

[5] The literature on this topic has been growing rapidly since the 1980s. See, for example, in the field of anthropology, James Boon, *Other Tribes, Other Scribes: Symbolic Anthropology in the Comparative Study of Cultures, Histories, Religions, and Texts* (Cambridge, 1982); James Clifford and George E. Marcus, *Writing Culture. The Poetics and Politics of Ethnography* (Berkeley, 1986); George Marcus and Michael Fisher, *Anthropology as Cultural Critique* (Chicago, 1986); and Vincent Crapanzano, *Hermes Dilemma and Hamlet's Desire* (Cambridge, 1992).

it was the process of encountering others that contributed to the intellectual change within cultures. In Europe, the Renaissance forms and tropes of observation and evaluation seen in Columbus's journal, or the report of Pero Vaz de Caminha on the first contact with the peoples of the Americas, mix marvel and wonder with negative evaluations of technology, carrying forward classical ideas of civility and barbarism that differ considerably from the universalizing concepts of the eighteenth century. The impact of the Reformation, with its plurality of interpretations raising questions about the authority of scripture, combined with the increasing dependence on observation and experience to bring about important changes in the way Europeans saw the world and its inhabitants after the sixteenth century.[6]

Enlightenment thinkers came to view human differences as stages in a universal story. As Denis Diderot formulated it, Tahitians were closer to nature and the world's origins, Europeans represented old age, but all civilized people had been savages and all savages could become civilized.[7] The tension between such ideas of universality and the recognition of real human and cultural diversity troubled European observers in the past and continues to plague all peoples in the present as a formula is sought for a means of understanding and for action.

The problem is a universal one. While the 1980s and 1990s have produced a flood of literature about changing European concepts of alterity and an increased appreciation of their impact, it is important to recognize that such changes occurred in other cultures as well. Sinologists who agree that neo-Confucian concepts in the Sung and Ming periods were an attempt to confront the penetration of foreign Buddhist ideas debate whether neo-Confucian doctrines created a universalist ideology that made all peoples potentially acceptable or whether they reinforced Chinese ideas of distinctiveness. Certainly by the nineteenth century, the desire to acquire European technology led to changes in the perception of and interaction with Westerners. In Southeast Asia, a different pattern developed at a different pace. Longstanding regional diversity was challenged between 1400 and 1700 by the spread of universalist religions, Islam in the Indonesian archipelago, Confucianism in Vietnam, Theravada Buddhism from Burma to Cambodia, and Catholicism in the Philippines. The spread of these faiths created new opportunities and needs for contact and

[6] Anthony Pagden, *European Encounters with the New World* (New Haven, 1993), 54–87.
[7] Peter Hulme and Ludmilla Jordanova, eds., *The Enlightenment and its Shadows* (London, 1990), 1–16.

alliance with outside forces.[8] Outsiders were often seen as allies in regional struggles. In the Middle East, the Muslim indifference to Europe, conditioned by a negative evaluation of Christianity as a superseded revelation and by the conviction that European culture had little to admire, began to change in the late eighteenth century as Europe became increasingly dangerous to the Islamic world.[9] All these instances underline the fact that understandings and evaluations were changing on both sides of the equations of contact.

The very act of using concepts such as "European" and "other peoples" creates categories that determine the way in which we tend to approach the study of these topics. Edward Said's *Orientalism* (1978) made a vigorous attempt to demonstrate that such categorizations in the West's view of the Orient had been tied to political programs and attitudes of cultural superiority, and others have carried his argument from the specific case to general principles.[10] That argument has been seriously questioned both specifically and generally, but in a variety of fields concern with the problems of definition and distinction and an awareness of the dangers of "essentializing" other cultures have shaped current practice in writing about and representing other cultures.[11]

Many of the contacts between Europeans and other peoples were forged in a context of unequal power and subordination, but not all of them, as the essays in this book on China, Japan, and Southeast Asia make clear. If one views cultural encounters and evaluations as governed by a perspective of power and hegemony, as Said and others have done, there is the danger of falling into the reductionist argument in which ultimate goals determine cultural understandings in a somewhat simplistic fashion. Many of the essays here demonstrate that the process of cultural contact and reporting was often "messy" and undirected, that it changed over time, and that it was interactive in the sense that perceptions and actions influenced each other on both sides of the equation of a cultural encounter. None of this denies the

[8] Anthony Reid, ed., "Introduction: A Time and Place," in *Southeast Asia in the Early Modern Era* (Ithaca, 1993), 5–6.

[9] See Bernard Lewis, *The Muslim Discovery of Europe* (New York, 1982), 295–309.

[10] Edward Said, *Orientalism* (New York, 1978); see also Gyan Prakash, "Writing Post Orientalist Histories of the Third World," *Comparative Studies in Society and History*, 32:2 (April, 1990), 383–408, and the critique of that article by R. O'Hanlon and D. Washbrook, "After Orientalism: Culture, Criticism, and Politics in the Third World," *Comparative Studies in Society and History* 34:1 (January, 1992), 141–67, and Prakash's response, pp. 167–84. Said's book was criticized on factual and ideological grounds by Bernard Lewis in *New York Review of Books*.

[11] Carlos Monsivaís, "Travelers in Mexico: A Brief Anthology of Selected Myths," *Diogenes* 125 (Spring, 1984), 48–74.

importance of power, or the fact that Europeans were peculiarly prone to using cultural observation of others as a means of self-knowledge and self-congratulation or as an element of imperial strategy. But power by itself is too crude an instrument for measuring all the subtleties that make up cultural interaction.[12]

A somewhat extreme formulation of the representational argument has sometimes emphasized language and representation as the equivalent of power and possession.[13] The ability to name, describe, and portray are in some ways an appropriation that constitutes an essential step toward control and exploitation. But I remain unconvinced that Columbus's naming an island Española had a great impact on the inhabitants, who called it Quisqueya. At the least, it had far less impact than the firearms, steel, missionaries, and microbes Columbus brought with him. Here the deconstructionists and the empiricists might part company altogether, but perhaps unnecessarily. We may, if we wish, see an unbridgeable chasm here between those who would "deconstruct" the apparent content of an encounter narrative and those who would treat the text as a transparent filter for reliable empirical observations. But the temptation to think in either/or terms should be resisted. Stephen Greenblatt has urged us to abandon the dream of "linguistic omnipotence, the fantasy that to understand the discourse is to understand the event." But at the same time he exhorts us not to abandon words and meanings. Events, weapons, and even sickness are always set in cultural contexts and are intimately bound up with discourse – "the stories that a culture tells itself."

It is the intersection between the objective or culturally created realities and their perception and representation that constitutes the underlying theme of this book. The authors here disagree on where the emphasis should be placed, and some may even doubt whether there is any epistemological grounds for such an idea as events unconditioned by perception, but the project itself is common. The fact that the issue is unresolved in this book reflects the present state of scholarly debate about the study of cultures and how we see ourselves and the world around us.

Another theme that emerges in these essays is the gradations of "otherness" recognized by many cultures. Diane Bell notes that Australian aborigines could certainly distinguish between outsiders from

[12] See Anthony Pagden, *European Encounters with the New World. From Renaissance to Romanticism* (New Haven, 1993), 183–189. On the political dimensions of anthropology, see Talal Asad, *Anthropology and the Colonial Encounter* (New York, 1973).

[13] Tzvetan Todorov, *The Conquest of America: The Question of the Other*, trans. Richard Howard (New York, 1984).

other aboriginal groups and those people who came from beyond the sea and who constituted a quite different category of alterity. James Lockhart argues that for the Nahuas of central Mexico, those kind of distinctions were not so important, and that the Nahuas already had a well-developed system for dealing with the new and strange that could be applied to the arrival of the Spanish. Europeans certainly recognized degrees of "otherness," as Seymour Phillips's essay makes clear, but Europeans, a relatively homogeneous lot, already had long experience with two Asian peoples, Jews and Gypsies, who, as "internal others," influenced the gradations and distinctions that Europeans would develop in their ethnographic observations.

Also characteristic of the Early Modern era was the increasing presence in Europe and its colonies of another internal other, the African slave. While in Antiquity and during the Middle Ages assessments of the character of Africans had varied and had not been entirely negative, from the fifteenth century on, with the increasing enslavement of Africans, that situation had changed. The blackness of the "Ethiope" became synonymous with slavery and a metaphor for their moral and spiritual benightedness and savagery.[14] Race and a perceived lower level of cultural attainments became a justification for enslavement, which survived the ideas of the Humanists, the arguments of the seventeenth-century rationalists, and the program of the Enlightenment. In fact, the freeing of European thought from theology in the eighteenth century in some ways opened the door to evaluations based on physical or mental attributes that contributed to a newly invigorated argument for enslavement. This added dimension of color or race used in making cultural evaluations became particularly acute in Europe, although it was not entirely absent in other parts of the world such as Asia. For Europeans both at home and in the American colonies, however, the presence of the African other cast a shadow over cultural assessments and other encounters and made up some portion of the European implicit ethnographies of other peoples.[15] Columbus used his African experience and Africans as a comparative reference point, and many Europeans later did the same. The

[14] See Winthrop Jordan, *The White Man's Burden. Historical Origins of Racism in the United States* (Oxford, 1974) for a good summary. Cf. A.J.R. Russell-Wood, "Iberian Expansion and the Issue of Black Slavery: Changing Portuguese Attitudes, 1440–1770," *American Historical Review* 83:1 (February, 1978), 16–42.

[15] The most thorough discussion of this problem and the transformation of European attitudes is found in David B. Davis, *The Problem of Slavery in Western Culture* (Ithaca, 1966). On the Enlightenment, see especially pp. 391–421.

African in Africa, but also as a bondsman or woman in Europe or its colonies, became Europe's "Banquo's ghost" of cultural encounters.

The book is organized into four parts. Part I examines the way in which European experiences and European visions of history and cosmology influenced concepts of self and other. Seymour Phillips demonstrates that the contact between Europeans and other peoples, particularly Asians and Arabs, during the Middle Ages set the stage for the more extensive contacts after 1492. This was especially true after the Mongol conquests of the thirteenth century reopened Asia as an area of interest for European merchants, missionaries, and politics. Europe was not closed within itself, but Phillips demonstrates that European images of the physical world and of other peoples who inhabited it were based only to some extent on experience and observation. European understandings, dreams, and fantasies in the form of wild men, monstrous races, or Christian princes in Asia also drew on classical authorities, myth and misunderstanding, and on religious beliefs, which included an apocalyptic vision of history moving from East to West. Wildness could represent either the goodness of natural man or the dangers of animal nature, and both images were reinforced by European experiences in the late Middle Ages.[16] Phillips presents a sweeping survey of the geographical, climatic, and ethnographic ideas that formed the basis of European visions of the world beyond their frontiers. Among these ideas were the attitudes of superiority that accompanied distinctions between Christians and "infidels" (Jews and Moslems), or between civilized English and Germans and "barbarians" on the periphery such as the Irish, Welsh, and Baltic peoples. Phillips notes that after the thirteenth century, European attitudes hardened toward the outside world with the exception of Asia, which continued to provide an image of wonder. In this sense he provides a historical background to the development of asymmetrical concepts that marked off Europeans from other peoples in ways that helped to determine subsequent interaction.[17]

John Friedman reinforces many of these observations by examining

[16] For comparison, see Hayden White, "The Forms of Wildness: Archaeology of an Idea," in his *Tropics of Discourse. Essays in Cultural Criticism* (Baltimore, 1978), 150–182. See also Margaret T. Hodgen, *Early Anthropology in the Sixteenth and Seventeenth Centuries* (Philadelphia, 1964), 17–78.

[17] Reinhardt Koselleck, "The Historical-Political Semantics of Assymetric Counterconcepts," in his *Future Past: On the Semantics of Historical Time* (Cambridge, Mass., 1985), 159–198.

the use of images in the European portrayal of the world, in this case cartographic images of the physical world contained in medieval world maps. For those of us who grew up in schoolrooms dominated by world maps in which North America was always in the center and the Soviet Union invariably divided and placed on both sides of the map, his observations that medieval maps were ethnocentric in their conception will come as no surprise. He demonstrates that these maps are texts that in their form and execution indicate ideas about the centrality of Christianity and of Europeans and often reflect the nationality of the mapmaker as well as an evaluation of other places or other peoples. The changing form of these maps indicated changes in the concept of the world.

From these general statements, we move to the specific case of Spain presented in the next three chapters. Iberia, with its long history of ethnic and religious contact, conviviality, and conflict between Christians, Muslims, and Jews, and then its impulse toward overseas expansion in the fifteenth century, presents a precocious example of the forces that moved European expansion in the Early Modern Era. At the same time, Iberian peculiarities in the creation of strong centralized monarchies, the early development of state bureaucracies, experience from the reconquest in the control and integration of conquered peoples, and the fusion of crusading zeal, missionary impulse, and economic motivation prepared Spain and Portugal in peculiar ways for their role as initiators of the new maritime expansion.

These themes form the spine of Miguel Angel Ladero Quesada's succinct and penetrating survey of Spain in 1492. His own previous research on the incorporation of Muslim Granada into the crown of Castile and on Spanish medieval history in general gives him a solid footing for his overview of Spanish society, polity, and economy on the eve of Columbus's voyage.[18] His view of an expansive, urbanizing Castile, in the process of political integration and mercantile accumulation accompanied by the last stages of a "prophetic millenarianism," suggests a direct background and continuity to the development of colonial Latin America. But Ladero is also careful to point out that seeming precedents for the conquest of America in the reconquest of Granada, the Castilian forays into North Africa, and in the conquest of the Canaries are sometimes more apparent than real. To some extent, the differences were due to the actions and reactions of the peoples encountered. As Ladero points out, the conquistadores

[18] For example, his *Castilla y la conquista del reino de Granada* (Granada, 1988); *Granada después de la conquista. Repobladores y mudéjares* (Granada, 1988).

clearly recognized the difference between the Muslims of Granada and the peoples of the Americas and acted accordingly.

The Iberian conquest and settlement of the Atlantic islands provided another seeming precedent for the subsequent European invasion of the Americas. The conquest, evangelization, and settlement of the Canary Islands preceded and paralleled in many ways the later experience of the Spanish in the Caribbean, not only because of the similarities in Spanish motives and techniques, but also because the material life and social organization of the indigenous inhabitants were closer to those of the Indians of the Caribbean than these were to the Muslims of Granada or North Africa. While a number of authors have recognized the importance of the Canary Islands as a geographical, mental, and institutional stepping stone in the process of the European encounter with other peoples, Eduardo Aznar Vallejo's essay demonstrates that the process of conquest and settlement was complex, depending not only on the conflicting interests of Normans, Mallorcans, Portuguese, and Castilians, and on royal, ecclesiastical, and private interests, but also because of the diversity of culture and political organization from island to island among the indigenous inhabitants. Aznar emphasizes the stages and variation in the European projects of slaving, conquest, colonization, and conversion, and in the Canarian forms of resistance and acculturation. The conquest of the Canary Islands thus provided not one but a number of models of how Europeans might proceed in the conquest of previously little-known or unknown lands and their peoples, and by extension the forms in which those peoples might respond.[19]

The Canaries also figure prominently in Peter Hulme's sweeping essay, which closes Part I. Hulme's goal is to demonstrate the way in which the insular Canaries at the margins of Europe "ethnographically as well as geographically became the zero degree of European culture." Their inhabitants, pagan, underdressed, and "bestial," served to help Europeans make distinctions between themselves and others and provided a mental and military proving ground for European expansion. As Hulme points out, the fact that Columbus sailed from the island of Gomera in the Canaries provides a historical and a metaphoric continuity between these Atlantic islands and those of the Caribbean on whose beaches other pagan, underdressed peoples were to be encountered. Hulme's essay then concentrates on the distinctions made in the Caribbean and the way in which Columbus's

[19] See also Felipe Fernández-Armesto, *Before Columbus. Exploration and Colonization from the Mediterranean to the Atlantic, 1229–1492* (Philadelphia, 1987).

language employed in naming and describing peoples and places was a form of possession and invention that created facts in the process, a factuality of discourse. Whether the cannibalism of the Caribs was a reality, a way in which Arawaks defined their "others," or a figment of European imagination and a justification of Columbus's actions has become a matter of modern dispute.[20] In any case, the putative differences between Caribs and Arawaks assigned to them by Columbus and other early observers created a "gendered" vision of the aggressive, thus "masculine," cannibal Caribs and the more docile, thus "feminine," Arawaks in ways that elicited another set of European understandings. These techniques allowed Columbus to transform entirely strange lands and peoples into ones that could be made "familiarly strange" in his description.

This essay serves to remind us that the early descriptions of encounters are partial accounts often passed off as the whole story. It appropriately concludes a section showing that European perceptions of self and other were formed out of a long series of previous contacts and the development of an ideology of difference, both of which were inscribed in a language that then determined the way in which these contacts and the people they involved were represented and appropriated.

The seemingly obvious but too often neglected need to recognize that the cross-cultural encounters of the early modern world always had at least two sides forms the central theme of Part II. To understand the nature of the non-European visions and responses to the Europeans it is necessary to examine the implicit ethnographies embedded in those cultures, to try, however imperfectly, to grasp the concepts and categories of thought that ordered their perceptions and actions, and to examine the process of contact within specific historical and cultural contexts. This kind of analysis leads to both surprises and cautionary tales. David Morgan's essay parallels the earlier essay by Phillips by dealing with the medieval contacts of Europeans beyond Europe. By focusing on Muslim Persian perceptions in the twelfth century, however, Morgan demonstrates how secondary was Persian concern with Christian Europe at a time when far more important to them were relations with the conquering Mongols, whose actions were viewed by Persian historians in an Islamic context as divine retribution for Persian sins. This attitude reflected not only cur-

[20] See Jalil Sued Badillo, *Los Caribes. Realidad o fabula* (Rio Piedras, Puerto Rico, 1978); Richard Moore, "Carib Cannibalism: A Study in Anthropological Stereotyping," *Caribbean Studies*, 13 (1973), 117–135.

rent political realities, but until the fourteenth century a perception of Europe in the Islamic world as a "remote and barbarous backwater."[21] Morgan also raises the question of sources, both because some of the major historians he uses wrote while under Mongol rule and because the views of women, common folk, and other social groups were not reflected in the available accounts. As he suggests, the available sources are also limiting because "ordinary" Muslim knowledge of Europe and elsewhere created by trade, travel, and contact with visitors may have been far more extensive than surviving evidence indicates.

The question of sources is much in the mind of James Lockhart in his revisionist view of Spanish-Nahua (Aztec) interactions in the century after contact. Making extensive use of Nahuatl language sources and vocabulary, Lockhart points out that most of these were created only after the second generation post-conquest, and then by particular segments of Nahua society, so that what we have is not *the* Nahua view but *a* Nahua view. This is nowhere better seen than in the post-conquest accounts of the fighting that reflect the ethnic and political divisions of pre-Columbian central Mexico. Lockhart suggests, however, that the basic structures of thought are apparent in the corpus of Nahua writings in European script, so that much can in fact be inferred about the first twenty-five years of contact and about subsequent adjustments thereafter. By a close reading of language use and change, Lockhart suggests that the arrival of the Spaniards was nowhere near as disruptive and bewildering to the inhabitants of central Mexico as has sometimes been asserted, and that discernible stages in the transformation of Nahua vocabulary and usage reflected the intensity of Spanish impact and frequency of contact. The ability of the Nahua to incorporate a panoply of new plants, animals, tools, and concepts within their own linguistic terms indicates the resilience of their culture, and the pattern by which this was done provides Lockhart a key to understanding the historical process of contact. To a great extent, the Nahua vision of "we" and "they" did not become "Indians" and "Spaniards" but rather maintained the traditional distinctions based on independent political units and their peoples to which the Castilians were subsumed.

[21] For similar views on the Islamic world in general, see Bernard Lewis, *The Muslim Discovery of Europe* (New York, 1982). A somewhat different tack is taken in Aszziz Al-Azmeh, "Barbarians in Arab Eyes," *Past and Present* 134 (February, 1992), 3–18. See also Jacqueline Kaye, "Islamic Imperialism and the Creation of Some Ideas of 'Europe,' " Francis Barker, et al., *Europe and its Others*, 2 vols. (Colchester, 1985), I, 59–71.

Unlike the post-encounter literacy of Nahua society or the pre-encounter literacy of various Asian peoples which provides a written record, the reconstruction of the implicit ethnography or the native anthropology of preliterate societies presents peculiar methodological and epistemological problems. Wyatt MacGaffey confronts these problems in his discussion of the early Portuguese relations with coastal West Africa, and especially the Kongo kingdom in the sixteenth century. His essay pays considerable attention to the political and religious underpinnings of Portuguese perceptions and understanding of African cultures, but similarly he seeks to use modern understandings of later Kongo cosmology and cultic practice in order to understand the original interaction between the Kongo kingdom and the Portuguese, especially in terms of the adoption of Christianity. MacGaffey argues that what resulted was a "dialogue of the deaf," in which serviceable misunderstandings on both sides allowed for interaction in a process of "double mistaken identity." Since the understanding of the Other depended on self-perception, the implicit ethnography was really of Self.

The remaining three essays of this section examine indigenous understanding and categorization of, and response to, Europeans by South Asians, Southeast Asians, and Japanese. In each of these cases, traditional cultural reference points and concepts of "us" and "them" structured the new interaction after 1500. The arrival of Europeans was neither shocking nor disruptive to the world vision of these peoples. In much of Asia where interaction between peoples of different religions, languages, and cultures was a relative commonplace, the nature of the meeting with Europeans took on a different character than in the Americas and Africa. Moreover, as Anthony Reid shows for Southeast Asia, the previous reception of foreign Muslims and the historical relationship between them and the Christians shaped the ways in which the *feringgi* or "Franks" were viewed when they arrived in the lands "below the winds." Neither color, creed, nor language determined the reception of the Portuguese and Dutch so much as their own actions, which over time earned them the distrust and fear. Chandra Richard de Silva finds a similar pattern in South Asia, where the Portuguese were at first accepted like the Arab merchants as simply another group of traders. But in India and Sri Lanka, Portuguese commercial competition and Portuguese religious intolerance, especially toward Muslims, led to a more negative view of the Europeans, and this developed over time as knowledge and experience accumulated. De Silva underlines the important point that local divisions and interests created a variety of responses to the European presence.

The Japanese also turned to traditional categories in order to situate and represent the Europeans. While Chinese, Korean, and Manchurians had constituted the "other" for the Japanese before the sixteenth century, the "men from Inde," the Portuguese who first arrived in Japan coming by way of Goa, were seen as coming from *Tenjiku,* the ancient, somewhat mystical home of the Buddha. Ronald Toby's essay demonstrates how traditional ways of depicting others were used to represent the Europeans and their servants, and also how the novelty of their appearance created a popular sensation and a peculiar iconography in Japanese art. Toby also emphasizes the importance of historical circumstance in molding this response. The fact that the Europeans arrived not long after the arrival of large numbers of Korean forced immigrants led to a popular identification of Europeans with them. As official policy toward Christianity changed toward the negative, the representation of, and masquerading as, Europeans became dangerous and increasingly less frequent. Toby's observation serves as a fitting reminder that visions of alterity are not culturally determined but constrained, and are subject always to various interests and to historical circumstance.

The concept of implicit ethnography suggests that the original period of encounter is limited on both sides by prior understandings of self and others, but that these understandings are themselves modified or transformed by the reality of interaction. As the contact then becomes continual, a series of adjustments to the encounter and to the interpenetration of cultures is worked out by individuals, states, and societies. These adjustments constitute the organizing theme of Part III, in which essays on the Americas, China, and India present studies of living with or in other cultures.

Mary Helms first presents a general theoretical discussion about the importance of objects and their collection as a way of incorporating and understanding other cultures. She concentrates on the Renaissance and post-Renaissance European habit of collecting objects from classical antiquity because of their aesthetic and thus moral qualities, as well as on foreign and strange things organized in *wunderkammer* designed to find divine order in the heterogeneity of the world. Objects of encounter – Aztec jewelry, Polynesian featherwork, African masks – were included because of their curiosity not because of their beauty, since aesthetic qualities could not be perceived in works whose creators were viewed as "uncivilized." Helms points out that not only Europeans collected objects of encounter, but that things from afar were valued for their craftsmanship and their strangeness and therefore their power in many societies. Things and their collection became a means of reaffirming cosmologies and incorporating the other, and served purposes beyond their immediate function.

The other essays in Part III present case studies of adjustment in various situations of cultural contact. Rolena Adorno examines the writings of hispanized Indians and *mestizos* in colonial Spanish America who were faced with the problem of interpreting their indigenous heritage while seeking to make these interpretations understandable to culturally European readers. They were, she states, "twice ethnographers," working between two worlds as cultural mediators. Rather than creating an "Indian" interpretation of the past, their histories invariably express their own personal and ethnic viewpoints and interests, which are usually reconciled with the standards and expectations of Hispanic society. But their role was contradictory, needed by colonial society yet held in suspicion and disregard. Their accounts of past glories were, in Frank Salomon's phrase, "chronicles of the impossible," since their Indian readers could not hope to reproduce them. The *ladino* writers were ethnographers of their own intermediate situation, and as such were able to discern the artificiality of boundaries between identities.

The essays by Willard Peterson and Ann Waltner discuss one of the most remarkable and sustained early modern cultural interactions – the Jesuit missionary presence in China which began after 1583. The Jesuit attempts to use European science and analogies between Christian and Chinese concepts of virtue and religion in order to spread their doctrine met with both sympathetic reception and entrenched opposition in China, depending on Chinese views of the universality of the doctrine or Chinese understanding of the inherent contradictions of Christianity with traditional Chinese culture.

The missionary success depended to some extent on an ability to adapt to the everyday realities of Chinese life as well as on the effectiveness of doctrine to convince and convert. In the case of China, where literacy and books were so widely diffused, the literate traditions on both sides became a field of interchange and encounter.[22] Willard Peterson deals with the missionaries' growing understanding of Chinese social and religious life. He shows how, within Chinese

[22] Jacques Gernet, *China and the Christian Impact* (Cambridge, 1985), 1–7. See also Jonathan Spence, *The Memory Palace of Matteo Ricci* (New York, 1983); and Charles E. Ronan and Bonnie B.C. Oh, eds., *East Meets West: The Jesuits in China, 1582–1773* (Chicago, 1988).

society, clothing carefully signified rank and how early missionaries like Matteo Ricci learned that if clothing did not make the man, it surely made the message of the man more palatable. The Jesuit shift from a style of appearance akin to Buddhist monks to dress more like that of the Confucian literati reflected a growing understanding of tradition, power and politics in the Middle Kingdom.

Ann Waltner's essay on the Spanish Jesuit Diego de Pantoja's *The Seven Victories* (1604) and its reception in China is a case study of how such encounters might cause each side not only to examine the "other," but to reexamine itself. Pantoja's book was written in Chinese to convey Christian ideas of virtue and morality in an attempt to convert, but some in China were able to separate its Christian message from its moral teachings and viewed it as a work in the popular tradition of Ming moral tracts. Pantoja framed his message in a form intelligible to his Chinese audience, but by doing so allowed the strength of traditional thought and categories to accept it without necessarily accepting its underlying doctrine. Like Peterson, Waltner sees the Jesuit attempt to achieve an ethnographic understanding of the Chinese and to use that knowledge for specific religious goals.

Clearly, over the course of the Early Modern Era, changes in knowledge, perceptions, and belief transformed the nature of new encounters and an understanding of self and others. The Enlightenment stands as a shorthand for this eighteenth-century transformation in European thought. While not alone, the islands and peoples of the Pacific provided an archetypical scenario, or in Greg Dening's formulation a *theatrum mundi* for new encounters and representations, and at the same time for struggle for empire between European nations. Part IV contains a group of essays that center on the Pacific and on the changes in the way Europeans perceived and represented cultural differences in that age.[23]

Dening makes a personalized, self-reflective, and generalizing analysis of the eighteenth century Pacific and of European observation of its inhabitants. His essay is a commentary on observing – by explorers, ethnographers, historians, and beachcombers – and on a specific historical moment of observation. He notes that the "observer is always reflected in the observed" and that ethnography should always be self-conscious, or as he puts it, "theatrical." We observers never stand apart from the reality we try to represent. His tour of Pacific history from beachcombers in the Marquesas to Cook's voyage to Australia allows him to argue that whatever the intention of captains, mission-

[23] Marshall Sahlins, *Islands in History* (Chicago, 1985).

aries, and scientists, knowing and "collecting" the "other" invariably led to the advantage of the knower and the "massive dispossession and transformation" of the "native." His remark suggests knowledge is a frame for power, and raises in a disturbing way the relationship between understanding others and controlling them. How observations are transformed or are codified into discourse more about ourselves than about others is an underlying theme throughout.

Peter Wood's study of three different North American Indian encounters with Europeans in the eighteenth century reminds us that what Columbus had initiated in the fifteenth century, the explorations of James Cook continued in the eighteenth, and by that time Europeans conceived differently of the project of "discovery" and the nature of cultural contacts. Wood also reminds us that the Americas presented a tremendous variety of indigenous cultures and that the differing nature of encounters complicated the developing implicit ethonography of Europeans. Moreover, by the time of the meetings of the eighteenth century, Europeans and indigenous peoples from Labrador to the Carolinas to the northwest Pacific coast often had a history of knowledge of encounters to draw upon. Wood argues that in each of the cases he examines, the options for action were never predetermined or inevitable. Encounters in place always left some room for creativity and surprise.

Diane Bell continues this observation of the observers in the context of early contacts between Europeans and Aboriginal peoples in Australia. She emphasizes the variety of Aboriginal responses, a variety due in part to previous external contacts with outsiders such as men from Macassar who visited the coast of Arnhemland long before the first European contacts. By a careful reading of the European texts of encounter, and attention to differences between the observations of the seventeenth and eighteenth centuries, she plots changes in attitude and intention, but she also uses an understanding of Aboriginal concepts of gender, territoriality, and social organization to explain the nature of the encounters. The overall effect is to emphasize the complexity as well as the variety of the encounter experiences. Her analysis is also self-reflexive and frank in its recognition of her own feminist readings of the materials she uses.

How did the means of observation and the ways of describing others change for Europeans during the early modern era? The problem of distinction occupies James Boon in the final essay of the book. He examines circumcision and its absence as "an enacted and inscribed semiotic" means of distinguishing "us" from "them." He traces the changes in perception of circumcision from the early modern hermeneutics of Montaigne, in which the variety and specificity of the world is seen through an act such as circumcision, to an Enlightenment focus that placed it on a universal scale to be judged by absolute standards. The Enlightenment did make a difference in observation and representation of the remote, the different, and the exotic. In this case, the European implicit ethnography had been transformed by the historical process.

Whether we have now entered into a post-Enlightenment age of observation and representation is a matter of considerable discussion and dispute. While few of the authors represented here would fully subscribe to the scientific and objective claims of a Cartesian intellect, stripped of emotion, prejudice, and other such limitations, the extensive and sometimes heated discussions that accompanied the first presentation of many of these essays demonstrated that profound differences exist among scholars over the nature and recoverability of the past. Those who emphasized the analysis of texts and the forms and categories of representation of the observers as the essential way to deal with the history of cultural encounters met firm opposition from those who continued to believe, despite the haze of linguistic and cultural assumptions that limit observation, that other cultures existed outside the mind of the observer, and that these can be observed and understood in an admittedly imperfect approximation of a reality. The tension between these two philosophical positions in the study of the past complicates and enriches any study of the formation of the modern world and our multiple understandings of it.

PART I

European visions of others in the late Middle Ages

CHAPTER 1

The outer world of the European Middle Ages

SEYMOUR PHILLIPS

I. COLUMBUS

ALTHOUGH the final significance of the discovery by the Genoese navigator Christopher Columbus of a series of islands previously unknown to Europeans in the western Atlantic during the autumn of 1492 is still a matter of dispute, there can be little doubt that this event proved to be a turning-point in the history both of the discoverers themselves and of the peoples whom they discovered. Even before Columbus had finished his fourth and final voyage in 1504, the Florentine businessman, explorer and self-publicist Amerigo Vespucci was writing about his own discovery of a "new world," while perceptive observers, like the Italian humanist Peter Martyr d'Anghiera, were beginning to realize that it would now be necessary to add a new continent to those of Europe, Asia, and Africa into which the land mass of the world had conventionally been divided since classical antiquity; and in 1507 the German cosmographer Martin Waldseemüller, named this new discovery as America in honour of Vespucci.[1] Within thirty years of the first voyage of Columbus, the conquest of the New World had been begun by the Castilian adventurer Hernán Cortés, and the globe itself had been circumnavigated by the few survivors of the expedition of Magellan. It is even possible that as early as the 1520s the shores of the continent of Australia had been sighted by Portuguese explorers.[2]

The profound upheaval in European understanding of the physical nature of the world that these events initiated and that was brought to a conclusion only at the time of the voyages of James Cook in the

[1] *The Letters of Amerigo Vespucci*, ed. C.R. Markham, Hakluyt Society, First Series, vol. 90 (London, 1894; repr. New York, n.d.), pp.xvi–xviii.

[2] H. Wallis, "The enigma of Java-la-Grande," in *Australia and the European Imagination*, ed. I. Donaldson (Canberra, 1982); idem, "Java la Grande: the enigma of the Dieppe maps," in *Terra Australis to Australia*, ed. G. Williams & A. Frost (Melbourne, 1988).

eighteenth century was accompanied by an equally profound transformation in European experience and understanding of mankind itself. Edmund Burke, writing in 1777, was to characterize the change as the unrolling of the "Great Map of Mankind," so that "there is no state or Gradation of barbarism, and no mode of refinement which we have not at the same instant under our View. The very different Civility of Europe and of China; the barbarism of Tartary, and of Arabia. The Savage State of North America, and of New Zealand."[3] This process, the "clash of cultures," "the fall of natural man," or, in a more neutral phrase, "the discovery of man,"[4] had begun both literally and symbolically the moment that Columbus set foot on the island he named San Salvador on 12 October 1492.[5] Indeed, the very act of crossing beaches in order to land on islands has been shown to be one of the most potent metaphors available for the historian wishing to describe the encounters between peoples of different cultural backgrounds.[6]

However, the intention here is to explore some of the assumptions about the world and its peoples that may already have been implicit in the mind of Columbus in 1492 as well as in those of other European explorers of the late fifteenth century. Some important clues can be found in the letter that Columbus wrote early in 1493 while still at sea on the return from his momentous first voyage:

> Since I know that you will be pleased at the great success with which the Lord has crowned my voyage, I write to inform you how in thirty-three days I crossed from the Canary Islands to the Indies, with the fleet which our most illustrious sovereigns gave me. . . . . When I reached Cuba, I followed its north coast westwards, and found it so extensive that I thought this must be the mainland, the province of Cathay'; ' . . . . . . From there I saw another island eighteen leagues eastwards which I then named 'Hispaniola' . . . . . . In

[3] Cited on the title page of P.J. Marshall & G. Williams, *The Great Map of Mankind: British Perceptions of the World in the Age of Enlightenment*, (London, 1982).

[4] B.F. Fagan, *The Clash of Cultures* (New York, 1984); J.H. Elliott, "The discovery of America and the discovery of man," in idem, *Spain and its World, 1500–1700: Selected Essays* (New Haven & London, 1989); A. Pagden, *The Fall of Natural Man: the American Indian and the Origins of Comparative Ethnology* (Cambridge, 1982); idem, "Dispossessing the barbarian: rights and property in Spanish America," in idem, *Spanish Imperialism and the Political Imagination: Studies in European and Spanish-American Social and Political Theory, 1513–1830* (New Haven & London, 1990).

[5] P. Hulme, *Colonial Encounters: Europe and the Native Caribbean, 1492–1797* (London & New York, 1986), ch. I, "Columbus and the cannibals"; L. Olschki, "What Columbus saw on landing in the West Indies," *Proceedings of the American Philosophical Society*, 84 (Philadelphia, 1941), pp.633–59.

[6] G. Dening, *Islands and Beaches: Discourse on a Silent Land: the Marquesas, 1774–1880* (Hawaii, 1980).

this island of Hispaniola I have taken possession of a large town which is most conveniently situated for the goldfields and for communications with the mainland both here, and there in the territories of the Grand Khan, with which there will be very profitable trade.[7]

Despite his observation that on the island of Cuba "one of these provinces is called Avan, and there the people are born with tails," Columbus also remarked,

I have not found the human monsters which many people expected. On the contrary, the whole population is very well made"; .... "Not only have I found no monsters but I have had no reports of any except at the island of 'Quaris', which is the second as you approach the Indies from the east, and which is inhabited by a people who are regarded in these islands as extremely fierce and who eat human flesh.[8]

The references by Columbus to "the Indies," "the province of Cathay," the "territories of the Grand Khan," and to the city of "Quinsay" and the island of "Chipangu" (which Columbus mentions in his journal[9]) are a clear demonstration that he was, initially at least, convinced that the destination he had reached by a long and hazardous westward voyage across the mysterious Atlantic ocean was essentially the same one that had been reached by Marco Polo of Venice by the land route eastward across Asia in the 1270s, and his search for monsters in human form has obvious parallels in the narratives of Marco Polo and of other thirteenth- and fourteenth-century European travelers such as Giovanni di Piano Carpini, William of Rubruck, and John of Marignolli. None of this is at all surprising because it is well known that Columbus had read and annotated one of the early printed editions of the travels of Marco Polo, from which he had learned about the wonders of the dominions of the Great Khan in Cathay as well as about the island empire of Japan (Chipangu), which Marco Polo described but had not actually seen. Together with his assiduous readings of other fourteenth- and fifteenth-century authors and of newly published editions of classical authors, such as Claudius Ptolemy, Columbus's mind was therefore well stocked with ideas and impressions about the wider world around him.[10]

[7] *The Four Voyages of Christopher Columbus*, ed. J.M. Cohen (London, 1969; repr. London, 1992), pp.115–16, 120.

[8] Ibid., pp.119, 121.

[9] Ibid., pp.71–3.

[10] J.R.S. Phillips, *The Medieval Expansion of Europe* (Oxford & New York, 1988), pp.77–8, 194–5, 201. On these monsters in general, see the very important book by J.B. Friedman, *The Monstrous Races in Medieval Art and Thought* (Cambridge, Mass., 1981). For a more detailed discussion of Columbus's ideas about "places and peoples," see

II. PLACES

Despite the extensive contacts that existed between medieval Europe and other parts of the world, with the lands of the eastern Mediterranean, with large areas of Asia, with parts of Africa and its adjoining oceans, and with the North Atlantic and even North America,[11] understanding of what lay out in this wider world was not always accurate, and older ideas frequently coexisted with and sometimes took precedence over new and more reliable information.[12] Thus we find the persistent search, in which Columbus was only the latest participant, for strange races of men, descriptions of whom can be traced back to the writers of classical antiquity.[13] Or, to take a more recent example, there was from the twelfth century the quest for Prester John, the supposed ruler of a Christian realm of immense power and wealth lying somewhere in the East, who was allegedly awaiting only the opportunity to come to the aid of a beleaguered Christendom against its Moslem opponents.[14] But erroneous as they were, such ideas were

P. Hulme, ch. I, "Columbus and the cannibals"; and Mary B. Campbell, *The Witness and the Other World: Exotic European Travel Writing, 400–1600* (Ithaca & London, 1988), ch. 5, "The end of the East: Columbus Discovers Paradise." For the sources of his geographical ideas, see F. Fernandez-Armesto, *Columbus* (Oxford, 1991), pp.24,34–43; Delno West, "Christopher Columbus and his enterprise of the Indies: scholarship of the last quarter century," *The William and Mary Quarterly*, April 1992; W.G.L. Randles, "Le projet asiatique de Christophe Colomb devant la science cosmographique portugaise et espagnole de son temps," *Islenha*, no.5, July-December 1989 (Funchal, Madeira, 1989), pp.73–88.

[11] See Phillips, *The Medieval Expansion of Europe*, and the bibliographies supplied for each chapter. I have discussed some possible explanations for European expansion in a forthcoming paper, "European expansion before Columbus: causes and consequences," in *The Haskins Journal*, vol. 5 (Woodbridge, 1994). See also A.R. Lewis, *Nomads and Crusaders, 1000–1368* (Bloomington & Indianapolis, 1988). This has much to say of interest about European relations with the outer world but is restricted by the choice of terminal date and by the concentration on Asia.

[12] Phillips, ch. 10, "Scholarship and the imagination"; see also Campbell, *The Witness and the Other World;* M. Helms, *Ulysses' Sail: an Ethnographic Odyssey of Power, Knowledge, and Geographical Distance* (Princeton, 1988); J.K. Hyde, "Real and imaginary journeys in the later Middle Ages," *Bulletin of the John Rylands Library*, 65 (Manchester, 1982–3), pp.125–47; F. Fernandez-Armesto, *Before Columbus: Exploration and Colonisation from the Mediterranean to the Atlantic, 1229–1492* (London, 1987). ch. 9, "The mental horizon"; and the important collection of essays, *Discovering New Worlds: Essays on Medieval Exploration and Imagination*, ed. S.D. Westrem (New York & London, 1991).

[13] See Friedman, *The Monstrous Races.*

[14] Phillips, pp.60–2, 77–9, 190–2. The most thorough survey of the Prester John theme is V. Slessarev, *Prester John, the Letter and the Legend* (Minneapolis, 1959); but see also C.F. Beckingham, *Between Islam and Christendom: Travellers, Facts, Legends in the Middle Ages and the Renaissance* (London, 1983); B. Hamilton, "Prester John and the three kings of Cologne," in *Studies in Medieval History Presented to R.H.C. Davis*, ed. H. Mayr-Harting & R.I. Moore (London, 1985).

part of the spur and the incentive for would-be explorers, and they were probably as influential in the fifteenth century as they had been in the twelfth or thirteenth.

A twentieth-century student of medieval Europe's relations with and perceptions of the outer world can have a much broader view of the subject than his medieval predecessor: No thirteenth- or fourteenth-century traveler, for example, would necessarily know even what his own contemporaries had discovered about the world. Although it is possible that John of Monte Corvino might have heard reports of Marco Polo's stay in China, which had ended shortly before his own arrival in Peking in 1294, there is no reason to suppose that Marco Polo knew anything of John. Similarly, it is most improbable that Ibn Battuta of Tangier, one of the greatest of all Moslem travelers, who visited India in the 1330s, probably visited China in 1346 and also crossed the Sahara in the early 1350s, and whose career is often compared with that of Marco Polo, ever heard of the Venetian's exploits.[15] A number of European travelers wrote about their experiences in Asia soon after the event: In some instances, like those of Giovanni di Piano Carpini in 1247 and Odoric of Pordenone in 1330, their accounts were widely read; in other cases, narratives that are now regarded as of great historical importance, such as those of the Franciscans William of Rubruck, who visited the court of the Great Khan at Karakorum in Mongolia in 1253–4, and John of Marignolli, who was in China in the 1340s, were either little known or were altogether unknown at the time they were written.[16] But all these travelers did at least visit various parts of a continent whose existence was a familiar part of European knowledge: In the case of the Viking navigators from Iceland and Greenland who discovered and explored a part of the North American continent in the early eleventh century and who perhaps continued to go there as late as the fourteenth century, there is very little evidence that anyone outside their own ranks even knew of their exploits, let alone was influenced by them.[17]

Another difficulty arises from the nature of the records of medieval travel. Although it is possible for us to conclude that some contemporary or near-contemporary accounts were written with a consider-

[15] Ross E. Dunn, *The Adventures of Ibn Battuta* (London & Sydney, 1986). There is, however, some doubt about Ibn Battuta's visit to China.

[16] William of Rubruck's account was known to Roger Bacon but does not appear to have been widely read; John of Marignolli's account was contained in the chronicle of the kingdom of Bohemia, which he composed in Prague and was not rediscovered until the early nineteenth century.

[17] Phillips, ch.9, "Medieval Europe and North America," ch. 12, "Fresh start or new phase?"

able degree of objectivity and that others contain a substantial amount of imaginative writing, such distinctions would have been less apparent to a medieval reader and would probably have had little meaning. Outstanding examples are the narratives produced by Giovanni di Piano Carpini, who was sent as a papal envoy to the Mongol Great Khan in 1245, and William of Rubruck who wrote about the Mongols a few years later. Although both men were traveling at a time when the terrors of the Mongol attacks on Europe were fresh in their minds and were describing a society that was alien almost beyond imagining, they nonetheless succeeded in treating the Mongols with sympathetic understanding.[18] However, in other cases, most notably perhaps the works commonly known as *Marco Polo's Travels* and *The Travels of Sir John Mandeville,* their form is both an attraction to the reader and a barrier to a full understanding of the material they contain. It is well known that Marco Polo's description of his travels was written for him around 1300 by a professional author, Rustichello of Pisa, who did not hesitate to incorporate highly colored passages to make his story more interesting, and also on occasions reused material from earlier works of his own. Exactly where Marco Polo's contribution began and ended is difficult, if not impossible, to ascertain.[19] On the other hand, there is no reason to suppose that Marco Polo did not actually go to India and China as he claimed. By contrast, the eponymous Sir John Mandeville did not visit any of the lands described in his travels, and probably never existed. Here we are faced with a skilfully written and very popular piece of literature by an unidentified author who probably intended both to entertain and to improve the minds of his readers and who made use of a wide variety of sources, representing both real and imaginary travels. It is also significant that of the four examples cited, *Mandeville's Travels* was probably the best known and most widely read in the fourteenth and fifteenth centuries.[20]

Although the spherical shape of the earth was well understood and serious attempts were made by classical writers, notably Claudius

[18] Phillips, pp.73–82; Dawson; Mary B. Campbell, ch. 3.

[19] Phillips, pp.112–20, 204–6; J. Heers, *Marco Polo;* Marco Polo, *The Travels,* trans. R.E. Latham (London, 1958); Campbell, ch. 3; *Marco Polo and his Book: China and Europe in the Middle Ages.*

[20] Phillips, pp.206–11; *The Travels of Sir John Mandeville,* ed. C.W.R.D. Moseley (London, 1983); Campbell, ch. 4; J.W. Bennett, *The Rediscovery of Sir John Mandeville* (New York, 1954). The most recent major work on Mandeville is C. Deluz, *Le livre de Jehan de Mandeville: une "géographie" au XIVe. siècle* (Louvain-la-Neuve, 1988). See also J.R.S. Phillips, "The quest for Sir John Mandeville," in *The Culture of Christendom: Essays in Medieval History in Memory of Denis L.T. Bethell,* ed. M.A. Meyer (London, 1993).

Ptolemy of Alexandria in the mid-second century A.D. to supply details of latitude and longitude for all the important places on the earth's surface, the inaccuracy of their results meant that throughout the classical and medieval periods there was a fundamental imprecision in spatial relationships. In the fifteenth century, for example, there was no agreement among European scholars on either the measurement of the circumference of the earth or on the East-West extent of Asia and Europe: The two most common estimates of the latter were 180 degrees of the earth's circumference (a figure derived from Ptolemy) and 225 degrees (a figure quoted in the early fifteenth century by Pierre d'Ailly but derived ultimately from Marinus of Tyre, a predecessor of Ptolemy). Both calculations were overestimates, the true figure being about 130 degrees. The consequences for the calculations of Christopher Columbus, who also accepted Ptolemy's considerable underestimate for the earth's circumference, are well known.[21] No classical or medieval European traveler, not even one as

[21] Phillips, *The Medieval Expansion of Europe*, pp.4–5, 213–6; Ptolemy provided a figure of 180,000 Greek stadia (c. 18,000 nautical miles) rather than the more accurate 250,000 stadia calculated by Eratosthenes in the third century B.C. The concept of a spherical earth would have been known to anyone who had received a university education through such works as the textbook, *De Sphaera Mundi*, written by John Holywood at the university of Paris in the 1220s, which continued to be cited as late as the sixteenth century. It seems to have been a commonplace scholarly and literary theme that the spherical earth could in principle be circumnavigated: this notion can be found in such diverse contexts as the *Opus Maius* of the thirteenth-century English Franciscan scholar Roger Bacon and the anonymous fourteenth-century literary work known as *The Travels of Sir John Mandeville*. In the 1370s the French scholar Nicholas Oresme even calculated that a circumnavigation would take exactly four years, sixteen weeks, and two days. (See "A fourteenth-century argument for an international date line," in C. Lutz, *Essays on Manuscripts and Rare Books* (Hamden, Connecticut, 1975.) Whatever the views of the unlettered about the shape of the earth may have been, educated Europeans were not Flat-Earthers and Columbus was not making any revolutionary claims when he argued for the possibility of a westward voyage to Asia. The real problem lay in the fact that there was no general agreement on the actual circumference of the earth, on the extent of the inhabited landmass, and, just as important, on the breadth of the ocean separating the Far Western from the Far Eastern extremities of the land. Here there was ample room for debate, and it is not surprising that Columbus did not win immediate acceptance for his scheme. As late as 1538 the *Libro de Cosmographía* by Pedro de Medina, who was one of the cosmographers employed by the Casa de la Contratación in Seville and an expert on practical navigation, included many references to and simple proofs of the spherical earth without any attempt to calculate its dimensions: Phillips, pp.184, 188–90, 197, 208–9, 215, 245; *A Navigator's Universe: The Libro de Cosmographía of 1538 by Pedro de Medina*, trans. & ed. Ursula Lamb, The Monograph Series of the Society for the History of Discoveries (Chicago, 1972). The best studies of medieval geographical ideas are G.H.T. Kimble, *Geography in the Middle Ages* (London, 1937; repr. New York, 1968); and J.K. Wright, *Geographical Lore of the Time of the Crusades* (New York, 1925; repr. New York, 1965); to these should now be added the very important *History of Cartography*, vol. 1, *Cartography in Prehistoric, Ancient and Medieval Europe and the Medi-*

much traveled as Marco Polo, actually succeeded in traversing the full extent of Eurasia from ocean to ocean. But even if someone had done so, his conclusions would have been of little help because the separation of places was seen not so much in degrees of latitude or of longitude or in miles as in the time taken to cover the distance. For instance, it took Giovanni di Piano Carpini over a year in 1245–46 to travel by land from Lyons to the vicinity of Karakorum in Mongolia and John of Monte Corvino took over two years to travel by sea from Iran to China between 1291 and 1293–94, whereas Marco Polo's land journey to China took about three and a half years from 1271 to 1274–75.

Although the compass was available for use at sea in the thirteenth century, and by the end of that century portolan charts were beginning to make it possible to navigate by following a compass bearing, long journeys on land were commonly made by the use of itineraries of the kind that had originally been designed for travel around the provinces of the Roman world. In principle, all the traveler needed to know was the place he was currently situated in and where to go next, and so on until the ultimate destination was reached. The thirteenth-century English chronicler Matthew Paris produced such an itinerary for the journey to Jerusalem, although it has also plausibly been suggested that some of the most elaborate *mappae mundi*, such as the Ebstorf Map of c.1240 and the Hereford Map of c.1300, which were put on display in great churches, were designed in part to act as itineraries for potential pilgrims to Santiago, Rome, or Jerusalem.[22]

However, not all destinations were as easily found as these. Then, as now, there was no questioning the existence in some specific location of a city such as Rome or Jerusalem, even if that location could not be described with mathematical precision. On the other hand, what may appear to us as well-defined geographical regions or countries were frequently very inexact in medieval usage. "Ethiopia" or "Sudan" or "Guinea," all of which have a context today as the names of African states, originally all meant more or less the same thing, "the land of the black people" to the south of the Sahara desert, each being expressed in a different language, Greek, Arabic, or Berber. In the case of Asia, the term "India" was very imprecise. A distinction between "India Major" and "India Minor" had already been made in

terranean, ed. J.B. Harley & D. Woodward (Chicago & London, 1987), together with future volumes in the series; D. Woodward, "Reality, symbolism, time and space in medieval world maps," *Annals of the Association of American Geographers*, 75 (1985).

[22] Phillips, p.217; M. Jancey, *Mappa Mundi: the Map of the World in Hereford Cathedral* (Hereford, 1987).

classical writings, but from about the twelfth century no less than three different usages of "India" were current: "Nearer" or "Lesser" India (roughly the northern part of the subcontinent of India as it is now understood); "Further" or "Greater" India (which referred to the southern part of India and also to the regions farther to the east which would now be called South-East Asia and Indonesia); and finally "Middle" India, which was often applied to Ethiopia, with all the further imprecision associated with that expression. "Middle" India should probably be understood as meaning "Intermediate" India or "on the way" to India proper. Although the modern analogy of "Near," "Middle," and "Far" East may help us to appreciate these different forms of "India," there is no doubt that ambiguity is inherent in any medieval writings that refer to India. It is equally significant that the classical and medieval varieties of "India" prepared the way for the multitude of "Indies" and "Indians" that European observers conjured into being in the fifteenth and sixteenth centuries. As late as the eighteenth century, "Indians" were still being found as European navigators explored the mysterious islands of the Pacific.[23]

The main features of medieval geography were derived almost entirely from classical sources: the spherical earth; the division of the earth's surface into equatorial, temperate, and cold ματα or zones; and the three continents of Asia, Africa, and Europe, which were surrounded by the all-embracing world ocean. All the known world was located north of the equator, but the belief that there might be an inhabited southern continent beyond the equator meant that there was an intellectual niche into which Australia and Antarctica could be fitted when these were discovered many centuries later. The southern continent did, however, create problems for Christian theologians, who had to consider whether its inhabitants could have received the blessings of Christianity and, if not, whether they were fully human. There was no such intellectual niche in classical writings for the undiscovered and unsuspected American continent, but the question of the humanity of its peoples was to be a very real problem when America finally was discovered in the early decades of the sixteenth century.[24] However, rather than examining the theoretical framework of

[23] Phillips, pp.203–4; Beckingham. *Between Islam and Christendom,* "The achievements of Prester John," pp.16–19; Marco Polo, *The Travels,* pp.210, 233, 268, 277–8.

[24] On geographical ideas, see Phillips, ch.1, "Classical discoveries and Dark Age transformations," ch. 10, "Scholarship and the imagination"; and also G.H.T. Kimble. On the "antipodes," see Friedman, pp.38–48. One of the ways in which Columbus formulated his objectives before 1492 and before he settled on an Asian destination was probably as a search for the antipodes; after his return from the New World in 1493 the royal and papal chanceries "inclined to the view that the explorer had found an

medieval geography, which was mainly the province of scholars, it will be convenient to take two commonplace forms of discourse in medieval European geographical thought that may broadly be described as a "western" and as an "eastern" view.[25] Apart from their obvious associations with the rising and the setting of the sun and symbolically with birth and death, these views also reflected the fact that the known world consisted of a broad band of territory in the northern hemisphere of the earth stretching from the shores of the Atlantic ocean in the west to an indeterminate point somewhere in eastern Asia.

The western view was strongly influenced by the proximity of the Atlantic. Some commentators, such as the twelfth-century Moslem geographer Al-Idrisi, regarded the Atlantic as an empty desolation, "a green sea of darkness" in the familiar phrase. As the most westerly known part of Europe, Ireland was frequently regarded as lying at the end of the world,[26] a perception that gave a peculiar and special sense of adventure to those pilgrims from all over Europe who went between the twelfth and fifteenth centuries to one of the strangest and most remote places of pilgrimage in medieval Europe, St. Patrick's Purgatory located on an island in Lough Derg in the north-western corner of Ireland.[27] It is ironic, though certainly coincidental, that the suppression of the pilgrimage was ordered by Pope Alexander VI in 1497 at the time that other European travelers were beginning to reveal the reality of a larger and more complex world. However, the fame of the Purgatory also effectively illustrates the very important point that a distant location on the earth's surface, whether in the far west or the far east, might nonetheless be very widely known either at firsthand or from common report. In this case the location happened to be a real one, but it is easy to understand how less well-attested places could also come to have an existence, if only in the imagination.

The desolation of the Atlantic and the remoteness of the western shores of Ireland were, however, tempered to some extent by knowl-

antipodal continent," an opinion that received support from Peter Martyr and other Italian humanists: Fernandez-Armesto, *Columbus*, pp.32, 43–4, 63, 96–8.

[25] Phillips, ch.10, "Scholarship and the imagination"; cf. M. Helms, *Ulysses' Sail*, ch. 6, "The outer realms of Christendom," especially pp.211–26.

[26] Phillips, pp.183–4; D. Metlitzki, *The Matter of Araby in Medieval England* (New Haven & London, 1977), pp.123–4; V.H. Cassidy, *The Sea around Them: the Atlantic, c.1250*, (Baton Rouge, 1968).

[27] M. Haren & Y. de Pontfarcy, ed., *The Medieval Pilgrimage to St. Patrick's Purgatory: Lough Derg and the European Tradition*, Clogher Historical Society (Enniskillen, 1988).

edge of the existence of numerous islands in the ocean. Irish monks, like the historical St. Brendan in the sixth century, had explored and established hermitages on many of the remote islands off the shores of Britain and Ireland: The monastic settlements on the Scottish island of Iona and on the rocky pinnacle of Skellig Michael off the coast of Kerry are two of the most famous. Irish navigators had also visited the Faeroes by 700 A.D. and Iceland (which they identified with the Ultima Thule of classical tradition) before the end of the eighth century, paving the way for the Viking discovery and settlement of the latter after about 870. Iceland remained as a European outpost in the Atlantic throughout the medieval period, although regarded as a northern rather than a western location.[28] The discovery and partial exploration of other groups of islands – the Canaries, Madeira, and the Azores in the fourteenth and early fifteenth centuries – added a large number of other Atlantic destinations.

The real possibility that still more islands were awaiting discovery provided ample scope for the curious and the ambitious fifteenth-century navigator. Just as important in stimulating ambitions were several other islands, which we would regard as having no substance outside the imagination but which were widely accepted as genuine. The island of Antilia (probably meaning "the island opposite" or on "the other side" of the ocean), which Columbus hoped to find on his way to Cathay, was one example, with its origin in the Iberian Peninsula. Two more were of Irish inspiration but became very widely known throughout Europe because of the circulation in manuscript of such works as the tenth-century *Navigatio Brendani* in which St. Brendan in his mythological guise wandered from island to island, each more remarkable than the last. The island of St. Brendan and its companion the island of Brasil (Hy-Breasail, "the land of the Blest") had their origins in pre-Christian Irish voyage literature on the search for a western paradise that was later influenced by Christianity and became a spiritual quest. When maps for navigation began to be drawn in the thirteenth and fourteenth centuries, these two islands were duly included along with the island of Antilia. Apart from an appearance off the coast of Newfoundland in a seventeenth-century chart, St. Brendan's island quickly fell victim to the progress of Atlantic discovery after 1500, but the island of Brasil lasted even as late as the eight-

[28] Phillips, ch.9, "Medieval Europe and North America"; G.J. Marcus, *The Conquest of the North Atlantic* (Woodbridge, 1980); G. Jones, *The Norse Atlantic Saga* (Second edition, Oxford, 1986); on the Irish knowledge of Iceland, see Dicuil, *Liber de Mensura Terrae*, ed. J.J. Tierney (Dublin, 1967).

eenth century as a testimony to the power of the medieval Irish imagination.[29]

Islands appear to have a special place in the history of human relations with and perceptions of the outer world. Each was in a sense a closed world in its own right, which was entered by the highly significant act of crossing the beach; the ship that took the explorer there was in itself a floating mobile world that took its origin from the society that constructed it, but that operated according to rules of its own.[30] Because real islands might hold many surprises for the outsider, it is hardly to be wondered at that islands have a place in the imaginative literature. The islands of St. Brendan and Brasil are two of the most evocative medieval examples: It is even possible that the enthusiastic descriptions of Vinland in twelfth- and thirteenth-century Icelandic sagas as a land of vines and self-sown wheat owed something to literary exemplars like the *Navigatio Brendani*.[31] In the fourteenth century the multitude of islands existing in the seas beyond India, to which Marco Polo and Odoric of Pordenone gave eloquent testimony, provided the author of *Mandeville's Travels* with locations for his dog-headed men and other wonders, secure in the knowledge that few travelers were likely to attempt to check his tales at firsthand. The literary role played by islands can readily be extended via Shakespeare's *Tempest* and Robinson Crusoe's island to the imaginary worlds of modern science fiction.[32]

By contrast with the "western view," which was heavily influenced by impressions of the Atlantic and its islands, the "eastern view" was connected with the land mass of the continent of Asia, which had been partly explored in classical antiquity and on which there was therefore a considerable amount of information available. The "East" was also the source of material goods of high monetary and prestige value. For Christians, the East was the direction from which salvation had come, and one very special part of it contained their Holy Places, which were given pictorial representation by the appearance on *mappae mundi* of Jerusalem as the symbolic center of Christendom.[33] In general, how-

[29] H.P.A. Oskamp, *The Voyage of Mael Duin: a Study in Early Irish Voyage Literature* (Groningen, 1970); T.J. Westropp, "Brasil and the legendary islands of the North Atlantic: their history and fable," *Proceedings of the Royal Irish Academy*, 30, Section C (Dublin, 1912–13), pp.223–60; P. Mac Cana, "The voyage of St. Brendan: literary and historical origins," and D.B. Quinn, "Atlantic islands," in *Atlantic Visions*, ed. J. de Courcy Ireland & D. Sheehy (Dun Laoghaire, Ireland, 1989).

[30] Cf. G. Dening, *Islands and Beaches*.

[31] R. Boyer, "The Vinland sagas and Brendan's Navigation," in *Atlantic Visions*.

[32] See P. Hulme, *Colonial Encounters*, chs. 3, 5; or, for example, James Blish's novel, *A Case of Conscience* (London, 1958).

[33] The central location of Jerusalem should not be seen as an example of European

ever, European impressions of the East were subject to the imprecision in spatial relationships that was discussed earlier, and also to the association of the East since classical times with many tales of marvels and of wondrous races of men, with the result that it was a location within the European imagination just as much as a real (and very large) location upon the face of the earth. For the inhabitants of medieval Europe, all these uncertainties about the East meant that there was plenty of scope for the exercise of imagination: If the wonders of the East, were not found in one place, then they might be somewhere more distant again, perhaps beyond the empire of Cathay or in the kingdom of Prester John. For many people, the East probably began almost as soon as they left familiar ground, after which any strange experience might be expected to befall them. In the early thirteenth century, Jacques de Vitry, the bishop of Acre in the kingdom of Jerusalem, remarked that "some light-minded and inquisitive persons go on pilgrimage not out of devotion, but out of mere curiosity and love of novelty. All they want to do is travel through unknown lands to investigate the absurd, exaggerated stories they have heard about the east."[34] It is not perhaps all that surprising that such views of the East could be dominant even at times when firsthand information was in principle readily available.[35]

Medieval European images of the East were founded in the writings of classical authors. These referred to the most distant parts of Asia either as the land of the "Sinae," whose name may correspond to the first ruling imperial dynasty of China in the third century B.C., or as the land of the "Seres," which adjoined that of the Sinae and was the place from which silk was thought to come. Other than these very vague impressions, the country that we think of as China was very little known to the civilizations of either Greece or Rome, and this continued to be the situation in Europe until the time of the Mongol conquests in Asia during the thirteenth century.[36]

Instead, the most enduring impressions of the East were focused

ethnocentricity comparable with the Chinese portrayal of their own land as the center of the world. Because of Jerusalem's key role in the history of Christianity, it was natural that it should be the center of attention for European Christians. Since Jerusalem also lay more or less at the point of focus of the three continents of Asia, Africa, and Europe, its Christian significance was easily grafted onto the classical idea of the *orbis terrarum:* see Phillips, pp.188–90, and D. Poirion, ed., *Jerusalem, Rome, Constantinople: l'image et le mythe de la ville* (Paris, 1986).

[34] Cited in J. Sumption, *Pilgrimage* (London, 1975), p.257.

[35] Phillips, ch. 10, "Scholarship and the imagination"; see also the detailed treatment of the theme in Campbell, *The Witness and the Other World*

[36] H. Yule, ed., *Cathay and the Way Thither,* 2nd edition, vol. I, Hakluyt Society, 2nd. series, 38 (London, 1915), Introduction and pp.183–97.

upon India. The earliest known references in Greek sources are in the writings of Herodotus in the middle of the fifth century B.C. and of Ctesias of Cnidos in about 400 B.C. Ctesias named his work *Indica*, gave great attention to the marvels of India, and so established a genre of geographical writing that was followed by many later Greek and Roman authors, such as Pliny the Elder in the first century A.D. and Solinus in the third century.[37] Although it is doubtful whether even Ctesias ever visited India, there were many points of contact between Europe and Asia, through military conquests like those of Alexander the Great and his successors and through trade. With the collapse of Roman power, little opportunity for direct relations between western Europe and Asia remained, but the marvels of India lived on and received a new lease of life from such works as the *Cosmography* by the mysterious figure of Aethicus Ister, the so-called *Letter of Alexander to Aristotle*, and the Old English and Latin texts known as *The Wonders of the East*.[38]

The spread of Christianity added a number of new perceptions and sources of interest in the East. One idea that became familiar was that of the terrestrial paradise, from which the four great rivers of the world began their course, and that was usually located in the easternmost reaches of Asia.[39] Although paradise was inaccessible to mankind, the supposed attempt by Alexander the Great to reach it became a part of the Alexander legend that was very familiar in medieval Europe. One of Alexander's exploits, which derives from material in both the Old and the New Testament, was the enclosure behind a wall or mountain range of the savage tribes of Gog and Magog, whose escape would herald the coming of Antichrist. Alexander's wall is usually identified with the Caucasus mountains, but it is just possible that the story contains an echo of one of the precursors of China's Great Wall far to the east.[40] Another tradition of

[37] J.B. Friedman, *The Monstrous Races in Medieval Art And Thought*, passim; R. Wittkower, "Marvels of the East," *Journal of the Warburg and Courtauld Institutes*, 5, 1942. For a collection of classical references to India, see the various works by J.W. McCrindle, e.g. *Navigation of the Erythraean Sea* and *Ancient India as Described by Ktesias of Knidus* (Calcutta & London, 1879; repr. Amsterdam, 1973)

[38] Phillips, pp.10–11; Friedman, op. cit., pp.5–7; Campbell, op. cit., pp.57–74; S. Rypin, ed., *Three Old English Prose Texts*, Old English Text Society, 161 (London, 1924, for 1921).

[39] J.K. Wright, *Geographical Lore of the Time of the Crusades*, pp.771–2, 261–5.

[40] Wright, op. cit., pp.72–4; G. Cary, *The Medieval Alexander* (Cambridge, 1956), pp.130–1; P. Noble, L. Polak & C. Isoz, ed., *The Medieval Alexander Legend and Romance Epic* (London, 1982). No European traveler to China in the thirteenth and fourteenth centuries made any mention of the Wall, which was constructed in its present form only

Christian inspiration was the legend of St. Thomas, which existed from about the third century A.D. and was based in part at least on the perfectly genuine spread of Christianity to parts of India. Although the legend underwent a revival in the twelfth century, after which a number of European pilgrims visited the shrine of St. Thomas at Mailapur on the east coast of India,[41] it was soon overshadowed by the much more powerful tale contained in the fictitious *Letter* of Prester John, the eastern king who was preparing to come to the aid of Christendom.[42] Once the *Letter* began to circulate, every European traveler who had the chance to travel in the East was almost bound to divert some of his energies to a search for the elusive Christian ruler.[43]

A great many ideas and impressions about the East were therefore already current in Europe even before the thirteenth-century Mongol conquests provided an unexpected new opportunity for European travel in Asia. The Mongols did not conquer India at this time,[44] but European merchants like the Genoese Benedetto Vivaldi and Percivalle Stancone and the Venetian Marco Polo, and missionaries such as John of Monte Corvino, John of Marignolli, Odoric of Pordenone, and the French Dominican, Jordan of Séverac, who became bishop of Quilon in 1329, did succeed in going there through Mongol-controlled territory in Iran at various times in the late thirteenth and fourteenth centuries.[45] Although they were sometimes skeptical of some of the old tales about India, they were never able to shake off all the ideas received from the past. John of Marignolli, for example, wrote several pages of reasoned argument against the existence of the monstrous races, while remaining convinced that while he was visiting Ceylon he had heard the waters issuing from the fountain of Paradise.[46] Jordan of Séverac's account of India, written in about 1330, contains much that is recognizable but was significantly entitled *Mirabilia Des-*

in the fifteenth and sixteenth centuries: see A.N. Waldron, *The Great Wall of China: from History to Myth* (Cambridge, England, 1990).

[41] Phillips, pp.59–61, 96, 116, 192; Wright, op. cit., pp.74, 272, 275–9; P.W. Brown, *The Indian Christians of St. Thomas* (Cambridge, 1956).

[42] For the literature on Prester John, see fn 14 above.

[43] Phillips, pp.60–2, 77–82, 117, 151–3, 161, 184, 191–4, 200, 209, 227, 246, 251–3, 258.

[44] A leader of Mongol descent did, however, create the Mughal empire in India in the early sixteenth century. See D.O. Morgan, *The Mongols*, ch.8, "What became of the Mongols?"

[45] Phillips, pp.96–100, 109–10.

[46] Phillips, pp.194–5, 201–2; *Cathay and the Way Thither*, vol. III, ed. H. Yule, Hakluyt Society, Second Series, 37 (London, 1914; repr. Nendeln, 1967), pp.232–5, 254–61.

cripta,[47] whereas one of the most elaborately illuminated manuscripts of the account of Marco Polo's travels begins as follows:

> Ci commence li livres du graunt Caam qui parole de la graunt Ermenie de Persse et des Tartares et dynde, et des granz merveilles qui par le monde sont.[48]

To Europeans, the reality of the extreme climate of India, the strange plants and animals, and the customs of its peoples were genuine sources of wonder, and it is likely that their written accounts and the fictional ones, such as *The Travels of Sir John Mandeville* and the *Itineraries* of Johannes Witte of Hese (1389), which were based upon them, succeeded all too well in reinforcing the old stereotypes about the East.[49]

By contrast, European understanding of the region of east Asia, which we think of as China, was transformed in the thirteenth and fourteenth centuries. In this case there was very little classical precedent to go on, beyond the vague references to the land of the Seres. China was in some ways superficially familiar to a European traveler from the Mediterranean: In both there were great cities, extensive commerce by land and sea, and a highly organized money economy; Christianity existed and was tolerated. It is not surprising, for example, that the city of Kinsai, with its many canals and bridges, should seem very like Venice both in Rustichello of Pisa's version of Marco Polo's travels and in Italo Calvino's modern act of imagination, or that Marco Polo should compare the trade of the port of Zayton with that of Alexandria. But there the comparisons ended.[50] Everything about China was on a scale unknown in Europe: If Zayton were comparable with Alexandria, its trade according to Marco Polo was a hun-

[47] *Mirabilia Descripta: The Wonders of the East by Friar Jordanus*, ed. H. Yule, Hakluyt Society (London, 1863).

[48] Bodleian Library, Oxford, Bodley Ms. 264, f.218r. The illuminators of manuscripts sometimes added wonders that were not in the text: see R. Wittkower, "Marco Polo and the pictorial tradition of the wonders of the East," in *Oriente Poliano* (Rome, 1957).

[49] The literary phenomenon of the imaginary journey has been studied by a number of scholars: see, for example, J.K. Hyde, "Real and imaginary journeys in the later Middle Ages," *Bulletin of the John Rylands Library*, 65 (1982–3), pp.125–47; J. Richard, "Voyages réels et voyages imaginaires, instruments de la connaissance géographique au moyen âge," in *Culture et travail intellectuel dans l'Occident médiéval*, ed. G. Hasenohr & J. Longère (Paris, 1981); J. Richard, *Les récits de voyages et de pèlerinages*, Typologie des sources du moyen âge, ed. L. Genicot, Fascicle XXXVIII (Turnhout, 1981).

[50] Marco Polo, *The Travels*, pp.213–31; Italo Calvino, *Invisible Cities* (London, 1974), pp.68–9.

dred times more than that of the great Egyptian port; the money in circulation was not made of silver or gold but of paper stamped with the emperor's seal and was accepted without question; China was to outward appearances a land of peace and order, unlike Europe; the local languages were very strange to European ears and were rarely mastered by them; Christians were very much in the minority and many of them were heretical Nestorians, descended from converts made centuries before, who were often hostile to the missionaries from Rome. Nonetheless, Europeans were and remained deeply impressed: Nothing like China had been seen or imagined before.[51]

Although true on one level, this is also a deceptive account of medieval European relations with China. To begin with, Europeans who went to the Far East in the thirteenth or fourteenth centuries were in a sense not going to China at all but to a land that had recently been conquered by nomadic invaders from the north. China, which under normal conditions would have been largely closed to foreigners, was now accessible to outsiders from other parts of Asia and from Europe whose services were needed by the ruling Mongols and who were more trustworthy than their Chinese subjects.[52] The "real China" was therefore temporarily in suspense during the rule of the Mongol Great Khans of the Yüan dynasty between 1272 and 1368. Second, China was known in medieval Europe as "the land of Cathay" and the great city of Peking/Beijing as Cambaluc (from the Turkish words "Khanbalik":"City of the Khan"). Strictly speaking, "Cathay" referred to

[51] Phillips, pp.87–92, 115–19; J. Heers, *Marco Polo* (Paris, 1983); *Marco Polo and his Book: China and Europe in the Middle Ages:* Abstracts of papers delivered at the Second International Congress on Marco Polo, Venice, 1989 (published by University of New Hampshire, 1989); Marco Polo, *The Travels*, pp.40 (languages), 147–9 (paper money), 237 (Zayton). Paper money, which was remarked upon by many foreign visitors to China, was a system of currency inherited by the Mongols from their Chinese predecessors. Lack of knowledge of the local languages was a major problem for the European missionaries in China: see C. Dawson, *The Mission to Asia*, p.233. Marco Polo is said to have known four languages, but whether these included Chinese is not clear. On the early history of Christianity in China, see A.C. Moule, *Christians in China before the Year 1550* (London, 1930). The peacefulness of Mongol-ruled China was probably more apparent to later European travelers than it was to Marco Polo, since the latter arrived in China just as the Mongol conquest of the south was being completed. For a recent detailed study of medieval European conceptions of the "wonders of the East" and of actual travel in East Asia see F. E. Reichert, *Begegnung mit China: Die Entdeckung Ostasiens im Mittelalter* (Sigmaringen, 1992).

[52] For information on China under the Mongols, see especially D.O. Morgan, op.cit., ch. 5; I. de Rachewiltz, *Papal Envoys to the Great Khans* (London, 1971); *China under Mongol Rule*, ed. J.D. Langlois, Jr. (Princeton, 1981); *China among Equals: the Middle Kingdom and its Neighbors, 10th.-14th. Centuries*, ed. M. Rossabi (Berkeley, Los Angeles & London, 1983); M. Rossabi, *Khubilai Khan* (Berkeley, Los Angeles & London, 1988).

northern China, whereas southern China was known as "Manzi," but Cathay was the familiar and most commonly used word.[53] The name Cathay derived not from either the Chin or the Sung dynasties, which had ruled the north and south of China before the Mongol invasions, but from a people called the Khitans who had ruled Mongolia and northern China from the tenth to the early twelfth centuries. Their name had evidently survived the end of their rule in these regions, but it was also preserved in the empire of Kara Khitai, which had been founded in Central Asia in the twelfth century. The victory of their first emperor over the Turks near Samarkand in 1141 may have been one of the sources of the Prester John legend; more recently, in 1218, Kara Khitai had been destroyed by Ghenghis Khan in the course of his own empire building.[54]

The first European sources to refer to Cathay in a sense that clearly refers to northern China are the narratives composed in the late 1240s and in the mid-1250s by Carpini and Rubruck, both of whom wrote from information they had picked up at the court of the Great Khan in Mongolia. Rubruck was the first to realize that Cathay was probably the classical land of the Seres from which silk had come, and was followed in his conclusion by the Franciscan scholar Roger Bacon, who made use of Rubruck's writings in his *Opus Maius* composed soon after 1266.[55] Marco Polo's narrative of around 1300 is the first account of Cathay (and of Manzi as well) by a European traveler who had seen these countries at firsthand.[56] From then on, Cathay was a familiar part of all writings about the Far East, such as the *Flor des estoires de la terre d'orient* composed at the papal curia in 1307 by the exiled Armenian prince Hayton, the *Livre de l'estat du Grand Caan* written in 1330 by John of Cori, the Dominican Archbishop of Sultaniyeh in Iran, as well as those of Odoric of Pordenone in 1330 and John of Marignolli in the 1350s.[57] Cathay also bulked large in the highly imag-

[53] Morgan, op. cit., pp.48, 63, 196. To confuse matters further, the official name for the Mongol capital was "Ta-tu" rather than "Khan-balik": Morgan, p.123.

[54] Morgan, op. cit., pp.47–50, 108–9, 123.

[55] C. Dawson, ed., *The Mission to Asia*, pp.21–2, 42, 62, 64, 121–2, 143–4, 184; *The Opus Maius of Roger Bacon*, trans. R.B. Burke (New York, 1962), vol. I, pp.387–8.

[56] Marco Polo, *The Travels*, passim.

[57] There is an extract from Hayton's work in H. Yule, ed., *Cathay and the Way Thither*, vol. I, Hakluyt Society, Second Series, 38 (London, 1915), pp.260–2 (the full text is published in *Recueil des Historiens des Croisades, Documents Arméniens*, II (Paris, 1906)); the sixteenth-century English translation has been edited by G. Burger: *Hetoum: a Lytell Cronycle: Richard Pynson's Translation (c.1520) of La Fleur des Histoires de la terre d'Orient (c.1307)* (Toronto, 1988); for John of Cori (or Cora), see *Cathay & the Way Thither*, vol. III, Hakluyt Society, Second Series, 37 (London, 1914), pp.89–103; for

inative *Travels of Sir John Mandeville,* which was composed in either the 1350s or 1360s and then circulated widely in manuscript in many European languages.[58]

By the time *Mandeville's Travels* was written, Mongol rule in China was near its end but it and other popular works like Marco Polo's *Travels* ensured that just as the name Khitai had survived the demise of its original owners in the early thirteenth century, so "Cathay" and its ruler the "Great Khan" survived the ejection of the Mongols from China in 1368. "Cathay" was given a further lease of life by its inclusion in maps, such as the famous Catalan World Atlas of about 1375, which is still preserved in Paris, or the world map of Fra Mauro of Venice, which was made for the Portuguese in 1459,[59] and by the appearance of Mandeville and Marco Polo in printed editions from the early 1480s.[60] No European is known to have been to China in the fifteenth century, but the Castilian ambassador Clavijo who visited the court of the new Mongol conqueror, Tamerlane, at Samarkand between 1403 and 1406 was there at the same time as a Chinese envoy and probably learnt something about current conditions,[61] and the Venetian traveler Nicolo Conti included a description of Cathay in an account of his travels after he returned to Europe in 1444.[62]

Given the continuing European fascination with Cathay, it is hardly surprising that someone as suggestible as Christopher Columbus should become obsessed by it in his turn. What is more interesting is that "Cathay" survived even the discovery of America. Whereas India became increasingly familiar to Europeans in the sixteenth century,

Odoric of Pordenone see ibid., vol. II, Hakluyt Society, Second Series, 33 (London, 1913); and for John of Marignolli see ibid., vol. III, pp.213–16.

58 *The Travels of Sir John Mandeville,* ed. C.W.R.D. Moseley (London, 1983), pp.137–60. There are several other available editions. For the diffusion of Mandeville in manuscript and in printed editions, see C. Deluz, *Le Livre de Jehan de Mandeville: une "Géographie" au XIVe siècle,* Annexe V, pp.416–21. For a discussion of the problem of authorship see J.R.S. Phillips, "The quest for Sir John Mandeville," in *The Culture of Christendom: Studies in Medieval History in Memory of Denis L. T. Bethell,* ed. M. A. Meyer (London, 1993).

59 Phillips, *Medieval Expansion of Europe,* pp.220–2; *Cathay and the Way Thither,* vol. I, pp.299–302; there is an excellent facsimile reproduction of the Catalan map in *Mapamundi: The Catalan World Atlas of the Year 1375,* ed. G. Grosjean (Zürich, 1975).

60 *Mandeville's Travels,* for example, was published in German, French, and Latin editions between 1478 and 1483.

61 *Narrative of the Embassy of Ruy Gonzalez de Clavijo to the Court of Timour at Samarcand, A.D. 1403–6,* ed. C.R. Markham, Hakluyt Society, First Series, 26 (London, 1859; repr. New York, 1970), pp.171–4; M. Rossabi, *China and Inner Asia from 1368 to the Present Day* (London, 1975), pp.13–17, 61–2.

62 *Cathay and the Way Thither,* vol. I, pp.266–7; for other fifteenth-century references to "Cathay" by Toscanelli and Barbaro, see ibid., pp.267–70.

Cathay remained a mystery. It was suspected by the Jesuit missionaries who entered China from the sea at the end of the century that this was the country recorded in earlier European writings, but proof did not become available until 1606 when the Portuguese Jesuit Benedict Goes completed a four-year journey from India and was met by a colleague from Peking just before he died at Suchow.[63] Even then, some people were not convinced: As late as 1682 an edition of Peter Heylyn's *Cosmography* "assumed that there was still a Great Cham ruling over Cathay from a city called 'Cambalu,' although it admitted that nothing had been heard of him for over a hundred years"; and *Mandeville's Travels* was reprinted ten times in English alone in the late seventeenth and early eighteenth centuries.[64]

Meanwhile, in America the very vastness and intractability of much of the continent led to hopes of discovering a way round it or a short cut through it to the East. Of the fifty-two expeditions sent out by the French in Canada between 1603 and 1751, no less than half had the East as at least one of their objectives. Jean Nicolet dressed in robes of Chinese silk, standing on the western shore of Lake Michigan in 1634 in the hope that he would meet a representative of the Great Khan, is symbolic of the whole European involvement with the East since classical times.[65] Distant "Cathay," like "India" before it, had become firmly embedded in the European imagination, and in a curious fashion the "western" and "eastern" views had come full circle, to meet in the heart of the New World.

III. PEOPLES

In July 1241, three months after the great battles of Liegnitz and Mohi in which the latest and one of the most ferocious invaders of Europe, the nomadic Mongols, had destroyed the armies of Poland and Hun-

[63] B. Penrose, *Travel and Discovery in the Renaissance, 1420–1620* (Cambridge, Mass., 1952; repr. New York, 1962), pp.268–70; *Cathay and the Way Thither*, vol. IV, Hakluyt Society, Second Series, 41 (London, 1916), pp.x–xii, 169–259.

[64] P.J. Marshall & G. Williams, *The Great Map of Mankind*, pp.8–9, citing Heylyn, Book 3, p.204; Peter Heylyn (1599-1662), first published his book in London in 1652 under the title, *Cosmographie: Foure Bookes contayning the Chorographie and Historie of the Whole World, and All its Principall Kingdoms, Provinces, Seas and Isles Thereof*. Although Heylyn had a section on Cathay in Book 3 of his work (pp.185-205), he was aware that there was some distinction to be drawn between "Cathay" (in the north) and the rest of China and also included a section on the latter in Book 3, pp.206–12.

[65] *Historical Atlas of Canada*, vol. I, *From the Beginning to 1800*, ed. R. Cole Harris (Toronto, 1987), Plate 36; Phillips, p.259.

gary and their German allies,[66] Emperor Frederick II of Hohenstaufen wrote to Henry III of England and to his fellow sovereigns recounting the horrors of the Mongol attack and appealing for aid to resist their expected advance into western Europe. In doing so, the Emperor listed the military virtues of the countries of Europe – from Germany, *furens ac fervens ad arma,* France, *strenuae militiae genitrix et alumpna,* Spain, *bellicosa et audax,* and England, *virtuosa viris et classe munita,* through Denmark, Italy, Burgundy, and Apulia, and ending with the nations bounding the western ocean, which he dismissed merely as *cruenta Hibernia, cum agili Wallia, palustris Scotia, glacialis Norwegia.*[67] The language employed is highly rhetorical and the descriptions of the various peoples of Europe are restricted to their supposed fighting abilities, but the letter is nonetheless of considerable interest, because it suggests that there was a perceived pecking order among the nations of thirteenth-century Europe, while at the same time it also firmly opposes Europeans to a group of outsiders who are both alien and terrifying. The Emperor's letter is in fact but one illustration of the forms of ethnographic description that were current in medieval Europe. Some were the product of classical theories and perceptions whereas others were Christian in inspiration; but these did not exist in a vacuum, and were also influenced by specific situations both within and outside Europe in which peoples of different cultural, religious, and political traditions came into contact or into conflict and were forced to develop at the very least some practical working explanation or justification or narrative to describe their relations with one another.[68]

[66] For a general account of these dramatic events, see Phillips, ch. 4, "Europe and the Mongol invasions"; but see also D.O. Morgan, *The Mongols,* ch. 6; J.J. Saunders, *The History of the Mongol Conquests* (London, 1971).

[67] Matthew Paris, *Chronica Majora,* ed. H.R. Luard (Rolls Series), vol.IV, pp.270–7 (this letter forms part of a collection of documents on the Mongol invasions that was made by Matthew Paris); for the historical context, see P. Jackson, "The Crusade against the Mongols (1241)," *The Journal of Ecclesiastical History,* vol. 42, No. 1, January 1991, pp.1–18.

[68] I am attempting to avoid overprecise definition here. However, I am in agreement with Anthony Pagden's argument that the "Cartesian belief in the fundamental innocence of the observer's eye" cannot be sustained and that "observers of anything ultimately unfamiliar for which there exist few readily available antecedents had to be able to classify *before* they could properly see, and in order to classify in any meaningful sense they had no alternative but to appeal to a system that was already in use": *The Fall of Natural Man* (Cambridge, 1982), p.2. My only disagreement with this excellent book is that while it gives full treatment to medieval theoretical precedents drawn from Aristotle and Aquinas, it does not take sufficient account of the complexity and variety of medieval experience–for example, the relations between Christian and heathen in the Baltic lands or between English Christians and Irish Christians in Ireland.

Theories about the origins and distribution of the earth's peoples owed much both to classical and Christian ideas. The traditional classical division of the world into the three continents of Asia, Africa, and Europe was given new meaning by the story in the Book of Genesis of the peopling of the earth by the sons of Noah, Shem, Japheth, and Ham. By the seventh century this idea had been developed to the point at which

> Europe was the land of Japheth, of the Gentiles, the Greeks, and the Christians; Asia was the land of Semitic peoples, glorious in that they had produced the patriarchs and prophets, the chosen people and Christ himself; but – as the land of the circumcised adherents of older laws – condemned to an inferiority which was stated in the scriptures. . . . . . . As for Africa, the lot of the unhappy descendants of Ham, the Hamitic subjection was equally clearly laid down: Canaan was to be the servant both of Shem and Japheth.[69]

This distribution clearly implied the preeminence of Europe and its peoples over those of the other two continents and might have become a powerful idea in itself if "Europe" had not been overlaid so deeply for much of the medieval period by "Christendom." Although the whole world was visibly not Christian in allegiance, it was firmly believed that the world had been divided up and preached to by the immediate followers of Christ.[70] This idea was sometimes shown in pictorial form in the symbolic world maps that accompanied the commentary on the *Apocalypse* by the eighth-century Spanish monk Beatus. However, from the time of the papal reform in the eleventh century, the papacy saw itself as the leader of Christendom, which claimed in effect a superiority for Europe over the rest of the world, and which was given practical material effect in 1099 through the consummation of the Crusader[71] movement in the capture of Jerusalem.

European superiority was also implied in the belief that civilization had gradually moved westward after its beginnings in the East, but that when it reached the uttermost limits of the West the human race would meet its doom and extinction. This idea has been traced through Christian writings from Severian of Gabala in the fourth century to Hugh of St. Victor and the German bishop and historian Otto of Freising in the twelfth. In the prologue to his *Chronicon*, Otto remarked,

[69] D. Hay, *Europe: the Emergence of an Idea* (Edinburgh, 1957), ch. I and especially p.14; Friedman, p.39.
[70] Hay, pp.27–36, 40.
[71] Hay, pp.34–42.

What great learning there was in Egypt and among the Chaldeans, from whom Abraham derived his knowledge! But what now is Babylon, once famous for its science and its power? . . . . . . And Egypt is now in large part a trackless waste, whence science was transferred to the Greeks, then to the Romans, and finally to the Gauls and Spaniards. And let it be observed that because all human learning began in the Orient and will end in the Occident, the mutability and disappearance of all things is demonstrated.[72]

The effect of environment on the characteristics of peoples was another theme with a classical origin that was taken up by medieval writers. Aristotle, for example, had remarked that

those who live in a cold climate and in Europe are full of spirit, but wanting in intelligence and skill; and therefore they keep their freedom but have no political organization, and are incapable of ruling over others. Whereas the natives of Asia are intelligent and inventive, but they are wanting in spirit, and therefore they are always in a state of subjection and slavery. But the Hellenic race, which is situated between them, is likewise intermediate in character, being high-spirited and also intelligent.[73]

In the seventh century A.D., Isidore of Seville wrote that "In keeping with the difference in climate, the looks of men, their color, and their stature vary, and different dispositions appear. Consequently, the Romans are stately, Greeks shifty, Africans sneaky, Gauls warlike by nature and plunge into things, all because the climates they live in differ."[74] The thirteenth-century English scholar Roger Bacon noted, for example, in his *Opus Maius* that according to classical sources the Hyperboreans who lived in the far north were "a very happy race, which dies only from satiety of life" and that Claudius Ptolemy was correct in supposing "that nature requires that there be two races of Ethiopians (i.e. black people)," one on either side of the equator.[75] Bacon's contemporary, the German Dominican Albertus Magnus, had a considerable amount to say on the subject in his *De Natura Locorum.* He argued that people born in the hottest places were very hot themselves and became "wrinkled like pepper seeds from too much dryness," whereas the black color of their skin was the result of the thinner parts of the semen boiling away in the womb. People living

[72] J.K. Wright, *The Geographical Lore of the Time of the Crusades*, pp.233–5; cf. Hay, op. cit., p.51; see also C.J. Glacken, *Traces on the Rhodian Shore: Nature and Culture in Western Thought from Ancient Times to the End of the Eighteenth Century* (Berkeley and Los Angeles, 1967), pp.276-82.

[73] Quoted in Hay, p.5; see also p.33.

[74] Friedman, pp.39, 43.

[75] Roger Bacon, *Opus Maius*, tr. R.B. Burke (New York, 1928; repr. New York, 1962), vol. I, pp.325, 327.

in the regions of great heat, like the Ethiopians and Indians, were "quick-witted in invention and outstanding in philosophy and magic." On the other hand, people living in areas of cold were white "because of the cold which constricts the blood"; they were energetic but "dull-witted and untutored," although "they could be aroused to better things by study." The peoples of temperate climates however, existed under ideal conditions. They lived to old age, their works "as natural as they are spirited," were most praiseworthy and they had good customs. The temperate people "live easily among themselves, practice justice, keep their word, respect peace and the society of men."[76]

One of the best known and typically "medieval" forms of ethnography is the belief in monstrous races of men who "were always far away, in India, Ethiopia, Albania, or Cathay, places whose outlines were vague to the medieval mind but whose names evoked mystery."[77] As is well known, the monstrous races were originally another aspect of the fascination of the classical world with the wonders of the East. Altogether about forty such races have been identified in the writings of Greek and Roman authors from Ctesias in the late fifth century B.C. to Pliny the Elder in the first century A.D.: They include such beings as *Amazons* ("without breast"), *Anthropophagi* ("man-eaters"), *Antipodes* ("opposite-footed": supposedly people living on the opposite side of the world), *Blemmyae* ("headless men"), *Cynocephali* ("dog-head"), *Ethiopians* ("burnt face"), and so on.[78] J.B. Friedman has pointed out in his remarkable study of the monstrous races that many of them were not monstrous at all in the sense of being anomalous and deformed births. "They simply differed in physical appearance and social practices from the person describing them. Some took their names from their manner of life, such as the Apple-Smellers, or the Troglodytes who dwelt in caves; some were physically unusual but not anomalous, such as the Pygmies or Giants; and some were truly fabulous, such as the Blemmyae or men with faces on their chests. Even the most bizarre, however, were not supernatural or infernal creatures, but varieties of men, whose chief distinction from the men of Europe was one of geography."[79] Some of the "monstrous

[76] This passage is a paraphrase and quotation of Glacken, pp.267–9; see also ibid., chapter 6, "Environmental influences within a divinely created world," and Friedman, pp.51–3.
[77] Friedman, p.1.
[78] Friedman, ch. 1, 'The Plinian races', especially pp.5–22.
[79] Ibid, pp.1, 3.

races" are clearly the result of attempts to describe the unfamiliar: it has been suggested, for example, that the *cynocephali*, who are one of the most frequently met with, may be derived from hirsute-faced human beings or from cynocephalic monkeys, or from sightings of men dressed in animal skins.[80] It has also been argued that the monstrous races were the result of a form of xenophobia,[81] but this argument is weakened by the fact that the monstrous races usually seem to have been located in distant places in which they posed no immediate threat. It is interesting, however, to discover that many of the monstrous races known to classical writers also appear in Chinese sources, such as the work known as the *Shan Hai Ching* ("Classic of the Mountains and Rivers," 6th century B.C. to 1st century A.D.), which contains, for example, a lively illustration of a "headless man" brandishing an axe in his hand. Various explanations for this coincidence have been put forward, but none that is wholly satisfactory. Whatever the reason, it is apparent that for the Chinese the "wonders of the East" were instead the "marvels of the West."[82]

With the Christian gloss that they were the children of Cain, who had been sentenced to deformity and exile as punishment for their ancestor's sin,[83] the monstrous races passed into the medieval European imagination along with other aspects of the East, and they are to be found regularly in works of scholarship, cartography, and literature. In the early thirteenth century, Jacques de Vitry, the bishop of Acre in the kingdom of Jerusalem, described the monstrous races in his *Historia Orientalis* as if they were among the inhabitants of the Holy Land; the Ebstorf *mappa mundi* of c.1240 contained twenty-four of the races and the Hereford map of c.1300 includes a total of twenty.[84] The author of the mid-fourteenth-century *Travels of Sir John Mandeville* peopled some of the many islands in the East with dog-headed men, one-eyed giants, headless men, men who sheltered from the sun beneath their enormous upper lip, and beings with the genitals of both sexes, and Johannes Witte of Hese, who set out for Jeru-

[80] Needham, vol. III, p.507; Friedman, p.15.

[81] Needham, vol. III, p.507. Some of the races may also represent the projection of subconscious fears of the observers, but that perhaps is to get into too deep psychological waters.

[82] Needham, vol.III, pp.503–7 (see illustration on p.506).

[83] See Friedman, ch. 5, "Cain's kin."

[84] Friedman, pp.42,46,77. On the Hereford *mappa mundi* see M. Letts, *The Pictures in the Hereford Mappa Mundi* (8th.edition, Hereford, 1979); M. Jancey, *Mappa Mundi* (Hereford, 1987). On *mappaemundi* in general see the chapter in J.B. Harley & D. Woodward, ed., *History of Cartography*, vol.1.

salem in 1389, and claimed to have visited both Purgatory and Paradise, also "found" many of the monstrous races along his way.[85] On the other hand, a number of the European travelers in Asia in the thirteenth and fourteenth centuries expressed great skepticism about them. Although Marco Polo claimed that the Andaman islanders were as fierce as mastiffs and had heads like dogs, he also noted that some of the inhabitants of the island of Java tried to deceive unsuspecting travelers by claiming that the dried and shriveled bodies of monkeys were those of pygmies. John of Marignolli, for example, concluded that "no such peoples do exist as nations, though there may be an individual monster here and there," and also argued that the Indian use of parasols to keep off the sun was the origin of the *sciapods*, who were said to shade themselves with their one large foot. To prove his point he even took a parasol back with him to Florence.[86]

Almost by definition, the monstrous races existed in distant and inaccessible parts of the world and usually seemed to recede into every greater obscurity whenever any outsider went in search of them. However, on a few occasions they came closer to home. One example is that of the "wild man," who appears in various eastern forms in classical and medieval literature, but who also had a place within European traditions and folklore. He was "a hairy man compounded of human and animal traits, without, however, sinking to the level of an ape," who was particularly to be found in remote places in the mountains and forests of many parts of Europe. He was an ambiguous figure, often regarded as threatening to normal human beings, and with strongly erotic associations, but sometimes seen as a benevolent creature whose behavior could provide useful moral lessons for civilized humanity, becoming in the process a prototype "noble savage."[87] Another group of savages who were anything but noble were the tribes of Gog and Magog, whose escape from captivity behind Alexander's Gate somewhere in the East would herald the ending of the world.[88] It was naturally hoped that the tribes would stay there indefinitely, but it was almost inevitable when the Mongols appeared

[85] *The Travels of Sir John Mandeville*, ed. Moseley, pp.134–7; Friedman, p.143. For the marvels included in Mandeville and their geographical distribution, see C. Deluz, Annexe IV, pp.402–15.

[86] Phillips, pp.78, 94–5; C. Dawson, *The Mission to Asia*, p.170; Marco Polo, *The Travels*, pp.258, 253–4; *Cathay and the Way Thither*, vol. III, pp.254–6.

[87] Friedman, pp.15–16, 200–7 & Ch. 8, "Monstrous men as noble savages," especially pp.104–7; R. Bernheimer, *Wild Men in the Middle Ages: a Study in Art, Sentiment and Demonology* (Cambridge, Mass., 1952; repr. New York, 1970), p.1. Both these books contain illustrations of "wild men."

[88] On Gog and Magog, see fn 40.

in the 1240s from the prophesied direction, with little warning and without any indication of their true identity, that many Europeans should be influenced in their descriptions of the invaders by existing ideas of the monstrous races and their supposed characteristics, and so identify them with Gog and Magog.[89]

Recent work on the chronicles composed by writers such as Thomas of Spalato in Dalmatia who experienced the Mongol attacks at first hand has shown that although they contain ample evidence of the destruction caused by the Mongols, they do not present an apocalyptic interpretation of these events.[90] It has also been demonstrated that some of the best known material on the Mongols, particularly that recorded by Matthew Paris in England, far from the scene of events, was probably edited to produce a more dramatic effect.[91] But whether edited or not, a dramatic effect was achieved. The Mongols were commonly referred to as "Tartars," with the implication of infernal origins; some writers claimed that (like the *anthropophagi*) the Mongols indulged in cannibalism, and Matthew Paris even included a drawing of them committing this atrocity.[92]

The Mongols could also readily be identified with another form of

[89] C.W. Connell, "Western views of the origin of the 'Tartars': an example of the influence of myth in the second half of the thirteenth century," *Journal of Medieval and Renaissance Studies*, 3 (1973), pp.126–33.

[90] Connell, pp.126–7; James Ross Sweeney, "Thomas of Spalato and the Mongols: a thirteenth-century Dalmatian view," *Florilegium*, 4 (1982), Carleton University Annual papers on Classical Antiquity and the Middle Ages, pp.156–8, 163–71; the text of Thomas of Spalato's chronicle is published in *Der Mongolensturm: Berichte von Augenzeugen und Zeitgenossen, 1235–1250*, ed. H. Göckenjan & J.R. Sweeney (Graz, Vienna & Cologne, 1985), vol. 3 in the series *Ungarns Geschichtsschreiber*, ed. T. von Bogyay.

[91] For details of the material recorded by Matthew Paris, see J.J. Saunders, "Matthew Paris and the Mongols," *Essays in Medieval History presented to Bertie Wilkinson*, ed. T.R. Sandquist & M.R. Powicke (Toronto, 1969). For critical remarks on Matthew Paris, see Sweeney, "Thomas of Spalato," pp.157, 172, nn.3,4; and P. Jackson, "The Crusade against the Mongols (1241)", pp.2, 8–9.

[92] Connell, pp.115, 117–18; W.R. Jones, "The image of the barbarian in medieval Europe," *Comparative Studies in Society and History*, 13 (1971), pp.399–400; J.A. Boyle, "The last barbarian invaders: the impact of the Mongol conquest upon East and West," *Memoirs and Proceedings of the Manchester Literary and Philosophical Society*, vol. 112 (1969–70), pp.5–8; G. Guzman, "Reports of Mongol cannibalism in the thirteenth-century Latin sources: Oriental fact or Western fiction?," in Westrem, ed., *Discovering New Worlds;* M.R. James, "The drawings of Matthew Paris," in *The Fourteenth Volume of the Walpole Society* (Oxford, 1925–6), pp.15–16 and drawings nos. 75, 86; see also the more recent work by Suzanne Lewis, *The Art of Matthew Paris in the Chronica Majora*, California Studies in the History of Art, 21 (Aldershot, 1987). It should however be pointed out that the derivation of "Tartar" from "Tartarus," the classical Hell, was not universally argued by thirteenth-century writers and has been hotly debated by modern scholars: see J.R. Sweeney, "Thomas of Spalato," pp.177–8. On the other hand, whatever the origin of the name, it probably produced the appropriate "infernal" effect on many of those who read accounts of the Mongol invasions.

ethnography, the image of the barbarian, which was a familiar concept in antiquity in regions as far apart as Greece, India, and China. The barbarian was distinguished by such features as his lack of an ordered urban or rural existence, his inability to manufacture and to employ the material artefacts of more advanced civilizations, and by the absence of a sophisticated spoken and written literary culture.[93] Barbarism was, needless to say, in the eye (and in the mind) of the beholder and was particularly ascribed by the members of settled civilizations to neighbors whose way of life was conspicuously different from the accepted norms. When the "barbarian" was not simply someone of a different culture but was also perceived as a threat, the idea became a very emotive one.[94] The image of the barbarian outlived the classical world that had given birth to it. For the descendants of the former barbarians who took over the western Roman provinces in the fifth and sixth centuries A.D. and became partly Romanized in the process, there were other peoples living beyond the new frontiers who could now be classified as barbarians. But barbarism was also redefined to make adherence to paganism or to a Christian heresy rather than to Roman Christianity one of the most significant distinguishing marks. By these criteria the unconverted Slavs, Germans, Magyars, and Scandinavians were obvious barbarians, especially if like the latter two they were also a cause of terror and devastation to Christian Europe.[95] In this guise the barbarian was bequeathed by classical antiquity to medieval Europe.

The medieval European idea of the barbarian can also be understood more clearly through the modern concept of the "core and periphery," as expressed in the relations between areas like Anglo-Norman England and Germany on the one hand, which considered themselves as the natural repositories of civilization, and on the other the societies with which they came into contact and sought to dominate, Wales and Ireland to the west and the Baltic lands and the Slav territories beyond the Elbe to the east.[96] The perceived contrast be-

[93] Based on the definition of "barbarian" given in W.R. Jones, "The image of the barbarian in medieval Europe," *Comparative Studies in Society and History*, 13 (1971), p.376. This is a very important paper to which I am much indebted for this paragraph. See also A. Pagden, *The Fall of Natural Man*, ch. 2, "The image of the barbarian."

[94] Jones, pp.377–8.

[95] Jones, pp.385–8.

[96] This idea is very well expressed in A. Simms, "Core and periphery in medieval Europe: the Irish experience in a wider context," in *Common Ground: Essays on the Historical Geography of Ireland presented to T. Jones Hughes*, ed. W.J. Smyth and K. Whelan (Cork, 1988), p.22; see also the very important collection of essays in *Medieval*

tween the core and periphery is clearly stated in a much-quoted passage about the Irish by the twelfth-century historian Gerald de Barri, better known as Giraldus Cambrensis because of his shared Norman and Welsh ancestry:

> The Irish are a rude people, subsisting on the produce of their cattle only, and living themselves like beasts – a people that has not yet departed from the primitive habits of pastoral life. In the common course of things, mankind progresses from the forest to the field, from the field to the town, and to the social condition of citizens; but this nation, holding agricultural labour in contempt, and little coveting the wealth of towns, as well as being exceedingly averse to civil institutions – lead the same life their fathers did in the woods and open pastures, neither willing to abandon their old habits or learn anything new.[97]

Gerald's remarks are typical of many that could be cited from twelfth- and thirteenth-century English and German authors about the inhabitants of the European periphery. Their pastoral existence was contrasted unfavorably with that of the settled "normal" societies; the richness of their land and their supposed failure to put it to proper agricultural use were stressed; and for good measure they were regularly accused of "ferocity, cruelty, and bloodthirstiness" and "faithlessness and disregard for good laws and customs." Otto of Freising spoke for many of his contemporaries when he said of the Hungarians: "Fortune is rightly to be blamed or, rather, the divine patience is to be wondered at, which exposed a land as delectable as this to such, not men, but human monsters."[98] Clearly such debased and degraded peoples as these were fit only for conquest, and all the more so if religion or the lack of it could be used in further justification. This was the case, for example, in 1155 when Pope Adrian IV was induced to send his famous bull *Laudabiliter* to Henry II of England urging him as a Catholic prince to go to Ireland "to enlarge the boundaries of the church, to reveal the truth of the Christian faith to unlearned and savage peoples, and to root out from the Lord's field the vices that grow in it." Despite the recent reforms in the Irish Church that were bringing it into line with the new standards of organization and au-

Frontier Societies, ed. R. Bartlett & A. Mackay (Oxford, 1989); and R. Bartlett, *Gerald of Wales, 1146–1223* (Oxford, 1982), especially ch. 6, "The face of the barbarian."

97 Cited in Glacken, p.281; Simms, p.24.

98 Bartlett, pp.158–65; Simms, p.24. See also R.C. Hoffman, "Outsiders by birth and blood: racist ideologies and realities around the periphery of Europe," *Studies in Medieval and Renaissance History*, n.s. 6 (Vancouver, 1983); W.R. Jones, "England and the Celtic fringe: a study in cultural stereotypes," *Journal of World History*, 13 (1971), pp.155–71.

thority elsewhere in Europe, the core's view of the periphery (the core in this instance being probably the Church of Canterbury) had its customary effect.[99]

Where the objects of hostility were heathens the need to convert them to Christianity was an additional argument for intervention. From the time of the expedition against the Wends in 1147 until the final conversion of Lithuania in 1386, a series of Crusades was fought against them and other Baltic peoples. The question regularly arose as to whether conversion could properly be carried out by force. The papacy regularly stated that it could not, but this made little difference to the brutality of the eastern campaigns.[100] A twelfth-century bishop of Lübeck once "explained to the Slavs that he was not surprised that the Saxon princes had treated them badly because it was generally believed that it was not a serious sin to maltreat heathen, and in their own interests he encouraged them to convert to Christianity."[101] In the late thirteenth century an anonymous writer in Bohemia remarked: "May God deign to listen and reveal to his Christian people a Czech king such as he (Alexander the Great); I hope that before long the Latvians, Tartars, Turks, Prussians and the schismatic Russians will experience such terror that they will adopt the Christian faith and relinquish their idols."[102]

The fact that these words were written by a member of a Slav people (albeit one that had been converted three centuries earlier) is a sign that the periphery could fight back, verbally at least. In 1282, for example, the Welsh princes protested to the Archbishop of Canterbury that the English had failed to keep treaties, had devastated and burnt churches, and had slaughtered priests, monks, and nuns, as well as women and children at the breast.[103] In the early fourteenth century, when Edward I of England was trying to conquer Scotland, both the English and the Scots attempted to convince the papacy of the justice of their cause by presenting rival versions of mythical history, one employing the widely used Trojan legend while the other went one

[99] On *Laudabiliter*, see M.T. Flanagan, *Irish Society, Anglo-Norman Settlers, Angevin Kingship: Interaction in Ireland in the Late Twelfth Century* (Oxford, 1989), pp.7–8, 52–4, 277–8.

[100] The standard work on these conquests is E. Christiansen, *The Northern Crusade: the Baltic and the Catholic Frontier of Christendom, 1100–1525* (London, 1980), especially chs. 5, "The theocratic experiment, 1200–73," 6, "The interminable crusade, 1283–1410." See also R. Bartlett, "The conversion of a pagan society in the Middle Ages," *History*, 70 (1985), pp.185–201; J. Muldoon, *Popes, Lawyers and Infidels: the Church and the Non-Christian World, 1250-1550* (Liverpool, 1979).

[101] A. Simms, p.24, citing the chronicler Helmold of Bosau.

[102] A. Thomas, "Czech-German relations," in *Medieval Frontier Societies*, p.203.

[103] D. Douie, *Archbishop Pecham* (Oxford, 1952), pp.238–40.

better and claimed descent from ancient Egypt; in 1317 the Irish tried the same approach in a document that was also filled with examples of alleged English injustice and villainy since the time of Henry II.[104]

Usually such complaints had little or no practical effect: Wales was conquered and Ireland remained under a kind of English rule. However, a hundred years later an impassioned debate took place at the Council of Constance in which the Teutonic Knights were accused of unjustly attacking the newly converted Lithuanians. The Lithuanians won their case.[105] The last barbarians had finally been absorbed. In future, Europe would have to look for them elsewhere.

IV. CONCLUSION

Medieval Europeans had acquired a very varied experience of the world and of its peoples well before the opening of the New World by Columbus and his successors. In a few rare instances, notably Iceland, they found and settled lands that were empty of people or, like Greenland, were so vast that for most practical purposes they were unoccupied. In North America they also found a land of vast potential, but of which they learned little and which was moreover already settled by a people to whom the Vikings referred as "wretches" (*skraelings*) who were almost certainly the "Indians" encountered by a later generation of European explorers. The *skraelings* conformed to the image of the barbarian but they had a local superiority in numbers that helped to prevent any permanent European settlement on this occasion. Geographical distance from home bases was another factor both in the failure of settlement in North America and in the final disappearance of the Greenland colony in the fifteenth century. In the latter case, climatic change and southward migration by the native *inuit*, another candidate for the status of barbarian, were also responsible. But so too was the failure of the European settlers to adapt their way of life to local conditions by making full use of the rich fishing grounds around Greenland. Like some of the earliest English settlers in Virginia, they may in effect have "starved in the midst of plenty."[106]

[104] J.R.S. Phillips, "The Irish Remonstrance of 1317: an international perspective", *Irish Historical Studies*, vol. XXVII, no. 106, November 1990, pp.112–29; idem, "The Remonstrance revisited: England and Ireland in the early fourteenth century," in *Men, Women and War: Studies in War, Politics and Society, Historical Studies*, XVIII, ed. T.G. Fraser & K. Jeffrey (Belfast, 1993).

[105] Muldoon, pp.107–19, especially p. 118; Christiansen, pp.223–32.

[106] On North America, see Phillips, *The Medieval Expansion of Europe*, ch.9, but see also G. Jones, *The Norse Atlantic Saga* (2nd. edition, Oxford, 1986); E. Guralnick, ed., *Vikings in the West* (Chicago, 1982); L. Rey, ed., *Unveiling the Arctic* (Calgary & Fair-

In Asia, which was the continent most visited by medieval Europeans and that left the deepest impression on them, Europeans were rarely in a position of even local superiority. The merchants and missionaries who went to Iran, India, and China in the thirteenth and fourteenth centuries were few in number, surrounded by people of alien culture and dependent for their survival on the continued favor of the local rulers, who were themselves often foreign to these regions. No doubt partly because they were so dependent, European relations with the Mongols, who controlled much of Asia at this time, underwent a transformation. From being the almost supernatural bringers of doom, the Mongols became in European eyes benign and trustworthy and a potential ally against the world of Islam.[107] Marco Polo's idealization of Kubilai Khan is a good example of this change in outlook, only a generation or so after the latter's near relatives had sown terror in Europe.[108] The Mongols were almost "homogenized" and made safe for domestic use. There are examples of noble families in the city of Genoa naming their sons after the Mongol rulers of Iran with whom they did much diplomatic and commercial business, while in 1344 Edward III of England held a tournament at which the participants were dressed as Tartars. Only a few years before Columbus's first voyage of discovery, a citizen of Genoa bore the name Casano, possibly unaware that he was named after Ghazan Khan who ruled Iran at the end of the thirteenth century.[109] In the fourteenth century, female Tartar slaves were a common sight in the households of the great cities of northern Italy, and sometimes, as in the case of Gregorio Dati of Florence in 1391, had children by their masters.[110]

But the Mongols were only one aspect of European relations with Asia. There is no doubt that in the broadest sense European views of Asia were colored by a form of "orientalism," which was the result of the accumulated experiences and perceptions of both classical an-

banks, 1984). I have examined this and other situations involving the movement of populations of European origin in a forthcoming paper, "The medieval background," in *In Search of a Better World: Migration from Western Europe, 1500–1800*, ed. N. Canny (Oxford, 1994).

[107] Phillips, Part II, "Europe and Asia," especially ch. 7, "The lost alliance: European monarchs and Mongol 'crusaders.' "

[108] Marco Polo, *The Travels*, passim.

[109] Phillips, pp.109, 198; the information on "Casano" was obtained from the Italian Government travelling expedition on Christopher Columbus, Dublin, 1989.

[110] *Two Memoirs of Renaissance Florence: the Diaries of Buonaccorso Pitti and Gregorio Dati*, ed. G. Brucker (New York, 1967), p.112. On Tartar slaves, see I. Origo, "The domestic enemy: eastern slaves in Tuscany in the fourteenth and fifteenth centuries," *Speculum*, 30 (1955); and W.D. Phillips, *Slavery from Roman Times to the Early Transatlantic Trade* (Minneapolis, 1985), pp.97–106.

tiquity and medieval Europe. But, with the important exception of Moslems, this orientalism was not the product of an attitude of antagonism or superiority on the part of Europeans.[111] The wealth in goods and spices was well appreciated, as were the technical achievements of the land of Cathay in such things as porcelain manufacture and ship design. But the East was also seen as the abode of virtuous peoples whose conduct compared favorably with that of many Christians at home. Indian holy men, such as the Brahmans, were often described in this way. In 1247, after his return from Mongolia, the papal envoy, Giovanni di Piano Carpini, who was probably confused by reports of Chinese Buddhism, recorded that the people of Cathay "worship one God, they honor Our Lord Jesus Christ, and they believe in eternal life, but they are not baptized." Carpini also wrote with some admiration of the standards of honesty and justice of the Mongols in their dealings among themselves. It is also possible that one of the intentions of the author of *The Travels of Sir John Mandeville* in the fourteenth century was to draw a contrast between the corrupt state of Europe and the justice of the East.[112] As soon as the favorable conditions created by the Mongols changed, direct European contacts with Asia virtually ceased: Only on the periphery of the continent, on the shores of the Black Sea, and in Egypt did direct relations continue for any length of time. On the other hand, there was no doubt that Europeans were determined to resume relations with the East at the earliest opportunity.

For roughly two centuries, between 1099 and 1291, European colonists held a position of local dominance in Syria and Palestine in the crusader states of Antioch, Tripoli, and Jerusalem. But here their situation was complicated by the existence of neighboring Moslem powers that were frequently hostile and that in the end conquered the European enclaves. The society of the crusader states was itself very mixed. European settlers were few in number, being restricted to a select aristocracy, a small urban population of European origin, here and there a few peasant landholders, and a constantly changing contingent of merchants and pilgrims who visited the Holy Land but usually did not stay for long. The native population was a mixture of Moslems and Jews, who were viewed with the distrust reserved in medieval Europe for the "infidel," and Christians, whose allegiance

111 Cf. Edward W. Said, *Orientalism* (London, 1978); idem, "Orientalism revisited," in *Europe and its Others*, ed. F. Barker, P. Hulme, et al. (Colchester, 1984), vol. I.

112 Friedman, pp.167–70; C. Dawson, ed., *The Mission to Asia*, pp.21–2, 15–17 (Carpini also wrote extensively about the bad points of the Mongols' character); *The Travels of Sir John Mandeville*, ed. Moseley, pp.22–9.

and traditions did not endear them to Rome. Greatly outnumbering the colonists, these local communities were inferior to them in legal status and in practice there seems to have been little attempt to win their loyalty.[113] The attitude of the colonists was set from the first. In 1098 the conquerors of Antioch informed the pope: "We conquered the Turks and pagans, but we could not defeat the heretics, the Greeks, Armenians, Syrians, Jacobites" and hoped that "all the heresies, whatever they might be, you will eradicate and destroy by your authority and our valour."[114] There is no doubt that crusading as an ideal long outlived the crusader states and helped to inspire the European expansion at the end of the fifteenth century, but as possible examples of sympathetic understanding of complex cultural situations the European settlements in Syria and Palestine were poor precedents for the future.

In regions like Wales and in the Baltic lands, conquest and settlement were more complete and enduring; and a colonial population was also permanently established in Ireland, although the entire island was not conquered until the sixteenth century. In all of these cases there were fundamental differences in the status of colonists and of native peoples. In Ireland the natives were excluded from the English common law courts unless expressly granted the privilege; after 1284 the Welsh were allowed to retain their own civil law for cases involving property and inheritance although coming within the bounds of English criminal law.[115] But this was no concession on the part of the English monarch, who preserved only those parts of the Welsh legal system that were "just and reasonable" and consonant with "God and justice." In 1277, Edward I had gone even further and

[113] There is an enormous literature on the society of the crusader states. There is a summary of the general situation in Phillips, ch. 3, "Commerce and the crusades"; but for a more detailed treatment, the most recent work is *A History of the Crusades*, ed. K.M. Setton, vol. 5, *The Impact of the Crusades on the Near East*, ed. N.P. Zacour & H.W. Hazard (Madison & London, 1985), especially the section by Joshua Prawer, ch. 3, "The 'Minorities,' " and ch. 4, "The Franks." See also the important collection of essays, *Muslims under Latin Rule, 1100–1300.*, ed. J.M. Powell (Princeton, 1990), which deals with the situation in the crusader states, the Iberian peninsula, and Sicily.

[114] *A History of the Crusades*, vol. 5, p.72.

[115] The relationship between England, Ireland, Scotland, and Wales in the medieval period can readily be approached through two important new books: R. Frame, *The Political Development of the British Isles, 1100–1400* (Oxford, 1990); R.R. Davies, *Domination and Conquest: the Experience of Ireland, Scotland and Wales, 1100–1300* (Cambridge, 1990); and also R.R. Davies, ed., *The British Isles, 1100–1500: Comparisons, Contrasts and Connections* (Edinburgh, 1988). On the Baltic lands the standard work is E. Christiansen, *The Northern Crusade: the Baltic and the Catholic Frontier of Christendom, 1100–1525* (London, 1980).

described native Irish law as "detestable to God . . . and not to be deemed laws."[116] In practice there was a much greater degree of coexistence in Wales and Ireland than would appear at first sight, but there were nonetheless accumulations of grievances that awaited only the right moment for expression in revolt.

The only part of Europe in which a relatively harmonious mixed society was created was in the Iberian peninsula, where the kingdoms on both the Moslem and Christian sides of the frontier contained mixed populations of Moslems, Christians, and Jews, and various intermediate groups resulting from conversion or from acculturation to one group or another. The traditional view of the history of the peninsula in the medieval period has been conditioned by the notion of the *reconquista*, the opposition between Christian and Moslem Spain, which was expressed in unending warfare until the final Christian victory over Granada in 1492. The conclusions of recent research, however, have suggested that those who did the fighting were as inclined to fight Christian opponents as they were Moslems and that the Christian expansion of the period down to about 1300 "was rather a conquest than a reconquest" and "was propelled by more earthy impulses than earlier and more fastidious scholars chose to contemplate: demographic pressure, climatic change, developing military technology, the needs of an emergent aristocratic elite, the appetites of sheep and cattle." The papacy's attempt to dignify this process by the name of crusade in the twelfth century was really the implanting of an alien concept, which took root only slowly.[117] In place of conflict, greater emphasis has been placed on the practical recognition through *convivencia* of the different religious and cultural traditions, on, for example, the pride of Alfonso VI of Castile in the late eleventh century "on being emperor of the two laws, Christianity and Islam," or on Alfonso X's ability in the thirteenth century to write poetry in Moslem verse forms.[118]

The intermingling of cultures is particularly well illustrated in the transmission of texts from Arabic to Latin in the twelfth century. When Peter the Venerable, the abbot of Cluny, visited Spain in 1142,

116 Davies, *Conquest, Coexistence and Change*, p.367.

117 R.A. Fletcher, "Reconquest and crusade in Spain, c.1050–1150," *Transactions of the Royal Historical Society*, 5th. series, 37 (1987), pp.46–7.

118 R. Highfield, "Christians, Jews and Muslims in the same society: the fall of *convivencia* in medieval Spain," in *Religious Motivation: Biographical and Sociological Problems for the Church Historian, Studies in Church History*, vol. 15 (Oxford, 1978), ed. D. Baker, pp.121, 123; A. Mackay, *Spain in the Middle Ages: from Frontier to Empire, 1000–1500* (London, 1977), p.90. There is also valuable material on medieval Spain in *Medieval Frontier Societies*, ed. R. Bartlett & A. Mackay (Oxford, 1989).

the four scholars whom he recruited to make a translation of the Koran were two foreigners, Herman of Carinthia and Robert of Chester; Peter of Toledo, who was a Mozarab (an Arabic-speaking Christian); and Muhammad of Toledo, a Moslem. In another case, one of the works of the Arab philosopher Avicenna was first translated from Arabic into Castilian by a Jewish scholar and then by another scholar from Castilian into Latin. It has been aptly concluded that such people, Jews and Mozarabs, were "hinge men" who could both translate and mediate between the different cultures."[119]

The relations between cultures both in Spain and elsewhere in Europe and in the wider arena of Christendom were also influenced, if never fully controlled, by such features of papal ideology as the just war, the crusade, the universal mission to spread Christianity, and the treatment to be accorded to Moslems, Jews, and pagans, subjects that overlap and intertwine but can only be treated very generally here. By the thirteenth century the debate on the possible justification of war, which had begun with St. Augustine in the fifth century and had been completed by the canon lawyers and theologians, had led to the conclusion that warfare was licit provided that it was conducted by properly constituted authority (a king or an emperor) in defense of legitimate rights.[120] In the special case of the crusade the pope or his representative put himself at the head of an armed forced for the defense of Christians and for the recovery of their property.[121] In theory a war should not be fought solely for aggressive purposes: Even infidels and pagans were entitled to their possessions. The homelands of pagans could be invaded and occupied only for the purpose of spreading Christianity, but the inhabitants should not be dispossessed, and their conversion should be carried out by preaching and persuasion, not by the "iron tongue" of force.[122] This latter view was strongly argued by Pope Innocent IV in the 1240s.[123] Also by the thirteenth century the papacy had conceived the mission to preach Christianity in every accessible corner of the world. Gregory IX's bull *Cum hora undecima* expressed this very clearly in 1235. Already, in 1233, Gregory

[119] Mackay, *Spain in the Middle Ages*, p.88.
[120] On the just war, see F.H. Russell, *The Just War in the Middle Ages* (Cambridge, 1975); *The Church and War, Studies in Church History*, 20, ed. W.J. Sheils (Oxford, 1983).
[121] See L. & J. Riley-Smith, ed., *The Crusade: Idea and Reality, 1095–1274* (London, 1981), Section B, "The just cause," Section C, "Right intention."
[122] Muldoon, pp.34–8; R. Bartlett, "The conversion of a pagan society," pp.186, 196.
[123] Muldoon, pp.10, 21–2, 29–48. The idea of the "virtuous pagan," who might achieve salvation through divine grace, although denied the knowledge of Christianity, was also sometimes expressed: see C.L. Vitto, "The virtuous pagan in Middle English literature," *Transactions of the American Philosophical Society*, 79 (Philadelphia, 1989).

had sent a number of Franciscan missionaries to the sultan of Egypt and other Moslem rulers and even to the caliph in Baghdad, each with a written exposition of Christianity and with an injunction to listen to it; and one of the purposes of the papal envoys who were sent to the Mongol khans later in the same century was to try to convert them to Christianity.[124] It was hoped too that even the Jews might one day be induced to see the true light of Christianity.[125]

In all its policies, however, the papacy was essentially trying to square a circle. Crusading was supposed to be conducted with the minimum of violence, but there was no escaping the fact that it often led to atrocities, such as those that occurred after the capture of Jerusalem in 1099. The language in which preachers presented the crusade was frequently highly colored and an incentive to extremes of violence. In a sermon delivered (c. 1216–25) to one of the military orders, who were professed religious trained specifically for war, Jacques de Vitry, bishop of Acre, informed his audience that "If we were not resisting the Church's enemies, the Saracens and heretics would have destroyed the whole Church. For this reason the poisonous limbs must be cut off and the decayed flesh must be cut out, so that the sound part is not corrupted."[126] Although the suggestion has been made that the church's simultaneous encouragement of crusading and of peaceful missionary activity involved contradictory aims and that the latter only really came into its own after the loss of Acre and the apparent military failure of the crusades in 1291, such a contradiction was not generally perceived at the time. Peter the Venerable, for example, who commissioned a translation of the Koran and composed a refutation of Moslem doctrine, *Liber contra sectam sive haeresim Saracenorum*, and believed in a policy of peaceful conversion of the Moslems, was also fully in support of the crusade.[127] Nonetheless the crusade was extensively criticized in the thirteenth century on such grounds as the bloodshed involved, or the waste of resources, or through fears by some secular rulers that a successful crusade would make the papacy too powerful. Criticism became so strong that

[124] Muldoon, pp.36–45; Phillips, ch. 5, "The eastern missions"; I. de Rachewiltz, *Papal Envoys to the Great Khans* (London, 1971). The standard work on the subject is J. Richard, *La papauté et les missions d'Orient au moyen âge* (Rome, 1977). See also R.I. Burns, "Christian-Islamic confrontation in the West: the thirteenth-century dream of conversion," *American Historical Review*, 76 (1971), pp.1386–1434; B.Z. Kedar, *Crusade and Mission: Europe Approaches towards the Muslims* (Princeton, 1984).

[125] Muldoon, pp.30–2.

[126] L. & J. Riley-Smith, p.68.

[127] See B.Z. Kedar; E. Siberry, "Missionaries and crusaders, 1095–1274," in *The Church and War*.

Humbert de Romans, the Master General of the Dominicans, was commissioned by Pope Gregory X to write a treatise refuting the critics for use at the Council of Lyons in 1274.[128]

In general, little attempt was made to understand the beliefs of Moslems on their own terms. Studies of their religion or of the Arabic language were usually made with a view to refutation or conversion rather than comprehension, while the scholarly works that were translated from Arabic into Latin were in fields like philosophy, medicine, and mathematics rather than religion.[129] Relations between Christians and Moslems were characterized for the most part by mutual hostility and suspicion.[130] Unlike Moslem communities, which were concentrated in the Iberian peninsula, Jewish communities were widely spread through Europe. The general principle in Christian-Jewish relations was one of toleration by the Church and protection by the secular authorities. But toleration and protection were gained at a price. The Fourth Lateran Council of 1215, for example, laid down regulations that Jews should wear distinguishing marks and attacked their role as suppliers of capital: "The more the Christian religion curbs the taking of usury, the more does Jewish perfidy become used to this practice, so much so, that in a short time, the wealth of Christians will be exhausted." The protection offered by rulers was predatory in nature: In England, for example, the monarchy made such extensive demands on the financial resources of its Jewish subjects that by the middle of the thirteenth century these were greatly diminished and some of the most prominent Jews close to ruin.[131]

Medieval Europe has been described with some reason as taking on the character of a "persecuting society."[132] This was certainly true in relation to open heretics or those who were regarded as deviants from standard Christian belief and practice, all of whom were treated with growing severity from the thirteenth century onward. The institutions of the Inquisition, which were first established at this time to deal

[128] E. Siberry, *Criticism of Crusading, 1095–1274* (Oxford, 1985); L. & J. Riley-Smith, pp.103–17; J.H. Mundy, *Europe in the High Middle Ages* (London, 1973), p. 76.

[129] See N. Daniel, *The Arabs and Mediaeval Europe* (Beirut and London, 1975); C. H. Haskins, *Studies in the History of Medieval Science* (Cambridge, Mass., 1927).

[130] See J. Kritzeck, *Peter the Venerable and Islam* (Princeton, 1964); R.W. Southern, *Western Views of Islam in the Middle Ages* (Oxford, 1962); R.M. Thomson, "William of Malmesbury and some other western writers on Islam," *Medievalia et Humanistica* New Series 6 (1975); J.H. Mundy, op. cit., pp.75–81; M.A. Ladero Quesada, "El Islam, realidad e imaginación en la Baja Edad Media castellana," in *Las utopias*, Casa de Velásquez (Madrid, 1990), pp.215–40.

[131] Mundy. pp.81–92. See also R. Chazan, *Church, State and Jew in the Middle Ages.*

[132] R.I. Moore, *The Formation of a Persecuting Society: Power and Deviance in Western Europe, 950–1250* (Oxford, 1987).

with the Cathars in southern France, were potentially available to be used elsewhere if needed. The "demonization" of groups like the Cathars or the Templars was another indication of the possible extremes of intolerance.[133] Some missionaries, like Ricold of Monte Croce at the end of the thirteenth century, spoke of the need to understand the beliefs and languages of their opponents,[134] but such niceties were little in evidence in practice. The Lithuanians may have won the argument at Constance in 1416, but this did nothing to improve relations between them and their bitter enemies, the Teutonic Knights.[135] Anti-Semitism, which had already shown itself in the massacres in Germany that accompanied the beginning of the First Crusade in 1095–6, was evident in thirteenth-century attempts at forced conversion, in the expulsion of the Jews from England in 1290, and in the breakdown in *convivencia* in the Iberian peninsula that led to the pogroms of 1391.[136] The "intensification of lordship" in areas such as Wales and Ireland,[137] the brutalities of warfare in many regions of Europe, and the prevalence of urban and rural revolts were other signs of a society that was not at peace within itself.

Such conditions did not augur well for European relations with the non-European world in the fifteenth century. In the Ottoman Turks the Europeans encountered a new set of barbarians whom they could fear but could not overcome; in the native peoples of the Canary Islands, whose occupation began in 1402, European adventurers found a more feasible objective.[138] Although the papacy intervened in 1434 to ban further settlement because of attacks on native converts to Christianity, two years later Eugenius IV issued the bull *Romanus pontifex*, emphasizing the fullness of his power as Vicar of Christ and, in consequence of this power, authorizing the Portuguese to convert all the remaining infidels in the islands. In persuading the pope to make this concession, the king of Portugal had uttered pious sentiments and intentions, but he had also described the native inhabitants in terms that are reminiscent of earlier images of the barbarian: "The nearly wild men who inhabit the forest [of these islands] are not united by

[133] N. Cohn, *Europe's Inner Demons* (London, 1976).
[134] Phillips, pp.85–6.
[135] Christiansen, pp.232–4.
[136] J. Riley-Smith, "The first crusade and the persecution of the Jews," in *Persecution and Toleration, Studies in Church History*, 21, ed. W.J. Sheils (Oxford, 1984); J. Highfield, "The end of *convivencia*"; A. Mackay, "Popular movements and programs in fifteenth-century Castile," *Past & Present*, 55 (1972); M.A. Ladero Quesada, *Historia de America Latina*, vol. I, *España en 1492*, ch. 6.
[137] The phrase is that of R.R. Davies in *Domination and Conquest*, ch. 5.
[138] F. Fernandez-Armesto, *Before Columbus*, pp.175–92, 203–12; Quesada, ch.8.

a common religion, nor are they bound by the chains of law, they are lacking in normal social intercourse, living in the country like animals"; they had "no contact with each other by sea, no writing, no kind of metal or money."[139] The final conquest of the Canaries was achieved after great brutality in 1496. At one level the near coincidence of this event with the conquest of Moslem Granada, the expulsion of the Spanish Jews, and the first voyage of Christopher Columbus, all of which took place in 1492, is no more than that. But at another and deeper level the coincidence is symbolic both of the "persecuting society" that had developed within medieval Europe and of an aggressive continent, now starting to think of itself self-consciously as "Europe" rather than as part of Christendom, which was ready to transfer its aggression overseas.[140]

Europeans entered the new age of expansion at the end of the fifteenth century with a variety of ethnographic models, from the "noble savage" and the "cannibal" and the whole panoply of the "monstrous races" to the "barbarian" and the "infidel." Where knowledge already existed of a particular place or people, such as India before the sixteenth century, it was possible that the old stereotypes, many of which were of great antiquity, would in time be overlaid and to some extent replaced by more objective observations.[141] Even then, ideas were slow to change, as the long quest for "Cathay" after 1500 illustrates.[142] But the New World and its peoples were so totally unfamiliar and unexpected to their first discoverers, indeed almost like another planet, that the latter had little alternative but to fall back on the ethnographies that were already implicit. It was no wonder, as Lewis Hanke has remarked, that America began as fantasy or that the caption to a woodcut of 1505 could depict the natives as naked cannibals living without disease for a century and a half and lacking rulers and personal property.[143] Neither was it surprising that, as with the "antip-

[139] Muldoon, pp.119–29, especially pp.120–1.

[140] Hay, *Europe: the Emergence of an Idea*, ch.5, "The emergence of Europe."

[141] See, for example, D.F. Lach, *Asia in the Making of Europe*, vol. 2, *The Century of Wonder* (Chicago, 1972).

[142] See G. Williams & P.J. Marshall, *The Great Map of Mankind* (London, 1982).

[143] L. Hanke, *Aristotle and the American Indians* (1959), ch. 1, "America as fantasy"; cf. A. Pagden, *The Fall of Natural Man* (Cambridge, 1982), ch.1, "The problem of recognition"; P. Hulme, *Colonial Encounters: Europe and the Native Caribbean, 1492–1797* (London & New York, 1986), ch.1, "Columbus and the cannibals"; H.M. Jones, *O Strange New World* (New York, 1964), ch. 1, "The image of the New World"; Friedman, op. cit., Epilogue; V.I.J. Flint, "Monsters and the antipodes in the early middle ages and enlightenment," *Viator*, 15 (1984), pp.65–80; L. Olschki, "Ponce de Leon's fountain of youth: history of a geographical myth," *Hispanic American Historical Review*, 21 (1941), pp.361–85. See also the very important new book by Anthony Pag-

odal" people who caused such problems to medieval theologians, the humanity and origin of the peoples of America were seriously questioned.[144] America became a laboratory for the reexamination of basic problems. But a cynic might argue that the consequences of this reexamination were not much different from those of the past: Given a contest, "natural man" had little chance against his "civilized" rival.

den, *European Encounters with the New World: from Renaissance to Romanticism* (New Haven & London, 1993). In its way, the superficial familiarity of China when it was first visited by Europeans in the thirteenth century, which was alluded to earlier, was just as misleading as the total strangeness of mainland America when it was first explored in the sixteenth century. In both cases, Europeans fell back on existing models, one derived from the material civilization of the Mediterranean world and the other from the mental images inherited from classical antiquity.

144 Friedman, pp.47–8; B.M. Fagan, *The Great Journey: the Peopling of Ancient America* (London, 1988); W.E. Washburn, *The Indian in America* (New York, 1975).

CHAPTER 2

Cultural conflicts in medieval world maps

JOHN B. FRIEDMAN

THE reevaluation of medieval cartography during the last twenty years has suggested that world maps are works of art of a didactic and cultural sort, rather than rigid and unsuccessful attempts to portray geographical features.[1] For example, the great cathedral and monastic tabella maps like those of Hereford and Ebstorf[2] were conceived as gigantic detached illustrated leaves of the book of the world. In-

[1] For the older view, see for one of many examples, C. Raymond Beazley, *The Dawn of Modern Geography* (London, 1897–1906) especially Vol.III, 528; "Revisionist" works include David Woodward, "Medieval Mappaemundi," in J.B. Harley and David Woodward, eds., *The History of Cartography: Cartography in Prehistoric, Ancient, and Medieval Europe and the Mediterranean* (Chicago, 1987), I, 286–370, and the same author's "Reality, Symbolism, Time and Space in Medieval World Maps," *Annals of the Association of American Geographers* 74, no.4 (1985):510–52. Recent studies particularly sensitive to the question of maps as works of art are those of Catherine Delano Smith, "Maps as Art and Science: Maps in Sixteenth Century Bibles," *Imago Mundi* 42 (1990): 65–83; the same author's "Art or Cartography?: the Wrong Questions," *History of the Human Sciences* 2 (1989):89–93; and David Woodward, ed., *Art and Cartography: Six Historical Essays* (Chicago and London, 1987).

[2] See on the Hereford map Peter Barber, "Visual Encyclopedias: The Hereford and other Mappae Mundi," *The Map Collector* 48 (1989):2–8; and Meryl Jancey, *Mappa Mundi: The Map of the World in Hereford Cathedral: A Brief Guide* (Hereford, 1987). Though the Ebstorf Map was destroyed in World War II, a reproduction made by Rudolf Wienke on parchment and exact as to size and colors can be see in Lüneburg at the Museum für das Fürstentum. In the last few years, this map has excited much scholarly interest. On its milieu, see Bernd Ulrich Hucker, "Zur Datierung der Ebstorfer Weltkarte," *Deutsches Archiv für Erforschung des Mittelalters* 44 (1988):510–538; Birgit Hahn-Woernle, *Die Ebstorfer Weltkarte: dem Kloster Ebstorf und seinen Konventualinnen gewidmet* (Ebstorf, 1989); Hartmut Kugler, "Die Ebstorfer Weltkarte: ein europäisches Weltbild im deutschen Mittelalter," *Zeitschrift für deutsches Altertum und Deutsche Literatur* 116 (1987):1–29; Armin Wolf, "Neues zur Ebstorfer Weltkarte: Entstehungszeit-Ursprungsort–Autorenschaft," in Klaus Jaitner and Ingo Schwab, eds., *Das Benediktinnerkloster Ebstorf im Mittelalter: Vorträge einer Tagung im Kloster Ebstorf vom 22. bis 24. Mai 1987* (Hildesheim, 1988), 75–109 and Horst Appuhn, "Datierung und Gebrauch der Ebstorfer Weltkarte" and Renate Kroos, "Über die Zeichnungen auf der Ebstorfkarte und die niedersächsische Buchmalerei," in Hartmut Kugler, ed., *Ein Weltbild vor Columbus: Die Ebstorfer Weltkarte. Interdisziplinäres Colloquium vom 1–5 Juni 1988 in Kloster Ebstorf* (Weinheim, 1990).

deed, as David Woodward points out in his discussion in *The History of Cartography*, "the vast majority of the maps that survive were produced as ipso facto book illustrations."[3] These magnificent wall maps with their intermixture of large blocks of text with pictures are very like other and more portable medieval picture books where text and image are inseparable.[4] In fact, one of the few theoretical texts about medieval world maps, that of Boccaccio's friend, Paulinus of Venice, makes just this point:

> I think that it not merely difficult but impossible without a world map to make for oneself an image of or even to hold in the mind, what is said about the generations of Noah and the nations and areas of the earth, as these are mentioned by doctors and divines. What is necessary is a twofold map containing both painting and writing. Nor can one be sufficient without the other, because painting without writing indicates regions of nations unclearly, and writing without the assistance of painting does not delineate an area's boundaries for them to be taken in at first sight.[5]

Thus, far from being the poor relation of manuscript painting or literary texts – for *mappaemundi* partake equally of both worlds – as transmitters and reflections of cultural conflicts that arise when a relatively advanced and ethnocentric society encounters other societies physically, socially and technologically different from itself, medieval world maps must be seen in the forefront and rank among the most expressive and ideological of all cultural objects. These maps describe not only the world spaces of the Middle Ages as these were variously depicted from the Carolingian period to the age of the great discoverers, but, more important for students of contemporary culture, they chart their makers' minds and values.

To develop further the analogy between medieval maps and medieval literature and manuscript book painting, I suggest that two terms that have usefully been applied to these more familiar arts are also extremely helpful for the study of cartography. These are "cultural other" – anybody whose appearance or habits differ from one's own – and "marginalization" – the process by which people perceived

[3] Harley and Woodward, eds., *The History of Cartography*, 286.

[4] See Catherine Delano Smith, "Cartographic Signs on European Maps and their Explanation before 1700," *Imago Mundi* 37 (1985):9–29.

[5] Paulinus of Venice, *Satyrica Historia*, Prologue, Vatican Library MS Lat. 1960, fol. 13. On Paulinus, see Alberto Ghinato, *Fr Paolino da Venetia OFM, Vescovo di Pozzuoli* (Rome, 1951); von den Brincken, "Ut describeretur," 260–263, 272, and the same author's " 'Quod non vicietur pictura.' Die Sorge um das rechte Bild in der Kartographie," in *Fälschungen im Mittelalter. Internationaler Kongress der Monumenta Germaniae Historica München 16–19 Sept. 1986* (Hannover, 1988), I, 587–599.

as cultural others are relegated to realms sufficiently mythic to contain them and to insulate the holders of power from their dangerous or guilt-inducing presence.[6]

As has been well known since the publication of Edward Said's *Orientalism* in 1978, "orientalism" as a description of a particular space on the globe is really a source for ideas about the world and serves as precisely the insulator I have just mentioned.[7] To orientalize then, as Said would argue, is to push something eastward until either it recedes from consciousness or becomes a judgment of the worth of the thing so orientalized. Orientalism creates an "us" and a "they" who can easily become not only physically and morally different from us but not even fully human. The orient then, according to Said, had become a sort of negative image of Europe and was what Europe was not. In short, it was a space for the cultural other, whose physical "deformities" from the standards of western European appearance and manners reflected the moral deformation of Islam.

In a somewhat less documented way, Africa has had much the same function as a repository for, and home of, cultural others, and even the most superficial acquaintance with medieval world maps that show peoples will indicate that Africa and India are the chief homes of monstrous races of men, cannibals, mannish women, and other aberrant species. Thus, both orientalism and Africanism are words relating to "away" directions rather than to locations involving a "here."

The purpose of this chapter is to show how ethnocentrism and marginalization mirror cultural conflicts in the portrayal of the spaces of medieval world maps. The large wall maps referred to earlier, with their insets of didactic text explaining and glossing the images, immediately reveal their makers' cultural values. Representations such as the magnificent Ebstorf map, the Hereford Cathedral world map, which was nearly sold at auction in 1988,[8] and its apparent copy in

[6] Mary Helms, *Ulysses' Sail: an Ethnographic Odyssey of Power, Knowledge and Geographical Distance* (Princeton, 1988); A.R. Lewis, *Nomads and Crusaders, 1000–1368* (Bloomington and Indianapolis, 1988); J. K. Hyde, "Real and Imaginary Journeys in the Later Middle Ages," *The Bulletin of the John Rylands University Library* 65 (1982–1983):125–147; D. Constantine, *Early Greek Travellers and the Hellenic Ideal* (Cambridge, 1984); Hayden White, "The Forms of Wildness," in Edward Dudley and Maximillian Novak, eds., *The Wild Man Within: An Image in Western Thought from the Renaissance to Romanticism* (Pittsburgh, 1972); and J. Richard, "Voyages réels et voyages imaginaires, instruments de la connaissance géographiques au moyen âge," in Geneviève Hasenohr and Jean Longère, eds., *Culture et Travail intellectuel dans l'Occident médiéval* (Paris, 1981).

[7] Edward W. Said, *Orientalism* (N.Y., 1978).

[8] See, for an interesting discussion of the recent vicissitudes of this map, Tony Campbell, "Chronicle for 1989," *Imago Mundi* 42 (1990):121.

the Duchy of Cornwall paste down fragments now in the British Library,[9] as well as the small psalter map in the same collection, show many of these implicit preoccupations with ethnocentrism and marginalization of alien peoples.

On these maps, monstrous races of men in Africa and India, the peoples of Gog and Magog safely isolated from European contact by the Caucasus mountains, and so on pose few problems for one who wishes to study ethnocentrism as a justification of the colonial impulse. I have already discussed these maps in some detail elsewhere.[10]

More difficult of access are the broad cultural implications of space,[11] which can be profitably examined in the group of maps known to cartographers as quadripartite. They are developments of the T-O or tripartite maps, which divide the world according to Noah's post-diluvian allotment of Asia, Europe, and Africa to his sons Japhet, Shem, and Ham. Japhet as the eldest got the largest part, for generally Asia on such maps is equal in land mass to the other two continents.[12]

To these three continents was added a fourth or austral continent by quadripartite map makers. This area, boldly separated from Asia, Europe, and Africa, was a separate *oecumene* for the people most unlike westerners, often with its own sun shining on the inhabitants there.[13] A well-known example is the map in manuscripts of Beatus

[9] See Harley and Woodward, *The History of Cartography*, 14, 307, and a paper by Graham Haslam given at 12th International Conference on the History of Cartography, Paris 7–11 Sept. 1987; see *Imago Mundi* 40 (1988):121.

[10] John B. Friedman, *The Monstrous Races in Medieval Art and Thought* (Cambridge, MA, 1981). More recent treatments are those of Seymour Phillips, *The Medieval Expansion of Europe* (Oxford and New York, 1988); Mary B. Campbell, *The Witness and the Other World: Exotic Eastern Travel Writing 400–1600* (Ithaca and London, 1988); and F.M. Snowden, Jr., *Before Color Prejudice. The Ancient View of Blacks* (Cambridge, MA, 1983). Though Claude Lecouteux's essay, "Bestiaire et monstres Fabuleux," in M. Meslin et al., eds., *Le Mervéilleux, l'imaginaire et les croyances en occident* (Paris, 1984), 84–107, is uncritical, it has some fine pictures, as does the rest of this volume, largely a coffee table book.

[11] I have found Edward Relph, *Place and Placelessness* (London, 1986) helpful in my thinking about this subject. See also D. Lowenthal, "Geography, Experience and Imagination: Towards a Geographical Epistemology," *Annals of the Association of American Geographers* 51 (1961):241–260.

[12] See on this subject, Jonathan T. Lanman, "The Religious Symbolism of the T in T-O Maps," *Cartographica* 18 (1981):18–22, and an expanded form of this material in Lanman, *Glimpses*, 32–37; Harley and Woodward, eds., *The History of Cartography*, 301–302; and Woodward, "Reality, Symbolism, Time and Space in Medieval World Maps," 511.

[13] See, for example, Lambert of St. Omer, *Liber Floridus*, Wulfenbüttel, Herzog-August Bibliothek, MS Guelf. 1, Gud. Lat. Cat. 4305, folios 69v–70r. For reproductions, see Danielle Lecoq, "Le mappemonde du *Liber Floridus* ou la vision du monde de Lambert de Saint-Ômer," *Imago Mundi* 39 (1987): Frontispiece and 9–49, and A. Derolez,

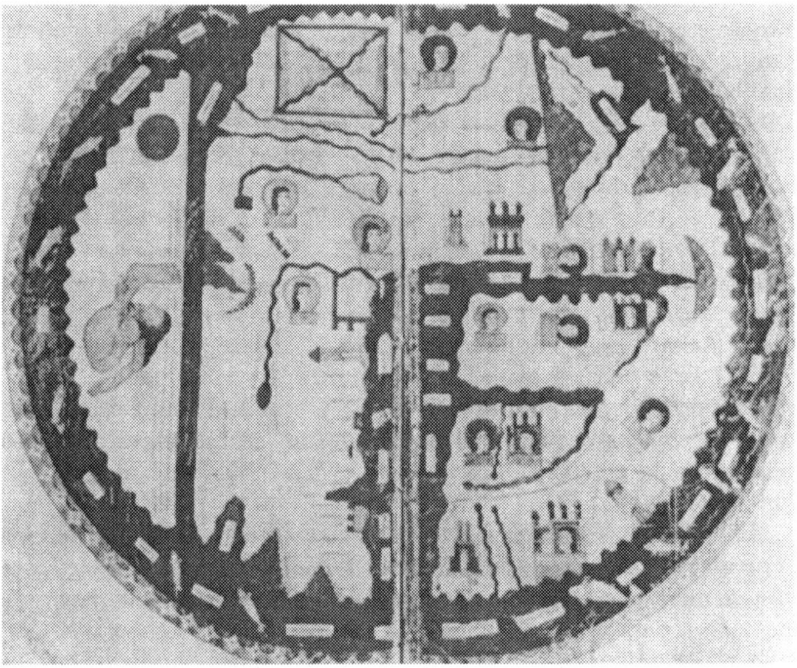

Figure 2.1. Quadripartite map. Beatus of Liébana, Commentary on the Book of Revelations, Cathedral of Burgo d'Osma, Archivo de la Catedral, MS 1, folios 35v–36, 1086.

of Liébana's commentary on Revelations. A Beatus map dating from 1086 in the Cathedral of Burgo d'Osma (Figure 2.1) shows a radical separation of the west from all that is not the west, as well as the antipodal region with its own cosmography. Though the known world portion of the map contains names of peoples, and features of the earth's surface such as mountains and rivers, the antipodal region contains nothing but a text of western description, exported there as if to fill a void.[14] This antipodal region of the world is neatly separated

ed., *Lamberti Audomarensis canonici Liber Floridus codex autographus Bibliothecae Universitatis Gandavensis* (Ghent, 1968).

[14] Beatus of Liébana, Commentary on the Book of Revelation, Cathedral of Burgo d'Osma, Archivo de la Catedral MS 1, folios 35v–36. See the recent discussion in Harley and Woodward, eds., *The History of Cartography*, 303–3–4, and that of L. Vasquez de Parga, "Un mapa desconocido de la serie de los "Beatos"," in *Actas del simposio para el estudio de los codices del Comentario al Apocalipsis del Beato de Liébana* (Madrid, 1978), 271–278.

from the civilized westerner by a vast and uncrossable body of water. In the antipodal space defined by the edge of what separated us from them, and ringed by the river of Ocean believed to circle the very edges of the earth, is a cultural other, a sciopode or shadow-footed man, whose single great foot protects him from the heat of the sun. He is then a projection of what this barely imaginable emptiness contains. And he is peculiarly appropriate to our discussion of space, for he differs from westerners precisely in spatial orientation; his essence is to lie with his foot over his head.[15] The sciopode has been placed as a titulary deity or guardian angel of the margin at the very borders of the world. His physical form defines the oddness beyond the border, for he is half like us and half like them. This map encloses the cultural other and renders him a harmless anecdotal representation like a gargoyle, who symbolizes the realm of the earth that must have been for the Middle Ages like the fourth dimension for us.[16]

Maps without such representations of human beings, however, pose different and interesting sorts of problems for the student of cartography, because at first glance they do not show ethnocentrism and the impulse to marginalize and the like on the part of their makers, often seeming to the viewer to be merely a hodgepodge of circles and pie-shaped slices imposed on the earth's surface. Yet even the simplest and most schematic maps are early forms of artistic and scientific evidence of a culture's value system, and one way this is shown is by the mapmaker's use of space.

Not only do these schematic maps insulate the known or imaginable world from the unknown or inconceivable other, they also illustrate a desire to control space. Such maps make place one-dimensional, unanimated, and quite lacking in the sacral and magical. The space within the circle is a void in which objects float at random; it is not an expressive space. No passage of time occurs, for time has become spatialized; these maps purify time of process and fluidity, for things do not become, they are. For instance, a biblical event such as the Flood is shown by an ark on a mountain after the flood has receded.[17]

As the schematic maps acquire more and more data, they become arranged according to economics, rather like a cross-section of a house

[15] See Valerie Flint, "Monsters and the Antipodes in the Early Middle Ages and the Enlightenment," *Viator* 15 (1984):65–80.

[16] See also a similar sciopode in a similar position in a Beatus map now Bibliothèque Nationale, NAL. MS 1366, folios 24v–25r.

[17] Admittedly this may also result from the lack of an artistic vocabulary by which to show the process. See Otto Pächt, *The Rise of Pictorial Narrative in Twelfth-Century England* (Oxford, 1962) for general discussion.

or an ant hill, where there are rooms and chambers in which work takes place. Sometimes Adam and Eve outside the paradisal garden boxed off from map space hold shovel and distaff. Nor should this seem odd, for of course the more developed maps were the means to the circulation and acquisition of goods and the delimitation of property. It is hard to imagine venture capitalism and colonialism without maps.

Let us move from theory to text by considering the two main types of primarily peopleless schematic maps, the T-O and the Macrobian or climatic maps, which illustrate some of these rather abstract ideas of space and show us much about attitudes toward the people who do not appear on their surfaces at all.

Originally the T-O maps seem to have developed as illustrations for Sallust's *Jugurthine Wars*.[18] A "T" whose vertical bar is the Mediterranean, which bisects Europe and Africa, its horizontal cross-bar made of the river Tanais or Don to the west – traditionally the border between Asia and Europe – and the Nile to the east, divides Asia from the other two continents. A ring encircles the T's extremities, separating the known from all that is unknown or beyond speculation, and often a circle in the very center of the disk indicates Jerusalem – and by extension, Christianity – as the hub of the universe.[19] Asia, or the east, is almost always at the upper half of the map as it is oriented on the page.

Much as the Quadripartite map had imposed a European conception of space on the austral continent in the act of describing it, so the world in T-O maps is a page from a European book. Thus, though the disk is theoretically flat and viewed as if by a bird above, it is in fact imagined on the page of the manuscript in which it appears, vertically, with its top at the top of the page. The world thus takes on the human and vertical orientation of the codex on the reading stand. Figure 2.2 is an example of such a map at its most simple and linear. This map, now in the Beinecke Rare Book and Manuscript collection of the Yale University Library, is of fifteenth-century date, but is very typical of even the earliest maps of its type.[20]

[18] See for discussion, Harley and Woodward, eds., *The History of Cartography*, 343, and Bernhard Brandt, "Eine neue Salluskarte aus Prag," *Mitteilungen des Vereins der Geographen an der Universität Leipzig* 14–15 (1936):9–13.

[19] See generally, Werner Müller, *Die heilige Stadt. Roma quadrata, himmlisches Jerusalem und die mythe vom Weltnabel* (Stuttgart, 1961), and Robert Konrad, "Das himmlische und das irdische Jerusalem im mittelalterlichen Denken," in Clemens Bauer et al., eds., *Speculum Historiale . . . Festschrift Johannes Sporl* (Munich, 1965), 523–540.

[20] Sallust, *De bello Jugurthino*, MS 358, folio 74v. See Barbara Shailor, *Catalogue of Medieval and Renaissance Manuscripts in the Beinecke Book and Manuscript Library, Yale*

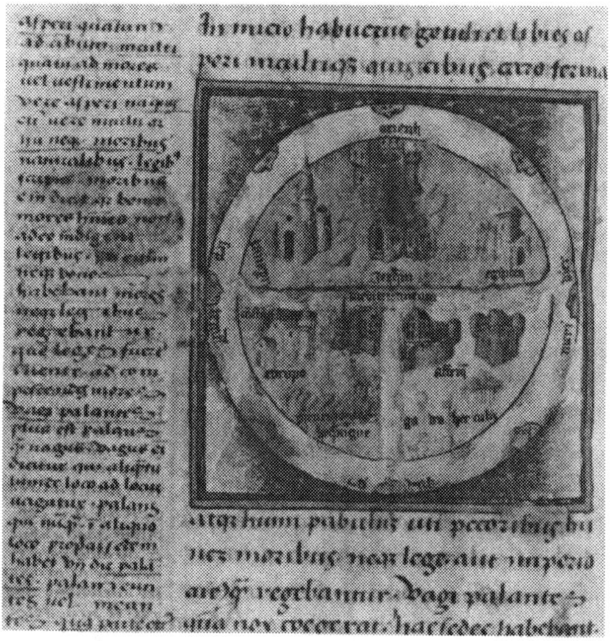

Figure 2.2. T-O map, Sallust, *De Bello Jugurthino*, New Haven, Conn., Beinecke Library, Yale University, MS 358, folio 74v, fifteenth century.

Even the relatively schematic T-O maps, which do not represent people, show ethnocentricity and marginalization. If our European habitable zone occupies more or less the center of the world, it then gives worth to the center and subtracts it from the nations of the edge. A new paradigm develops then, of a center and a circle at some distance from it, that contains and locates all that is the farthest not only geographically but culturally from that center. One world map ca. 1130, now in Oxford[21] (Figure 2.3), places Thule outside the river of Ocean, in an area of space scarcely to be comprehended. Britain is placed just at the edge of the circle of the known, as far from the center as possible; beyond it in the realm of Ocean is Ireland. What is known, for this mapmaker, is Asia Minor, where the regions evan-

University (Binghamton, NY, 1987), II, 201–202, and Marcel Destombes, *Mappamondes A.D. 1200–1500* (Amsterdam, 1964), no. 31, 72.

21 Oxford, Saint John's College, MS 17, folio 6. See Anna-Dorothee von den Brincken, "Mundus Figura Rotunda," in Anton Legner, ed., *Ornamenta Ecclesiae. Kunst und Künstler der Romanik in Köln* (Cologne, 1985), Vol. I, 103–105.

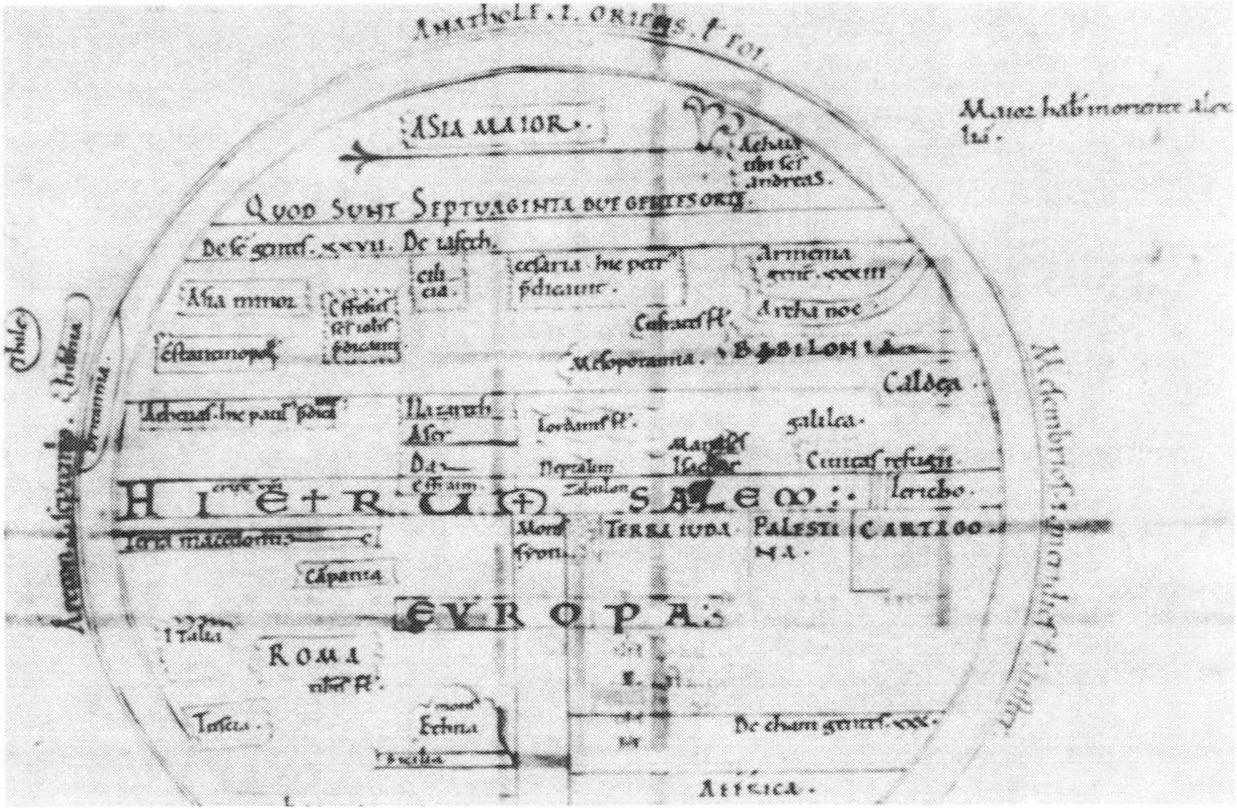

Figure 2.3. T-O Map, Oxford, Saint John's College, MS 17, folio 6, *ca.* 1130.

gelized by various apostles are listed. As the map is really intended to celebrate apostolic influence and the power of Christianity, those lands where Christianity came relatively late are given short shrift.

Let us think for a moment about some of the attitudes toward space shown here. Typically, in Graeco-Roman and Judaeo-Christian cultures, height or the space above the head was the space of political, social, and divine power. The temple, the Capitoline hill, and the stronghold at once come to mind. In like manner, wisdom and revelation come from above as in late antique author portraits, or Evangelist portraits where God speaks to man from above his head. In the ninth-century Lothair Bible from Tours (Figure 2.4), John the evangelist looks up to the sky for inspiration as he writes.[22] On the other hand, the space below the feet was to be disdained; insignificant, frightening, or dangerous existences were marginalized there. Indeed, it is hard to characterize this space below the level of man's eyes without using words such as inferior or lowly with all their attendant moral denotations. In eastern and western art of the Middle Ages, one might think of Byzantine *proskynesis* – the humbling of one person to ground level before another person, or the way St. George or Christ tread down the dragon of Satan and sin below their feet in many paintings, as well as the way in which the virtues in various sculptural programs deriving from the *Psychomachia* of Prudentius conquer by standing on or abasing their corresponding vices. A miniature of the virtues crushing the vices beneath their feet from a manuscript of Johannes Andreas, *Novella in Libros Decretalium*, painted by the eminent artist Nicolo di Bologna in 1354, now in the Ambrosian Library in Milan,[23] is nearly contemporary with some of the maps discussed here (Figure 2.5). The social is the space ahead of man; it corresponds to the center, and the space behind him is that of mystery or danger. Typically, then, power inheres in the space above his line of sight, and is that toward which he raises his eyes.

Christian history and the spatial relationships of the codex form in which most of these schematic maps are found give worth to the kinds of space they depict. For example, in a somewhat more detailed version of the typical T-O map in a tenth-century copy of Isidore of Sev-

[22] Paris, Bibliothèque Municipale MS lat. 266, folio 171v. See for color reproduction and discussion, Florentine Mutherich and Joachim E. Gaehde, *Carolingian Painting* (New York, 1976), item XII and plate 26.

[23] Milan, Biblioteca Ambrosiana B 42 inf., fol. 1. See on this manuscript, Renate Cipriani, *Codici Miniati dell' Ambrosiana* (Milan, 1968), 171–172. I am grateful to Louis Jordan of the Ambrosiana Microfilm Collection, University of Notre Dame Library, for information on this codex. See also Adolph Katzenellenbogen, *The Allegories of the Virtues and Vices in Mediaeval Art* (New York, 1964), 1–21.

Figure 2.4. St. John the Evangelist, Lothair Bible, Paris, Bibliothèque Nationale MS lat. 266, folio 171v, ninth century.

ille's *Etymologiae*, now in Madrid, Royal Academy of History, MS 25, folio 204 (Figure 2.6), the three continents are labeled with the names of Noah's sons, and there is a good deal of geographic detail, names of rivers, numbers of Roman provinces, and the like. But the focal point of this map is the boxed area at the east labeled Paradise from which the four rivers emerge to run all through the world.[24] This box both delimits sacred history and makes it become the history of the world, for life forces flow out of it into the unorganized space of the rest of the map.

A cross at the top indicates worth from a Christian point of view here, for patristic thought had placed Eden and the creation story in the east. Isidore of Seville, in his *De Natura Rerum*, had noted, in a metaphor of the world as an anthropomorphized body, that "the world's head, and so to speak, its face, is the eastern region."[25]

Several reasons for this belief come to mind, both of an anthropological and of a more textual kind. Cosmography, geography, and prayer direction had long been related, and the cardinal points had had symbolic as well as geographic significance. The Old Testament contains a number of injunctions that men should pray to the east because God is to be found there. In Ezekiel 43:2 we learn that "the glory of the God of Israel came by way of the east." And indeed the Hebrew word indicating the easterly direction also indicates that which is in "front" of man.

That the sun rises in the east was paralleled with the east as the source of Christianity and the place of monotheism as well as of the creation of man. Such an idea is well portrayed in the third century *Apostolic Constitutions*. There the author exhorts an ideal congregation "let all rise up . . . and looking towards the east, . . . pray to God eastward, who ascended up to the heaven of heavens to the east."[26]

In a similar fashion, the alignment of sacred architecture exemplified these beliefs. The early Christian church was a form of cosmography, with the altar a paradise oriented toward the east and the congregation facing the altar aligned in an easterly direction. And the *Apostolic Constitutions* just cited commanded that churches belong with their heads to the east.[27] A well-known sixth-century map in the

[24] See Jack J. Boies, *The Lost Domain: Avatars of the Earthly Paradise in Western Literature* (Lanham, MD, 1983).

[25] Jacques Fontaine, ed. *Isidore de Seville, Traité de la Nature* (Bordeaux, 1960), IX, 3, 207, and Wesley M. Stevens, "The Figure of the Earth in Isidore's 'De natura rerum,'" *Isis* 71 (1980):268–277.

[26] Alexander Roberts and James Donaldson, trans., *The Apostolic Constitutions in The Ante-Nicene Fathers* (New York, 1907), VII, Book II, sec. vii, 421.

[27] Loc. cit.

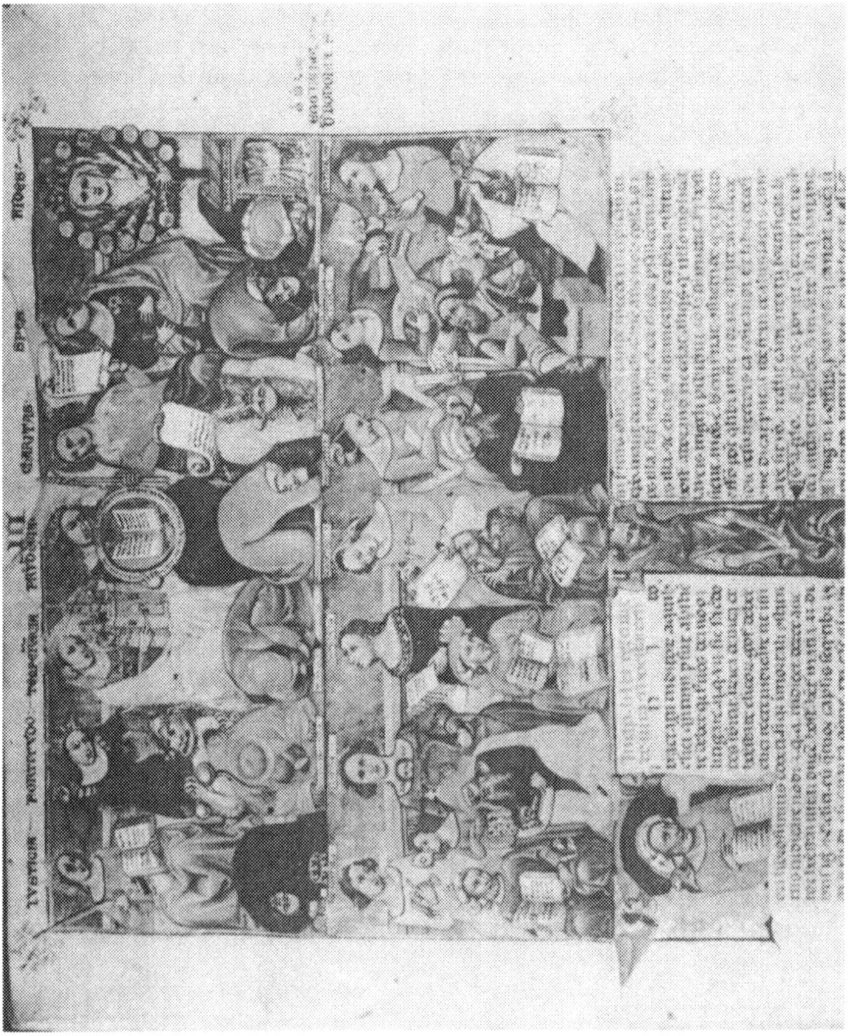

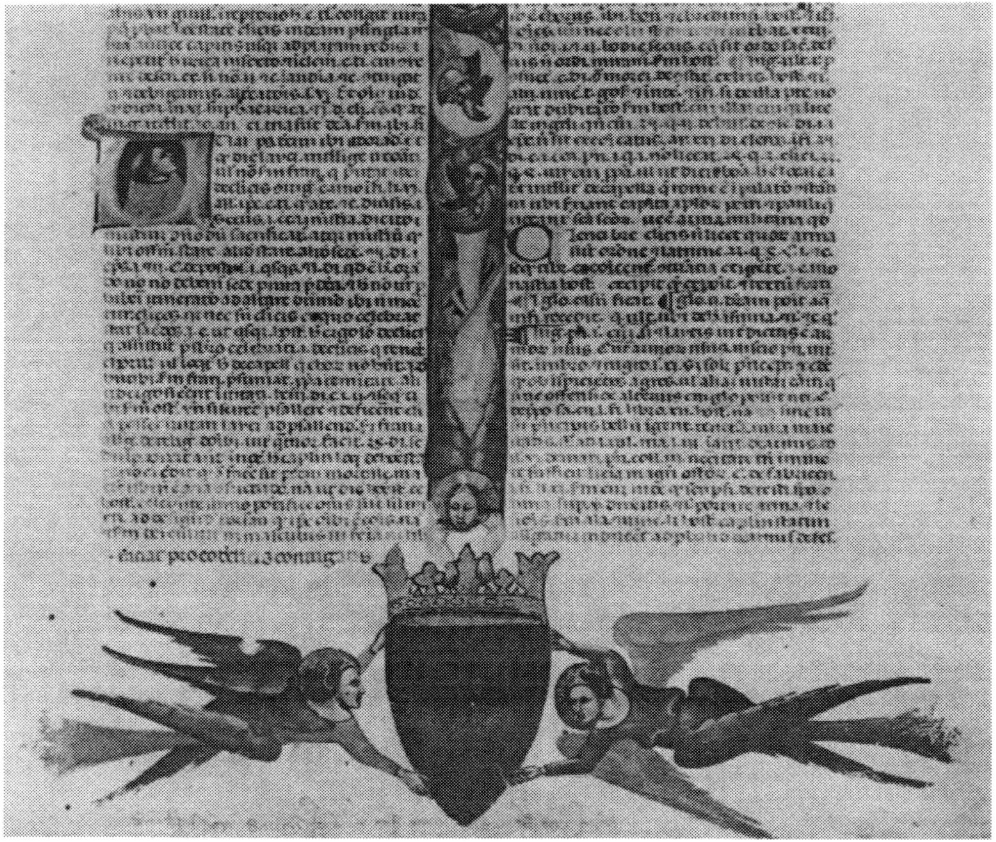

Figure 2.5. Virtues overcome vices, Johannes Andreas, *Novella in Libros Decretalium*, Nicolo di Bologna, Milan, Biblioteca Ambrosiana, MS B.42 inf., folio 1, 1354.

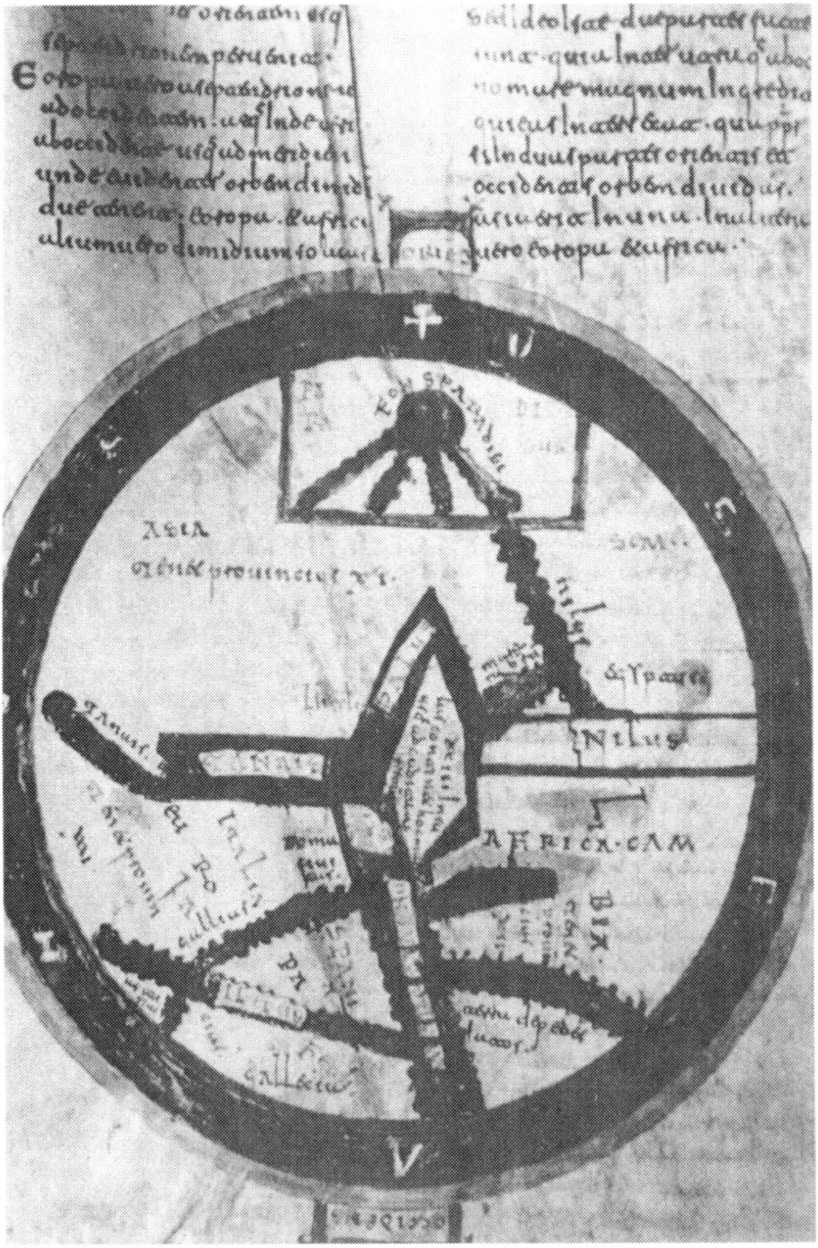

Figure 2.6. T-O map, Isidore of Seville, *Etymologiae,* Madrid, Royal Academy of History, MS 25, folio 204, tenth century.

form of a floor mosaic in the church of St. John in Madaba, a town in Jordan, represents the Holy Land with east at the top, as in the maps we have seen.[28] Jerusalem in the mosaic falls at the center of the cross-shaped structure of the building. Thus the liturgical center of the church and the centers of Christian and cartographic history are the same, and the map illustrates how the Church gives meaning to history as well as to space. Later Christian maps would naturally reflect such practices.

Typically, then, divine power is centered in the east of the map,[29] the area that is above the center or at the top of the page where a reader of a book might look for the instruction of a running head. In some world maps, this relationship of power or authority in the east is made clear by the way God holds the world disk on his body, with his head at the east or top of the disk and his feet at the west, often treading down sin, personified in the form of several dragons. The magnificent Ebstorf world map shows the first form; Christ's head is the east.[30] A similar scene occurs on the back of a map found in a thirteenth-century psalter now in the British Library, London (Figure 2.7), where a tripartite map is surmounted by a bust of God whose extremities mark off the cardinal points and whose feet tread down sin in the west.[31] West traditionally was the direction Christ was believed to have faced at his passion, and thus newly baptized converts were taught that by their action symbolically they look toward the sunset, renouncing the ruler of darkness. For example, Lactantius in the *Divine Institutes* contrasted east and west, saying that out of the one direction God rose and flourished, because He Himself was the source of light, as is shown in all things, and that thus rising, He brings us to eternal life. But the west is ascribed to that disturbed and

[28] See Michele Piccinillo, *Chiese e mosaici della Giordana Settentrionale* (Jerusalem, 1981), and the same author's "Chiese e mosaici di Giordania. Una comunità cristiana dalle origini bibliche," *Antonianum* 58 (1983):85–101, as well as C. Andresen, "Betrachtungen zur Madeba-Karte in Göttingen," in Ernst Dassmann and K. Suso Frank, eds., *Pietas. Festschrift für Bernhard Kötting* (Münster, 1980), 539–45. More recently, see Harley and Woodward, *The History of Cartography*, plates 7 and 8 and for discussion and bibliography, 264–266.

[29] See Anna-Dorothee von den Brincken, "Christen des Orients auf abendländischen Karten des 11. bis 14. Jahrhunderts," in Werner Diem and Abdoldjavad Falaturi, eds., *XXIV. Deutscher Orientalistentag vom 26. bis 30. September 1988 in Köln* (Stuttgart, 1990), 90–98, and B. L. Gordon, "Sacred Directions, Orientation, and the Top of the Map," *History of Religions* 10 (1971):211–227.

[30] See Walter Rosien, *Die Ebstorfer Weltkarte* (Hanover, 1952). A good representation from this part of the map appears more accessibly in Harley and Woodward, *The History of Cartography*, fig. 8.2, 291.

[31] London, British Museum MS Additional 28681, folio 9v.

Figure 2.7. Tripartite map, London psalter, British Library, MS Additional 28681, folio 9v, thirteenth century.

depraved mind that conceals the light, brings darkness, and makes men die in sin.[32]

Some of these ideas about the cardinal points and their power can be illustrated by the fascinating sketch of the world as a space for the conflict of man with the devil that occurs in the manuscript of the English morality play *The Castle of Perseverance* now in the Folger Library[33] (Figure 2.8) The cardinal points are associated with temptation and salvation. Thus, south at the top of the sketch is *caro* or flesh, west, as we have seen, is connected with *mundus* or the things of the world, north with the devil, and east with god.

Even maps of the city of Jerusalem, often but not always conceived of as the center of the earth,[34] are microcosms whose cardinal points are gates. In one such twelfth-century example from a collector, perhaps from St. Bertin, now in The Hague (Figure 2.9), the city is imagined as the world and titled "locus quadragesime."[35] The miniature serves not only as a detailed map of Jerusalem but also as crusade propaganda. At what would be the westerly point, an erect St. George in white surcote, white shield with prominent red cross, and riding a white palfrey spits on a lance with white cross-bearing gonfalon – a Moslem warrior in dark surcote and on a dark horse – driving him in the direction of Africa. This knight inclines his head and torso toward the ground. Islam is thus Africanized and marginalized at the same time.[36] The whole pairing echoes the Ecclesia-Synagoga iconography of upright church and downcast synagogue in contemporary art.

[32] Lactantii, *Divinarum Institutionum*, Book II, c. 10, *PL* 6.507.

[33] See David Bevington, ed., *The Macro Plays: The Castle of Perseverance, Wisdom, Mankind* (New York, 1972), 152.

[34] See Harley and Woodward, eds., *The History of Cartography*, 340–342, on this point.

[35] The Hague, Royal Library MS 76 F 5, folio 1r. See for discussion Franz Niehoff, "Umbilicus mundi – Der Nabel der Welt. Jerusalem und das Heilige Grab im Spiegel von Pilgerberichten und-karten, Kreuzzügen und Reliquiaren," in Legner, ed., *Ornamenta Ecclesiae*, III, 77; J. Wilkinson, *Jerusalem Pilgrims before the Crusades* (Warminster, 1977), 149; R. Röhricht, "Karten und Pläne zur Pälastinakunde aus dem 7. bis 16. Jh.," *Zeitschrift des deutschen Palastina-Vereins* 159 (1892):34–37; Müller, *Die heilige Stadt*, 54; Zev Vilnay, *The Holy Land in Old Prints and Maps* (Jerusalem, 1963); S. de Sandoli, *Itinera Hierosolymitana Crucesignatorum (Saec. XII–XIII)* (Jerusalem, 1980), II, 413; and more generally R. Rubin, "Old Maps of Jerusalem as Historico-Geographical Sources," *Studies in the Geography of Israel* 12 (1986):52–64.

[36] On this idea, see the varying points of view presented by Richard C. Hoffman, "Outsiders by Birth and Blood: Racist Ideologies and Realities around the Periphery of Medieval European Culture," *Studies in Medieval and Renaissance History* NS 6 (1981): 1–34; B. Z. Kedar, *Crusade and Mission: European Approaches towards the Muslims* (Princeton, 1984); and R.I. Moore, *The Formation of a Persecuting Society: Power and Deviance in Western Europe, 950–1250* (Oxford, 1987). That such colors had a symbolic function is clear from the comment of a later map maker, Andreas Walsperger, who in 1448 observed of the colors he used for Christian and Moslem cities "red marks

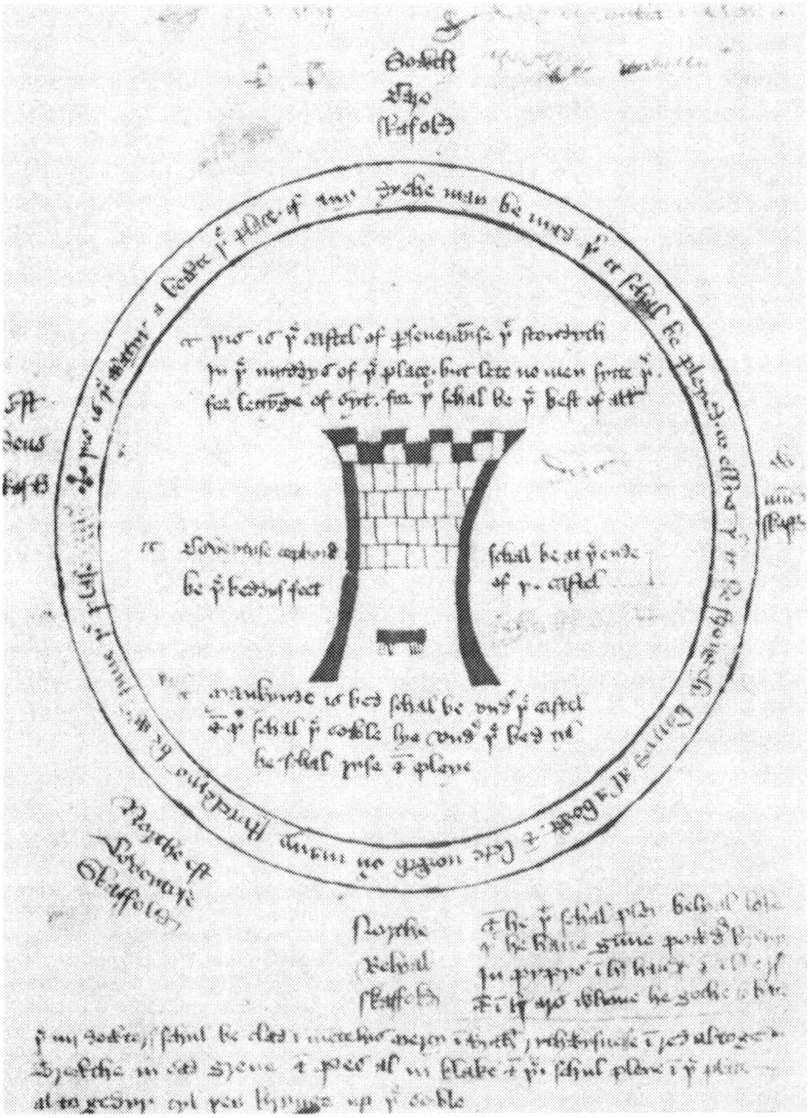

Figure 2.8. Moralized map, *The Castle of Perseverance*, Washington, D.C., Folger Shakespeare Library, fifteenth century.

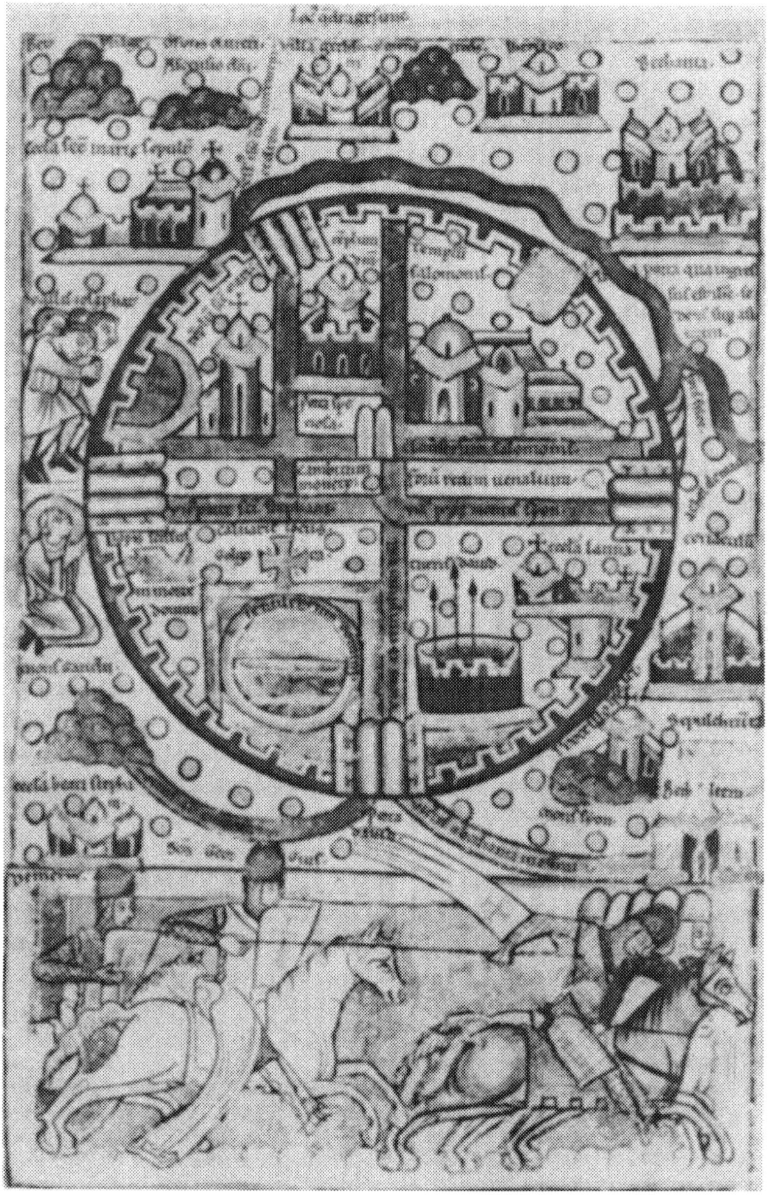

Figure 2.9. Saint George vanquishes a Moslem, city of Jerusalem map, collector, St. Bertin?, Netherlands, The Hague, Royal Library, MS 76 F 5, folio 1r, circa 1180.

In the Macrobian maps, so called because the type first appears in manuscripts of the fifth-century A.D. author Macrobius' *Commentary on the Dream of Scipio,* five habitable and uninhabitable zones or parallels of latitudes divide the globe.[37] Because of the mechanical difficulties in projecting such a figure, however, the world is more usually a disk divided in five climates from north to south, though such maps have no dominant vertical orientation, and do not necessarily relate either to the codex or to the religion of which the codex is a symbol. They are really more abstract than the T-O types, dealing with principles of organization rather than with locations of peoples. An example of the type occurs in a volume of William of Conches' *De Philosophia Mundi,* now a Ludwig manuscript in the J. Paul Getty Museum.[38] (Figure 2.10). The zone or climate *frigida australis* is separated from a temperate southern zone and that from the northern half of the world by the Mediterranean, imagined here as girdling the earth. An area called "our habitable zone" comes next, and then the frigid north pole.

The disk is symmetrical; no area is to be preferred on theological grounds, and the extremes of the world appear equally uninhabitable. As close to the center as it is possible to be with the Macrobian map, however, we find a rubric "nostra zona habitabilis." There is, of course, no corresponding "their habitable zone," and indeed the map is a perfect example of geographical solipsism, for the only evidence of human life on it is that offered in the maker's point of view. That is to say, the maker's culture is the only one this map recognizes, though it certainly implies antithetical cultures, inherent in the antipodean structure of the map. In some variants of this idea, such as in that depicted in illustrations for Raoul de Presles' translation of St. Augustine's *City of God,* people stand upside down from the viewer's perspective at the bottom of the southern hemisphere.[39]

A climate map of John of Wallingford now in the British Library

the cities of the Christians, black those of the infidels." This map is now in Rome, Biblioteca Apostolica Vaticana MS pal. lat 1362 b.

37 See Macrobius, *Commentary on the Dream of Scipio,* William Harris Stahl, ed. and trans. (New York, 1966), ch.5, 201–202, and Stahl, *Roman Science* (Madison, 1962), 158–169.

38 Now Malibu, California, J. Paul Getty Museum MS XV 4., folio 217v. See Anton von Euw and Joachim Plotzek, *Die Handschriften der Sammlung Ludwig* (Cologne, 1984). Some color photographs of miniatures from this manuscript appear in Joachim M. Plotzek, "Mirabilia Mundi," in Legner, ed., *Ornamenta Ecclesiae,* I, 112–13.

39 See, for example, the miniature in A. de Laborde, *Les Manuscrits à peintures de la Cité de Dieu de Saint Augustin* (Paris, 1909), III, pl.102c, and discussed in II, 443. The miniature is from Nantes, Bibliothèque Municipale MS Fr. 8, folio 163v. See also Sharon Dunlap Smith, "New Themes from the *City of God* around 1400: The Illustrations of Raoul de Presles' Translation," *Scriptorium* 36 (1982):68–82.

Figure 2.10. Macrobian climate map, Malibu, California, J. Paul Getty Museum, MS XV.4, folio 217v, thirteenth century. Author's photograph.

mixes these Macrobian and tripartite forms. This thirteenth-century representation (Figure 2.11) makes Jerusalem the middle climate, just as in the purely spatial maps that city is the center of the world. On the extreme edge of the Wallingford map, without even an image, is the familiar area of marginalized peoples bearing the rubric "*monstruosi homini.*"[40]

This process of marginalization occurs in a rather unusual map

[40] London, British Library MS Cotton Julius D.vii, folio 46v. See on this map, Destombes, *Mappamondes*, 168, and Anna-Dorothee von den Brincken, "Die Klimatenkarte in der Chronik des Johann von Wallingford–ein Werk des Matthaeus Parisiensis?" *Westfalen* 51 (1973):47–57, and the same author's "Das geographische Weltbild um 1300," *Zeitschrift für Historische Forschung* 6 (1989):9–32. An excellent discussion in English appears in Nigel Morgan, *Early Gothic Manuscripts*, 1190–1250 (Oxford, 1982), item 91, 141.

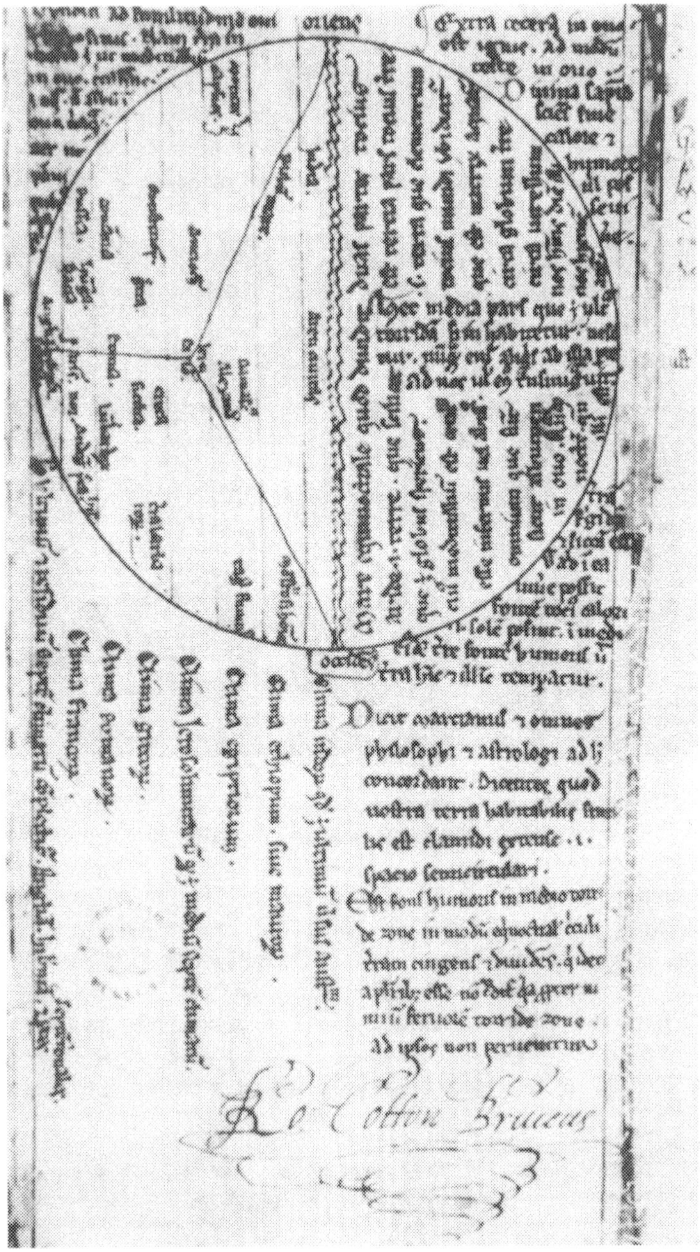

Figure 2.11. Climate map, John of Wallingford, London, British Library, MS Cotton Julius D.vii, folio 46, thirteenth century.

found in a volume of Pomponius Mela's treatise on cosmography. Mela, active in the first half of the first century A.D., had a climatic or zonal conception of the world. Not a Christian, he would of course have had no interest in Hebraic conceptions of the earth, nor in spaces intended to show the favor of a creator shed upon a chosen people. A volume of Mela published in 1417, now in the Reims Municipal Library (Figure 2.12), contains a map in which the artist seemingly ignored the climatic idea of the world found in the book for which the map was an illustration, and created one with the three continents assigned by Noah to his sons labeled in red.[41] The river Ocean enclosing them contains at its edge fabulous geography. Not only distant lands, but lands where the inhabitants differ profoundly in culture and appearance from westerners, are appropriately marginalized.

At the far right of the map in Africa is a rubric indicating the land of Prester John, a fabulous region belonging to the tall travel tales of Mandeville and others; it is placed at the very edge of the known world, and opposite at the far left of Europe is a region called *terra incognita*.[42] Another element of fabulous geography appears here in the form of the Hyperborean mountains, also at the extreme or marginalized edges of the world.

A little known but extremely curious T-O map that combines a number of features of the planispheres we have been talking about can be used to end this discussion of space (Figure 2.13). This map occurs on the flyleaf as the frontispiece for a work on world and British history, Paris, Bibliothèque Nationale MS Lat. 4126,[43] compiled and partly written in York by the Carmelite Robert de Popilton. Most probably the map was conceived and perhaps even drawn by Robert, who in 1368 was Prior of the Carmelite convent of Hulne on the north-

[41] Reims, Bibliothèque de la Ville, MS 1321, folio 13.

[42] On The Land of Prester John, see Anna-Dorothee von den Brincken, "Presbyter Iohannes, Dominus Dominantium-ein Wunsch-weltbilt des 12. Jahrhunderts," in Legner, ed., *Ornamenta Ecclesiae*, I, 83–97; L. N. Gumilev, *Searches for an Imaginary Kingdom: The Legend of the Kingdom of Prester John* (Cambridge, 1987); C.F. Beckingham, *Between Islam and Christendom: Travellers, Facts, Legends in the Middle Ages and the Renaissance* (London, 1983); and Bernard Hamilton, "Prester John and the Three Kings of Cologne," in Henry Mayr-Harting and R.I. Moore, eds., *Studies in Medieval History Presented to R.H.C. Davis* (London, 1985), 177–191.

[43] Folio 1v. On the codex itself, see François Avril and Patricia Danz Stirnemann, *Manuscrits enluminés d'origine insulaire VIIe-XXe Siècle* (Paris, 1987), no. 204, 163–164, who date it as second half of the thirteenth century and second half of the fourteenth century. The map is described by them as a celestial and terrestrial map of the fourteenth century with Jerusalem at the center, drawn in red ink. Several names have been added in black ink and the planets indicated in green ink. The map is mentioned briefly by Destombes, *Mappamondes*, 159, and Charles Samaran, et al., *Catalogue de Manuscrits en écriture Latine Datées* (Paris, 1962), II, 488.

Figure 2.12. World map, Pomponius Mela, *De Chorographia*, Reims, Bibliothèque de la Ville, MS 1321, folio 13, 1417.

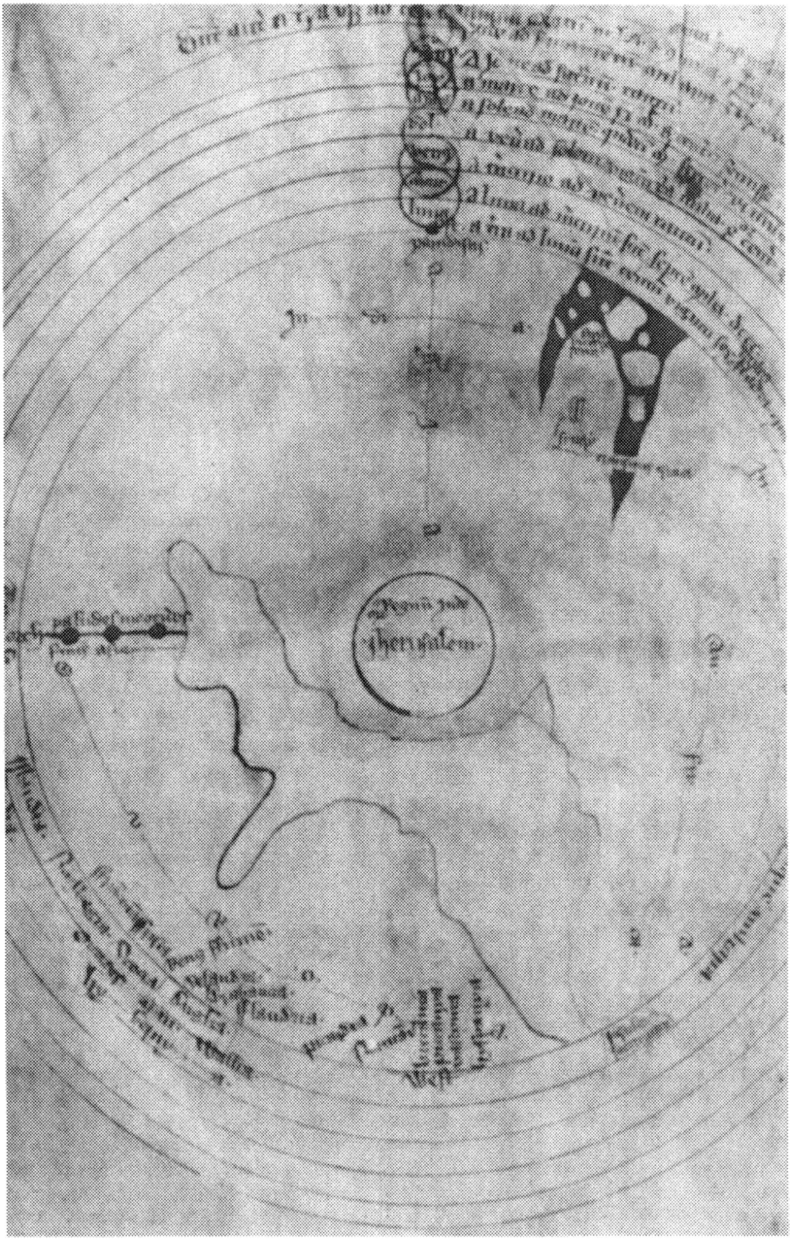

Figure 2.13. T-O map, Robert de Popilton, geographical and historical miscellany, Paris, Bibliothèque Nationale, MS lat. 4126, folio 1, *ca.* 1368.

ern outskirts of Alnwick in Northumberland.[44] Fascinated by both geography and early British history, he chose texts of writers such as Orosius, Geoffrey of Monmouth and Alfred of Beverley, editing them with marginal cross-references and comparative comments.[45]

Robert seems to have come from one of two very small villages, Nether and Upper Popiltoun, both within the ainsty of the city of York.[46] Ordained subdeacon on 21 May 1345, deacon on 24 September 1345, and priest on 17 December 1345 in the church of the Carmelites at York, Popilton's first ordination describes him as of the York convent. In 1351-2 he was licensed as a confessor and was still described as of the York convent, so that the association with Hulne seems to have begun later in his life.[47] He was apparently quite successful as a prior, as he managed to obtain a large gift of lead for repair of the roof of the house from the Percy family, whose seat was only a few miles from the convent.[48]

The Paris volume was apparently written at York under Popilton's direction – "*ora pro Popilton, qui me compilavit Eboraci.*"[49] Though Popilton's name appears in nine *explicits* marking the ends of stints, these seem to have been written by several hands, and only the signatures at folios 13v and 211v seem to be his. Thus he functioned chiefly as an overseer and editor for the volume, as well as an occasional scribe.

That Popilton was a well-to-do book owner with an attraction to works on British history and scientific knowledge before becoming the Prior of Hulne is clear from the catalogue of this library, which has just been republished by Kenneth Humphreys. The catalogue,

44 See David Knowles and R. Neville Hadcock, *Medieval Religious Houses: England and Wales* (New York, 1972), 235, and Keith J. Egan, O. Carm., "Medieval Carmelite Houses, England and Wales," *Carmelus* 16 (1969):179–180.

45 A detailed treatment of Robert de Popilton as scribe, compiler, and editor occurs in my study, *Northern English Books, Owners and Makers in the late Middle Ages* (Syracuse University Press, 1995). See also Kenneth W. Humphreys, ed., *The Friars' Libraries* (London, 1990), xxxiv, and Edward J. Cowan, "The Scottish Chronicle in the Poppleton Manuscript," *The Innes Review* 32 (1961):3–21.

46 See Samuel Lewis, *A Topographical Dictionary of England* (London, 1831), III, 555.

47 See Borthwick Institute of Historical Research, York, Register 10A, Zouche, folio 11, folio 13, and folio 13v for ordinations and folio 280 for licensing to hear confessions.

48 See generally, G. Davis, *Medieval Chartularies of Great Britain* (London and N.Y., 1958), 3; W.H. St. John Hope, "On the Whitefriars or Carmelites of Hulne, Northumberland," *Archaeological Journal* 47 (1890):116–17; W. Dickson, "Contents of the Cartulary of Hulne Abbey," *Archaeologia Aeliana* ser. 1,3 (1844):46–7; George Tate, *History of the Borough, Castle and Barony of Alnwick* (Alnwick, 1866–1869), II, 49, 51–53; and Charles Henry Hartshorne, *Feudal and Military Antiquities of Northumberland and the Scottish Borders* (London, 1858), 268 and Appendix xcv, ci.

49 Folio 213v

dated 1366, indicates that Robert gave a bible worth three marks to the house, as well as the sermons of Hugh of St. Cher, a Peraldus, *Summa de Virtutibus*, a Bartholomeus Anglicus, *De Proprietatibus Rerum*, a sermon, Bede's prose life of St. Cuthbert, and another of Saint Silvester. He also owned a Henry of Huntingdon, *Historia Anglorum*. This is a well-written codex of mid-fourteenth-century date, now at Trinity College, Cambridge MS R. 5.42, bearing the *ex libris* "Liber fratris Roberti de Popultoun precij 20s" on the first folio in what I take to be the prior's secretary's script.[50]

As can quickly be seen, his map combines a T-O structure of a very Christian kind, with a representation of the heavens and the distances between the planetary spheres based on Moses Maimonides' account of these, a popular bit of astronomy that appears in the *Pricke of Conscience*, the *Book of Sidrak and Boccas*, and other didactic works.[51] In the original Moses Maimonides text, the distances are calculated by how many thousands of days it would take a man to walk from one sphere to another, but Popilton uses a system of miles.

Such maps offer a geocentric view of the world imagined as at the bottom of the spheres; man looks upward from his place on the disk toward the heavens and the *primum mobile*. In Popilton's map, the spheres rise above the disk of earth, with the individual planets indicated in them by small circles of green ink. But the use of space in this map is quite complex, because we have both the idea of the world as part of the heavens and as well a conception of the world as a plane surface rather than as a ball within an inverted dome. Though the sons of Noah are not mentioned on this map, the T-O structure associated with them is clearly in the maker's mind as the rubric "*finis Asie*" shows that he imagines the upper portion of the map as Asia. The map's spatial perspective is also very interesting, for we have the world seen at the bottom of the heavens, so that we look up at the sky rather than up at the top of the page. There is thus a tension between an astronomical world sphere idea where power inheres in

[50] Humphreys, *The Friars' Libraries*, publishes a photograph of the first page of the catalogue, figure 5. See items 9, 30, 32, 33, 37, 43, 44, [pp. 168, 171, 172, 173]. See M.R. James, *A Descriptive Catalogue of the Western Manuscripts in the Library of Trinity College, Cambridge* (Cambridge, 1900–1904), II, 210–211. The twenty shillings was the price paid by Robert either for the book secondhand or to have it written.

[51] See Theodor Graesse, ed., *Jacobi a Voragine Legenda aurea vulgo historia lombardica dicta* (Rp. Osnabrück, 1969), C. LXXII, 321. See generally S.S. Pines, "Maimonides," in *The Dictionary of Scientific Biography* (New York, 1974), IX, 27–32, and Wolfgang Kluxen, "Literargeschichtliches zum lateinischen Moses Maimonides," *Recherches de théologie ancienne et médiévale* 21 (1954):23–65.

the *primum mobile,* and a vertical or page orientation, where in some maps an anthropomorphic God the father looks downward from the east.

A rubric shows us Paradise, and the cross typical of maps with an eastern orientation at the top is formed by the intersection of the words India and Asia. Jerusalem in the center is labeled as the land or kingdom of the Jews in a theological sense, but the Red Sea at the upper right contains important landmarks of actual rather than theological geography, Arabia Deserta, and Mount Sinai with the tables of the Law. Though the areas belonging within the Judeo-Christian cultural boundaries are labeled in Latin, interestingly, three of the four cardinal points are clearly indicated in English, the language of the maker's perspective as we shall see. South, located in Africa and India at the extreme right, appears to have been cut off in binding.

Only the Judeo-Christian offers landmarks in what is a significantly entitled space – Arabia Deserta – for all traces of the Islamic world are lacking. The specificity and particularity of the northern European labels, however, indicate that the maker was perfectly capable of adding geographic detail but that he did not choose to do so. What is present is fabulous. At the north are Ultima Thule and the Paludes Moetides. These marshes, in the area around the Sea of Azov, reveal the gradual silting-up process there, because in the work of antique cosmographers such as Mela and Solinus they are called the Moetican lakes.[52]

The artist seems to have had an unusually good knowledge of northwestern geography and to have been particularly interested in this area, since the cultural perspective of the rubrics makes it seem that no other part of the world – except the Holy Land – exists. Thule is placed at the outermost reaches of northern exploration, with Iceland and Vinland marking the edges of the inhabited world. Norway, the Orcades, Franconia, Frisia, the river Danube (or flumen Retius here in red),[53] Zeeland, Belgium, and Flanders, Scotland, England, the Aran isles, Wales, and Ireland all attest to the mapmaker's particular interests. Moving southward, Brittany, the Poitou, and Spain mark what he considers significant, and at the extreme southern reaches and appropriately marginalized like Thule are the Fortunate or Canary Islands. There is, oddly, no representation of Italy or the capital of Christianity, Rome. As Rome was a constant of the *mappaemundi,* its omission here is surprising.[54]

[52] See on this point, Harley and Woodward, eds., *The History of Cartography,* 328, 345.

[53] See Eric Christianson, *The Northern Crusade: The Baltic and the Catholic Frontier of Christendom 1100–1525* (Minneapolis, 1980).

[54] See Harley and Woodward, eds., *The History of Cartography,* 330.

All of this is relatively unexceptional. What is striking is the presence of a water outline or a land mass stretched on a roughly northeast southwest axis. I think the mapmaker may have intended this to be an enormous representation of England, with the thumb of Land's End at the tip of Cornwall unusually distorted and sticking out. Though he has already labeled Britain, he seems to have had an afterthought and drawn in this land mass.

The shape of England, if this is what the artist intended, in its vast and truly ethnocentric scale,[55] belongs to the moralized geography of the period that we find in maps of Pavia by Opicinis da Canistris,[56] or of Venice by some of the mapmakers so ably studied by Juergen Schulz.[57]

Popilton is not unusual in his geographic ethnocentrism, for Matthew Paris before him, in his own enlargement of Britain, said of his map that if he had had a larger page he would have made England even longer.[58] The unusual proportions of England may reflect one of the texts of the compilation. At folio 26v the compiler incorporates the twelfth-century "De situ Albanie, que in se figuram hominis habet." This is because "pars namque principalis eius id est capud est in Arregarchel . . . pedes autem eius sunt supra mare Northwagie . . . corpus vero ipsius est mons qui Moinid uocatur . . . brachia autem eius sunt ipsi montes qui dividunt Scociam ab Arregarchel" (folio 26v), and so on. Such an idea of the shape of Scotland derives from the fact that in some accounts the region took its name from a legendary Albanactus, who was imagined to give the region its outline. It is probably similar thinking that accounts for the size of England.[59]

Typically the gigantic has been a metaphor for the geographic, and the miniature for the domestic environment. Opicinus da Canistris,

[55] For an example of this sort of thinking in a different geographic context, see Susan Gole, "Size as a Measure of Importance in Indian Cartography," *Imago Mundi*, 42 (1990):99–105.

[56] See R. Salomon, ed., *Opicinus de Canistris, Weltbild und Bekenntnisse eines Avignonesischen Klerikers des 14.Jahrhunderts* (London, 1939) and his more recent studies, "A Newly Discovered Manuscript of Opicinus de Canistris," *The Journal of the Warburg and Courtauld Institutes* 16 (1953):45–57, and "Aftermath to Opicinis de Canistris," *The Journal of the Warburg and Courtauld Institutes* 25 (1962):137–146.

[57] Juergen Schulz, "Jacobo de' Barbari's view of Venice: Map making, City Views, and Moralized Geography before the Year 1500," *Art Bulletin* 60 (1978):425–474.

[58] See British Library MS Royal 14. C.vii and Richard Vaughan, *Matthew Paris* (Cambridge, 1958), 243, as well as W.R. Tobler, "Medieval Distortions: The Projections of Ancient Maps," *Annals of the Association of American Geographers* 56 (1966):351–360.

[59] This text is briefly discussed by Marjorie O. Anderson, "The Scottish Materials in the Paris Manuscript, Bibliothèque National Latin 4126," *SHR* 28 (1949):34, and the full text is printed by Anderson, *Kings and Kingship in Early Scotland* (Edinburgh, 1973), 240–45.

with his Mediterranean countries in the forms of enormous men and woman, looks forward to Swift's Brobdignagians and later landscapes, which are the projections of a vast human body or parts of that body. We speak easily of mouths of rivers, foothills, the finger lakes of upstate New York, and the heartland of America, and virtually every region has its own Giant City, showing the perennial fascination of magnified human and animal bodies.[60]

The gigantic in landscape as in human scale evokes nostalgia, the loss of some larger or finer quality of life, as in the common literary metaphor of the Renaissance and eighteenth century in which modern writers are dwarfs standing on the shoulders of giants. Thus the gigantic forms a part of the romantic primitivism often associated with the literature of wonders and marvels as in Mandeville, the *Letter of Prester John* and the Alexander narratives.

The appeal of the gigantic to Robert de Popilton can be located in the overall conception of his book. For the history it relates is either that well before the compiler's time – the last date is 1326–or it is the apocalyptic history of the future in the *Oraculum Cyrilli* and the prophecies of Hildegarde of Bingen with which the work ends.[61] Popilton's fascination with the mythical history of Scotland and early Britain, and the nostalgia of loss that accompanies it, are in keeping with his moralized geography.[62]

Popilton's map, indeed, is an extreme form of some of the tendencies I have been outlining. Rather than representing the area from which the maker surveys the rest of the world as bigger or more significant than those countries or regions not his own, Popilton simply ignores the existence of large areas of the known world, including all of Islam.[63] And his concentration of rubrics in the northwest makes

[60] Susan Stewart, *On Longing: Narratives of the Miniature, the Gigantic, the Souvenir, the Collection* (Baltimore and London, 1984), 70–80, 105–111, and see William G. Niederland, "The Pre-Renaissance Image of the World and the Discovery of America," in Howard F. Stein and William G. Niederland, eds., *Maps of the Mind: Readings in Psychogeography* (Norman, 1989), 104–113. I am grateful to Peter H. Wood of Duke University for this reference.

[61] See Kathryn Kerby-Fulton, "Hildegard of Bingen and the Anti-Mendicant Propaganda Tradition," *Traditio* 43 (1987):381, 391–393, and Jeanne Bignami-Odier, *Etudes sur Jean de Roquetaillade* (Paris, 1952), 53–112.

[62] For an overview of Popilton's interest in Pictish mythic history, see R. Frame, *The Political Development of the British Isles 1100–1400* (Oxford, 1990) and R.R. Davies, ed., *The British Isles, 1100–1500: Comparisons, Contrasts and Connections* (Edinburgh, 1988).

[63] Though its focus is rather later than mine, J. B. Harley's "Silences and Secrecy: the Hidden Agenda of Cartography in Early Modern Europe," *Imago Mundi* 40 (1988): 57–76, is full of valuable insights relevant to the maps discussed here.

all that is not within the purview of the English appropriately so marginalized that it does not even appear on the surface of the map.

In sum there is much that can be learned about cultural conflicts from even the most schematic of medieval maps. Relative size and position reveal value just as they do in the manuscript paintings of the period, and in their own way these maps can be virtually as narrative as the programs of illustration accompanying more conventional texts. Nor is the seemingly empty space of the simplest of these maps mute. As we have seen in what is a fairly representative body of medieval world maps, the marginalized cultural other has had a very long and honored history. Indeed, just as much as in the west, which conceived these beings in the first place, such persons and places are ideas that form part of the larger study of the history of mentalities; they have their own traditions, their own images, and it could be said that the west needed all that was the non-west to define its own identity. Many of the configurations of power and domination that we see as early, for example, as the binary oppositions of pagan and Christian in the *Song of Roland,* were in fact equally visible in the world maps that begin to be made at about the time that poem was first composed, and express many of its attitudes. World maps of the Middle Ages are texts; they can be read in much the same way we interpret the books in which they are often found, and their minimal, geometric spaces, just as much as their random and chaotic collections of labels for peoples, mountains, and rivers, figure a language of their makers that can give valuable insights into the cultures that produced them.

CHAPTER 3

Spain, circa 1492: Social values and structures

MIGUEL ANGEL LADERO QUESADA

THIS chapter is a reflection on the country that discovered the New World and peopled a good portion of it for more than three hundred years. What were Spain's kingdoms and regions, its social and political organization, and its world of mental values? In short, I seek to explore the historical background with which explorers, conquistadors, missionaries, and colonizers faced the new and unique challenges, often of tremendous dimensions, upon their arrival in America.[1]

Perhaps at no other time in human history was a handful of men so compelled by both the desire to maintain their historical reality and by the need to transform it in the face of new and unforeseen circumstances within the span of two generations (1492–1550). The chronicler López de Gómara captured the spirit of this paradox: "Never has a nation extended its customs, its language and arms like the Spanish, nor has any nation gone as far as Spain by sea and land with weapons on their backs." Years later, in the same vein, but from the perspective of a navigator and explorer, Belmonte Bermúdez reaffirmed that: "We named the ocean and the rivers/measuring the skies, adjusting the compass."[2]

"With weapons on their backs" is suggestive of the bellicose and violent Hispanic medieval society, while the other phrase – "we

[1] For those with an interest in a more detailed bibliography, here are some general works on the history of Spanish America: F. Morales Padrón, *Historia del Descubrimiento y conquista de América*, 3d ed. (Madrid, 1981); M. Hernández Sánchez-Barba, *Historia de América Latina* (Madrid, 1985), 1: 269–371 (Dir. N. Sánchez-Albornoz); *El Descubrimiento y la fundación de los reinos ultramarinos hasta fines del siglo XVI* (Historia General de España y América), vol. 7 (Madrid, 1982) (Dir. D. Ramos Pérez); James Lockhart and Stuart B. Schwartz, *Early Latin America: A History of Colonial Spanish America and Brazil* (Cambridge, 1983).

[2] The citations in this chapter about America from chroniclers and authors of the sixteenth century are taken from F. Morales Padrón, *Los conquistadores de América*, 2d ed. (Madrid, 1974).

named the ocean" – guides our thought toward the ancient southward colonizing movement during the Middle Ages in the peninsula itself. For this reason, the question of the medieval antecedents of the conquest and colonization of the Spanish Indies occupies an old and central place in the minds of historians of America.

Regarding the medieval antecedents, historians have paid more attention to the long period of the Reconquest (ninth to thirteenth centuries) rather than to the late medieval period that molded the experience of those who lived through the Columbian moment and its aftermath. The majority of men who arrived in the Indies came from Andalusia, Extremadura, and the two Castiles, and very often came from noble families (*hidalgo* and *caballeros*) as younger sons or from commoner (artisan and peasant *pechero*) backgrounds. These two dimensions, geographic and social, direct our attention toward certain realities of the fifteenth century perhaps more characteristic of the Kingdom of Castile than of the other Spanish lands.

Castile overcame the late medieval crisis through an early process of expansion that reached its height around 1492. It was an advanced and renovated feudal society, capable of incorporating certain aspects of an incipient capitalism and of making them compatible with the effects of the "modern state" that emerged out of previously established power relations and the old *reconquista* impulse that was renewed at the end of the fifteenth century. This was also a land where people still praised the values of knighthood and held an intense Christian religiosity, reformed by means that were not always comparable to those of northwestern Europe. This religiosity is another matter that cannot be overlooked.

CONQUEST AND COLONIZATION: THE RENEWAL OF A MEDIEVAL HERITAGE

From the vantage point of 1492, the medieval enterprise of conquest and colonization was not part of the distant past. Drawing on the base of experiences accumulated from the eleventh and the thirteenth centuries, Castile was able to take over the Moorish kingdom of Granada (1482–1492) and the Canary Islands (1478–1496).[3] Both provided models for the colonization of the Indies, in administrative organization as well as in the contact and conversion of the indigenous inhabitants.

[3] For some general introductions to the period of the Catholic Kings, see my books, *Los Reyes Católicos: la corona y la unidad de España* (Madrid, 1989); *España en 1492* (Madrid, 1978). See also L. Suárez Fernández, *Los Reyes Católicos*, 5 vols. (Madrid, 1989–90); J. Pérez, *Isabelle et Ferdinand. Rois Catholi ques d'Espagne* (Paris, 1988).

This was less so in Granada, where the Muslims continued to live for some years under the old medieval formula of coexistence as *mudéjares* recognized by the treaties or *capitulaciones*, but it was more true in the Canaries where the native peoples were not infidels, but pagans. During the reign of the Catholic kings, relations between Castile and Africa also reached their peak in both mercantile and military terms, especially with the Muslim kingdom in the Maghreb. One aspect of these contacts was the growth of the phenomenon of slavery in the cities of Atlantic Andalusia as Moors, Guineans (Black Africans), Azeanegues (Berbers and North Africans), and Canarians arrived in increasing numbers. This tradition of modern slavery evolved from medieval precedents, but was greater in scope than in the past.[4]

There is no doubt that all this influenced the behavior of the Spaniards in the Indies, but one should not exaggerate the parallel. Both conquests provided models for the subsequent colonization of the Indies, as much in terms of the administration of new territories as in the contact with indigenous peoples and their evangelization. These earlier conquests were valuable in themselves because they contributed to the consolidation and creation of certain attitudes and Hispanic social values dealing with war and the integration of new territories that were less applicable in the New World.

There are considerable differences between the conquest and the repopulating of Granada by Spaniards and that of the Americas. Despite the invocations of Santiago on the battlefield and their frequent references to Indian temples as "mosques," the Indians seemed little like the Muslims that the conquistadors knew so well. Indeed, the evangelization campaigns were very different. Whereas success accompanied the missionary effort in the Americas, the Moors in Granada, although baptized between 1500 and 1502, remained alienated from the religious and cultural worlds of the Hispano-Christians until Philip II expelled their descendants, the *moriscos*, from his lands in 1571.[5]

[4] On the repopulation in general S. de Moxó, *Repoblación y sociedad en la España cristiana medieval* (Madrid, 1978), and J. A. García de Cortázar, et. al., *Organización social del espacio en la España medieval. La Corona de Castilla en los siglos VIII a XV* (Barcelona, 1985). On Granada my books, *Granada. Historia de un país islámico (1232–1571)*, 3d ed. (Madrid, 1989); *Castilla y la conquista del reino de Granada*, 2d ed. (Granada, 1987); *Granada después de la conquista. Repobladores y mudéjares* (Granada, 1988). On the Canary islands see Eduardo Aznar Vallejo, *La integración de las Islas canarias en la Corona de Castilla (1478–1526)* (La Laguna, 1983); F. Fernández Armesto, *The Canary Islands after the Conquest* (Oxford, 1982); and his *Before Columbus: Exploration and Colonization from the Mediterranean to the Atlantic, 1229–1492* (London, 1987).

[5] For English-speaking readers it will be useful to wait for the full edition of C. Smith and C. H. Melville, *Christians and Moors in Spain*, 3 vols. (Warminster, England, in press).

On the other hand, it is only a partial truth that the Canary Islands were a testing ground for the colonization of the Indies. The situation prevailing at the time of the Canarian conquest, its dimension and the nature of the indigenous society, even the objectives being pursued, were different, although the initial image of the Antilles as "the overseas Canaries" might have initially invited comparison of the two cases. It is certain, nevertheless, that the continuous and intense relationship between the Canaries and America in later years would create other ties that do not pertain to this chapter.

The Crown engaged in the Canarian campaign – begun in 1402 under seigniorial initiative – to prevent a likely Portuguese intervention as a result of the 1475–1479 war. At that time, the three "major islands" – Gran Canaria, Tenerife, and La Palma – had not been conquered or integrated into Castile, and the Crown assumed the task. However, the conquest, achieved by captains with contractual ties to the Crown, was irregular, at times difficult, and engendered a peculiar type of repopulation and territorial organization. Such a process was necessary to combine the interests of the Crown and those of the conquistadors and their associates in an area much smaller and farther away than Granada. The sparse indigenous population of the Canaries had to choose between baptism and assimilation – the prevailing norm – or enslavement.[6] From the beginning in the Canaries, as in Granada, the Crown hoped to integrate both territories on an equal footing with the others that it governed, as part of the same community. The two were given the title of "kingdom," so that the "colonial" situation referred to the circumstances of the arrival of Christian settlers and the commencement of mercantile activity, but not to political authority.

We must consider carefully the case of the incorporation of the emirate of Granada because it exposes the breadth of the social and political traditions of medieval conquest and colonization and the great importance that they had for Castile. For a decade, both the Crown and Castilian society thoroughly immersed themselves in the conquest of Granada, putting into play all of their military, financial, and institutional resources. The enterprise was considered the culmination of a secular process of *reconquista* against the Muslims, the recovery of the entire peninsula through the elimination of the last Islamic political power and of the frontier that it had sustained before Castilian Andalusia for two and a half centuries.

The conquest of Granada was, consequently, an event of exceptional importance, without doubt the principal legacy that that epoch left to

[6] A. Rumeu de Armas, *La política indigenista de Isabel la Católica* (Valladolid, 1969).

the times and in the consciousness of the people that would follow in Spain. Studying its development one finds not only singular deeds, but also an opportunity to clarify our understanding of numerous historical structures of late medieval Castile, from those of *mentalité* to those of colonization, social, political, and economic organization, all of which were dynamized and employed in the huge effort of that war.

The means for the conquest of Granada were procured from all parts of Castilian society. By continuous and energetic political action, the Crown utilized all the processes of mobilization available to medieval Castile. These proved to be superior to those employed in any other enterprise of conquest and colonization during the sixteenth and seventeenth centuries. Castile succeeded in forming armies of 12,000 knights and 40,000 foot-soldiers, plus the non-combatant personnel and 200 pieces of artillery in the principal campaigns. The Crown had to accumulate extraordinary financial resources in order to raise the 5 million *ducados* of expenditures incurred directly by the war.

The enterprise in Granada involved ten years of clashes against an enemy known for centuries, and the conquest of a territory of 30,000 square kilometers populated by some 300,000 people and well-endowed with walled cities and castles. In this respect it is difficult to establish parallels or relationships between the events in Granada and those that occurred in America. But another question presents itself: What was the relationship between the acts of surrender and the treatment of the conquered?

There was a fundamental difference. The indigenous peoples of America, like those of the Canaries, were pagans to whom one could apply either a criterion of evangelization and freedom, or another of war and enslavement. On the other hand, the Muslims were infidels with whom Castilians had had a long medieval tradition of coexistence, including both diplomatic and commercial relations as well as physical proximity. Therefore the Muslims were often allowed to live like *mudéjares* with their own religious law and judicial system in the dominions of the Christian kings. This situation, however, occurred much more frequently in Aragon and Valencia than in Castile.

For the majority of the Granadans the conquest signified their passage to the condition of *mudéjares* regulated by the terms of the *capitulaciones,* treaties that were signed at the end of hostilities. All of these treaties, in diverse degrees, maintained the tradition of tolerance with respect to religion, personal liberty, and property ownership, at least of household goods, that had characterized a good part of the medieval coexistence between Christianity and Islam in the peninsula.

However, the Castilians acceded to these favorable conditions in order to accelerate the surrender and the end of the war. In the majority of the known texts of the *capitulaciones* one observes that the inhabitants of unfortified villages and towns carefully guarded the ownership of their real estate. On the other hand, those of the cities and strongholds that had been the objects of sieges and military action abandoned them, the townsfolk as well as the country people. Only in the city of Granada did they stay, despite the long siege. There were a few cases, like Alhama and Málaga, where the conquest was by force, without surrender, and all the inhabitants were taken captive. However, these were isolated although important situations.

In spite of the *capitulaciones,* the Muslim population diminished rapidly, in part because of the war and the confinements, in part because of the ruin, the loss of property, and because of emigration to the Maghreb, an act chosen especially by directed groups and cults that aggravated the indefensibility and the cultural impoverishment of those who stayed. By 1530 there were only 100,000 *moriscos,* but they had organized the revolt of 1500–1501 that accelerated the flow of emigrants, and had already completed the process of colonization along with Christians who came from other parts of Andalusia and Castile.

This colonization of the population also had medieval precedents. The Crown utilized the techniques for distribution of land and other property that it had perfected around the middle of the thirteenth century in the valley of the Guadalquivir. The Crown organized the population directly. First, it decided the number of inhabitants to establish in each locality. It decided on the exemptions and fiscal advantages – more abundant when there was an interest in attracting colonists – and the distribution of property to be divided. All the cities of the interior were completely repopulated: Ronda, Alhama, Loja, Baza, Guadix, and Vera, as were the coastal towns of Marbella, Málaga, Vélez Málaga, Amuñécar, Salbreña, and Almería. In the city of Granada there were *avecindamientos* (grants of citizenship and land) and purchases of territory. *Mudéjares,* however, could sell, but not buy. By 1497, five years after the surrender, the Christian population had grown considerably and the *mudéjares* were concentrated in Albaicín and other suburbs.

Between 1485 and 1499, 35,000 to 40,000 colonists entered the kingdom of Granada, the majority with families. In 1530 there were some 100,000 old Christian inhabitants, more than the *moriscos.* Thus, a massive, effective colonization followed the conquest completed by settlers who frequently came from nearby regions. The differences with the situation in the Indies did not end here. The majority of the colonists were, naturally, farmers (between 50 and 75 percent), and they received their *vecindad* or allotment of lands as commoners, stimulating medium and small property ownership. There were also contingents of artisans and merchants, mostly in the major cities, and many *escuderos* of the Royal Guard, knights, and other military people. The Crown mandated that they receive a double allotment as a minimum.

Although the inhabitants were obligated to reside with an open house and family a minimum of five or ten years, it happened, as in previous times, that little by little the number of large property owners grew with much of the populace becoming renters or tenants – as it was with many *mudéjares*. Simultaneously, local powers fell into the hands of oligarchies that were more closed than in the rest of Castile. Often this situation prevailed from the beginning owing to the abundance of royal grants (*mercedes regias*) in some localities that favored already privileged or dominant groups and persons. In contrast the Crown authorized few seignorial jurisdictions, or at least few of any importance. These jurisdictions were always located in rural interior areas populated by *mudéjares* over which the lord acquired the responsibilities of government and intermediate administration. Royal power remained dominant and maintained its capacity as arbiter.

The administration of the kingdom of Granada was organized according to models employed in the rest of the kingdom of Castile but without the remnants of a previous evolution; this permitted it to accentuate the exercise of regal authority, something indispensable in that initial moment. The military command of the kingdom and responsibility of *capitán general* belonged to the Count of Tendilla, Iñigo de Mendoza, who resided in the Alhambra, of which he was governor. Iñigo de Mendoza had been a royal confidant. He had been, among other things, ambassador to Rome in 1486, and was one of the great organizers of the recently conquered kingdom before his death in 1515. Throughout the territory of Granada he maintained hundreds of castles, towers, and rural and urban fortresses, and organized a system of coastal vigilance to prevent any incursions from the Magreb, paid for by the *mudéjares* through a special tribute, or *farda*.

The municipal administration, organized and headed by *corregidores* and magistrates, was based on closed municipal councils or *regimientos* of a few people who initially were named directly by the kings. Over time they established the legal model, initially inspired by the law of Seville and regulated in many populations after 1494–95 by the *Fuero Nuevo*, a royal ordinance, the same law that applied in Las Palmas de Gran Canaria, to which soon was added the ordinances issued by each municipality.

In the first years the presence of organizers delegated by the Crown were fundamental. They were the *repartidores* (tax assessors) and the reformers of the *repartimientos,* such as Juan Alfonso Serrano in and around Málaga. The prime example was the efficient royal secretary, Hernando de Zafra, who had lived in Granada since 1492 and who, jointly with the Count of Tendilla, the Archbishop Hernando de Talavera, and the *corregidor* Andrés Calderón, formed the directive team of the new Castilian organization of Granada.

The papal concession of the *Patronato Real* (Royal Patronage) permitted the Crown to act with great liberty in the organization of the Granadan Church through its *colaboradores,* initially Cardinal Pedro González de Mendoza, Hernando de Talavera who arrived at the peak of his career as archbishop of Granada, and the suffragan bishops of Málaga, Almería, and Guadix. In spite of the evangelical mildness of Talavera, it was a conquering and triumphant church that was installed in Granada. The dedication of many temples to the Incarnation – one of the Christian dogmas most inassimilable to the Islamic mentality – demonstrates clearly the firmness with which the Church wanted to cement the new religious edifice that it understood as the restoration of the Christianity that had existed on the peninsula prior to the Islamic invasion.

In the colonization and organization of Granada, techniques and institutions already known in medieval Castile were put into play. Some of them also were applicable in America, in different ways according to the place and the moment. However, this does not mean that the Granadan model directly influenced behavior in America except for the advantage of creating a common pool of knowledge. Although, as we will indicate later, the Crown's tight control of both political and ecclesiastical organization was a novelty in many respects, the case of Granada was an experience that was very useful for what would follow in America.

The Spanish relationship with the Muslims developed in ways substantially different from that with the indigenous peoples of America. The Muslims were part of a religion and civilization that dominated all the southern shore of the Mediterranean and was much better structured than that of the Amerindians. Thus, in order to frame this question adequately, one would have to allude to the entirety of the reciprocal relations and images that affected Islam and Europe in the Middle Ages. But without leaving the example of the Hispanic world, we can see that this relationship oscillated between hostility and mutual acceptance. This included a limited, but very ancient, cultural contact that explained the *capitulaciones,* which served to maintain tranquility for some years, when their provisions were enacted, although always with the understanding that conquest remained incomplete so long as Christian colonization was not consolidated. With the memory of the war and the past hostility weighing upon consciences and attitudes, the situation of the Muslims, already impoverished, worsened, sometimes inevitably.

In the political situation of the "modern state" inaugurated by the Catholic kings, the unity of religious faith was an indispensable condition of the social order and a premise for the exercise of power. In America, the alternatives were either war or the evangelization of the indigenous peoples; in Spain, the expulsion or the baptism of Jews and *mudéjares*. There is a parallel between the cases, produced by the novelty of the political/religious program, but the process and the results were very different and depended, in large part, on the religious-cultural cohesion of the human groups affected, something that the Spanish governors and conquistadors perceived very well.

Thus in 1492 the great majority of Spanish Jews opted for emigration. Those who were baptized were, despite being recent converts, given no leniency. There were scarcely campaigns of evangelization, but instead application of the punishments of the Inquisition.

With the *mudéjares*, on the other hand, persuasion was attempted, although with very few positive results, either in Castile and Aragon, or in Granada. Nevertheless, there was more flexibility and the alternatives of baptism or expulsion were not available until much later. The Granadan revolts of 1500 and 1501 were neither foreseen nor desired by the Catholic kings, but the political result was mass conversions, although some thousands of Granadans emigrated. In 1502 the measure extended to all of Castile and in 1526 to Valencia. However, the *conversos* or *moriscos* were rarely investigated by the Inquisition for many years, although in Granada their cultural assimilation into the customs of the old Christians was attempted in 1511 and 1526.

The *moriscos* nevertheless preserved their culture and with it, their religion, although secretly. It was not possible to break this identity or to combine it with the European one, in contrast to what would happen in America, and the political and religious leaderships developed a very clear understanding in this regard. Thus it happened that in the first half of the sixteenth century there were surely parallels in the methods of evangelization employed in Moorish Granada and in America, but the results were very different. The *colegio* of San Miguel and the Casa de la Doctrina of Granada had few successes, nor did the rural missions of the Franciscans, the Dominicans, and the Jesuits. When tension heightened during the reign of Philip II, the result was the war and expulsion of 1569 and 1571, the antithesis of the religious acculturation and racial mixing that in spite of many excesses and difficulties had just triumphed in America. The main reason was perhaps the different perception of the Muslims by the Christians, and vice versa. Their reciprocal rejection was profound – to accept nothing or almost nothing from each other, convinced as they were of the superiority of their respective religions and their whole cultural worlds. Moreover, both prohibited mixed marriages, and although the *morisco* was formally Christian, such marriages were never frequent, and the family, together with the rural community, became the strongest bastions of their separate cultural identity.

The intensification of Spain's relations with the Maghreb provided another field of experiences and modes of behavior in the decades before and after 1492. This was particularly true in the realms of peaceful trade, piracy and the zeal for luxury and booty, and the bellicose hypersensitivity toward the infidels, who responded in kind. This relationship generated conflict in the form of raids, uprisings, enslavement, and the establishment of strategic forts on the coast to dominate or at least monitor the interior. The "Berbería de Levante" was more interesting than the "Pennant" – Ferdinand the Catholic was above all a Mediterranean-oriented ruler – yet to some extent the Atlantic expansion took interest away from the Hispanic campaigns in the Magreb. However, the Spanish efforts in North Africa also furnish some keys toward a better understanding of events in America despite the great differences between the two scenarios and the objectives that were pursued in each of them.[7]

Above all, the Seville-Cádiz commercial axis acquired invaluable expertise in trade and navigation in the mid-Atlantic, thanks in large part to the relations with the Barbary Coast. We are now aware of the importance of the two import commodities that would soon be important in the commerce with or toward the Indies: gold – in this case from south of the Sahara – and the slaves from Guinea and the Sahara. Acquired in the Atlantic ports of Morocco, the slaves did not include the captives supplied by naval forays on the Magreb coasts led by Andalusian sailors on their own initiative.[8] Plunder, hostility and conquest more than commerce loomed large in the spirit of both Portuguese and Andalusians in this period.

After the occupation of Ceuta in 1415, the Portuguese conquered

[7] For an analysis of questions with bibliography in my work, "Castilla, Gibraltar y Berbería (1252–1516)," in *Los mudéjares de Castilla y otros estudios de historia medieval andaluza* (Granada, 1989), 169–219.

[8] A. Franco Silva, *La esclavitud en Sevilla y su tierra a fines de la Edad Media* (Sevilla, 1979).

some coastal African sites. The Andalusians, for their part, engaged in plunder for captives and booty from which the Crown got the royal fifth (*quinto real*) according to medieval custom. The step from trade to plunder and vice versa must have been an everyday practice for those sailors to the extent that Jerez, El Puerto, Sanlúcar, and other places along the Andalusian Atlantic coast specialized in these activities. Such raiding foreshadowed the most sordid episodes of the conquest of America. These things had also occurred in Granada. For example, during the *mudéjar* revolts in Sierra Bermeja in 1500–1501, the "Christian commoners began to plunder and take the Moors' belongings the moment the Moors abandoned their quarters, taking as much as each one could. . ."[9]

However, these depratory and brutal practices were definitely incompatible with the dominance of institutionalized royal authority and the objectives of colonization.

Many of the men who were children at the time of the Catholic monarchs later on themselves experienced or narrated in their old age the deeds of the Castilians in the New World. Gonzalo Fernández de Oviedo exemplifies this as much in his life as in his written works, which embrace everything from the literary portraits of personages at court to the great *Historia . . . de las Indias*, a work of his old age.[10]

In the experience of these men there was no transition from the medieval reconquest to the discovery of the New World. Even though they quickly realized the large differences between the two realities, it was inevitable that they would appeal to the same arguments and justifications. We read in López de Gómara:

> Upon finishing the conquest of the Moors, that lasted over 800 years, the one of the Indies was begun so that the Spaniards could always wage war against the infidels.

Hernán Cortés knew, used, and certainly assimilated the religious arguments that had stimulated the medieval conquests and crusades. His own ensign of war was the Labarum, surrounded by the Latin motto composed by himself, which reads "amici seguamur crucem et si nos fidem habemus vere in hoc signo vencemus." It is certain that

[9] A. Bernáldez, *Historia de los Reyes Católicos*, cpa. CLXVI, en *Crónicas de los Reyes de Castilla*, III (Biblioteca de Autores Españoles, 70 [Madrid, 1953]).

[10] G. Fernández de Oviedo, *Historia General y Natural de las Indias*, ed. J. Pérez de Tudela Bueso, 5 vols. (Madrid, 1959); *Batallas y Quinquagenas*, ed. J. Pérez de Tudela Bueso, vol. 1 (Madrid, 1983); J. B. Avalle Arce, *Las memorias de Gonzalo Fernández de Oviedo*, 2 vols. (Chapel Hill, 1974); *América y la España del siglo XVI. Homenaje a Gonzalo Fernández de Oviedo*, eds. F. Solano and F. del Pino (Madrid, 1982).

Cortés possessed a literary and historical culture shared by very few conquistadors, but it did not take much knowledge to invoke Santiago during the battle – "Santiago y a ellos" or "Santiago y cierre España" – as they did many times or to ascribe victory to the help of the Apostle also mounted on horseback or to the Virgin Mary. These customs and beliefs dominated the Middle Ages and were slow to disappear. Their resilience is shown by the celebration in sixteenth-century Mexico of the "fiestas de Moros y cristianos," and more recently by the use of the term "reconquista" to refer to the operations against hostile Indians in eighteenth-century New Mexico.[11]

Yet frontier and conquest were just the first steps toward the colonization of a territory during the Spanish Middle Ages, as well as in the Indies, because as López de Gómara wrote:

> Failure to settle will not lead to a successful conquest, and failure to conquer will not lead to conversion of people. Thus the maxim of the conquistador is to populate.

This is precisely what Pedro de Valdivia did during the difficult conquest of Chile:

> Having seen the wolf's ears, it seemed to me that in order to keep this territory for your majesty it was necessary to eat from the product of our labor, as in the old times, everybody taking two roles, digging, ploughing and sowing at the right time, but keeping ourselves well-armed and our horses ready.

Since the colonizing efforts were built beginning with the possibilities and the experience offered by the social and economic structures of the Hispanic fifteenth century, it is fitting to devote some attention to them.

THE APOGEE OF MERCANTILE ECONOMY AND URBAN CENTRALITY

Let us first consider demography. At the end of the fourteenth-century, depression appeared in many areas of the kingdom of Castile long before other parts of Western Europe. It sparked a marked growth in population, and the population doubled throughout the

[11] L. Weckmann, *Le herencia medieval de México*, 2 vols. (México, 1984), a work very rich in ideas, interpretations and information. The debate about the character of the "conquistador" in *Proceso histórico al conquistador*, ed. F. de Solano (Madrid, 1988), and *Simposio sobre la ética en la conquista de América* (*Corpus Hispanorum de Pace*, 25) (Salamanca, 1983). Also, R. Romano, *Les mécanismes de la conquête coloniale: les conquistadors* (Paris, 1972).

fifteenth century until it reached approximately 4.5 million around the year 1500.[12]

In order to understand the importance of population growth and its influence over Castilian dominance and expansion one has to set it in its proper context. The population of Castile comprised 70 percent of the peninsular population in an area that, including Granada, amounted to 385,000 square kilometers or 65 percent of the territory. Over 50 percent of the population lived to the north of the Sistema Central, despite the rapid growth of Andalusia, Extremadura, and Toledo that permitted, for example, the flood of colonizers toward the kingdom of Granada in the years that followed the reconquest. Their descendants grew to more than 100,000 around 1530 as did the rapid movement to the Canaries – some 25,000 inhabitants around 1525 – of whom only one-quarter were of indigenous origins. Thus it is very likely that some areas in Baja Extremadura, in the sierras to the north of Seville, and on the plains and coast of Huelva were facing the problem of surplus population at the beginning of the sixteenth century, which in an indirect way served to stimulate migration to the New World.

Portugal, whose territory amounted to 91,500 square kilometers, had about 1 million inhabitants; the territories of the Crown of Aragon had 850,000 in an area of 110,000 square kilometers, and Navarra had 120,000 in an area of 11,700 square kilometers. Population size and rapid growth worked in favor of Castile by supporting a political authority that was notably stronger than that possessed by the other Spanish kingdoms with the possible exception of Portugal.

The late medieval crisis unleashed in Castile, as in other countries, complex demographic transformations, both rural and urban. Of the changes in the countryside we know very little. There are some examples of depopulation in Tierra de Campos and the Duero basin, while in Andalusia several attempts to populate the area failed in the fourteenth century due as much to the direct effects of epidemics as to the indirect effects of population decline and the reduction or adaptation of cultivated areas to new economic conditions. In contrast, the new settlements established during the fifteenth century in Baja Andalusia, for example, almost all took root. This attests as much to the success of the demographic expansion as to the new agrarian and colonizing enterprises that flourished at the end of the century.

Perhaps the most significant phenomenon was the triumph of the

[12] I summarize and update my work in *Historia General de España y América*, 5 (1982): 3–103, entitled, "Población, economía y sociedad."

city both as a response to the crisis and as a motor of post-crisis expansion. Throughout the fifteenth century there was a steady increase in urban population, reaching approximately 20 percent toward the end of the century, an impressive figure at the time if one takes into account that only Flanders and northern Italy, the sites with the greatest urban densities in Europe, would fully surpass this figure.

One has to suppose that many cities, often with new suburbs, grew more than the rest of the country during the fifteenth century and assumed command over various social, economic, and political functions to become the fundamental basis of the *realengo*, territory under direct royal jurisdiction.

However, the urban phenomenon varied according to the geohistorical regions of the Crown of Castile. On the Cantabrian frontier, these were small but active regional capitals with populations of between 2–3,000 inhabitants, such as Santiago, Oviedo, Tuy, Santander, and Bilbao. These regional capitals were surrounded in turn by a dense rural settlement composed of small villages, hamlets, and *villas*, towns that enjoyed particular privileges (*fueros*) by charter, had local markets, and contained no more than 1,000 dwellers.

South of the Cordillera Cantábrica to the Tajo River was a vast territory characterized by an ancient urban tradition and dense settlement. There were a number of old royal and episcopal civitates (León, Palencia, Zamora), mercantile towns such as Valladolid, old frontier cities from the *extremaduras* of Castile and León and even some Muslim cities. Toward the end of the fifteenth century, Toledo and Valladolid were the two most important urban centers in the region, with as many as 25,000 inhabitants. These sites were followed by other important cities in the range of 10–20,000 inhabitants (Segovia, Salamanca, Medina del Campo) and 10 or so intermediate cities containing somewhere between 3–10,000 inhabitants. Burgos was at the head of this group given its extraordinary economic situation.

The third zone consisted of the lands conquered and occupied in the thirteenth century. The largest urban settlements in the country were found in this area, but also the greatest concentration of rural settlements, so that in towns of less than 5,000 inhabitants the agrarian tended to replace the specifically urban. Seville was the largest metropolis, with more than 40,000 inhabitants by the end of the fifteenth century. It was larger than Barcelona but similar to Lisbon and Valencia. Córdoba was also a city of the first order, with a population in the neighborhood of 25,000. In addition, there were another half-dozen important cities with populations between 11,000 and 18,000 (Jaen, Ubeda, Murcia, Ecija, Jerez de la Frontera). Below the 10,000 level were a dozen intermediate cities in Extremadura and Andalusia (Cáceres, Badajoz, Carmona, Marchena, for example), and the majority of the important Andalusian seaports, such as Huelva, Cádiz, Sanlúcar de Barrameda, Puerto de Santa María and Lepe, had fewer than 5,000 inhabitants.

Therefore we see the image of a country where the cities formed a dense and wide network, with the population and force necessary to lead economic life on the eve of an incipient mercantile capitalism.

The realities and changes in economic activity have to be understood not only from the perspective of the crisis but also from the vantage point of the conditions that allowed them to overcome it and begin a new period of expansion. The effects of depression and the convulsions produced by catastrophic epidemics on price and wage levels were similar to other European countries. Likewise, there were similarities in the evolution of the monetary system, even though certain conditions favored Castile over other regions.

It appears that Castile experienced the same general decrease in agricultural prices and the increase in wages and the price of manufactures that took place in the second half of the fourteenth century all over Europe. However, it has not been possible to construct long-term wage and price series including the fifteenth century. After a period of stability that lasted until the 1420s, the prices of agricultural goods and of primary materials tended to decline until the end of the century, although this downward trend was halted briefly in the 1460s. In a country undergoing demographic growth, this meant that production rose even more rapidly and that the cost per unit or of commercialization fell due to a better organization of internal markets in Castile. Available data on salaries for construction work reveal that purchasing power showed some stability, maybe a slight decrease, during the period 1420–1480. This is in marked contrast to the labor shortage problem that prevailed throughout Europe that forced wages up until the 1460s or 1470s.

Research on currency has shown a clear increase in the amount of circulating money in the form of gold, silver, and vellón (copper) coins as well as in its capacity as a means of exchange, despite the strong devaluations to which the vellón was subject after Alfonso X's reign (1266–1287), but especially during the first Trastámara rulers (1369–1398). Shortage of gold supplies was not as serious in Castile as in other western countries (silver is another story), but this did not exempt it from suffering a scarcity crisis between 1395 and 1415 and again between 1440 and 1460. The observation of currency trends confirm not only a steady and strong increase of mercantile activities, but also the greater ease with which operations of capital accumulation and credit were carried out.[13]

The study of prices, wages, currency, and other indicators serves to trace the overall evolution of the Castilian economy in the late medieval period. It is very possible that after some brief periods of recovery (1325–1340, 1353–1362, and 1389–1380), the economic and demographic depression reached its depth around 1390. However, by that time the structures that allowed growth to occur in the fifteenth century had already consolidated. As mentioned, this was a period of demographic growth, and in terms of Castilian institutions there were important conditions that would lead to the early development of the monarchical state.

It is clear that in this process of growth the interests of landowners, cattle raisers, the aristocracy, and the large merchants, both Castilian and foreign, were carefully guarded. Although no significant economic archaisms were witnessed in the fifteenth century, the basis for their emergence and entrenchment was laid out. This is evidenced by new patterns of land ownership and the corresponding social relations, the boom in transhumant herding, the development of external trade based on the exportation of agricultural goods and raw materials, the limits on further expansion of manufactures, and the complacent attitude about greater access to gold supplies.

Nevertheless, Castile during the fifteenth century lived in a period of great expansion that eventually allowed it to become a European pioneer at the beginning of the so-called Atlantic civilization. After an initial phase of recovery until approximately 1420, one can see another stage of rapid economic growth until 1460. The outcome of the 1462 crisis was much more favorable to Castile than to the rest of the Hispanic kingdoms, despite the civil wars and turmoil during the final years of Enrique IV. For this reason, the Catholic monarchs were able to introduce in the 1480s energetic policies that threatened important economic interests, such as the foundation of the Inquisition, the conquest of Granada, and the expulsion of the Jews. In the last decade of the fifteenth century, renewed economic expansion was halted by the 1503–1507 agrarian and demographic crisis. Little is known about the immediate aftermath of the crisis, but everything seems to indicate

[13] A. MacKay, *Money, Prices and Politics in Fifteenth-Century Castile* (London, 1981); and my work, "La política monetaria en la Corona de Castilla (1369–1497)," *En la España Medieval*, 11 (1988): 79–123.

that it was overcome by 1515 and that the previous rhythm of growth was recovered.[14]

Some features of the economic transformation in Castile directly influenced the models applied to the Indies. Certainly, the fifteenth century witnessed the ruin of traditional agricultural practices, specifically in the dry lands. Yet the Mediterranean agrarian typology lent itself to experimentation with methods effective enough to increase productivity or to combine agriculture and mercantile-financial activities. Therefore, both subsistence agriculture and cash-crop production for urban and external markets did very well. This was the case of Andalusian wheat exports, the wines of Andalusia and other regions, Mediterranean crops such as fruits and sugar cane, fiber for textiles, and *grana* (cochineal) for dyes. From the mid-fifteenth century, the diffusion of new forms of agricultural credit, especially the *censo consignativo,* fueled investments in some zones that helped production to rebound.[15]

The most remarkable development occurred in livestock-raising and its byproducts (wool, leather, meat, and cheese). The most studied aspect is the famous organization of transhumant livestock raisers, the *Mesta,* created in 1270. It has been suggested, and not unreasonably, that the demographic crisis was behind the expansion of the livestock industry given the limited demand for labor in this kind of activity. However, the roots of transhumance in Castile were much older and its causes more varied, and its expansion was due above all to a peak in the demand for wool both internally and externally, especially in Flanders from the second half of the fourteenth century.[16]

As a result, the herds and flocks belonging to the *Mesta* doubled in size during the fifteenth century. Besides the *Mesta* there was another migratory pattern of smaller dimensions as well as a stationary livestock industry, bigger in size that grazed on the *ejidos* and communal lands administered by the municipal governments. It has been estimated that Castile had about 6 million head of cattle and sheep in

[14] See also my work, "El crecimiento económico de la Corona de Castilla en el siglo XV: ejemplos andaluces," in *Los mudéjares de Castilla . . . ,* 257–282.

[15] Examples in M. A. Ladero Quesada and M. González Jiménez, *Diezmo eclesiástico y producción de cereales en el reino de Sevilla (1408–1503)* (Sevilla, 1978). M. Borrero Fernández, "Efectos del cambio económico en el ámbito rural. Los sistemas de crédito en el campo sevillano," *En la España Medieval,* 8 (1986): 219–244.

[16] Among the recent studies the work of Me. Cl. Gerbet stand out: "La Orden de San Jerónimo y la ganadería en el reino de Castilla desde su fundación a principios del siglo XVI," *Boletín de la Real Academia de la Historia,* 179:2 (1982): 219–314, and "Les Ordres Militaires el l'élevage dans l'Espagne médiévale," *En la España Medieval,* 8 (1986): 413–445.

1492. How can it be that livestock raising was expanding at the same time that there was an increase in population and demand for foodstuffs? No matter how you look at it, the answer must be that Castile was at that time an underpopulated country.

The problem of achieving a balance between agriculture and livestock raising did not become serious until the end of the fifteenth century as the first colonizers began to emigrate. These people mastered the techniques of extensive land-use combining agriculture and livestock, and making the most of expansive territory and moderate labor resources.[17]

The maritime fishing industry also showed significant development along the Cantabrian, Galician, and Andalusian coasts and the Canaries-Saharan banks. One must never forget the role played by the Andalusian fishermen in the European discovery of the Indies.[18]

Although the economic system on a whole continued to be procapitalist, Castile stands out as an example of a country that linked its well-organized network of internal markets to external trade via maritime routes. The vitality of its urban centers and its fluid monetary system certainly worked to its advantage. Equally important was Castile's double outlet to the ocean: the north by the Cantabrian Sea and the south by way of the Andalusian Atlantic. These two outlets were far more advantageous than the Italy-Flanders routes.[19]

The Cantabrian outlet had Bilbao as its main port and Burgos as its economic center. Its location allowed for a steady commerce with all ports in the Bay of Biscay, the English Channel, and the North Sea. The second outlet was served by several Andalusian ports organized around Seville as their economic center. Seville lay in the middle of the Mediterranean-Atlantic route and also served as the bridge to North African markets.

Geographic position and a well-established merchant marine were two major assets of Castile. Especially in the Cantabrian Sea area, the merchant marine was often freighted by foreign merchants. Moreover,

[17] See the recent study of K. W. Butzer, "Cattle and Sheep from Old to New Spain: Historical Antecedents," *Annals of the Association of American Geographers*, 78:1 (1988): 29–56.

[18] A. Rumeu de Armas, "Las pesquerías españolas en la costa de Africa (siglos XV–XVI)," *Hispania*, 130 (1975): 295–319, his book *España en el Africa atlántica*, 2 vols. (Madrid, 1956), and *Cádiz, metrópoli del comercio con Africa en los siglos XV y XVI* (Cádiz, 1976).

[19] Bibliographic references referred to in my work, "L'Espagne et L'Océan à la fin du Moyen Age," *L'Europe et l'Océan au Moyen Age. Contribution à l'histoire de la navigation* (Nantes: Société des Historiens Médiévistes de l'Enseignement Supérieur-Cid Editions, 1988), 115–130.

there was a large and active internal market, organized around the fairs at Medina del Campo since 1407, which could supply a wide variety of agricultural goods and raw materials: wool, leather, cereal, fruits, wines, salt, iron, and even African gold in Andalusia.

From Bruges and other marketplaces, Castilian, English, and Italian traders imported to Castile all kinds of products including woolens, linens, tapestry, silk, metallurgy, and Levantine spices. Castile also demanded experts in trade and the capital that accompanied them. Therefore it is not strange that Italian merchants took leading economic roles, especially in Andalusia. Indeed, the presence of Genoese traders in Seville, which became rather intense after the mid-fifteenth century, set the precedent for their eventual involvement in the Atlantic expansion.[20]

The same patterns of trade witnessed in late medieval Castile influenced the organization of commerce with the New World. It has been argued that during the fifteenth century Castile had a colonial economy because of its foundations in the exchange of raw materials for manufactures. However, such a statement is inadequate because those trade relations took place within an incipient mercantile capitalist system alien to any industrialization process in which wealth lay in the largest countries with moderate populations and abundant agricultural resources much like Castile.

However, there is no doubt that certain economic sectors were affected negatively or were limited by these circumstances, as in the case of textile manufacture, although it experienced considerable expansion during the fifteenth century in cities such as Segovia, Cuenca, Ubeda, Córdóba, and Murcia. And it is no less true, as we will soon see, that some sectors fared better than others.

Although different in area and scale, the economies and trade of Aragon and Valencia did not differ much from the Castilian model. Aragon exported wheat, oil, wool, and livestock to Catalonia and Valencia, and received in turn many manufactures from Catalonian markets. Valencia, on its part, furnished a variety of Mediterranean agricultural goods of great speculative value. Valencia was also a great port for the redistribution and reexportation of commodities. It attracted foreign capital and traders from Lombardy, Florence, Genoa, Germany, and Catalonia. Nevertheless, it never attained manufactur-

[20] For more on the state of the question, see E. Otte, "Il ruolo dei genovesi nella Spagna del XV e XVII secolo," *La repubblica internazionale del denaro tra XV e XVII secolo*, Annali dell'Istituo storico italo-germanico, 20 (Bologna, 1986), and in my work, "Los geneoveses en Sevilla y su región (siglos XIII–XVI): elementos de permanencia y arraigo," in *Los mudéjares de Castilla*, 283–312.

ing comparable to Barcelona, and neither the local merchant marine nor financiers flourished, despite the fact that some artisanal goods such as silk, pottery, leather, and paper had potential as exports. Proximity to Castilian mercantile interests improved Valencia's economy during the reign of the Catholic monarchs, as the city grew to as many as 50,000 inhabitants.[21]

The situation in Catalonia was quite different. Here the civil war of 1462–1471 produced the collapse of the "empire of Catalonian merchants" in the Mediterranean whose decadence had begun in the previous decades. The restoration begun in 1480, and based on the plans of Alfonso V was successful in markets such as Sardinia, Sicily, and Naples, where Catalan manufactures were afforded special protections. Trade with the eastern Mediterranean was renewed. Contacts with North Africa and the ports of the western Mediterranean also occurred. But Catalonia was unable to recoup the western route, which, although it had been secondary in earlier times, became the most promising trade route toward the end of the fifteenth century.

The population of Barcelona grew from 20,000 to 35,000 during the reign of the Catholic monarchs, but its *redreç* at the levels of manufacture and commerce was simply not enough for the adequate accumulation of capital needed to meet new challenges, despite the expertise of Catalan merchants. This explains the absence of Catalonia in the incipient trade with the Indies centered in Seville.[22]

ARISTOCRATIC PREDOMINANCE

In the West, the late medieval crisis and the transformations that ensued culminated in the consolidation of the prevailing social system, although at the expense of great internal changes through which the European aristocracy was able to reaffirm their domination. The Castilian aristocracy – both the high nobility and the small or middle patriciate or urban oligarchy – also participated in this process. How did this process take place? What were its consequences for the social organization that the Spanish established on the other side of the Atlantic in the sixteenth century?[23]

[21] J. Guiral, *Valence, port méditerranéen au XVe siècle (1410–1525)* (Paris, 1986).

[22] C. Martínez Shaw, "Catalunya i el comerç amb América: final d'una legenda," *L'Avenç* (15 abril 1979): 19–23. Other aspects in M. Batllori, "Cataluña y América. Precedentes, descubrimiento y período colombino," *Humanismo y Renacimiento* (Barcelona, 1987), 73–99.

[23] Diverse examples and points of view in M. Cl. Gerbet, *La noblesse dans le royaume de Castille. Etude sur les structures sociales en Estrémadure de 1454 à 1516* (Paris, 1979), and in my article, "Aristocratie et régime seigniorial dans l'Andalousie du XVe siècle,"

One has to evaluate the Castilian aristocracy's flexibility and capacity to renew its sources of income as a fundamental aspect of the maintenance and perpetuation of its domination. As in other countries, the late medieval depression provoked the decline or loss of traditional forms of seigniorial rent – for example, the *solariegas* generally paid by dependent laborers. Nevertheless, many landowners benefited from these changes in the agricultural sector, enlarging their properties and participating indirectly in the sale of their products. This included laying the groundwork, already begun in the fifteenth century, for some forms of pre-capitalist agriculture.

However, the most striking phenomenon was the growth of seigniorial authority and the notion of income, which drew on the principle of public jurisdiction exerted by the high and middle nobility upon peasant vassals. This did not constitute a second servitude of the peasantry, but rather greater control over a portion of public finances by the nobility and a significant increase in the number of jurisdictional lords in Castile between 1329 and 1475. This occurred without inciting any general or permanent state of tension between lords and peasants, even though for a number of reasons it may have produced some resistance and episodes of rebellion.

Thus seigniorial lands frequently enjoyed as much or more prosperity than the royal lands, although this might have been made possible by seigniorial abuses and by levying duties over economic transactions and trade involving royal goods. Involvement in commerce was the key to overcoming the depression and stimulating the peasant economy.

In summary, there was not a collapse of seigniorial rents but a change in their sources and in the relative importance of each type of rent. Moreover, during this period new procedures of maintaining and concentrating the noble patrimony via familial and hereditary means became more generalized.

The "new nobility" of the late medieval period organized itself in strong lineages and passed down to the principal heir the bulk of the family's belongings and rents. This was done according to the custom of *terce de mejorar* in the case of inheritance or to the new practice of *mayorazgo* (entail). *Mayorazgo* gained some diffusion during the fif-

Annales E.S.C., 6 (1983): 1346–1368. The state of the question in M. C. Quintanilla Raso, "Nobleza y señoríos en Castilla durante la Baja Edad Media. Aportaciones de la historiografía reciente," *Anuario de Estudios Medievales*, 14 (1984): 613–639, and "La nobleza en la historia política castellana en la segunda mitad del siglo XV. Bases de poder y pautas de comportamiento," *Congresso Internacional Bartolomeu Dias e a sua época*, 1 (Porto, 1989): 181–200.

teenth century, but did not become widely accepted until the Cortes of Toro (1505) also extended its use to the urban patriciate. In this way, the aristocracy as a group attained a new-found stability and crystallized itself into strong lineages capable of defending its social position through the centuries despite the continued entrance of new members into its ranks during the fifteenth century.

The third factor that explains the strengthening of the aristocracy during this period involves the pre-crisis attitudes toward the ancient methods of exercising political power and their ability to serve in behalf of the new methods. The late medieval situation in Europe can be described in a few comments that affected above all the western European monarchies: a crisis of local power built on feudal relations, the reemergence of the idea of the state as embodied by the Crown and its public institutions for administration, justice and finance, the acceptance of civil (Roman) law and, consequently, the growth of a new and equitable juridical system out of many ancient ones.

Castile partook of these changes, but had its own particularities as well. First, royal power was stronger here than anywhere else, and King Alfonso X (1252–1284) had definitively contributed to the development of the principle of sovereignty and the increase of royal power. Following the extended late medieval strife between the great nobility and the monarchy over ways of exercising and sharing the power institutionalized in the Crown, the aristocracy finally acquiesced to the superior authority of the monarch, but continued to maintain considerable power as the main collaborators with the Crown of Castile.

This applied both to the jurisdictional seignioralities as well as to the ample zones of *realengo*. The nobility occupied high public offices and got a good deal of royal income in the forms of grants or payment of services due to the expansion of the fiscal resources of the state since the mid-thirteenth century. All in all, the aristocracy continued as the main beneficiary of the prevailing institutional and juridical order until the end of the *Antiguo Régimen*.

The same situation held true at the local level and in a less complete form in the urban municipal oligarchies and the patriciates that dominated municipal life in every city, especially after the *regimiento* reform implemented by Alfonso XI from 1337 to 1348. This social group adopted the same aristocratic forms of income-earning, family organization, inheritance rights, power-holding, and even the nobility's social conventions and the cult of lineage.

The urbanization of the high nobility and their relations with the urban patriciate increased their influence. One can argue that the low aristocracy did not have an alternative to the social values of the high nobility. This would become important precisely because in other European countries the trend toward modernity was impelled by the urban patriciate, which had more of a noble outlook than a bourgeois outlook.[24]

Of course, there were bourgeois elements and middle classes in Castilian cities of the fifteenth century but never a consolidated bourgeoisie distinct from the ranks of the aristocracy, except at times in Burgos and some other towns, which continued to serve aristocratic interests. In addition, the persecution and marginalization of Jewish *conversos* since mid-century made it even more difficult for an alternative social order to emerge. Moreover, the highest aspiration of the bourgeois class was to enter the aristocracy by becoming a knight or, if possible, a *hidalgo* (nobleman). Even well-to-do peasants and landowners shared these social goals.

In summary, at the end of the Middle Ages we find that the force behind the Hispanic expansion was a renovated feudal society in which the aristocracy had increased its social influence and its leadership role, adapting itself to new economic and political conditions. Despite attacks against idleness, the disdain for manual labor, and economic parasitism made by people like Bartolomé de las Casas from the beginning of the sixteenth century, these aristocratic conventions and attitudes were not modified.

In contrast to the Castilian model that prevailed in America, the aristocracy and urban patriciate of the Crown of Aragon were less dynamic and more conservative. The most evident difference between the lesser nobility of Aragon, Catalonia, and Navarra and their Castilian counterpart was the small degree of integration of the former into urban life, dominated as it was by the urban patriciate with its distinct interests. Thus the Aragonese and the Navarese *infanzones* led a rural life much influenced by the late medieval crisis. The *cavallers* of Catalonia were in a similar position. Their main sources of wealth, land rents, and feudal control over the peasantry had been affected above all by the civil war and later, by the concessions granted to cultivators (*payeses de remensa*), who were freed from servitude and

[24] M. C. Gerbet, "Accès á la noblesse et renouvellement nobiliaire dans le royaume de Castille (de la Reconquête au XVe siècle)," *Arquivos do Centro Cultural Português* (Lisbon-Paris), 26 (1989): 359–387. M. Asenjo González, "Oligarquías urbanas en Castilla en la segunda mitad del siglo XV," *Congresso . . . Bartolomeu Dias*, 4 (Porto, 1989): 413–436, and my work in publication (Bordeaux, Maison des Pays Ibériques), "Linajes, bandos y parcialidades en la vida política de las ciudades castellanas (siglos XIV y XV)." Also, A. MacKay, "The Lesser Nobility in the Kingdom of Castile," *Gentry and Lesser Nobility in Late Medieval Europe*, ed. M. Jones (New York, 1986).

ties to the land. Toward the end of the century, the *cavallers* living in some cities like Barcelona and Lérida were granted citizenship, forming a part of the urban patriciate, although this was not a widespread phenomenon.

On the contrary, the high nobility was able to renovate itself and to maintain its socioeconomic domination in diverse political contexts. In Catalonia, the *ric homens* lost much as a result of the 1462 war, while in Valencia the great nobility ruled over solid manorial estates, often comprised of *mudéjar* peasants. In Aragon, the nobility achieved maximum power due to the absence of strong monarchical authority. This set of contrasts vis-à-vis the Castilian model would become even more acute in the sphere of politics, serving to explain the heterogeneous development of monarchical power in these areas.

In spite of regional differences, aristocratic domination required the practice and widespread acceptance of certain social and mental values, especially the medieval customs of chivalry forged in the eleventh century. One has only to recall the influence of chivalric literature on the perception of the New World by the conquistadors. One author has coined the term "Amadises de América" to refer to the conquistadors in a study of the juxtaposition of chronicles of the conquest and with the texts of the novels.[25] Upon seeing Tenochtitlán, Bernal Díaz del Castillo wrote: "We were amazed and said that this was like the enchanted things that they tell of in the story of Amadís." One hundred years later, around 1621 in Mexico, a masquerade in the streets included such characters as "Don Belianés of Greece, Palmerín de Oliva, Febo the Knight, Melia the Witch, Adrian and Bucendo the enchanted dwarves, and Urganda the Unknown." Furthermore, *Sergas de Esplandián* provided the name for California.

In a feudal society, a knight was expected to be a worthy man, to behave in an honorable and courageous way with those of his own class. Such behavior would bestow glory and honor on oneself as well as contribute to the well-being of society. Such behavior was further legitimated by the Christianization of the knightly class. These ideas were deeply ingrained in the mentality of the conquistadors, who were seeking not just wealth and power, but glory, a belief as medieval as it was Renaissance. Hernán Cortés provides the clearest statement about this:

[25] I. Rodríguez Prampolini, *Amadises de América. La hazaña de Indias como empresa caballeresca* (Mexico, 1948). M. Hernández Sánchez-Barba, "La influencia de los libros de caballería sobre el conquistador," *Anuario de Estudios Americanos,* 19 (1960). A. Sánchez, "Los libros de caballería en la conquista de América," *Anales Cervantinos,* 7 (1968): 237–270.

I inspired them telling that the Spaniards were a flawless breed and that we were willing to gain for Your Majesty the greatest kingdoms and *señoríos* of this world. As we are obligated as Christians ... we would gain glory in the heavens and such honor that nobody has even experienced in this world.

We will lead a just war, of great glory ... to redress wrongs ... and do away with any tyranny.

These words of Cortés, who conceived of himself as an armed knight (*caballero de armada caballería*), are reminiscent of many late medieval Castilian texts. Two texts from the early fifteenth century about *adelantados* of Andalusia relate the following:

He died having spent a lifetime waging wars, the kind of deeds that immortalize men.

In Roman writings a lot is said about honor and the marks of victory granted to consuls and princes who had conquered lands and provinces for Rome. The same thing happened in the summer of this year ... [26]

The content of this story is not as important for our purposes as the circumstances that inspired its writer.

Chivalry was above all a profession of arms, and one had to be prepared to execute it. In both America and in Spain, the performance of paramilitary equestrian drills was relatively frequent. The activities consisted of single matches, tournaments, fake skirmishes, parades, bullfighting, hunting on horseback, and games of skill. Furthermore, some of the obligations of the knightly class to the Crown that had been regulated for centuries were applied to the *encomenderos* in the Indies. They were required to muster occasionally and later on to pay a *derecho de lanzas* for an exemption from direct military duties. As in the case of late medieval knights, the widow, the single daughter, and the youngest son were entitled to inherit the father's privileges and tax exemptions as long as a squire performed the regular duties.

This is why the Castilians in the New World, at least at the beginning of the conquest, behaved in a feudal manner and used a seigniorial vocabulary distinctive to fifteenth-century Castile. They used the term *vasallos* to refer to persons under the jurisdiction of the king or of a lord – that is, subject to someone else's authority and fiscal exactions. The *encomenderos*, however, never became *señores* in the Castilian sense of the word. As was written in the mid-sixteenth century, "The Indian is free and a vassal of Your Highness." Yet this feudal-seigniorial vocabulary as applied to a new setting does not obscure

[26] See my work, "De Per Afán a Catalina de Ribera. Siglo y medio en la historia de un linaje sevillano (1371–1514)," *En la España Medieval*, 4 (1984): 347–397. R. Sánchez Saus, *Caballería y linaje en la Sevilla medieval* (Sevilla, 1989).

the reality of personal dependence and actual subjugation of many Indians.

This medieval legacy also explains the words and actions of the conquistadors in the exercise of their power. The acquisition of new territories was based on the medieval procedure regarding possession of seigniorial lands. The oaths of homage are also no different from fifteenth-century Castilian ones, serving as a vehicle for both political and personal loyalty.

The ancient Castilian custom of requesting royal permission to build a castle or a fortress was maintained. Likewise, two ancient customs regarding distribution of wealth gained widespread recognition. The *regalía,* based on Roman roots, consisted of a royal monopoly on mining, and the Islamic *quinto* contained the obligation to deliver 20 percent of captured booty and treasures to the king.

Nobility and the knightly class were, in the last instance, ostentatious and generous in a world of scarcity. Magnanimity was characteristic of the aristocrat who saw himself as the father/protector of his subjects. Once again the Middle Ages came to the fore. In the New World, the descriptions of political celebrations, both viceregal and seigniorial, resembled those of the high nobility of Castile. Hospitality toward their peers reveals a mentality akin to former times. Their servant and staff were also similar to those of the Castilian aristocracy. As the case of Hernán Cortés aptly illustrates, in his Cuernavaca palace he maintained a chief waiter, a baker, a falconer, running footmen, squires, a head groom, muleteers and jugglers.[27]

THE MONARCHY AND THE STATE

Many of the peculiarities of the conquest and colonization of the New World may be explained because they took place under the political authority of a strong, yet complex, monarchical state, rooted in the actions of the Catholic monarchs, King Ferdinand and Queen Isabel (1474–1516). The "Columbian moment" is also the historical moment of Ferdinand and Isabel, which is why we must inquire as to the substance and the bases upon which their political program was carried out, and its major consequences.[28]

[27] I. Beceiro Pita, "Los estados señoriales como estructura de poder en la Castilla del siglo XV," *Realidad e imágenes del poder. España a fines de la Edad Media* (Valladolid, 1988), 292–324, on the diverse aspects of the seignorial regime.

[28] See chapters 3 and 4 ("Ideas, proyectos y realidades políticas" and "Los medios de gobierno") of my book, *Los Reyes Católicos: la Corona y la unidad de España,* 71–163, and the volume *Realidad e imágenes del poder,* cited in previous note (ed. A. Rucquoi).

The dynastic union of the crowns of Castile and Aragón in 1480, into which Navarre was incorporated in 1515, was a unique event both in circumstances and characteristics, yet it must be added that it came about not by chance but by the historical weight of more than two centuries of relations between the Spanish kingdoms, starting in the middle of the thirteenth century, when the great territorial conquest of the coast of Al-Andalus was concluded. From then on, centered around the Crown of Castile and León, which was, furthermore, the ancient heir to various "imperial" pan-Hispanic conceptions of state, several possibilities of dynastic union, or disunion, were put into play, often accompanied by wars in which the various peninsular kingdoms participated. Seen in this light, the year 1480 was a point of arrival, although hypothetically many alternative possibilities existed.

The union of the Crowns of Isabel and Ferdinand allowed for the superposition of an initial form of state on the historical reality of the kingdoms of medieval Spain; put another way, it allowed for the first firm step toward the formation of the Spanish state, parting from its own historical existence, of which its inhabitants were conscious. This was clearly expressed in medieval historiography, above all from the thirteenth century when, in the *Primera Crónica General,* Alfonso X (el Sabio) wrote:

> We have here this our general history of the Spains in which we have all the kings and their deeds they carried out in times past, and that which is happening in the present time in which we are, including the Moors as well as the Christians, and even the Jews, participating.

This tendency toward pan-Hispanic affirmation is accentuated in the fifteenth century, above all in the courtly and intellectual milieu of Castile, as an immediate precedent to the deeds of the Catholic monarchs.

This tendency did not give rise to the sudden appearance of a unified Spanish national state, as is sometimes anachronistically asserted. In Spain, as in other parts of Europe, between the old medieval notion of State and contemporary ideas, we may trace its development over several centuries, and fundamentally we find a complex transformation of national conceptions and sentiments. In this way, though we may affirm that there was a historical concept of Spain in the Middle Ages, it is equally true that in 1480 the various legal and political-administrative structures of the kingdoms remained intact. The Catholic monarchs did not alter this reality, which made the birth of a unifying national political consciousness more complex. This fact would become accentuated at times due to the dislocations and diverse rhythms of political evolution of the Spanish kingdoms that composed the common monarchy.

The Spanish Crown had to be constructed despite these diverse realities. Extra-peninsular kingdoms and seigniorial lands would have to be added to these. At the same time that the Crown stimulated the sentiments of fidelity toward it as the nucleus of the emerging idea of State, it offered fields of common interest across the kingdoms, as well as a unified foreign policy, and created unifying, though not uniform, bases of power, population, territory, and political consciousness. To this end, the Crown utilized doctrinal tenets, institutional means, and programs of political action.

Centuries of thought resulted on the one hand in elements of legitimation created by medieval Christianity that, along with ecclesiastical interests, played a fundamental role in the elaboration of projects and the decisions taken by the kings. On the other hand, we find respect for the hierarchical order, and therefore the social order expressed through it, as well as for its economic bases. The kingdom was considered a sort of body whose legitimate head was the king, with inequalities and hierarchies regulated for each stratum and for each level of political power exercised by its representatives – noblemen, bishops, and urban patricians. In the third place is the Roman principle, which referred to sovereignty, an exclusive attribute of the king, his legislative capacity, and his judicial and administrative preeminence: the basic principle for the construction of the State, which the Catholic monarchs utilized as energetic restorers of monarchical authority in their project of "order, govern, rule, and be lord."

Yet it is true that the institutional means – the structures of exercising political power – were different in Castile and Aragon. For centuries the kings of Castile refined and perfected the bases and instruments of their power, creating a relationship of forces amply favorable to the development of an absolutist monarchical State. Castile's departure on the road to modernity, perhaps precocious and undoubtedly exhausting in the very long run, led to the political construction of the Spanish State as we know it.

From that peculiarity derived the great achievements as well as the limitations and failures of the Spanish monarchy during several centuries. The brief but transcendent epoch of the Catholic monarchs took place after the process had begun in Castile two centuries earlier, *but* they had fed it, accelerated it, and carried the Castilian institutions toward the acceptance of responsibilities and charges on a peninsular and European level, converting the Crown of Castile into a platform for a policy that the monarchy understood as Spanish. It definitively shortened the assimilation and identification of pro-national Castilian sentiments that were in existence there, as well as in other kingdoms, upon assuming the costs of representation of the political ensemble that, given the circumstances, could not divide the Crown more equitably among its various members.

In order to better understand this point, a detailed analysis of the institutions and structures of power would be required, which is not possible at this time. Let it suffice to recall that with respect to the Castilian Crown, royal administration was exercised equally throughout the entire territory, such that the kingdoms that composed it were not, with a few minor exceptions, compartmentalized political realities. The monarchs ruled with great economic power free from the control of other political constraints. They exercised their legislative power supremely and had at their disposal a notable permanent armed force with an extremely effective capacity for military mobilization throughout the territory. In spite of the local predominance of the aristocracy and the extension of the seignorial regime, royal power was not limited hierarchically by the nobility and could intervene, in turn, as a superior judge in the seigniorial lands. In short, the cities did not reach political pacts with the monarchy, they utilized the courts and submitted themselves to the control of the *corregidores* sent by the kings.

In this way we can explain how the financial resources of "a Castile well-administrated but poorly defended against the fiscal demands of the Crown" (Elliot) were employed, toward the end of the fifteenth century, in the Naples enterprise, or in the defense of the Pyrenees county-states of Rosellón and Sardinia against France, both political issues in Catalonia and Aragon.

On the other hand, the institutional machinery of the Aragonese Crown was more complex and compartmentalized, as can be seen, for example, in the fact that each kingdom or country integrated within it maintained full control over its laws and private institutions, so that there were no common ties between the Aragonese, the Catalans, Valencians, and Balearic groups. For this reason, the monarchy, which kept them together permanently, found it difficult to increase its effective power by modifying or making innovations in the institutional framework which reflected a fixed social structure. Within this social structure the king occupied the apex but saw his power limited in every direction, and the diverse sectors of "political society" maintained a considerable degree of power and could oppose the Crown via legal means. This was achieved by following a "contractual" model that impeded evolution toward other forms of State and blocked the full union toward larger political entities while fostering conservative attitudes incompatible with royal absolutism.

In those circumstances, Ferdinand the Catholic acquired almost all his power from having been also king of Castile, while Isabel was not able to rule, effectively, in Aragon. The political ordering could not be modified except in the sense of rejecting the attempts by individual protagonists to utilize it to further their ambitions: Such was the reach of the new procedure of balloting or lot-drawing for municipal positions, which extended throughout Aragon during the fifteenth century.

The dynastic union would thus culminate, inevitably, in a certain Castilianization of the state, but from the outside this would not be perceived but rather seen as the development of a new common foreign policy whose design corresponded more in cases such as Italy and relations with France, to the interests of the Aragonese Crown, not to the Castilian. For the first time, the Spanish kingdoms with the greatest weight would show themselves as united, and in this area, more than in others, Spain began to act as a political entity. Contemporaries perceived it in this way and did not hesitate to confer upon Isabella and Ferdinand the titles of Spanish monarchs, titles not used by the royal chancellery, for together they represented to the rest of Europe the totality of what had been up to that time a geo-historical entity divided into various fronts and diplomatic attitudes.

The Castilian solutions of the late Middle Ages inspired those later adopted in the New World colonies that were incorporated into the Castilian Crown, and because these solutions were the most adequate for the designs of the monarchical power that, in some aspects, was able to construct the "Modern State" with greater clarity in America than was possible in its European kingdoms. The Crown, unconstrained by the need to respect prior circumstances, was able to control the forms of aristocratic social and economic domination, and could fit them into its political projects within a new institutional framework.

Thus, in America, two forms of organization of productive relations, based on the same principles as those of late medieval Castile, were consolidated, but adopted different institutional forms. On the one hand, was the formation of vast *haciendas* whose agrarian economy was linked to trade and the consequent dominance of an authentic territorial aristocracy. On the other hand there was the institution of the *encomienda*, a form of patronage over the indigenous worker that allowed an *encomendero* to obtain income and services through a form of feudalized personal domination, but limited by monarchical jurisdiction.[29]

In America, traditional aspects of feudal society that were the most damaging to monarchical political order were not allowed. There were hardly any jurisdictional lordships, nor hardly any titled nobility. Certainly, nobility was recognized and honored, and its judicial privileges were even respected, but economic or other exemptions were not permitted. Thus although in the private sphere and in the daily exercise of many powers the aristocratic organization of society remained intact, in the sphere of public law, aristocratic jurisdiction was blocked and marginalized to a great extent.

At another level, only the triumph of the late medieval city and its domination by the aristocracy allows one to comprehend the transference of the Castilian municipality to the Indies and the central role that the cities and the municipal regime had in the Spanish colonial process in the Americas. This included the greater vitality of the local institutions there than in the Castile of modern times because these local institutions facilitated the administrative control of the population under the best conditions from the perspective of royal power.

The acceptance of this new mode of carrying out political and institutional relations in the space of *res publica* was facilitated by lack of historical antecedents to maintain, by the smallness of the "Republic of the Spaniards" compared with the subjected "Republic of the Indians," by the enormity of the territory, and by the sheer arduousness of the tasks to be realized. Only in this way could they attain their fundamental objectives, which were to pass from the conquest to territorial permanence, and defend the organization and the basic values of the social system that the Spaniards brought with them.

This explains, then, the discipline with which the rapid implantation of institutions of monarchical governance were obeyed, although not always willingly. Their listing suggests several medieval antecedents: Admirals, *Adelantados*, or Frontier Governors, Governors and Captains General, Viceroys and Royal *Audiencias*, Mayors, Magistrates, and the *Hermandad* on the local level. A Royal Treasury, inspired by the Castilian one, and the Council of the Indies – one of the main councils of the monarchy – coordinated the ensemble from Castile only thirty years after the discovery of the New World. Similarly, we find the implantation of a legal system that was Castilian in its principles and its general norms, though complemented, little by little, by abundant legislation specific to the Indies.[30]

[29] S. A. Zavala, *La encomienda indiana* (Madrid, 1935).
[30] See, in particular, D. Ramos Pérez, *Historia de la colonización española en América* (Ma-

THE POWER OF THE CHURCH AND RELIGIOUS LEGITIMATION

The exercise of royal patronage (*Regio Patronato*) over the ecclesiastical institutions in the New World responded to the same organizing principle: It is true that its general norms of operation respected the Catholic Church and the evangelization mission as well as promoting religious expressions since these things were of general interest and widely respected. But ecclesiastical law and, even less, papal administration were not allowed to intervene and disrupt the supremacy of the royal jurisdiction. There were several medieval antecedents, and they were evident, just slightly earlier, in the *Regio Patronato* of Granada and the Canary Islands after 1486.[31] The Church in Spanish America would be, paraphrasing a well-known idea, "a social giant and a political dwarf," even though some ecclesiastics would occupy governmental positions, as was common at that time.

But it is even more interesting to discover the specific Christian religious beliefs and attitudes that passed to the New World after 1492. After all, people lived in an atmosphere of exaltation of the very values of the regime of medieval Christianity in the midst of heretics, infidels, and pagans, which allowed them to appreciate the theocratic justifications of the Conquest. The Pope, as universal authority, conceded to the Castilian monarchs and their subjects dominion over those lands whose pagan inhabitants were required to accept at the same time the sovereignty of the Christian prince and evangelization, as the only way short of war, to conserve their personal liberties.[32]

To what extent was this religious motivation sincerely felt? Though it always appears mixed with other issues, it must have had considerable weight, and not only to justify their own actions or promote those of others, but out of conviction as well. Without this motive,

drid, 1947). A. García Gallo, *Estudios de historia del derecho indiano* (Madrid, 1972). E. de la Torre Villar, *Las leyes del descubrimiento en los siglos XVI v XVII* (Mexico, 1948). L. García de Valdeavellano, *Curso de historia de las instituciones españolas de los orígenes a la Baja Edad Media* (Madrid, 1970). J. M. Pérez-Prendes, *Curso de Historia del Derecho Español*, 4th ed. (Madrid, 1989); and *La monarquía indiana y el Estado de Derecho* (Madrid, 1989).

31 J. Suberbiola Martínez, *Real Patronato de Granada. El arzobispo Talavera, la Iglesia y el Estado Moderno (1486–1516)* (Granada, 1985). A. de Egaña, "El regio patronato hispánico-indiano. Su funcionamiento en el siglo XVI," *Estudios de Deusto*, 6 (1958): 147–204. Cr. Hermann, *L'Eglise d'Espagne sous le patronage royal (1476–1834)* (Madrid [Casa de Velázquez], 1988).

32 P. Castañeda Delgado, *La teocracia pontificia y la conquista de América* (Vitoria, 1968). See the fundamental work of Ch. M. de Witte, "Les bulles pontifcales et l'expansion portugaise au XVe siècle," *Revue d'Histoire Ecclésiastique* (1954–1958), 210 pp., various paginations.

evangelization would not have been such a primary goal of the most gigantic enterprises of spiritual conquest that had ever been undertaken. This contrasts with the scant success of the medieval attempts to convert the Jews or Muslims in the Iberian peninsula, or the failure – contemporary with the American missions – to assimilate the Moors during the sixteenth century. Nevertheless, the transference of missionary methods and experiences elaborated in the West from the thirteenth to the fifteenth centuries to the New World remains to be studied.[33]

Without the force and vigor of the missionary spirit – understood in a mental and historical context very different from ours – the impulse to respect the indigenous population would not have been produced, which, in spite of everything, was based upon the idea that each and every member of the human race is made in the image and likeness of the Creator, and all are potential Christians.[34] The texts that indicate the religious motivations of the conquests abound, as do those that conceive of the evangelization as a continuation of the conquest in which priests take the place of soldiers. As Fray Jerónimo de Mendieta wrote:

> Soldiers of Christ who come to conquer . . . armed with the shield of the faith, with the armor of justice, with the sword of the divine word, with the helmet of salvation and with the lance of perseverance.

Those missionaries came from a church that had undergone important reforms during the fifteenth century, especially in the final decades. The Catholic monarchs followed a policy in relation to the episcopal seats of their kingdoms that combined political interests and control

[33] R. Ricard, *La "conquête spirituelle" du Mexique. Essai sur l'apostolat et les méthodes missionaries des ordres mendicants en Nouvelle Espagne de 1523–24 à 1572* (Paris, 1933). P. Borges, *Métodos misionales en la cristianización de América* (Madrid, 1960), and *Misíon y civilización en América* (Madrid, 1986). See also *Gran Enciclopedia de España y América*, dir. J. M. Javierre, vol. 7: *Las Creencias* (Madrid, 1986). And the study by A. Garrido Aranda, *Moriscos e indios. Precedentes hispánicos de la evangelización de México* (México, 1980).

[34] On the difficult road toward an understanding of human dignity of the indigenous peoples in this mental context, see L. Hanke, *La lucha española por la justicia en la conquista de América* (Madrid, 1959), and *La humanidad es una. Estudio acerca de la querella que sobre la capacidad intelectual y religiosa de los indígenas americanos sostuvieron en 1550 Bartolomé de las Casas y Juan Ginés de Sepúlveda*, 2d ed. (México, 1985), and also the conferences in Madrid (Instituto de Cooperación Iberoamericano) and in Toulouse celebrated in honor of the 500th anniversary of Las Casas (Madrid, 1986; Toulouse, 1987), and the book by M. Mahn-Lot, *Bartolomé de las Casas et le droit des indiens* (Paris, 1982), and also T. Todorov, *La conquête de l'Amérique. La question de l'autre* (Paris, 1982). In a broader sense, C. Esteva Fabregat, *La Corona española y el indio americano*, 2 vols. (Madrid, 1959).

by the monarchy of the appointments made by the popes, in a line that foreshadowed the *Regio Patronato,* with religious ideals relative to the personal conditions of the bishops. Azcona summarized these conditions in the following points: They were native to their kingdoms, residents in their seat, of an honest life and fulfilling priestly celibacy, "of the middle class, neither nobles nor bourgeois," and as literate as possible. There is no doubt that there was a gradual rise in the professional and moral standards of the high and middle clergy during those decades. However, the only studies available have examined the major prelates whose political activity was greater at times even than their religious activity, such as the Archbishops of Toledo Alfonso Carrillo and Pedro González de Mendoza, the Archbishop of Burgos Pascual de Ampudia, Archbishop of Santiago Alfonso de Fonseca, Archbishop of Granada Hernando de Talavera, or Diego de Deza and Francisco Jiménez de Cisneros, who were also Inquisitor Generals.[35]

The new Inquisition, which functioned from 1481, grew to support the policies of the monarchy, with the consequent exclusion of apostates, heretics, and non-Christian groups. It served to link governmental action to the defense of the orthodoxy, reinforcing previously mentioned ideological tenets common within Europe in that time and present in the conquest of America. Here, only one of its possible social effects is worth mentioning, the passing of Jewish conversos to the Indies and the attenuated transplantation, on the other side of the Atlantic, of socioreligious problems specific to fifteenth-century Spain.

In a much wider sense, the reformist propositions slowly diffused some new and deeper religious sensitivities with respect to the devotion to Christ and reflection on his life (*Vita Christi* of Ludolfo de Sajonia; *Contemptus mundi* of Thomas à Kempis) along the line marked by the *Devotio moderna.* This move culminated in the original works of Spanish authors such as the *Lucero de vida cristiana* of Pedro Ximénez de Prexano, or the *Exercitatorio de la vida espiritual* of García Jiménez de Cisneros, Abbot of Montserrat, which are the preambles to sixteenth-century Spanish mysticism. The diffusion of ethical thought from antiquity – Aristotle, Cicero, Seneca – as the best preparation for understanding of Christian morality accompanied this wave of new spirituality due to the development of the first Castilian and Catalan humanism during the fifteenth century.

The reforms found a greater audience in the monastic and religious orders, which counted upon their own authors and spiritual traditions

[35] T. de Azcona, *La elección y reforma del episcopado español en tiempo de los Reyes Católicos* (Madrid, 1960).

and which, as in the rest of Europe, were affected throughout the fifteenth century by observant movements that reached their peak during the epoch of the Catholic monarchs, or by the revival of the medieval hermetic spirit.

One of the most notable events in the revival of monastic life was the expansion of the Order of Saint Jerome, which was almost exclusively Spanish. It was founded in the period between 1373 and 1419, during which time thirty-two monasteries arose, and new ones continued to arise until the number reached fifty-seven in 1515. In their monasteries, among which Guadalupe stands out, the Jeronimites combined the practice of their hermetic ideals with opulent cult and choral forms, and they knew how to respond to the religious demands of kings and nobles, for which they enjoyed ample protection and patronage. Although their expansion into America would be minimal, with the exception of some notable intervention during the first years, it is difficult to comprehend some aspects of the religiosity of the conquistadors without knowing the history of this order in the fifteenth century.[36]

The success of the Observant movement among Franciscans and Dominicans had, on the other hand, a much greater influence in the Indies, since most of the missionaries came from the two Orders before the diffusion of the Jesuits. Most influential were the Franciscans because the expansion of the Order in Spain was enormous. It is estimated that a third of the Franciscans in Europe lived on the Iberian Peninsula. They relied upon prior missionary experience in the Canaries and in the Maghreb.[37]

There were also signs of greater religiosity within the laity during the fifteenth century: a systemization of the steps of preaching and catechism, with the publication of "tables" of Christian doctrine, catechisms, confessions, and sermon manuals that would be utilized and adapted by the missionaries in America. A new impetus was also given to the holding of councils and synods, there were forty-four in Castile between 1473 and 1511, which allowed for updating and re-

[36] A good introduction is R. J. Highfield, "The Jeronomites in Spain, Their Patrons and Successes, 1373–1516," *Journal of Ecclesiastical History* 34:4 (1983). See also my work, "Mecenazgo real y nobiliario en monasterios españoles: los jerónimos," *Príncipe de Viana, anejo 3* (1986).

[37] Essential works include the investigations by J. García Oro, *La reforma de los religiosos españoles en tiempo de los Reyes Católicos* (Valladolid, 1969), and *Cisneros y la reforma del clero español en tiempo de los Reyes Católicos* (Madrid, 1971). V. Beltrán de Heredia, *Historia de la reforma de la Provincia de España, 1450–1500* (Roma, 1939), and *Las corrientes de espiritualidad entre los dominicos de Castilla durante la primera mitad del siglo XVI* (Salamanca, 1941).

ordering of canonical legislation. Finally, from the middle of the fifteenth century there was a notable increase in the number of urban and rural confraternities, an expression of secular religiosity and, at the same time, of social and hierarchical values.[38]

There is another aspect that we should mention in this brief review of the elements of Spanish religious life that influenced the mission in the Indies. At the end of the fifteenth century the final waves of messianic and prophetic millenarianism of the late Middle Ages were being lived out, expressed, for example, in the *Libro de Anticristo* of Martín Martínez de Ampiés. The retaking of Granada in 1492 offered a case of "meaningful chronology" that Columbus himself would use in recalling that in that year the Jews were expelled from the kingdoms of Castile and Aragon and that a western route was discovered to lands where he and many others believed there was another hidden Christianity. The year 1492 came to be a "prefiguration," a prophetic announcement of the unification of the ecumenical whole of humanity under the flag of Christianity.[39] It seems that the Franciscans, due to the very tradition of the Order, best preserved and diffused those myths of reform and return to original purity as a preparation for the fulfillment of the millenarian hopes in the triumph of Christianity and the coming end of the world.

In sum, an experienced and renewed ecclesiastical organization was transferred to the New World with recent practice and a long medieval tradition of the creation of new dioceses and institutions. This tradition included beliefs and religious practices that included the deepest of medieval Christianity and therefore its remarkable capacity for absorption and utilization of pre-Christian elements compatible with the Christian faith in the course of the evangelizing process.

Thus we can understand why in Mexico, "New Spain," the last spurt of millenarianism arose, promoted by several "observant" Franciscans. There also arose the cult of Our Lady of Guadalupe, one of the greatest Marian movements of late medieval Castile, built upon the ruins of the formerly worshipped Tonantzin, indigenous "mother of the gods." The Mexican mission, as well as those of other parts of America, was often related in terms that reproduced episodes and

[38] J. Sánchez Herrero, "Los concilios provinciales y los sínodos diocesanos españoles, 1215–1550," *Quaderni Catanesi di Studi Classici e Medievali*, 5 and 7 (1981–1982), and "La literature catequética en la Península Ibérica, 1236–1553," *En la España Medieval*, 9 (1986): 1051–1117, also the general proceedings of *Primer Congreso Nacional de Cofradías de Semana Santa* (Zamora, 1987).

[39] A. Milhou, *Colón y su mentalidad mesiánica en el ambiente franciscanista español* (Valladolid, 1983). Also, the ongoing works of D. C. West (Northern Arizona University).

feats from the *Legenda Aurea* compiled by Jacobo de Vorágine three centuries earlier. This legendary quality did not, however, prevent evangelization from being accomplished with discipline and an extraordinary practical sense.

CONCLUSION

Many authors have emphasized the importance of the "late fruits" (*frutos tardíos*) that the Spanish medieval spirit produced well into the Modern Age.[40] This was due to the permanence of the ways of conceiving reality that corresponded to a situation where the most typical values of the Middle Ages became rooted firmly into the economic, social, political, and religious transformations of the fourteenth and fifteenth centuries.

In the longer term, this activity would produce a certain Spanish disjunction from the evolution of other countries of western Europe, but at the end of the fifteenth century it was shared by all of the Western countries. It was a viable, creative force, and had a major influence in the New World. As L. Weckmann states:

> The Spaniards, in a consummately medieval manner, were able to transmit . . . institutions and archetypal values from the Middle Ages. . . . The New World was seen in the dawn of its history as a perfect geographic theater in which to realize the great medieval expectations.

On the one hand, the conquistadors tended to designate and thus to assimilate the new realities they encountered with medieval terms. For example, in the New World there was the search for "the confirmation of the existence of the marvelous," such as had been imagined in the Middle Ages. The explorers acted at times on the basis of "imaginary geography" that was slow in changing and that skewed their vision of America during several decades.[41] On the other hand, the rapid diffusion of the intellectual values of humanism in the Spain of the Catholic monarchs facilitated the elements necessary for the peculiar and innovative "discovery of the world and of man" spearheaded by Spaniards in the New World through the work of the chroniclers,

[40] See, in particular, the reflections of C. Sánchez-Albornoz y Menduíña, *La Edad Media española y la empresa de América* (Madrid, 1983; 1st ed., La Plata, 1934), and A. Tovar, *Lo medieval en la Conquista y otros ensayos americanos* (Mexico, 1981).

[41] J. Gil, *Mitos y utopías del descubrimiento: I. Colón y su tiempo* (Madrid, 1989). D. Ramos, *El mito de El Dorado* (Madrid, 1988). J. P. Duviols, *L'Amerique espagnoles vue et rêvue. Les livres de voyages de Christophe Colomb a Bougainville* (Paris, 1986).

geographers, intellectuals of law, and missionary-anthropologists during the sixteenth century.[42]

The late medieval historical framework was a point of departure that would be deeply and rapidly transformed upon contact with the American reality. Nevertheless, little could be understood of those new societies without appreciating the medieval baggage from which they sprung and the influence it had on many aspects of their evolution. And, after all, the actions of the Spaniards in the New World, their results and limitations, would not be understandable without also understanding how they implanted on the other side of the Atlantic the historical reality of the previous centuries.

[42] The bibliography on this topic is abundant. See J. H. Elliot, *The Old World and the New, 1492–1650* (Cambridge, 1970). A. Gerbi, *La naturaleza de las Indias nuevas. De Cristóbal Colón a Gonzalo Fernández de Oviedo* (Mexico, 1978). F. Vicente Castro and J. L. Rodríguez Molinero, *Bernardino de Sahagún. Primer antrópologo en Nueva España (siglo XVI)* (Madrid, 1986). F. Rico, "El nuevo mundo de Nebrija y Colón: notas sobre la geografía humanística en España y el contexto intelectual del descubrimiento de América," *Nebrija y la introducción del Renacimiento en España* (Salamanca, 1983), 157–185. F. M. Cuesta, *Alonso de Santa Cruz y su obra cosmográfica*, 2 vols. (Madrid, 1983–1984). J. Brufau Prats, *La Escuela de Salamanca ante el descubrimiento del Nuevo Mundo* (Salamanca, 1989). A. M. Salas, *Tres cronistas de Indias: Pedro Mártir de Anglería, Gonzalo Fernández de Oviedo y Fray Bartolomé de las Casas*, 2d ed. (Mexico, 1986), and the classic work of F. Esteve Barba, *Historiografía indiana* (Madrid, 1964).

CHAPTER 4

The conquests of the Canary Islands

EDUARDO AZNAR VALLEJO

THE archipelago of the Canaries became the first Atlantic overseas colonies because of its proximity to the northern coasts of Morocco. From the point of view of European expansion, the early history of the Canaries can be divided into three historical moments: Rediscovery (1336–1401), "the Seigneurial epoch" (1402–1477); and "the Royal epoch" (1478–1526).[1]

The first period can be called one of "Rediscovery" because the archipelago had been known to the world of classical antiquity but was then forgotten during the Middle Ages. Knowledge of the islands became hazy, and references to the "Fortunate Isles" cannot be understood as referring only to the Canaries nor even always to real places. Therefore, in this period of rediscovery knowledge of the islands was not only renewed, but also deepened. This was accomplished by a series of expeditions, first by Mediterranean mariners (Genoese, Catalans, and Mallorcans) and then Atlantic (Portuguese and Castillian) mariners. The objective of these expeditions was not settlement but trade or plunder. Nevertheless, some sailors stayed in the archipelago, as did the Genoese Lanzarote Malocello on the island that bears his name (1336), or the few Mallorcan hermits who lived on Gran Canaria (1386–1393). These voyages made known some Canarian "products" (slaves, hides, and dyestuffs such as sangre de dragón and orchil). The papal investiture of the archipelago in Don Luis de la Cerda (1344) negated the concept of African expansion as an extension of the reconquest of Iberia and provoked the competition of Portugal and Castile over the islands. The Portuguese invoked their chronological claim, having organized an expedition to the islands as early as 1341. Castile, on the other hand, pointed to historical prece-

[1] An overview of these questions can be seen in Eduardo Aznar Vallejo, "La colonización de las islas canarias en el siglo xv," *VII Jornadas de Estudios Canarias-America* (Santa Cruz de Tenerife, 1985), 197–226.

dents, noting that the Mauritania-Tingitana had belonged to the Visigothic kingdom to which its kings proclaimed themselves heirs.

The so-called "Seigniorial epoch" witnessed the beginnings of colonization and can be divided into two periods: Franco-Norman (1404–1418) and Castilian-Andalusian (1419–1477) according to the origins of its titulars and the nature of lordship: exempt lordship in the first case, jurisdictional lordship in the second.

The establishment of effective sovereignty on the archipelago was marked by two characteristic phenomena of Europe at this historical moment: the decline of authority of a universal type and the growing power of the Atlantic countries. This explains why the colonization was attempted from Castile in competition with Portugal with little participation by the Papacy, whose role changed from dispenser of sovereignty to arbiter between the two kingdoms. Sovereignty passed, therefore, in a series of treaties of partition, inspired by earlier ones that had previously regulated the Iberian reconquest.

The military conquest took place within the claims of sovereignty and at least as one more element of these. During this period the conquerors were the lords, although they were aided by certain facilities granted by the crown. With such means, the Normans between 1402 and 1404 carried out the conquest of Lanzarote, Fuerteventura, and Hierro. Around the middle of the century, the Castilians incorporated Gomera, although this process was not based on military victory but rather on the establishment of superior power supported by the aid of one of the island's indigenous groups.

The direct intervention of the monarchy after 1478 was favored by the rising cost of military conquest since the kings controlled greater human and financial resources than the individual lords. The monarchs could count on the troops of the Santa Hermandad, on contingents supplied by royal cities and towns, and on groups of convicts who satisfied their judicial sentences by providing armed service. In the economic sphere, the crown controlled, apart from its own resources, property from confiscations and the funds of the Bull of the Canaries transformed from an instrument for "conversion" into a tool for "evangelizing conquest." Under its protection, individuals in charge of the conquest through an agreement *(capitulación)* with the crown could finance the payment of international companies of soldiers.

Between 1478 and 1483 the conquest of Gran Canaria was carried out by a war of attrition that wore down stiff aboriginal resistance. In contrast, the conquest of La Palma was carried out quickly (from the end of 1492 to mid-1493) thanks to bands of cooperative "peaceful" natives. Similar collaboration also existed on Tenerife, although in a more accentuated manner. There, a second landing was needed after the annihilation suffered by the first, and the military operations extended for three years (1494–96). On the administrative level, royal colonization assumed the direct intervention of the monarchy on three of the seven islands and its greater presence throughout the archipelago.

At the arrival of the Europeans, the Canarian archipelago was characterized by a notable cultural diversity that affected its material life, its social and political systems, its economic structure, and its religious beliefs.[2] This diversity was determined primarily by the variety of ethnic groups that had populated the islands in spite of their common North African background and their recent arrival (surely within the Christian era). It was also owed to their process of adaptation to a territory of differing ecological niches, despite certain similar traits among them such as the total absence of metallurgy.

We can briefly review the cultural differences of the islands. The island of Hierro had a political system based on a redistributive chieftain, an economy of agriculture and herding, housing in caves and cabins, burials in caves, and stone drawings of an epigraphic type. There was a dual society on Gomera divided into four sections. The economy was based on herding and to a lesser extent on agriculture and collecting, housing was in caves and cabins, and there were geometric rock drawings like those on Tenerife. On that island the political system was divided into nine tribes with a segmentary organization. People lived in caves and cabins and their dead were buried mummified (*mirlado*). They lived by herding and, to a lesser extent, by agriculture. That activity did not exist on La Palma, however, where herding and gathering formed the basis of the economy. Spiral form rock drawings marked this island as did its organization of segmentary tribes, which divided the island into nine distinct territories.

Of all the islands, Gran Canaria had the most advanced culture on the archipelago. Its hierarchical social structure and its political system, close to a proto-state, were manifested in the control of irrigated agriculture through collective silos, in important settlements of artificial houses and caves, and in a certain priestly hierarchy *(faicanes)*. These phenomena, along with their small idols and rich ceramics, had no parallel on the other islands.

[2] The details can be seen in A. Tejera and R. González, *Las culturas aborígenas canarias* (Santa Cruz de Tenerife, 1987).

On the two remaining islands of Lanzarote and Fuerteventura culture was less complex than on Gran Canaria. On Lanzarote there was a redistributive chieftainship centered on an important town that served as a model for settlement just as the caves served their funerary ritual. The island had a mixed economy of agriculture and livestock. We know very little about the social structure of Fuerteventura although we know about other aspects. The island lacked agriculture, which made herding and collecting very important. The islanders lived in villages of rough houses or natural caves, the latter serving also for burials.

Contact between these aboriginal cultures and Western medieval civilization was intimately connected to the process of European expansion in the Late Middle Ages. The diverse aspects of this expansion can be summarized by three techniques: creation of commercial enclaves, the establishment of protectorates or zones of political influence, and colonization. The first two techniques, which often appear together, exert pressure on existing structures but do not supplant them. The third attempts a substantial, complete transformation of existing conditions. It is necessary to differentiate the various approaches according to the means employed and the existing relations between the zones that are brought into contact. A distinction must be made between "territorial" colonization and "population" colonization according to the size of the prior population. Moreover, a distinction between "frontier" colonization and "foreign" colonization depending on the proximity and the similarity of the regions is also in order. All of these features had precedents, both on the Hispanic and the Germanic frontiers and on the Mediterranean coast of Spain. While the Early Middle Ages had been marked by the predominance of frontier colonization, if we exclude the exceptions like the Crusades, expansion became increasingly aimed toward foreign colonization, although examples of the frontier variety continued in such places like the kingdom of Granada.

These characteristics of expansion are best examined from the viewpoint of contact with other civilizations in terms of both their continuation from the past and their adaptation to new realities. A theory fashioned in this way can take into account the vision held of other peoples as well as their juridical situation and the understood right to conquer others. The transition in European thought from the symbolic to the concrete contributed to a sharpened conceptualization of exterior realities, especially in terms of individuals. The monsters of the fourteenth century, as they appeared in the *Libro de Conocimiento,* were replaced by the "noble savage" of the fifteenth century, characterized by a list of virtues.[3] These for the most part are physical (strength, beauty, and so on) although moral attributes are also bestowed on them, especially those qualities perceived as more intrinsic such as loyalty and bravery. Other attributes were denied them until their conversion, thus making moral turpitude a frequent accusation against them, especially in terms of their domestic life. This interest in persons extends to objects as well, as can be seen in descriptions of the landscape, dwellings, and diet. Although in some cases, especially in the evaluation of future economic possibilities, an overly optimistic view is expressed, the writers tend to opt for accuracy. This is shown in various passages from the chroniclers such as those collected in *Le Canarien*, a French chronicle of the conquest of the Canary Islands, when noting that information on the "red-skinned people" could not be verified "because we have not seen them in those regions" or on the origin of speech produced by the Gomerans' lips, an idea that was accepted because, "according to their way of speaking it seems credible."[4]

The theory of contact between Europeans and foreigners is also concerned with the juridical situation of these peoples. Although the political superiority of the Christians over those who were not Christian was commonly accepted (in spite of some purely theoretical considerations which do not support this), personal freedom, patrimony, and certain principles of organization depended on the division between the narrowly defined infidels (those who had sufficient knowledge of divine enlightenment but refused to accept it) and pagans or heathens (those who lacked access to enlightenment).[5] Faced with the first group (Jews and, largely, Muslims) the usual recourse was conflict until submission by the non-Christians, although extenuating circumstances led at times to periods of respite and some instances of evangelization promulgated by the Franciscan missionary spirit, as in the case of Ramón Llull or the bishopric of Morocco. The second non-Christian group was subjected to a process of indoctrination until their voluntary conversion. The Christians used force and denial of per-

[3] The transition from an "ideological" geography, a phrase used by Leo Olschki (*Storia letteraria delle scoperte geografiche.* Florence, 1937), to a realistic geography can be seen in the case of the Canaries in the comparison between M. Jiménez de la Espada, ed., *Libro del conoscimiento de todos los reinos . . .* (Barcelona, 1980) and Elias Serra Rafols and Alejandro Cioranescu, *Le Canarien: crónicas francesas de la conquista de Canarias,* 3 vols., *Fontes Rerum Canarium* vols. 8–9, 11 (La Laguna, 1959–65).

[4] *Le Canarien,* iii, chaps. 64 and 66 of the Gadifer de La Salle text.

[5] Antonio Rumeu de Armas, "Los problemas derivados del contacto de razas en los albores del Renacimiento," *Cuadernos de Historia. Anexos de la Revista Hispania,* I (Madrid, 1967).

sonal liberty when this process resulted in armed resistance; in this case the war was declared legitimate.[6]

The application of these considerations to the case of the Canary Islands enables us to distinguish two stages of acculturation that may be linked to either a process of pre-colonization or of colonization. The first concerns the archipelago in its totality throughout the fourteenth century and which was prolonged for the length of the fifteenth century on those islands which remained unsubmissive. The second developed in stages during the fifteenth century.

During the first phase, European expansion in the Canaries did not seek to replace indigenous structures, but to exert pressure on those already existing in order to create a situation favorable to European interests through commercial or missionary relations. Contacts between the two worlds were begun at this time.

We should bear in mind that it was at this moment that a fundamental role was played by organized evangelical efforts, crystallizing in the creation of the missionary bishopric of La Fortuna.[7] Christianization, the papal argument for the conversion of the Canary Islands into the kingdom of La Fortuna, developed through the efforts of the Mallorcans and Catalans. In 1351, the year in which the bishopric was founded, twelve natives of Grand Canary Island, proficient in Catalan, were educated on Mallorca. They probably formed part of an exchange of persons and products that was the result of an alliance and protection treaty. This appears to be alluded to in the statement from Hermmenlin who noted the delivery of "some couples of males and females of those people to whom it was indicated that they would return."[8] In 1352, 1370, and 1386, new missionary expeditions were organized. Traveling on the voyage of 1386 were some "pauperous hermits" who established themselves on Grand Canary. The bishopric lasted until the end of the fourteenth century. The martyrdom of the

[6] This formula was recognized in *Le Canarien*, chap. 27 of Gadifer which states the intention of the French to foment a rupture of the agreement between both populations, "if we find no other solution then we will kill the men who defend their country, and it will have begun; we will save the women and children and have them baptized and we will live as they do." During the "royal" conquest a distinction was made between slaves taken in "good war," or those of a "bad war," according to whether they belonged to factions which had offered armed resistance or to those that had capitulated. Many examples of this are found in Eduardo Aznar Vallejo, *Documentos canarios en el Registro de Sello* (San Cristóbal de La Laguna, 1981).

[7] Details on the bishopric can be found in Antonio Rumeu de Armas, *El obispado de Telde* 2nd ed. (Madrid, 1986).

[8] The text of Hermmenlin was published by A. Lutolf, "Acerca del descubrimiento y cristianización de las Islas del Occidente de Africa," *Revista de Historia de Canarias*, 64 (1942): 284–292.

last missionaries occurred about 1393, coinciding with a looting expedition by Basques and Andalusians.

Contacts such as these led to the first processes of acculturation. At the material level, historical tradition notes the Mallorcan influence on the construction of houses, excavation of caves, painted wood, and the introduction of fig trees.[9] This last point has been refuted by modern authors who base their argument on the reference to fig trees in the account of the Italian-Portuguese expedition of 1341, a year before the first known Mallorcan expedition.[10] It is a matter that cannot be resolved, however, since we do not know if it was the same type of tree, nor if previous expeditions had in fact occurred.

At the ideological level, the Mallorcan influence on systems of organization is notable. According to the chroniclers, the Mallorcans gave the inhabitants "the means to govern with great skill and propriety,"[11] and, above all, evangelization, which outlasted the physical presence of the Mallorcans. This fact appears to be supported in the so-called will of the thirteen brothers, included in an account by the Franco-Normans in the region of Telde in 1403.[12] The results of this influence were seen in later periods when the native islanders were used as "tongues" (interpreters) and trade was renewed. *Le Canarien* mentions these exchanges, noting the employment of two natives who were brought to France, and the search for others in Seville, and the exchange of figs and dragon's blood (dye) for fishhooks and old tools.[13]

These conditions were extended to the unsubmissive islands for a good part of the fifteenth century since colonization was preceded by precolonization here as well. On these islands, periods of confrontation alternated with periods of peaceful relations, with or without political sanction. The duration of these epochs could be fairly long, as is noted in the *Pesquisa de Cabitos,* which comments on the six years of "peace" with Tenerife.[14]

9 Tomás Arias Marin de Cuba, *Historia de la conquista de las siete islas de Canaria* (Las Palmas, 1986); J. de Viera y Clavijo, *Noticias de la historia general de las islas Canarias,* 2 vols. 8th ed. (Santa Cruz de Tenerife, 1982); Juan Abreu Galindo, *Historia de la conquista de las Siete Islas de Canarias* (Santa Cruz de Tenerife, 1955).

10 Elias Serra Rafols, "Los mallorquines en Canarias," *Revista de Historia de Canarias,* 54 and 55 (1941), pp. 195–209; 281–287; 66 (1944), 145–155. Buenaventura Bonnet y Reverun "Las expediciones a las Canarias en el siglo xiv," *Revista de Indias* 5:18 (1944–45), 577–610; J. Alvarez Delgado, "De la vida indígena, "*Revista de Historia de Canarias* 66 (1944).

11 Abreu Galindo, *Historia,* 41.

12 *Le Canarien,* iii, chap. 36 of Gadifer.

13 *Le Canarien,* iii, chaps. 24, 38 of Gadifer; ii, chaps. 36, 40 of Juan V. de Béthencourt.

14 *Información sobre cuyo es el derecho de Lanzarote y conquista de Las Canarias (Pesquisa de*

Trade with these islands is attested to by the products obtained from them: fish, orchil, and dragon tree.[15] It must also be noted that the stream of commerce destined for construction and the late provisioning of these fortress towers would seem unthinkable without a flow of returns. This can also be inferred from the very existence of these fortresses, the capacities of which indicate quite ample possibilities of storage.[16] It is also possible that these operations involving exchange gave rise to others tied to production. This appears to be indicated by a comment on the death of livestock that "the Christians had on the island."[17]

Relations of an evangelical character developed simultaneously with commercial ones. These were carried out either under the auspices of the fortresses or autonomously. With respect to the first possibility, *La Pesquisa* informs us of the celebration of mass in the towers and of the construction by Diego de Herrera of a church on Tenerife that we must suppose was next to – but not joined to – the Fortress of Añazo.[18] These relations reached their highest point in the moments of "peace" during which the islands were even visited by church officials. We know that during one of these visits, Bishop D. Diego López celebrated mass in Telde.[19]

Christianization operated at other times without the co-operation of these organizing centers and in fact often preceded them. We do not know how and when contacts were renewed with potential Christians of Grand Canary, although doubtless it was at an early stage since communities of neophyte Christians existed on that island and on Gomera in 1424.[20] Ten years later the mission was flourishing on both islands to the extent that it thought of transferring the cathedral of San Marcial del Rubicón to Grand Canary.[21] An important role was played in these missions, overseen by the Franciscan vicariate of the Canaries, by the indigenous lay brother Juan Alfonso Idubaren.[22] We

Cabitos), Eduardo Aznar Vallejo, ed. (Las Palmas, 1990), see testimony of Diego Martínez, 274.

15 Abreu Galindo, *Historia,* 135; *Pesquisa de Cabitos,* testimonial A; Rumeu de Armas, "El origen de las islas Canarias del licenciado Luis Melian de Betancor," *Anuario de Estudios Atlanticos* 24 (1978), 15–81, especially 53–54; Aznar Vallejo, *Documentos,* n.362.

16 *Pesquisa de Cabitos,* testimony of Juan Iñíguez de Atabe, 229–230.

17 *Pesquisa de Cabitos,* testimony of Alvaro Romero, 300.

18 *Pesquisa de Cabitos,* testimony of Juan Iñíguez de Atabe, 229.

19 *Pesquisa de Cabitos,* testimony of Martin de Torre, 294.

20 Bull of Martin V (November 20, 1424) published in Viera y Clavijo, *Noticias,* v. 2, appendix 7, 955–956.

21 Bulls of Eugene IV (January 12, 1435; August 25, 1435) in J. Wülfel, "La Curia Romana y la Corona de España en la defensa de los aborígenes canarios," *Anthropos* (Vienna) 25 (1930): 1011–1083; *Monumenta Henriciana,* 5, n.82 (Coimbra, 1962).

22 For further information on the Franciscan missions in the Atlantic see Antonio Ru-

have information that dates from the middle of the fifteenth century on the missionary center of Tenerife, also located at the south of the island.[23] We know that it was composed of three missionaries who lived among the native islanders and preached to them in their language. One of these missionaries, Fray Masedo, fled from the island, most likely due to the general deterioration in relations between Europeans and native islanders. A decisive role was played in the development of the hermitage by the discovery of an image of the Virgin of Candelaria between 1430 and 1450, according to both historic documentation and art scholarship.

The major obstacle to evangelization was the enslavement of the native islanders, which resulted in a hostile attitude toward the work of the missionaries. This antipathy led to the proclamation by Eugene IV in 1434 that freed all indigenous islanders within the area of evangelization.[24] This papal bull prohibited attacks on natives and made the freeing of captives mandatory under penalty of excommunication. Those who set their slaves free were promised plenary indulgence. Pius II went a step further to assure the freedom of the native islanders by guaranteeing that the agreements between the bishops and the aboriginal peoples would not be changed.[25] These edicts, called "peace bulls," also proclaimed the liberty of the natives, violation of which would be punished by excommunication.

The result of all this was formal Christianization, understood as the acceptance of certain rituals that were the symbols of fundamental truths but the fulfillment of which did not imply a substantial moral transformation. We find its most precise reflection in the administration of baptism that, according to the witnesses recorded in the *Pesquisa de Cabitos,* reached a great number of people but did not imply an actual change in a person's life.[26] This is explained by the ritual nature of the celebration in which merchants and other occasional visitors acted as the godparents. We know that on La Gomera formal evangelization ultimately collected tithes, and was compatible there with polygamy and other non-Christian prac-

meu de Armas, "La nunciatura castellana de Guinea, *Revista de Indias* 27: 109–110 (1967): 285–312.

[23] For details on this mission see Antonio Rumeu de Armas, *La conquista de Tenerife* (Santa Cruz de Tenerife, 1976).

[24] Bull of Eugene IV (October 29, 1434) in R. Torres Campos, *Caracter de la conquista y colonización de las Islas Canarias* (Madrid, 1901).

[25] Bull of Pius II (October 9, 1462), in Viera y Clavijo, *Noticias.* v. 2, appendix 15, 967–70.

[26] *Pesquisa de Cabitos.* Testimonial section, considerations of the seigniorial attorney, testimony of Gonzalo Rodríguez and of Ferrand Alfonso, 250, 271, 277.

tices.[27] In any case, evangelization was a basic element in acculturation. This is evident in Diego de Sevilla's interpretation of the situation following the rupture of peace, in which he affirmed: "Afterwards they were not pleased with the faith and they stopped being obedient."[28]

These processes were realized in a series of material borrowings and in a certain political effect on the aboriginal population. With regard to these visible results, the *Pesquisa de Cabitos* contains highly revealing testimony that indicates that the Canarians attacked the fortress of Gando with "carts" in order to burn it.[29] This statement confirms information from other sources such as *Le Canarien*, which mentions the use of metal utensils and arms captured from the Spanish.[30]

The second result, extended political influence, is supported by more numerous sources. The scope of that influence allows us to differentiate the two areas where its thrust was felt: Gomera and the rest of the islands. The effect for Gomera was incorporation of the island, achieved virtually without military conquest. This is explained by the support of Fernán Peraza, a large landowner of the islands, for one of the island's political factions. This support meant the imposition of control over the other factions and that the Portuguese, who had been supporting them, lost their hold on the island. This political agreement was then authorized by the native islanders in a pact of fraternity.[31] We do not know if this indigenous ceremony had its counterpart in a similar act on the part of the Europeans as was done in the so-called "Acta de Bufadero" (Buffoon's Ceremony) on Tenerife. The political agreement did not exclude armed conflict, as is shown in the *Pesquisa de Cabitos*, which mentions the confrontation between the leader of the faction aligned with Peraza, supported by members of his political group, and the other political leaders of the island; but the spread of violence to the other islands was deliberately avoided.[32]

The uniqueness of this conquest is demonstrated in the survival of a consolidated aboriginal population until the resumption of slavery in 1477 and, even more intensely, in 1488. The progressive character of the process of acculturation, shown by the denunciations of the Gomerans "who obeyed Fernán Peraza but in matters of their religion

[27] Aznar Vallejo, *Documentos*, n. 17 and those following.
[28] *Pesquisa de Cabitos*, testimony of Diego de Sevilla, 280.
[29] *Pesquisa de Cabitos*, testimony of Pedro Tenorio, 288.
[30] *Le Canarien*, chap. 36 of Gadifer; chaps. 40, 61 of Béthencourt.
[31] Juan Álvarez Delgado, "El episodio de Iballa," *Anuario de Estudios Atlanticos*, 5 (1959): 255–374.
[32] *Pesquisa de Cabitos*, testimony of Juan Iñíguez de Atabe, 228.

lived any way they wanted to," was marked by a separation from the other islands where Christianization was understood as one more, and very immediate, effect of the conquest.[33]

Political influence on the other islands was much less despite the optimistic interpretation of the peace agreements concluded with Tenerife. According to the *Pesquisa de Cabitos,* Diego de Herrera not only took possession of the island but also imposed law upon it.[34] The "*Acta de Bufadero*" more realistically indicates that this lord, Peraza, divided administration among nine faction chiefs (*menceyes*).[35] The surrender of hostages – who must have been members of a religious order, as was the case on Grand Canary – proves the lack of seigniorial control over the islands although it does show the stability of relations. This political agreement, symbolized by the ceremonial kissing of the lord's hands on the part of the *menceyes,* also existed on Grand Canary. This is recorded in the testimonies of Abreu Galindo and Melian de Betancor, and by the construction of a fortress inside of Telde because defense against attack from sea was impossible. The building of the fortress was, as in other cases, impossible without the agreement of the Canarians.[36] The possible peace agreements with La Palma were not documented in that era but delayed until just before the conquest. Once set forth, they must have been of minor import. In any case, the political agreements with these islands did not survive long enough to prove fruitful, and were always at the expense of the goodwill of the natives. This was exposed by Antón de Soria, who indicated that the peace agreements lasted "as long as the Canarians wanted." He also cited the existence of captives during the time of peace.[37]

The second phase was characterized by the process of colonization, which sought to create new structures for both the importation of new elements and for the transformation of what already existed. From the point of view of acculturation we can distinguish three groups of islands. The first, composed of Lanzarote, Fuerteventura, and Hierro, corresponds to the conquest launched by the Franco-Normans (1400–1404). Acculturation at this time came about rapidly, without major setbacks, and in such a way that the conquerors were designated "peoples of the islands," with no distinction made as to place of ori-

[33] *Pesquisa de Cabitos,* testimony of Juan Ruiz, 202.
[34] *Pesquisa de Cabitos,* cosiderations of the seigniorial attorney, 250.
[35] Real Sociedad Económica de Amigos del País de Tenerife. Archivo Rodríguez Moure 20/29 (copy of the existing transcript is in Archivo Histórico Provincial de Tenerife).
[36] Abreu Galindo, *Historia,* 115–116; Rumeu de Armas, *El orígen,* 15–81; *Pesquisa de Cabitos,* testimony of Gonzalo Rodríguez, 270.
[37] *Pesquisa de Cabitos,* testimony of Antón de Soria, 266.

gin. This situation was not present on Gomera which makes up the second island group. There European society and aboriginal society remained separate for generations. The cause of this singularity must be attributed, as we have seen, to the absence of a true military conquest until the natives' revolt in 1488. Grand Canary, La Palma, and Tenerife constitute the third group of islands. They are characterized by the most complex process of transculturation, fruit of the conjunction of three essential elements: the preservation of the most important native communities, the attraction of the greatest number of colonizers, and the substantial increase in slavery.

In the first group of islands the relation of forces between conquerors and conquered did not permit a pure and simple military occupation on the part of the Europeans.[38] The superiority of European weapons, and especially the absence of the bow among the natives, was offset by both the difficult conditions of climate and terrain, which made combat impossible while encumbered with overburdened horses, and the better knowledge of the land held by their adversaries, points commented on in *Le Canarien*. The islanders were able to hide and attack the Europeans by surprise but they were unable to dislodge them from their fortified positions. The conquest became a series of skirmishes in which both sides suffered defeats at times, and a series of political negotiations. In these, the Normans imposed their supremacy as "protectors" of the natives, who in turn claimed their supremacy as "hosts" of the foreigners, a role that allowed them to elevate their prestige in the context of their segmented organization. Proof of this was the attempt by Afche to displace the king of Lanzarote with the support of the Normans.

The shortage of settlers is related, in the first place, to the character of the occupied islands.[39] In attempting to settle on the islands that were most exposed to attacks by pirates and that offered the least potential for agricultural development, the aboriginal population suffered the greatest losses. To the group of survivors – more on Fuerteventura and Lanzarote, fewer on Hierro – the addition of some slaves from other islands (although their usual fate was to be exported) and hostages who were taken as a guarantee of peace accords must be recognized. The *Pesquisa de Cabitos* mentions the presence of this group in various passages. Juan of Grand Canary, who died in the revolt against the Portuguese, is an example. More striking, per-

[38] Details of this conquest are found in A. Tejera and Eduardo Aznar Vallejo, *El asentamiento franconormando de San Marcial del Rubicón* (Yaiza, 1989).

[39] Details found in Eduardo Aznar Vallejo, "La colonización de las Islas Canarias en el siglo xv," *En la España Medieval* V (1986), 205–208.

haps, is the account of the death of two natives in the fortress of Gando when it was attacked by the Canarians.[40] The presence of the hostages is seen in the peace negotiations that preceded the royal conquest. An example given in the testimony of Abreu Galindo states that Diego de Herrera delivered to Pedro Chemida and other ambassadors the Canarians of Lanzarote and Fuerteventura who wished to return with them.[41]

The limited agricultural possibilities of these islands also discouraged settlement on them. We have to consider, too, that this first period of colonization developed at the moment when European demographic rates had not yet stabilized, and would remain unstable until well into the fifteenth century when these islands would undergo competition with the larger ones.

The fusion of different groups around interests that they had in common did not exclude the establishment of a social hierarchy.[42] This was founded on the possession of lands, which was the source of wealth and of authority according to some clearly defined theoretical principles included in *Le Canarien*, which refer to apportionments of land. The superiority of the Europeans over the indigenous peoples was established by means of these principles since "it was quite reasonable to say they were better than the Canarians of the country." Among the Europeans, preeminence was accorded to holders of seigniorial titles and to those who held high posts in the government, chosen from among their relatives and supporters, and to scions of the gentry. This system depended upon the continuation of the resettlement of peasants as the main support of colonization through their work and contributions. Included in this group were the native islanders since there did not exist among them a solidified aristocracy that benefited from hierarchical integration in spite of some honorific considerations such as a greater concession of land and goods.

There were basically three paths toward integration: participation in common economic activities, mixed marriage, and evangelization. With respect to the first, the autochthonous population participated in distributions (*repartimientos*) of land after the conquest and cooperated, to a greater or lesser degree, in agrarian and military enterprises. *Le Canarien* refers, in this respect, to the French having sent the inhabitants of Fuerteventura and Lanzarote to work the land – some-

[40] *Pesquisa de Cabitos*, testimony of Juan Rodríguez de Gozón and Iñíguez de Atabe, 188, 229.
[41] Abreu Galindo, *Historia*, 173.
[42] Aznar Vallejo, "La colonización," 208–209.

thing that up until then had never been done – and to repair fountains and cisterns so that the cattle could drink from them. *Le Canarien* also indicates that the inhabitants of Lanzarote had become archers and soldiers. At the same time a series of family ties, some legal and others not, had been established between the two sectors of the population, a result of the shortage of women among the settlers. Suffice it to say that of the eighty fighters that Béthencourt brought as reinforcements, only twenty-three were accompanied by their wives. The available women married into their own class as is attested to by the union between Maciot de Béthencourt, nephew and lieutenant of the French conqueror, and Teguise, daughter of the "king" of Lanzarote.

Evangelization took on differing characteristics depending on whether the islands were those of "conquest" where the military victory had meant its de facto incorporation into the Christian community, or if they were islands of "penetration" where the acceptance of the new doctrine was matter of personal discretion. This lack of fervor on the part of the native population is attested to by Cabitos whose commentaries on Gomera include the justification put forward by Doña Beatriz de Bobadilla for enslavement of the island's inhabitants. She cited Fernán Peraza in her arguments, stating that he had complained to the king and to the bishop that the Gomerans refused baptism, used non-Christian names, did not wear clothes, and had eight to ten wives. Peraza arranged an accord with the Gomerans to dissuade them from their errors under penalty of imprisonment. In 1477, an order was issued for the return of Gomerans who had been sold by their owners, stating that "they are Christians or in the process of conversion."

A plan to evangelize this first group of islands did exist, as shown by the catechism contained in *Le Canarien*.[43] This catechism was an effective tool of evangelization, both for its simplicity and for its adaptation to the public to which it was directed. It was composed of a succinct *Story of Salvation* and a summary of three of the seven precepts of Christian doctrine. For example, only two of the Ten Commandments are presented, and but briefly – love God and one's neighbor, and of the seven sacraments, confirmation and extreme unction are left out. Adaptation to the specific conditions of the islands is seen in the insistence on the permanent character of marriage, em-

[43] *Le Canarien*, ii, chaps. 47–52 of Béthencourt. See the study of these chapters by J. Sánchez Herrero, "El tratado de doctrina cristiana incluído en *Le Canarien*," in *VI Coloquio de Historia Canario-Americana* (Las Palmas, 1988): ii, 2.

phasized on islands where polyandry was pervasive, and, again, in the use of the wind as an image that suggests destruction of what has been erected.

The best example of these processes of acculturation is the city of San Marcial del Rubicón, the first Norman settlement in the archipelago and the seat of its bishopric, known through archaeological excavations and references found in *Le Canarien*.[44] These sources have provided proof that the two populations lived together in one center, differentiated by type of dwelling and cultural loans between the two societies. With respect to diet, we have found adaptation by the Europeans of a diet based on cattle, complemented by fish, shellfish, and fowl. According to *Le Canarien*, necessity imposed the consumption of meat even during Lent. We have found variations to this diet since the Europeans were accustomed to slaughtering young animals, a practice unknown among the aboriginal peoples. Symbiosis took place at the technological level in which indigenous pottery was used beside imported ceramics and with European pottery produced in situ, of which we are ignorant as to the type of clay that was used. Wells also show evidence of transculturation, having developed through application of aboriginal technology – the "ere" or the collection of water through capillary attraction – combined with European engineering solutions. Engravings have been discovered of podomorphs and of the goddess Tanit, demonstrating the ritual character of water.

The native population of the third group of islands was not homogeneous, but rather consisted of four communities: [Gran] Canarian, Gomeran, Palman, and Guanche. Diverse social, economic, and juridical levels existed within each of these. Both of these conditions are closely related to the conquest, which at first generated a certain uniformity among the inhabitants of each one of the islands that then gradually disappeared as wider re-associations occurred. The redistribution of native islanders to different zones contributed to this realignment; especially noteworthy was the flow of Gomerans toward the royal islands.[45] Another factor was rising solidarity in the face of common problems such as restrictions on freedom of movement and free disposition of person and property.

The harshness and long duration of the conquest of Grand Canary (1478–1483) reduced the original population of that island.[46] Both those captured during the conflict and those who surrendered were

[44] Tejera and Aznar, *El asentamiento*.

[45] Eduardo Azar Vallejo, *La integración de las Islas Canarias en la Corona de Castilla (1478–1526)* (La Laguna, 1983), 76, 191, 207, 213.

[46] Aznar Vallejo, *La integración*, 199–200.

exiled from the island. The only exceptions to this practice were the Guanarteme of Galdar, one of the two factions that comprised the native leadership of the island. They and forty supporters were allowed to remain, although this concession later proved to be a ploy for the installation of groups from other islands. The remainder of the freed Canarians were settled in various parts of Castille, especially in Seville. The situation for the Canarians under the terms of the peace agreements fell short of the hopes aroused by official promises since some were enslaved immediately upon surrender and others suffered abuses in their island or peninsular exile. The situation of those settled in Castille is evident in the complaint lodged by Don Fernando de Guanarteme of mistreatment by the residents of Seville who didn't understand their language and accused the Canarians of not being Christians. These charges led to the royal decree of 1485 in which the mayor of Seville was entrusted with the responsibility of protecting the Canarians and assisting their integration, while at the same time preventing the Canarians from assembling, obliging them to look for a lord to serve, and separating the unmarried *in facie eclesiae.* Recommendations were also included to refrain from harsh punishment of those still ignorant of the laws and to facilitate their indoctrination. The remedy was counterproductive and served only to accelerate slavery, which had begun some time before. Those islanders established on Grand Canary also suffered abuses, either because they had been reduced to slavery or because their goods and property had been taken from them. In spite of these difficulties, the Canarian community was marked by a strong Hispanization, which differentiated it from the other indigenous groups. This change was convincing to the monarchs who authorized their transferral to Grand Canary. This integration was reinforced by the Canarians' participation in the conquest of La Palma and Tenerife, which elevated many of them to the position of "conquistadores." This action as allies of Castille encouraged the Canarians to consider themselves, and ask to be considered by others, as authentic Castilians.

The history of the Gomerans established on the royal islands dates from the slaving perpetrated against them from 1477 to 1488.[47] Unlike the case of the Canarians, the Gomerans' assimilation was very superficial. This situation caused them numerous difficulties despite their condition as free men. The authorities accused them of multiple offenses – extraction of honeycombs from beehives, cattle stealing, non-fulfillment of religious duties – the basis of which was always

[47] Ibid., 200–201.

their inability to adapt to the European way of life, a fact made vividly real by the Gomerans' nomadic life of following the herds, and, of course, their lack of cultivated fields. Opposition to them reached such a point that the town council of Tenerife decreed their expulsion in 1505. Only five persons were exempted from this ruling, significantly all landowners. The mandate was not put into effect then, however, nor was it later when the decree was revived in 1508; in 1511 it was replaced by another that obliged residency in settlements. Despite the resistance to this decree, which we can deduce from the reiteration in 1518 of a new ordinance, adaptation by the Gomerans did proceed, albeit slowly.

The conquest of La Palma was achieved with the support of a part of the Palman population.[48] The legal consequence of this act was the distinction between "pro-peace" factions, who enjoyed protection of their persons and property, and "pro-war" factions, who were at the disposal of the victors. We do not know what portion of the population was considered pro-peace since no data survives giving names or territory of the factions affected, although it must have been a major grouping to judge from the short duration of the military campaigns (September 1492–May 1493). In any case, the governor-conquistador ignored this factional division and acted with equal harshness against both groups. The result was the reduction to slavery of the major part of the population, as much within the island as outside of it.

Nonetheless, free Palmans did exit, having either maintained their freedom or having recovered it through judicial verdict known as *ahorramiento* or "being saved" (manumission). The freedom of the Palmans was long and painstaking. Although the first demands for liberty were voiced by Francisca Gamira – a native who had negotiated the peace agreements – and date from 1494, the first commission on this matter was not established until 1500. It lasted until at least 1514, when transferral of Palmans was outlawed until the conclusion of the dispute. We are ignorant of its outcome but we can infer from the absence of later news reports, the interest of the Crown in the legal activity of the attorneys for the poor, and from some individual verdicts in favor of the peace agreements of the Guanches – whose cause was viewed as part and parcel of the same question – that the verdict was favorable.

The conquistadores of Tenerife also counted on the support of the peace factions of the Guanches. These were Anaga, Güimar, Abona, and Adeje, who together composed the leadership of half the island's

[48] Ibid., 201–202.

territory although its population was inferior to that led by the remaining five factions.[49] The legal consequences of this division and their implementation were the same as on La Palma. Transgressions began even before the conquest, when allied Guanches were captured on "incursions" that took place at that time.

Slaving expeditions continued after incorporation had been completed. Reparation for these illegal actions was slow, not beginning until 1498. Subsequently, the struggle against slavery took the same path as it had for the Palmans. As in the case of the Gomerans, the adaptation of the Guanches to the new way of life was arduous. The beginning was particularly difficult given that many uprisings aroused the mistrust of the Castillians against the whole community. Suspicions that the slaves were cattle thieves also plagued them and led the town council of Tenerife to attempt to hinder manumitting slaves as well as to decree their expulsion, although neither of these measures was actually enforced. Freed men, for their part, were obliged to demonstrate their innocence by participating in squadrons attempting to conquer their countrymen. This did not get at the root of the problem, which was the lack of integration into society, the response to which was to order freed men to become wage earners and to live in designated areas. The obligation to participate in work gangs was repeated in subsequent years but without positive results; consequently, expulsion was also considered, and requested from the court by the town council of Tenerife. Receiving a negative response, the town council again insisted that free men live in the capital city. This demand was changed to residence in any of the ten to twelve designated villages then existing, and that possession of livestock be limited to cattle.

All these restrictions were ineffective means to achieve what could only be gotten through free acceptance. Besides, discrimination harmed groups that were on their way to integration. These began to make their protests heard and did accomplish some improvements. For example, following the prohibition by the town council of Tenerife against the carrying of arms by the Guanches, a group headed by Antón Azate won the modification that the law would apply only "to those who live in the mountains who do not dress or carry themselves as Castilians, but go about covered with markings." Others, like André de Güimar, brought their complaints directly before the king. Their grievances were the familiar ones: expulsions – or return not permitted, prohibition against carrying weapons, forced residence in

[49] Ibid., 202–205.

the capital, obligation to hunt criminals, and so on. The monarchs' response to these cases is illustrated by the legal upholding of the ordinance that granted freedom to the Guanches (the *ahorramientos*) and, by extension, to that of the Gomerans. On the one hand, the monarchs accepted some of the restrictions proposed by the local authorities; on the other, they supported verdicts in favor of the oppressed native population, even if these were opposed by the governor himself. However, the passage of time made these precautions unnecessary, and from 1519 on there is no mention made of interventions of this kind.

The circumstances outlined here were present at the economic and social levels of integration in each of the communities. The Canarians engaged in a wide range of agricultural occupations.[50] The principal activity was cattle breeding, combining the offspring of traditional species with that of imported cows. These efforts were possible through the contracting of herders who were either fellow countrymen or natives of other islands. Alongside cattle raising, the Canarians developed other agricultural occupations such as land cultivation, both irrigated and non-irrigated, and apiculture. Outside of these usual activities, the group was recognized for its military capability and used in the campaigns in the Indies, Italy, and Barbary. These expeditions caused wide loss of life as well as economic losses for which the Canarians requested – and obtained – an end to forced military participation outside of the archipelago, an exemption not extended to the Castilians. The Canarians were not, however, unwilling to participate in short and lucrative operations such as the *cabalgadas*, which were mounted raiding forays. The Canarians' military and agricultural contributions gave them considerable social and political prestige. In Tenerife, for example, the local governing official, the *Adelantado*, favored them generously, bestowing economic advantage on their lands and counting on them to extend his influence over the island. It is not strange, therefore, that some Canarians, such as Guillén García who became deputy constable, obtained posts of some prominence. The awareness that they were held in high esteem led Canarians who were established outside of their island to create homogeneous communities, clearly promoting regionalism from a geographic standpoint. This is not to say that they formed closed groups, since time narrowed differences and heightened similarities with other groups, especially the natives.

[50] Ibid., 200.

The fundamental activity of the Gomerans was stock raising.[51] The majority were owners or shepherds of sheep and goat flocks, although some pioneers in adaptation possessed large animals. This depended on the agricultural enterprise of some individuals, both on lands obtained through the early distributions or lands that they bought. The Gomerans also practiced apiculture.

As a result of the loss of legal documentation on La Palma and of the scarce records kept by the Palman colonies on other islands, much information is lacking on the way of life of this group.[52] Their chief occupation seems to have been, like the other indigenous groups, stock raising. Although some Palmans did collaborate in the conquest of Tenerife, no mention of any Palmans is made in the distributions of land nor in any official position of responsibility.

The duality existing in the degree of adaptation of the Guanches is reflected in their economic life.[53] This group that remained at a distance from population centers and was dedicated to migratory cattle raising conserved their language, customs, and traditional way of life. Of nineteen wills that we examined, four stated expressly that they were made in places at a distance from a populated area. In one of these an interpreter was present during confession, and was again present in the tutorship of the sons of Don Pedro de Adeje. These instances demonstrate the relatively late date at which the Guanche language was still spoken by a part of the native population. The accusations of refusal to give up traditional dress, nomadism, and lack of religious instruction were present in all the requests for restrictive laws. Yet, despite the survival of traditional practices, there was acceptance of some foreign influences, especially in those areas where the old and new could be combined easily and where an adaptation of ancient customs was possible. It is sufficient to note the will of a Guanche, even of Guanches who lived in isolated regions, to understand the force of certain religious practices and customs (alms, mass, . . .) despite the oft-repeated complaint of their ignorance of prayers and festivals.

According to reports, livestock raising based on goats and sheep continued to be the primary occupation of the Guanches, both for the residents of Tenerife and for those established on other islands. While some were ranchers (*señores de ganado*) others were mere shepherds of

[51] Ibid., 201.
[52] Ibid., 202.
[53] Ibid., 204–205.

flocks belonging to Canarians, Europeans, or even other Guanches. Since payment was in kind everyone participated in some manner in property-holding. On contact with the new way of life, some Guanches became involved in other types of livestock and in agriculture but did not give up traditional activities. A small number of islanders took up non-agrarian means of livelihood.

The position granted to the Guanches in the new social order lacked importance, as shown in the small number of landholders and their absence in official posts. Despite this, it is worth noting that the *menceyes* and their relatives, both those pro-peace and those pro-war, received a certain honorific position. This special treatment, evident in the title "don" and in a greater participation in the distributions of land, did not spare them abuses. The Queen of Adeje was raped, Don Diego de Adeje was imprisoned, and restrictions hindered Don Fernando de Anaga from transferring his estate to Grand Canary. Another group that enjoyed prestige was the Guanches of Güimar in whose territory the Virgin of Candelaria was worshipped. The exclusive right of this group to carry the Virgin's image provoked a strident dispute with the island's councilmen.[54]

A clearly defined program of evangelization, similar to the one developed on the royal islands before their integration or to the one established by *Le Canarien* for the islands occupied by the Normans, did not exist at this later time on the royal islands.[55] Here the idea that conversion was one more fruit of the conquest gained its clearest expression. This notion explains the Castilians' surprise that certain religious norms were unfulfilled by the native islanders. This is inferred from the declaration of Cristóbal de Contreras to the Inquisition in which he stated that he saw a Canarian recently buried in a cave and that "I get a bad conscience thinking that it's been 20 years since the island was taken and that all these Canarians are Christians." Christianization here was tied more to acculturation than to conversion and was oriented to the acquisition of certain religious habits by means of communal living. This explains the motivation for sending exiles from Grand Canary to live among families of Seville, and the insistence by the council of Tenerife that the natives reside in designated areas under the pretext that they would be able to attend mass on Sundays. The nature of their religion permitted greater adaptation than that of Jews and Moslems since the problem of apostasy was

[54] Archivo Casa Osuna. legajo. 90–2.
[55] Eduardo Aznar Valejo, "La religiosidad popular en los orígenes de Canarias," *VII Coloquio de Historia Canaria-Americana* (Las Palmas, 1990), II: 213–45.

non-existent. The Christianization of traditional practices was common as attested to by the transmutation of the names of two autochthonous gods to designate God and the Virgin, or the connection made between Calvary and other Christian historical events and specific trees.[56] This syncretism lends a different character to the religion practiced by these converts than in the communities cited here. In spite of the theoretical obligation to register the "newly converted," their actual presence was insignificant.[57] Aboriginal descent was not an obstacle to occupying government posts, even those of the Inquisition, and the synodic constitutions exempted them from "reserved cases" pertaining to sexual relations with a church person, Indian or Moor.[58] The problems of native islanders with the Holy Office represented a small percentage of the total and affected minor cases (funeral and dietary practices, domestic conflicts, blasphemies and some sacrileges) also common to Christians by birth. These were resolved with minor penalties for infringement.[59]

The legal order presented more major obstacles to integration than did the insistence on religious conversion.[60] Although enslavement of the aboriginal population soon gave way to other practices, the problem of rebels was endemic. These were slaves who fled from the domination of their owners, runaways who were predominantly native to the island, encouraged by their better knowledge of the terrain and by the possibilities of aid from their countrymen. As a result, the

[56] "E instruidos en la Fe aplicaron a Dios Nuestro Señor el nombre Eraoranzan y a la Virgen María el nombre de Moneyba (and instructed in the faith they gave to Our Lord God the name Eraoranzan and to the Virgin Mary the name Moneyba)," Abreu Galindo, *Historia*, 90. The clearest reference to the sacred nature of trees is that of F. López de Ulloa on Our Lady of the Pines in Teror in which he states: "in this pine, in the middle of which, according to what has been sworn to me by eye witnesses, is a piece of living stone, and on it are stamped two footprints." See *Historia de la conquista de las siete islas de Canarias* in Francisco Morales Padron, *Canarias, Crónicas de su conquista* (Las Palmas, 1978).

[57] Following the edict of 1525, only nine aborigines appeared before the Inquisition to declare themselves Christians, and these were 11 percent of the Christian converts who presented themselves. See Manuel Lobo Cabrera, "Los indígenas canarios y la Inquisición," *Anuario de Estudios Atlanticos*, 29 (1983): 63–84.

[58] Lobo Cabrera, "Los indígenas," Biblioteca del Museo Canario, Synodial decisions of Don Fernando de Arce, ms. [COTA, Signatura I-D-11.].

[59] Verdicts against them in the period between 1489 and 1526 are presumed to be about 4 percent of the total. In every case including sacrilege, disrespect for the host at mass, administration of communion with *gofio* (roasted corn cake) and wine, the penalty was a small fine or light penance. See Manuel Ronquillo Rubio, "Los orígenes de la Inquisición en Canarias," Ph.D. thesis (Las Palmas, 1991), 241.

[60] Aznar Vallejo, *La integración*, 192. For a global vision of slavery, see Manuela Marrero Rodríguez, *La esclavitud en Tenerife a raiz de la conquista* (La Laguna, 1966); Manuel Lobo Cabrera, *La esclavitud en las Canarias orientales en el siglo xvi* (Las Palmas, 1982).

quantitative evolution of the problem is in relation to the enslavement of natives and arises from it. The struggle against the rebels had a double focus: persecution of runaways and control over the remaining slaves so they would neither imitate the runaways nor help them. It was forbidden to shelter or give food to runaways, or to sell slaves who had been fugitives, although this injunction was systematically violated. The opposition of the councils to the purchase and sale of rebels was based on the fact that some buyers encouraged runaways as a means of lowering the price of slaves. This attitude is only comprehensible in cases of collusion between the slave and the new buyer since the possible lower price would not be worth the risk involved. It is possible that many of these sales hid a future granting of freedom to the slave. This situation is clearer if we look at the exchange of non-runaway slaves for insurrectionaries, who in some cases appear to have been planning their rescue through this means.

In conclusion, we can say that the native population of the islands did not disappear despite the devastation of war, slavery, and biological shock. Rather, their endurance permitted them to become a significant element of the population, making up, more or less, a quarter of the total. However, their physiognomy underwent important transformations, fruit of the traverses of the indigenous peoples and of the processes of fusion, both among groups of native islanders and between islanders and colonizers. The dominant imprint was European, as shown by the new economic, social, and institutional realities, but autochthonous traditions such as livestock raising survived in some features of life.

CHAPTER 5

Tales of distinction: European ethnography and the Caribbean

PETER HULME

ON THE BEACH: 12 OCTOBER 1492

I, he says, in order that they would be friendly to us – because I recognized that they were people who would be better freed [from error] and converted to our Holy Faith by love than by force – to some of them I gave red caps, and glass beads which they put on their chests, and many other things of small value, in which they took so much pleasure and became so much our friends that it was a marvel.[1]

THESE are the first words in the ethnographic discourse of the so-called New World, words written by Christopher Columbus in his journal, under the entry for Thursday 11 October 1492 (although not composed until the following day), and quoted verbatim by Bartolomé de Las Casas, with appropriate sense of occasion, in the course of his extensive summary of that journal, which is the only form in which the text has survived. In the beginning, then, the central distinction is clear, articulated through that simple grammatical differentiation between, on the one hand, the observing and writing "I," the first person singular, and on the other the observed "they," the third person plural.

When he wrote those words Columbus had only spent a few hours on the island of Guanahaní, but already a complex web of action,

[1] Christopher Columbus, in Oliver Dunn and James E. Kelley, *The Diario of Christopher Columbus' First Voyage to America:1492–1493* (Norman, OK, 1989), 65. All quotations are given in English. I have generally used existing translations, modifying them where necessary. Where the reference is to the original, the translation is my own (with acknowledgement of the help given by Lesley Theophilus). In the case of Peter Martyr, I have translated from the Spanish version in Juan Gil and Consuelo Varela, *Cartas de particulares a Colón y Relaciones coetáneas* (Madrid, 1984), but consulted the Latin original. In a run of references, the second and subsequent are simply to page number. Where appropriate, chapter or section numbers are included in square brackets.

reaction, and assumption is embedded in his language. Columbus's first announced action is the gift of red caps and glass beads. The introductory, but subsidiary, clause explains that this was "in order that they would be friendly to us." What is at issue, however, is not merely the "friendliness" appropriate to meetings on liminal spaces between residents and visitors from across the sea. Implicit within Columbus's reported action (in other words not accessible to the island recipients, but spelled out in his journal entry for the eyes of his King and Queen), is the ulterior motive of conversion "to our Holy Faith," better achieved, in this case, by love than by force. The key word in this sentence turns out to be "recognized," because this prior "recognition" has governed the choice of "love" over "force" and therefore set the agenda for the subsequent actions of Columbus and his party.

The native behavior that has brought about that "recognition" can only be inferred from Las Casas's summary of the earlier part of Columbus's entry. The island had been first sighted at two o'clock in the morning. At first light they had seen "naked people" on the shore. The Admiral had landed "in the armed launch" with his other captains, the *escrivano*, the royal banner, and the ships' standards, and had called on his companions to witness "that, in the presence of all, he would take, as in fact he did take, possession of the said island for the king and for the queen his lords, making the declarations that were required, and which at more length are contained in the testimonials made there in writing. Soon many people of the island gathered there [se ayuntó allí]."[2]

It is the action described in that last sentence that presumably governs Columbus's "recognition." "Ayuntarse" may have political over-

[2] The original Spanish is on the facing page of the Dunn and Kelley translation, ibid., 65. The most convenient Spanish edition is that of Consuelo Varela, *Cristóbal Colón: Textos y documentos completos* (Madrid, 1984). Significant recent readings of the journal include Noé Jitrik, *Los dos ejes de la cruz* (Puebla, Mexico,1983); Beatriz Pastor, *Discurso narrativo de la conquista de América* (Havana, 1983), 17–109; Gerald Sider, "When Parrots Talk and Why They Can't: Domination, Deception, and Self-Deception in Indian-White Relationships," *Comparative Studies of Society and History* 29 (1987), (pp. 3–23); Mary B. Campbell, *The Witness and the Other World: Exotic European Travel Writing, 400–1600* (Ithaca, 1988), 165–209. Recent work on Columbus relevant to my approach here includes José Juan Arrom, *La otra hazaña de Colón* (Santo Domingo, 1979); Alain Milhou, *Colón y su mentalidad mesiánica* (Valladolid, 1983); Pauline Moffitt Watts, "Prophecy and Discovery: On the Spiritual Origins of Christopher Columbus's 'Enterprise of the Indies'," *American Historical Review* 70, no.1. (1985); Stuart B. Schwartz, *The Iberian, Mediterranean, and Atlantic Traditions in the Formation of Columbus as a Colonizer* (Minneapolis, 1986). For a review of recent work, see John Larner, "The Certainty of Columbus: Some Recent Studies," *History* 73, no.237. (1988):3–23.

tones: a "gathering," rather than simply a collection of individuals. However, most important of all for Columbus, the people were not hostile. The Spaniards' launch was armed, the initial encounter presumably wary, but the tone quickly established as friendly. Columbus's "recognition" is based upon that initial absence of hostility. Absence of hostility therefore governs the next move – the distribution of caps and beads "and many other things of small value," as a result of which the islanders become "so much our friends that it was a marvel." There is an element of calculation in even this very first sentence of American ethnography. The degree of friendliness that results from the gifts is a "maravilla" (one of the key words of the journal); and that "tanto" in "tantos nuestros" (so much our friends) is related to the "poco" in "de poco valor" (of small value). In other words, it comes as a pleasant surprise to Columbus that the warmth of the welcome is in excess of the value of the items distributed, which were, after all, only a "loss leader" rather than any kind of gift.

The element of calculation suggested by Columbus's words hints at a cultural economics. Implicit – if tightly embedded – in that "poco"/"tanto" couplet is the language of investment and accounting with which Columbus was familiar through his early years working in Genoese trade, and through his continuing connection with his Genoese backers. Accountancy is lodged at the very beginning of the European colonial venture, and intimately entwined with that accountancy is the question of power. After all, trade per se does not necessarily involve any great degree of cultural encounter: The famous "silent barter" for African gold, whether it actually happened or not, is an eloquent symbol of the possibility of trade without interaction. More commonly, trade is dependent on an atmosphere of minimal tolerance – perfected by generations of medieval Christian and Muslim traders around the shores of the Mediterranean. The "amistad" with which Columbus begins his statement augurs well for business as well as for peaceful conversion, but the unexpected success of the caps and beads is ultimately to be gauged by the sort of relationship established. "Amistad" is a relationship of mutuality, in which trade and other forms of exchange can develop. It is entered into by equals, a point often emphasized in traditional societies by the ritual exchange of names. But by the end of Columbus's sentence the relationship has altered: In the original Spanish, "tanto" governs not "our friends" but simply "ours" – "tantos nuestros," the possessive adjective signaling a relationship in which trade is not going to be necessary because everything and everyone will rapidly become "ours"; ours to exploit as we will. In fact, all the recent English translations return to the notion of "friend" or "friendliness" at the end of this sentence, softening the starkness of the original formulation.[3]

Three initial and tentative points might be made about the assumptions implicit in the native behavior described here by Columbus. On this first occasion – the only "pristine" moment of contact that we can be sure was not preceded by news of the caravels conveyed by native travelers – the islanders approach the Spaniards in what seems to have been a spirit of friendliness, curiosity, and hospitality. It is worth making this point because "flight" is so often later interpreted as evidence of the natural timidity of the native inhabitants. Second, the open acceptance of the visitors' gifts (which is probably how the islanders would interpret them), along with their subsequently described visit to the ships with gifts of their own, suggests a traditional economy of the kind classically described by Marcel Mauss, one of many "economies of the gift" disrupted by European ideas of "trade." But, and this is the third point, we should hesitate before moving too quickly to Columbus's own implicit conclusion that the islanders' failure to cut the cloth of their friendship according to the value of the handouts indicated any lack of understanding on their part of the principles of value or exchange, a point later to be made much of because of native "liberality" with items of "valuable" gold. After all, value is relative, and glass beads may well have quickly been assimilated into a possibly sophisticated economy of barter and prestige about which we know very little.[4]

Columbus's opening sentence refers back, then, to his "recognition" of the implications of the immediate native attitude. In Las Casas' summary of the Journal it seems as if the islanders "gather" after the drama of "taking possession" has been enacted. Las Casas' own account in his *Historia de las Indias,* is slightly different and more detailed:

[3] The translations of the journal referred to are Cecil Jane, *The Journal of Christopher Columbus* (London, 1960); Robert H. Fuson, *The Log of Christopher Columbus* (Southampton, 1987); J.M. Cohen, *The Four Voyages of Christopher Columbus* (London, 1988); Dunn and Kelley, *The Diario of Christopher Columbus' First Voyage to America* (1989). For further comments on recent translations see Peter Hulme, "The Log of Christopher Columbus: A Review Essay," *Culture and History* 6 (1989):25–36.

[4] Mary W. Helms, *Ulysses' Sail: An Ethnographic Odyssey of Power, Knowledge, and Geographical Distance* (Princeton, NJ, 1988), 207–8, quoting unpublished work by George Hamell. On the economy that Columbus encountered in the Caribbean, the best recent work is Francisco Moscoso, *Tribu y clases en el Caribe antiguo* (San Pedro de Macoris, Dominican Republic, 1986).

The Indians, who witnessed these actions in great numbers, were astonished when they saw the Christians, frightened by their beards, their whiteness, and their clothes; they went up to the bearded men, especially the Admiral since, by the eminence and authority of his person, and also because he was dressed in scarlet, they assumed him to be the leader, and ran their hands over the beards, marvelling at them, because they had none, and carefully inspecting the whiteness of the hands and faces.[5]

Many of the difficulties in reading Caribbean ethnography are implicit in this passage. Las Casas did not witness this scene so, despite the vividness of his account, his words are at best a transcription with grammatical changes of Columbus's own written words. His position as a historian outside the encounter is a construct, a fiction. No one observed who was not part of that encounter. Perhaps the words are originally Columbus's, in which case they immediately assume a different tone – "by the eminence and authority of my person"; or they are Las Casas's version of another eye-witness account – though we have no evidence of him talking to any participants, at least in the months immediately following the first voyage; or they are a poetic fiction elaborated by Las Casas. Most likely they are some combination of these possibilities – although we have no way of gauging the various proportions.

What then *can* be said about Las Casas's words? Ethnography stems from the observation of such actions and appearances as put to the test prior assumptions and expectations. Those assumptions may be confirmed or modified or overthrown, but there is nothing that might be called ethnography if they are not tested through interaction. Ethnographers of all kinds have therefore little to gain by not describing: The work of their texts, what holds together the *ethnos* and the *graphein*, comes in the interpretations that are offered of the actions and appearances described. The distinction between description and interpretation is not hard and fast. Indeed one of the best places to look for implicit ethnography is precisely in the area of interpretations that offer themselves as "merely" descriptions.

So, whatever the provenance of Las Casas's material, what can be said about the passage is that it offers a description and interpretation of the actions of the inhabitants of Guanahaní on first encountering strange beings from across the seas. Spanish expectations – insofar as they can be judged – were probably of flight or aggression. To be

[5] Bartolomé de Las Casas, *Historia de las Indias*, Agustín Millares Carlo, ed. (Mexico, D.F., 1965), I, 202 [xl].

touched was a surprise, and the unexpected always carries more verisimilitude in an ethnography precisely because writers have no prior interest in its occurrence – though they may demonstrate their ethnographic skills in subsequent explanation of such unexpected acts.

In situations of this kind where there is no immediate linguistic communication possible, much depends on the interpretation of gesture and facial movements. For Columbus and Las Casas gesture is not a language, or, at least, if so, it is a universal language in which emotions are expressed transparently through body movement: There is no difficulty in recognizing astonishment, fear, and wonder – although we are not told what gestures correspond to such reactions. Assuming that astonishment and wonder are not unlikely in the circumstances, it is not clear how fear is consonant with the touching and inspection that immediately ensue. The process of interpretation embedded in this seeming description of the encounter of two sets of bodies is also apparent in the short list of things that occasion both fear and marvel: "their beards, their whiteness, and their clothes." Beards and clothes can be touched, and we are told that both were. Both stand in manifest opposition to the first adjective offered in description of the islanders – "naked," and therefore mark the distinctive features of the Spaniards' appearance in which we might assume the islanders to take an interest. "Whiteness," though, is a quality that cannot be touched, and it is difficult to imagine how interest in it – whether of fear or wonder – could be manifest through gesture or expression. What had actually to be touched – as Las Casas's final words make clear – was hands and faces, not the parts of the body on which "whiteness" is most easily observed at the best of times (even allowing the term as accurate to describe the color of southern Europeans), let alone given the beards and the five weeks crossing the Atlantic, the last part in tropical weather. We obviously have no way of knowing what – assuming the "actions" to be as described – the islanders were in fact astonished by: Perhaps by the weatherbeatenness, or the hair on the hands. Most likely they were just assuring themselves that there really was some skin, however little, on these gigantic wingless parrot-men with their ridiculous plumage.

Las Casas's words speak not in any unproblematic way of native reaction to Spanish appearance, but rather of Spanish interpretation of such reaction, an interpretation that addresses not just "distinctions" between islanders and Spaniards, but the kinds of distinctions that matter to the Spaniards: In other words, what they see as marking themselves out as different from the islanders – even if the description is couched in terms of the islanders' astonishment or fear at what they are *assumed* to perceive as the distinctive features of their visitors. From the passages so far analyzed, two sets of oppositions can be drawn. The islanders are "naked" – a crucial term, as can be gathered by its range of antonyms: armed, bearded, clothed. And the islanders are not white. As yet they have no color, which is strange since their nakedness would reveal their color more easily than the Spaniards' clothes would reveal theirs. But the text's insistence on the whiteness of the Spaniards makes it clear that whatever color the islanders are, it is not white.

Columbus's opening statement moves on to quite detailed descriptions of the bodies of the natives with some general remarks on aspects of their culture, these sentences being prefaced by the remark that "it seemed to me that they were a people very poor in everything," where "poor" registers in the discourses of both economics and anthropology:

> They are very well formed, with handsome bodies and good faces. Their hair is coarse – almost like the tail of a horse – and short. They wear their hair down over their eyebrows except for a little in the back which they wear long and never cut. Some of them paint themselves with black, and they are the color of the Canarians, neither black nor white, and some of them with red, and some of them with whatever they find. And some of them paint their faces, and some of them only the eyes, and some of them only the nose. They do not carry arms nor are they acquainted with them, because I showed them swords and they took them by the edge and through ignorance cut themselves. They have no iron. Their javelins are shafts without iron and some of them have at the end a fish tooth and others of other things. All of them alike are of good-sized stature and carry themselves well.[6]

This is closer to description, though still shot through with "implication." "Nakedness" makes its second appearance, a cultural marker of real significance, rife with sexual and theological connotations, and is followed by descriptions of what are very clearly not meant to qualify it – in this case paint on the face, elsewhere feathers in the hair or ornamentation on the upper body or legs. The aesthetics of the native body are also of interest. Generally speaking, adjectives such as "well-formed," "handsome," "good" can be taken to signify "like us," either in the sense of "with no threatening features" (such as circumcision or cicatrization) or with the implied reassurance that these are indeed human beings rather than the wild men or monsters who might well have occupied such an island off the coast of Asia. The one bodily feature

[6] Christopher Columbus, in Dunn and Kelley, *The Diario of Christopher Columbus' First Voyage to America*, 65, 67.

apart from their nakedness that does not merit aesthetic approval is the hair, and the field of comparison introduced – again, for the first but not for the last time – is the animal kingdom: "coarse, almost like the tail of a horse."

The question of color is pursued, although we should again be clear that actual skin-tones are of secondary importance to the cultural markers laid across the spectrum: "They are the color of the Canarians, neither black nor white." Three categories are made available: "white," by which Columbus means "us," the Spaniards and Italians; "black," the Africans, usually slaves, common enough in both Mediterranean and Atlantic worlds in the late fifteenth century; and "Canarians," intermediate in color, appropriate because of their "nakedness," cultural "poverty," and intermediate geographical location – between white Europe and black Africa – since Columbus had, according to his calculations, sailed almost due west from the Canary Islands and similar skin-color could, it was thought, be found on similar latitudes.

The absence of iron, and therefore of serious weapons, is described without comment. The interest of that fact for the Spaniards could presumably be twofold. Lack of arms would hinder any possible resistance to Spanish domination of the natives. But ignorance of weaponry is also a characteristic of the Golden Age. Taken alongside their supposed innocence of economic values and their lack of clothes, the picture is growing of a set of simple and innocent pagans. From the repertoire of non-European figures available to fifteenth-century travelers, the inhabitants of Guanahaní are here beginning to most resemble the Hellenic primitives. But this is no simple Golden Age world. It carries the scars of a political process: "I saw some who had marks of wounds on their bodies and I made signs to them asking what they were; and they showed me how people from other islands nearby came there and tried to take them, and how they defended themselves; and I believed and believe that they come here from *tierra firme* to take them captive."[7]

For this to be credible, a dumb-show of some complexity must lie behind Columbus's words, but there is no indication as to what body-movements could convey such a message. The suspicion must remain that the "marks of wounds" were sufficient in themselves for Columbus to arrive at his conclusion. If this was not Cathay, then what could

[7] Ibid., 67. Cf. the subsequent discussion of this passage in David Henige's remarkable *In Search of Columbus: The Sources for the First Voyage* (Tucson, 1991), and my comments in a forthcoming article.

be more logical than that a nearby and powerful kingdom would make use of the island for its supply of slaves: Guanahaní must be to Cathay as, say, the Canaries are to Spain. What follows carries an air of inevitability:

> They should be good and intelligent servants, for I see that they say very quickly everything that is said to them; and I believe that they would become Christians very easily, for it seemed to me that they had no religion. Our Lord pleasing, at the time of my departure I will take six of them from here to Your Highnesses in order that they may learn to speak. No animal of any kind did I see on this island except parrots.[8]

The kind of relationship to be established is one of master and servant, with the ideal quality for the subsidiary role proving to be mimicry. Implicit in these remarks is that there will be no cultural resistance, no local growth to contest the field: no religion and no language, since six natives will be taken to Spain "in order that they may learn to speak." The most embedded assumption is that the European has the immediate power to control the lives of these islanders. They will be removed; their willingness or otherwise is not even an issue. That the one comment on the fauna should end this speech seems highly appropriate: The parrot is the implicit template by which the Indians' abilities will be judged.

This dramatic encounter on the beach at Guanahaní elicited no expressions of surprise from Columbus. The appearance and behavior of the islanders may have been in various ways a "marvel" but marvels were, so to speak, within the horizon of expectations. Implicit within Columbus's account, governing his comments though never explicitly discussed, was the very clear distinction between Columbus and his men on the one hand and the islanders on the other. Much of that opening passage is concerned with specifying the exact differences, but of the central gulf between them there is no doubt, at any rate from the first glimpse of their "nakedness." This "distinction" was one for which there was significant precedent in the attempts made, during the fourteenth century, at least by southern Europeans, to come to terms with the questions posed by the Canarians, a subject to which I will return later. Toward the end of that passage, Columbus introduces the first sign of a further distinction: the marks of wounds on the bodies of the islanders. In some ways this is the more significant "encounter." Columbus looking at the wounded body of a Guan-

[8] Christopher Columbus, in *The Diario of Christopher Columbus' First Voyage to America*, 69.

ahanian islander foreshadows the ternary relationship that will dominate subsequent White-Indian encounters throughout the continent, a relationship with very different internal dynamics from the dualism of this initial encounter.

During his first month in the Caribbean, Columbus reports that the native inhabitants (of Cuba) speak of a land to the east called "Bohio,"

> which they said was very large and that there were people on it who had one eye in their foreheads, and others whom they called cannibals, of whom they showed great fear. And when they saw that he was taking this route, he says that they could not talk, because the cannibals eat them, and that they are people very well armed. The Admiral says that well he believes there is something in what they say, but that since they were armed they must be people of intelligence; and he believed that they must have captured some of them and because they did not return to their own lands they would say that they ate them. They believed the same thing about the Christians and about the Admiral when some Indians first met them.[9]

By late November 1492, an associative chain has been established, linking what Columbus had heard about the island of "Bohio" with these "canibales" who attacked their neighbors to the west, and the Great Khan whose soldiers these canibales are presumed to be. In early December a strange new element is added: It all begins to remind Columbus of home. On Thursday 6 December: "That big island appeared to be very high land not closed in by mountains, but level like handsome and extensive farmland; and all, or a large part of it, appeared to be cultivated, and the planted fields looked like wheat in the month of May in the farmlands of Cordova."[10] These references become increasingly insistent. Many of the trees are "of the kind found in Spain"; or, more specifically, "native . . . to the land of Castile." Later, "he saw inland very large valleys and farmlands and extremely high mountains, all very similar to Castile." On the 9 December he even has rain that reminds him of "Castile in October." This entry goes on to describe a harbor and ends with these words: "Facing it there are some fields, the most beautiful in the world, and almost comparable to the lands of Castile; rather these have an advantage, because of which he named the said island the Spanish Island."[11]

It may be significant that in the long run two of the large islands of lesser importance to Columbus retained versions of their native

[9] Ibid., 167.
[10] Ibid., 203.
[11] Ibid., 207, 209, 211, 213, 215.

names (Cuba, Jamaica), while Columbus's seeming investment in the similarities between the island on which he built his capital and the topography of Spain may have motivated the retention of "La Isla Española," although only in its abbreviated form, La Española, anglicized as Hispaniola. The foreign is here possessed in language through domestication: There is, discursively, hardly any difference between Castile and the largest island in the Caribbean. The process of naming clearly has various determinants. Columbus no doubt "takes possession" in some formal sense by naming, and it may be that Hispaniola was distinguished by its name the better to assert its closeness to its metropolitan original. It is "secondary" and yet also has "advantages" over. This rich and fertile land was, the name implies, to be the eldest daughter of *la madre España*. To name is also to make familiar, and the string of European place names reproduced down the whole Atlantic coast of America suggests the force of this motive in the early period of European colonization. But still more seems involved in this particular example. The island of Bohio (as Columbus misunderstands its native name) is dreaded by his Lucayan guides from the smaller islands to the north, who "had the greatest fear in the world of the people of that island."[12] This is the home of the canibales, people who eat people. Columbus is prepared to be skeptical: canibales must mean "soldiers of the Can." Ignorance must be responsible for stories of anthropophagy – after all, at first, these people even thought the Admiral would eat them; and these canibales are well armed ("son gente muy armada"), so they must be people of reason ("gente de razón"), an impression confirmed by their extensive cultivations. In other words, the subtext insistently suggests, they are rather like us – well-armed, intelligent, cultured, inspiring fear: based in a beautiful and cultivated landscape, from which they journey in search of labor, rather like the Spaniards do to the Canary Islands. This identification underlies the naming of Bohio as Hispaniola. Yet the identification cannot speak its name. The canibales are feared – and the Spaniards happy to be so too: Yet they need also to present themselves as protectors. However, it soon becomes apparent that the canibales are not men of the Grand Khan: Neither group is evident on Bohio, despite Columbus's attempt to locate the court of the Khan. The canibales then take on a different dimension as marauders against whose depredations Columbus will protect those who are seen as the weak and peaceful natives of Española. The emphasis changes from the signs of cultivated fields to the traces of gold-bearing rivers. The Cubans' fear

[12] Ibid., 207.

of the inhabitants of "Bohio" becomes invisible when set alongside the distinction between the "indians" of the northwest Caribbean met on the first voyage and the supposedly ferocious "canibales" or "caribes" to the southeast, a distinction that was to have a lasting effect on European perceptions of the area.[13]

After a short stop on an island that seemed uninhabited, Columbus's second voyage through the Caribbean reached the large and impressive island of Guadeloupe. The Sevillian physician, Diego Alvarez Chanca, tells the story:

> When we came near, the admiral ordered a light caravel to coast along looking for a harbour. It went ahead and having reached land, sighted some houses. The captain went ashore in the boat and reached the houses, in which he found their inhabitants. As soon as they saw them [our men] they took to flight, and he entered the houses and found the things that they had, for they had taken nothing away, and from there he took two parrots, very large and very different from all those seen before. He found much cotton, spun and ready for spinning, and articles of food; and he brought away a little of everything; especially he brought away four or five bones of the arms and legs of men. When we saw this, we suspected that the islands were those islands *of Caribe*, which are inhabited by people who eat human flesh. For the admiral, in accordance with the indications as to the situation of those islands which the Indians of the islands which they had previously discovered had given to him on the former voyage, had directed his course to discover them, because they were nearer to Spain and also because from there lay the direct route by which to come to Española, where he had left people before. To these islands, by the goodness of God and by the good judgment of the admiral, we came as directly as if we had been sailing on a known and well-followed route.[14]

Columbus's skilled navigation (possibly aided by the returning islanders) allowed him to take up his exploration of the islands almost exactly where he had left off earlier that year. Chanca's letter – addressed to the municipality of Seville – is as close to an official version of the second voyage as has survived. There is a clear continuity of discourse: as soon as they see the bones "we suspected that. . ." Chanca can "suspect" because he has already been told what to expect. The hearsay and hypotheses of the first voyage have hardened into the "truth" of the second. The details of the encounter do not, as

[13] Peter Hulme, *Colonial Encounters: Europe and the Native Caribbean, 1492–1797* (London, 1986), 45–87.

[14] Diego Alvarez Chanca, "Dr. Chanca's Report" [1494], in Peter Hulme and Neil Whitehead, eds., *Wild Majesty: Encounters with Caribs from Columbus to the Present Day* (Oxford, 1992), 32. The original of Chanca is in Gil and Varela, eds. *Cartas de particulares a Colón y Relaciones coetáneas*, 152–76.

it happens, seem to match that "truth" very well. The exchange of goods on the beach at Guanahaní, unequal as it may have been, has been replaced by open pilfering: "He took away a little of everything." The supposed cannibals are again present only in their absence; this time the tell-tale sign is the bones of their supposed victims – in all probability the drying bones of family members midway through extensive mortuary rituals. And, whereas the "docile" natives of Guanahaní had approached the strangers without fear, these supposedly "fearless" inhabitants run away, an action rather unconvincingly "explained" by Peter Martyr: "When they saw our men, moved by terror or by remorse at their crimes, looking at one another and murmuring among themselves, they suddenly fled in disarray as fast as they could, like a flock of birds, towards the wooded valleys."[15]

An added complexity is that the relationships are now gendered. The fleeing Indians leave behind women prisoners. The Spaniards ask the female captives who their captors were, and they reply that they were "caribes." Having been told that the Spaniards hate these people because of their anthropophagous habits, the women then proceed to act as native informants, secretly telling their rescuers whether captives are caribe or not. The triadic relationship with the indigenous population is confirmed. The language of chivalry provides the script through which the Spaniards insert themselves into the political process of the native Caribbean as protectors of the women and enemies of what has now become, within this emergent ethnographic discourse, an ethnic group: the Caribs.

The "invention of the Caribs" is a crucial move in European writing because the establishment of the triadic relationship made possible by that invention enables the European observer to enter into a series of antagonisms and identifications with non-Europeans. This process is simultaneously ethnographic and, for want of a better shorthand, political: It is both word and deed, although the actual relationship between the two is as complex as ever. But, as such, that move is situated on the center-stage of the colonial "theater" of which Greg Dening speaks. It is at the heart of the performance of colonialism. In the example of the women prisoners it is possible to see how this performance is implicitly gendered. It has become something of a commonplace in writing about the Spanish chronicles to reflect on the inspiration found by those early travellers and writers in the books of chivalry: Miguel Angel Ladero quotes the example of Bernal Díaz remembering how, faced with the city of Tenochtitlán, he and his com-

[15] Gil and Varela, eds., *Cartas de particulares a Colón y relaciones coetáneas*, 53.

panions said to each other that such wonders seemed like the enchantments found in the books of Amadís. The problem with the argument about the influence of the books of chivalry, despite its intuitive attraction, is that the actual evidence is so slight – which is why everybody quotes the same example. A real breakthrough on this issue was made several years ago in a paper by Rolena Adorno in which she pointed out that what Bernal Díaz actually says is not that Amadís inspired his actions as a conquistador, nor that the spectacle of Tenochtitlán made him feel like a knight errant, but rather that he, as a reader of novels of chivalry, could now, as a writer, make use of that reference in order to translate for his potential readers the utterly strange into what we might call the familiarly strange.[16] This focus on the strategies of writing is a tremendous advance both over the stale notion of literary "influence" and over the intuitive idea that the books of chivalry in some unspecified way "inspired" the *conquistadores*.

If, however, the argument is broadened from the books of chivalry to something like the *code* of chivalry, then two other avenues are opened. One is that pursued by Ladero in his pages on Cortés and his self-fashioning as a knight, a self-fashioning both behavioral and discursive since Cortés was the Benengeli to his own Quixote. The other avenue concerns the deeply embedded cultural codes of chivalry that are put to use both in action and in writing by Columbus and others in these early years of the conquest, through which one group of islanders is "feminized" and another "masculinized," irrespective of the actual proportion of men and women involved in either case. In some sense, this is a matter of the taking advantage of circumstance: The existence of a group of women prisoners *authorizes* (or, better, is *permitted* to authorize) an ethnic distinction between prisoner and captive that is "really" gendered inasmuch as the three groups involved – captives, prisoners, rescuers – in this case correspond to their ideologically gendered categories.[17] However, this particular circumstance has been taken advantage of because of the "match" it offered between the coded categories of chivalric behavior and an "actual" situation. Only with hindsight is it possible to see the deep investment in "feminizing" the Arawak, of which these sentences form the earliest indication. The "innocent" islanders would often show remarkable martial qualities in the years to come but, having been ideologically gendered within the chivalric discourse that interpreted

[16] Rolena Adorno, "Literary Production and Suppression: Reading and Writing About Amerindians in Colonial Spanish America," *Dispositio* XI (1986):1–25.

[17] Captured Arawak men are often described as castrated.

their significance to a European audience, the Arawak-Taino went down in history as the passive victims of both Caribs and Spaniards.[18]

The psychic dimension is elusive but inescapable. On one level the Caribs are "recognized" by the Spaniards as their equals, both groups occupying the "masculine" position within the chivalric code: rivals for the possession of the lady. Traces of this unconscious identification remain in the journal and elsewhere. But once the caribes are disassociated from the world of the Grand Khan, that identity has to be denied in order to preserve the central distinction between civilized and savage, with the Caribs demonized into the equivalent of the animal opponents of knights.

The fleet eventually arrives back at Hispaniola, home of the friendly islanders encountered on the first voyage. Here they find the building put up for those who had stayed behind burned to the ground, and the Indians going about "very stealthily."[19] They are eventually told that the Christians were killed in an attack on the village by "the king of Caonabo," and that their protector Guacanagarí is lying wounded in another village. The latter is tracked down and his bandaged thigh found to be apparently undamaged. Chanca reports "many different opinions" among the Spaniards as to the likelihood of Guacanagarí's involvement with the deaths. Columbus's decision was "to dissemble" (disimular).[20] There is a certain symmetry here. The visible wounds seen during the first voyage are traces of violent attack from elsewhere (by the unseen Caribs). The invisible wound uncovered on the second voyage is also the trace of violent attack from elsewhere.[21] What then would *not* speak of violent attack from elsewhere? What would count as evidence of violence *here?* Not seeing the absence of Guacanagarí's wound is a sign of the investment already made in the ethnographic distinction between here and there, our Indians and those that attack from elsewhere. Such a distinction has nothing to do with "evidence," but everything to do with maintaining the clear lines of the discursive division established at the end of the first voyage. As for Guacanagarí,

[18] Skepticism about the conventional anthropology of the pre-Columbian Caribbean can be found in Jalil Sued Badillo, *Los Caribes: realidad o fábula?* (Río Piedras, Puerto Rico, 1978): Peter Hulme, *Colonial Encounters*, 45–87; and Francisco Moscoso, *Tribu y clases en el Caribe antiguo.* On one example of Taino resistance, see Francisco Moscoso, "La conquista española y la gran rebelión de los Taínos," *Pensamiento Crítico* XII, no.62 (1989, "Documentos"):1–16.

[19] Gil and Varela, eds., *Cartas particulares a Colón y Relaciones coetáneas*, 167.

[20] Ibid., 169–71.

[21] In Ridley Scott's film *1492: Conquest of Paradise* (1992), Guacanagarí blames the killings on the Caribs, a fine example of stereotypes being applied retrospectively to tidy up the unfortunate details of historical complexity.

he may have adapted himself well to the demands of the colonial theater by telling Columbus the story he wanted to hear: When the bandage was taken off, the reluctance to "see" the absence of the wound probably suited them both.

Colonial tales of distinction, read differently, can also be revealed as stories of secret identification, speaking more of the truth about colonial violence than their writers dreamed of. Even in later versions an undercurrent of identification forms part of the stream of condemnatory accusations directed at the canibales, those raiders from the east who kill and capture and eat, but whose military prowess is so admirable. Take, as a last example, this passage from Peter Martyr:

> The tame Indians complain that the cannibals are always overrunning their islands with frequent raids, just like hunters pursue the wild beasts in the woods with violence or traps. They castrate the young boys they capture, just like we do the cocks or pigs that we want to grow fatter or more tender for eating; once they are big and fat they eat them; when older men fall into their hands they kill them and quarter them, and they have a banquet with their intestines and the fresh extremities of their limbs: they keep the limbs for another occasion by salting them, just as we do with hams. Eating women is regarded as sacrilegious and monstrous; if they capture a young girl they take care of her and keep her to have children, just as we do with hens, sheep, cows and other animals; they keep the old women as servants. The men as well as the women on the islands that we can now call ours, when they realize that the cannibals are approaching, seek salvation only in flight. Although they use sharpened cane arrows, they found out that these were little use in putting a stop to the outrages and excesses of the cannibals; in fact, the natives recognize that ten cannibals could easily overcome one hundred of them in open battle.[22]

The surface rhetoric compares cannibal practices with Indians to our practices with animals: The intention is therefore to contrast savagery with husbandry. Yet the repetition of "just as we do" (ut nos pullos . . . ut nos pernas . . . atque nos gallinas) works against the contrast, insistently bringing closer together what the surface argument wants to hold apart. Distinction through comparison is the strategy of colonial discourse that I want to investigate here.

ATLANTIC PRECEDENTS

On the basis of the fundamental relationship established between two sets by the significant difference between them, a rhetoric of otherness may be de-

[22] Gil and Varela, eds., *Cartas particulares a Colón y Relaciones coetáneas*, 44.

veloped, to be used by narratives that tell, primarily, of "others," travelers' tales in the widest sense of the expression. A narrator who belongs to a group tells the people of a about b; there is one world in which one recounts, another that is recounted. How can the world in which one recounts be introduced in convincing fashion into the world where it is recounted? That is the problem facing the narrator: a problem of translation.[23]

Ethnographic writing must find the techniques to make the strange comprehensible without making it too familiar. The principal technique is that of comparison, often used in its negative form – "these people are unlike us in their actions, habits and so on," but also found in positive statements. The first positive comparison that Columbus makes is between the islanders of Guanahaní and the Canarians: "They are the color of the Canarians, neither black nor white."[24] The general significance of the conquest of the Canary Islands to the conquest of America is a large and many-faceted question. But with respect to implicit ethnography, there would seem no doubt that the Canary Islands provided a catalyst for anthropological thinking and a crucible for actions toward a set of islanders who did not easily fit into existing categories, and who were involved in a long and punishing guerrilla campaign that did not end until the "pacification" of Tenerife in 1496.[25] Columbus's references to the Canarians are unsurprising given that he actually left his known world from Gomera, one

[23] Francois Hartog, *The Mirror of Herodotus: The Representation of the Other in the Writing of History* (Berkeley, 1988), 212.

[24] Columbus, in Dunn and Kelley, eds. *The Diario of Christopher Columbus' First Voyage*, 67.

[25] On the conquest of the Canaries, a good recent summary is Felipe Fernández-Armesto, *Before Columbus: Exploration and Colonization from the Mediterranean to the Atlantic, 1279–1492* (Philadelphia, 1987):151–222. See also Florentino Pérez Embid, *Los descubrimientos en el atlántico y la rivalidad castellano-portuguesa hasta el tratado de Tordesillas* (Seville, 1948); Antonio Pérez Voituriez, *Problemas jurídicos internacionales de la conquista de Canarias* (La Laguna, Canary Islands, 1958); Charles Verlinden, "Lanzarotto Malocello et la découverte portugaise des Canaries," *Revue Belge de philologie et d'Histoire* XXXVI (1958):1173–1209; Elías Serra Ráfols, "El redescubrimiento de las Islas Canarias en el siglo XVI," *Revista de Historia Canaria XXVII (1961):219–32*. On the economic connections between the Canarian and Caribbean enterprises, see Manuel Giménez Fernández, "América, 'Isla de Canaria por ganar'," *Anuario de Estudios Atlánticos* I (1955):309–36, and Francisco Morales Padrón, *El Comercio Canario-Americano* (Seville, 1955); on the ideological continuity, Fermín Del Pino, "Canarias y América en la historia de etnología primigenia: usando una hipótesis," *Revista de Indias* 36 (1976):99–156, and Felipe Fernández-Armesto, *Before Columbus* (1987):223–52. On Gomera, John Mercer, *The Canary Islanders: Their Prehistory, Conquest, and Survival* (London, 1980), 180–4; Antonio Rumeu de Armas, "Cristóbal Colón y Beatriz de Bobadilla en las antevesperas del descubrimiento," *El Museo Canario* XX, no.2 (1960):255–79; María Rosa Alonso, "Las 'endechas' a la muerte de Guillén Peraza," *Anuario de Estudios Atlánticos* II (1956):457–71; Antonio De la Torre, "Los canarios de Gomera vendidos como esclavos en 1489," *Anuario de Estudios Americanos* VII (1950):47–72.

of the most westerly of the Canaries. Columbus may have suspected from his extensive experience of the Atlantic that the Canaries would offer the best entry into the wind-systems; he may even have had a prior arrangement, financial or sexual, with the formidable Beatriz de Bobadilla, then fighting to retain control of Gomera. Columbus reports the residents of Gomera as saying that every year they could see land to the west, so there was always the expectation that more Atlantic islands would be found, stepping stones to the Asian mainland.[26] What is certain is that Gomera was the site of the Atlantic frontier, the island most recently reduced to Spanish rule after the murder of Beatriz's husband, Hernán Peraza, by native Gomerans in 1488 had provoked savage reprisals.

But from the perspective of implicit ethnography, in some ways more important than the facts of conquest is the general significance attached during this period to the Atlantic as a whole, and to the Canaries in particular. The connotations of the western islands were clearly quite different from those pertaining to the lands of the Orient. For the Christian Middle Ages the central axis of the world ran from its center in Jerusalem to the east. Mappae mundi were, so to speak, oriented to the east, with the head of the map occupied by the figure of Christ or a depiction of the last judgment or of the Garden of Eden, which sometimes featured as an island. That axis was, however, mainly symbolic in that the routes of communication through the known world – the arms of the T on the so-called T-O maps – were the Tanais (Don), the Nile, and the Mediterranean. If this was the world's body, then the Pillars of Hercules were its anus.[27] This Chris-

[26] Columbus, in Dunn and Kelley, eds., *The Diario of Christopher Columbus' First Voyage*, 25.

[27] On the significance of the Atlantic, Helms's *Ulysses' Sail* is indispensable. See also, on various aspects, George Boas, *Essays on Primitivism and Related Ideas in the Middle Ages* (New York, 1978 [1948]); Howard R. Patch, *The Other World, According to Descriptions in Medieval Literature* (Cambridge, MA, 1950); Louis-André Vigneras, *La búsqueda del Paraíso y las legendarias islas del Atlántico* (Valladolid, 1976); William H. Babcock, *Legendary Islands of the Atlantic* (New York, 1922); Stephen Clissold, *The Seven Cities of Cíbola* (New York, 1961); Harry Levin, *The Myth of the Golden Age in the Renaissance* (New York, 1972); Arthur Lovejoy and George Boas, *A Documentary History of Primitivism and Related Ideas in Antiquity* (New York, 1965 [1935]), 290–303; Ronald Sanders, *Lost Tribes and Promised Lands: The Origins of American Racism* (Boston, 1978), 3–38; Juan Alvarez Delgado, "Las 'islas afortunatas' en Plinio," *Revista de Historia Canaria* XI (1945):26–51; Ernst R. Curtius, *European Literature and the Latin Middle Ages* (Princeton, 1979 [1948]), 195–200. On the relevance of these ideas about "the West" to the conquest of America, see Stelio Cro, *Realidad y utopía en el descubrimiento y conquista de la América Hispana, 1492–1682* (Troy, MI, 1983), and Juan Gil, *Mitos y utopías del descubrimiento: I. Colón y su tiempo* (Madrid, 1989).

tian world-view had sacralized classical geography. For Greece the center of the world had been Hellas, and the arms of the T divided the known world into three: Europe, Asia, and Africa (a division taken over and explained in the Christian tradition by one of the best-known Noachid stories). But for the classical world there was no symbolic significance in direction, and no axis: There was, as it were, a civilized center surrounded by a series of concentric circles as the world became more and more unknown and more and more barbarous. The trading and colonizing impetuses of the classical world had been toward the west, along the coast of the Mediterranean, so it was natural that its mythological spaces lay beyond the exit from that known sea: the island of Geryon visited by Hercules, the Elysium mentioned by Homer, the islands of the blessed that feature in Hesiod as the home of the heroes. As the most fundamental of metaphors, the west was a place of repose at the end of life's journey. According to Loren Baritz, happiness and death "formed the dialectic of the west."[28] As against the positive features of the Orient, the islands of the west presented negatives: no laws, no worries, no toil. If the islands had a positive feature, it was their fertility: "The grain-giving earth bears honeyed fruit, flourishing thrice a year."[29] The islands' status as the westernmost point of the known world is confirmed by the authority of Claudius Ptolemy, the most important geographer in the ancient world, who used them as his prime meridian for the calculation of longitude: Everywhere was east of the Canaries.[30] Columbus's postil C 314 to Pierre d'Ailly's *Imago Mundi* reads "De situ Fortunate insule; nunc dicitur Canarie," confirming the conventional identification of the rediscovered islands with those hymned by classical writers.[31]

In the Christian world the East was a place of substance, with a series of attendant signifiers; the West was a tendency, a direction, less substantial, at best a series of hazy islands.[32] (This distinction may lie behind Columbus's paranoid insistence that Cuba is not an island. To his mind he had not really arrived anywhere unless he had reached terra firma.) Only the East was invested with temporal significance.

[28] Loren Baritz, "The Idea of the West," *American Historical Review* 66 (1960–61):620.

[29] Hesiod, *Works and Days*, quoted in Lovejoy and Boas, *A Documentary History of Primitivism and Related Ideas in Antiquity*, 290.

[30] Ptolemy, *The Geography of of Claudius Ptolemy*, Edward L. Stevenson, ed. (New York, 1932), 40–41 [I, xxiv].

[31] Quoted in Gil and Varela, eds., *Cartas de particulares a Colón y Relaciones coetáneas*, 40, n.46.

[32] See Helms, *Ulysses' Sail*, 220, and A. Bartlett Giamatti, *The Earthly Paradise and the Renaissance Epic* (Princeton, 1966).

As the location of the Garden of Eden it signified the past, but also through Gog and Magog, whose loosing on the world was the occasion of apocalypse, the future:

> For all its wonders and riches, the East in the medieval mind was a fearsome place – immense and wild, a place of an Edenic paradise forever lost to man, and a place from which ultimate destruction would rage forth in the final apocalypse. Western islands, in contrast, though still the domain of the miraculous, the strange, and the curious, were generally envisioned in far gentler terms, as blessed settings for peaceful health and happiness that might be sought and even possibly obtained in a future characterized not by chaos but by perfected utopian existence.[33]

As Helms suggests, utopias were situated in the west: Oceana, Utopia itself, New Atlantis, and were either literally or metaphorically islands, a point Thomas More emphasizes by having the Utopians cut the causeway that links them to the mainland. It is on this basis that the island becomes a metaphor for so much of importance in colonial history, from Prospero to Fletcher Christian, with Robinson Crusoe as the ultimate explorer of its ambiguities: a place of sexual temptation, a natural fortress, but perhaps above all a crucible of manageable proportions in which to act out the fantasies of colonial power.[34]

THE SHEEP AND THE FOLD

> When I came a little out of that part of the island, I stood still a while as amazed; and then recovering my self, I looked up with the utmost affection of my soul, and with a flood of tears in my eyes, gave God thanks that had cast my first lot in a part of the world where I was distinguished from such dreadful creatures as these. . . – Daniel Defoe, *Robinson Crusoe*[35]

Christian discourse necessarily works with a clear dichotomy between those who are saved and those who are not. That dichotomy finds its expression in several of the key stories in *Genesis:* Esau and Jacob, Sarah and Hagar, and especially one of the earliest and most powerful, Cain and Abel. But these stories could also be interpreted as allegories of political and cultural (rather than simply individual) distinctions, providing a repertoire of explanatory genealogical narratives in which the development of religious, cultural, ethnic, and eventually colonial distinctions could be inscribed. The very brief development of the

[33] Helms, *Ulysses' Sail*, 217.
[34] On islands and colonialism, see Diana Loxley, *Problematic Shores: The Literature of Islands* (London, 1990).
[35] Daniel Defoe, *Robinson Crusoe*, Angus Ross, ed. (Harmondsworth, 1965), 172.

story of Cain and Abel in the fourth chapter of *Genesis* left plenty of scope for interpretation. One kind of division clearly being articulated was that between the pastoralism associated with Abel and the tilling of ground and building of cities, both connected with Cain, the slayer of his brother. Abel "was a keeper of sheep," who offered the firstlings of his flock to the Lord; Cain "was a tiller of the ground" who brought its fruit as an offering: "And the LORD had respect unto Abel and to his offering: But unto Cain and to his offering he had not respect" (4.4–5). Cain, expelled from the presence of the Lord after killing his brother, went to dwell in the land of Nod, to the east of Eden: "and he builded a city, and called the name of the city, after the name of his son, Enoch" (4.16–17). No reason is given for God's preference for Abel's offering over Cain's, and nothing more is said of the city that Cain built, but the impression left is that one way of life, even one mode of production, has here been validated over others. Abel's pastoralism will become a rich source of imagery for the New Testament.

In the early centuries of the Christian era there was a strong ascetic strain of piety associated with a rejection of the city as emblem of this-worldly concerns: After all, the builder of the first city was Cain, the Bible's first murderer. A Christian was a pilgrim in this world and therefore in temporary exile from the true "self," which was to be found in the afterlife. Pilgrimage on earth was a hallowed activity, but it was not always pilgrimage to a holy place: Wandering without destination was more common. The eventual association of Christianity with an imperial civilization committed to urban settlement and political life was bound to test Christian commitment to the ideals of the world outside the city. Augustine's *Civitate Dei* is principally an attempt to synthesize these two incompatible traditions, and an index of what has to be done in order to establish the *City* of God is the way in which the Cain and Abel story must be retold to play down God's apparent preference for Abel's pastoralism over Cain's agriculture, for wandering with herds over settlement and cultivation. Cain was the builder of cities, but he can be seen by Augustine as the archetypal pagan: concerning the city of God against the pagans. Pagan comes from the Latin word for countryside, so already in Augustine Cain is removed *outside* the settlements of civilized life: a wanderer, a fugitive, a vagabond – which is how he enters European literature on the basis of a couple of very ambiguous lines in Genesis. His role as builder of cities is largely forgotten.[36]

[36] On the relevant developments within Christian thought: Charles N. Cochrane, *Christianity and Classical Culture: A Study of Thought and Action from Augustus to Augustine*

Paganism is still then a significant term in the language of distinction, but in the thirteenth and fourteenth centuries its referent is much less clear than in the case of the *City of God*, where the pagans of the book's full title represented a still powerful religion against which Augustine had to direct his argument.[37] As far as Christian Europe was concerned, the four centuries before Columbus were dominated by the idea (and reality) of the Crusades against Islam. Augustine's division into two cities was therefore perpetuated by the Crusades: the ideological dividing-line between Christian and infidel dominated the spiritual geography of the known world. European communication with Asia declined during the fourteenth and fifteenth centuries and, in any case, a deep-seated Christian belief visualized much of the world beyond Islam as also Christian – a myth powerfully represented in the figure of Prester John.[38]

The Jews offer a particular and clearly very important case of distinction, arguably as important in the long run of European history as any contact with people outside Europe. But their importance stems from their very closeness, both physical and religious, to Christian Europe. Roger Bacon wrote in the thirteenth century of the idolaters outside Christianity, but knowledge of these "sects" was restricted, in whichever way idolater was defined.[39] However, during the course of the fifteenth century various candidates emerged as pagans in something like Columbus's sense of having no religion and, consequently, no culture. Black African slaves in Spain and Portugal were clearly pagan in the required sense (where not Muslim), but they were individuals rather than representatives of a known nation, so questions of dominion did not arise; and they were long familiar in Europe,

(New York, 1957 [1948]); and the recent books by Judith Herrin, *The Formation of Christendom* (Princeton, 1987); Peter Brown, *The Body and Society: Men, Women, and Sexual Renunciation in Early Christianity* (New York, 1988); and Elaine Pagels, *Adam, Eve, and the Serpent* (New York, 1988). On Biblical discourse, William McKee Evans, "From the Land of Canaan to the Land of Guinea: The Strange Odyssey of the 'Sons of Ham'," *American Historical Review* 85 (1980):14–43; John B. Friedman, *The Monstrous Races in Medieval Art and Thought* (Cambridge, MA, 1981), 86–130. Note the possibilities in the phonological continuum that runs from Cain and Canaan to Canarians and Cannibals.

[37] Augustine, *Concerning the City of God Against the Pagans*, Henry Bettenson, trans. (Harmondsworth, 1972). Cf. Peter Brown, *Augustine of Hippo* (London, 1967), 291–312.

[38] On Europe and non-Europeans, see Henri Baudet, *Paradise on Earth: Some Thoughts on European Images of Non-European Man* (New Haven, 1965); Francis Rogers, *The Quest for Eastern Christians: Travels and Rumor in the Age of Discovery* (Minneapolis, 1962); and J.R.S. Phillips, *The Medieval Expansion of Europe* (Oxford, 1988).

[39] Roger Bacon, *The Opus Majus*, 2 vols., Robert B. Burke, trans. (New York, 1962), II.: 788–90.

their position clearly "established."[40] The popular and literary traditions concerning "wild men" and "monstrous races" provided an endless stream of pagans but, again, these were almost by definition individuals living on the margins of the known world. They did, however, provide a rich source of language and imagery. That leaves two groups, each on the edge of the expanding European world, the Lithuanians and the Canarians, both conquered during the course of the fifteenth century, and both crucial to the developing discussion about the rights of non-Christians to govern themselves. For obvious reasons of geography, the Canarian case bears closest on the extension of Spanish interests in the Caribbean and the Americas more generally. Columbus, as we have seen already, left his known world from a Canarian island.

The discussion of the Canarians took place within the context of the medieval debate on the proper extent of papal sovereignty. As far as canon law was concerned, the crucial question had been asked as early as the thirteenth century by Sinibaldo Fieschi, Pope Innocent IV (1243–54), in his commentary on the question: "Is it licit to invade the lands that infidels possess, and if it is licit, why is it licit?" That question had obviously arisen out of the experience of the Crusades, but it was not addressed to the capture of the Holy Land because that, it was universally agreed (in Christendom), was validated by the theory of just war, as was the reconquest of Spain. The more difficult question related to land not previously possessed by Christians and that could not therefore be reclaimed. And Fieschi's answer was that under the law of nations all "rational creatures" had the right to select their own rulers, whether they were infidels or not. It was not licit for the pope or anyone else to wage a campaign to deprive infidels of their property or their lordship simply because they were infidels: "Both infidels and the faithful belong to Christ's flock by virtue of their creation, although the infidels do not belong to the sheepfold of the Church." That pastoral metaphor of the flock and the sheepfold is the touchstone of Christian discourse throughout these centuries, from the thirteenth to the sixteenth. Bartolomé de Las Casas used it to defend the American Indians from the attentions of the Spanish colonists, and Pope Paul III deployed it in his bull, *Sublimis Deus,* when Las Casas and his supporters finally succeeded in forcing the Church to respond to the genocide of the native population of the Caribbean in the early sixteenth century.[41]

[40] Cf. Frank F. Snowden, Jr., *Blacks in Antiquity* (Cambridge, MA, 1970).

[41] It is possible to find Fieschi's metaphor of the flock in classical texts, but only in

The earliest surviving European account of the Canarians themselves was originally written by a Genoese merchant, Niccoloso da Recco, in 1341. The letter describing his expedition was sent from Seville to Florence, where Giovanni Boccaccio eventually made a manuscript version under the title *De Canaria et insulis reliquis ultra Hispaniam noviter repertis.* Italian scholars see *De Canaria* as a translation from a presumed Italian original into Latin, and from a presumed reportage on prospective trade into a kind of ethnography. They also see its very presence as emblematic: One critic writes of this "unique inruption of the world of contemporary action into pages otherwise concerned with traditional learning."[42] The notebook that contains *De Canaria* is otherwise full of copies of and commentaries on classical texts. *De Canaria* tells how two ships supplied by the King of Portugal and with men from Florence, Genoa, Catalonia, and various parts of Spain on board set sail from Lisbon "carrying with them horses, arms, the machines of war, to destroy cities and castles, and they went to seek out these islands commonly said to have been found."[43] They did not destroy any cities or castles but did bring back four inhabitants of the islands, and a selection of produce, including goat and sealskins, tallow, fish-oil, brazil wood, and redwood dye.

Their first extended sight of the islanders came when the Europeans saw gathered on a beach "a large multitude of men and women, almost all of them naked; some of whom seemed important, dressed in goat-skins dyed yellow and red and as far as one could tell from a distance soft and delicately embroidered with great skill with gut-thread."[44] This first "encounter" did not proceed very far because the sailors were too frightened to disembark. Some of the islanders swam out to the ship – and were taken prisoner. The north of the island seemed more cultivated than the south, with reports of houses, fig-trees, palms, and vegetable gardens. The houses "were made of dressed stone, marvellously constructed, covered in large and beautiful wood." The doors were locked and the Europeans wanted to see

deeply heterodox ones such as Zeno's *Politeia.* This is Plutarch's account: "That our life should not be based on cities or peoples each with its own view of right and wrong, but we should regard all men . . . as our fellow-countrymen and fellow-citizens, and that there should be one life and one order, like that of a single flock on a common pasture feeding together under a common law," quoted in H.C. Baldry, *The Unity of Mankind in Greek Thought* (Cambridge, 1965), 159.

42 J.K. Hyde, "Real and Imaginary Journeys in the Later Middle Ages," *Bulletin of the John Rylands University Library* 65 (1982):138.

43 Giovanni Boccaccio, "De Canaria et Insulis Reliquis" [1341], *Monumenta Henricina* I (1960):202.

44 Ibid., 203.

what was inside, so they knocked down the doors with stones. They also found a small temple (templum) "where there was no painting or ornament other than a stone statue of a naked man with a ball in his hand, his shame covered with branches of palm, according to the customs of the country. They stole the statue, loaded it on the ship and took it to Lisbon."[45]

The major ethnographic interest then comes from the long description of the four native "prisoners" taken back to Lisbon:

> The four men they took with them were young, beardless and handsome; they wore a loin-cloth and had a belt around the hips of cord from which hung thick, long strips of palm-leaves of at least one or two hands (in length) with which to cover their shame in front and behind, unless the wind or something else lifted it. They are not circumcised, and have long blond hair down to their waists, and they cover themselves with their hair, and walk with bare feet. The island from which they were taken was called Canaria, the most inhabited of them. They cannot understand anyone else's language, as they were spoken to in various languages. In height they do not pass ours. They are strong-limbed, lively, and very robust and of great intelligence, in as much as one can judge. We speak to them through gestures, and with gestures they respond, in the manner of the dumb. They have respect for each other, but particularly towards one of them; this one has a loin-cloth of palm and the three remaining have loin-cloths tinted yellow and red. They sing sweetly and they dance almost in the manner of the French; they are merry and agile and quite domesticated, more so than many Spaniards. They were shown gold and silver coins but did not recognize them. Nor with perfumes of any kind, nor necklaces of gold, etched vases, sabres and swords of any sort, the like of which it seems that they have never seen nor had. They also showed enormous faith and loyalty towards each other, in as much as one can judge, principally because when any one was given anything to eat, before eating he would divide it into equal portions and give the others their portions.
>
> They marry, and their women wear the loincloth in the same manner as the men. The unmarried women go naked, giving no signs of shame as they walk around like this.[46]

Boccaccio's version of the letter describing the 1341 voyage was probably not made until about 1350, by which time a substantial claim

[45] Ibid., 204.

[46] Ibid., 205–6. Boccaccio's De Canaria is translated from the original version reprinted in *Monumenta Henricina* I (1960). The first publication is Boccaccio, "Della Canaria e dell'altre isole oltre Ispania nell'oceano novamente ritrovate," in *Monumenti d'un Manuscritto Autografo de Messer Gio. Boccaccio da Certaldo*, Sebastiano Campi, ed. (Florence, 1827), 60–66. An Italian translation is in Rinaldo Caddeo, ed., *Le Navigazioni Atlantiche di Alvise da Cá da Mosto, Antoniotto Usodimare, e Niccoloso da Recco* (Milan, 1928).

had been made to the Canary Islands by a European prince called Luis de la Cerda, who was actually invested with the title King of the Canary Islands by Pope Clement VI at a ceremony in Avignon in 1344. Several years later (and possibly with knowledge of Boccaccio's transcription), Petrarch wrote a section of his book *De vita solitaria* about the Fortunate Islands, in which a very different kind of language is at work. He calls the islands,

> a land famed through the writings of many men but chiefly through the lyric song of Horace, and whose repute is both very old and quite fresh. For within the memory of our fathers the warships of the Genoese penetrated to them, and recently Clement VI gave a prince to that country, a man of noble stock mixed of the royal blood of Spain and France, who I once saw. You remember how, on the day when he went out to display himself in the city with crown and sceptre, a great rain suddenly poured out of the sky and he returned home so completely drenched that it was interpreted as an omen that the sovereignty of a truly rainy and watery country had been imposed upon him. How he succeeded in that dominium situated outside of the world I have not learned, but I do know that many things are written and reported in view of which its fortune does not appear fully to square with the designation of the Fortunate lands. For the rest, its people enjoy solitude beyond nearly all other men, but are without refinement in their habits and so little unlike brute beasts that their action is more the outcome of natural instinct than of rational choice, and you might say that they did not so much lead the solitary life as roam about in solitudes either with wild beasts or with their flocks.[47]

Petrarch here takes his distance from the classical tradition. The augury of the rain parodies the islands' famously moderate climate, and there are hints at the falseness of the occasion as Luis goes out "to display himself" in his finery. In retrospect we can see a note of modernity in the reference to the Fortunate Islands: Name and reputation do not match, ancient confusions can now be clarified by Italian expeditions. But these touches are really preliminary notes before the main theme. The relevance of the Canary Islands to Petrarch is as a land of solitude, though not of course the kind of solitude in which he is primarily interested. Indeed the Canarians stand as an anti-type. He comes to the solitary life, or at least is prepared to defend solitariness, as a "rational choice"; they lead it as "the outcome of natural

[47] Petrarch, *The Life of Solitude*, Jacob Zeitlin, trans. (Chicago, 1924), 267. For the original Latin see Petrarch, *De Vita Solitaria*, Antonio Altamura, ed. (Naples, 1943), 125–6. On Petrarch's solitude in its classical and Renaissance context, Michael O'Loughlin, *The Garlands of Repose: The Literary Celebration of Civic and Retired Leisure* (Chicago, 1978). Cf. Giorgio Padoan, "Petrarcha, Boccaccio e la scoperta delle Canarie," *Italia Medioevale e Umanistica* VII (1964):263–77.

instinct," almost incorporated into their flocks or into groups of wild animals. But there is a difficulty here, perhaps signaled by that uneasy double negative, "so little unlike" (non absimilem beluis). According to Aristotle, since man's natural disposition is to form cities, these wild men who roam beyond the city must be looked upon as either beasts or gods: In other words, there is a deep ambivalence about their position.[48] Petrarch's language is very different: "To belong to yourself in all seasons and, wherever you are, to be ever with yourself."[49] This kind of secular egoism has that distinctively "modern" tone that has led to Petrarch being seen as a foundational figure in the development of European thought and attitudes. In this sense he inhabits a different world from Aristotle. Yet in other ways that classical ambivalence is itself not alien to Petrarch's intentions.

One way of understanding his interest in solitude, at least read metaphorically, would be to see it as a recreation of the cosmopolitanism of Zeno, in the strict sense of being at home in no city, standing alone, sufficient for himself, a Stoic conception not alien to the Christian idea of man as a mere sojourner on this planet, not fully "belonging" to this world (though "sufficient for himself" would be a contradiction in terms for a Christian.) However, Benedict's reorganization of the monasteries had more or less put an end to the tradition of "wandering" in the west, and had been used by the Carolingians as a stabilizing force, underpinning what Sumption calls the "cultural colonialism" of the ninth century – the process that has been seen as an early stage of the "internal" European colonialism that preceded (and then accompanied) the external form.[50] The "nomadic" and "itinerant" had gradually been placed outside the pale (except within the increasingly rigorous structures of "the pilgrimage" or later "the voyage of discovery"). "Wandering" had become exclusively Eastern; vagabondage socially disreputable. Cain has to be emphasized through his curse, rather than as the founder of cities. In another way, though, Petrarch is less ambivalent than Aristotle. Aristotle had been talking about individuals; Petrarch's discourse is at least incipiently ethnographic in that he is

[48] "The proof that the state is a creation of nature and prior to the individual is that the individual, when isolated, is not self-sufficing; and therefore he is like a part in relation to the whole. But he who is unable to live in society, or who has no need because he is sufficient for himself, must be either a beast or a god: he is no part of a state," in Aristotle, *Politics*, Stephen Everson, ed. (Cambridge, 1988):4 [1253 a 25-9].

[49] Petrarch, *The Life of Solitude*, 70.

[50] Jonathan Sumption, *Pilgrimage: An Image of Mediaeval Religion* (London, 1975), 96–7; Michael Mann, *The Sources of Social Power, Vol. I: A History of Power from the Beginning to AD 1760* (London, 1980), 373–415.

talking about Canarians as an ethnos. The problem is that although Petrarch seems to be aware of speaking about a nation here, the Canarians over whom de la Cerda has been granted dominion, he has no way of speaking about their polity without losing them as his antitype. The compromise formation is to have them roam in solitary *places* rather than leading solitary *lives* ("in solitudinibus errare"), and to deny polity through having them roam with wild beasts or herds, damning them through the company they keep. In the Canarians Petrarch found the type of non-European man against which to define his ideal of secular individualism. The Canary Islands proved to be, ethnographically as well as geographically, the degree zero of European culture.

Petrarch's language shocked Las Casas, but by this time it was common currency. One way around the consequences of the Aristotelian argument about dominion was to assert that the Canarians were too "bestial" to have dominium at all. This was not an argument that could be made about the Muslims – who all too clearly exercised political power (if in some places "illegitimately"), nor about the Mongols – who responded to western overtures by making their own assertions of universal dominance. But the Canarians, like the Irish – also western islanders – were often conceptualized as "wild men" living the life of beasts. The clearest papal statements of this position came in Clement VI's bull *Sicut exhibitae*, issued in November 1344, granting the Canary Islands to Luis de la Cerda, and in his sermon given at the investiture of de la Cerda as King of the Canary Islands, recalled by Petrarch. The discourse of "bestiality" came close to identifying its object as outside culture altogether: The association with beasts that Petrarch raises betokens behavior against natural law, or even against nature itself.[51]

The coming together of Judaeo-Christian and classical elements meant that the trope of nakedness deployed by both Boccaccio and Columbus had a complex set of significations. In the classical tradition

[51] For Las Casas's shock at Petrarch's language: Las Casas, *Historia de las Indias*, I, 117–8. For Clement VI's sermon, see Elías Serra Ráfols, "Sermón de Clemente VI acerca de la otorgación del Reino de Canarias a Luis de España, 1344," *Revista de Historia Canaria* XXIX (1963–4):88–111; and cf. Felipe Fernández-Armesto, *Before Columbus*, 230–4. On "wild men" in general, see Richard Bernheimer, *Wild Men in the Middle Ages: A Study in Art, Sentiment, and Demonology* (Cambridge, MA, 1952); Timothy Husband, ed., *The Wild Man: Medieval Myth and Symbolism* (New York, 1980); Susi Colin, "The Wild Man and the Indian in Early 16th-century Book Illustration," in *Indians and Europe*, Christian Feest, ed. (Aachen, 1987).

"naked" often implied an unalloyed truth contrasted with the deceit made possible by the cunning garments of rhetoric: A truth personified by the Gymnosophists of India, whose naked spokesperson Dindimus was allowed to have bettered Alexander himself in their debates. This nakedness was assimilable to the simple truths spoken by Christ, and some Christian writers like Abelard and Dante were prepared to see these "virtuous heathens" as proto-Christians, living their lives in a way that foreshadowed Christianity.[52] But various other kinds of nudity could also find doctrinal sanction including what was called nuditas temporalis (the shedding of all worldly goods), which again had an important place in the early Christian tradition, especially amongst Franciscans. When the Canarians or Caribbean islanders were looked at from this tradition, being "naked" and without culture meant that nothing was already growing in either native fields or native hearts. This was seen as an advantage: That lack of contamination by other faiths or idols left them as pure as the supposedly unused soil – purer, so Las Casas and others could argue, than the nominally Christian Europeans who killed and enslaved them. But of course purity of heart could only be built on total denial of existing culture: the fundamental trope of colonial discourse.

The most familiar reading of nakedness is probably as nuditas criminalis, the nakedness of the sinner, taken as a sign of vice, powerfully established through the Augustinian association of sexuality with original sin. *Genesis* had suggested that the very concept of nakedness stems from the eating of the fruit of the tree of knowledge: "And the eyes of them both were opened, and they knew that they were naked; and they sewed fig leaves together, and made themselves aprons" (3:7). On this foundation Augustine established the connection between original sin and sexuality: Adam and Eve had spontaneously covered their sexual organs after the fall, and that shame was hereditary. Only animals felt no sexual shame. Boccaccio emphasizes the Canarian covering of the genitals, thereby demonstrating their full humanity in the Christian sense. Much of his description is of a clas-

[52] The tradition of the "naked philosopher" (Thomas Hahn, "Indians East and West: Primitivism and Savagery in English Discovery Narratives of the Sixteenth Century," *Journal of Medieval Renaissance Studies* 8 [1978]:77–114, and "The Indian Tradition in Western Medieval Intellectual History," *Viator* 9 [1978]:213–34) needs to be set within the general context of what came to be called "perennial philosophy": Louis Capéran, *Le problème du salut des infidèles* (Toulouse, 1934); Charles B. Schmitt, "Perennial Philosophy: From Agostino Steuco to Leibnitz," *Journal of the History of Ideas* 27 (1966): 505–32. Cf. Anthony Pagden, "The Savage Critic: Some European Images of the Primitive," *The Yearbook of English Studies* 13 (1983):32–45.

sical Golden Age, but the stone statue, classical in outline, has a woven apron of palm leaves covering the genitals. The Canarians are here assimilated to the tradition of the virtuous pagans, naturally modest.

One common reading of the famous debate between Bartolomé de Las Casas and Juan Ginés Sepúlveda is that it turned on whether the Amerindians were to be regarded as human beings or not. In one sense that view is wrong since Aristotle, on whom Sepúlveda based his case, made it clear that the natural slave is a man: His humanity was not in question. In a broader sense, too, Amerindian membership of the human species can hardly have been in ultimate doubt: The "problem" only existed in the first place because of human beings behaving in what were understood by European observers and commentators to be inhuman ways – in Fieschi's traditional image (above, p. 179) – there are sheep outside the sheepfold of the church but they must still be regarded as sheep if the possibility of them entering the fold is seriously entertained. The difficulty lay in defining the relevant terms and, once again, it is possible to perceive an underlying tension between the basic Judaeo-Christian position and the relatively subtle scale of humanity that classical writers had elaborated.[53] Rhetorically, one way of negotiating such tensions (though perhaps also perpetuating them) is through the use of metaphor. Certainly the commonest metaphors used to describe both the Canarians and the Amerindians come from the animal kingdom.

What had enabled Augustine's recasting of the story of Cain and Abel was the double positioning of Cain, on the one hand a founder of cities – and therefore associated with settlement in contrast to Abel's pastoralism; on the other, eternal wanderer, allowing Abel's pastoralism to take on – through contrast – an association with settlement itself. With Cain in the first position, Abel and his dogs could be seen – as pastoralists often have been in European history – as dangerous predators. With Cain in the second position, Abel becomes (metaphorically) protector of the flock against the threat from outside posed by the true predator. Two animals clearly play the key roles in this story: sheep, who signify the same in both versions, and dogs who, in the second version of the story, become split into two – the domesticated sheep-dog who assists the shepherd and the external predator (wolf-dog) who threatens the flock. The later imagery surrounding Cain includes animalization through the attribution of a

[53] Anthony Pagden, *The Fall of Natural Man: The American Indian and the Origins of Comparative Ethnology* (Cambridge, 1986), 18.

horn.[54] The pastoral metaphor acted as a serious restraint on what could be said directly about Canarians (or, later, Amerindians). Explicit accounts – especially ones that claimed legal status – had to pay attention to Christian principles. Implicitly, though, many ethnographic assumptions were carried by the kinds of comparisons offered. In 1436, for example, King Duarte I of Portugal called on Pope Eugenius IV to lift the papally imposed ban on further European colonization of the Canary Islands. The King's argument was basically that colonization was going to go ahead anyway, so it was better in the long run to authorize scrupulous colonizers such as himself, rather than leaving the field open to the unscrupulous who would pay no attention to papal bans:

> O most blessed Father, among the countless islands which the sea encompasses, there are included seven islands close to one another in the ocean south of Portugal which are popularly called the Canary Islands. The nearly wild men who inhabit the forests are not united by a common religion, nor are they bound by the chains of law, they are lacking normal social intercourse, living in the country like animals. They have no contact with each other by sea, no writing, no kind of money or metal. They have no houses and no clothing except for coverlets of palm leaves or goat skins which are worn as an outer garment by the most honored men. They run barefoot quickly through the rough, rocky and steep mountainous regions, hiding... in caves hidden in the ground.[55]

Despite their shared use of the vocabulary of deprivation, the ideological implications of Duarte's description are very different from those of the classical language of the "Golden Age," later deployed in famous passages by Montaigne and Shakespeare. Here the negatives are used to strip the Canarians of all forms of recognizable cul-

54 Ruth Melinkoff, *The Mark of Cain* (Berkeley, CA, 1981), 59.

55 James Muldoon, ed., *The Expansion of Europe: The First Phase* (Philadelphia, 1977), 54. On Duarte's letter and its consequences, James Muldoon, *Popes, Lawyers, and Infidels: The Church and the Non-Christian World, 1250–1550* (Philadelphia, 1979), 120ff. Eugenius sought advice from canon lawyers who replied through commentaries on Innocent IV's *Quod super his*. Both questions and answers were cast in very general terms, not mentioning the Canarians by name, but nonetheless this was a turning-point of some importance: the debates about dominium of pagan lands, thus far conducted in the abstract, now had a specific referent, as knowledge of the Canarians allowed pagan to regain its specific meaning, quite different from infidel. See also P.E. Russell, "El descubrimiento de las Canarias y el debate medieval acerca de los derechos de los príncipes y pueblos paganos," *Revista de Historia Canaria* XXXVI (1978):10–32, and James Muldoon, "A Fifteenth-century Application of the Canonistic Theory of the Just War," in *Proceedings of the Fourth International Congress of Medieval Canon Law*, Stephan Kuttner, ed. (Vatican City, 1976), 467–80.

ture. The single comparison offered by the King is "like animals," the simile carrying the comparison, which – formally at least – stops short of identity. Duarte's single but telling comparison reappears half a century later in the official letter that Columbus wrote on his return from the Caribbean, where he uses the phrase "like animals" (como bestias) to describe the way the Indians give everything they have in return for things of little value.[56] *Like* animals is not of course the same as saying that they *are* animals: They share with animals this one characteristic (although the ethological basis of Columbus's comparison is far from clear), but then the theory of natural law in its Aquinian form certainly recognized that humans and animals shared certain kinds of behavior so, strictly speaking, such comparisons did not carry great ideological weight. Nevertheless, the metaphor associated the Canarians and Amerindians with animals. It was ideologically then a short step to the accusations of bestiality that were frequent in fifteenth-century Portuguese accounts of the Canarians.[57] Alternatively, the animal metaphor could be developed. A conventional Franciscan view is stated by Motolinía, noting the meekness (and therefore natural goodness) of the Indians who go to their destruction in the mines "like great flocks of sheep."[58] A more revealing example is that of Francisco Ruiz (also a Franciscan) who turned the pastoral imagery of the Psalms onto its head by affirming (around 1516) that Caribbean Indians were incapable of receiving the faith, an opinion he supported by saying that they lived like sheep, unable to see beyond what they held in their hands, and that they therefore needed to be controlled by Christians, "just as a horse or other animal is controlled by a rein or halter."[59]

Implicit within such a metaphor it is possible to find assumptions that are basically economic: Ruiz has recourse to the idea of human control of domesticated or semi-domesticated animals used for transport or other heavy labor. It is hardly accidental that these animals were not available in the Caribbean, nor that the absence of such beasts of burden – which the Spaniards needed for building and mining – meant that de facto the Indians were treated as such.[60] Carl Sauer points to the fact that the first census in the New World was a statistic

[56] Columbus, "Letter to Santangel," in Consuelo Varela, ed., *Cristóbal Colón: Textos y documentos completos*, 142.

[57] See Fernández-Armesto, *Before Columbus*, 233–4.

[58] Quoted in Mario Góngora, *Studies in the Colonial History of Spanish America*, Richard Southern, trans. (Cambridge, 1975), 210.

[59] Quoted in Pedro Borges Morán, *Misión y civilización en América* (Madrid, 1987), 28.

[60] Frank Moya Pons, *Después de Colón: Trabajo, Sociedad y Política en la Economía del Oro* (Madrid, 1987), 31.

of native numbers as to age suited to labor.[61] Set alongside such facts, the philosophical subtleties of the arguments of Sepúlveda and the others seem less important. Nobody in Seville or Salamanca may have considered that the Caribbean Indians were not really human. In the Indies they were treated *as if* they were not human, and the metaphorical field in which they were placed at least enabled and encouraged such treatment. The mark of the success of this tactic is the shock occasioned by Montesinos's simple question, posed in 1511 from the pulpit of the cathedral in Santo Domingo: "Are these not men too?," which led eventually to the restatement of the traditional Christian terminology by Pope Paul III in his bull of 1537, *Sublimis Deus*, where the devil is seen as responsible for blinding men to the implication in that primary instruction "Go ye and teach all nations" that all are capable of receiving the faith:

> The enemy of the human race, who opposes all good deeds in order to bring men to destruction, beholding and envying this, invented a means never before heard of, by which he might hinder the preaching of God's word of Salvation to the people: he inspired his satellites who, to please him, have not hesitated to publish abroad that the Indians of the West and the South, and other people of whom We have recent knowledge should be treated as dumb brutes created for our service, pretending that they are incapable of receiving the catholic faith.
>
> We, who, though unworthy, exercise on earth the power of our Lord and seek with all our might to bring those sheep of His flock who are outside, into the fold committed to our charge, consider, however, that the Indians are truly men and that they are not only capable of understanding the catholic faith but, according to our information, they desire exceedingly to receive it.[62]

Bartolomé de Las Casas, the most outspoken critic of the Spanish colonizers, was deeply aware of the significance of this metaphorical field, which he also upheld in its most traditional form with the native Americans as sheep outside the fold who needed to be brought within by peaceful means. Unfortunately, the Spanish had behaved instead, according to Las Casas, like the beasts of the field, preying upon these errant sheep rather than leading them into the fold: "Amongst these tame sheep, gifted with the aforementioned qualities by their Maker and Creator, came the Spaniards, who behaved, as soon as they knew

[61] Carl O. Sauer, *The Early Spanish Main* (Berkeley, CA, 1966), vii.

[62] In J.H. Parry and Robert G. Keith, eds., *The New Iberian World: A Documentary History of the Discovery and Settlement of Latin America to the Early 17th Century*, 5 vols. (New York, 1984), I.:387; cf. Lewis Hanke, "Pope Paul III and the American Indians," *Harvard Theological Review* XXX (1937):65–102, and Edmundo O'Gorman, "Sobre la naturaleza bestial del indio americano," *Filosofía y Letras* I (1941):152–3.

them, like wolves and tigers and lions made cruel by many days' hunger."[63] These tigers, lions, and wolves often appear together, elsewhere supplemented by bulls, dogs, and dragons: Spanish cruelty takes many different shapes. But throughout the *Brevíssima Relación* the innocent or tame sheep always appear on their own, at least consistent in their powerlessness. Confirmation of Las Casas's care with these metaphors comes in Book III of *Historia de las Indias*, where the terms dog, tiger, and lion are sometimes applied to the Indians, but never the term wolf. The Indians are allowed to be angry and courageous and to take on the appropriate animal characteristics; the cruelty of the wolf – enemy par excellence of the sheep – is reserved to describe the Spaniards.[64]

This vocabulary was highly charged and difficult to ignore: It needed to be incorporated and reworked in order to blunt its critical edge. The key moment, discursively speaking, comes in Peter Martyr's account of Columbus's second voyage. Columbus returns from Jamaica to Hispaniola and repairs his ships "with the intention again of destroying the islands of the cannibals and burning all their canoes, so that those rapacious wolves could not harm their neighboring sheep."[65] Ironically, Las Casas, willing to support Columbus in the spite of all evidence, suggested that "destruir" might be a mistake for "descubrir," a reading that appears in Fernando's biography of his father.[66] It was argued earlier that Columbus's willingness not to see the absence of Guacanagarí's wound presupposed a disposition toward the presence of a division within the native Caribbean world, a disposition for which – on one level – the ground had been laid in the latter stages of the first voyage, but that was also deeply embedded in what the next section will discuss as an emergent European ideology. Here, in Peter Martyr, the pastoral language of the Bible is inflected in such a way that the relationship between sheep and wolf is a relationship between different divisions of the native population. This pastoral image underlies the dualism that has dogged Caribbean anthropology (and that is a staple of all colonial discourse). It may even have contributed to the identification of the natives of the eastern Caribbean as cannibals, and therefore to the legislation that permitted

[63] Las Casas, *Brevíssima Relación de la Destrucción de las Indias* [1552], André Saint-Lu, ed. (Madrid, 1987), 77.
[64] See André Saint-Lu, *Las Casas indigeniste: Etudes sur la vie et l'oeuvre du défenseur des Indiens* (Paris, 1982), 35–43.
[65] Columbus in *Decades* III, 19; in Gil and Varela, eds., *Cartas particulares a Colón y Relaciones coetáneas*, 77.
[66] Ibid., 77, n.118.

their enslavement. For present purposes, though, the important point is that the rhetorical move should be understood as completing a triadic structure: In the light of Las Casas's indictment it can be seen that the ethnic dualism of the Caribbean is achieved by the creation of a relatively neutral, third space, that can be occupied by the Christians. Implicit within Peter Martyr's analogy is the suggestion that Columbus occupies the role of shepherd, protector of the sheep against the predators, or even that of hunter, active enemy of the rapacious wolves: It was, after all, on this second voyage that the Spaniards first took dogs to hunt the Indians, a move that has its own implications.[67]

EUROPE'S ETHNOGRAPHIC AUTHORITY

> Neither affection for my son, nor duty
> To my old father, nor the proper love
> Which should have given Penelope happiness,
>
> Could overcome, within me, the desire
> I had to have experience of the world,
> And of the vices and virtues of mankind;
>
> I put out on the deep and open sea
> With one boat only, and the company,
> Small as it was, which had not deserted me.[68]

The previous sections of this chapter have largely dealt with the distinctions made between different kinds of "other peoples," whether on religious or cultural grounds. That process can properly be regarded as growing in complexity over time, and as issuing into the full-blown project of comparative ethnology. It is, though, a process founded upon the distinction between "self" and "other," that initial (and often implicit) splitting that constitutes the entity that sees itself (again often implicitly) as authorized to make distinctions, as occupying what we think of as the ethnographic position, as assumed, for example, by Peter Martyr at the end of the previous section. Distinctions were made within Caribbean culture by Europeans: That third space – the position of ethnographic authority – has long presented itself as transparent, neutral, "white." I want to end by giving the

[67] Antonello Gerbi, *Nature in the New World: From Christopher Columbus to Gonzalo Fernández Oviedo*, Jeremy Moyle, trans. (Pittsburgh, 1985), 325.

[68] Dante Alighieri, *The Divine Comedy*, C.H. Sisson, trans. (Manchester, 1980), 113 [*Inferno* XXVI, 94–102].

term "Europe" a little color.[69] The briefest of historical sketches will have to suffice. "Europe" has a long history as a word, although it only acquired anything like its current significance relatively recently. Europe, Asia, and Libya were the traditional parts of the tripartite world according both to classical geography and later to the Noachid story of racial origins that was featured on medieval maps. However, the significant geographical markers were the rivers that ensured contact between those three parts, or at least between those areas closest to the defining center, whether Athens or Jerusalem. The more distant areas were unknown, and there was certainly no strong sense of any of the three as "continent" in the modern sense: In the *Politics*, Aristotle actually has the Hellenic race as "intermediate," combining the best characteristics of Europe and Asia.[70]

Christianity inevitably worked against the significance of such territorial division: Its missionary impulse made it ecumenical in scope. The shift in emphasis from Christianity to Christendom was, though, in large part a territorial move, and by the time of Urban II's speech at Clermont (1095) Christendom was in actuality, if not in aspiration, fairly closely aligned with a geographical area we could recognize as Europe. Denys Hay's magisterial survey offers some key moments, some markers in what was inevitably a slow process. The first stage was the limitation imposed upon the universal aspirations of Christianity by the successful expansion of Islam northward and westward from its Arabian base. In the west, in consequence, there emerged the notion of Christendom, a territorially bounded faith that gradually consolidated its hold on what we now think of as the continent of Europe, a process effectively completed by the conversion of Lithuania in 1386. Although the word "Europe" is not at all common until the fourteenth century, Hay cites a telling early example:

> . . . the contemporary alarm and its significance for the emergence of a sense of unity can be seen in the invention by the eighth century chronicler Isidor Pacensis of a term to describe the composite forces—Romano-Gallic and barbarian – which under the leadership of the Frankish chief Charles Martel defeated the Moslems at the battle of Tours in 732: he calls them "Europeans" – *Europeenses*.[71]

1291 can stand as a suitably symbolic date. The brothers Vivaldi broke the mold of "Mediterranean" sailing when they boldly set out

[69] On "ethnographic authority," see James Clifford, *The Predicament of Culture: Twentieth-Century Ethnography, Literature, and Art* (Cambridge, MA, 1988), 21–54.
[70] Aristotle, *Politics*, Stephen Everson, ed. (Cambridge, 1988), 165 [1327b].
[71] Denys Hay, *Europe: The Emergence of an Idea* (Edinburgh, 1957), 25.

from Genoa through the Pillars of Hercules into the Ocean Sea, never to be heard of again, an incident that Dante may have used when he has Ulysses recount his death in the 23rd canto of the *Inferno:* Such a moment symbolizes the movement from Mediterranean patterns to what the Belgian historian Charles Verlinden has called the "Atlantic Mediterranean," the extension of Mediterranean models of settlement, colonization, and trade into a new geographical area, prior to the development of a fully "Atlantic" system.[72] In the same year the loss of Acre indicated the decline of Christianity outside Europe. This is close to what Hay offers as a threshold when he says that one can count the score or so of references to Europe in Dante, while in Petrarch they are too frequent to enumerate.[73] Certainly, by the early fourteenth century there were separate maps of the three parts of the world, a crucial move toward the idea of "continent."[74]

There is clearly a dialectical process at work here. Christianity provided the ideology of a territorially bounded area that came to be known as Europe, but that "Europe" also had a shared economic and cultural and legal base in part supplied through its having been the western half of the old Roman Empire. Equally, though, to use Michael Mann's recent formulation, "if Europe was a 'society,' it was a society defined by the boundaries of ideological power, Christendom."[75] Christendom only gradually lost its force as a descriptive category to be replaced by "the civil world," "civilization," "European civilization," and, simply, "Europe."[76] More important than the details of the changing terminology is the sense that some kind of unity, above and beyond the national, was perceptible. Norman Daniel sees the experience of the Crusades as strengthening the notion of a "European" cultural and ethnic identity on the grounds that western European crusaders found non-European Christians –

[72] Charles Verlinden, *Les origines de la civilisation atlantique* (Paris, 1966), and *The Beginnings of Modern Colonization,* Yvonne Frecero, trans. (Ithaca, 1970).

[73] Hay, *Europe: The Emergence of an Idea,* 59.

[74] Supporting evidence is also found in Gregory X's decision to hold the Ecumenical Council of 1274 at Rouen rather than Rome: "When Gregory X decided to hold the council, he had no clear idea of the limits of Christendom, but as planning proceeded it became increasingly clear that the curia's conception of the Christian realm was essentially European. For Gregory the primary purpose of the Council was to have been the provision of aid to the Holy Land, but the preparations proved that the actual frontier of Christendom lay not in Jordan but in Eastern Europe," in Jacques Le Goff, *The Medieval Imagination,* Arthur Goldhammer, trans. (Chicago, 1988), 61–2.

[75] Michael Mann, *The Sources of Social Power, Vol. I,* 338.

[76] See also Franklin Le Van Baumer, "The Conception of Christendom in Renaissance England," *Journal of the History of Ideas* VI (1945):127–56, and Denys Hay, "The Concept of Christendom", in *The Dawn of European Civilization,* David T. Rice, ed. (New York, 1965), 327–43.

Greek, Syrian, Coptic, Arab – just as alien as Muslims.[77] Evidence for a secular sense of such unity is apparent in the first epic of European colonization, Camöes's *Lusiads,* published in 1572. And certainly by the time of Samuel Purchas's collections in the early seventeenth century there is the strong hint of a superiority that is cultural (in the widest sense of the word) rather than simply religious, and coextensive with what was now perceived as a continent: Purchas, for all his anti-Catholic animus, still speaks about "us" and "ours" in an unmistakably European sense, echoing the Latin formulation "nostra Europa" found as early as Apian's *Cosmographia* of 1533.[78] As Voltaire would later put it: "One sees among all nations a mutual correspondence; Europe is like one great family."[79] The formulation might sound trite, but its genealogical metaphor rehearses a deeply exclusive ideology, still powerfully at work in the 1990s.

To generalize about this Europe is a problematic exercise, to say the least, but it is also, I would argue, a necessary exercise for a book of this kind, whose span from, say, the end of the thirteenth century to the end of the eighteenth, from Dante Alighieri to Edmund Burke, covers the period in which Europe consolidated into a meaningful and even seemingly self-evident formulation. Europe has, after all, often enough been considered an actor in the historical process: Examine almost any modern history book for examples of Europe as the grammatical subject governing verbs of action. There may be problems with such formulations, but if historical processes are to be read in this way "the mind of Europe" must be allowed its unconscious, those implicit assumptions that act so powerfully in the telling of its stories of distinction.

The first volume of Michael Mann's impressive history of the sources of social power locates itself within a European assessment of the rise of European capitalism that goes back over fifty years to the seminal work of Max Weber. Mann notes that historians have constantly used the word "restless" to characterize the uniqueness of "western civilization": William McNeill's *The Rise of the West* (1963) is an influential example. Such analysis certainly has its historiographical limits: The language of "dynamism" and "motors of develop-

[77] Norman Daniel, *The Arabs and Medieval Europe* (London, 1979), 117.

[78] Samuel Purchas, "A Brief and Generall Consideration of Europe," in *Purchas His Pilgrimes* [1625], 20 vols. (Glasgow, 1905); cf. Denys Hay, *Europe: The Emergence of an Idea,* 117–21.

[79] Quoted in Percy G. Adams, *Travel Literature and the Evolution of the Novel* (Lexington, KY, 1983), 77.

ment" inevitably sees an internal and self-propulsive history.[80] My interest, though, is not in the supposed "dynamic" itself, nor in the kinds of explanations that have been offered of it, but rather in its very constitution as a phenomenon in the first place, and in particular in what is acknowledged through negation in that constitution.

Weber himself was careful to speak of "rational restlessness," a psychological quality he located especially within Puritanism; Mann helpfully suggests, here following Durkheim, that it was the broader idea of Christendom itself that underlay the potential anarchy of this "rational restlessness," providing an "unseen hand" that would act as the "major regulatory agency."[81] This is certainly in line with the thread of implicit assumptions traced earlier in this chapter. Karl Ferdinand Werner, joining the stream of explanations of the "European miracle," points out that Wever's *Unruh* is a term that the Nuremberg inventors of the portable mechanical watch gave to its main part, the balance wheel. This is no doubt technologically appropriate – given, for example, the importance of time-keeping in Lewis Mumford's classic study *Technics and Civilization*. But Werner also remarks suggestively that *Unruh* denotes both perpetual movement and also anxiety or agitation, "restlessness" but also "unrest"; not, in other words, just a description of a supposed "European psychology" but a suggestion as to its pathological constitution.[82] In one sense there is a standard explanation for this phenomenon: Weber was himself drawing on Karl Marx's analysis of the dynamic of capitalism, which emphasized the revolutionary impetus of the bourgeoisie, restlessly destroying in order to create anew. Marshall Berman's innovative reading of *The Communist Manifesto* suggests that there has been an abiding contradiction between this intrinsic and destructive dynamic and the overt *ideology* of capitalism, committed to the establishment of lasting structures, whether they be those of familial and social institutions or those of more material fabric.[83] Underlying my analysis here has been the suggestion that this contradiction is foreshadowed by that between the "restlessness" implicit in the Judaeo-Christian search for salvation (embedded in the "mobile" imagery of pastoralism) and the classical

[80] Michael Mann, *The Sources of Social Power, Vol. I*, 373.
[81] Ibid., 376–7.
[82] Karl Ferdinand Werner, "Political and Social Structures of the West, 300–1300," in Jean Baechler, John A. Hall, and Michael Mann, eds., *Europe and the Rise of Capitalism* (Oxford, 1988), 173.
[83] Marshall Berman, *All That Is Solid Melts into Air: The Experience of Modernity* (London, 1983), 90–105.

ideal of the civic institutions of the polis: the city of this world. Europe may have "resolved" these contradictions, at least to its own satisfaction, but the colonial project has always tended to stretch them again to breaking point: It is never easy to speak convincingly in favor of the values of "settlement" when you have just traveled three thousand miles across an ocean.

The psychic anxiety shadowing the European colonial project takes many forms. Its clearest manifestation is, as one might expect, in the literary texts – from *The Tempest* to *Heart of Darkness* – that have always reworked and ironized the discourses of empire. But it is important to realize that the worm of anxiety is also at the heart of the bud, serving to undercut and complicate the procedures of "distinction" even at their very beginnings.[84] This means turning again, for one last time, to Columbus's journal of his first voyage in order to highlight a final passage. On 3 December 1492, on the coast of Cuba, Columbus reports that his launch is approached by an Indian who proceeds to make "a big speech" (una grande plática). Columbus does not understand a word and presumes that it is a speech of welcome until he sees the face of the Indian by his side "turn yellow as wax" and understands, from the signs made by this Indian, that the speech threatens the Spaniards with death. It is a small moment and the threat is soon dispelled. Its significance lies in its being the first reported verbal resistance to Europeans in America, and in the complex but basically internal method of communication. Columbus does not understand the words spoken to him, nor does he understand the gestures with which the speaker accompanies his words: He needs to interpret the response of another Indian in order to assume comprehension of the original words. The mechanisms of ethnography are already in

[84] There are relatively few studies of the psychic dimension of the colonial project: the two best are probably Frederick Turner, *Beyond Geography: The Western Spirit Against the Wilderness* (New York, 1980), and Joel Kovel, *White Racism: A Psychohistory* (New York, 1984). Hahn's brief paragraph is telling: "When we receive routine details of a voyage, initial encounters with natives, construction of an outpost, punitive liquidation, journeys into the interior, body counts of thousands, and an uneventful return–all in an undifferentiated series, as if no one of these actions clashed more than another with the prevailing Christian ideology and European morality–all of this suggests considerable internalization, however schizophrenic, of new values concerning aliens." (Thomas Hahn, "Indians East and West," 107). An early example of the "savage critic" is the Muslim question, posed in *De expugnatione Lyxbonensi*, the anonymous chronicle of the conquest of Lisbon, significantly achieved by a pan-European army: "Do your possessions give you no pleasure at all, or have you incurred some blame at home, that you are so often on the move? Surely your frequent going and coming is proof of an innate mental instability, for he who is unable to arrest the flight of the body cannot control the mind" (quoted in James Muldoon, ed., *The Expansion of Europe*, 209).

place at this early moment. But it is also possible to glimpse here the trope of the "savage critic," that figure who appears as a constant troubling presence within colonial discourse, allowed to voice the anxieties that accompany the colonial project, anxieties that almost always relate to the violence that implicitly underwrites that enterprise.

PART II

Europeans in the vision of other peoples

CHAPTER 6

Persian perceptions of Mongols and Europeans

DAVID MORGAN

I

THROUGHOUT its long history, Persia has had to come to terms with the fact that it is on everyone's invasion route: Whether the invader is heading west or east, he is likely to pass through Persia, even if he does not stop there for long. Without going back as far as the Indo-Europeans, we might begin with Alexander the Great, invading from the west and bringing to Persia and points well beyond a period of Hellenistic cultural influence. But certainly the most momentous of all the invasions was that of the Muslim Arabs in the seventh century A.D. As a result, Persia acquired a new religion and became part – indeed, a formative part – of a new and great civilization, that of medieval Islam.

Persia was not, however, swallowed up. Unlike much of the rest of the Middle East, it in no way lost its unique identity. The Syrians, the Egyptians, and the Iraqis not only (eventually) became Muslims, but adopted the language of the Qur'ān, Arabic. They became Arabs, in fact, in every meaningful way except that of their ultimate descent. Persia was the great exception. Islam certainly became the majority faith, reducing the official pre-Islamic religion, Zoroastrianism, to numerical insignificance. And for some while the language of literature in Persia, as of law and theology, was Arabic. But Persian did not disappear. It continued to be spoken, and in due course it reemerged as a written language: now in an adapted form of the Arabic script, and with a large quantity of Arabic vocabulary, but still an obviously Indo-European language in its grammatical structure, a fact that has deceived many an English speaker, at least for a year or two, into thinking it an easy language to learn. So the Arab conquest did not destroy the sense of *īrāniyyat*, of Persian-ness. The country of today is still, in ways that are intangible but nevertheless real enough, the country of Cyrus the Great.[1]

This cultural resilience was to stand Persia in good stead in the centuries to come. From the eleventh century there was another major ethnic and political influx, that of the Turks. At some risk of oversimplification, one might say that not only in Persia but throughout the Middle East, the next nine centuries were a period during which the Turks supplied the rulers and the soldiers. Certainly there were no ethnically Persian rulers of the whole of Iran between 1040 and 1925, apart from a few decades during the eighteenth century when the Zand dynasty ruled most of the country.

The Persians took the Turks, almost effortlessly, in their stride. The Seljuk invasions were not especially destructive, and before long the Turkish sultans, already converted to Islam, were fully reliant on the administrative skills of the traditional (and apparently indestructible) Persian bureaucracy. In many ways the Seljuk period saw a flowering of Persian culture, especially in architecture and literature.[2]

But the greatest test still lay ahead. In the thirteenth century the most successful military conquerors the world had yet seen, the Mongols added Persia to their empire. The principal successor to the Seljuks in the eastern Islamic world had been the Khwārazm-shāh, who by 1215 ruled much of what is now Iran, Afghanistan, and former Soviet Central Asia. This large empire had been put together in a very few years, and the seams were still showing. The Khwārazm-shāh ᶜAlā' al-Dīn Muḥammad needed above all a period of peace during which he could consolidate the territorial gains he had made in the fifteen years of his reign.

Unhappily for him and for his subjects, those fifteen years had coincided with the rise to power in east Asia of Chinggis (Genghis) Khan, who after unifying the steppe tribes and campaigning in north China, invaded and devastated the Khwārazm-shāh's empire between 1219 and 1223. A confused period followed, during which much of northern Persia was ruled by Mongol viceroys. But when the Great Khan Möngke, Chinggis Khan's grandson, ascended the Mongol throne in 1251, he determined that not only should the whole of China be subjugated, by armies under the command of his brother Qubilai, but that another brother, Hülegü, should march westward to incorporate the whole of Persia, together with Iraq and other territories, into the Mongol Empire.

[1] See further, David Morgan, *Medieval Persia 1040–1797* (London 1988), ch. 1.
[2] On the Seljuk impact on Persia, see *ibid.*, pp. 32–3.

Hülegü's advance was halted in Syria in 1260, as much by Mongol internal disputes as by the armies of the Mamlūks of Egypt, but from that time Persia, Iraq, and eastern Anatolia became a semi-independent Mongol kingdom, known to historians as the Ilkhanate, which survived until its still mysterious collapse in the late 1330s.[3]

The Mongol conquest was the greatest shock Persia had had to endure since the coming of the Arabs. This was for at least two reasons. First, the Mongols were infidels. Islamic theory divided the world into two parts: the *Dār al-Islām*, the Abode of Islam, and the *Dār al-ḥarb*, the Abode of War. In the former, Islam ruled, though all the inhabitants would not necessarily be Muslims: many might well be *ahl al-kitāb*, people of the book – Jews and Christians whose religions were considered a true if incomplete and distorted divine revelation. In the latter, infidel rule prevailed, but only temporarily. Whatever brief truces might be necessary, war was the natural state of relations between Islam and the infidel. In due course it was to be expected that the *Dār al-Islām* would include the entire world. The problem was that the theory contained no provision for the process to go into reverse, for the *Dār al-ḥarb* to expand at the expense of the *Dār al-Islām*. Yet this is what the Mongol conquest of so large a part of the central lands of Islam implied.

Second, there had never been anything of the scale and ferocity of the Mongol invasions. Persia became only a part, and by no means the most important, of a world empire of unequaled dimensions. And this was an empire founded upon what were until that time unparalleled effusions of blood. Persians knew of nothing in their historical experience to compare with the massacre and destruction inflicted on them by the Mongols during their initial conquest.[4]

The period of the Mongol invasions was for Persia, then, a truly traumatic experience with which it was by no means easy for Persians to reconcile themselves. And there seem few grounds for arguing that it was not a wholly negative experience: Silver linings have to be searched for very hard if they are to be found in the Mongol cloud. But this is not to say that things did not eventually improve, that there was not a positive side to the Mongol era. One of the most remarkable results of the fact that most of Asia came, for a time, under the rule of a single family was an opening up of the continent, the establish-

[3] For accounts of the Mongol invasions of Persia and the history of the Ilkhanate, see J. A. Boyle (ed.), *The Cambridge History of Iran V: The Saljuq and Mongol Periods* (Cambridge 1968), ch. 4; David Morgan, *The Mongols* (Oxford 1986), ch. 3 & 6; *Medieval Persia*, ch. 6–8.

[4] See further, Morgan, *The Mongols*, pp. 73–83; *Medieval Persia*, pp. 79–82.

ment of direct contacts across it and as far as Europe. Europeans traveled across Mongol Asia as far as Mongolia and China: Ambassadors like John of Piano Carpini, missionaries like William of Rubruck, merchants like Marco Polo.

In Persia, too, there was a broadening of horizons. Chinese motifs found their way, most beneficially, into Persian art, especially miniature painting and ceramics. Some of the Persian historical writing of the Mongol era shows a breadth of interest and knowledge on the part of its authors that had not been shown by their predecessors and was not, regrettably, to be evident either in the work of their successors. Europe played a small part in this new world view, and some evidence does survive of how the Persians may have seen the Europeans, both in historical writing and in the account of Europe written by the one known Asian equivalent of Carpini, Rubruck, and Marco Polo: the Nestorian monk Rabban Ṣaumā.

II

How could a Muslim hope to explain, to the satisfaction of himself and his coreligionists, the loss to the infidel of lands that had formed part of the *Dār al-Islām* since the earliest days of the Islamic expansion? What was he to say about the Mongols? The problem was, in a rather different form, to recur in the twentieth century, when Muslims found that they had fallen to an unacceptable extent under the cultural and political domination of the West. The solution found by some has been what is most misleadingly called Islamic Fundamentalism – a feeling that God has (apparently) abandoned His people because they have themselves abandoned true Islam: that what is necessary is the finding of authentically Islamic answers to the difficulties that beset the Muslim world.

Some Persian contemporaries of the Mongol invasions saw their predicament in terms of divine judgment on the sins of the Muslims. As an explanation of the catastrophe this had two advantages: it provided a satisfactory solution so far as Islam was concerned, and it went some way toward legitimizing the Mongols. Persian writers under Mongol rule inevitably had to exercise a degree of caution when writing about their conquerors and masters (and in some cases employers), who could hardly be represented, without qualification, as mere brutal mass murderers.

The major historian of the early Mongol period in Persia was Juwaynī, who died in Ilkhanid service as governor of Baghdad and Iraq in 1283. His brother, until his fall from office and death in the following year, had for many years been chief minister of the Ilkhanate; and their ancestors had had a long tradition of government service to whoever happened to hold the reins of power in Persia. Juwaynī completed his *Ta'rīkh-i Jahān Gushā*, "The History of the World Conqueror" (Chinggis Khan) in 1260, and he covered the period up to the fall of the north Persian Assassin castles to Hülegü in 1256.[5]

Juwaynī's "Islamic" explanation of the Mongol cataclysm was as a divine judgement on the sins of the Persian people. It is in his history that a celebrated story of Chinggis Khan's invasion is to be found. After his capture of Bukhārā, Juwaynī tells us, Chinggis mounted a (Muslim) pulpit and addressed the Bukharans in these words:

> O people, know that you have committed great sins, and that the great ones among you have committed these sins. If you ask me what proof I have for these words, I say it is because I am the punishment of God. If you had not committed great sins, God would not have sent a punishment like me upon you.[6]

That Juwaynī's own views are accurately represented in this anecdote is made clear enough in many remarks of his own, especially in the introduction to his history. Here is a characteristic example: "For the admonishment and chastisement of every people a punishment hath been meted out fitting to their rebellion and in proportion to their infidelity, and as a warning to those endued with insight a calamity or castigation hath overtaken them in accordance with their sins and misdemeanours."[7] So it is, then, that the Mongol conquest is rendered legitimate, since the Mongols are – even consciously, Juwaynī will have us believe – the instruments of God's judgment. It followed, it may not be unreasonable to suggest, that in the eyes of Juwaynī and those who thought like him, there was nothing discreditable about entering Mongol service. It also followed that the Mongols, for reasons of both theological theory and personal prudence, could not be directly criticized for their barbarity.

This did not mean, however, that Juwaynī's attitude toward his Mongol masters was necessarily "nauseating" or "servile," as was

[5] On the Persian historians of the Mongols, especially Juwaynī, Jūzjānī and Rashīd al-Dīn, see further, Morgan, "Persian historians and the Mongols," in Morgan (ed.), *Medieval Historical Writing in the Christian and Islamic Worlds* (London 1982), pp. 109–24; *The Mongols*, pp. 16–23.

[6] Juwaynī, *Ta'rīkh-i Jahān Gushā*, ed. M. M. Qazwīnī, I (Leiden & London 1912), p. 81; tr. J. A. Boyle, *The History of the World-Conqueror* 2 vols (Manchester 1958), I, p. 105.

[7] Qazwīnī, p. 12; Boyle, I, p. 16.

suggested twenty years ago.[8] E. G. Browne, writing much earlier, was nearer the mark when he suggested that Juwaynī's circumstances "compelled him to speak with civility of the barbarians whom it was his misfortune to serve."[9] What we get from this historian is not criticism of the Mongols, but a sober and detailed account of what he quite evidently regards as a series of disasters, horrors that he clearly views with revulsion. He says of some areas that "every town and village has been several times subjected to massacre and has suffered this confusion for years, so that even though there be generation and increase until the Resurrection the population will not attain to a tenth part of what it was before."[10] Whatever this is, it is not flattery of the Mongols.

That Juwaynī did in fact feel, or feel obliged to express, admiration for the Mongols is not, however, in doubt. He was, after all, a courtier, and a remarkably successful one. And he does appear to have believed that if he had to administer flattery, he might as well do the job properly and lay it on heavily. When he visited the court of the Great Khan Möngke, he writes, "I beheld the effects of that justice whereby all creation hath recovered and bloomed again; . . . wherein I fulfilled the commandment of the Lord—'Look to the effects of God's mercy, how He maketh the earth to live after its death' (Qur'ān, xxx, 49) . . . The breezes of the north wind of his comprehensive equity perfumed the entire world and the sun of his royal favours illumined the whole of mankind. The blast of his shining sword cast fire into the harvest of the abject foe. . . " etc., etc.[11] In fairness to Juwaynī it should be pointed out that he was not only a government servant and a historian, but also a distinguished exponent of the art of Persian prose composition. The style of this passage, in Persian would have been much admired, and perhaps this consideration almost as much as the actual subject matter helps to determine what Juwaynī says.

As we try to weigh up how the Persians of Juwaynī's generation saw the Mongols, it is instructive to turn from him to a historian who, though a much older man, finished writing his history in the same year, 1260, that saw the completion of Juwaynī's book. This is Jūzjānī, who was born in what is now Afghanistan, experienced the first Mongol invasion, and fled to the Delhi Sultanate, where he was to spend the rest of his life, in 1226. His *Ṭabaqāt-i Nāṣirī* is a long general his-

[8] See D. Ayalon, "The Great Yāsa of Chingiz Khān: a reexamination," A, *Studia Islamica* 33 (1971), p. 133.
[9] *A Literary History of Persia*, II (Cambridge 1928), p. 473.
[10] Qazwīnī, p. 75; Boyle, I, pp. 96–7.
[11] Qazwīnī, p. 2; Boyle, I, pp. 4–5.

tory, of which the most important part is perhaps the account of the former Ghurid rulers of Afghanistan, some of whose generals had founded the Delhi Sultanate. The work ends with a section on the Mongols, which is the only significant Persian account written outside the Mongol Empire and hence immune from accusations of pro-Mongol bias.

Not that Jūzjānī has ever been so accused. For him, Chinggis Khan is always *mal^cūn*, the Accursed. His account of the Mongol invasion includes every atrocity he can lay his hands on – though it is interesting, and encouraging, to observe that the general impression he gives is not so very different from Juwaynī's. He tells us, for example, that when the Khwārazm-shāh's ambassadors to Chinggis Khan reached Peking, they saw a large pile of bones outside the city walls. They were told that these were the remains of 60,000 young girls who had thrown themselves to their deaths rather than risk falling alive into Mongol hands.[12]

Yet even for the refugee Jūzjāni, things are not quite as simple as that. Like Juwaynī, he has a theological explanation of the Mongol invasions. For him they are not a divine judgment but a Sign of the Times. Prophecy makes it clear, he says, that the end of the world will be heralded by the coming of the Mongols. So for him too, the Mongols were part of the divine plan. Further, and perhaps more surprisingly, they were not wholly evil: They had their good points. In particular they placed great emphasis on an austere code of sexual morality: Widows were fair game, but married women were not. Hence, "If any woman they took from Khurāsān and Persia had a husband, no creature would form a relationship with her: and if an infidel set his eyes upon a woman who had a husband, he would [first] kill the husband of the woman, and then would form a relationship with her."[13]

It seems that the Mongols also had the habit, whatever the cost to themselves, of telling the truth. Jūzjānī tells us of two sentries who fell asleep while on duty. This, a capital offense, was reported by a single witness. The sentries neither denied their guilt nor complained when they were marched off to execution. Jūzjānī's Persian informant, who had observed this incident, expressed his amazement to the Mongol commander, who replied: "Why are you astonished? You Tājīks [Persians] do such things, and tell lies, since telling lies is you Tājīks'

[12] Jūzjānī, *Ṭabaqāt-i Nāṣirī*, ed. ^cA. Ḥabībī, 2 vols (Kabul 1964), II, pp. 102–3; tr. H. G. Raverty, 2 vols (London 1881), II, p. 965.
[13] Habībī, II, pp. 144–5; Raverty, II, p. 1079.

occupation. But a Mongol, were a thousand lives at stake, would choose being killed, but would not speak false; and it is on account of this that God Most High has sent a calamity like us upon you"[14] – a clear echo of Chinggis Khan's sermon at Bukhārā, though the Mongol commander presumably did not, like a good Muslim, say "God Most High," but probably the Shamanist equivalent *Möngke Tenggeri*, the Eternal Heaven. Is there perhaps a faint pre-echo here in Jūzjānī's perspective of that later European notion, the Noble Savage, which comes across so strongly in Gibbon's account of the Mongols?

So Jūzjānī is torn two ways. The Mongols had driven him from his home and they had devastated the lands of Islam and killed enormous numbers of Muslims. Chinggis Khan was "a killer. . . , sanguinary and bloodthirsty"; but he was also, there was no denying it, "possessed of great energy, discernment, genius and understanding . . . just, resolute."[15] And the source of such qualities was clear: "Such was the energy, constancy and intrepidity which God Most High had implanted in the nature of Chingiz Khān and the Mongol army."[16]

Important though Juwaynī and Jūzjānī are, there can be no doubt that the major Persian historian of the Mongol period is from a later generation: Rashīd al-Dīn, joint chief minister of the Ilkhanate for twenty years, whose career (like those of all Ilkhanid chief ministers but one) ended on the scaffold, in his case in 1318, at the age of seventy. He was the author of, among other books, the *Jāmiʿ al-tawārīkh*, the "Collection of Histories." This he was commissioned to write by his master, the Mongol Īlkhān Ghazan (r. 1295–1304). It is a history of the Mongol and Turkish tribes, of the Mongol conquests and of their empire up to the time of writing. Ghazan's conception seems to have been that it would serve as a permanent *aide-memoire* for the Mongols of Persia, who were perhaps in some danger of forgetting who they were and where they had come from. Ghazan's brother and successor Öljeitü (r. 1304–16) asked Rashīd al-Dīn to add to his history accounts of the various peoples with whom the Mongols had come into contact – the Chinese, the Indians, the Jews, and so on. As this "world-history" section includes a history of the Franks, we shall return to it later in this chapter.

For Rashīd al-Dīn, the shock of the Mongol conquests had worn off. The Mongol Empire and the Ilkhanate were long-established facts: He was writing some eighty years after Chinggis Khan's invasion. Not

[14] Habībī, II, p. 146; Raverty, II, pp. 1080–1.
[15] Habībī, II, p. 144; Raverty, II, p. 1077.
[16] Habībī, II, p. 105; Raverty, II, p. 969.

only that, but Ghazan had announced his conversion to Islam, and the rest of the Mongols of Persia had declared that they too had become Muslims (whatever they may have thought that that meant). There was therefore no need to justify a regime that was firmly ensconced and that had restored Persia to the *Dār al-Islām*. Indeed, the writing of Rashīd al-Dīn's history at Ghazan's instigation might be taken to indicate that by the end of the thirteenth century it was a Mongol rather than a Persian identity that was in danger of disappearing (and in fact the Mongols do seem ultimately to have been fairly painlessly absorbed into the population of Persia).

As the circumstances of its composition make clear, the *Jāmiᶜ al-tawārīkh* was "official history." We will search it in vain, therefore, for a critical view of the Mongols. For Rashīd al-Dīn, the rise of the Mongol Empire, of which he was the chronicler, was of momentous importance. "What event or occurrence," he asked rhetorically, "has been more notable than the beginning of the government of Chingiz Khān, that it should be considered a new era?"[17] His attitude to the empire reflected that of his Mongol masters: It and the world were coterminous – those countries that were not part of it had simply not yet submitted. Of Chinggis Khan he writes: "He gave the [whole] world one face; and the same feelings to all hearts. He purified the territories of the countries, in delivering them from the domination of perverse usurpers and the oppression of proud tyrants."[18] Where there is criticism of the Mongols, it is self- (or rather Ghazan-) serving. Ghazan had instituted a series of major administrative reforms, designed to repair the ravages of the first seventy years of Mongol rule in Persia. Rashīd al-Dīn's account of the nature of Mongol rule under Ghazan's (infidel) predecessors is an unflattering one, and it may well in large part be accurate. The consideration that has, however, to be borne in mind is that the greater the chaos before Ghazan, the greater Rashīd al-Dīn's master's achievement in remedying the situation. Rashīd al-Dīn the chief minister inevitably casts a long shadow over Rashīd al-Dīn the historian.

For many years another important book has been attributed to Rashīd al-Dīn: a volume of letters, published as *Mukātabāt-i Rashīdī*. Here, as it happens, it is possible to see a much more directly critical view of the Mongols being expressed. We find in the letters such phrases as "the time of the tyrannical Turks [Mongols in this context]

[17] Rashīd al-Dīn, *Histoire des Mongols de la Perse*, ed. & tr. E. Quatremère (Paris 1836; repr. Amsterdam 1968), pp. 60–2.
[18] *Ibid.*, pp. 62–3.

and the oppressive *bitikchis* [Mongol scribal officials]."[19] on another occasion one of Rashīd al-Dīn's correspondents calls the Mongols "mere deceivers and accomplices of the Devil."[20] But we would be unwise to make very much of this. The authenticity of the letters has long been disputed: It can be demonstrated, for example, that one of them shows knowledge of Tamerlane's Anatolian campaign of 1402– a century after the supposed time of writing.[21]

So far as we can tell, then, if Rashīd al-Dīn's writings represent his "true" opinions and if he was at all typical, Persians in the last decades of the Ilkhanate viewed the Mongols as legitimate rulers who could be fitted, if not entirely effortlessly, into the Muslim scheme of things. By the long survival of their regime and because of their conversion to Islam, they had become acceptable, even respectable. Their reputation rose even higher after the collapse of the Ilkhanate following the death of Öljeitü's son Abū Saʿīd in 1336. Persia was plunged into political chaos, not to be resolved for decades – and then by Tamerlane, a cure possibly as bad as the disease. Historians began as early as the 1360s to describe the Mongol period as the Good Old Days, when Persia was under good government. Abū Saʿīd in particular received an especially good press, perhaps because of what may well have been his very real qualities as a ruler, perhaps because the contrast with the absence of coherent government that followed his death made him seem in retrospect more impressive than he did at the time (compare views of the late Shah of Iran expressed in the late 1980s with those of around 1979!). "The time of his government," wrote Abū Bakr al-Quṭbī al-Aharī, "was the best period of the domination of the Mongols."[22] The Mongols had come into Persia like a lion; they went out rather more like a lamb.

III

For most of the Middle Ages, writers in the Islamic world did not rate western Europe very highly, if indeed they thought about that part of the world at all. For Islam, Europe was a remote and barbarous backwater. Civilization ended at the Pyrenees. Muslim geographers some-

[19] Rashīd al-Dīn (attrib.), *Mukātabāt-i Rashīdī*, ed. M. Shafīʿ (Lahore 1945), p. 33.

[20] *Ibid.*, p. 274.

[21] See A. H. Morton, "The letters of Rashīd al-Dīn: Ilkhanid fact or Timurid fantasy?," forthcoming in D. O. Morgan et al. (eds), *The Mongol Empire and its Legacy*.

[22] *Ta'rīkh-i Shaikh Uwais*, ed. & tr. J. B. van Loon (The Hague, 1954), text, p. 149, tr., p. 51.

times made an attempt to describe the area, but historians largely ignored it. The only historical account to survive from before the time of Rashīd al-Dīn is a list of Frankish kings from Clovis to Louis IV, written in the mid-tenth century by Masᶜūdī.[23]

Rashīd al-Dīn's "History of the Franks" is then of rather considerable historiographical interest.[24] Yet even here there is a very significant contrast between his treatment of the Franks and what he has to say about the other peoples in his world history. For one thing, other areas – notably China and India – are incorporated into the text of his main history: the lands of the Franks, never. For another, he generally gives us details about the identity of his informants – a Buddhist monk in the case of the history of India, for example. He tells us nothing about his informants on the Franks. The History is divided into two parts: a description, geographical and political, of Europe, and an annalistic account of European history, arranged under the reigns of popes and emperors, and concluding with the Emperor Albert I and Pope Benedict XI, both alive at the time of writing. Where Rashīd al-Dīn obtained the information in the first part is anyone's guess. The basic source of the annals has, however, been identified by Professor Karl Jahn, the editor and translator of the two editions of the History. That source appears to be the chronicle of Martin of Troppau, a Dominican bishop otherwise known as Martinus Polonus, who died in 1279 (hence his material had to be updated by Rashīd al-Dīn), and whose chronicle was evidently very popular, still surviving in an unusually large number of manuscripts and having inspired (for reasons apparently unconnected to its less than remarkable quality) many continuations by other hands.[25]

The annalistic section, being no more than a version of Martin's material, is of little inherent interest. It is the survey of Europe preceding it that (though slapdash and superficial compared with Rashīd al-Dīn's accounts of India or China) contains more that is worthy of attention. I have discussed some of these points elsewhere.[26] They include a remarkably accurate Arabic-Persian terminology to express the precise nature of the offices of pope, emperor, and king of France, and the differences between them; a striking account of what is al-

[23] See further, B. Lewis, *The Muslim Discovery of Europe* (London 1982), pp. 141–2.
[24] There are two editions, both ed. & tr. K. Jahn: *Histoire universelle de Rašīd al-Dīn Fadl Allāh Abul Khair. I.Histoire des Francs* (Leiden 1951), and *Die Frankengeschichte des Rašīd al-Dīn* (Vienna 1977).
[25] See D. Hay, *Annalists and Historians* (London 1977), pp. 49, 64.
[26] See *The Mongols*, pp. 189–93.

leged to happen at an imperial coronation, which places the pope very much in the position of supreme ruler, and tit-bits of information such as that there are no snakes in Ireland, but 100,000 students in Paris.

One would never guess from reading this History that there were extensive contacts between Europe and Mongol Persia during Rashīd al-Dīn's time. Yet there were. The Mongols were always very conscious of the importance and profitability of trade, and the capital of the Ilkhanate, Tabrīz in north-west Persia, was a major entrepôt. Merchants passed constantly from Europe to the east and back. There were longstanding Italian colonies in the city, and some Italians rose high in Mongol service, even acting as Ilkhanid ambassadors to the European powers. When the Īlkhān Öljeitü moved the capital southeast to Sulṭāniyya, the Papacy found it worthwhile to establish a Catholic archbishopric there. Merchants, then, and churchmen: It seems very probable that Rashīd al-Dīn's principal European informant may have been one of Martin of Troppau's fellow-Dominicans who had brought a copy of Martin's chronicle with him to Persia and who provided Rashīd al-Dīn with information for his survey of Europe. This would explain the pervasive papal bias of the information. There were, too, many diplomatic envoys passing to and fro. For decades after the first contacts were established around 1262, vigorous attempts were made to form an offensive alliance between the powers of western Europe and the Ilkhanate, the object being to defeat the Mamlūks and retake the Holy Land. Probably mainly for logistical reasons, these attempts never came to very much, but the project was not easily given up, and there seems to have been complete sincerity on both sides about the alliance's desirability and practicality.[27]

No one, then, who lived in Tabrīz and moved in the more elevated social circles would have had the slightest difficulty in obtaining adequate, indeed copious and accurate information about Europe and its history, had he so wished. In addition, Rashīd al-Dīn was chief minister of the Ilkhanate. He must have known about all the diplomatic manoeuvrings; indeed, he must surely have been directly involved in them. But there is no reference to any of this in any of his works. Professor J.A. Boyle once published a very short article, "Rashīd al-Dīn and the Franks,"[28] in which he discussed what is to be found on the subject in Rashīd al-Dīn's works other than the "His-

[27] See further J. A. Boyle, "The Il-Khans of Persia and the princes of Europe," *Central Asiatic Journal* 20 (1976), pp. 25–40; J. Richard, "The Mongols and the Franks," *Journal of Asian History* 3 (1969), pp. 45–57; Morgan, *The Mongols*, pp. 183–7.

[28] *Central Asiatic Journal* 14 (1970), pp. 62–7.

tory of the Franks." It had to be short because despite Boyle's painstaking sifting of the material there was so little there to be found.

We can only deduce, therefore, that Rashīd al-Dīn deliberately chose not to bother himself unduly about Europe. This cannot be ascribed simply to Muslim prejudice regarding other religions, since no such prejudices deterred Rashīd al-Dīn from providing much fuller accounts of non-Muslim societies like those of India, China, and the pre-Islamic Mongols. There is, however, an element of religious prejudice involved. For centuries, as we have seen, western Europe had been the Islamic world's poor relation, in terms both of civilization and (in Muslim eyes) of religion. Europe was regarded with a contempt and lack of interest that might perhaps during the Dark Ages, when the lights shone brightly in Córdoba, Damascus, and Baghdad, have been justified. This view had not been much revised by the early fourteenth century, though possibly by then, for the future good of the Islamic world, it ought to have been. Rashīd al-Dīn was a remarkable man, and a remarkable historian, in many ways. The fact that he wrote a history of the Franks, however inadequate it may have been, is significant. But so far as his basic attitude toward the Franks was concerned, even Rashīd al-Dīn was not able to rise above the prejudices and misconceptions of his contemporaries: prejudices and misconceptions which, it should be said, were paralleled on the European side, but which Europe was quicker to disabuse itself of, at least up to a point.

Rashīd al-Dīn is, then, a singularly untypical Persian historian but typical enough in his attitude toward the Franks. To find a more appreciative view we have to look at the travel narrative of Rabban Ṣaumā.[29] Whether this can legitimately be called a Persian view is open to discussion: The narrative was originally written in Persian, and in Persia. But its author was a Turk who had come from north China, and the only version we have of his narrative is a translation into Syriac. Still, if we had the original (and it may yet turn up) we might contend that it is as much Persian as the novels of Joseph Conrad are English literature.

The Mongol period saw a last efflorescence of the Nestorian church in Asia. Indeed, it has been argued in a recently translated book

[29] There are two English translations of this account: E. A. Wallis Budge, *The Monks of Ḳûblâi Khân Emperor of China* (London 1928), which includes the whole document; and J. A. Montgomery, *The History of Yaballaha III* (New York 1927), which stops at the end of the travel narrative. There is now a valuable study of Rabban Ṣaumā: Morris Rossabi, *Voyager from Xanadu: Rabban Sauma and the First Journey from China to the West* (Tokyo and New York, 1992).

(though not in my opinion very convincingly) that the role of the Nestorians was absolutely crucial in the rise of the Mongol Empire.[30] Whatever the truth of that, there can be no denying that Nestorianism was influential among many of the Mongol and Turkish tribes, and that some Nestorians, especially women, achieved positions of very considerable influence in the Mongol political world. In addition, the Mongols were, at least until the end of the thirteenth century, highly tolerant in matters of religion: a feature that is frequently adduced in their favour by their apologists. It is indeed the case that anyone who managed to avoid being massacred during the Mongol invasions was unlikely subsequently to be persecuted for his religious beliefs. The Nestorian church, always a strongly missionary organization, was able to take advantage of this situation and for a time to spread more or less unhindered across the Asian continent.

It was in these circumstances that the Nestorian monk Rabban Ṣaumā and his disciple Mark decided to travel from China on pilgrimage to Jerusalem. They never reached their goal, for Jerusalem, apart from two brief moments, remained obstinately outside the boundaries of the Mongol Empire. Instead, Mark was elected to the supreme office in the Nestorian church, that of Catholicus, in which post he had the misfortune to survive long enough to have to cope with the persecutions that followed the conversion of the Persian Mongols to Islam. Rabban Ṣaumā, too, was given high office, and in 1287 he was sent to Europe by the Īlkhān Arghun as Mongol ambassador (it was a Mongol custom to despatch envoys whom they thought might be acceptable to the recipients – in this case a Christian envoy was sent to Christian monarchs).

Rabban Ṣaumā, to judge from his narrative, was completely awed by what he found in Europe. This was essentially a religious wonderment. He seems to have been quite unaware that, strictly speaking, he was in Catholic eyes a heretic, and he was happy to acknowledge the pope as head of the church, and Europe as the headquarters of Christendom. In particular, he was overwhelmed by the wealth of religious relics to be found; he even persuaded a grudging Pope Nicholas IV to give him some to take back to Persia. Ṣaumā visited Constantinople, Naples, Rome, Genoa, Paris, and Gascony, and talked with kings, emperors, and cardinals wherever he went. But what can we deduce from all this? There is some vivid observation, fascinating

[30] See L. N. Gumilev, *Searches for an Imaginary Kingdom: the Legend of the Kingdom of Prester John*, tr. R. E. F. Smith (Cambridge 1987), and my review in *Journal of the Royal Asiatic Society* 1989/1, pp. 161–2.

because of its uniqueness. But it is doubtful that any wider conclusion can be drawn. Ṣaumā represented the Īlkhān diplomatically, but so far as his pro-European attitudes were concerned, if he represented anyone it was only a minority group, the Christians, in a vast Islamic sea: a group that had less than a decade of official favor left to it when Ṣaumā returned to Persia. It might be possible to speculate that we have in Ṣaumā's account of Europe a flavor of what might have happened had the Mongols been converted to Christianity, as at one time seemed possible. As Sir Richard Southern has commented, this "was a noble prospect, and one which, if only a fraction of it had come true, would radically have altered the history of the world."[31]

It did not happen, of course. Rabban Ṣaumā is very far from being a typical Persian of the Mongol period. Rashīd al-Dīn is nearer to being one, though he showed an untypical degree of interest in Europe even when he wrote his somewhat throwaway "History of the Franks." If the attitudes of those Persians in the Mongol Empire whose writings have come down to us are characteristic, the peoples of Asia were not, in the thirteenth and fourteenth centuries, on the way to being mentally prepared to deal with the expansion of Europe. Yet perhaps a caveat should be entered here. As we have seen, northwest Persia in the Ilkhanid period was very familiar to European, and especially Italian, merchants and churchmen. For the most part they have left us no record of their travels. But this does not necessarily mean that Persians who came into contact with them did not learn a good deal about Europe, or that what such travelers told people when they returned to Italy had no effect on contemporary European notions of the world.[32] "Ordinary" knowledge on both sides may conceivably have been rather more extensive than the surviving written evidence would lead us to suppose.

This is speculation, but one indication of possible contact at other than historiographical and diplomatic levels may be mentioned. The finest architectural memorial left by the Mongols in Persia is the mausoleum of the Īlkhān Öljeitü at his capital, Sulṭāniyya. Its most remarkable structural feature is its double-skinned dome; and it has been suggested that knowledge of this may have had an influence on the design of Brunelleschi's dome for Florence Cathedral, in many respects similar in construction, built around a century later. Direct evidence of a connection is of course wholly lacking, but it is perhaps not entirely inconceivable that Italians at the Ilkhanid capital might

[31] *Western Views of Islam in the Middle Ages* (Cambridge MA 1962), p. 65.
[32] See Morgan, *The Mongols*, pp. 195–8.

have taken home detailed knowledge of how the city's finest building had been designed.[33]

We shall probably never know with any degree of certainty, and it may after all be that Persian historians' lack of interest in Europe was not untypical of their compatriots. Perhaps they found that the Mongols were quite enough to have to cope with, and if that is so, who are we, whose ancestors through no virtue of their own escaped incorporation in the Mongol Empire, to blame them?

IV

What does all this tell us, in more general terms, about Persians' perceptions of themselves and of others? Did they, at this or at other times, see themselves as *Persians* (or, as they would have said, *īrānī*, Iranians), and if so, as opposed to what? What is certain is that there was no concept of national identity in the sense popularized by nineteenth-century Europeans, and that has ever since exercised so maleficent a worldwide influence. Nor was the notion of ethnic identity, which has torn apart what used to be Yugoslavia, something of which medieval Persians would have felt much understanding. But as I suggested at the beginning of this chapter, there is a Persian identity, based on cultural and linguistic continuity, that has in some sense survived for 2,500 years. Until very recently, many Persians, even if – perhaps especially if – illiterate, could recite from memory vast tracts of the great Persian epic poem, the *Shāh-nāma* of Firdawsī, which was written in the Islamic period but whose subject matter is the legendary and pre-Islamic Persian past and its heroes. The twentieth-century Pahlavi shahs, Reza Shah and his son Mohammed Reza, made much of this heritage, choosing to emphasize the Persian monarchical tradition and the glories of the Achaemenian and Sasanian empires, and deliberately downplaying the Islamic element. The ultimate fate of the Pahlavi regime should perhaps make us wonder, however, if this can really be the whole story.

It has indeed been suggested that if a Persian, say, a century ago, had been asked what he was, how he identified himself, he would probably have said that he was a Muslim. All very well, and likely to be true, but in what way, then, would he have differentiated himself from a fellow-Muslim in Egypt, Syria, Turkey, or India? – assuming, that is (a rather large assumption) that the question had occurred to

[33] For a discussion of the structural features of both domes, see R. J. Mainstone, *Developments in Structural Form* (London 1975), pp. 123–6.

him. From the sixteenth century the Persians had been distinguished from their immediate neighbors, especially from the Ottoman Turks and their subjects, by the fact that the official religion of Persia was Shīʿi Islam, as opposed to the Sunnism which was and remains the form of Islam professed by the great majority of Muslims. Western historians, in my view somewhat anachronistically, have often argued that the first Safavid shah, Ismaʿīl I (r. 1501–24) imposed Twelver Shīʿism on the Persian people *in order* to differentiate Persia from its hostile neighbors, the Ottomans and the Uzbeks, and to provide his subjects with a distinctive sense of identity. An improbably twentieth-century motivation; but whether intended or not, that was in fact the ultimate effect.

I conclude, then, that the Persian sense of identity was based on specifically "Persian" cultural elements, but was also very heavily influenced by Islam and the Islamic world-view. It has recently been suggested[34] that the period of Mongol rule may have played an important part in creating a sense of "Iran" that endured to modern times: But we need to remember that in Rashīd al-Dīn's history, the Mongol ruler who converted to Islam, Ghazan, is always *Pādishāh-i Islām*, the King of Islam, not of Iran. Hence the Mongols were acceptable once they became Muslims; the Europeans, who remained infidels, were not. I suspect that, as the Ayatollah Khomeini perceived, most Persians were usually Muslims first and Iranians second, and that this was the principal factor that determined their attitude toward other peoples.

[34] By Professor Bert Fragner, in an as yet unpublished paper.

CHAPTER 7

Sightings: Initial Nahua reactions to Spanish culture

JAMES LOCKHART

BEFORE speaking directly of how the Nahuas first viewed the Spaniards, I should mention that I have recently brought to a provisional conclusion a project of many years, the aim of which was to survey the cultural and social organization of the Nahuatl speakers of central Mexico over most of the three centuries after European contact, on the basis of records produced by themselves in their own language.[1] I have no intention of attempting to summarize the results in any detail, but since my examination of first-generation Nahua impressions of Spanish culture takes place within that larger context, I must say something on the subject.

One of the more central aspects of the work I have been doing (and in this I am supported by the findings of a different type of research by my predecessor Charles Gibson and my contemporary William Taylor)[2] is to highlight the extent of the similarities between the cultural systems of the Europeans and the Nahuas (probably the Mesoamericans generally). As a people with a sedentary life, intensive agriculture, dynastic rulers and tax systems, territorial polities, a well-developed religious apparatus of pantheon, priesthood, and ritual cal-

[1] James Lockhart, *The Nahuas After the Conquest: A Social and Cultural History of the Indians of Central Mexico, Sixteenth through Eighteenth Centuries* (Stanford: 1992).

[2] See especially Charles Gibson, *Tlaxcala in the Sixteenth Century* (New Haven: 1952) and *The Aztecs Under Spanish Rule: A History of the Indians of the Valley of Mexico, 1519–1810* (Stanford: 1964), and William B. Taylor, *Landlord and Peasant in Colonial Oaxaca* (Stanford: 1972) and *Drinking, Homicide and Rebellion in Colonial Mexican Villages* (Stanford: Stanford University Press, 1979). Also see Stephanie G. Wood, "Corporate Adjustments in Colonial Mexican Indian Towns: Toluca Region" (Ph.D. dissertation, UCLA, 1984); S. L. Cline, *Colonial Culhuacan, 1580–1600* (Albuquerque: University of New Mexico Press, 1986); Rebecca Horn, "Postconquest Coyoacan: Aspects of Indigenous Sociopolitical and Economic Organization in Central Mexico, 1550–1650" (Ph.D. dissertation, UCLA, 1989); Robert Haskett, *Indigenous Rulers: An Ethnohistory of Town Government in Colonial Cuernavaca*. (Albuquerque: University of New Mexico Press, 1991); and Matthew B. Restall, "The World of the *Cah:* Postconquest Yucatec Maya Society" (Ph.D. dissertation, UCLA, 1992).

endar associated with those polities, and social distinctions between nobles, commoners, and intermediate groups, the Nahuas had reasonably close analogues of the concepts structuring nearly all facets of European life. Each side was able to operate for centuries after first contact on an ultimately false but in practice workable assumption that analogous concepts of the other side were essentially identical with its own, thus avoiding close examination of the unfamiliar and maintaining its own principles. The truce obtaining under this partial misconception allowed for a long period of preservation of indigenous structures of all kinds while intercultural ferment went on gradually, hardly attaining the level of consciousness. I have called the phenomenon the process of Double Mistaken Identity.[3]

Within a broad comparability between the two cultures in contact, Nahuatl-language documents show us a world of well-defined indigenous concepts, far from identical with their closest Spanish parallels, embodied in special vocabulary; as a corpus these fixed ideas organized sociopolitical, economic, and household life (and art as well), often making large use of the principles of cellular subdivision, rotation, numerical ordering, and symmetry. Most of this lore and its vocabulary survived for more than a hundred years after the conquest, and large and basic parts were still operative at the time of Mexican independence. The Nahuas continued to be primarily self-centered, judging things within the framework they had developed for themselves, concerned above all with life inside the local ethnic states that had always been their primary arena. Yet they did not shy away from contact with things Spanish, readily adopting any new artifacts, practices, or principles that struck them as comprehensible and useful for their own purposes. Clearly they had maintained their balance past the cataclysms of first contact in a way that many less sedentary peoples, who had less cultural common ground with the intruders, did not. Every year brings us new monographs and philological publications further reinforcing the proposition that the postconquest Nahuas were self-centered realists and corporate survivors.

Surely they were the same people during the generation that first met and dealt with the arriving Spaniards. Yet the picture of the Na-

[3] First enunciated in James Lockhart, "Some Nahua Concepts in Postconquest Guise," *History of European Ideas*, 6 (1985): 465–82; also mentioned in Lockhart, *The Nahuas*, 445. A similar notion will be found in Richard White, *The Middle Ground: Indians, Empires, and Republics in the Great Lakes Region, 1650–1815*. (New York: Cambridge University Press, 1991) in relation to French-indigenous relations in the Great Lakes region in the seventeenth and eighteenth centuries; for a brief statement of his view, see p. x.

huas arising from the massive written evidence they produced in their own language stands in stark contrast to the reigning image of them during the first moments of contact. In the version dominant since at least the mid-nineteenth century, the indigenous inhabitants of central Mexico were overwhelmed and dumbfounded by the Spanish advent, immobilized by fear and fatalism, expecting the Spaniards to carry out prophecies of their own doom and the disappearance of their culture. I am convinced that this by now traditional view of the matter is illusory. No only does it go against my understanding of the Nahua nature, but it is very thinly documented. Most of the little evidence for it is posterior by at least a full generation, often more, and is found in texts that, I would maintain, reflect the backward-looking imperatives of the time of writing rather than the thinking of the contact generation.

But if positive evidence is slim and flimsy, evidence to the contrary has been equally lacking. My own work, and that of other scholars studying Nahuatl materials, perforce centers on the period when they were written: the late 1540s into the 1570s. That it would be the task of a generation for a Nahuatl orthography to be devised and for a critical mass of Nahuas to learn how to use it in actual recordkeeping is not surprising. It is more surprising, perhaps, that the surviving corpus of administrative and mundane documents in Spanish concerning central Mexico in the conquest period is also very slight; one is forced back upon a few chronicles and some reports of high officials, as stingy in mentioning Nahua ideas, attitudes, and motivations as they are unreliable and uninformed in the little they do say on such matters.

I do not mean, however, to rely on plausibility and deduction alone to throw light on initial Nahua reactions to Spanish culture, but will make every effort to find and analyze the most direct evidence available on the Nahua side, though it remains far less contemporary and multidimensional than what we have for later decades. To date I have found two main approaches to the Nahuas of the first generation beyond deduction from patterns obtaining in succeeding generations and use of statements by Spaniards. These approaches rest on quite different bodies of material and use distinct methodologies, so I will present my results in two separate parts before treating very briefly the question of how the two can be combined.

The first part takes the approach of examining the ways in which Spanish phenomena are described in the earliest Nahuatl texts and dictionaries. Though the materials originate at the very end of the first generation or even a bit later, they enable us to make a systematic reconstruction of the linguistic reaction of Nahuatl speakers. This is the one field of first-generation studies where I was able to make substantial inroads in the course of the larger project mentioned above. The section relating to language is indeed largely a summary of the relevant portion of Chapter 7 of my book, *The Nahuas after the Conquest* (Stanford, 1992). It asserts, in essence, that during the first postcontact generation the Nahuas hardly entered into the substance of Spanish culture at all, viewing it as a set of discrete sensually observable phenomena (mainly visually observable) to be integrated into their own conceptual-linguistic framework, in which no change is detectable. The denomination of Spanish things took place within the limits of the normal mechanisms of the Nahuatl language, not only in the same ways human beings in their languages have generally named new things, but the way they name anything at all, the way language evolves wherever and whenever it is spoken.

The second body of material bearing on the conquest generation is of a very different nature. It purports to speak directly of actions, speech acts, and emotions of the Nahuas during the first year or two after the arrival of the Spaniards in central Mexico. It is thus more obviously to the purpose, and as such has been copiously used by several generations of scholars; at the same time it is highly suspect, for the versions we have were written down at least a generation after the events and show many signs of legend formation, as well as other distortions – distortions, that is, if we are interested in Nahua reactions of 1520 or 1525, as opposed to the attitudes of certain Nahuas in certain places writing between 1545 and 1565 for the most part, and looking back to the events of the earlier period. The small literature of this type is dominated by Tenochtitlan, the leading power of the Triple Alliance of the Valley of Mexico, which in itself says a great deal about who reacted most intensely to the intrusion, and beyond that by writings of the Tlatelolca, the junior cousins and partners of the Tenochca and their immediate neighbors on an island base in Lake Tetzcoco. The single most well-developed and well-known account is Book 12 of Sahagún's Florentine Codex, composed by Tlatelolca under Sahagún's sponsorship, and it is that on which I will concentrate.

LANGUAGE AND VISION

One of my main strategies in attempting to establish the patterns of Nahua reaction to Spanish culture has been to comb through Nahuatl texts for the presence or absence of Spanish lexical items and Spanish-influenced phonological, syntactic, and semantic features.[4] What emerged from such surveying was an evolution proceeding across the centuries in three quite clear-cut stages. Stage 1 – about a generation (1519 to about 1540 or 1545) during which change in the Nahuatl language was minimal, in a sense entirely absent except for the incorporation of some Spanish proper names (of which the overwhelming majority were Christian names received at baptism). Stage 2 – nearly a hundred years (to about 1640–50) during which Spanish nouns were borrowed in large quantities and fully naturalized, and a certain amount of semantic change in Nahuatl vocabulary occurred in response to common Spanish words, but change was still restricted in scope. Only nouns came into Nahuatl, and native pronunciation and syntax remained unaffected. Stage 3 – the time from mid-seventeenth century until today, wherever Nahuatl is still spoken. The barriers fell, and Spanish influence penetrated all aspects of the language. Spanish verbs and function words came in, in addition to new types of nouns. Spanish idioms were translated. Syntax was now substantially affected, and Spanish sounds were acquired. Nahuatl was still Nahuatl, but now it could readily reproduce any Spanish notion, expression, or construction.

Looking across the sweep of this centuries-long process, the conclusion I draw is that Stage 1 corresponds to and in some sense is caused by a virtual absence of routine contact between the Nahuatl-speaking and the Spanish-speaking populations. Stage 2 corresponds to corporate contact, with a prominent role for interpreters and other intermediaries. Stage 3 corresponds to massive individual contact between the two populations, with concomitant widespread bilingualism. We could say then that Stage 1, however transcendent and earthshaking the events that accompanied it, brought very little cultural readjustment, Stage 2 involved significant corporate change, and Stage 3 saw pervasive changes centered on the individual.

Stages 2 and 3 are relatively easy to study, because of the exuberant, many-sided documentary legacy the Nahuas have left us. The prob-

[4] In the beginning, this effort was carried out in conjunction with Frances Karttunen; its main product was Frances Karttunen and James Lockhart, *Nahuatl in the Middle Years: Language Contact Phenomena in Texts of the Colonial Period*, University of California Publications in Linguistics, 85. (Berkeley and Los Angeles: University of California Press, 1976). Frances Karttunen, "Nahuatl Literacy," in George A. Collier et al., eds. *The Inca and Aztec States* (New York: Academic Press, 1982), 395–417, is a succinct and readable restatement, bringing out the chronological pattern more clearly than the earlier work. Chapter 7 of Lockhart, *The Nahuas*, goes back over the whole ground in considerable detail, on the basis of further research, not only restating but extending, supplementing, and updating.

lem in studying Stage 1 – indeed one might say the prima facie impossibility of it – can be succinctly stated: Alphabetic writing in Nahuatl is a Stage 2 phenomenon. Although one can remain in doubt, as I in fact have, just where in the years 1540–50 to place a rough boundary between Stages 1 and 2, and it is entirely plausible to imagine that the change took place in some subregions and with some individuals rather earlier than with others, precisely those Nahuas who began to write alphabetically were the ones who had entered the second stage.

Fortunately, one large exception exists. Considerable portions of a very early set of house-to-house censuses and tax inventories from the Cuernavaca jurisdiction (in the modern state of Morelos, south of the Valley of Mexico) have come down to us. Two substantial sections have been published in transcription and translation.[5] The records depart from the rule for Nahuatl alphabetic texts in several ways. They are written on indigenous paper, not the imported Spanish paper that was virtually universal by the later 1540s. Not only are they not assimilated to any Spanish documentary genre, they are without the date specification that is the common denominator of all Nahuatl mundane documentation. They are so early that they precede the integration of pictorial and alphabetic modes characteristic of writing in indigenous genres in early Stage 2. Estimates of their time of composition have fallen in the general range of 1535 to 1545 (they were not necessarily all done simultaneously, and some were maintained current for a time).[6] Very close to 1540 would be my own best guess, and one must keep in mind that the Spanish impact in the relatively isolated Cuernavaca region would have been less at that time than in the Valley of Mexico or the Tlaxcala-Puebla area, so that there is every likelihood that the texts represent a very early phase indeed of Nahuatl adaptation to the Spanish presence.

The language of the Cuernavaca censuses is, naturally enough, not very discursive or elaborate, but the corpus is so extensive that variety is not entirely lacking, and some conversations and discussions of exceptional situations do occur. What stands out is the general absence of Spanish words or constructions, aside from numerous proper

[5] Eike Hinz, Claudine Hartau, and Marie-Luise Heimann-Koenen, eds., *Aztekischer Zensus. Zur indianischen Wirtschaft und Gesellschaft im Marquesado um 1540: Aus dem "Libro de Tributos" (Col. Ant. Ms. 551) im Archivo Histórico, México,* 2 vols. (Hannover: Verlag für Ethnologie, 1983); S. L. Cline, ed. and tr., *The Book of Tributes: Early Sixteenth-Century Nahuatl Censuses from Morelos (Museo de Antropología e Historia, Archivo Histórico, Colección Antigua, vol. 549),* Nahuatl Studies Series, 4. (Los Angeles: UCLA Latin American Center Publications, 1993).

[6] See Cline, *Book of Tributes,* 8.

names, and the use of indigenous neologisms for the one or two Spanish phenomena that are central to the texts' subject matter.[7] The Cuernavaca censuses thus give us a pattern strongly contrasting with the great mass of Stage 2 Nahuatl documents, a base line from which we can measure the degree of change in later times and start to explore the characteristics of Stage 1.

The greatest single resource in approaching Stage 1 language strategies is the lexical work of fray Alonso de Molina, resident in the Mexico City area from childhood and one of the most productive of the Franciscan philologists. The definitive version of his great *Vocabulario*, the one most accessible from the date of its publication through the eighteenth century and on until today (and the one I have used), came out in 1571, years into Stage 2.[8] It was preceded, however, by an edition with only Spanish-to-Nahuatl entries published in 1555, relatively few years after the time I postulate for the transition between Stages 1 and 2. The 1555 edition contains the core of the later version, which does add and elaborate but rarely changes anything and drops little. The 1571 volume thus contains Nahuatl renderings of Spanish introductions from different time periods, sometimes in the same entry. The accretive process can be projected back to the genesis of the first edition, which must have taken many years to develop and then produce in print. Surely the collection of items must have begun in the mid-1540s, if not earlier.

Molina was one of the greatest Spanish masters of Nahuatl, spoken and written, in a time of intense indigenous-language philological activity in the mendicant orders. He did not write his dictionaries entirely by himself, however. Like all his colleagues, he relied heavily on native speakers as aides. It was essentially they who provided Nahuatl glosses of Spanish words in the project's first incarnation. Along with the cases where Nahuatl and Spanish semantics coincide reasonably – the great bulk – and a liberal sprinkling of Stage 2 Spanish loan vocabulary, one finds many entries in which new Spanish phenomena are rendered with Nahuatl vocabulary; these represent the best and most copious evidence on Stage 1 that is presently available. And despite the fact that all the different responses are side by side in the

[7] It is true that some Spanish vocabulary is found in the corpus, a good deal of it apparently involving code switching (i.e., going over briefly to Spanish) and some of it highly whimsical, deviant loans of a type that later times were to avoid. I judge these aspects to relate to the fact that the writers had been subjected to quite intensive instruction by Spanish ecclesiastics. See the discussions in Karttunen and Lockhart, *Nahuatl in the Middle Years*, 40–41, and Lockhart, *The Nahuas*, 284n.

[8] Fray Alonso de Molina, *Vocabulario en lengua castellana y mexicana y mexicana y castellana* (1571) (México: Porrúa, 1970).

same book, one can deduce something about sequence. Thus Nahuatl *maçatl*, "deer," the Stage 1 rendering of "horse," no longer appears as an independent word in that meaning in Molina, having been displaced before the time of publication by the popular Spanish loanword *caballo*, but it still is found in many compound words having to do with equine matters. From Molina alone we can confidently postulate a time when *maçatl* was dominant, entering into a large number of complex constructions as well as appearing independently. As an independent word it gave way quickly to the onslaught of loan nouns at the beginning of Stage 2, but held on for a time in larger constructions in which it had become embedded and was harder to replace.

The glosses proffered by Molina's aides can always be taken as in some sense authentic expressions of those particular speakers. But if we had the dictionary alone, we might wonder whether any of the expressions were ever current. Indeed, some have the earmarks of ad hoc solutions found for arcane words explained by Molina to the aides, probably never thought of again—thus for "corsair" *acalco tenamoyani*, "someone who robs people on boats."[9] A certain number of Stage 1 expressions took hold and stayed in the language for centuries, appearing in texts of all time periods and confirming Molina's material as to its currency, if not as to chronology. Mundane Nahuatl documents of the first decade or so after their appearance (circa 1545–55) are a great help because they contain, along with Stage 2 phenomena, native-vocabulary names for Spanish things identical with or similar to entries in Molina. With time, such expressions largely fade out in the documentary corpus, leaving us to deduce that they were vestigial in early Stage 2 documentation, left over from the preceding stage. All through the second half of the sixteenth century, certain (usually abstract, difficult, or exotic) loanwords in Nahuatl texts are routinely found accompanied by another version in Stage 1 style; by the seventeenth century such pairing becomes rare, revealing its nature as another aspect of the transition between stages. A most useful text is Book 12 of Sahagún's Florentine Codex, a narration of events taking place early in Stage 1. Direct speeches by the actors use Stage 1 expressions almost exclusively, whereas the narrators, who wrote at various times in Stage 2, readily use Spanish loanwords, even when speaking of the same things mentioned in other terms by the actors.[10]

We thus have ample reason to believe in the existence of a linguistic

[9] Ibid., Spanish to Nahuatl section, f. 31v.

[10] See James Lockhart, ed. and tr., *We People Here: Nahuatl Accounts of the Conquest of Mexico* (Berkeley and Los Angeles, University of California Press, 1993), introduction.

Stage 1, roughly the first generation after contact, going to approximately 1540 or 1545, and we have a fair amount of material elucidating its nature.

Presented with a Spanish introduction that was perceptibly different from anything known to them, the Nahuas of the first generation resorted to several devices doubtless already existing in their language (and common to virtually all languages, for that matter). The most straightforward strategy may be termed identification. That is, the new thing was simply called by the name of something similar, as though the two things were the same. As we have seen, horses were called deer; iron or steel was called *tepoztli*, "copper." Such identifications are open to various interpretations. They can be taken as metaphors that became frozen (and Nahuatl was full of metaphor, though the identifications are not of the normal Nahuatl type, in which a symmetrical pair of words stands for something not fully or directly named by either). They can be taken as extensions of meaning of a more normal type. The horse, like the deer, ate grass, had hooves and soulful eyes, and was notably fleet; surely, sharing so much, the creatures could share a name. Or the identifications can be taken as the result of imagining the Nahuatl word in its generic sense rather than its specific sense. "Maçatl" would mean ultimately fleet herbivorous quadruped, the deer happening to be the only example known in the vicinity of the Nahuas. Something of this nature is especially likely to have been involved with *tepoztli*, which by its etymology appears to have referred originally to metallic ores in general, and probably meant "workable nonprecious metal" before it meant "copper." Essentially no adjustment at all was required to apply it to iron and steel; it was used also for bell metal and the metal of printers' type.[11]

But as subtle and ambiguous as the background of identifications is, one aspect is clear. They bear no relation to the corresponding Spanish vocabulary; they are not interlinguistic and are barely intercultural. They rest on the direct perception of a phenomenon, the appellation of which was then formulated entirely within the framework of the Nahuatl language and the culture it bore. The great bulk of early Nahuatl linguistic reactions to the Spanish presence had the same character.

When the new phenomenon was perceived (following principles I have not yet managed to systematize) as too distinct from its local equivalent for a simple identification, one solution was to modify the word bearing the identity, noting both the sameness and the difference

[11] For a detailed treatment of the word see Lockhart, *The Nahuas*, 272–76.

(or rather one striking difference; a name had to be succinct to take hold). This type of construction I call a qualified identification. Spanish candles were quite similar to Nahua pine torches (*ocotl*) in their purpose and effect, but notably different in appearance and in other qualities. The expression the Nahuas hit upon and used for a time was *xicocuitlaocotl*, "beeswax torch."[12] The preconquest war club, inset with obsidian blades, was a *macquahuitl* (literally "stick in the hand"). A Spanish sword was called a *tepozmacquahuitl*, a "metal war club."[13] One of the most widely used and long-lasting expressions of this type was *tlequiquiztli*, "fire trumpet (horn, whistle)" for firearm.[14] Note that the emphasis falls on the sensory impression rather than on the lethal impact.

Direct description was another way to arrive at neologisms, but many such renderings suffered from excessive length and never found favor. An appropriately compact expression could sometimes be attained by indicating function, using Nahuatl's deverbal instrumental construction, the effect of which was something like English *-er*. Thus a key was a *tlatlapoloni*, an "opener," and a lock a *tlatzaqualoni*, a "closer."[15] Synecdoche also provided telling and usable expressions. A cart was a *quauhtemalacatl*, "wooden wheel," named after the outsized wheels that dominated the Spanish model.[16]

In language contact generally, grammar makes itself strongly felt. Nouns are the items most frequently borrowed; various kinds of constraints and morphological complexities impede other types of loans. Nahuatl in Stages 2 and 3 is an excellent example. But in the prelinguistic, hermetic Stage 1, there was nothing to keep neologisms from being verbs describing observed actions. The best known are from the religious sphere: *quaatequia*, "to pour water on someone's head," "to baptize"; *quailpia*, "to tie (a ribbon on) someone's head," "to confirm"; *tetlamaca*, "to give something to someone, to serve someone," "to give someone communion." The visuality, the lack of connection with the Spanish cultural framework and symbolic system, is especially clear here. In the same way, a characteristic Nahuatl expression (which

[12] Molina, *Vocabulario*, Spanish to Nahuatl, f. 24. Some of the most popular identifications may have begun with qualifications that were dropped in the name of streamlining once the new reference was sufficiently familiar. The expression for iron is sometimes found listed as *tliltic tepoztli*, "black copper" (ibid., Spanish to Nahuatl, f. 71), but in actual texts the modifier is hardly seen.

[13] Ibid., Spanish to Nahuatl, f. 59.

[14] See Lockhart, *The Nahuas*, 267–68.

[15] Molina, *Vocabulario*, Spanish to Nahuatl, ff. 34v, 79v.

[16] *Temalacatl* was itself a neologism in this sense, an identification with the round flat sacrificial stone of preconquest times. See Lockhart, *The Nahuas*, 268.

smacks of Stage 1 but cannot be tied to it with documentary evidence) was to "see" rather than "hear" mass.[17]

Language in general minimizes innovations, and Stage 1 Nahuatl was no different. Each successful neologism was used to the hilt, avoiding the necessity of further neologisms in that semantic vicinity. All the accoutrements of horses, firearms, carts, and the like were denominated by compounding the neologism with a familiar term, creating a complex of secondary qualified identifications. Thus a stable was a *maçacalli,* a "deer house," horseshoes *maçacactli,* "deer footwear," and so on.[18]

In every case, the Nahuas judged what they perceived by the criteria of their own culture, forcing the new into their own framework whether it fit well or not. A prime example is the Nahuatl reaction to European musical instruments. The Nahuas' two main categories were winds and drums, differentiated by two manners of performance, blowing and beating. These modes the Spaniards shared, but they also brought instruments in a new category, the strings (during the time period in question, plucked strings only). The Nahuas, however, recognized no new category. They took guitars and lutes to be drums, inventing a qualified identification for the purpose, *mecahuehuetl,* "cord drum," and to play such an instrument was called beating.[19]

The general impression of Stage 1 language adaptations is, as we have seen, of no properly linguistic contact at all. Yet the Nahuas were already picking elements of one type out of the to them meaningless chaos of Spanish speech: proper names. Even during the first generation, a large number of local people received baptism and along with it a Spanish Christian name. The mere introduction of a name, however, did not change the overall Stage 1 context; here too the story was much the same, of indigenous interpretation of something perceived within the existing framework. The Spanish personal names were opaque, not consisting of transparent lexical words like Nahuatl names, so they were close to simple sounds. Moreover, the Nahuas, as people of the world normally do in such situations, failed to hear those Spanish sounds that differed from their own, hence naturalized the names by pronouncing them with substitute sounds according to their own phonological system.

A few names of prominent Spaniards (and also the Spanish name of the famous indigenous interpreter Marina) appear to have become

[17] See ibid., 269–70.
[18] See these and other such terms in Molina, *Vocabulario,* Nahuatl to Spanish, f. 50.
[19] See Lockhart, *The Nahuas,* 281–83.

generally known around this time, as well as one very important place name, Castilla (Castile), the homeland of the outsiders. This too was brought within the local framework, for the Nahuas not only adapted the word to their own pronunciation, they found a place for it in Nahuatl morphology, identifying the last syllable with a common Nahuatl locative suffix. In Nahuatl the word became Caxtillan, with a *-atlan/ -lan* ending as in Tlaxcallan (Tlaxcala); from this form was derived *caxtiltecatl*, "inhabitant of Caxtillan" – that is, Spaniard. Caxtillan itself served mainly not as a place designation but as a prominent element in the general Stage 1 system of naming Spanish introductions. It was heaven sent as an all-purpose modifier for use in qualified identifications. (Its only remote rival was "tepoztli," "iron, metal," which could be used with all the many new metal artifacts the Spaniards brought.) *Caxtillan centli*, "Castile maize," for "wheat," was but one of a host of such constructions. It never ceases to bemuse me that the expression is virtually the same thing, seen from the other side, as the first formulation of the English in North America for maize: "Indian corn."[20]

The language of the first generation of Nahuas after contact, even and especially when dealing with contact phenomena, fully retained its normality and regularity. It used long-standing Nahuatl mechanisms and elements of the traditional lexicon to construct new expressions for things emanating from the Spaniards that were deemed worthy of notice. The interpretation came entirely from the Nahuas; each new thing was denominated and described in relation to existing words and concepts, as a discrete item within the unchanged indigenous framework, as with the "string drums," unaffected by the Spanish interpretive frame. The raw materials for the new lore being formed were not understood Spanish words and instructions but direct sensory impressions, visual or sometimes aural.

WRITING, SEEING, AND THE CONQUEST

If reconstructing the general Nahuatl linguistic reaction to the Spanish presence in the first generation requires a great deal of detective work, the conditions for discovering their more specific view of the Spaniards and the Spaniards' actions during the conquest epoch are even less propitious.[21] It is notorious that opinions on cataclysmic events –

[20] See ibid., 275–79.

[21] Much of the following section parallels portions of the introduction to Lockhart, *We People Here*, often summarizing or casting in a different light according to the present purpose, but in several cases entering into more detail.

not only value-judgments and interpretive frameworks, but also beliefs about the narrative skeleton of what happened – evolve drastically during succeeding decades. As we have seen, Nahuatl alphabetic writing did not mature as a vehicle capable of capturing conquest narratives until twenty or twenty-five years after contact. And complex conquest narratives did not necessarily blossom the moment the technical capacity to write them came into existence. One important text, the annals of Tlatelolco, may date from around 1545, some twenty-five years after the events related, but most relevant writings are the product, in their present form, of the 1560s and 70s, and that includes the most formidable and well known of all the conquest narratives, Book 12 of Sahagún's Florentine Codex.[22]

The main preconquest historical genre, by all indications, was a form that can reasonably be called annals, organized by calendar year in the indigenous system, invariably taking the home *altepetl* or local ethnic state as the arena (some hundreds of entities of this type made up the Nahua world). Dates and names were reliably expressed through pictographic writing, and some other conventional glyphs, aided by direct depiction, hinted at events and conversations which had to be kept in the recorder's mind for full oral presentation. Pictorial documents with an oral component continued to be produced after the conquest and even on into the time of alphabeticism. The writers of the very first alphabetic documents, of which very few examples remain, did not yet know how to incorporate the pictorial element. After some years, however, a mode of doing annals evolved in which the pictorial component, though stylistically affected by European artistic techniques, was somewhat as in preconquest times, accompanied by an alphabetic text transcribing the oral component. In this form, annals writing took hold all over central Mexico in the second half of the sixteenth century, and several texts have been preserved. They are of special interest in that they are in an indigenous genre and were written by indigenous people on their own initiative and for their own purposes, without the Spanish encouragement that was at least a factor in the evolution of Nahuatl notarial records or the actual Spanish supervision seen in the production of ecclesiastical texts in Nahuatl.[23]

In general, however, such annals tell us quite little about Nahua views of the conquest, or rather, perhaps, they tell us much by what they fail to say. They are usually much more concerned with precon-

[22] See ibid., introduction.
[23] For a study of the annals genre, see Lockhart, *The Nahuas*, 376–92.

quest than with postconquest happenings; their central purpose is the exaltation of the local altepetl, its legacy, and its rights, especially in relation to neighboring indigenous groups. Not much is made of the Spanish conquest, nor is ink lavished on the Spaniards. Portrayal of the countrywide aspect of the campaign and subsequent transformations is weak or entirely lacking. The Spaniards receive mention primarily as they physically move into or past that particular altepetl and later as they bring about changes in the jurisdictional arrangements of the altepetl or alter its tribute arrangements. Both types of changes were, and were seen as, adjustments in already existing systems. The introduction of the Christian sacraments is also recorded, again in relation to that particular entity, generally without comment (overt authorial comment was not indeed a normal part of annals style). Most postconquest entries continue to have to do with the installation, removal, or death of local altepetl authorities, and with other local news, a good deal of it meteorological, astronomical, or epidemiological. The overall impression is of a continuation of the preconquest entity and its autonomous governance. Concern with the Spaniards and their doings is minimal, limited to direct impact on the local entity.[24]

We must remember that in most parts of Nahua in central Mexico, what passes for conquest involved at most brief skirmishing or no hostilities at all, and a large body of Spaniards was present for a few days or never. Small wonder that most of the Nahuas were not moved to write at length about the first phase of Spanish contact. Prolonged, bitterly contested combat and catastrophic defeat were seen only in the immediate vicinity of Tenochtitlan and its junior partner (and rival) Tlatelolco, the two island altepetl in Lake Tetzcoco which were the base of the Mexica (known to many as the Aztecs). It is only in Tenochtitlan/Tlatelolco that we find major Nahuatl historical writings narrating in some detail the events of the conquest, especially, of course, events involving the Mexica themselves (for as we will see, these texts share the overwhelmingly local orientation of the rest).

The three most salient Mexica sources are very unequal in extent and unbalanced by provenience. Book 12 of Sahagún's Florentine Codex, a full-scale treatment of how the Spaniards overcame the Mexica, is more bulky than all the rest of the relevant Nahuatl literature put together. The annals of Tlatelolco, the second most extensive source, are mainly preconquest in subject matter, with only one substantial

[24] See the excerpts from the annals of Cuauhtinchan and Cuauhtitlan in Lockhart, *We People Here*, and the comments on them in the introduction.

section devoted to the conquest and after. The Codex Aubin, primarily postconquest, contains only some suggestive fragments.[25] The two more copious texts are both from Tlatelolco, perhaps because the Tlatelolca were so intent on denying their lesser status compared with the Tenochca (a major thrust of their writings), but perhaps also because Tlatelolco was the epicenter of the massive campaign in Nahuatl philology carried on by the Franciscan order in central Mexico. Book 12 was done under frankly Spanish auspices and even ostensibly in a Spanish genre. The annals of Tlatelolco approach the traditional indigenous form more closely and bear no overt indications of Spanish participation, but given the place and the apparent time of writing, Franciscan influence must virtually be assumed. The third text, the Codex Aubin, is Tenochca; it was done independently of Spanish sponsorship, although the writer had close connections with the Franciscans. Much of the material of Book 12 was apparently first put on paper in the 1550s; it continued to evolve, however, not taking the exact form in which we know it until the 1570s. The annals of Tlatelolco, the earliest of the whole corpus, may, as mentioned above, be dated around 1545. The Codex Aubin was not begun until the 1560s; the conquest portion is material then circulating in some form that the writer collected and reproduced to all appearances quite uncritically.

The corpus left to us, then, is late, tainted with Spanish influence and participation, and comes mainly from groups atypical not only of the mass of Nahuas spread around the country in their various less affected altepetl, but atypical even of the Mexica, among whom Tenochtitlan was dominant and much larger than Tlatelolco (as it continued to be after the conquest). Yet we must use what we have, and indeed there is no reason to despair. The Mexica were, after all, Nahuas, with the same proud localism and self-absorption as the rest,

[25] Details in ibid., introduction. See also fray Bernardino de Sahagún, *Florentine Codex: General History of the Things of New Spain*, trans. by Arthur J O. Anderson and Charles E. Dibble, 13 pts. (Salt Lake City, Utah, and Santa Fe, New Mexico: University of Utah Press and School of American Research, Santa Fe, 1950–82), especially pt. 13 (Book 12), and Sahagún, *Códice Florentino*. MS 218–220 de la colección Palatina de la Biblioteca Medicea Laurenziana, facsimile edition, 3 vols. (Florence: Giunti Barbera and the Archivo General de la Nación, 1979), as well as *Historia de la nación mexicana*, ed. by Charles E. Dibble (México: Porrúa, 1963), "Unos Annales Históricos de la Nacion Mexicana. Teil I. Die Handschrift nebst Übersetzung," ed. by Ernst Mengin, *Baessler-Archiv: Beiträge zur Völkerkunde*, 22. (Berlin: Dietrich Reimer, 1939), and "*Unos Annales Históricos de la Nacion Mexicana.*," ed. by Ernst Mengin, Corpus Codicum Americanorum Medii Aevi, vol. 2 (Copenhagen: Einar Munksgaard, Det Berlingske Bogtrykkeri, 1945). Some other Nahuatl texts from the region have passages or sections bearing on the conquest; it is not my intention to be exhaustive.

and though they bore the brunt of the Spanish attack and were the great losers, and hence cared much more intensely about the process, many facets of their attitudes, reactions, and general outlook must have been widely shared. And if Spanish friars had something to do with the records being put in alphabetic form, still evidences of authentic indigenous forms, impulses, and expressions abound. They are especially clear where a tension exists between Spanish aims and what is to be found in the Nahuatl texts.

Sahagún wanted to cap his great enterprise of an encyclopedia of preconquest culture with a volume on the conquest of Mexico, partly, as he explains, so that things unknown to Spaniards would be told, and partly to record the Nahuatl vocabulary of war. His vision clearly embraced at least all of central Mexico, as shown in one of the Spanish titles he composed for Book 12; in a spirit of realism, however, he qualified the broader thrust, admitting that the story concerned Mexico City.[26] But what we read in the body of the book is not even that broad; things Tlatelolcan are given the majority of the space, and the perspective is Tlatelolcan in the most pervasive manner, to the point that the Tenocha appear in a negative light more often than not. One of Sahagún's purposes, part of Franciscan political posturing, was to exalt the figure of Hernando Cortés, leader of the conquest. Yet Cortés is mentioned much less frequently in the Nahuatl than in Sahagún's Spanish translation. Sahagún had in mind the Spanish chronicles of the conquest; it was because of their influence that the work had a title at all, and he cut up the text into titled chapters following the same model. But even a cursory examination of the text shows that it existed in a more fluid form before Sahagún inserted the chapter divisions, which often conflict with the course of the narrative. One chapter break divides a war cry in two; at one point, a long chapter contains several separate major episodes.[27]

A search in Book 12 for things congruent with the results of the general linguistic inquiry sketched here will not go unrewarded. Visuality, pragmatism, normal processes, the retention of the traditional framework are all found here as well. All older Nahuatl narrative known to us, if indeed narrative is the term, is episodic, consisting of a series of fully realized scenes rather than an even, connected flow of events. Book 12 is the same, and the manner of bringing the scenes to life is highly visual. It is, of course, the scenes involving Spaniards that most interest us here.

[26] Sahagún, *Códice Florentino*, Book 12, unnumbered introductory folios and f. 1.
[27] See Lockhart, *We People Here*, introduction.

One very suggestive episode takes place toward the end of the Spanish campaign against the Mexica, when the latter were hemmed into an enclosure on the north end of the island holding both Tenochtitlan and Tlatelolco. Unable to come to grips, the Spaniards resorted to a device of siege warfare with which they had little experience, a catapult. Book 12 tells how they set it up on an altar platform, gesticulating to one another to show where to aim it, then placed in a stone, drew the arm back, and shot, missing the target. Thereupon, as the arm went back and forth like a pendulum until it righted itself, the Spaniards angrily jabbed their fingers in one another's faces. Seeing the operation of the instrument, the Mexica hit upon calling it a *quauhtematlatl*, a "wooden sling," a typical qualified identification as treated above.[28] Here, then, the Nahuas were by no means privy to the discussions of the Spaniards; they watched from afar, drawing their own conclusions from what they saw, on the presumption that the Spaniards were like themselves. This purely visual and deductive interpretation of Spanish actions, cast in words, represents the entire rendering of the episode, and so it is with a great many others. Sometimes the visuality (and aurality) are even more pronounced than in the first example, and the culture-free perceptions more noticeable. The passage on the first horses to enter Tenochtitlan does indeed mention the high-spirited prancing, rearing, and neighing associated in the European tradition with the noble steed, but it goes further, putting things in a quite different light by fastening on the holes made in the ground every time a horse puts its foot down, the noise like throwing stones when several go by, and their sweat lathering up so that it falls to the earth like soapsuds splatting.[29] Many passages are tinged with pragmatism. Observing the action of Spanish guns and crossbows, the text graphically describes their effect on indigenous boats and on individuals, distinguishing, though, between types of wounds as to their likely mortality, and goes on to explain how the Mexica soon began to zigzag, to hit the ground, and to clear out entirely when they could see a cannon (*huei tlequiquiztli*, "big fire trumpet") was about to go off.[30]

My belief is that passages like these, that give the tone to the entire core of Book 12 on the siege proper, represent authentic oral tradition

[28] Nahuatl text and a translation in Sahagún, *Florentine Codex*, pt. 13, 113. Also in Lockhart, *We People Here*.

[29] Nahuatl text and a translation in Sahagún, *Florentine Codex*, pt. 13, 40. Also in Lockhart, *We People Here*.

[30] Nahuatl text and a translation in Sahagún, *Florentine Codex*, pt. 13, 86. Also in Lockhart, *We People Here*.

preserved in relatively unchanged form from the time of events. Only someone who had actually been there and seen (though not heard) could, it seems, have originated such an item as the story of the catapult. The language of these sections is a relatively normal colloquial Nahuatl different from the elaborately repetitive style of so many parts of the Sahaguntine corpus. As I will have occasion to mention again, it is in those parts of the Florentine Codex which are most European in genre, or where we have other reasons to suspect that Sahagún or his trained Nahua aides/transcribers/authors intervened more directly, that this easily recognizable style makes its appearance.

The Stage 1 aura of the language of the siege sections (with a splendid example in the already mentioned name for the catapult) is another piece of evidence pointing to their eyewitness nature. A hierarchy is observable. Direct quotes from the actors are in a virtually impeccable Stage 1 Nahuatl. Third-person narrative is mainly the same, and does contain typical qualified identifications as opposed to loans, not only "wooden sling" for catapult and "fire trumpet" for firearm, but "metal war club" for sword, "metal dart" for crossbow bolt and by synecdoche for crossbow, and others. Yet the writers do not hesitate to insert loanwords of their own time (Stage 2) into their narrative. Thus the narrative usually says *caballo*, "horse," whereas the actors in direct speech always say *maçatl*, "deer."[31] In fact however, "deer" occurs a couple of times in the third person narrative as well. When I first noticed the distinction between narrative and direct speech, I thought it meant that the writers were aware of the distinction between Stage 1 and Stage 2 and showed it in the speeches they composed for the actors. I have not given up that view of the matter entirely, but I increasingly think that the Stage 1 phenomena originated primarily with the Nahuas who, whether eyewitnesses or not, were possessed of the oral tradition going back to the events. The aides would have felt freer to use their own normal vocabulary in narrative than in direct address (on the exact and unabbreviated reproduction of which the whole Nahuatl tradition lays stress). The Stage 2 words in the narrative would thus be a superficial overlay, explaining the largely Stage 1 feel of the text.

Ironically, in view of the degree of visuality of the core of the alphabetic text, the pictorial component of Book 12, though extensive, gives every indication of not being the primary, generative kind of element that it was in the older Nahua recordkeeping system. The pictures (incorporating some glyphs) deserve study from many points

[31] See ibid., introduction, and Lockhart, *The Nahuas*, 283–84.

of view, study they have not yet received and which I am hardly equipped to give them, but it is already clear enough that they were made by someone who was inspired by the text, rather than having existed first, with the text as an extended commentary upon them. My contention may be a bit hard to demonstrate conclusively. The fact that the pictures contain virtually nothing not in the text and sometimes echo relatively peripheral textual details can be interpreted in various ways. Most convincing is the fact that an earlier version of Book 12, minimally different from it in its alphabetic text, lacks illustration entirely.[32] Together with the annals of Tlatelolco and the corpus of early censuses from the Cuernavaca region, it hints at something we have only begun to realize, that the first alphabetic productions in Nahuatl were not yet accompanied by pictures.

There may well have been a pictorial-oral version produced by Tlatelolcans themselves in the years immediately after the events, and they may have drawn on it when in the 1550s they told their tales to Sahagún's aides, who wrote down some amalgam of what they heard and what they might have said themselves. But if pictures corresponding to the strong visuality of the perceptions had their part in the generation of the alphabetic text, they are now lost to us and escape analysis.

Impressive though it is to find visuality so resoundingly confirmed in the largest of the Nahuatl conquest accounts, one must ask if the lesser versions are the same. In fact, they are not exactly the same. Although the annals of Tlatelolco and the Codex Aubin do contain a revealing visual detail here and there, picturing is not among the main techniques used. These texts are, however, episodic, to an even larger degree than Book 12. The way they realize scenes is primarily through dialogue. One result is an even greater emphasis on the Nahua linguistic, rhetorical, and conceptual framework and more attention to internal matters. In both texts, a good deal of the conversation revolves around internecine struggle, pushing the Spaniards yet further into the background than they are in Book 12. In none of the texts is curiosity about the newcomers the driving force; primary interest in all cases falls on one's own group and how it fared in a context that, it is true, included the Spaniards as a major new factor. In the lesser texts, the Spaniards appear to a large extent through their words. But the words are not in Spanish; they have been translated into Nahuatl, whether by the Spaniards' ubiquitous interpreter doña Marina or by

[32] The so-called Codices matritenses. See Sahagún, *Florentine Codex*, pt. 1, 11–12.

someone else, and no doubt they have been further naturalized in the process of retelling. The speeches of Cortés and others in the annals of Tlatelolco – and there are not many of them – sound very much like the utterings of the Nahuas. By the time they reach Nahua awareness, they have been transformed into idiomatic, expectable Nahuatl statements, much as the visual data were interpreted, and little of anything that is specific to Spanish culture and language adheres to them. Whether the Spanish phenomena were aural or visual, words, actions, or things, they first came to Nahua attention in neutral terms shared by both populations and both cultures (else they could not have been perceived at all), and then were immediately given meaning by being placed within Nahua interpretive frames, hence changed and naturalized. Even if some of the interpreters of the first generation had an excellent understanding of both languages, which is far from impossible, no means yet existed to render culture-specific Spanish meanings and modes into Nahuatl.

The system of identifying corporate groups, whether one's own, other indigenous groups, or the Spaniards, is the same in all three of the Mexica texts we are discussing (and indeed in the whole corpus of annals and in all the documents Nahuas generated in the sixteenth century). A blanket term for indigenous people as opposed to Spaniards, Europeans, or Old World inhabitants in general is essentially missing. That such should have been the case before contact and knowledge of the existence of the rest of humanity is understandable and predictable. The arrival of the Spaniards, as in so much else, failed to bring about a quick change in the indigenous way of viewing this matter. Only in the Florentine Codex does one find any terms at all attempting to describe the generality of the indigenous population of central Mexico in contradistinction to Spaniards, and they are used only a few times, as a last resort, when the turn of the narrative renders it imperative to find some word for the distinction. Considered strictly, there is only one such term, occurring a grand total of three times: *nican titlaca,* literally "here we-people," best translated perhaps as "we people here" or "we local people." The term *macehualtin,* "commoners," originally "human beings," is more frequent, with the clear implication that an indigenous, non-Spanish population is being spoken of, but it is always limited in its scope to the inhabitants of a specific altepetl or small ethnic realm.

It is the altepetl (or to a much lesser extent its constituent parts) that defines indigenous identity, as in precontact times, despite the Spanish presence. References to any larger ethnic or linguistic affiliation are very rare and mainly limited to enemies and (indigenous) foreigners.[33] Book 12 does recognize the subordinated language group the Otomis, interspersed among the Nahuas in many parts of central Mexico, over and above altepetl organization. There are some terms for the inhabitants of whole regions, such as the *tlatepotzteca*, the "people from behind (the mountains), or the *chinampaneca*, "the people of the chinampa area." Overwhelmingly, though, indigenous groups are described by the altepetl name, whether there be only one or a whole list is needed. The altepetl is also the criterion for assigning the all-important "we" and "they," "we" being citizens of our altepetl and "they" all others, whether Spanish or indigenous.

The Spaniards, on the other hand, are specifically recognized and named in all the texts. In the Florentine Codex they uniformly receive the (apparently Stage 2) appellation *españoles*, the Spanish loanword. In the other texts, as in the sixteenth-century Nahuatl corpus generally, they are variously called: *caxtilteca*, "inhabitants of Caxtillan (Castile, Spain)"; *Caxtillan tlaca*, "Castile people"; *cristianos*, (the loanword) "Christians." Of these, the first two appear to be the oldest, bearing the signs of Stage 1 processes. Everything points to the Nahuas' having granted the Spaniards a name and identity from a very early time. The question is, what sort of identity was it? Since there was no overarching indigenous identity, there is no reason to imagine that the new category was a matching overarching intrusive or alien identity.

[33] One apparently very large exception will take a bit of explaining. An altepetl group was in itself an ethnic group, with cultural idiosyncrasies, its own history, and an awareness of itself as a people. It might, however, share much of its earlier history with the people of other altepetl. A unitary conquering group might take over and refound several contiguous altepetl, or found one from which segments would repeatedly hive off, and the whole set would recognize an affinity and share a supra-altepetl name. Thus several altepetl of the western and southwestern part of the Valley of Mexico referred to themselves as Tepaneca. Several such macro-groups existed in the Valley, of which Book 12 and the other Mexica texts make no mention. The most famous such group, however, consisted precisely of the Mexica, who are mentioned on almost every page. The Mexica merit supra-altepetl status because their island stronghold came to harbor such a formidable population, and above all because there were two Mexica altepetl, Tenochtitlan and Tlatelolco, the latter having left the rest and established a separate polity on the northern part of the island after a factional dispute early in the group's history. Yet since all the Mexica were confined to one compact island in Lake Tetzcoco, they hardly seem to qualify as a macroethnic group in most senses. In any case, in the two Tlatlelolcan texts which dominate the corpus of conquest narratives, one can detect a tendency to narrow the meaning once again. When the texts talk of the Mexica, more often than not they in fact mean the Tenochca, by the same process by which the United States tends to appropriate "American." Moreover, when the Tlatelolca call themselves Mexica, they seem more than anything else to be trying to cash in on Tenochca prestige.

The key, I think, is in the fact that, as already mentioned, the Nahuas of the contact period assimilated the Spanish word Castilla to their own altepetl names, producing Caxtillan and from it *caxtiltecatl* on the model of the names for many altepetl whose names ended *-tlan*/*-lan*. In effect, the Spaniards were viewed as constituting one more among many altepetl groups. The internal divisions, regional and otherwise, that were so important to the Spaniards themselves went unrecognized in Nahua categorization, just as the newcomers on the other side put all the indigenous people in their single category of *indios*. Nahuatl terminology did not set up a dichotomy between indigenous people and new arrivals or outsiders but retained the already existing dichotomy between members of the altepetl and all others, putting the Spaniards essentially on the level of a single, if powerful, altepetl group. No better expression of this view could be found than Book 12's frequent expression *toyaohuan*, "our enemies," which includes Spaniards and their indigenous allies alike.[34]

None of the conquest texts, neither those originating among the Mexica nor those from the rest of central Mexico, neither those made partially under Spanish supervision nor those written entirely independently and on indigenous initiative, contain any overt moralizing about the Spaniards of the kind prevalent among modern observers. This fact may be partly attributable to the noncommittal style of Nahuatl annals writing in general. But it also seems to result from the same attitude noticed before, of simply observing what the Spaniards do and drawing conclusions within one's own cultural expectations, on the unspoken assumption that the people observed are much like oneself. The texts speak in quite graphic detail of some Spanish massacres and of the execution of some Mexica leaders after the conquest, but in the same way and apparently the same spirit they tell of the Mexica capturing, sacrificing, and dismembering Spaniards. In Book 12, when defeat is near, the Mexica leaders consult about how much and what kind of tribute they should pay, taking it for granted that the Spaniards would want the same thing as the result of a martial victory that they would themselves; and they were right. I do not mean to say that Spanish warfare made no impression on the Mexica; it surely did. Especially, the first unexpected attack on the assembled celebrants during the Toxcatl festivities, the true beginning of the war between the Spaniards and the Mexica, seems to have left an indelible impression. As we will see, all three Mexica accounts essentially begin

[34] More detail and precise references on the terminology in the section just above in Lockhart, *We People Here*, introduction.

with that episode, which in the Codex Aubin is the occasion for the only full-page picture accompanying the conquest section.

In what has been said until now, I have been withholding discussion of one section of the corpus that I view as anomalous within it, although precisely that portion has been definitive in the rise of the general conception of the first Nahua reactions to the Spaniards. The commonly mentioned omens, prophecies, visions, belief in a Cortés as the returning god Quetzalcoatl, and a hopeless fatalism on the part of the indigenous people, especially Moteucçoma, all essentially go back to the first eighteen chapters of Book 12. They received their introduction to the modern world primarily through William Prescott and have been common currency ever since, not only in the public mind but in the writings of serious scholars in several disciplines. Only in the last few years has a reaction set in.

Prescott recounts some of the omens as simple historical fact, mentions the expected Quetzalcoatl several times, and above all homes in on Moteucçoma: "If we cannot refuse our contempt for the pusillanimity of the Aztec monarch, it should be mitigated by the consideration, that his pusillanimity sprung from superstition."[35] Book 12 of the Florentine Codex decisively shaped Prescott's thinking; though several other sources are mentioned in this connection, some of them derive from Book 12, and it was to that text that Prescott openly gave precedence in the matter of determining indigenous attitudes.[36] Most of his references go to the early chapters.[37] Prescott did not, of course, know Nahuatl, nor have most of the followers of his example, using Sahagún's Spanish paraphrase instead, but in this case the language aspect affects the results little, for the Spanish faithfully reproduces the essence of what the Nahuatl says, in terms of substance (not, needless to say, in terms of language-specific concepts and semantic ranges).

A second and more recent example is the work of Tzvetan Todorov, whose writing is far more sophisticated than Prescott's narrative, but rests on the same materials and makes much the same epistemological assumptions.[38] Todorov recognizes that the omens and the tales of the

[35] William H. Prescott, *History of the Conquest of Mexico and History of the Conquest of Peru* (New York: The Modern Library, n.d.), 438.

[36] Ibid., 280, n. 19, has "perhaps the most honest Aztec record of the period is to be obtained from the volumes, the twelfth book, particularly, of father Sahagun, embodying the traditions of the natives soon after the Conquest."

[37] See especially the fatalistic speeches on ibid., 289, with a note to chapter 13 of Book 12.

[38] Tzvetan Todorov, *The Conquest of America: The Question of the Other* (New York: Harper & Row, 1984).

trembling Moteucçoma are posterior, but he proceeds nevertheless to use them to interpret thoughts and actions at the time of the conquest, especially, again, in relation to Moteucçoma himself. His rationale is that though a given fact in a presentation of this type may not be literally true, it must have verisimilitude. I have no objection to this principle in many contexts, and I have often used it myself, especially in deducing the nature of basic, repeating patterns. But it will not serve across genres and across generations, and it is weakest in dealing with specific exceptional episodes. Verisimilitude amounts to meeting expectations, which would be one thing in a testament, another in annals; even within annals, expectations would be one thing in realistic battle reports and another in symbol-charged, legendary material like the first part of Book 12. And what an audience will accept as literally true for its own time is not the same as what it will believe about a time two generations back. I do take the introduction of Book 12 as full of meaning for Mexica attitudes and rationales two and three generations after the conquest, but that is quite another topic.

Todorov seems to have realized that the great majority of the inhabitants of central Mexico interacted and communicated meaningfully with the Spaniards in their own at least temporary self-interest, but he ignores them, basing everything on the exceptional Mexica alone, clearly because of their relatively large written legacy. Beyond following in the tradition of Prescott, Todorov attempts stylistic and other kinds of textual interpretation. Here lack of knowledge of the language and of its genres and conventions becomes a handicap. In Todorov's view, Spaniards were more adept in communicating with people than were the Nahuas, whose intercommunication was dominated by rigid ritualized statements of received lore.[39] Leaving aside the Spaniards (in effect, Todorov takes the Spaniards and especially Cortés at face value about what great communicators they were), the Nahuatl speeches of Book 12 do not have the implications that Todorov imagined. One could as well say that having things written down and solidified in books hampered the Spaniards. First of all, the set speeches of Book 12 do not imply that other modes of discourse did not exist; the Nahuas had a full panoply of discourse genres, including some notably straightforward, unambivalent, unadorned speech. The Mesoameri-

[39] Ibid., 123, asserts that indigenous people felt no need to impose their language on other groups. How does Todorov imagine that Nahuatl had come to be the dominant language of central Mexico? Even the Nahuatl annals tell of barbarous peoples learning Nahuatl along with civilization. On the other side, how is it that Portuguese, Galician, Catalan, and Basque coexist with Castilian in Iberia?

cans in general were masters of talking to each other. The reader of Tezozomoc's *Crónica mexicana* will soon see that preconquest wars consisted of singing, shouting, and blustering at the other side, a brief test of arms, and the weaker side subsequently running to high places and negotiating endlessly with the other.[40] Even within the ritualistic and frozen forms so full of elaborate conventions, communication goes on, for those who understand the system. Each speech is different from the last in its details, each abbreviates, expands, shades according to the situation and the audience. The Nahuas were as rhetorical as the old Greeks, sharp and subtle, in control, not overwhelmed by the formulas they manipulated so well.

It is true enough that a rhetoric must be understood within its own framework, by people accustomed to its conventions, and that outsiders may not grasp the subtleties. The problem surely existed with communication in both directions between Nahuatl and Spanish. One of the most transcendent impressions the Spaniards received (or claimed to have received) from the Mexica, that Moteucçoma was voluntarily handing over his kingdom to Cortés, may have originated in a too literal interpretation of a polite convention. When a king or other high dignitary visited a foreign altepetl, the ruler of the latter greeted the visitor with a speech that in another tradition might be taken as fawning, picturing himself and his people as dust beneath the visitor's feet and the visitor as a majestic high tree overshadowing all else and protecting all around it. The visitor would be granted all facilities, virtually be offered the realm. Within the Nahua framework, this performance was anything but fawning. Not only was it simply the polite and expected thing, but the extravagance of the speech and the gestures accompanying it were actually meant in a sense to put the visitor to shame with their magnificence.[41] If the translator doña Marina was at all literal in her renderings, it would be small wonder that the Spaniards could reach the conclusion that Moteucçoma was giving them the empire on a platter. Even when we look at the welcoming

[40] Don Hernando [Fernando] de Alvarado Tezozomoc, *Crónica mexicana* (together with *Códice Ramírez*, both introduced by Manuel Orozco y Berra), 2d. ed. (México: Porrúa, 1975), passim.

[41] *The Art of Nahuatl Speech: The Bancroft Dialogues*, ed. by Frances Karttunen and James Lockhart, UCLA Latin American Center Nahuatl Studies Series, 2 (Los Angeles: UCLA Latin American Center Publications, 1987) contains some speeches somewhat in this vein; others are in Sahagún, *Florentine Codex*, pt. 7 (Book Six). In *The Art of Nahuatl Speech*, see especially (154–55) the episode in which a Tetzcocan woman refers to a splendid feast prepared for a grand occasion as putting the Mexica to shame. The ceremonial inversion of meanings was a strong element in formal Nahuatl speech (see ibid., 43–45).

speech as reproduced in the first part of Book 12, where after decades of legend formation Moteucçoma's intention is (apparently) actually to hand over the altepetl to the rulership of a returning divinity, one could change a very few words and have a normal welcoming address. Indeed, with the usual expectations and allowing for maximum hyperbole, one could still read the speech that way.[42]

The welcoming address comes toward the end of the preliminary part of Book 12, before the fighting between Mexica and Spaniards begins. It is precisely this section that has, at least until the last few years, been definitive in determining modern commentators' views of early indigenous reactions to the intruders. Yet, in my opinion, it does not have the same status as the rest of the account, which by all indications substantially represents a tradition carried down by eyewitnesses and their successors from the time of the events. Rather it is the result of posterior reinterpretation and reconstruction, an explanatory process highly interesting in itself, but carried out by different people, with a different purpose, using the concepts and attitudes of a different time.

Surveying the annals of Tlatelolco, the Codex Aubin, and Book 12, one notices that the conquest-related portions of the first two essentially begin with the Toxcatl massacre, which clearly had an enormous impact on Mexica consciousness. Book 12 is apparently – but only apparently – an exception. A sharp break in style and orientation separates everything after Toxcatl from everything before it. Indeed, the break is within the episode, with the background description of the festivity belonging to the first part, and the second part beginning with the attack of the Spaniards.[43]

The second part, on which I have concentrated in my discussions above, is, by Nahuatl standards, in a very spare, straightforward, unmetaphorical narrative-colloquial prose. The first part is preponderantly in the specific style of the Sahagún corpus that I briefly characterized above. Like traditional Nahuatl elevated speech, it is full of metaphor and repetition. But whereas extant examples of Nahuatl speeches, songs, and polite conversation tend strongly to a symmetrical rhythm in phrasing, and especially to pairing at various levels, the specific Sahagún style goes beyond pairing to a piling up of close equivalents, at times giving every imaginable lexical and grammatical variant of expressions, as though the purpose were to create a working

[42] The speech is in Chapter 16. It is in Sahagún, *Florentine Codex*, pt. 13, p. 44. Also in Lockhart, *We People Here*.

[43] The second part begins with Chapter 20, p. 55 in Sahagún, *Florentine Codex*, pt. 13.

dictionary or language lessons. Such thoughts were in fact not far from Sahagún's mind.[44] The style is not uniformly present throughout the Florentine Codex. In large portions of the corpus, such as the set speeches of Book 6 or the stories about gods in Book 3, it is entirely absent. In other parts, such as the volumes on plants and animals, it is dominant. The connoisseur of the corpus gradually comes to expect it more in parts based on European genres, less in parts based on indigenous genres; more in materials more thoroughly processed by Sahagún and his aides, less where the presentations of Nahuas outside the Sahagún team were allowed to stand in something closer to their original form.

Following this line of evidence, I conclude that the second part corresponds more closely to a relatively older Mexica (Tlatelolca) tradition existing apart from the Sahagún circle, and that the first part, probably originating among second-generation postcontact Mexica intellectuals (a category including many of Sahagún's aides), underwent more extensive and conscious rewriting, if not full-fledged original composition. I do not mean to say that the division between the two parts is categorical and exceptionless. The Sahagún style reappears to an extent in the portions dealing with fighting the Spaniards after their disastrous exit from Tenochtitlan[45]; the very fact that the action takes place elsewhere, however, is most suggestive. It would appear that the Mexica (again, specifically the Tlatelolca) knew and cared less about matters affecting them less directly. They must have retained only a very skeletal record, which Sahagún's aides or others like them and of their generation filled out in their own fashion. Even leaving this section out of consideration, the distinction between the two parts of Book 12 is not absolute. A certain amount of the characteristic padding of the Sahagún style is to be found throughout the volume; on the other hand, some widely reported details of the first part seem to go back to an earlier tradition.

The two parts also share a strong visuality. Only in the second part, however, do we find episodes like that of the catapult, where the description could hardly have originated with anyone but an eyewitness. The highly visual renderings of horses and dogs in the first part, or of Spaniards sickened by the sight of blood on food offered them, could easily have been based on observations of phenomena visible in the everyday life of the post-contact period. The supremely detailed descriptions of the gods' or priests' outfits given to Cortés, and of the

[44] See Lockhart, *We People Here*, introduction.
[45] Portions of Chapters 25–27.

the appearance and raiment of the dough image of Huitzilopochtli, complete with colors,[46] give every indication of deriving from preconquest-style pictorial or pictographic documents, which need not have been, and doubtless were not, tied in any way to the specific story of the conquest.

Taking it, then, that a substantial divergence exists between the two portions of Book 12 as to style and as to time and manner of origin, we would expect thematic differences as well, and they appear as expected. Omens and prophetic epiphanies are restricted to the first part, as are the general dumbfounded acceptance of the inevitability of doom, the pusillanimous, vacillating, augury-ridden Moteucçoma, and the notion of the return of the god Quetzalcoatl. But these things, the reader will say, are the entire content of the version normally purveyed to us of how the population of central Mexico reacted to the coming of the Spaniards. Just so. The by now traditional view of the matter not only passes by everyone but the Mexica and fastens nearly exclusively on Book 12 among Mexica texts, but it draws only on the posterior first part, ignoring the earlier second part (actually much more to the purpose) and its decidedly more pragmatic, microethnic cast.

The omens are eight in number,[47] as one could have predicted, eight being canonical among the Nahuas for almost any set of things, from the verses of a song to the constituent parts of an altepetl. No other known Nahuatl sources mention the omens or anything like them. A few equally late sources in Spanish do.[48] Nearly all are connected in some way with Tenochtitlan; the Book 12 omens, as is normal in the Nahua annals tradition, refer entirely to the local scene. It is most telling that the Tlaxcalan mestizo chronicler Muñoz Camargo, who wrote in Spanish some years after the Florentine Codex project reached its definitive form and must have known it in some way, is reduced to quoting literally the same Mexica omens, very much against the spirit of the indigenous historical tradition.[49] Surely the omens are part of a posterior stocktaking in which the Mexica, well after the fact, tried to explain, or explain away, their dizzying fall from

[46] Chapters 4, 19.

[47] Chapter 1.

[48] See John E. Kicza, *Patterns in Spanish Overseas Encounters to 1600* (forthcoming, Albuquerque: University of New Mexico Press).

[49] Diego Muñoz Camargo, *Descripción de la ciudad y provincia de Tlaxcala.*, ed. by René Acuña (México: Instituto de Investigaciones Antropológicas, Universidad Nacional Autónoma de México, 1984), 209–212. Juan López y Magaña first pointed out to me the similarities and the probable origin of the passage in Muñoz Camargo.

dominance. Other Nahua groups had not undergone that experience and felt less need to explain.

Book 12's Moteucçoma is another aspect of the same explanatory enterprise, in this case the finding of a scapegoat. All over the Spanish Indies, a reaction sooner or later set in among indigenous groups against those who led them – often seized in the course of peaceful parleys – at the time the Spaniards came. The reaction is real enough, but we must be careful not to confuse it with the attributes of the leaders themselves. We have no reason to imagine that Moteucçoma was at all as the first part of Book 12 makes him. In addition to the effects of scapegoating and uninformed posterior reconstruction, the Moteucçoma of Book 12 suffers from the strong Tlatelolca orientation of its writers, who not only set up their own Itzquauhtzin as a near-equal of Moteucçoma in status and power but use the two as contrasts in virtue, wisdom, and popularity, needless to say to Itzquauhtzin's advantage. By a generation after contact, Moteucçoma, aside from matters of how he was evaluated, had become far more important to the Mexica than he had been at the time; he had become a symbol of the conquest. For the Spaniards, the same thing had meanwhile happened with Cortés. Note that in the second part no one leader stands out; the several Tenochca and Tlatelolca who are prominent are mentioned primarily for feats of arms. Moteucçoma's successor Quauhtemoc, who as the decades and centuries went on was to displace Moteucçoma as a Mexica symbol, this time a positive one, appears infrequently and neutrally.

As for the notion aired in the first part of Book 12 that Moteucçoma and others viewed Cortés as the god Quetzalcoatl, returning as prophesied across the eastern seas to reclaim his kingdom, recent scholarship has already cast doubt on the Quetzalcoatl identification as a phenomenon of the conquest years. Carefully surveying the corpus of relevant indigenous and Spanish writing, Susan Gillespie has come to the conclusion that the Quetzalcoatl myth only gradually took shape over the postconquest years, again as a posterior explanatory device, not reaching its full and definitive form until around the 1570s – when the Florentine Codex too was receiving the final touches.[50] Many Nahuatl texts having doubtless disappeared, an argument from the absence of a specific item in surviving early documents is perhaps not absolutely conclusive, but I find the evidence convincing and the sug-

[50] Susan D. Gillespie, *The Aztec Kings: The Construction of Rulership in Mexica History* (Tucson: University of Arizona Press, 1989), Chapter 6, especially 192–96, 200. See also Kicza, *Patterns*..

gested lateness congruent with all the other indications about the first part of Book 12.

Not that all references to the Spaniards in general or to Cortés specifically as gods can be relegated to the second generation. On the contrary, the Nahuatl word *teotl,* usually and properly translated "god," occurs as a designation of the Spaniards in both parts of Book 12, and also in the other texts that have been discussed here. Spanish testimony on the point exists as well. The usage seems to have been an authentic feature of the conquest period, and it further seems, on the face of it, to go against the pragmatism and realism I have detected in early Nahua responses. Perhaps it really does so; I do not insist that the reaction was wholly of one piece, either in a given individual or among the Nahuas in general. But much remains misunderstood. We do not know how widespread the usage was, nor for how long a time it was current. Most especially, we do not know exactly how the term was meant. Another part of the Florentine Codex asserts that in ancient and legendary Tula, men used it to address each other, presumably in extreme politeness.[51] In addition to denominating gods and divine things, "teotl" was used in connection with anything extraordinary, not only unusually large things, but oddities and monstrosities. Conceivably it had something of the thrust of Maya *dzul,* "outsider, non-Maya," which became the definitive word for Spaniard in Yucatan[52] (whereas "teotl" in the sense in question was current for at most a few years). Conceivably the word was meant ironically. Even if it did refer to divinity in the obvious way and, for a time, was intended seriously to recognize the newcomers as indigenous gods or their avatars, it would have been one more example of the tendency to place the new in one's own framework, using the resources of one's own culture.

At any rate, returning from my long digression on second-generation Mexica lore about the conquest, I repeat by way of conclusion that a strong congruity as to the view of the Spaniards and the conquest process exists that emerges from two very disparate bodies of evidence: texts containing aspects of the first-generation linguistic reaction to the Spanish presence, and the apparently older and less reworked portions of the relevant Nahuatl annals. In both bodies of material and in both modes of expression, the Nahuas see and assess the Spaniards, their things, and their ways from outside Spanish cul-

[51] Sahagún, *Florentine Codex*, pt. 11 (Book 10), Chapter 29. On this whole matter see also Lockhart, *We People Here*, introduction.

[52] Restall, "The World of the *Cah*," passim.

ture, feeding visual and other direct sensory impressions into the normal indigenous interpretive framework. Whatever cataclysms, shocks, epidemics, or technological and economic changes were going on, that framework itself did not yet change, nor was it yet in an internal crisis. The input of the Spaniards was absorbed as individual, separate elements each of which was in some way comparable to items in the Nahua cultural repertory. No stark indigenous-foreign polarity arose. The Nahuas seemed to recognize no new "other"; rather they continued to define themselves by altepetl, making the members of the altepetl "we" and all others, indigenous or Spanish, "they."

CHAPTER 8

Dialogues of the deaf: Europeans on the Atlantic coast of Africa

WYATT MACGAFFEY

If the encounter of Africans with Europeans in the early modern period is to be represented as two-sided rather than one-sided, special methodological problems must be faced. Of the other chapters in this section, four deal with Asian countries, and all of them with populations in which, at least within a short time of the arrival of Europeans, literacy was sufficiently established that indigenous chronicles were written, from which some idea of the local view of those Europeans can be gained. On the Atlantic coast of Africa, literates were relatively few until the nineteenth century, and apparently none of those who could write recorded their early impressions of Europeans in any document that has survived. The question of what Africans thought must be approached indirectly. With respect to history ("what happened"), the problem of the absence of documentation is not new in African studies, nor peculiar to Africa, but with respect to indigenous ethnography ("perceptions of the other") there has been very little discussion, largely because the indications of ethnographic knowledges among Africans have been classified as mythology and religious belief.[1]

It is traditional to assume that anthropology is a science peculiar to the modern West, where it arose in response to the European experience of other parts of the world then coming under European domination. Given a narrow sense of anthropology as a professional discipline, the tradition is obviously correct; even in Europe, museums of ethnology and professorships of anthropology were created only toward the end of the nineteenth century. Nevertheless, it is reason-

[1] An admittedly cursory survey of recent books about early Portuguese commercial and diplomatic activity in West Africa discovered none in which the question of what Africans thought is even mentioned.

able to assume that every people forms some conception of the difference between their own society and those of others.[2] It is a separate question whether and to what extent such a science is correct. Part of our own modern self-conception has been that our knowledge of others has been distinctively scientific – that is, intrinsically realistic and on the whole empirically correct – but in recent years this assumption has been questioned. It has become something of a cliché that the most sacred reports and concepts of traditional anthropology are "inventions," meaning at best interpretations if not actual fictions.[3] In the aftermath of this exercise in self-criticism, it may be appropriate to look again at the latent "anthropologies" of other societies, relating them to their social context as well as to our own standards of validity.

Part of the difficulty attending such an inquiry is that an exotic anthropology is likely to be unrecognizable as such – that is, formally untranslatable into a discourse that we would classify as anthropological. Our social sciences presuppose categories such as "religion," "government," and "economy," despite the difficulty we have in giving satisfactory definition to them and explaining the relationships among them. It can be argued that these terms of art seem compelling to us, despite their logical obscurity, because they correspond to the functional differentiation of our lives, in which "religion," "government," and "economy" are carried on in different buildings by different groups of specialized personnel. By analogy, we can expect that the categories in which an exotic social science is couched will be the folk concepts corresponding to the functional differentiation constitutive of the society in question, but lacking equivalents in our experience.[4] These concepts will seem "uniquely realistic" to the members of that society because they build "models of" and "models for" their social lives with them.[5] Their apparent incoherence and lack of correspondence with "reality" will lead us to dismiss them as elements of the local "religion," itself defined a priori as the domain of the unempirical and irrational.

Only recently have Africanists come to recognize that many African narratives that they had regarded as myths or perhaps as history are

[2] There is a parallel here with the vexed question of whether we can speak of "African philosophy" except when referring to the products of professional philosophers. See P.J. Hountondji, *African Philosophy: Myth and Reality*, H. Evans, trans. (Bloomington, IN, 1983).

[3] Originally the word "invention" meant simply "discovery."

[4] W. MacGaffey, "The Kongo Prophet as Social Theorist," *Cahiers de Religions Africaines* 18, no. 35 (1984): 31–44.

[5] Clifford Geertz, "Religion as a Cultural System", in M. Banton, ed., *Anthropological Approaches to the Study of Religion* (London, 1965), pp. 1–46.

in fact examples of sociological theory, of "what a society says, thinks, and feels about itself".[6] To take such materials seriously as social science obliges us to ask what categories of thought, what processes of reasoning, may have led the people in question to adopt them.[7] With respect to the early modern period, the hypothesis that categories of thought were related to social structure seems only to raise the further problem of knowing what was the structure of the society in question.

For the European side of the encounter, a whole library of documents is available, much of it taking the form of explicit ethnography, beginning with the reports of Portuguese sailors in the fifteenth century. Much of this writing increasingly takes the form, not simply of description, but of an explanation, why African culture is what it is. The origin and content of this theory, summed up in the word "fetish" (or, in its sixteenth century, Afro-European pidgin form, "Fetisso"), is being examined in detail in a series of articles by William Pietz, not yet completed.[8] Fetish was, precisely, a theory about African thinking. It was, says Pietz, "a pragmatically totalized and totalizing explanation of the strangeness of African societies and the special problems [Europeans] encountered in trying to conduct rational market activities with these benighted peoples" and "a bizarre phantasm wherein the new forces and categories of the mercantile world economy then reshaping African and European societies alike were read into a foreign social order and locale."[9]

This phantasm originated in the intercultural spaces of the Guinea coast, inhabited symbiotically by Europeans and by Africans alienated from their own societies. Fetisso was a vocabulary and a conceptual scheme that made possible trade and political relations between Africans and Europeans on the basis of a shared and double misunderstanding: by Europeans of Africa, and by Africans of Europe. As such it persists into modern times, where it has been called "a dialogue of the deaf."[10]

It is a useful fact in the present context that a considerable degree

[6] J. Vansina, "Traditions of Genesis", *Journal of African History* 15 (1974): 317–22; W. MacGaffey, "African History, Anthropology, and the Rationality of the Natives," *History in Africa* 5 (1978): 101–20.

[7] James W. Fernandez, "Fang Representations Under Acculturation," in Philip Curtin, ed., *Africa and the West: Intellectual Responses to European Culture* (Madison, 1972), 43–48.

[8] William Pietz, "The Problem of the Fetish, I," *Res* 9 (1985): 5–17; "The Problem of the Fetish, II: The Origin of the Fetish," *Res* 13 (1987): 23–45; "The Problem of the Fetish, IIIa: Bosman's Guinea and the Enlightenment Theory of Fetishism," *Res* 16 (1988): 105–23.

[9] W. Pietz, "The Problem of the Fetish IIIa," 116–17.

[10] A. Doutreloux, *L'Ombre des fétiches* (Louvain, 1967), 261.

of deafness continues on both sides in spite of intensifying "dialogue" over the centuries and the special opportunities that imperial rule gave to Europeans both to understand Africans and to explain themselves to them. We are dealing with systems of notable strength and stability.

PORTUGUESE EXPLORATIONS

Portuguese sailors reached the Gold Coast (modern Ghana) in 1470. Within a few years, West African gold was an important source of wealth for the Portuguese crown. But the Portuguese were also interested in spreading Christianity, and hoped to discover the legendary Christian kingdom of Prester John, whom they saw as a potential ally in their struggle with the Moors. The first substantial kingdom they encountered was that of Benin (in modern Nigeria); the Obas of Benin took no interest in Christianity, despite the fact that the first Portuguese captain to arrive sent "holy and most Catholic advisers with laudable admonitions concerning the Faith, strongly reproving the heresies and great idolatries and sorceries [feitiçarias] which the blacks practise in that country."[11] A few local converts became literate in Portuguese and acted as interpreters.

The only kind of document from this era to represent Europeans directly is a number of Benin bronzes in which Portuguese soldiers are shown; in other respects, "Benin reaction to these first twenty years of contact with an alien people and culture is poorly documented both in European records and in Benin tradition."[12] Whatever ethnographic understanding these figures refer to was lost, and the figures themselves gradually became a mere decorative motif.[13] In the absence of direct testimonies, we are forced to rely on inference from what Africans did.

Columbus visited the Gold Coast between 1482 and 1484, traveling in a Portuguese ship. Although the knowledge of the Guinea coast that he acquired was slight, his experience there shaped his expectations of what he would encounter on the other side of the Atlantic.[14] It is probable that envy of the new Portuguese wealth in African gold helped to motivate Spanish support for Columbus's search for Cathay.

Apparently the Portuguese had no great difficulty setting up trad-

[11] Rui de Pina, in A. Brasío, *Monumenta Missionaria Africana*, vol. 1 (Lisbon, 1952).
[12] Alan Ryder, *Benin and the Europeans, 1485–1897* (London, 1969), 39.
[13] Ibid.,
[14] P.E.H. Hair, "Columbus from Guinea to America," *History in Africa* 17 (1990): 113–29.

ing relations on the coast; it is remarkable, in view of later discussions, that their early reports make no mention of language problems. Their assumption that they could make themselves understood was borne out by their success in trade, but denied by the failure of their evangelical efforts. Only the Kongo kingdom, in what is now northwestern Angola, seemed to listen to the Gospel.

The sea captain Diogo Cao first arrived at the mouth of the Zaire in 1483. He did not visit the capital, Mbanza Kongo, but sent some of his sailors as messengers with gifts (it would be interesting to know what and how they communicated). When their return was delayed, he decided not to wait for them, but returned to Portugal with hostages taken from the coastal province of Soyo. It was in fact standard Portuguese practice to acquire Africans who could be taught Portuguese and serve as interpreters.[15] On his second voyage in 1485, Diogo brought back the hostages, who reported on their experiences in Portugal (once again, we have no idea what in fact they said), together with rich gifts for the Kongo king, Nzinga Nkuwu. Diogo Cao, following instructions from the Portuguese king, urged Nzinga Nkuwu to abandon his idols and to renounce sorcery. Nzinga Nkuwu's reply, as conveyed by Diogo and reported by the chronicler Rui de Pina, consists of conventional Portuguese sentiments and gestures: He kisses the hands of his Portuguese counterpart in gratitude for his kindness "not only in honoring his body in his lifetime, but also by advising him how to save his soul after death."[16] After more expressions of Christian piety, Nzinga requests that he be sent holy water for his baptism, and also carpenters and masons to build churches, farmers to domesticate cattle and teach agriculture, and women to show how flour is made. In all this, as in later missionary projects, the spiritual character of the Christian life is of a piece with the material practices of Europe, and both its utility in Africa and its intrinsic intelligibility are taken for granted.

Nzinga's appeal met with a full response in 1491. The governor of Soyo (the Mani Soyo) was so impressed by the riches, spiritual and material, intended for his suzerain, the Mani Kongo, that he insisted on being baptized himself, immediately, but refused to allow any of his subordinates this privilege, excluding them even from witnessing the ritual. Afterward, he ordered a holocaust of idols. The Portuguese expedition proceeded on to Mbanza Kongo, where an even grander version of the same scene unfolded. A stone church was constructed,

[15] Ibid., 118.
[16] Brasío, *Monumenta Missionaria*, 57.

but the king demanded baptism before it had been completed, because war had broken out on his eastern frontier. Under the name of João I, he was baptized with six of his nobles, explicitly denying the sacrament to all of lesser degree. Carrying a banner with the sign of the cross, given him with the assurance that it would bring him victory, the king set out to do battle, and was indeed victorious. The Portuguese, leaving behind a small detachment of clergy to give Christian instruction to the converts, returned home.

Within three years, however, the king had found intolerable his new religion's demand that he give up polygyny, and he lapsed from the faith. After his death in 1506, his oldest son, Mvemba Nzinga, baptized Afonso, who remained a Christian, defeated the successor elected by the nobles; according to near-contemporary Portuguese accounts, he overcame a greatly superior force with the aid of a body of celestial cavalry led by St. James. Afonso I, who reigned until 1543, became famous as the respected correspondent of his counterpart in Portugal, as leader and defender of his people in the face of the increasing depredations of the slave trade, and even as a satisfying realization of fabled Prester John. Like Captain Cook in Hawaii, Afonso was "a myth before he was an event," in this instance a Portuguese myth.[17] Development of the myth continued as missionary activity in Kongo intensified during the seventeenth century. It went on to become "one of the most durable myths of the history of central Africa."[18]

ANCIENT KONGO CHRISTIANITY: THE MODERN VERSION

The modern historians of Kongo are strongly skeptical of the adequacy of the foregoing account, passed on to them by the last generation of (by now) Belgian missionary historians. Basing themselves on modern ethnography of the BaKongo, they have argued that Nzinga Nkuwu, the Mani Soyo, and their followers interpreted the rituals they were offered as a new version of the sort of cult with which they were already familiar, itself a manipulation of a cosmic system of which the Portuguese were ignorant then and remained ignorant hundreds of years later. The more recent and bolder of these rereadings of the events is that of A. Hilton, who indicates confidence that sub-

[17] R. P. Toby in this volume, quoting M. Sahlins.
[18] J. Thornton, "Early Kongo-Portuguese Relations: A New Interpretation," *History in Africa* 8 (1981), 183.

stantial continuity exists between sixteenth and twentieth century Kongo cosmology, cultic practice, and social structure, despite massive political change in the seventeenth century and again in the early twentieth.[19] Such assertions of continuity are generally regarded by historians with professional skepticism, since to them non-change is non-history and may recall the embarrassing era, ended all too recently, in which Africa was said not to have any history. Change, however, must be change in something that itself continues.

Kongo cosmology

In the twentieth century, BaKongo have generally thought of the universe as divided into two worlds of the living and the dead, separated by water. Any real body of water serves for passage between the two, which can also be effected at certain other boundaries. Though the expression *nsi a bafwa* can be literally glossed as "land of the dead," "death" itself (*lufwa*) is understood as life continued in another place. The dead, being older, are more knowledgeable and more powerful than the living, whose lives they can influence in various ways. The dead also contrast sharply with the living in some respects, one of which is that they are white in color. The significances of this whiteness are subtle and complex, but it is ritually represented by white porcelain clay, found under streambeds; its name (*mpemba; luvemba,* "whiteness") is also one of the terms for a cemetery and for the land of the dead. This same whiteness, contrasting with the organic and domestic blackness of charcoal, appears on masks all over Central Africa.

All of the categories of the dead require appropriate kinds of gifts, homage, and obedience at times, but they can also confer some of their own powers on the living. All outstanding individuals among the living owe their special gifts, real or supposed, beneficent or evil, to some sort of special contract with the dead. In practice, this means that they have undergone an initiation for which they have paid the proper fee. Initiations include a more or less protracted sojourn "in the land of the dead," meaning in reality a special enclosure (*vwela*), often built away in the bush, from which the candidate eventually emerges, equipped with the insignia of his new powers and indica-

[19] A. Hilton, *The Kingdom of Kongo* (New York, 1985), x, 9, and passim; W.G.L. Randles, *L'ancien royaume du Congo des origines à la fin du XIXe siècle* (Paris, 1968). Hilton uses MacGaffey (1970-no ref.), but not his recent work on religion (*Religion and Society in Central Africa* [Chicago, 1986]). Her understanding of Kongo religion includes mistaken concepts that it is not pertinent to dispute in the present context.

tions that he is not as other men are. One such indication is the ability to speak in strange tongues understood only by fellow initiates. The color of initiates in cult context is usually white, that is, white clay applied to the body, often with details in red.

The categories of the dead are also the categories of cultic practice. All cultic initiation in Kongo involves a visit to the land of the dead. Descent groups address themselves to their forebears; local groups to *bisimbi*, spirits of the land and of terrestrial waters; individuals in trouble, or in search of special advantage, to *minkisi* (sing. *nkisi*), individual forces or personalities specializing in the matter in question; and ambitious scoundrels (witches), supposedly, to their counterparts in land of the dead, errant ghosts who were witches in their lifetime. Both descent groups and local groups are corporations serving public functions, with leaders; the other two categories, devoted to individual ends, are regarded as either criminal or potentially so.

The foregoing summary of Kongo religion can be extensively documented for the period 1880–1920 on the basis of contemporary texts, indigenous and European. Its modifications in subsequent decades up to the present have been described and analyzed by several anthropologists.[20] With its aid we can join the modern historians in their rereading of the conversion story. But what confidence can we have that this reading is not simply anachronistic?

A KiKongo grammar published in Rome in 1659, the first grammar of a Bantu language, attests to the stability of the Kongo language from the seventeenth to the twentieth century.[21] A similar degree of correspondence can be shown to exist in religious practices over the same period. We know that although many minkisi disappeared and others arrived, some of the great ones survived until 1900, and that the material packages in which these spirits were approached were composed in the same way with many of the identical ingredients. The contrast between local and lineal cults persisted, each ritually dependent on the other, as did the tension between occult practitioners deemed to be legitimate upholders of the public good and those regarded as subversive of it. As in the case of language, systematic continuity is a matter not simply of a sum of substantial similarities but of the persistence of systematic contrasts between categories.

[20] For a bibliography, see MacGaffey, *Religion and Society*. Many of the indigenous texts have not yet been properly published, but a digest of them can be found in K.E. Laman, *The Kongo*, vol.3 (Uppsala, 1962). See also MacGaffey, *Art and Healing of the BaKongo Commented by Themselves* (Bloomington, IN, 1991).

[21] H. Gratten Guinness, *Grammar of the Congo Language as Spoken Two Hundred Years Ago* (London, 1882).

A further index of stability can be derived from the fact that the system in question is not a local peculiarity of the BaKongo around the estuary of the Zaire but is found over the entire Central African rain forest and beyond, as far south as the Zambezi, though it contrasts specifically with other systems in the eastern savannas and on the Bantu borderland from Cameroon to Sudan. As not only a set of practices but a social theory (a "tradition"), it was a controlling factor in the economic and political adaptation of peoples speaking Western Bantu languages as they diffused through the rain forest for more than 2,000 years before the Portuguese contacted them.[22]

Kongo christianity reconstructed

It is well-documented from missionary reports that in the seventeenth century white people were believed to live under the ocean, and to belong specifically to the category of spirits of the soil and terrestrial waters (*bisimbi*), which were responsible for fertility and communal well-being. This belief persists to the present time; it is not derived from experience but is a fundamental postulate in terms of which experience is interpreted.

The critical event in the original reception of the Portuguese and their religion was probably the return of the hostages in 1485. The king and his court were exceedingly glad to welcome the return of the hostages, "as though they had seen them resuscitated from under the earth."[23] Clearly, they had survived a truly exceptional initiation into the powers of the dead. The baptism promised by the visitors was understood as an initiation into the powers of a new and improved version of the cult of local spirits. Nzinga Nkuwu's first ambassador to Portugal was therefore the Mani Vunda, *kitomi* of Mbanza Kongo.[24] Every candidate for lordship over a local cluster of clans was qualified by descent and by election, the electors being the heads of the ruling clans, related by marriage in such a way that they shared the office among themselves. The distinctive powers of all chiefs, symbolized by the leopard, were violent, but the candidate had also to be

[22] J. Vansina, *Paths in the Rainforests* (Madison, 1990); MacGaffey, "African Religions: Types and Generalizations," in I. Karp and C.S. Bird, eds., *Explorations in African Systems of Thought* (Bloomington, IN, 1979). Interpretations of particular ritual values by means of comparative materials should be restricted to materials drawn from the area of this tradition; Randles, presuming the unity of a pan-African culture, is led into error here.

[23] Brasío, *Monumenta Missionaria*, I: 56.

[24] Hilton, *The Kingdom of Kongo*, 50.

inaugurated by the kitomi, the priest of the fertility cult addressed to local bisimbi.[25]

Upon the third visit of Diogo Cao in 1491, the Mani Soyo organized a festival in which the people were naked to the waist, their skins painted in white and other colors, and with headdresses of parrot feathers.[26] They sang the praises of the king of Portugal, calling him Zambemapongo [*nzambi a mpungu*], a title also applied to Kongo kings.[27] According to Rui de Pina, it meant "Lord of the World," but in fact it means something like "greatest of the spirits."[28] The fact that the *kitomi* of Mbanza Kongo, the ambassador, had died on the voyage home did not dampen the excitement. The baptism of the Mani Soyo and his son, obviously not something to be shared with everyone, took place in a ritual seclusion, other people being forbidden to see the sacred objects of the cult. Secure in his new consecration, the governor then ordered the destruction of a large number of *nkisi*-objects, which as instruments for the pursuit of individual aims were always seen by central authorities as a threat.

When the turn of the Nzinga Nkuwu came, he was baptized with six of his nobles, clan heads at Mbanza Kongo who took the names of members of the Portuguese court; taking a new name is a standard feature of all important Kongo initiations and other personal successes and transitions. The king immediately tested his new powers in war, a demonstration of exceptional powers of violence being one of the standard means of authenticating the ruler's relation with the dead. One of his newly baptized associates, brother and possibly successor to the late *kitomi*, found a cruciform stone, thus fulfilling the corresponding test of successful contact with bisimbi, the guardians of fertility and well-being.[29]

Nzinga Nkuwu, now known as João I, soon ran into trouble. He was forced to allow most of his high officials to be baptized, so that the new powers were more widely shared than he intended. On the

[25] Ibid., 36.

[26] Brasío, *Monumenta Missionaria*, 61. Hilton, *The Kingdom of Kongo*, 51, says this was "clearly an nkimba cult assembly." In fact there is no means of saying what it was, except that it deployed elements from the symbolic vocabulary common to all Kongo cults, including the relatively well-known nkimba.

[27] Randles, *L'ancien royaume du Congo*, 31.

[28] Randles gets into difficulties trying to decide whether Nzambi Mpungu, who in Christian times became God Almighty, originally referred to a live or a dead person. In fact, the BaKongo do not, and presumably did not then, classify the dead as "dead"; they were reported by seventeenth-century missionaries as not believing in life after death (Hilton, *The Kingdom of Kongo*, 228), a view perhaps more accurately glossed as "not believing in death after death."

[29] Brasío, *Monumenta Missionaria*, 128; Hilton, *The Kingdom of Kongo*, 51.

other hand, these powers scarcely lived up to their promise; a drought ensued in the coastal region which the people there blamed on the new ritual. Lastly, the Portuguese clergy insisted that he abandon all but his principal wife. The older interpretation, based on the assumption that polygyny was an expression of unregenerate lust, saw João's reluctance in this matter and eventual lapse from the faith as simple moral failure; Hilton's explanation is more convincing. The marriages of chiefs were, as in Europe at that time, political alliances that distributed advantages then and in future generations. Royal monogamy would mean that a single clan had a prescriptive right to the succession; it may also have been the case that a member of the clan of this particular principal wife would have been ineligible under traditional rules.[30]

Upon the death of João I, his elected successor was challenged by Afonso Mvemba Nzinga, son of the principal wife. Afonso's victory is attributable to Portuguese support, the missionaries having abandoned the unfavorable environment of revived paganism at Mbanza Kongo for the province of Nsundi, of which Afonso was governor and which lay on what they presumed was the route to the as-yet-undiscovered Prester John. The Portuguese also helped Afonso to develop the trade in the excellent copper mined north of the Zaire at Mboko Nsongo and to channel it to Mbanza Kongo, where it became a valued commodity which the new king could exchange for European goods. These imports, in turn, allowed him to secure the loyalty of important nobles, the basis for a long and distinguished reign.[31] Afonso also developed the slave trade as a royal and aristocratic monopoly whose network reached not only to São Tomé, center of the entire West African slave trade, but even as far as Benin.[32]

Intercultural space

The history of Kongo accommodation to European presence parallels that of the Nahuas of Mexico, of whom Lockhart writes (in this volume), "Each side was able to operate for centuries after the first contact on an ultimately false but in practice workable presumption that analogous concepts of the other side were essentially identical with its own, thus avoiding close examination of the unfamiliar and maintaining its own principles. The truce obtaining under this partial mis-

[30] Hilton, *The Kingdom of Kongo,* 52.
[31] Ibid., 53.
[32] Thornton, "Early Kongo-Portuguese Relations"; Alan Ryder, *Benin and the Europeans, 1485–1897* (London, 1969), 39.

conception allowed for a long period of preservation of indigenous structures of all kinds while intercultural ferment went on gradually, hardly attaining the level of consciousness. I have called the phenomenon the process of Double Mistaken Identity."

We may suppose that similar processes went on in other parts of the Atlantic coast, but only in Kongo is there good evidence of what the African side of the phenomenon looked like. The special circumstances of Kongo conversion literally opened the interior to generation after generation of missionaries and other Europeans in whose reports an implicit African ethnography can be read. The explicit ethnography is silent. Afonso learned Portuguese, studied theological texts, and was praised for his erudition and devotion to study. He sent some of his young relatives to Portugal to study, where one became a bishop and another became a professor of humanities. But none of this literate learning resulted in any direct ethnography of the Europeans. Few missionaries learned KiKongo, but some did. The first catechism in KiKongo was written in 1556, the first of which a copy is still extant in 1624, and the first dictionary in 1652. These documents, besides showing us the stability of the Kongo language, reveal the development of the ambiguous vocabulary that mediated the dialogue of the deaf for centuries, in which religious terms carried "a range of meanings, from pagan to Christian, of which the former [were] known obscurely or not at all to the missionaries and the latter obscurely or not at all to Kongo Christians."[33] Well into the eighteenth century, missionaries were relied on to make rain; after their departure they were remembered as *bisimbi.*

Nevertheless, this picture of institutionalized misunderstanding requires serious qualification. In Kongo as on the Guinea coast, commercial and political relations highly satisfactory to both sides, on the whole, were established and maintained for centuries. In both areas, these relations were mediated by mixed Euro-African populations whose social and religious practices were similarly heterogeneous and whose commercial interests were not necessarily those of either their African or their European trading partners.

Thornton argues that it is a mistake to read the relations of the Portuguese with Kongo in modern, colonial terms. In the sixteenth century, Portugal and Kongo (or Portugal and Benin) were not unlike, as seen in a modern sociological perspective. Both had similar rates

[33] J.M. Janzen and W. MacGaffey, *Anthology of Kongo Religion* (Lawrence, KS, 1974), 16. Holman Bentley, the nineteenth-century missionary linguist, described the language of the catechism of 1624 as "Whiteman's Kongo" (F. Bontinck and D. Ndembe Nsasi, *Le catéchisme kikongo de 1624* [Brussels, 1978], 263).

of agricultural productivity and standards of living. Each would recognize in the other a monarchy dominating a political system organized by relations of kinship and clientage among the aristocracy. On the basis of these resemblances, King Afonso was not long in developing a good understanding of the Portuguese system of quasi-feudal land rents and commercial monopolies, in which he participated. BaKongo were sufficiently numerous in Lisbon by 1550 that one of them was appointed royal factor, something like a modern consul, to represent them in the courts and to arrange credit and the like; this person, "a Kongolese of noble blood, eventually married into the royal household of Portugal, an accepted right for a man of his status and position."[34] In short, the level of practical intercultural understanding was considerably higher than the available texts would indicate.

On the European side, where all of the texts originate (except for some of the correspondence of Kongo kings), what we see developing is a theory of African society that is to a considerable extent independent of actual experience, though it appears to be well grounded in ethnographic reporting, and which is implicitly revelatory of important features of European culture, from the sixteenth to the nineteenth centuries. This is the theory of Fetish.

FETISSO

Exploration and idolatry

The first Portuguese explorers in West Africa were equipped with conceptual categories with which they could confidently describe the communities they encountered; only later did African society and culture seem problematic. The basic categories were cannibalism, nudity, and idolatry, representing the inverse of civilization: respectively, right eating (production), right sexual practices (reproduction), and right religion and government. These categories remained basic to all subsequent ethnographic reporting of Africa into the twentieth century; they were so closely related that the presence of one could be adduced from the presence of another.[35]

The *Esmeraldo de Situ Orbis* of Duarte Pacheco Pereira, written in the first decade of the sixteenth century, gives detailed navigational instructions for the West African coast, together with information on the landscapes, the climate, and commercial opportunities, but its eth-

[34] Thornton, "Early Kongo-Portuguese Relations," 191.
[35] D. Hammond and A. Jablow, *The Myth of Africa* (New York, 1977), 36–7.

nographic accounts are summary and formulaic: "The negroes of all this coast are naked and are not circumcised, and they are idolaters."[36] "Sometimes these negroes eat one another, but this is less usual here than in other parts of Ethiopia; they are all idolaters and sorcerers and are ruled by witchcraft, placing implicit faith in oracles and omens."[37] "It is possible to buy some slaves here . . . but it is necessary to be on guard against the negroes of this country for they are very evil people and attack our ships."[38] In purpose and in its assumptions about what constitutes useful information, the *Esmeraldo* is the prototype of a genre represented more recently by a project of the United States Strategic Air Command, which in 1960 equipped its flight crews with information concerning all the tribes among whom a given crew might be forced down. According to a pamphlet distributed at the time by the Air Force, the information, printed on 5 × 8 cards to fit in the flight suit pocket, described each ethnic group

> in terms of population, range, environment, physical appearance, language, religion, social organization, economy, diet, transportation, and reputation for being friendly or hostile. In addition, each card bears a photograph of a typical male and female and a map which pinpoints the location and range of the particular ethnic group.

Ethnographic reporting improved rapidly in the next two centuries, freeing itself to a considerable degree from the heritage of Herodotus and the Bible, which had shaped the reported experiences of Pacheco. Information of great historical value is contained particularly in Pigafetta's account of the Kongo kingdom, based on interviews with the Portuguese sailor Duarte Lopez and published in 1591; Pieter de Marees' description of the Gold Coast (1602); Cavazzi's historical description of Kongo, Angola, and Matamba (1687); Olfert Dapper's great collection, the first to give space to Africans' own accounts of their history (1668; French edition 1686); a series of reports by Italian Capuchin missionaries to Kongo at the end of the seventeenth century; and Willem Bosman's highly influential *New and Accurate Description of the Coast of Guinea* (1703, published in English in 1705).[39]

[36] D. Pacheco Pereira, *Esmeraldo in Situ Orbis*, G.H.T. Kimble, ed. and trans. (London, 1937), 113.

[37] Ibid., 97.

[38] Ibid., 107.

[39] F. Pigafetta and D. Lopez, *Description du Royaume de Congo et des Contrées Environnantes* (Louvain, 1963); P. de Marees, *Description and Historical Account of the Gold Kingdom of Guinea*, A. van Dantzig and A. Jones, eds. and trans. (London, 1987); G.A. Cavazzi, *Descrição histórica dos treis reinos do Congo, Matamba e Angola*, 2 vols., G.

In the course of this accumulation of knowledge, the theory of Fetish was elaborated, but underneath it the categories of an older way of thinking persisted. It guides Randles in his interpretation of documents which he must use to reconstruct the story of the reception accorded to the first Portuguese at the Kongo capital. Noting, correctly, De Pina's desire to represent the BaKongo as humbly receptive of the Gospel, Randles charges him with omitting a significant detail found in another account, published in Rome in 1506:

> According to this author, the king of Congo made a gift to the Portuguese of seven men, who committed suicide on the spot. The Portuguese, aghast, having refused to eat their roasted heads, they were given to the people. This text shows that the Congolese were once cannibals.[40]

Along with mention that a seventeenth-century account flatly denies that the Congolese were ever cannibals, Randles repeats this story, saying that it shows that "the despotic conduct of Congolese kings did not differ from that of their neighbors."[41] In support, he quotes Dapper's statement that the Teke king (on Kongo's eastern frontier) slaughtered 200 slaves every day to provision the royal dinner table. In fact, nothing at all is "proved" by this story, and more like it, except the strength of European preconceptions.

Just as the accounts of cannibalism present themselves as reports of fact, so the new idea of Fetish appears in the texts not as a theory but as a descriptive account of African realities; so De Marees writes of the Fetissero, which "in their language . . . means as much as a Servant of their God."[42] The working misunderstanding developed in the Euro-African coastal communities included pseudo-African terms for European Christian concepts, such as *ngudi a nkisi,* supposed to mean "Holy Mother" in KiKongo but more accurately glossed as "source of magic." It also included a pseudo-African, but in fact Portuguese, vocabulary for African concepts. The remarkable fact is that these fictions worked; their success in practice served to guarantee their theoretical adequacy.

Graciano Maria de Leguzzano, ed. and trans. (Lisbon, 1965); Fondation Dapper, *Objets Interdits* (Paris, 1989); on Capuchin missionaries, see bibliography in Hilton, *The Kingdom of Kongo;* W. Bosman, *A New and Accurate Description of the Coast of Guinea* (London, 1967).

[40] Randles, *L'ancien royaume du Congo,* 95.

[41] Ibid., 140.

[42] P. de Marees, *Description and Historical Account,* 67.

From idolatry to fetishism[43]

The concept of idolatry, which the first Portuguese navigators applied to African cultures they encountered, was soon replaced by the concept of Fetish, itself derived from a Portuguese term for witchcraft. According to Pietz, idolatry had meant, since the time of such Church Fathers as Tertullian, voluntary contact with a demonic spirit through the medium of a material image representing it. Witchcraft (*feitiço*), on the other hand, was a much less well defined category involving "vain observances" and the misuse of fabricated composites of natural materials that nowadays we would call magical; such devices were not sharply distinguished from others that were accepted in ordinary use. In practice, the distinction was political: Talismans and remedies were acceptable if they were used within the framework of life as controlled by the Church, and came under suspicion when they were used by persons whose religious loyalty was doubtful.

The Portuguese soon saw that West African religion did not in fact center on idols, but rather on material composites that were supposed to produce concrete, material results. In consequence, *feitiçaria*, a term that had obscurely designated certain marginal practices in Christian Europe, was appropriated to characterize the entirety of African religion and the kind of social order it was believed to support.[44] The associated theory took some time to develop.

At first, African fetishes were not sharply distinguished as to their nature from Christian sacramental objects; in Kongo, both were called nkisi by the missionaries themselves. The difference was, once again, political. Objects consecrated by the church whose head was the Pope were approved, similar objects related to a rival hierarchy were disapproved. The use of one or the other kind of amulet became a marker of social affiliation, which in the intercultural spaces of the coast could be changed according to context.[45] In Kongo, Capuchin missionaries were called *nganga*, as were the local magicians, whose prescriptions the missionaries matched point for point: women about to give birth should wear Christian relics instead of the magicians' mats; instead of binding their infants with superstitious cords made by magicians, mothers should make cords from palm leaves consecrated on Palm Sunday; instead of planting a magic guard to save their corn crop and make it fertile, people should use consecrated palm branches.[46] Exten-

[43] Much of this section is based on the work of W. Pietz, here inadequately summarized.
[44] W. Pietz, "The Problem of the Fetish, II," 37.
[45] Ibid., 38.
[46] MacGaffey, *Religion and Society*, 205; J. da Sorrento Merolla, "A Voyage to Congo,

sive parallels of this kind have led Thornton to see the differences between Kongo Christianity and European Christianity of the day as simply a matter of competing political interests, but this view is surely exaggerated.[47]

A distinct turn in the definition of Fetish occurred when the Dutch replaced the Portuguese in West Africa in the first half of the seventeenth century. Dutch merchants, of Calvinist background, identified Catholic relics and African amulets alike as false religion. In addition, however, the Protestant attitude toward commerce, valuing regularity and rationality, demanded an explanation for the evident irrationality of the values Africans placed upon objects. Africans would exchange gold for what Europeans regarded as trifles, and attributed exaggerated religious value to objects apparently chosen at random: "some a Bird's Feather, some a Pebble, a Bit of Rag, a Dog's Leg; or, in short, any thing they fancy."[48] Africans were also said to regard European technology as inventions of the Devil. Europeans thought that mistaken notions of causality explained the false appreciation of the value of goods. "From this developed a general discourse about the superstitiousness of non-Europeans within a characteristically modern rhetoric of realism, which recognized as 'real' only technological and commercial values."[49] Part of this discourse described African society as likewise "based on the principles of chance encounter and the arbitrary fancy of imagination conjoined with desire."[50] Merchants found themselves obliged to take oath upon fetishes before they could conclude a commercial exchange, and even invented fetishes of their own. The unreliability of contracts reached in this way made Fetisso (the pidgin term in common use) synonymous with deceit, as in the notion of "fetish gold," gold mixed with base metals.[51]

In the *New and Accurate Account* (1703) by the Enlightenment skeptic Willem Bosman, said to be one of the most popular travelogues ever written,[52] the theory of Fetish culminated in a fully elaborated picture of African society that was itself an unconscious parody of European mercantilism. Whereas rational self-interest, and the correct estimation of the absolute value of material things, was the foundation of the

and Several Other Countries," in J. Pinkerton, ed., *A General Collection of the Best and Most Interesting Voyages and Travels in All Parts of the World* (London, 1814).

47 J. Thornton, "The Development of an African Catholic Church in the Kingdom of Kongo, 1491–1750," *Journal of African History* 25 (1984): 147–67.

48 Pietz, "The Problem of the Fetish, II," 41, quoting a text of 1744.

49 Ibid., 42.

50 Ibid., 43.

51 Pietz, "The Problem of the Fetish, IIIa," 111.

52 Ibid., 116, quoting A. van Dantzig.

mercantilist self-conception, Africans were supposed to be governed by irrational self-interest based on impulse rather than calculation. The idea that Africans, lacking reason, were totally subject to the random claims of natural events and the equally capricious demands of their rulers (the cannibalistic "African despots" of later historiography), implicitly legitimated the real enslavement of these same Africans by reasonable European traders.[53]

What Bosman and others reported was supposedly an empirical description based on observation. Bosman, who had lived on the Guinea coast for some time, cohabiting with an African woman, recited colorful anecdotes to support his view, and could quote local informants who would themselves expound the principles of Fetish. Such informants, like generations of Africans after them, had learned what terms and what kinds of statement of belief were acceptable to their European interlocutors.

What appeared to be ethnography, grounded in the practical experiences of merchants in West Africa, was picked up by a wide range of Enlightenment thinkers and converted into a general theory of the primitive mentality, the cornerstone of a developing evolutionary account of human civilization. In 1757, Charles de Brosses, having read Bosman, coined the term fétichisme. The human sciences that constituted themselves during the nineteenth century "did so in part by taking a position in the ongoing debate over the explanation of the history and nature of religion proposed by the theory of fetishism."[54]

CONCLUSION

On both sides of the encounter, ethnographies of the Other were developed whose categories derived from the self-conception of the societies in question. Each such ethnography therefore contained within it an implicit ethnography of Self. On the European side, we have vast resources enabling us to elaborate and critique that ethnography; on the African side, there is little to go on except what can be derived from a possibly anachronistic reading based on modern sources. The account we can now give of African thinking about Europeans in the fifteenth century is itself a palimpsest of successive interpretations, each layer related to the political context of its production. Europeans still largely control the production and evaluation of modern evidence, since they dominate the academic publishing industry, and

[53] Hammond and Jablow, *The Myth of Africa*, 23; Pietz, "The Problem of the Fetish, IIIa," 112.

[54] Pietz, "The Problem of the Fetish, II," 23.

their readings, no matter how sympathetic to African culture, continue to employ social scientific categories derived from the institutional form of "modern" society. To the extent that Africans participate in debate about African experience, they do so as "moderns" whose lives and language are shaped by much the same institutional forms. Responding to this dilemma, a number of African intellectuals argue that an independent African voice must necessarily speak an African language, but the foregoing discussion implies that language itself is dependent on social organization, including its constitutive ideology.

The anthropological understanding of Europe established in Kongo at the end of the fifteenth century, in which the Europeans were classed as *simbi* spirits from the land of the dead, may seem simply mistaken, if not downright irrational. The history of the next 500 years shows, on the other hand, that the theory worked, in that it effectively guided and interpreted Kongo experience. Its relation to what we would now regard as empirical fact was no more tenuous than that of the corresponding European theory, Fetish; but to focus on its obviously erroneous features is to exoticize Kongo thought and distract attention from the highly pragmatic elements evident – for example, in Afonso's diplomatic and commercial relations with Portugal.

Moreover, in modern applications of the theory we can readily see, behind the exotic categories and "mistaken" facts, a true understanding of African-European relations. A story current in Zaire in recent years describes the slave trade as a form of witchcraft in which the souls of Africans were transported to America by occult means, and put to work there making automobiles and textiles. This slave trade persists in modern times; European businessmen, missionaries, technical experts and the like are believed to take a few souls with them to trade when they go home on leave. The souls in question are those of Africans who have died in "industrial accidents" in the port of Matadi, for example; some of them are supposed to volunteer for the trip to the land of the dead, where they will change their skins and become prosperous, like other white people. Some even return to Zaire, where they can be identified by their willingness to associate with Africans and their ability to speak African languages. The story reveals an arguably better understanding of economic relations between the "developed" and "developing" countries than we find in the reports of many development agencies.[55]

[55] MacGaffey, "African History, Anthropology, and the Rationality of Natives." For a discussion of recent "aid" programs every bit as mythological as Fetish, see J. Ferguson, *The Anti-Politics Machine* (New York, 1990).

CHAPTER 9

Early Southeast Asian categorizations of Europeans

ANTHONY REID

CATEGORIES OF OTHERNESS

SOUTHEAST Asia was not "discovered" by world trade systems. It lay athwart the sea route between India and China. For centuries before 1500 it had exported spices to the whole of Eurasia, and imported cloth, political systems, and religious ideas from India; porcelain, technology, and people from China. A substantial sea voyage lay between these places and Southeast Asia, but for over a millennium there had been traders, adventurers, and pilgrims (to the holy places of India and Sri Lanka) who thought that effort justified.

Many Southeast Asians of the sixteenth century shared a religion (Buddhism, Islam, or for Vietnamese, Confucianism) with those outside. Within these larger worlds they distinguished themselves in geographical terms. Vietnamese saw themselves as a distinct "southern" country equal in civilization to China in the north, the constant point of reference.[1] The remainder of the people of coastal Southeast Asia, particularly those touched by Malay culture, identified themselves as "below the winds" in relation to India and all points west, which were "above the winds." Barros[2] was the first western writer to note this distinction, but William Marsden was more perceptive about its meaning.[3] As he noted, it was analogous to "us-them" distinctions such as Greeks and Barbarians, Jews and Gentiles, Arabs and others (*arabu ajem*), except that unlike these phrases, or similar distinctions made by Chinese, Christians, Muslims, and others, there was no presumption of moral or cultural superiority involved. The Malay-maritime

[1] The founder of the Lê Dynasty put it clearly after driving out the Chinese in 1427: "Our state of Dai Viet is truly a cultured land. Our mountains and rivers have long been different, as likewise have the customs of South [i.e., Vietnam] and North [China]." Quoted in John K. Whitmore, *Vietnam, Hô Quy Ly, and the Ming (1371–1421)* (New Haven, 1985), 128.

[2] João de Barros, *Da Asia* (Lisbon, 1777), Dec. II, bk. 6, II:4.

[3] *A Dictionary and Grammar of the Malayan Language* (London, 1812), 2:ix–xiii.

culture of coastal Southeast Asia was itself too ethnically varied, too open to external influences, to be inherently exclusive in that way. When conflict led to polarization against Europeans, as we will see later, the exclusive terminology of believer and infidel became more useful.

Chinese and Japanese were outside the "above the winds" category, since they came from a different direction, with different monsoon winds, and had cultures very distinct from those of the Indian Ocean. Europeans, however, even when they came across the Pacific as the Spanish did, were quickly understood to be part of that world "above the winds" in which Hinduism, Buddhism, Islam, and such powerful associated symbols as Alexander the Great and the empire of "Rum" all had their origin.

"Below the winds" located Southeast Asians geographically, notably in relation to a set of Indian Ocean ports that already had many points of reference in common. The same points of reference – commerce, cosmopolitanism, affluence, lavish dress, diplomatic decorum, a strong Islamic presence – implicitly juxtaposed the whole universe of Indian Ocean exchange against tribal shifting cultivators of the interior.

Foreign writers no doubt exaggerated the stories they heard in the cities about the savages of the hills. Ma Huan,[4] for example, distinguished three types of people in Java in the early fifteenth century. The Chinese residing temporarily, and the Muslim traders from every quarter who had taken up residence there more permanently, were both clean and civilized. The natives of the interior, however, were dirty, worshipped devils, and ate unclean foods. Chou Ta-kuan portrayed an even more stark gulf between the civilized lowland Khmers of Angkor and their slaves taken from savage highlanders.

> They constitute a race apart known as the *ch'uan* [Ch'ong] brigands. Brought into the town, they do not dare to come and go outside their houses. In town, if in the course of a dispute one calls one's opponent *ch'uong*, he is suffused with hatred to the marrow of his bones, to such an extent are these people despised by other men. . . . Males and females couple with each other, but their masters would never have sexual relations with them. If by chance a Chinese arrives and, after his long enforced celibacy, should inadvertently have intercourse just once with one of these women, and the master finds out, then the next day the latter will refuse to sit down in the newcomer's company, because he has had intercourse with a savage.[5]

[4] *Ying-yai Sheng-lan: "The Overall Survey of the Ocean's Shores,"* trans. J.V.G. Mills (Cambridge, 1970), 93.

[5] Chou Ta-Kuan, "Some Remarks on the Present State of Knowledge about Slavery in

A succession of visitors to northern Sumatra, from Marco Polo onwards,[6] made similar points about the contrast between the civilized Muslims of the ports and the savage cannibals of the interior who lived like beasts.

Although local residents must have been the sources for these sharp distinctions, Southeast Asian writers themselves were more ambivalent about the dichotomy. Almost every lowland people had to deal with adjacent upland people (and often also "sea-gypsies", usually Bajau-Samal) whom they regarded as lacking civilization and religion and therefore fit to be enslaved. At the same time they were seen as the original inhabitants, often in having a special (if servile) relation with the coastal ruler and mysterious, even magical, powers over the natural and supernatural forces of forest and sea. Their rare appearances in Archipelago sources, therefore, are chiefly as direct servants of the king[7] or as magically potent individuals.[8] The riverine kingdoms of mainland Southeast Asia all saw themselves surrounded by "wild" upland peoples, potentially able to be brought within the everchanging boundaries of lowland royal countrol and settled wet-rice agriculture.[9] The interdependence in trade between the upstream and downstream populations ensured that each side incorporated the other into the myths that expressed their world-view.[10]

Nevertheless, this dichotomy between civilized/cosmopolitan peoples of the cities and coasts and barbarous/isolated people of the interior or of remote islands was certainly part of the thinking of the former. It finds one form of expression in the contrast of the Javanese (and Thai and Cambodian) theater between *halus* and *kasar* – that is, the refinement proper to the court and city as against the gross appear-

Angkor," as translated from Pelliot's French by Ian Mabbett, in *Slavery, Bondage and Dependency in Southeast Asia*, ed. Anthony Reid (St. Lucia, Australia, 1983), 44.

6 *The Travels of Marco Polo*, trans. Ronald Latham (Harmondsworth, 1958), 225–7; A. de Gubernatis, *Storia dei viaggiatori italiani nelle Indie Orientali* (Livorno, 1875), 35.

7 V. Matheson and M.B. Hooker, "Slavery in the Malay Texts: Categories of Dependency and Compensation," in Reid, *Slavery*, 192–9.

8 *De Hikajat Atjéh*, ed. Teuku Iskandar (The Hague, 1958), 91–2.

9 See, for example, *The Royal Orders of Burma, A.D. 1598–1885*, trans. Than Tun (Kyoto, 1983), 1:13, 127, 137.

10 The upstream-downstream symbiosis was set out by Bennet Bronson, "Exchange at the Upstream and Downstream Ends: Notes toward a Functional Model of the Coastal State in Southeast Asia," in Karl Hutterer, ed., *Economic Exchange and Social Interaction in Southeast Asia* (Ann Arbor, Mich., 1977), 39–54. It has been sensitively explored in a Sumatran context in two studies: Jane Drakard, *A Malay Frontier: Unity and Duality in a Sumatran Kingdom* (Ithaca, NY, 1990); Barbara Andaya, "Cash-cropping and Upstream/Downstream Tensions: The Case of Jambi in the Seventeenth and Eighteenth Centuries," in Anthony Reid, ed., *Southeast Asia in the Early Modern Era* (Ithaca, NY, 1993), 91–122.

ance and behavior of rustic folk, people from the *sebarang* (places outside Java), and demons. It also helps account for the credence given to stories of bizarre savages in some more distant island or mountain valley, whom nobody had seen but all had heard tell about. Some had tails; others had ears so long they could wrap themselves up in them at night; in one mysterious island there were only women, who became pregnant by the wind and put their male children to death.[11]

In this context, one can also understand the response of Raja Soliman, the Muslim ruler of Manila, to the aggressive approach of the first Spanish fleet under Legazpi, in 1570. Manila was already the most important port of the Philippines, but a somewhat tenuous Muslim enclave in an animist archipelago. Its commercial links with China and the other Muslim ports of the Archipelago were as vital as those with its unruly hinterland. When the Spanish somewhat peremptorily summoned Soliman to talks, therefore:

> Soliman assumed an air of importance and haughtiness, and said that he was pleased to be the friend of the Spaniards, but the latter should understand that the Moros [Muslim Tagalogs] were not painted Indians [i.e. tattooed Visayans]. He said that they would not tolerate any abuse, as had the others; on the contrary they repay with death the least thing that touched their honour.[12]

FIRST CONTACTS: "WHITE BENGALIS" AND "IRON HEADS"

Europeans were often astonished at what they found in Southeast Asia, a place of fabulous wealth, mysterious herbs and poisons, and strange sexual customs. It was certainly no less remarkable to them than Africa, the Pacific, or the New World of the Western Hemisphere.

But the surprise was not reciprocated. In a region of enormous diversity, accustomed to having its ports crowded with people of every kind, Europeans represented just another element. Foreign ships were always welcome, for they represented wealth and power. Every coastal ruler wanted to have them calling at his own port and not his rival's. The initial reception Europeans encountered was therefore uni-

[11] Local informants of Pires put the people with long ears in Papua and the island women off the west coast of Sumatra; those of Pigafetta put the former in the lesser Sundas and the latter south of Java. *The Suma Oriental of Tomé Pires* [c. 1515], trans. A. Cortesão (London, 1944), 222, 162; Antonio Pigafetta, *First Voyage Round the World*, trans. J.A. Robertson (Manila, 1969), 93, 95.

[12] "Relation of the Voyage to Luzon," 8 May 1570, translated in E.H. Blair and J.A. Robertson, *The Philippine Islands, 1493–1898* (Cleveland, 1903–09), 5 vols., 3:95.

formly agreeable. Even in relatively remote Samar, Magellan's first Southeast Asian landfall in the eastern Philippines, "their chief went immediately to the captain-general, showing signs of joy because of our arrival."[13]

Foreign merchants were acknowledged and honored figures in the diplomatic practice of the region. They were allowed to build temporary houses on shore, to acquire temporary wives, to mingle freely in the marketplace. Their leading figures had much better access to the ruler and his circle than did most natives, for they brought him extra prestige. If they carried a message from their ruler, as most substantial merchants took care to do, they were mounted on richly decorated elephants or galleys to ride in solemn procession to the palace, where they were entertained with feasting and dancing.

Language was not a major barrier. Linguistic diversity was part of the everyday experience of Southeast Asian commerce, and virtually all had to resort to some lingua franca. Arabic was one of them, because of Islam, and provided a key for the earliest European visitors – Italians traveling overland through the Middle East, Portuguese and Spaniards with a long history of interaction with "Moors." The most valuable lingua franca was however Malay, which foreign traders including the Europeans were quick to pick up. The first two non-Portuguese expeditions to reach the region already had Malay-speaking interpreters on board who facilitated their early encounters. The Spanish fleet in 1521 made use of Magellan's Sumatran slave as interpreter in the Philippines,[14] while the French expedition of the Parmentier brothers in 1529 carried two Malay-speakers who had been in the East with the Portuguese.[15]

Women were the crucial cultural intermediaries with the earliest Europeans, as with other "above the winds" and Chinese traders before them, though their role is seldom acknowledged in the literature of either side. It was not simply that temporary marriage was accepted in Southeast Asia, that divorce could be readily undertaken by either party, and that wealthy foreigners were acceptable marriage partners in most coastal centers (except for high-born women). Retailing, small trade, and money-changing were seen as the domain of women and some very large commercial transactions were handled by them. In all the ports of the region it was accepted practice that visiting traders

[13] Pigafetta, *Short Voyage*, 23.
[14] Ibid., 26.
[15] *Le discours de la navigation de Jean et Raoul Parmentier de Dieppe* (Paris, 1883), 63, 67.

took a temporary local wife, who was at the same time a commercial partner able to provide local market information, sell foreign goods in the market, and buy and sell trade goods on behalf of her partner during the monsoon period when he was away.[16] As a seventeenth-century Chinese visitor to Hoi An (Central Vietnam) put it matter-of-factly: "The women are very good at trade, so the traders who come here all tend to marry a woman to help them with their trading."[17] This practice was especially highly developed by Chinese, but there is no doubt that Europeans also profited from it.

Such relationships began very early, and provided the mechanism whereby Portuguese learned the language and culture of their Asian environment, and the local community domesticated newcomers and learned their languages. Among the tiny proportion of such relationships that have found their way into the literature, two occurred at the very beginning of Portuguese contact. The first European fleet to reach Southeast Asia, that of Lopes de Sequiera in 1509, was reportedly saved from a Malay surprise attack by the timely warning of a local Javanese woman who swam out to alert her lover on one of the Portuguese ships.[18] Among the Portuguese captured in Melaka from that fleet, nine escaped the city with the help of the daughter of the aristocrat to whose custody they had been assigned.[19] The first Portuguese Captain in Maluku, the "Spice Islands" proper, was Francisco Serrão sent there by Albuquerque in 1511. Pigafetta, who arrived two years after his death there in 1521, happened to report that he left two children by a woman he had married in Java, presumably during that first voyage from Melaka in 1511.[20] We have to assume that the harshness of the initial Portuguese irruption into Southeast Asia was very quickly modified by relationships such as these.

Regrettably few indigenous documents have survived from the early sixteenth century, and later reconstructions often carry the burdens of another age. Moreover, the impact of the early encounters appears to have been far greater on the Europeans, for the reasons sketched out. Except in the cases where they achieved spectacular military victories, Europeans are largely ignored by indigenous chronicles

[16] See Anthony Reid, *Southeast Asia in the Age of Commerce. I: The Lands below the Winds* (New Haven, 1988), 155–6.
[17] Da San, *Hai Wai Ji Shi* (N.p., 1699), 4:9, as translated for me by Li Ta Na.
[18] *The Commentaries of the Great Afonso Dalboquerque*, trans. W. de Gray Birch (London, 1877), 2:74.
[19] Barros, *Da Asia*, Dec. II, bk. 6, II:28.
[20] Pigafetta, *Short Voyage*, 66–7.

until the eighteenth century. What follows, therefore, is limited to a narrow range of Southeast Asian literature, supplemented by European descriptions.

The few Europeans who reached the region before Vasco da Gama, like the Jews of Cairo or the Armenians of Persia, usually traveled with Persian or Arab vessels, and were grouped with them. Nicolo Conti, for example, was a Venetian who learned Arabic as a young merchant in Damascus, traveled to Baghdad in an Arab caravan, and subsequently learned Perisan in the ports of Ormuz and Calacatia. There he threw in his lot with some Persian merchants, "having first taken a solemn oath to be faithful and loyal companions to one another."[21] He sailed with them to India and eventually Southeast Asia in the 1430s. Towards the end of the century, Hieronomo di Santo Stefano of Genoa traveled overland from Cairo to the Red Sea port of Cosseir with an Arab caravan, and then sailed in Arab vessels to India and Sumatra. The people he identifies as having rescued him from disasters were the Muslim *kadi* of Pasai (Sumatra) (presumably a learned Arab trader) who knew some Italian as well as Arabic, and some Arab merchants from Damascus whose service he entered in India.[22] In the first decade of the following century, Ludovico di Varthema learned his Arabic in Damascus, and must have passed himself off as Muslim, since he joined a caravan to Medina and Mecca. He found the Persian merchants of Shiraz, however, "the best companions and the most liberal of any men who inhabit the earth," and formed a contract with some of them to explore the world together. Thus in Burma, for example, he was simply a Persian.[23]

Europeans may typically have been a shade paler than Arabs and Persians, but the physical dividing line was not a fundamental one. Both the Russian Athanasius Nikitin and Ludovico di Varthema claimed that their relative whiteness was a source of interest in southern India and Burma. There were places, not easy to locate from their accounts, where women were said to offer themselves readily to the white men, or be offered by their husbands. Whatever the truth of such stories, it is significant that both authors granted that no distinction was made between themselves and their Muslim traveling companions.[24] The Portuguese conquistadors routinely described their Gujerati or Arab antagonists as "white," as well as the Chinese and

[21] "The Travels of Nicolo Conti," in R.H. Major, ed., *India in the Fifteenth Century* (London, 1857), 5.
[22] "Account of the Journey of Hieronomo de Santo Stefano," in Major, *India*, 8–9.
[23] *The Travels of Ludovico di Varthema*, trans. J.W. Jones (London, 1863), 102–3, 220–2.
[24] Ibid., 202–4; "The Travels of Athanasius Nikitin, of Twer," in Major, *India*, 10.

Ryukyuans with whom they had better relations,[25] implying that European skin-color was not seen as novel by either side.

The early Portuguese fleets, carrying hundreds of Portuguese with little prior experience of non-Christians, were of course perceived differently from individual traders. The Portuguese began by attacking Muslim ships, which confirmed the earlier idea of Muslims in the Indian Ocean that these were "Franks," the same people who had attacked the holy places during the Crusades. They now demanded to be classified as distinct from other visitors, especially Muslims. Some Malay accounts of their arrival grant this distinctiveness, though it has to be remembered that none date from before 1536, a generation after the Portuguese had demonstrated a certain uniqueness by conquering and fortifying Melaka.

The first direct impact of these "Franks" (Malay: *Feringgi*) in Southeast Asia was the mission of Diego Lopez de Sequeira, arriving in Melaka in September 1509. The chronicle of Malay kings, *Sejarah Melayu,* has this to say of the occasion:

> Then there came a Feringgi ship from Goa, and it came to trade in Melaka. The Feringgi saw that the city of Melaka was magnificent, and its port was exceedingly crowded. The people crowded round to see what the Feringgi looked like, and they were all surprised at their appearance. The Melaka people said, "These are white Bengalis!" Dozens of Melaka people surrounded each Feringgi; some twisted his beard, some knocked his head, some took off his hat, and some grasped his hand. The Captain [*kapitan*] of the ship then presented himself to the Bendahara [Chief Minister], Sri Maharaja. The Bendahara adopted him as his son, and gave him honorific cloths [the normal honour for ambassadors]. The ship's Captain presented Bendahara Sri Maharaja with a golden chain studded with jewels. He himself put it around the neck of the Bendahara. At that everybody was angry at the Feringgi Captain, but they were stopped by the Bendahara, who said, "Don't get carried away, for these are people who know nothing of manners [*bahasa*]."[26]

Though any European who has visited rural Southeast Asia will recognize the chaotic scene, we cannot be sure it all happened in 1509. The Malay account is primarily concerned to put the blame for the

[25] *Afonso Dalboquerque,* 3:69; *Lettera di Giovanni da Empoli* [1514], ed. and trans. A. Bausani (Rome, 1970), 132; *Tomé Pires,* 130.

[26] I have translated this from the Shellabear text, *Sejarah Melayu [The Malay Annals],* 10th ed. (Singapore, 1961), 248. The Raffles text, better known through Brown's translation, is almost identical except for the omission of the final sentence of this paragraph. R.O. Winstedt, ed., "The Malay Annals or Sejerah Malayu," *Journal of the Malayan Branch of the Royal Asiatic Society* 16, no. 3 (1938): 181–2 [Malay text]; C.C. Brown, trans., "Sejarah Melayu or 'Malay Annals'. A translation of Raffles MS 18," *Journal of the Malayan Branch of the Royal Asiatic Society* 35 (1952): 157.

loss of Melaka on Sultan Mahmud, particularly by his execution of its hero, the Bendahara of the above account. According to the numerous Portuguese chroniclers,[27] the respectful initial reception of Sequeira quickly turned sour, and he was lucky to escape with his life, leaving about sixty of his men ashore who were killed or kept captive. The *Sejarah Melayu* however turns this into two separate incidents, with Sequeira returning to Goa to explain the wonders of Melaka, and the Viceroy (*wazir*), Albuquerque, then sending a fleet to try to take the city, which fails. Albuquerque wants at once to send a larger fleet, but is warned against this by his admiral (*Kapitan Mar*), who states prophetically, "Melaka will not fall if Bendahara Seri Maharaja is still there; no matter how great the force sent against Melaka, it will not fall."[28]

Nevertheless there is much of interest in this account about Malay perceptions of the Portuguese in the sixteenth century. In likening them to Bengalis rather than Arabs, an insult may have been intended. Arabs had to be respected on religious grounds, however much they were laughed at privately, but Bengalis were more numerous and more resented in Melaka. Tomé Pires noted, "When they want to insult a man, they call him a Bengali," since these were a mercantile rather than a military people, alleged to be sharp-witted but treacherous.[29] At all events the Portuguese seemed a variation on the Indian theme. They were a substantial group of overdressed male traders (Malays and Javanese carried women in their ships) coming from above the winds in well-equipped ships. The earliest Burmese references to the Portuguese also describe them as a kind of Indian – *Kala-pyu* (white Indians) or later *Kala-bayin-gyi* ("feringgi" Indians).[30]

After the conquest, some Malays made an analogy the Portuguese found more to their taste – with the Ryukyu traders who carried Japanese goods from Okinawa to Melaka. "The Malays say to the people of Melaka that there is no difference between Portuguese and Ryukyus, except that the Portuguese buy women, which the Ryukyus do not." Their country had wheat, meat, and "wines after their fashion" as well as rice; they were truthful, non-Muslims, and far too proud to

[27] See Barros, *Da Asia*, II:i, 400–7; *Tomé Pires*, 254–7.

[28] Shellabear text of *Sejarah Melayu*, 248–9; Winstedt, "The Malay Annals or Sejarah Melayu," 182; Brown, "Sejarah Melayu or 'Malay Annals'," 157–8.

[29] *Tomé Pires*, 93.

[30] Saya Lun, "Life of Bayin-naung," trans. Maung Ba Kya, *Journal of the Burma Research Society* 10, no. 3 (1920): 116–17; J.S. Furnivall, trans., "The History of Syriam," *Journal of the Burma Research Society* 5, no. 2 (1915): 53; V. Lieberman, "How Reliable is U Kala's Burmese Chronicle? Some New Comparisons," *Journal of Southeast Asian Studies* 17, no. 2 (1986): 244n.

sell a fellow-countrymen into slavery. "They are white men, well dressed, better than the Chinese, more dignified . . . If they are lied to when they collect payment [for sales on credit], they collect it sword in hand."[31]

The other area where the initial Portuguese impact could not be ignored was Maluku (the Moluccas or "Spice Islands"). Again there is a Malay account, written more than a century after the events by Rijali, a Muslim Ambonese taking refuge against Dutch depredations at the court of Makassar. He describes the arrival in Nusa Telu, Ambon, of a small group of Portuguese under Francisco Serrão, shipwrecked nearby in 1512 after having made the first Portuguese voyage to Banda, further south:

> At one time a vessel from Sakibesi Nusa Telo went fishing to the Puluh Tiga Sea. Then they came and brought news to the Chief Minister [of Hitu] Jamilu, saying "In all our lives in this world we had never encountered people who looked like these. Their bodies were white, and their eyes were like cats-eyes. Then we enquired of them, but they did not know our language,[32] and we did not know their nationality." Jamilu said to them, "Go, and bring them here." So they went back and brought them to the town, to Chief Minister Jamilu. He asked them, "Where do you come from and what is the name of your country?" They replied, "We come from *negeri* Portugal with the intention of trading. The reason we came here was that we were lost and didn't know the route. So we were cast upon the coast. . . . What will our fate be here?" Then they were given a place they could build a house. After some time they asked that half should stay and maintain the house, while the other half should take the news back to their superiors. When the time of the west monsoon came they arranged for a ship to come every year without interruption. So the market became busy at Hitu, and the whole of Ambon became renowned. . . . At that time the name of Kapitan Hitu was famous from *negeri* Ambon to *negeri* Portugal. The King of Portugal gave him two names, the first Kapitan Hitu and the second Don Jamilu.[33]

Just as the Bendahara was the central figure of the Sejarah Melayu account, Jamilu holds center stage here, though he eventually comes to a bad end through pride, drunkenness, and irreligion. Yet the Portuguese are clearly portrayed as an exceptional windfall, as Chinese and Javanese had been before them to the ports they had frequented. The Portuguese accounts of the early contact in Maluku are more

[31] *Tomé Pires*, 130.
[32] The fishermen were therefore portrayed as simple folk who knew only their local language, and not the lingua franca, Malay, in which the Portuguese would have conversed to Jamilu.
[33] Z.J. Manusama, "Hikayat Tanah Hitu" (Thesis, Leiden University, 1977), 167–8.

graphic in showing the enthusiasm of the Malukans, much tested in later years, for alliances with the powerful foreigners. Portuguese chroniclers depict the rulers of Ternate and Tidore, rival centres of clove production, trade, and political influence, competing to bring Serrão's men to their capital, and thereafter to play the Portuguese card against their rivals. The same enthusiasm greeted the Dutch, the next unpredictable new factor in Malukan politics a century later.

Commercial wealth was one reason for this enthusiasm, but military prowess was the other. Galvão's view was that small-scale warfare was the favorite sport of the Malukans: "They are always waging war; they enjoy it; they live and support themselves by it."[34] Foreign traders, with large ships, firearms, and experienced fighters, were often a crucial factor in these wars. The Portuguese immediately acquired a reputation everywhere as formidable warriors, but nowhere more than in Maluku, where armor and firearms had previously been virtually unknown:

> Formerly, upon seeing a man with a helmet, they said, "Here comes an iron head," and all of them ran away presuming that we were invincible and not subject to death. But at present they know that under that helmet there is a head that can be cut off, and a body that is not immortal. And seeing us fire muskets, they imagined that our mouths breathed out a deadly fire; and at hearing bombards shooting and the Portuguese being mentioned, pregnant women had a miscarriage because among them artillery was unknown nor had they any inkling of it. But for a long time now [1544], they make war with us and do not hold us in much esteem. . . . They are men expert at arms.[35]

Other Portuguese chroniclers relate that the Ternate ruler maximized the effect of his new Portuguese allies by claiming they were the fulfillment of a prophecy: "That the time would come, when Iron Men should arrive at Ternate, from the remotest parts of the world, and settle in its Territory; by whose power the glory and dominion of the Moluco islands should be far extended."[36]

In the bigger ports of the region, firearms were already known, and

[34] *A Treatise on the Moluccas (c.1544).* Probably the preliminary version of António Galvão's lost *História das Molucas*, trans. Hubert Jacobs (Rome, 1971), 169.

[35] Ibid., 171.

[36] Leonardo de Argensola, *The Discovery and Conquest of the Molucco and Philippine Islands* (London, 1708), 3, 6. A similar allegation is made by the major Burmese chronicler U Kala, with similar skepticism, that Mon monks had claimed that de Brito's advent had been prophesied in their religious texts, which foretold that "strangers with white faces and teeth [Southeast Asians blackened their teeth] and cropped hair" would have a period of ascendance. Victor Lieberman, "Europeans, Trade, and the Unification of Burma, c. 1540–1620," *Oriens Extremus* 27, no. 2 (1980), 218.

the surprise factor cannot have been as great. The Portuguese claimed, probably with exaggeration, to have taken 3,000 guns in their conquest of Melaka, where "the gun founders were as good as those of Germany."[37] These guns appear to have been highly ornamented bronze culverins, introduced both from Gujerat and China. They may have been intended to intimidate rather than to injure. In reality it can only have been the way the Portuguese *used* their artillery so effectively that surprised the defenders. The *Sejarah Melayu* account takes this further, making play of the strangeness of the guns:

> On arrival at Melaka the ships forthwith opened fire with their cannon. And the people of Melaka were astonished at the sound of the cannon, and they said, "What sound is this, like thunder?" When the cannon balls began to arrive and struck the people of Melaka, some had their heads shot away, some their arms and some their legs. The people of Melaka were more and more amazed to see how these guns were made, and they said, "What is this weapon called that is round, yet is sharp enough to kill?"[38]

There is confirmation in letters from two Italians in Albuquerque's fleet that the fire from 400 shipboard cannon was indeed exceptionally intense, especially from a specially fortified junk that the Portuguese anchored in the Melaka river, near its central bridge, in order to bombard the town from very close quarters, "day and night" for twenty days before the assault proper began. According to these accounts, the fearful novelty of this did encourage the defenders to treat for peace.[39] Yet it is curious that the Malay writers make this alarming bombardment part of the fictional Portuguese attack between Sequeira's visit and Albuquerque's conquest, and make the outcome of it a Portuguese defeat. They wanted to show the Portuguese as a new and different element in Malay history, but clearly they did not find their modern weapons a satisfactory explanation for the loss of Melaka.

In short, Europeans were initially perceived as another kind of people from "above the winds," who were distinguished primarily by the effectiveness of their shipboard cannon, armor, and firearms. Although most indigenous sources took little account of them, they did have a major effect on the military balance in a number of areas and they greatly speeded the transformation of Southeast Asian warfare. In some areas such as Maluku and the Straits of Malacca, the Portu-

[37] *Afonso Dalboquerque*, 3:128. The more balanced account by the Italian Giovanni da Empoli confirms that Melaka did defend itself with cannons. *Giovanni da Empoli*, 136–7.

[38] I translate from the Raffles text, p. 182, with some deference to Brown, p. 158. The text is very similar in Shellabear, *Sejarah Melayu*, 248.

[39] *Giovanni da Empoli*, 137; de Gubernatis, *Storia*, 375–6.

guese state enterprise became a significant player in interstate rivalries. Elsewhere, Portuguese individuals were much in demand as mercenary gunners. In 1550, for example, a Portuguese arquebusier killed one of the leading contenders for the throne of Pegu (lower Burma), and Portuguese mercenaries subsequently helped Bayinnaung to unite Burma by conquering the old heartland around Ava. A firsthand Burmese account of Bayinnaung's five-day bombardment of Ava city in 1555 makes no mention of Portuguese as such, but its amazement at the intensity of the bombardment ("cannon and muskets reverberated like Indra's thunderbolts. . . . detonation followed detonation till it seemed a man's ears would burst") is comparable to the Malay depiction of Albuquerque's onslaught at Melaka.[40]

POLARIZATION

Despite the disaster the Portuguese inflicted on Malay kingship, Malay accounts of their arrival are morally quite neutral about the newcomers. The wars fought by the first generation of Portuguese were described as if they were fair contests between two honorable parties. The real villains of the story are not the Portuguese, but the Malays who let the side down – Sultan Mahmud himself, and Raja Abdullah of Kampar who foolishly believes Portuguese promises that they will help him become king of Melaka.

The contrast is striking with the reaction of their fellow Muslims "above the winds," notably the Arabs of the Red Sea area:

> The vessels of the Frank appeared at sea [in 1502] en route for India, Hormuz and those parts. They took about seven vessels, killing those on board and taking some prisoner. This was their first action, may God curse them.[41]

The Portuguese wasted no time in attacking the shipping of the "Moors," beginning with Arabs but quickly extending to the Gujerati Muslim traders who were a far bigger factor in Southeast Asia. Their reputation as fanatical enemies of Islam was carried ahead of them to the ports of the Straits of Malacca region. When Lopes de Sequeira arrived in Melaka in 1509, according to Tomé Pires,

> first the Gujeratis went to the said king Mahmud with a great present, and also the Parsees and Arabs and Bengalis and many of the Klings [South Indians] reported to the said king together, that the Portuguese had reached the

[40] *Nidana Ramadhipati-katha*, translated in Lieberman, "Europeans," 215.

[41] Serjeant's translation of the Arab chronicle of Hadhramaut, cited in K.N. Chaudhuri, *Trade and Civilization in the Indian Ocean* (Cambridge, 1985), 65.

port, and consequently were bound to come there every time, and that, besides robbing by sea and land, they were spying in order to come back and capture it [Melaka], just as all India was already in the power of the Portuguese—whom they call *Framges* here—that because Portugal was far away they ought to kill them all here.[42]

The first "ethnography" of the newcomers was undoubtedly provided to local rulers by Muslims in this way, and was not flattering. When Magellan's men reached the Philippines the same thing happened, a Muslim merchant in the port of Cebu explaining to its raja that these were the same *Feringgi* who had conquered Calicut and Melaka.[43] It was this Muslim term for Frank (Arabic *Faranj*, Malay *Feringgi*) that came to characterize the Portuguese (and Europeans in general) almost everywhere, carried by Malay or other Muslim traders. In Burma the term was *Balang-gyi*, as we have seen, in Thai it became *Farang*, in Khmer *Barang*, and in Chinese *Fo-lang-ji*. Only Vietnam encountered the Portuguese without this Muslim mediation, through Macao-based trade, and used geographical terms such as "people from the sea" (*Yang Ren*) or "western sea people" (*Yang Tây Duong*). In the Philippines the Muslim filter was very temporary, and the Spanish were soon called by their own preferred term, *Castila*.

It by no means followed, however, that Southeast Asians, even when they were Muslim, would necessarily share the negative view of the Gujeratis and Arabs. The initial reaction was much more neutral, or even positive, as we have seen. Only as Portuguese plundering appeared to confirm the unflattering picture given by the foreign Muslims did Southeast Asians range themselves in opposition to them. An Italian serving a Portuguese cause for which he had no special love, Giovanni da Empoli, gave a graphic account of this mounting hostility in northern Sumatra, where Albuquerque selected the reluctant Florentine as his trouble-shooter:

The General [Albuquerque] was sending me to enemy territory [at Pedir] where there were, as well, people whose boats and belongings had been seized, and whose fathers, sons and brothers, etc. had been killed by us; . . . and he commanded this like a man who had little regard for me. . . . And while I was there, many people came by night with lights to see me, as if I were a monster; and many asked how we made so bold as to pass through other peoples' territory plundering peoples and harbours.[44]

[42] *Tomé Pires*, 255.
[43] Pigafetta, *Short Voyage*, 33.
[44] *Giovanni da Empoli*, 125.

At both Sumatran ports Albuquerque visited on his way to Melaka, da Empoli was sent ashore to spy out the land and talk to the ruler, and in both cases he received a lecture on how foreign traders ought to behave: "That whoever seized his ships coming to his ports could not be deemed a friend, and that if he desired his friendship what had been seized should be returned."[45]

The *Hikayat Hang Tuah* is the most timeless because it is the most popular of Malay epics. Its earliest versions must have been recited in the fifteenth century, but the versions that survive in written form were adapted and reworked in the following century and a half. It is the story of a warrior hero of the Melaka Sultanate who is the epitome of Malay bravery, loyalty, cultivation, physical attractiveness, and mastery of the spirit world. All the other peoples with whom Melaka had to do are brought into this great epic. Hang Tuah travels to India, China, and "Rum" (Byzantium/Turkey) to show the greatness of these countries, and the high respect they have for the Malays and their king. He is sent to Siam and Java to get the better of civilized and formidable rivals who have designs on the independence of Melaka. Europeans (*Feringgi*), however, appear only as antagonists for the Malay culture hero.

Chronological sequence is not of great concern in the story, and Hang Tuah first meets the Portuguese on his voyages on Melaka's behalf to India and China. In both cases the local harbormaster (*syahbandar*) asks the Malays to berth their ships adjacent to the Feringgi, who become angry at the approach of the Melaka vessels. The Malays reply: "Why should you forbid us? We too are merchants; wherever we are told to go, there we anchor. However if you want to fight with us . . . so be it."[46] In China the enmity appears more patent, and the Malays respond that they are ready to fight, "for the Feringgi and the Malays are enemies."[47] It is forbidden to fight in a neutral Chinese port but the Portuguese, further humiliated by the magnificent reception given by the Chinese court to Hang Tuah, lie in wait for the Malays when they leave. The Portuguese guns prove useless when Hang Tuah reads his magic spell (*membaca pustaka-nya*), and the Portuguese are all killed or put to flight.[48]

News of these humiliations eventually reach the "Gebernador of Manila" [meaning this story at least postdates 1571], who reports in

[45] Ibid., 127–8.
[46] *Hikayat Hang Tuah*, ed. Kassim Ahmad (Kuala Lumpur, 1966), 346. Almost the same wording is used on p. 364.
[47] Ibid., 364.
[48] Ibid., 369–72.

person to the King of Portugal. The latter sends a fleet of forty well-armed galleys to attack Melaka in revenge. Although sick, Hang Tuah is there to drive them away with terrible casualties, including the Portuguese commander.[49] Only after Hang Tuah's death do the Portuguese succeed in taking the city by stratagem. Not surprisingly, there are many to advise the ruler not to deal with them at all, because "the Feringgi are evil people."[50]

The Portuguese, it seems, were simply like that – born enemies of the Malays. There is nothing in this or other early Malay sources to point to religion as the reason for this antagonism. Some early Portuguese sources, on the other hand, do impute the same religious motive to the Malays as to themselves. Tomé Pires, for example, related that Sultan Mahmud eventually sided with the anti-Portuguese lobby in Melaka in 1509, and told his ministers that the Portuguese "go about conquering the world and destroying and blotting out the name of our Holy Prophet. Let them all die."[51] But indigenous sources only picked up this theme in the second half of the sixteenth century, if at all.

A religious polarization between Islam and its enemies became established in Southeast Asia only after 1550. One reason may have been the Catholic Counter Reformation, the arrival of Francis Xavier and his Jesuit followers in 1542, and the beginning of a serious attempt by the Iberians to make conversion one of their major goals in the region. Another was the revival of the Islamic spice-trading route, shipping cloves, nutmeg and pepper directly from Aceh (Sumatra) to the Red Sea ports with increasing efficiency from the 1530s, in direct competition with the Portuguese route to Europe. A third factor was the rise of Turkey as a great Islamic power commanding the western termini of this route, and able to challenge Portuguese dominance of the Indian Ocean in the name of Islam. Factors internal to Islam must nevertheless be given the greatest weight. In India, as in Southeast Asia, there was a steady shift toward militant orthodoxy between 1550 and 1650. Orthodox Sunni Islam became the state religion not only of the Mughals, but also of southern states such as Bijapur, Golconda, and parts of Kerala.[52] In Southeast Asia, states such as Aceh, Brunei, Banten, Makassar (Muslim from 1603), and Ternate were visited by a

[49] Ibid., 428–35.
[50] Ibid., 487.
[51] *Tomé Pires*, 256.
[52] Richard Eaton, *Sufis of Bijapur, 1300–1700. Social Role of Sufis in Mediaeval India* (Princeton, 1978), 83–134, 193–9; Aziz Ahmad, *Studies in Islamic Culture in the Indian Environment* (Oxford, 1964), 182–90.

stream of reformist preachers and teachers from the Middle East, and began to generate revered teachers of their own, some of whom had spent long periods in Mecca and Medina.

Having arisen by uniting the northern coast of Sumatra against the Portuguese, the Sultanate of Aceh set the pace for this militant trend throughout the sixteenth century. Sultan Ala'ad-din Ri'ayat Syah al-Kahar (1539–71) was hailed by the Muslim historian Raniri a century later as "the very first who fought against all the unbelievers [*kafir*] to the point of going himself to attack [Portuguese] Melaka."[53] He was also the chief beneficiary of the direct spice trade to the Red Sea, now a Turkish lake. Through this connection he received not only a succession of Muslim scholars, but also guns and men with which to fight the infidel.[54] We should take with caution the militant speeches that Mendez Pinto put into his mouth, for example after having ferociously executed the king of Aru for having so far forgotten his religion as to ally with "those accursed dogs of the other end of the world, who for our sins and through our negligence, have with notorious tyranny made themselves lords of Melaka."[55] We also have an idea of his thinking, however, from a letter he wrote to the Sultan of Turkey in about 1565 which is recapitulated in the extant Turkish response of 1567.

> The Sultan of Aceh says that he is left alone to face the infidels. The infidels have captured islands, and taken Muslims. Merchant and pilgrim ships going from these islands towards Mecca were captured one night, and the ones they couldn't capture they fired upon, causing many Muslims to drown. And infidel rulers have conquered Ceylon and Calicut, where most of the inhabitants are Muslims. If we (Turkey) would send a fleet, all the infidel subjects of those lands would come to the true faith.[56]

There is no doubt that a militant Muslim "ethnography" of the Iberian Christians was making rapid headway here. A literature developed during the seventeenth century exhorting Muslims to make holy

[53] Nuru'd-din ar-Raniri, *Bustan as-Salatin, Bab II, Fasal 13,* ed. T. Iskandar (Kuala Lumpur, 1966), 31–2.

[54] Anthony Reid, "Sixteenth Century Turkish Influence in Western Indonesia," *Journal of Southeast Asian History* 10, no. 3 (1969): 395–414; Naimur Rahman Farooqi, "Mughal-Ottoman Relations . . . 1556–1748" (Ph.D. diss., University of Wisconsin, 1986), 267–9.

[55] *The Voyages and Adventures of Ferdinand Mendez Pinto,* trans. Henry Cogan (London, 1897), 65–6.

[56] Letter of Sultan Selim II, in Saffet Bey, "Bir Osmanli Filosofunun Sumatra Seferi," *Tarihi Osmani Encumeni Mecmuasi* 10 (1912), 606–8. I am grateful to Professors Salih Ozbaran and Cornell Fleischer for the outline translation of this letter.

war against them.[57] Similar ideas suffuse Rijali's chronicle about Maluku, the other area of intense Portuguese influence, written about 1650. After the good fortune represented by the initial Portuguese arrival, described earlier, the *Hikayat Tanah Hitu* changes mood to describe the constant wars against the infidel, and the succession of war leaders who distinguished themselves in them. Although the introduction of Muslim-Christian hostility in many respects continued the pattern of warfare between rival Ambonese *negeri* (village communities), the chronicle portrays a situation of constant holy war (*perang sabilu'llah*) in the second half of the sixteenth century. All the dead who fell on the Hitu (Muslim) side were martyrs (*syahid*) guaranteed immediate entry into heaven.[58] The Iberians appear as the inevitable enemies of the faithful, now giving a wider meaning to the ancient cleavages within Maluku.

Muslim-Christian conflict affected most parts of the region in this period, with Catholic missionaries, and to some extent Europeans in general, seen by the mercantile Muslims of the cities as inveterate enemies of Islam. A Franciscan missionary, Francisco de Santa Maria, was killed by a militant Muslim group in Brunei in the 1580s, while the first Dominicans to arrive in the Siamese capital in the 1560s were set upon by a Muslim mob who killed one and badly injured the other.[59] In the leading Islamic capitals such as Aceh, Banten, Brunei, and Makassar, Europeans who broke laws or offended rulers were given the choice of conversion to Islam or death. Some of the Muslim scholars whose job it was to convince such Christians to accept Islam showed from their arguments that they had considerable knowledge of Christianity through an Islamic prism.[60]

The Theravada Buddhists of mainland Southeast Asia had a tradition of tolerating the religious practice of others, and the friendly initial approach of the Iberians gave them no reason to change it. By the end of the sixteenth century, however, Spanish intervention in Cambodia and Portuguese activity in Burma changed the perception of the Europeans.

[57] The oldest known version of the popular Acehnese *Hikayat Perang Sabil*, a rhymed chronicle of the Holy War, is dated 1710 although there were probably oral predecessors. Ibrahim Alfian, *Perang di Jalan Allah* (Yogyakarta, 1987), 109–14.

[58] Manusama, "Hikayat Tanah Hitu," 169–71.

[59] Marcelo de Ribadeneira, *History of the Philippines and Other Kingdoms* [1601], trans. Pacita Fernandez (Manila, 1970), 457–60.

[60] Frederick de Houtman's account of his captivity in Aceh is in *De oudste reizen van de Zeeuwen naar Oost-Indie, 1598–1604*, ed. W.S. Unger (The Hague, 1948), 96–100. A more fatal Catholic experience in Aceh is chronicled in Philippe de la tres-saincte Trinité, *Voyage d'orient* (Lyon, 1652), 496–515.

Burmese chronicles have nothing good to say about Europeans, despite the crucial role Portuguese mercenaries played in helping Tabinshweti and Bayinnaung reunite the country and bring it to its greatest pinnacle of power. Of Tabinshweti (1531–51) it was recorded that "he gave himself up to the company of his favorite, a *Kala-pyu* adventurer, from whom he learned the habit of drinking. Addicted to hard drinking he began to lose his sense of morality, and had no scruple to commit adultery with the wives of his ministers."[61] More severe judgments were passed on Felipe de Brito, the enterprising Portuguese who captured the port of Syriam (opposite modern Rangoon) on behalf of the King of Arakan in 1599, and managed to turn it into a powerful independent kingdom with some local Mon support. The Mon chronicle of Pegu, very Buddhist in spirit, was mainly concerned at de Brito's inability to earn merit and ensure the kingdom's welfare because he was not Buddhist: "The ship commander, the *kala* Kappitan Jera [Captain General], was king again in Syriam. Because he was of Devadatta's company, a heretic, he had no opportunity of enshrining at the relic chamber of the pagoda."[62] On the other hand, the chronicles of the Burmese Toungoo dynasty, which took Syriam and executed de Brito in 1613, were unambiguous in their condemnation of the foreigner. Although acknowledging that he made Burmese and Mon allies, including the ruler of Martaban whose son married his daughter, the major chronicles portray de Brito (whom they call the *kala baringyi* Nga-zinga) as plundering the Buddhist shrines and temples of their riches. "He removed the precious stones with which the images were adorned, melted down the gold and silver, and beat them into leaves which he sold to traders calling at the ports. Thus, he waxed very rich by this nefarious trade, and with riches came power and authority."[63]

After Toungoo had conquered Syriam, de Brito was publicly impaled in the town square because he was "a man who had destroyed religion". Between 400 and 500 of his *kala baringyi* followers were sent to Ava as captives, where they eventually served the Burmese kings

[61] Saya Lun, "Life of Bayin-naung," 118–19.

[62] "Slapat Rajawan Datow Smin Ron: A History of Kings," trans. R. Halliday, *Journal of the Burma Research Society* 13, no. 1 (1923): 59.

[63] "Intercourse between Burma and Siam, as recorded in Hmannan Yazawindawgyi," trans. Phra Phraison, in *Selected Articles from the Siam Society Journal* (Bangkok) 5 (1959): 153. See also U Kala, *Mahazawingyi*, vol. 3, ed. Saya U Khin Soe (Rangoon, 1961), 106–111. I am grateful to Maung Maung Nyo for translating this last source for me.

as soldiers.[64] According to Furnivall, de Brito was still remembered as "the destroyer of religion" in Syriam early in the twentieth century.[65]

The disinterest of the Dutch in spreading their own religion, together with their readiness to ally with all enemies of the Portuguese, undermined the simple polarization between Muslim and Christian. Yet because Dutch did establish a degree of military and economic hegemony that the Portuguese did not, opposition to them quickly became even more universal. One of the greatest Dutch East India Company (VOC) empire-builders in the east, Rijklof van Goens, conceded in 1655 that "there is nobody who wishes us well in all the Indies, yea we are deadly hated by all nations."[66] English observers make the same point,[67] and a Chinese memorialist, noting that of all barbarians Europeans alone should be feared as "the most evil and intractable," singled out the Dutch as especially insatiable.[68]

A good example of the mood of those who suffered from Dutch expansion was the *Sja'ir Perang Mengkasar*, a verse epic in Malay celebrating the fierce wars of the 1660s through which Makassar lost its independence to the Dutch (with much Bugis help). Its author uses the terms Hollander (*Welanda*) and infidel (*kafir*) interchangeably to suit his meter. Each term is invariably accompanied by some colorful epithet – "cursed," "devils," "fiendish," "renegade," "perfidious," "greedy," "thieving," "insane."[69] As others have pointed out, the term *kafir* was not in itself necessarily abusive.[70] In referring to the English who supported the Makassar side as far as they could, the Malay writer noted, "their minds were as sharp as a *kris;* although they were crass *kafir;* they were unwavering, with upright hearts."[71] On the Dutch, however, his judgment is clear:

> Listen, Gentlemen, to my request
> never make friends with the Dutch

[64] "Hmannan Yazawindawgyi," 158; Furnivall, "The History of Syriam," 53.
[65] "History of Syriam," 57.
[66] Quoted in C.R. Boxer, *The Dutch Seaborne Empire, 1600–1800* (London, 1965), 84.
[67] William Dampier, *Voyages and Discoveries* (London, 1931), 82–3.
[68] Quoted in a letter from Beijing by the Jesuit de Mailla, 5 June 1717, *Lettres edifiantes et curieuses, écrites des missions etrangères*, vol. 19 (Paris, 1781), 10–12. See also memorial of 17 January 1684 by Shih Long, trans. in Lo-Shu Fu, *A Documentary Chronicle of Sino-Western Relations* (Tucson, 1966), 60–1.
[69] *Kutuk, syaitan, iblis, murtad, dusta, bacil, pencuri, gila*, respectively.
[70] C. Skinner, *Sja'ir Perang Mengkasar, by Entji' Amin* (The Hague, 1963), 11n. Skinner quotes Snouck Hurgronje on the same point.
[71] Ibid., 144.

they behave like devils
when they are about no country is safe[72]

EMULATION

The Southeast Asian sources of the period show both neutrality and hostility toward the Europeans, with hostility gaining ground over neutrality. Positive remarks about Europeans are extremely hard to find before the nineteenth century. Yet that cannot have been the whole picture. In the first century and a half of intense contact, before the gulf in power and wealth had become substantial, there were numerous Southeast Asians who responded enthusiastically to the new ideas introduced by Europeans. King Narai of Siam, Karaeng Pattenggalloang of Makassar, and Raja Laut of Mindanao were three seventeenth-century statesmen known from European sources to have read European books and creatively mediated European scientific and historical knowledge to their people.[73] The conversion to Christianity of the great majority of lowland Filipinos and substantial numbers of Moluccans and Vietnamese in the short period 1570–1650 is evidence of a positive response at a mass level. How did such converts perceive the Europeans who presented the gospel to them? For the most part we can only guess, on the basis of missionary accounts, that they saw them as having the keys to a great source of power.

The only Filipino author who wrote in Tagalog and touched on the issue was Tomas Pinpin, a Tagalog printer whose *Librong Pagaaralan nang manga Tagalog nang uicang Castila* [Book with which Tagalogs can learn Castilian] was published in Manila in 1610. He took for granted that his fellow-countrymen wanted to emulate the Spaniards:

> No doubt you like and imitate the ways and appearance of the Spaniards in matters of clothing and the bearing of arms and even of gait, and you do not hesitate to spend a great deal so that you may resemble the Spaniard. Therefore would you not like to acquire as well this other trait which is their language? . . . it is this [Castilian] that is the source of a lot of other things and it is like the inside of things, and everything else is only its external covering.[74]

The prologue of this work promised that learning Spanish would help or "cure" Tagalogs, and was sure to give pleasure. Vicente Rafael's intriguing analysis argues that Pinpin and his readers saw Spanish as

[72] Ibid., 214.
[73] Reid, *Southeast Asia*, 232–4.
[74] Translated in Vicente Rafael, *Contracting Colonialism. Translation and Christian Conversion in Tagalog Society under Early Spanish Rule* (Ithaca, 1988), 58.

a source of protection against the unpredictable shocks of the hierarchic system the Spanish sought to impose.[75] However Pinpin's complex text is read, it is almost the only extant Southeast Asian statement to the effect that the Europeans had introduced something of real importance.[76]

EXPLAINING EUROPEAN POWER

In every culture, perhaps in every soldier, there is a curious mixture of belief in technology and belief in fate. Few soldiers neglect to sharpen their swords or keep their powder dry before the battle, but equally few will explain their own survival or their comrade's death in purely material terms. In saying that Southeast Asians of the sixteenth century believed power to be essentially spiritual in nature, therefore, we are placing them on a continuum, not in opposition to Europeans. Portuguese too attributed their victories to divine help and the intervention of Santiago (St James). Their early victories were, however, partly attributable to the stronger conviction among their Southeast Asian antagonists that there was no use fighting if spiritual forces favored the other side. Southeast Asian wars had often been decided like trials by ordeal, by an initial skirmish or battle between individual champions or leaders. If the spiritual preparation, moral worth, and reading of the signs were superior on one side than the other, one death could be enough to show it.[77]

As we have seen, Southeast Asian sources refused to attribute defeat to inferior technology, even when they described the superiority of European firepower. As European power grew and the memory of its origins faded, progressively more symbolic explanations were developed to explain it.

The royal chronicle of Melaka, in the post-conquest versions that have come down to us, can be seen as a moral text on the theme that Melaka was made great by virtue and destroyed by vice. The dying testament of the penultimate ruler to his successor is that if you put

[75] Ibid., 55–83.

[76] As has been shown by Ileto, Filipino borrowing of Spanish motifs extended to the popular myths through which they expressed their longing to be free in later centuries. The holy week drama of the passion of Christ, and the heroic struggle of the Spanish millennial hero Bernardo Carpio, were rendered in Tagalog verse so emotionally powerful that they provided the language for nineteenth-century liberation movements. R.C. Ileto, *Pasyon and Revolution* (Manila, 1979); "Tagalog Poetry and Image of the Past During the War Against Spain," in *Perceptions of the Past in Southeast Asia*, ed. A Reid and D. Marr (Singapore, 1979), 379–400.

[77] Reid, *Southeast Asia*, 121–9.

your people to death when they have done no wrong, "your kingdom will be brought to nought." It is then made crystal clear that Albuquerque's conquest of the city was only possible because the great Bendahara Sri Maharaja and others were unjustly executed by the Sultan.[78] The best of nineteenth-century Malay historians, Raja Ali Haji, retold this story more simply: "According to the story, when His Majesty Sultan Mahmud killed Bendahara Sri Maharaja without just cause, by the decree of God Almighty the Portuguese came and attacked Melaka."[79]

In Malay texts intended more for popular entertainment than for royal instruction, explanations in the tradition of the beloved trickster tales play their part. These have nothing to do with the facts of Albuquerque's conquest in 1511, but draw inspiration from the tortuous attempts by later European companies to build permanent stone dwellings in the trading cities. Up until 1619 their requests were sometimes granted in return for favors rendered, but in that year the Dutch made themselves impregnable in their fort in Jakarta, which they renamed Batavia and established as the headquarters of their Asian trade empire. The same mistake was not made again.

The main Javanese chronicle of the kings of Banten, suzerains of Jakarta, tells this story in realistic terms. Kapitan Jangkung [Jan (Pieterszoon) Coen] requested a piece of land from the Pangeran of Jakarta, and built a strong wooden fence around it. When goods were stolen, he was allowed to strengthen this fence. A large Dutch ship then sank in the harbor, and the Dutch received permission to unload it into their factory. Trade goods were unloaded by day and, unknown to the Javanese, arms by night. Approval was sought from Banten for this increasing strength, and the Banten authorities accepted Jangkung's argument that the Dutch would be a buffer against the greater threat of Mataram (which ruled central and east Java). However, several ministers gave the prophetic warning: "The Dutch now were like a spark no bigger than a firefly. They must be smothered now lest that spark become a great fire which would destroy all."[80]

The Batavia experience seems the likeliest origin for a trickster story that quickly spread around Southeast Asia. This has the Europeans requesting and receiving a plot of land no bigger than an oxhide. They then cut an oxhide into long strips, so that it embraces enough ground

[78] Brown, "Sejarah Melayu or 'Malay Annals'," 124–5, 156–71.

[79] Raja Ali Haji ibn Ahmad, *The Precious Gift: Tuhfat al-Nafis*, trans. Virginia Matheson and Barbara Andaya (Kuala Lumpur, 1982), 17.

[80] Hoesein Djajadiningrat, ed., *Critische beschouwing van de Sadjarah Banten* (Haarlem, 1913), 43–4.

for them to build a great fort. This story is told of the Dutch occupation of Jakarta by several Javanese histories.[81] It is also told of the Portuguese conquest of Melaka by a number of Malay texts, including the popular *Hikayat Hang Tuah*.[82] While the borrowing of stories between Malay and Javanese texts is to be expected, it is surprising to find exactly the same story told in the Burmese chronicle of Syriam about Felipe de Brito's capture of that city. De Brito made the Burmese ruler numerous presents so as to

> be allowed to found in our town of Syriam a village such as might be included in a hide. When this request had been granted, he drew out the hide like a wire and on the North, South, East and West, he measured out land.[83]

Classicists will not need reminding that this is exactly the tale told by Virgil about how Dido established Carthage, by purchasing from the King of Libya as much land as an oxhide would cover, and then stretching the hide out in narrow strips. I have no explanation to offer as to how this legend traveled so far. Southeast Asians may have heard it from Portuguese themselves, or it may have spread much earlier through the long-established Middle Eastern connection. At all events it must have been thought appropriate as well as entertaining, explaining as it did how a handful of people coming from the other side of the world, ostensibly to trade, could have ended by making themselves impregnable and strangely powerful.

In the colonial era, the mental world of businesslike Dutchmen and mystical, hierarchic Javanese seemed poles apart, and theories of dualism were popular to explain how they coexisted without influencing each other. Looked at in the longer term, however, this dualism can be seen as an historical construct which suited the VOC very well. The earliest Dutch descriptions give no suggestion of such an opposition – indeed the Dutch were known to complain that a Javanese would "sell his own grandmother" for a profit. But under Jan Pieterszoon Coen's guidance the VOC showed itself on the one hand absolutely ruthless toward its commercial competitors in the spice trade; on the other hand, indulgent toward the symbolic claims of rulers in the interior to divinely ordained and universal power. VOC factors at Semarang and Padang sent regular tribute to the "Emperors" of Mataram and Minangkabau, respectively, addressed them in appropriately humble terms, and supported them against their more

[81] Ibid., 165; T.S. Raffles, *The History of Java* (London, 1817), 2:154.

[82] *Hikayat Hang Tuah*, 486–8. See also A.L.V.L. van der Linden, *De Europeaan in de Maleische Literatuur* (Meppel, 1937), 31–7.

[83] "The History of Syriam," 53.

commercially oriented local antagonists. Although the military power of the Dutch was far beyond that of their Iberian predecessors, they used it for calculated commercial advantage, never for symbolic or spiritual victories. In effect, if not in deliberate intent, they encouraged Southeast Asian rulers to retreat from economic and military concerns to symbolic and spiritual ones, where they did not compete with Dutch ambitions.

Java was the principal battlefield where this symbiosis was hammered out, and it is to Javanese literary tradition we should look for how it was perceived at the end of the day. The writing in question (though inheriting much from earlier traditions) dates almost entirely from *after* the Gianti Treaty of 1755, whereby the Mataram kingdom was divided under Dutch sponsorship between Surakarta and Jogjakarta. To that extent it can be seen as a literature making the best of a critical defeat.

A story widespread in this literature, including the major court tradition known as the *Babad Tanah Jawi*, legitimated Dutch power in Batavia through marriage to a princess of the Sundanese kingdom of Pajajaran, in west Java. This Hindu kingdom, defeated in the sixteenth century by the rising Muslim power on the coast, was seen by Javanese as legitimately distinct from Javanese kingdoms (indeed, early Portuguese maps, based on Javanese information, placed a waterway through the island separating Sundanese territory from Javanese territory). At the same time its dynasty was believed to possess great spiritual powers. From their line came the Queen of the South Sea (*Nyai Loro Kidul*), mystical bride of all legitimate Javanese rulers. The common element in all the stories in question is a beautiful Pajajaran princess so sacred (or perhaps accursed) that flames issue from her genitals whenever a normal mortal attempts to sleep with her.[84] Other rulers having failed to conquer her, she is exiled to the island of Onrust (off Jakarta), where a Dutch captain arrives and marries her – or more commonly buys her for the price of three magically powerful cannon. Their union is the origin of all Dutchmen, or at least of the Governors-General of Batavia, and explains why the Dutch are appropriate rulers of western Java and allies of the Javanese kings.[85]

While this story is usually but a small episode in mythical histories of Java, one cycle of stories set out explicitly to explain in extraordi-

[84] An established theme in Javanese mythology, since Ken Dedes in the 16th century *Pararaton* had the same miraculous power, which only the legitimate ruler Ken Anggrok could cope with.

[85] Th. G. Th. Pigeaud, *Literature of Java* (The Hague, 1968), 2:249, 333, 361, 463; Djajadiningrat, *Sadjarah Banten*, 285–6.

nary complexity who the Dutch were and why they were powerful. This is the story of Baron Sakender, whose name appears to unite a Dutch aristocratic title (familiar only from the time Baron van Imhoff became Governor-General in 1743) and the Javanese name of Alexander the Great.[86] In this text the princess with the flaming genitals is married by Sakender's brother, Baron Sukmul, who returns with her to Holland after his successful trading expedition to Java. The son of this union is the previously mentioned Jangkung (J.P. Coen), here seen as a famous warrior who determines to avenge the insult to his mother and her loss to the Muslims of her Pajajaran kingdom.

It is Baron Sakender who dominates the story, however, with a succession of superhuman exploits worthy of Ulysses or the Monkey King. Though these are too numerous even to summarize, some of them reveal much about the then perception of the Dutch. The first Dutch ruler is called Nakhoda (shipowner or supercargo), who has eleven other sons besides Sakender and Sukmul, all of whom have the names of prominent Dutchmen in the east such as Speelman, van Imhoff, and [again!] Coen. After obtaining various magical powers and assistants, Sakender saves the kingdom of Spain from attack by all the other known kings of the world above the winds (Persia, England, France, China, the Arabs), and marries the king's daughter. The Spanish throne, now suzerain over all these countries, is repeatedly offered to Sakender, but he seeks more adventure so bestows it instead on his father, the king of Holland, Nakhoda. Nakhoda regulates this great kingdom to be governed by his other twelve sons, who are the founders of the *Edele Heren*, the members of the Dutch *Raad van Indië* which ruled Batavia. He tells them:

> Suffer no misfortune in what you desire,
> even though it comes to thievery,
> These worldly goods I name, "The Company."[87]
> But to be consulted over by [you] twelve are all of its affairs:
> Commerce, war, the destroying of cities.
> These worldly goods be salaries then,
> But omit not to calculate,

[86] The only scholarly edition of this epic is by A.B. Cohen Stuart, *Geshiedenis van baron Sakéndhèr* (Batavia, 1850), which uses a text dated 1845. The same text was published with an Indonesian translation in Jakarta in 1978. I am indebted for what follows, however, to the lengthy summary and analysis provided by M.C. Ricklefs, *Jogjakarta under Sultan Mangkubumi, 1749–1792. A History of the Division of Java* (London, 1974), 377–407, based on an earlier British Museum text circa 1810.

[87] *Kumpeni* was a term by which the Dutch were known throughout Indonesia until early this century.

write up precisely
the profits and losses.[88]

This is the foundation of the curious power of the VOC, so utterly at odds with eighteenth-century Javanese ideas of what kingly power should be. The Company was ruled by a committee of men equal in rank, yet it was heir both to Dutch mercantilism and the world-empire of Philip II of Spain.

Baron Sukmul and his son Coen carry this power to Batavia to claim the inheritance of Pajajaran. It is not their firepower that gains them victory, but the characteristic trick of firing coins from their cannon, causing the defenders to become so distracted they can easily be killed. The truly powerful figure and hero of the story, Baron Sakender, appears to play no further part in advancing the cause of Holland or Europe. He flies off to see the wealthy land of Java, together with his magically powerful companions, the eagle Garuda and the horse Sembrani. In Java they appear to meet their match. Their powers of flight are negated by some more powerful force. Alarmed, they disguise themselves in new curious forms and go to meet Senapati, the first ruler of Mataram [ruled 1600–13], whose service they enter. Attention then switches to Senapati, and a prophecy about the greatness of his dynasty, which will nevertheless fall after three generations.

By the time this tale was written, the power of the Europeans could not be ignored. Javanese attempted to domesticate it through myth; others saw it as a punishment by God, or a sign of the approaching end of the world. Curiously, it was not until European colonial power was at its arrogant peak, after 1890, that Southeast Asians could see in the ideas behind it a great source of new hope.

[88] Ricklefs, *Jogjakarta*, 396.

CHAPTER 10

Beyond the Cape: The Portuguese encounter with the peoples of South Asia

CHANDRA RICHARD DE SILVA

I. AN OVERVIEW

THE "first encounter" of the Portuguese with the people of "Asia" was in some ways very different from the European encounter with the peoples of the Americas and with the inhabitants of parts of southwest and southeast Africa. Beyond Sofala, in the area called Asia by the early Portuguese writers, the situation was different. Although those who had traversed the whole distance from the West to China and vice versa were very few in number, many traders – Greeks, Romans, Arabs, Armenians, Jews – had linked India with the Mediterranean for centuries. Vasco da Gama's Portuguese were certainly not the first Europeans in these regions and European visits to South and Southeast Asia across the Islamic world continued into the fifteenth-century and beyond. Nicolo di Conti, a Venetian merchant, traveled for twenty-five years in West, South, and Southeast Asia between 1416 and 1441. Venetian envoys like Josafat Barbaro, who returned to Europe in 1478, and Genoese emissaries like Girolamo da Santo Stefano, who ventured to Sumatra between 1493 and 1499, certainly added to what learned Europeans knew of the East.[1] Indeed, the Portuguese came to the East precisely because they had heard so much about it.

As has been pointed out repeatedly by many scholars, the first man that Vasco da Gama sent ashore at Calicut was taken to two North African Muslims who could speak Castilian and Genoese.[2] It was not only a question of preexisting knowledge. The Indian Ocean and the

[1] Donald F. Lach, *Asia in the Making of Europe. Volume I: The century of discovery* (Chicago, 1965), 5–86, especially 59–65.

[2] *A Journal of the Voyage of Vasco da Gama 1497–1499*, trans. and ed. E. G. Ravenstein (London, 1898), 28. See also João de Barros, *Asia de João de Barros. Primeira Década*, ed. Hernani Cidade (Lisboa, 1945), I-iv-vi. 48–9, 143.

China Sea littorals were areas where there was constant interaction among diverse groups of peoples to a much greater extent than in the Americas or South Africa. The port cities of Asia were cosmopolitan and characterized by ethnic plurality and religious diversity. In the case of South Asia, for instance, the Portuguese were initially just one more group of visiting foreigners with fleets that were puny by comparison with the huge Chinese fleets of Admiral Zenghe (Cheng Ho).[3] Indeed, throughout the sixteenth century, except in the area of maritime commerce, Portuguese power was limited to a few small localities. What to the Portuguese signaled the opening of the fabulous Orient was for many Asian powers simply the arrival of yet another trading group, although one that unfortunately did not conform to existing practices and conventions.

On the other hand, the activities of a few European traders and travelers in the Indian Ocean in the fifteenth century cannot really be compared to the impact of the continuous presence of the Portuguese – soldiers, sailors, administrators, and priests – in forts and trading posts all along the Ocean littoral during the period that followed the voyage of Vasco da Gama.[4] Moreover, in the early encounters of the period after 1497, each side's knowledge of the Other was very sketchy. For the Portuguese, all Muslims were Moors (*Mouros*), so named after the Moors of North Africa, and for many Asian peoples the Portuguese were Franks (*faranghis*), the foresworn enemies of the Muslims. Prolonged interaction led to a cumulative accumulation of knowledge of the Other, a knowledge that was, as we shall see, mediated by preconceptions and prejudices, but one that also engendered new perceptions.

In the study of this interaction between the Portuguese and the "Other," it is sometimes necessary, due to the nature of the evidence available, to regard the Portuguese as a single group. Yet they were, in some respects, very diverse. Virtually all Portuguese shared at least outwardly the strong religious bond of Christianity, but there was among them a minority of "New Christians," recent and often reluctant converts from Judaism. Not all were Portuguese. The early expeditions carried a number of Italians, Castilians, Germans, and other Europeans as traders, gunners, and sailors. Perhaps more signifi-

[3] This idea and several others presented in the introductory section of this chapter have been anticipated in Michael Pearson, *The Portuguese in India* (Cambridge, 1987), 10–13.

[4] Ibid., 13. For instance, Pero da Corvilham, the Portuguese king's spy, visited many ports in the Arabian Sea (1487–1493) but he, like many Western travelers, traveled disguised as a Muslim.

cantly, the cultural background of the Portuguese nobleman (*fidalgo*) differed in many ways from that of the Portuguese sailor who, unlike the former, would have, as a rule, sat on the floor at home and eaten his food without the use of cutlery. On the other hand, in contrast to the extraordinary diversity of the people they encountered in Asia, the Portuguese do appear as a cohesive group. Even among the Muslim traders of the Indian Ocean there was great ethnic diversity, Arabs, Turks, Persians, Mughals, Gujaratis, Mappillas, Navayats, Ilappal, each speaking a different language. When one adds the Hindus, Jains, and Buddhists of different regions as well as the many ethnic groups in India alone, it is clear that the picture is one of many different interactions, even if one does not consider the caste and other social differences within these groups.[5] Finally, one needs to keep in mind that interaction involves differential integration.[6] Asian groups adjusted to the Portuguese presence differentially, which, in turn, led to a reevaluation of their self-perception and of their relations with other groups within the same social system.

A similar transformation occurred within the Portuguese community settling in the East. When the Portuguese first came to the East they brought with them a tradition of hostility to Islam. They hoped to find the kingdom of "Prester John," a Christian ally who would help turn the flank of the Islamic assault on Christendom. Instead, they found Muslim merchants, including some of their old enemies, the "Moors" of North Africa, dominating the trade of the Indian Ocean. The initial reaction was one of caution, but fear, suspicion, and distrust were not far behind. After clashes in the East African ports of Moçambique and Mombasa, da Gama refused to land at Malindi to see the Sultan in person.[7] When, after his arrival in India, the Samudri (ruler, or literally, sealord) of Calicut poured scorn on the poor gifts that da Gama presented to him, the Portuguese suspected that the Samudri's mind had been poisoned by the Muslims. As an account of the voyage relates: ". . . the captain said that he begged as a favour that as the Moors wished him ill and might misinterpret him, a Christian able to speak Arabic should be sent for. . . . " As the trading con-

[5] On the social diversity in the Indian Ocean ports, see Duarte Barbosa, *The Book of Duarte Barbosa*, trans. and ed. M. L. Dames (London, 1918–1921), 2 vols. passim; Geneviève Bouchon, "Les Musulmans du Kerala à l'époque de la découverte Portugaise," *Mare Luso-Indicum* 2 (1972): 18–19; Jean Aubin, "Le royaume d'Ormuz au début du XIVe siècle," *Mare Luso-Indicum* 2 (1972): 77–179, especially 138–150, 175–179.

[6] Marshall Sahlins, *Historical Metaphors and Mythical Realities: Structure in the Early History of the Sandwich Islands Kingdom* (Ann Arbor, Mich., 1981), 67–72.

[7] *Voyage of Vasco da Gama*, 41–5; *Asia de João de Barros*, I-iv-vi, 150. Negotiations were conducted with the Sultan's son who came to the Portuguese ships in a boat.

tinued to falter, largely because the goods that the Portuguese had brought were not marketable in India, Portuguese suspicions of the Muslims grew: "... they bore us no good will, and when one of us landed they spat on the ground, saying 'Portugal, Portugal.' Indeed, from the first they had sought means to take and kill us. ..."[8]

Contemporary Muslim accounts do not give us an inkling of the preconceptions that Islamic peoples of the region had about the Christians of Europe. But while they too might have been cautious at first, there is no reason to conclude that there was inveterate hostility to the Portuguese among all Muslims of India at the time of the arrival of da Gama's fleet.[9] As we have seen, the Muslims of the Malabar coast of India were made up of diverse groups, but all of them had been trading peacefully with the Syrian Christian inhabitants of the region. The Portuguese accounts themselves do not indicate blanket hostility toward them. A Tunisian Muslim who met the first member of da Gama's crew to go ashore at Calicut is said to have come on board with the words: "A lucky venture, a lucky venture! Plenty of rubies, plenty of emeralds! You owe great thanks to God, for having brought you to a country holding such riches!"[10] When da Gama wanted to rest after his first audience with the king of Calicut, it was a Muslim who provided him with a night's lodging in his own house. On the other hand, it is quite reasonable to conclude that the Arab, Persian, and Gujarati merchants who handled the trade between the Malabar coast of India and West Asia (the *Mouros de Meca* as the Portuguese called them) were not enamored of fresh trading rivals, and were glad enough to be able to ridicule Portuguese pretensions to wealth and power.[11] Genevieve Bouchon suggests that there is reason to believe that at least the locally resident Muslims (*Mouros da terra*) were not averse to the emergence of a competitor whose trading activities might well raise the prices of local produce.[12] In fact, there is reason to believe that even the locally resident merchants were themselves divided between the elite Maraikkayar families who maintained close links with the Arab and Persian centers of trade and pil-

[8] *Voyage of Vasco da Gama*, 62, 68.

[9] Shaikh Zeen-ud-Deen [Zain-ud din] *Tohfut-ul-Mujahideen*, trans. M. J. Rowlandson (London, 1833). The account was written around 1581 and reflects three generations of warfare between the Portuguese and Muslim traders of the Malabar coast.

[10] Ibid., 49, 59–60; *Asia de João de Barros*, I-iv-viii, 159.

[11] *Asia de João de Barros*, (I-iii-ix), 161–165; Fernão Lopes da Castanheda, *História do descobrimento e conquista da India pelos Portugueses*, ed. Pedro de Azevedo (Coimbra, 1924–1933), 9 vols., 1: 50–1.

[12] Genevieve Bouchon, *"Regent of the Sea": Cannanore's response to Portuguese expansion, 1507–1528* (New York, 1988), 53.

grimage (and thus were more hostile to the Portuguese) and the local Muslim traders who were engaged in small scale trade.[13]

The reaction of the Samudri, the Hindu ruler of Calicut, can be gleaned from Portuguese accounts. Initially, the Portuguese were warmly welcomed as one more group of traders. In tolerant Calicut, the action of the Portuguese in praying at a Hindu temple, which the Portuguese themselves mistook for a Christian church, might have been favorably construed. It was when the ruler of Calicut saw the paltry presents he was offered from a ruler who, according to the Portuguese, "... was lord of many countries and the possessor of great wealth of every description, exceeding that of any king of these parts...,"[14] that the respect accorded to the strangers evaporated. Still the Portuguese were not yet perceived as a threat to the ruler. They were allowed to travel freely, and once lost their way and "wandered far inland." The people welcomed them and fed them. Many visited the Portuguese vessels. It was when Vasco da Gama, on the point of departure, sent another paltry present to the Samudri accompanied by a request for a bahar of cinnamon, a bahar of cloves and samples of other spices as a present to the king of Portugal that the ruler of Calicut finally lost patience. The Samudri of Calicut, like other rulers of the area did not himself participate in trade. Such mundane matters were left to the merchants of his kingdom for whom the ruler provided protection and facilities. The traders in turn gave presents to the ruler and paid him customs dues. The demand of a group of men from a faraway land that he should grant them valuable presents in exchange for some worthless gifts must have seemed presumptuous indeed. The Portuguese refusal to pay customs dues for the goods landed was an equally significant issue. Here was one more reason to believe the tale spread by some Muslims that these newcomers "had nothing to give but would rather take away and that thus his country would be ruined." The Samudri's rejection of the present and his demand that the Portuguese should pay customs duties was therefore an assertion of his position as ruler to this apparently unsophisticated group of strangers.[15]

[13] Susan Bayly, *Saints, Goddesses and Kings: Muslims and Christians in South Indian society 1700–1900* (Cambridge, 1989), 79. Bayly provides evidence for this on the neighboring Coromandel coast.

[14] *Voyage of Vasco de Gama*, 58, 60. The presents offered to the Samudri consisted of 12 pieces of striped cloth, 4 scarlet hoods, 6 hats, 4 strings of coral, 6 hand-wash basins, a case of sugar, 2 casks of oil and 2 casks of honey.

[15] Ibid., 63–72; *Asia de João de Barros*, 240, refers to a similar difficulty arising with the ruler of Cannanore in 1502. After meeting with de Gama, retired leaving commercial

The importance of the Indian conception of the state and of the role of the king in assessing the attitude of Indian monarchs toward the newcomers has been highlighted by Michael Pearson.[16] The ideal of the Indian king was to be *chakravarthi* or world conqueror, and the world in this context was the subcontinent of South Asia. Land revenue was the basis of royal power of all major South Asian states. The sea was the arena of merchants and of lowly fishermen, and as long as the merchants paid their dues, the king did not interfere in overseas trade. Of course, this attitude was modified by royal concern for trade in the smaller principalities such as Calicut, Cochin, and Cannanore where a substantial portion of royal revenue was derived from trade. However, this attitude explains why the major kingdoms of India made no real military effort against the Portuguese and why the *Mirat-Sikandari*, a Persian history of the kingdom of Gujarat, dismisses the naval battle of Chaul (1507) as a pacification exercise conducted with the aid of some Turks against some disorderly *faranghis*.[17]

Yet the Portuguese did alienate the principal ruler on the Malabar coast. How much of this rift was due to ignorance of local conditions by the Portuguese? Clearly the Portuguese, having geared themselves for so long to the needs of African trade, had not foreseen the need for costly presents to win the favor of Eastern rulers. They had had no clear idea of what could be sold in India. Some gaps in their knowledge were easily filled. When Cabral appeared in the East with the next Portuguese fleet, he brought valuable presents of silverware and precious cloth.[18] Social nuances proved more difficult to master. In 1500, Cabral sent as his first messengers to Calicut five persons of the fisher caste together with a Muslim all of whom had been taken by da Gama from India to Portugal. The Samudri agreed to meet the Muslim (now turned Christian), but refused to receive the "low-caste" fishermen.[19] Cabral caused further aggravation during the negotiations with the king of Calicut by insisting on keeping some of his "high-caste" Nair hostages on board despite being informed that they "could not eat, drink, or sleep at sea" because of their caste

matters to be discussed by the merchant representatives. See Bouchon, *Regent of the Sea*, 59–60.

[16] Michael Pearson, *Merchants and Rulers in Gujarat: The Response to the Portuguese in the Sixteenth Century* (Berkeley, 1976).

[17] See translation by Edward C. Bayley published as *The Local Muhammadan Dynasties: Gujarat* (London, 1886), 222.

[18] *The Voyage of Pedro Alvares Cabral to Brazil and India*, trans. W. B. Greenlee (London, 1938), 74; *Asia de João de Barros*, 192; Castanheda, *História do descobrimento*, 80–81; Bouchon, *Regent of the Sea*, 52.

[19] *The Voyage of Pedro Alvares Cabral*, 71, 110.

status.[20] Negotiations were broken off by the Samudri and did not resume until the Nair hostages were replaced by Muslims.[21] In January of the next year, Cabral was loading his ships off Cochin with two Hindu hostages on board when a hostile fleet arrived from Calicut. By this time Cabral had learnt of the fear of pollution among high-caste Hindus and had agreed to change the hostages daily, but when the enemy squadron appeared, Cabral, to the despair of the two Nairs on board, set sail for Portugal without releasing them.[22] A decade later, the incident still rankled in the mind of the king of Cochin.[23]

It has been suggested by some analysts that some of the initial misunderstandings might have been eased if there had been greater proficiency by at least one of the parties in the language of the other.[24] In most cases the Portuguese used translators who knew Arabic to communicate with Asian rulers.[25] This was adequate for the areas of Islamic dominance in East Africa and West Asia, but south of Goa in India the local rulers did not speak Arabic. For example, in Calicut, there had to be two separate translations to convey a proposal – Portuguese to Arabic and Arabic to Malayalam – and the reverse process was needed to obtain a response. On the other hand, the very presence of a third mutually comprehensible language must have made the acquisition of knowledge about the "other" a much swifter and more complete process than in other encounters.[26] Even with better communications there would have been the problem of adjusting to different behavior patterns arising from different cultures. The Portuguese killed and ate cows; the Hindus venerated them.[27] The

[20] Ibid., 74. 171–2, 174–6. In fairness to Cabral it should be pointed out that he had explicit instructions from his king on the need to take and keep hostages while his men were on land.

[21] Ibid., 75–6.

[22] Ibid., 86–87; Castanheda, *Historia do descobrimento,* 90; *Asia de João de Barros,* I-v-viii, 208.

[23] [Afonso de Albuquerque], *Cartas de Afonso de Albuquerque* (Lisboa, 1894–1935), 7 vols., 3:73, 77, 81.

[24] Bouchon, *Regent of the Sea,* 53–4; *The voyage of Pedro Alvares Cabral,* xxvi.

[25] See Jean Aubin, "L'ambassade du Pretre Jean a D. Manuel," *Mare Luso-Indicum* 3 (1976): 28; *The Voyage of Pedro Alvares Cabral,* 66, 71.

[26] One of the better known of the translators and guides that the Portuguese used was Gaspar da India, a Jew from Granada (in Spain) who was a Muslim when da Gama on his return journey met him at Anjediva. Gaspar da India became a Catholic and returned with Cabral to India. A few years later he wrote to the Portuguese king offering the services of his son, Balthezar, who, according to his father, spoke several languages.

[27] As the king of Cochin wrote to D. Manuel, King of Portugal (1509?), "*e o Visorey matar muytas vacas e eu mandava me queixar a elle . . . E esta mor deshonra que nesta terra. . .*", Albuquerque, *Cartas,* 4:44. Bouchon relates the story of how those who were besieging the Portuguese fort sent two cows as decoys. The Portuguese caught

people of India chewed betal, a habit that at least some Portuguese found repulsive.[28] Shah Jahan, much later on, is reputed to have said: "In truth the Franks would be a great people but for their having three most evil characteristics: first, they are Caffars, secondly they eat pork, and thirdly, they do not wash that part from which replete Nature expels [its] superfluities of. . . ."[29]

Yet communities with divergent cultural traditions (for example, Hindus and Muslims,) had lived amicably for centuries in the Malabar coast of India. It is clear that some of these adverse views of each other were a result of a conflict that stemmed from the Portuguese decision to use force to monopolize the import of spices from Asia. Cabral was instructed to request the Samudri of Calicut to expel (foreign) Muslims from his ports and that ". . . if you encounter ships belonging to the aforesaid Moors of Mecca at sea, you must endeavor as much as you can to take possession of them, and of their merchandise and property and also of the Moors who are in the ships, to your profit as best you can and to make war on them and do them as much damage as possible as a people with whom we have so great and so ancient an enmity. . . ."[30] The Portuguese demand that sovereign rulers of the area should provide hostages as proof of their "good intent" was another factor that would have poisoned relations at the very outset.

There are numerous instances of excessive violence by the Portuguese. Cabral's bombardment of the township of Calicut left bitter memories, as did the plunder of Muslim ships in a region long accustomed to peaceful trade. Among the best known of such seizures was that of the large Calicut ship *Meri,* captured by the Portuguese under da Gama after three days of fighting in August 1502. The ship was plundered and set on fire with passengers (including pilgrims returning from Mecca) and crew still on board. Twenty children who were spared were baptized and sent to Portugal. One of the few adult survivors was later despatched to the Samudri with a threatening letter.[31] This kind of episode partly explains the sentiments about the Portuguese expressed in Zain-ud-din's writings:

the cows but were shown up, to the Hindus, as a group committing sacrilege. Bouchon, *Regent of the Sea,* 95. See also *Asia de João de Barros,* 35.

28 Albuquerque poured scorn on his Portuguese enemies as *"cheos de betele e de negras."* Letter to D. Martinho, n.d., in Albuquerque, *Cartas,* 1:468.

29 Sebastien Manrique, *Travels of Fray Sebastien Manrique 1629–1643,* trans. E. Maclagen (Oxford, 1927), 2 vols., 2:219.

30 *The voyage of Pedro Alvares Cabral,* 180. The Muslims were soon aware of Portuguese policy: see Zain-ud-din, *Tohfut-ul Mujahideen,* 79.

31 Castanheda, *História dos descobrimento,* 1:97–98; *Asia de João de Barros,* 237–9.

... they tyrannized and corrupted the Muslims and committed all kinds of ignoble and infamous acts. Their acts of violence were countless. ... They hindered the Muslims in their trade, above all in their pilgrimage [to Mecca]. They robbed them, burnt their cities and mosques, seized their ships and dishonored the Sacred Book [Qu'ran], desecrated the sacred precincts of the mosques and incited the Muslims to apostasy. ... They tortured the Muslims with fire, sold some and enslaved others, and against others, practiced deeds of cruelty which indicated a lack of all humanitarian sentiment.[32]

On the other hand, there were many Muslims (as well as those of other faiths) who proved willing to assist the Portuguese for their own profit. Among the traders of the port cities of Asia, the Portuguese found collaborators who were quite willing to serve them if, in the process they also served themselves.[33] The ruler of Cochin saw in the Portuguese the means of freeing himself from the dominance of the neighboring Samudri of Calicut. Among the earliest Portuguese envoys to Ethiopia was Sidi Muhammed, a Tunisian Muslim. Malik Aiyaz, who held the strategic island of Diu for the Sultan of Gujarat, was quite willing to work with the Portuguese to retain his wealth and power.[34] In economic and political self-interest, Asians proved to be much like the Portuguese. If collaboration was limited in the early stages, it was often because common ground did not always prove easy to find.

One of the factors that overshadowed possibilities of political and economic cooperation was the divergence of the Portuguese attitude toward religion from that of the Hindus, Buddhists, and Jains. At the outset, the Portuguese, unaware of the existence of religions other than those stemming from the Judeo-Christian tradition and seeking the fabled Christian kingdom of Prester John, thought that the Hindus were Christians. By the time da Gama returned to India in 1502 they knew better. Yet all along the Portuguese brought with them the idea that political allegiance and at least nominal adherence to the religion of the ruler went hand in hand. Afonso de Albuquerque argued that the ruler of Cannanore had no authority to mediate in a dispute between Mamale, the ruler's own Muslim vassal, and the Portuguese over the Maldive Islands because the ruler of Cannanore was a Hindu

[32] My translation from Zain-ud-din (Zinadim), *História dos Portuguêses no Malabar por Zinadim*, trans. David Lopes (Lisboa, 1898), 44–5.

[33] For later instances, see Michael Pearson, "Indigenous dominance in a colonial economy: The Goa rendas 1600–1700," *Mare Luso Indicum* 2 (1972): 61–72.

[34] See, for example, Bouchon, *Regents of the Sea*, 53, 55–56, 80, 86, 90; Pearson, *Merchants and Rulers*, 67–70; Aubin, "L'ambassade du Preste Jean," 5–7; Jean Aubin, "Cojeatar et Albuquerque," *Mare Luso-Indicum* 1 (1971): 123–33.

and the islands were Muslim.[35] The very acceptance of conversion to Christianity was taken as prima facie evidence of a shift of allegiance to the Portuguese king. This was how the submission of the Syrian Christian community to da Gama (1502) was interpreted.[36] Conversion was also a means of liberating oneself from the caste obligations of Hindu society. Within a dozen years of the first arrival of the Portuguese, the ruler of Cannanore was complaining that converts no longer felt that they owed obligations to the Hindu community.[37] The refusal of "low-caste" converts to continue to provide obligatory services to the "high-caste" Hindus must have roused deep resentment. A few years later, Portuguese Governor Afonso de Albuquerque ordered that no one should be baptized without making certain that he was free of obligations.[38] This order was soon forgotten. As the king of Kotte in Sri Lanka complained to the Portuguese governor of India in the 1540s,

> . . . they do not become Christians except when they kill another or rob him of his property or commit other offences of this nature which affect my crown and in their fear they become Christians and after they become unwilling to pay me my dues and usual quit rents in consequence of which I am not so satisfied with their becoming Christians. . . .[39]

In fact, the zeal for missionary work and greater intolerance that came in the 1540s with the Counter Reformation aggravated the problem. Hindu temples in Goa were destroyed and Hindu ceremonies forbidden. Although economic and political realities persuaded the Portuguese to allow non-Christians to remain in the areas they ruled, they lived essentially as second-class citizens who were legally disadvantaged vis-à-vis the Christians. The Syrian Christians were gradually forced to adhere to the Roman rite and to accept the authority of Catholic bishops.[40]

However, religion was also significant in terms of the differential integration of Asian communities in the European universe. Charles R. Boxer's work has made it abundantly clear that the Portuguese, especially the fidalgos and the clergy, were not without color preju-

35 Albuquerque, *Cartas*, 1:87–8.
36 *Asia de João de Barros*, I-vi-vi, 249.
37 Albuquerque, *Cartas*, 3:335 (summary of undated letter), 2:402.
38 Ibid., 4:67. Jorge de Melo to the King, 28 December 1514.
39 P. E. Pieris and M. A. Hedwig Fitzler, eds., *Ceylon and Portugal: Kings and Christians, 1539–1552* (Leipzig, 1927), 86–7.
40 Pearson, *The Portuguese in India*, 109, 116–9; C. R. de Silva, *The Portuguese in Ceylon, 1617–1638* (Colombo, 1972), 245–6.

dice,[41] it seems clear that those who accepted the new faith gained greater social status and new economic opportunities. As in the case of Islam, many of the early converts were those at the lower end of the social ladder. In 1514, almost half the converts in Cannanore were from the Tiyan and Mukkuvan castes.[42] In Sri Lanka and on the neighboring pearl fishery in south India, the converts were largely fishermen – Karaiyars and Paravars. Recent scholars have attempted to trace the rise of the social status of these groups to their conversion to Christianity in the sixteenth century.[43] In the course of time, in the areas controlled by the Portuguese, Christianity was accepted by some members of higher castes as well. Differential integration of the Portuguese to Asian society was the other side of the coin. While the Portuguese religious and political elite kept aloof from the Asians, many of the soldiers and sailors proved to be less inhibited. Women in Indian ports included many who were willing to set up house with foreign traders; indeed, this had been a frequent practice of Muslim traders. Portuguese women in the East were few in number, and Portuguese men began to live with local women. By 1514, in Cannanore alone there were thirteen children from such unions.[44] In the context of the lax enforcement of canon law in early sixteenth-century Europe, it was not surprising that priests were not far behind. In 1510, chaplain Julião de Nunes wrote to the king of Portugal about two priests who had lived with local women and had fathered children.[45] Such instances became rare after the 1540s, but thriving communities of married Portuguese and Eurasians began to appear in the sixteenth century, not only within Portuguese territory but also in other Asian port cities.[46] These groups began to think of their settlements as home and had no expectation of returning to or traveling to Portugal. They often lived as traders and artisans in Portuguese lands but supplemented these activities with work as mercenaries and pirates.[47]

Differential integration with the indigenous peoples led to changes

[41] C. R. Boxer, *Race relations in the Portuguese colonial empire 1415–1825* (London, 1963).

[42] *Documentação para a história das missões do padroado português do Oriente*, ed. António da Silva Rego (Lisboa, 1947–1958), 12 vols., 1: document 113. Letter of Alonso to the King, 27 December 1514.

[43] See Michael Roberts, *Caste conflict and elite formation: The rise of a karava elite in Sri Lanka, 1500–1950* (Cambridge, 1982).

[44] *Documentação*, 1: document 113.

[45] Albuquerque, *Cartas*, 3:309–11. Letter dated 14 October.

[46] Pearson, *The Portuguese in India*, 83–84, gives information on some of these communities: Cambay in Gujarat, S. Thomé on the Coromandel coast (100 casados by 1545), Hughli in Bengal and Chittagong and the Arakan (2500 including descendants by 1598).

[47] Ibid., 94.

in Portuguese social stratification within the colonial possessions. Those born in Portugal (*reinões*) considered themselves superior to those born to Portuguese parents in Asia (*Indiaticos*) and both considered themselves to be above the Eurasians (*mestiços*) or those of Portuguese and African parentage. The Asian converts came next, and those who were not Christian were followed at the bottom of the order by the slaves. These social barriers were not completely impermeable,[48] but the new context did introduce new social gradations. In Portuguese Asia, as in the Americas, tensions between *reinões* and *casados* (married Portuguese settlers) surfaced from time to time. In the second half of the sixteenth century there was increasing evidence of cultural exchange. This exchange was evident in the impact of European illustrations and paintings on Mughal art. Emperor Akbar invited Jesuit missionaries to his court and was presented with a polyglot Bible illustrated by Italian and Flemish artists.[49] The missionaries also presented Akbar with several paintings. The best known of these was a copy of the Byzantine Virgin now in the Borghese chapel of the Basilica of Santa Maria Maggiore at Rome.[50] This painting was hung at the Jesuit chapel at Fatehpur Sikri. By the 1580s, Mughal artists were copying European paintings. There were adaptations as well. Paintings with European themes were drawn with Indian costumes or European figures were drawn on an Asian background.

Other more widespread instances of the intermingling of artistic traditions can be seen in the use of Asian decorative motifs in Indo-Portuguese furniture and household goods.[51] Language was even more significant in terms of the continuing interaction. By the end of the sixteenth century, Portuguese seems to have become one of the languages of communication between traders in the Indian Ocean littoral.[52] Many of the terms used by the people of the Indian Ocean littoral to describe the novelties brought by the *faranghi* were derived from Portuguese words. These borrowed terms include words for items such as shoes and tables but also Christian concepts.[53] Words

[48] Ibid., 96.

[49] Ahsan Jan Quaisar, *The Indian response to European technology and culture A. D. 1498–1707* (Delhi, 1982), 86.

[50] What was presented to Akbar was probably a copy of a copy. See *Letters from the Mughal Court: The First Jesuit Mission to Akbar*, ed. John Correia Affonso (Bombay, 1980), 31, 48.

[51] See Carlos de Azevedo, *Arte Christã na India Portuguêsa* (Lisboa, 1959).

[52] David Lopes de Melo, *A expansão da lingua portuguêsa no Oriente durante os séculos XVI, XVII, e XVIII* (Barcelona, 1936).

[53] Sebestião Rodolpho Dalgado, *Influencia do vocabulário português em linguas asiáticas (abrangendo cêrca de cinquenta idiomas)* (Coimbra, 1913).

and terms bring conceptual baggage with them. For example, the term *asianu* in Sinhalese (*asiano* in Portuguese) seems to indicate that the very concept of Asia as distinct from Europe came with the Portuguese impact.[54] There was a comparable acquisition of Oriental words by the Portuguese.[55] Much more work needs to be done on this subject.

Another area that has shed light on the extent of cultural interaction is the study of Portuguese creole languages. David Jackson and others have unearthed evidence that Portuguese creoles in Asia have African as well as European and Asian elements, the African element coming through soldiers and slaves brought by the Portuguese.[56] The oral texts transmitted in verse and song in different regions seem to indicate the spread of such texts from one area to another and the merging of Portuguese imagery with local background and custom. The song "Singelle nona" (Sinhalese Lady), for instance, was known in Southeast as well as South Asia.[57] These hybrid texts have to be evaluated in the context of their performance through equally hybrid musical forms and instrumentation, and it is this picture of a vanishing communal identity that scholars are trying to capture today.

Obviously in the long run the extent of the accommodation varied according to location, class or caste, and religion. In territory directly under Portuguese rule, where European culture was constantly reinforced by arrivals from Europe, the tendency, especially among the elite, was to try to conform to the then current Western norms. Yet, even in such areas, the Portuguese themselves were always in a minority, and there was a process of absorption of some local practices, some of which were loaded with values. No wonder that the Goa Inquisition (established 1560) was suspicious of practices such as the refusal to eat pork, the wearing of Indian dress (*dhotis* and *cholis*), or

[54] Instance given in D. E. Hettiaratchi, "Influence of Portuguese on the Sinhalese Language," *Journal of the Ceylon Branch of the Royal Asiatic Society* 9 (1965):229–239, especially 234.

[55] D. Fransisco de S. Luis, *Glossario dos vocabulos portuguêses derivados das linguas orientais e africanos, excepto o arabe* (Lisboa, 1837).

[56] Kenneth David Jackson, "Canta sen vargonya: Portuguese creole verse in Sri Lanka," *Journal of Pidgin and Creole Languages* 2, no. 1 (1987):31–48; Kenneth David Jackson, "Um conto folclorico no crioulo Indo-Portugues," *Boletim do Instituto Menezes Bragança*, no. 154 (1988):1–14.

[57] Jackson gives one version: "Singelle nona, Singelle nona,/ Veeanda lava,/Savam nuthen, bolsa nuthen,/Korpuper roosa." (Sinhalese girl, Sinhalese girl,/I saw you going to bathe,/Without soap, without a bag,/ Your body blushing.) Jackson, *Canta* 33, gives references to other versions in his *Sing Without Shame: Oral Traditions in Indo-Portuguese Creole Verse with Transcription and Analysis of a Nineteenth-Century Manuscript of Ceylon Portuguese* (Philadelphia, 1900), 6.

even of cooking without salt (Hindu practice).[58] Even in sixteenth-century Goa, the center of Portuguese culture in the East, the majority of the indigenous people remained recognizably South Asian. They chewed betal, drank from vessels without touching them with their lips, washed frequently, drank arrack rather than wine, and anointed themselves with sandalwood.[59]

Beyond the pale of Portuguese power the impact of their culture was certainly limited; its greatest impact came through religion. Even those Portuguese who ate rice with the fingers of their right hand were brought up in the belief that those other than Christians were idolaters. A century of Portuguese writing on the wonders and novelties of South Asia include some comments on Hinduism, Buddhism, and Jainism but indicate no real understanding of any of these religions. Long after political conflicts were resolved, religious prejudice and historical memories on either side kept peoples apart.

II. A CASE STUDY: SRI LANKA

The interaction between the Portuguese and the people of the Kingdom of Kotte, located on the southwestern plain of the island of Sri Lanka, provides a rare example of a "first encounter" that is described by both indigenous and Portuguese sources. In this case, two accounts – one Portuguese and one indigenous (Sinhalese) – allow us to discover how each side interpreted the incidents of the initial encounter and trace how memories and traditions relating to the "first encounter" were modified by later contacts and experiences. The two documents chosen are very different in nature. The Portuguese description is drawn from the long, rambling, and detailed *The temporal and spiritual conquest of Ceylon,* written by a Jesuit priest, Fernão de Queyroz.[60] Queyroz, born at Canavezes (Portugal) in 1617, entered the Jesuit Order in 1631 and lived in India from 1635 till his death in 1687. He never visited Sri Lanka (Ceylon), but assiduously collected data relating to Portuguese activities in Sri Lanka after his countrymen were expelled from the island by the Dutch. His major motivation in writing this work seems to have been the fact that a fellow Jesuit whom

[58] A.K. Priolkar. *The Goa Inquisition* (Panjim, 1961), 120.

[59] John Huyghen van Linschoten. *The voyage of John Huyghen van Linschoten to the East Indies,* ed. A.C. Burnell (London, 1885), 2 vols., 1:207–8, 212–3.

[60] This work was first published as *Conquista temporal e espiritual de Ceylão* (Colombo, 1916), xxx, 994. The English translation by S.G. Perera, *The temporal and spiritual conquest of Ceylon,* from which I have extracted the quotations, was published in Colombo, 1930. xxviii, 1274.

he admired, Pedro de Basto,[61] had predicted that some day the Portuguese would regain control of Sri Lanka. Queyroz, in his book, believed that the loss of Sri Lanka was simply God's punishment of the Portuguese for the inequities of their rule in Sri Lanka. Therefore he had no compunctions about exposing Portuguese misdeeds; indeed, evidence of them was essential to prove his own thesis. On the other hand, as a Portuguese and a missionary, Queyroz could not but regard the conquest of Sri Lanka as a laudable and glorious achievement, both for the King and for the Faith.

In this respect, Queyroz is squarely in the tradition of the Portuguese historians such as João de Barros, Diogo do Couto, Fernão Lopez de Castanheda, Gaspar Correa, João dos Santos, Francisco de Souza, and Paulo de Trinidade, who recorded the deeds of their compatriots in Asia in great detail.[62] Like them, Queyroz, anxious to find out what had actually happened, spent a great deal of time talking to those who had been to Sri Lanka, reading all the published histories and chronicles he could obtain and making full use of the access he had to the archival material at Goa. This is what makes his book a veritable gold mine for later historians despite its obvious disadvantage of having been written over 150 years after the events it describes. The less complete accounts of Castanheda and of Gaspar Correa written in the mid-sixteenth century and the chronicle of Barros composed some fifty years later in the early seventeenth century must all be used to supplement Queyroz.[63]

The Sinhalese account is much harder to define. As its very name – *Rajavaliya* (*List of Kings*) – suggests, it is a chronicle. It begins with the very origins of kingship and gives some geographical details relating to India, but about seven-eighths of this book of approximately one hundred printed pages traces the linear succession of the rulers of Sri Lanka from the sixth century B.C. onward. The account is of course interspersed with descriptions of the achievements of some of these kings.[64] It seems clear from internal evidence that the Rajavaliya

[61] Queyroz wrote a biography of Pedro de Basto: *História da vida do veneravel irmão Pedro de Basto S.J.,: coadjutor temporal da Companhia da Jesus, e da variedade de successos que Deus lhe manifestou* (Lisboa, 1689), xxviii, 594.

[62] Queyroz also began writing a more comprehensive work on the Portuguese in the East, *Conquista temporal e espiritual do Oriente*. This work was never completed and an incomplete version was published as an anonymous account in *Documenta Ultramarina Portuguêsa* [Lisbon] 1 (1960): 267–632.

[63] Gaspar Corrêa, *Lendas da India*, ed. Rodrigo José de Lima Felner (Lisboa, 1858–1866), 4 vols.; *Asia de João de Barros*, I-x-v, 414–6; Castanheda, *História do descobrimento*, 11: chs. 22–3, 258–63.

[64] A. V. Suraweera, ed., *Rājāvaliya* (Colombo, 1976), xii, 278. The text and the notes on variant readings occupy pages 146–265.

is not the work of any one person. The chronicle was updated from time to time apparently without a conscious effort (as we shall see later) to provide a stylistic or philosophical consistency to the whole work. While many versions of the *Rajavaliya* end in 1685, others continue the story to the mid-eighteenth century, and one version goes up to the conquest of the interior of the island by the British in early the nineteenth century. However, we know now that the portions of the *Rajavaliya* relating to the fifteenth and sixteenth centuries have been taken almost entirely from another chronicle called the *Alakeshvara Yuddhaya* (*The war of the Alakeshvaras*), which was completed around 1581.[65] Thus, we have an indigenous source compiled within three generations of the first encounter.

The main events of this first encounter in Sri Lanka have been carefully examined by many generations of historians. It seems clear that in the year 1506, Dom Lourenço de Almeida, son of the then Portuguese Viceroy, Dom Francisco de Almeida, was patrolling the area of the Maldive Islands to the south of Sri Lanka when his ships were driven by storms to the coast of Sri Lanka and made their way to Colombo. Colombo was the port nearest to Kotte, the capital city of the major kingdom of Sri Lanka. Fernão de Queyroz describes the arrival of the fleet as follows:

> ... there set out from Cochin D. Lourenço de Almeyda in the November of 1505 [sic] of our redemption with nine baxeys [Arab vessels] ... making for the Maldives which are 61 leagues from that port, to await the ships of the South which sail between those islands to the strait of Meca; and being driven by contrary winds and finally by a violent storm ... when they least expected it, they came in sight of the port of Gale[66] ... there he had speech with [the people of the] land and some refreshment and with the scanty information of one who ill understood them, they went coasting up to the port of Colombo, where they anchored ... causing much astonishment to the natives as grief to the Moors [Muslims] there resident for the loss which they foresaw. They prudently dissembled this their distrust by visiting our squadron and inquiring from the Captain-Major what spices he wished to buy and giving withal such information about the country and its people that though for the nonce it seemed deceitful, the future proved it to be true.[67]

[65] This conclusion is derived from the fact that the *Alakéshvara Yuddhaya* does not record the death of King Mayadunne of Sitawaka while the *Rājāvaliya* in taking up the thread of history beyond what was given in the *Alakéshvara Yuddhaya* starts by recording his death (1581).

[66] Corrêa, *Lendas da India*, 1:643 says that he landed in Colombo.

[67] The Muslims "... in order to secure their property, pretended to desire peace with us ... had spread the report that the Portuguese were sea pirates." *Asia de João de Barros*, 415.

Forthwith King Paracrame-Bau [Dharma Parakramabahu IX] learnt of the arrival of the Portuguese, of whom he had already heard of before, and when our men meanwhile relying on the fair words of the inhabitants of Columbo sent for wood and water, they tried to hinder them. But as they had so far had no experience of firearms, so great was their astonishment at the balls, that they stopped only in the interior, and the King of Cota [Kotte], which is one short league from Columbo, at once sent his Ambassadors the next day to give satisfaction and to offer peace and friendship to D. Lourenço with vassalage to the King of Portugal. They brought presents of value, expressed how much the King was pleased that the Portuguese should come to his ports and carry on commerce with that island. For as he had already had tidings of our arms, he thought it better counsel for a while to submit rather than run the risk of perishing.[68]

This description, while revealing few specific details of the first impressions that the Portuguese themselves had of the people of Sri Lanka, provides many clues relating to the preconceptions that they held. They were suspicious of the Muslim traders and distrusted the information they gave. They were by this time confident that news of their power at sea would have spread so widely that the rulers in India would not dare to defy them, and obviously they were convinced of their right to use arms to enforce their dominance in the East. Let us now examine the story of the first encounter as narrated by the *Rajavaliya/Alakeshvara Yuddhaya:*

When in the year 1522 [sic] of our Lord Jesus Christ, a ship left the Portuguese territory in Jambudvipa [India] and traversing the immeasurable ocean without harm through the power of God [alternative reading-of the gods], arrived at the harbour of Colombo [Kolontota], the people who were at the port reported thus to King Parakramabahu; there is in our port of Colombo a race [*jati*, which also means a kind, a caste] of people very white in colour and of great beauty; they wear jackets and hats of iron and pace up and down without resting for a moment. Seeing them eat bread and grapes and drink arrack, they reported that these people devour stone [*kudugal*, which also means meat] and drink blood.[69] They said that these people give two or three pieces of gold or silver for one fish or one lime. The sound of their cannon is louder than thunder at the end of the world.[70] Their cannon balls fly many leagues

[68] Queyroz, *The Temporal and Spiritual Conquest*, 176–8. Corrêa and Castanheda also say that tribute was agreed to. Barros thinks that the Portuguese never met the king because the Muslims took them to meet an imposter.

[69] The possibility of translating this phrase as "devour meat" instead of eat stone was first suggested by Michael Roberts, "A Tale of Resistance: The Story of the Arrival of the Portuguese in Sri Lanka," *Ethnos* 54, nos. 1–2 (1989):70–4.

[70] For this sentence I have taken the text from the older *Alakésvara Yuddhaya*, ed. A.V. Suraweera (Colombo, 1965), 28. The *Rājāvaliya* text reads "The sound of their cannon is louder than thunder on the rock of Yughandhara."

and shatter forts of stone and iron. These and countless other details were related to the King.

On hearing this news, the King Dharma Parakramabahu summoned his four brothers to his city and having informed them and other chiefs and wise ministers, inquired "Should we make peace with them or fight them?". Thereupon, Prince Chakrayudha said "I will go myself and after observing what kind of people they are, will inform as to which of these two courses of action should be adopted." He went to the port of Colombo in disguise and having observed and understood the ways of the Portuguese, he returned to the city and reported back that it was not worth [*kam natha*, which could also mean that it was useless] fighting them and that it was better to grant them an audience [*dakva ganima*]. [Thereupon] one or two Portuguese were granted audience by the King who gave them presents and made them bring presents and curiosities to him. The King also granted innumerable honors [*nathak sammana deva*, granted innumerable tokens of esteem] to the King of Portugal and became his true friend. Let it be known that from that day the Portuguese lived in the port of Colombo.[71]

The interpretation of Sinhalese attitudes toward the Portuguese as portrayed in this quotation from the *Rajavaliya* depends partly on the author or source of information for this section of the chronicle and the possible transformations the text might have undergone during transmission. Most scholars agree that the "second part" of the *Rajavaliya*, starting from the account of the arrival of the Portuguese, is distinct linguistically from the earlier one. B. Gunasekera, who has provided us with an English translation of the *Rajavaliya*, further argued that linguistic evidence indicates that at least some sections of the book (obviously referring to those quoted here) were written by a Christian.[72] A.V. Suraweera's counter that the author of that section was not a Christian and was simply following the calendar current at the time[73] is not convincing because a close examination of the *Rajavaliya* indicates that the description of events from the arrival of the Portuguese [1506] to the return of the ambassadors of the King of Kotte from Portugal [1543] has a more favorable view of the Portuguese and of their allies than the later sections. We are therefore left with the conclusion that this section of the *Rajavaliya* (1506–1543) is a composition originally drafted by a Christian convert.[74] The date of

[71] *Rājāvaliya*, 213–4. (My translation).

[72] B. Gunasekara. *The Rājāvaliya or a historical narrative of Sinhalese kings from Vijaya to Vimala Dharma Surya II* (Colombo, 1900). iii.

[73] *Rājāvaliya*, 39.

[74] The theory that the section of the *Rājāvaliya* dealing with the period 1506 to 1545 came from a different source, first expounded here, is also supported by the fact that

the original composition of this section cannot be fixed with precision. However, it is possible to conjecture that it was probably recorded as early as the late 1540s,[75] but in any case at least by 1581, the date when the whole of the *Alakesvara Yuddhaya* appears to have been completed.

The description of the first meeting has elements of drama and the story, in time, entered the folk memory of the Sinhalese. The newcomers are described in graphic terms, and their differences – appearance, dress, food, wealth, and power – are all carefully noted. It appears that the impression the author seeks to give is a favorable one. It is a picture of attractive and active people of great wealth and power confronting a group of locals who were struck with amazement at the physical beauty, strange food, and carefree liberality of the strangers and were awed by their armor and cannon.[76] This is indeed the picture that one would have expected a Christian convert to draw. Historian Michael W. Roberts has contended that within this very description is a less complimentary vision of the Other.[77] As the Portuguese soon found out, wearing full armor in tropical heat was totally counterproductive. The picture of a soldier clad in iron in tropical South Asia is thus also a picture of ridicule. Restless pacing is the opposite of the Buddhist ideals of serenity and of calm detachment. Is the story of the Portuguese seeming to drink blood intended to hint that they were a people "polluted" in the Hindu sense of the term? It can be argued that there is no reason to believe that the Portuguese, after almost a decade of experience in Asia, were continuing to pay exorbitant prices for fresh fruits (limes) and fish.

What the recent reexamination of the text has done is to open up the possibility that the text might have been reinterpreted (and even subtly altered in the process of copying) in later times. As Gadamer put it, "The meaning of a text surpasses its author, not occasionally

the next section does not simply take up the story from the late 1540s but starts off by going back in time to give the lengths of the reigns of the two kings of Kotte who preceded Bhuvanekabahu (1521–1551). Compilers of chronicles such as the *Rājāvaliya* often strung different accounts together without much conscious editing.

[75] The error in the date of the first arrival of the Portuguese in the *Rājāvaliya*, which seems to militate against its being a near contemporary account, could have been a later insertion because the earlier versions of the account in the *Alakesvara Yuddhaya* do not have any specific date for the first Portuguese visit.

[76] Note that the Portuguese account of Fernão de Queyroz also mentions the fear aroused by the firing of artillery. Portuguese chronicles give many instances when their joyous firing of guns was regarded as evidence of hostile intent by Asians.

[77] Roberts, "A Tale of Resistance," 69–82. The idea that the *Rājāvaliya* description contained a scornful view of the "other" was first raised with me in 1984 by Michael W. Roberts of the Department of Anthropology, University of Adelaide.

but always. Thus understanding is not a reproductive procedure but rather a productive one."[78] Thus the fact that the original account might have been intended to paint a favorable picture would not have prevented it from being reinterpreted in later times. In fact, the recent work of Michael Roberts might well represent an extension of this process. Writing at a time of ethnic conflict in Sri Lanka and concerned with the attitudes of the Sinhalese majority vis-à-vis the minority groups, he tends to go further than the text seems to permit at first glance. His argument that the story of eating stones and drinking blood could be interpreted as a denigration of the Eucharist is perhaps within the boundaries of reasonable interpretation. However, he also attempts to link the Portuguese offer of high prices for limes with the fact that they were used by the Sinhalese in exorcism, thereby concluding that the Sinhalese equated the Portuguese (foreigners) with demons. While it is possible to agree that the *Rajavaliya*, like all texts, might contain potential "alternative readings," it is less plausible to argue that these readings were those which were really intended by the author. Some of them might well be twentieth century reinterpretations.

A further analysis of the *Rajavaliya* account of events that followed shows a distinct difference in perception between its author and the Portuguese chroniclers. According to the *Rajavaliya* it is the Sinhalese who take the initiative. A royal prince sent to observe the conduct of the Portuguese reports that it was useless [not worth?] fighting them. The king grants them a *dâkum*, a word that implies a grant to a subordinate for the right to appear before the royal presence. The vassal then offers gifts to the ruler who could, if he wished, bestow favors and material benefits on him. While the Sinhalese accounts thus try to somehow preserve the authority of the king and convey a somewhat ambiguous view of the Portuguese, the descriptions by Queyroz and by other Portuguese historians pinpoint the Sinhalese fears. For example, there is the description of the way in which the first Portuguese envoy was conducted to Kotte, only five miles from the port city of Colombo. The king of Kotte wanted to conceal the vulnerability of his capital from attack by sea, perhaps recalling that a previous ruler of the region had been captured by a Chinese naval force less

[78] Hans Georg Gadamer, *Truth and Method*, trans. Garret Barden and John Cumming (London, 1975), 264. It should perhaps be noted that my own approach to theory is closer to Jurgen Habermas, *Theory and Practice*, trans. John Viertel (Boston, 1973), than to Gadamer's.

than a century before.[79] As Queyroz relates the story of the first visit:

> . . . the envoy set out and though the way was very short, through the industry of the Chingalaz he spent three days on the journey, going up hill and down dale and crossing the same river several times. But as everything was foreseen and it had been agreed that a gun would be fired at every hour glass, he knew very well that the distance was short. He remonstrated with those who guided him. but in reply they laughed outright making fun of his ignorance of the lie of the land, for their intention was merely to secure themselves from any danger.[80]

Here is a story of Sinhalese cunning thwarted by Portuguese foresight. Yet the reality might well have been different. The Sinhalese folk tale about this attempted deception does not mention the periodic firing of the cannon and implies that the Portuguese were actually deceived. Even today, there is a Sinhalese proverb meaning "to go by a circuitous route" (*Parangiya Kotte giya vagei*) that literally means "in the way the Portuguese travelled by Kotte." The Portuguese historian Barros, writing some eighty years before Queyroz, states that the journey "through such dense thickets that they could scarcely see the sun, is taking so many turns that it seemed to them more like a labyrinth than a direct route" took a whole day but also makes no mention of the firing of cannon.[81] As for the conduct of the Portuguese at the first encounter, Queyroz reports: "At the proper distance he made due obeisance in the European and Portuguese fashion, which the King was pleased to see, though the bystanders noticed the little abasement which we show to Kings, for as they treat them like their Pagodes, they want our manners to be accommodated to theirs. . . . " Once again, the earlier Portuguese chroniclers make no mention of this reluctance to adopt Asian modes of showing respect.[82] Clearly, a "Portuguese history" of the encounter was being elaborated in the seventeenth century to match contemporary pretensions to dominance.

This was woven into the picture of cowardly and deceitful Asians. From the outset the Portuguese accounts depict the Muslim traders as being cowardly. When Dom Lourenço ordered the firing of cannon to

[79] K. M. M. Werake, "A re-examination of Chinese Relations with Sri Lanka during the 15th century A.D.," in *K.W. Goonewardena Felicitation Volume*, eds. C. R. de Silva and Sirima Kiribamune (Peradeniya, 1989), 89–102.
[80] Queyroz, *The temporal and spiritual conquest*, 178.
[81] *Asia de João de Barros*, 415.
[82] Queyroz, *The temporal and spiritual conquest*, 180.

celebrate the successful return of his first envoy to Kotte, "The Moors did not understand that this was a courteous demonstration of joy, but thought it was [a manifestation] of hostilities owing to an unsatisfactory reply; and in fact it drove such fright into them, that they began to cross over to the opposite coast on the mainland, preferring to quit their fatherland than their lives."[83]

The Portuguese view of the Sinhalese as cunning and deceitful was reinforced in time by the numerous wars and uprisings against Portuguese dominance. On the other hand, experience did teach the Portuguese to have a better appreciation of the martial qualities of Asians. Duarte Barbosa writing in the second decade of that century thought, "... the natives of this island, as well Moors as Heathen, are ... extremely luxurious and pay no attention to matters of weapons, nor do they possess them. ..."[84] Thirty years later, the Portuguese historian Castanheda concurred,[85] but later Portuguese experience was very different. Diogo do Couto (1542–1616) tried to explain this: "... at that time there was not a single firelock in the whole island and after we entered it with the continual use of war that we made on them, they became so dextrous as they are today and came to cast the best and handsomest artillery in the world and to make the finest firelocks and better than ours. ..."[86] In fact, experience was giving the Portuguese a more realistic estimate of the abilities of their opponents.

Then again, the Portuguese did begin in time to make distinctions between various indigenous peoples. Non-Muslims were all still considered "heathens" and there was very little effort made to study the doctrines of Buddhism or Hinduism. However, caste distinctions were slowly recognized, and those who were converted to Christianity were shown special favor. Indeed, they were the only group considered even partially reliable. The evolution of the Sinhalese attitudes is even more interesting. It seems clear that conversion to Roman Catholicism often made a great difference in perspective. The *Kusthanthinu Hatana*, a war poem composed by Alagiyawanna (born 1552), a famous Sinhalese poet,[87] is a good example illustrating this tendency; the hero of

[83] Ibid., 178.

[84] Duarte Barbosa, *The Book*, 1:110. Varthema writing a few years earlier had said much the same thing. Ludovico di Varthema, *The Itinerary of Ludovico di Varthema of Bologna from 1502 to 1508*, trans. J. W. Jones (London, 1928), 189.

[85] Castanheda, *História do descobrimento*, 2:261: "*... eles sam homẽs que entedẽ pouco em feyto d'armas; porque afora serẽ mercadores sam muyto dados a boa vida e effeminados. ...*"

[86] Diogo do Couto, "Asia, Decada IV" (trans. D. Ferguson), *Journal of the Royal Asiatic Society* (Ceylon Branch) 20 (1909): 72.

[87] See text edited by M. E. Fernando and S. G. Perera (Colombo), 1932.

Kusthanthinu Hatana was not a Sinhalese king or a rebel leader fighting the Portuguese but Constantino de Sá de Noronha, the Portuguese Captain-General of Sri Lanka (1618–1621 and 1623–1630). The poem of 175 stanzas transforms what was merely a successful ambush of the Sinhalese advance-guard by a retreating Portuguese army into a great victory.[88]

The Sinhalese Buddhist tradition, or at least one version of it, seems to be reflected by the section of the *Rajavaliya/Alakeshvara Yuddhaya* dealing with the events from about 1550 to 1581. King Bhuvanekabahu of Kotte (1521–1551), ally of the Portuguese, is repeatedly condemned, chiefly for bringing harm to Buddhism:

> Bhuvanekabahu who lived in intimacy with the Portuguese committing foolish acts, was killed by them as a consequence [due to the *karma*] of his foolish act in entrusting the prince he had brought up [his grandson] to the Portuguese. It should be known that Bhuvanekabahu brought misfortune on future generations in Sri Lanka and that, due to him, harm befell the *Buddha Sasana* in later times.[89]

This section clearly shows disillusionment with the traditional policy of religious tolerance that Sri Lankan monarchs had followed. There are many indications that Bhuvanekabahu himself remained a Buddhist. As he wrote to the king of Portugal in 1548, " . . . Your Governor wrote to me that you are displeased that I have not become a Christian as my ambassador promised in the *Regno*, but I did not say this . . . I would not follow a double course because there are in this world, your friendship and my god. . . . "[90] This did not save him from being held responsible for the failure to defend his faith. Nevertheless, the *Rajavaliya* still attempts to be fair to the Portuguese. When King Bhuvanekabahu died of a gunshot wound inflicted by a Portuguese soldier, the author remarks that "God [the gods] alone knows"[91] as to whether the death was due to assassination or accident, though it is clear from other remarks he makes that he believed that it was an assassination. In fact, the main complaint that the author of this section has against King Bhuvanekabahu is that he allowed his grandson and heir to fall into Portuguese hands, paving the way for his conversion to Christianity. Hostility to the Portuguese is now grounded in religion and is linked with contempt for the converts:

[88] For an analysis of this campaign, see C. R. de Silva, *The Portuguese in Ceylon 1617–1638*, 39–41.
[89] *Rājāvaliya*, 218–21. (My translation.)
[90] *Ceylon and Portugal: Kings and Christians. 1539–1552*, 219.
[91] *Rājāvaliya*, 219. (My translation.)

From that day many women of Kotte became subject to the Portuguese and people of low castes, servile castes, the Karava caste, the tailor caste, the Salagama caste, Durawa caste and Goyigama caste and the chief people of Kotte became covetous of the wealth of the Portuguese and became subject to them and became converts and intermarried with them. . . . [92]

Later portions of the *Rajavaliya,* composed in the seventeenth century, also strongly condemn the misdeeds of the indigenous converts:

Simankure Rala [Simão Correa], paying no respect to the Four Temples nor to the *Buddha Sasana* which is the most revered in the world, was committing sins by making [children] orphans and by killing innumerable animals, when by the power of the deities who protect Sri Lanka his body became inflamed and he died. . . [93]

The *Mandarampurapuwatha,* a local history of a small portion of the central highlands of Sri Lanka that never came under Portuguese rule, offers a much more critical view of the Portuguese. The first 308 verses of this poem giving the history of this region up to 1635 were composed by Archarya Wickrama in 1647. Much of the later work was by Unambuwe in 1702. Portuguese oppression is vividly described:

[The Portuguese] having seized and destroyed temple lands, temples, libraries and sacred Bo-trees in Lanka, established false doctrines by imposing heavy punishments and created unrest by oppressing many people in a number of areas. The many low-country folk who refused to accept Christianity were imprisoned with their wives and children and burnt to death. Punishing the people with penalties derived from unjust laws [they] caused them to lose their worldly goods. . . [94]

Unlike the parts of the *Rajavaliya* dealing with the first encounter, the *Mandārampurapuwatha* is unabashedly partisan. The action of the King of Kandy [Vimaladharmasuriya, 1591–1604] in suddenly turning his arms against his Portuguese allies is justified on the grounds that the Portuguese had broken faith with him earlier.[95] Those holding office under the Portuguese are described as "wicked people committing evil deeds."[96] The poem is clearly written from a Sinhalese Buddhist viewpoint.

The argument that the attitude of the Sinhalese Buddhist toward the Portuguese grew increasingly bitter with the continued oppression

[92] Ibid., 220. (My translation.)
[93] Ibid., 239. (My translation.)
[94] Labugama Lankānanda, ed., *Mandārampurapuwatha* (Colombo, 1958), stanzas 316–317. The Portuguese ar e also described as cruel and "infidel": stanzas 318–319.
[95] Ibid., stanzas 72–78.
[96] Ibid., stanza 340.

and warfare in the sixteenth and early seventeenth centuries is borne out by other Sinhalese documents such as the *Parangi Hatana,* or *Rajasiha Hatana.* This work was probably composed soon after 1638. Paul Pieris' free translation has preserved (and indeed, heightened) the spirit of the poem:

> And many a sacred shrine and palace proud and the very temple of the Sacred Tooth were consumed in the devouring flames, while many a fertile land of fruit and flowers, mango and plaintain, jak and arecanut, betal and coconut were ravaged by this devouring host and our gentle herds of kine were slain to fill the maw of these devouring ogres and many a wanton deed they wrought. . . [97]

This kind of hostility could explain a seemingly deliberate copying error in the *Rajavaliya,* which ridicules Christianity. The Sinhalese term *Khristu Samaya* [Christian Faith] is copied as *Khristu Samayama* [Christian farce] in several versions of the text.[98] The historical tradition on each side often built an interpretation of events that fitted in with existing knowledge and preconceptions of the Other. This in turn reinforced existing prejudices. A good example of this is the story of the second visit of a Portuguese squadron to Colombo. In 1517, a Portuguese fleet of seventeen ships arrived in Colombo under Governor Lopo Soares and demanded permission to build a fort. The king of Kotte agreed. We know from contemporary Portuguese documents that as soon as the walls of the fort were up to a defensible height, the Governor wanted all the cinnamon available in the royal storehouses of Kotte to be handed over to the Portuguese at a fixed price. The king refused, and the Portuguese, having defeated the Sinhalese forces, imposed tribute.[99]

[97] P.E. Pieris. *Ribeiro's History of Ceilao,* 2nd ed. (Colombo, 1909), stanzas 28–31. A slightly different Sinhalese version has been published as *Rajasiha Hatana,* ed. H.M. Somaratne (Kandy, 1968). A literal translation of the same verses is given here to indicate the liberties that Peiris has taken with the content to give (and perhaps enhance) the flavor of the original: " . . . Having put to flames and destroyed many temples of Ganesha, residences of monks, palaces and the treasured Temple of the Tooth, displaying their prowess throughout the land by swiftly cutting down all mango, plantain, jak, arecanutna, and coconut trees, having killed and devoured cows, cattle and buffaloes and devastating the land as if devils had been there. . . " *Rajasiha Hatana,* stanzas 24–26. For evidence of Portuguese excesses in mid-sixteenth century Sri Lanka, see C. R. de Silva, "The rise and fall of the Kingdom of Sitawaka (1521–1593)," *The Ceylon Journal of Historical and Social Studies* 7, no. 1 (1977):13–14.

[98] *Rājāvaliya,* 220. Professor K.W. Goonewardena suggested in a personal communication to me that the word *samayama* might not necessarily have had pejorative implications at the time the documents were copied.

[99] For details, see C. R. de Silva, "The kingdom of Kotte and its relations with the Portuguese in the early sixteenth century," *Don Peter Felicitation Volume,* ed. E. C. T. Candappa and M. S. S. Fernandopulle (Colombo, 1983), 35–50.

The Sinhalese war poem composed in the late seventeenth century, the *Maha Hatana*, relates how the Portuguese arrived from Goa with presents for the king of Kotte, and at his feet asked for permission to lay as much merchandise as could fit on a cowhide to show their goods. The king agreed to this request because it was customary to allow all traders who came to Colombo to sell their goods. The very wise (very cunning?) Portuguese tore the cowhide to hair-thin strips, and enclosing an area, built a fort after promising to pay tribute to the King of Kotte and began to think of conquering the country.[100] The *Rajavaliya* treats this episode in the same way with no mention of war, defeat or treaty:

> During the reign of Vijayabahu another ship arrived from Portugal and seeing forces with arms they fired their cannon. On seeing a cannon ball strike the branch of a *jak* tree, the forces fled and reported this to King Vijayabahu at Jayawardhanapura [Kotte]. King Vijayabahu called four or five Portuguese to his presence in the city and gave them permission to leave after giving them presents. It should be known that in the reign of Vijayabahu the Portuguese were trading and resident at the port of Colombo.[101]

What seems to emerge from this examination of the first encounter is that while images of the "Other" at the time of contact could well be multiple in time, each community created a composite image of the Other by concentrating on what seemed to be new and different among the strangers. As a rule, the image seemed to be a negative one, especially in times of misunderstanding or conflict; but in any case, the image of the Other is often influenced by self-perception. To the Portuguese who saw themselves as conquerors, the Sinhalese were timid and unwarlike. To the Sinhalese Buddhists to whom self control and contentment were noble ideals, the Portuguese were simply rapacious. On the other hand, even in literate societies where some accounts of the first contact were recorded within one or two generations, the traditions came to be embroidered or altered in subtle ways to explain current realities. The emergence of new social divisions, such as the growth of a Christian community in Sri Lanka, resulted in efforts to modify the image of the newcomer. As Greg Dening reminds us: " . . . The Past and the Other are two of humanity's main preoccupations. Rendering significant what has happened

[100] *Kirimatiyāwe Matiwarayāge Maha Hatana*, ed. T. S. Hemakumar (Colombo), 1964. stanzas 3–12. The words *puraa nämäthi* mean "very wise" but are not used in a laudatory sense here.

[101] *Rājāvaliya*, 215.

is a daily, seasonal, celebratory, generational activity, done in private and in public, personally and institutionally. . ."[102]

III. CONCLUDING THOUGHTS

In the closing years of the fifteenth century and in the early years of the sixteenth, the explorations of the Europeans brought them into contact with diverse groups of peoples. It is not necessary to belabor the point that in all these interactions, the two sides in each encounter saw each other through a cultural filter and that in each case the reactions to first contact also depended on historical memories of earlier contacts with other "Others" modified by ongoing experiences.

By the time the Portuguese reached Asia they had already met many different groups in Africa. They already had some inkling of the riches of the East. When they arrived they found a mutually comprehensible language in Arabic. The linguistic competence of some early converts to Christianity provided other links. It seemed as if there were sufficient preconditions for a swift acquisition of knowledge about the Other. The Portuguese were often amazed at the complexity of Asia, its bustling port cities and its wide variety of peoples, each group with its own language, dress, and modes of social conduct. Chroniclers and missionaries, nobles and soldiers spent much ink and paper describing these "wonders" but they were seen as part of a Portuguese achievement, something that they had "discovered," all part of an *Asia Portuguesa*. It was a land to be conquered. The inhabitants? They were to be converted to the only "True Doctrine" and thereby "saved." That is why, a century after their arrival, the most learned among the Portuguese had only a vague idea of the tenets of Buddhism, Hinduism, or Jainism, and indeed could barely distinguish the one from the other.

The destruction of the court archives of all of the coastal states of South Asia and the disappearance of many local traditions have made it difficult for us to make detailed evaluations of the Asian reactions. However, it is clear that at the outset the Portuguese arrival was seen as the coming of yet another trading group. There were many strangers in every busy seaport in Asia. It was their readiness to use force to control trade in an area where trading competition had traditionally been peaceful,[103] and their ability to establish command over the high

[102] Greg Dening, *History's Anthropology: The death of William Gooch* (New York, 1988), 4.

[103] C.R. de Silva, "Muslim traders in the Indian Ocean in the sixteenth century and the Portuguese impact," *Muslims of Sri Lanka: Avenues to antiquity*, ed. M.A.M. Shukri (Beruwala, Sri Lanka, 1986), 147–165.

seas, that marked the Portuguese as a group apart just as the exclusiveness of their brand of Christianity identified them as different. Indeed, in terms of their belief in religious exclusivity, there are interesting parallels between the Portuguese intrusion and that of the Muslims in northern India.

Interaction between two different groups also involves the interaction of individuals. The perception of the Other by an individual could depend on the position in society, the degree of acculturation, the personality, and the personal experiences of that individual. Obviously, the greater the degree of division within a community and the more diverse the interests of the individuals within it, the more likely it will be that there will be differential reactions to the newcomers. Of the many different interpretations of the first encounter, we can hope to have a glimpse of just a few.[104]

[104] Professors K.W. Goonewardena and Steven Kemper read through earlier drafts of this paper. I am most grateful for the numerous insights and suggestions they offered.

CHAPTER 11

The "Indianness" of Iberia and changing Japanese iconographies of Other

RONALD P. TOBY

Miranda
O! Wonder!
How many goodly creatures are there here!
How beauteous mankind is! O brave new world
That has such people in't.

The Tempest, v.1, 182–185

Caliban
Do not torment me! O!

Stephen
What's the matter? Have we devils here? Do you
put tricks upon me with salvages and men of Inde?

The Tempest, II. ii, 56–58

*nos disserão chensicus(. . . [the Japanese] call us "Tenjiku" [Indians] . . .)

Fr. Cosme de Torres, writing from Japan, to Fr. Francisco Xavier, 1551

JAPAN'S most significant Other, China, as well as Japan's other Others, Koreans, Mongols, and Ainu (Japan's indigenous northern tribes) and "devils" and "salvages and men of Inde" had populated the universe of Japanese consciousness for centuries before the "European expansion" brought Iberians and Italians, English and Dutch, Blacks, Indians, and Amerinds to Japan.[1] Chinese, Koreans, and Manchurians

[1] The literature on China in Japanese consciousness is too vast for complete inclusion here. See especially, David Pollack, *Fracture of Meaning: Japan's Synthesis of China, from the Seventh to the Eighteenth Centuries* (Princeton, 1985), who examines the literary trope of China over a millennium. Other recent important studies, looking particularly at the seventeenth to nineteenth centuries, include Harry D. Harootunian, "The Function

had voyaged to Japan from at least the third century of our era,[2] and Japanese had ventured abroad. Chinese and Koreans, especially, had migrated permanently to Japan, either in communities or as individual Buddhist missionaries. And the Mongols had twice attempted (and failed at) invasions of Japan.

These old Others inhabited – indeed constituted – a world of Japanese iconography and representation, of performance, and of rich oral and written literatures. Yet despite the large numbers of Others in Japan prior to the Iberian irruption in the sixteenth century, the Other of Japanese representation was overwhelmingly marked as "Chinese" and Chinese in ultimate referent. Other was nearly invariably represented as being "out there," in China or India (the land of the Buddha, and venue of much Buddhist representation, hence inherently Other) rather than "here" in Japan. Save for visual representations of the thirteenth-century Mongol invasions, there are precious few representations of Other in Japan in art (drama, or literature) of the Japan that greeted Xavier on his arrival in 1549. Typically, Japanese artists depicted their Chinese figures in Chinese landscapes, and indeed, in profoundly Chinese painterly styles, like Sesshū's *Winter Landscape*, or Shūbun's *Studio of the Three Worthies*.[3]

The Iberian irruption transformed all this. Other was no longer safely "out there." Japanese art and festival masquerade responded to the "salvages and men of Inde" who arrived by the hundreds, if not thousands, after 1549, with a new interest in, a new excitement with, the "Southern Salvages,"[4] who were depicted with great zest in the vibrant genre painting of the late sixteenth and early seventeenth centuries. Portuguese and Spaniards, and their African and Indian slaves, peopled Japanese cityscapes, as well as being represented in an imagined Iberia of the Japanese artist. After an initial infatuation, Japan's nearly allergic reaction to Counter Reformation Catholicism brought the Iberian interlude to an end after less than a century, and

of China in Tokugawa Thought," in A. Iriye, ed., *The Chinese and the Japanese* (Princeton, 1980), 9–36; Kate Wildman Nakai, "The Naturalization of Confucianism in Tokugawa Japan: The Problem of Sinocentrism," in *Harvard Journal of Asiatic Studies*, 40, no. 1 (1980): 157–199.

2 I use the terms "Japanese," "Korean," and "Manchurian" strictly as geographic markers when speaking of an age before the peoples inhabiting those regions had coalesced from multi-tribal and multi-ethnic local societies or states into the ancestors of their modern nation-states.

3 For Sesshū (1420–1456), Robert Treat Paine and Alexander Soper, *The Art and Architecture of Japan* (Baltimore, 1955), 78; for Shûbun (15th century), ibid., 77.

4 *Nanban* (Ch. *nanman*); *nanban*, though usually translated "southern barbarians," can as well be parsed "savages," for the character *ban/man* means "fierce, savage, uncivilized," as well as "foreigner."

a wave of Christophobia and attendant Iberiophobia obliterated the image of Iberians from Japanese art and performance – indeed, from nearly all modes of discourse. By 1650, Christianity was a capital offense, and the representation of Iberians taboo.

Yet the disappearance of the Iberian (read Catholic) Other from the painter's palette, the performer's stage, and the masquer's dance did not mean reversion to an iconography in which Other was only "out there." Rather, as the new Other was cast out of Japan, nearly expelled from consciousness, and totally obliterated from view, the niche it had carved for itself in the Japanese landscape was appropriated by other Others, the old Others of Korea, the Ryukyus, and China.

This absence of Other from the iconographic/cognitive landscape of Japan prior to the Iberian irruption, the intensity with which Japanese art and masque adopted the Iberian trope during the *Nanban* (Iberian) interlude, 1543–1640, and the assumption by old, familiar Others (formerly excluded from the Japanese landscape) of the place the Iberians had made for themselves are suggestive of transformations in consciousness wrought by Japan's experience of Other in the *Nanban* century.

THE IMPLICIT OTHER AND MANIFEST MEN OF INDE

"During the reign of Emperor Gonara-no-in [1526–1557]," wrote a Japanese chronicler nearly a century later,[5]

[5] *Kirishitan monogatari* (Tales of the Christians), in *Zokuzoku qunsho ruijū*, 12 (Zoku Gunsho Ruijū Kanseikai, 1970): 531–550. For a full translation, see George Elison, *Deus Destroyed: The Image of Christianity in Early-Modern Japan* (Cambridge, MA, 1973), 319–347. Elison translates this passage somewhat differently, p. 321; he regards "[t]his alien apparition [as] altogether unnatural" (p. 30), but it is unlikely that the realm of demons and goblins, of fox- and badger-spirits capable of assuming human form, were entirely un-"natural" to most Japanese of the sixteenth and seventeenth centuries, who rather saw an animate continuum, from "Japanese human" at the least remove, through "alien human" on one axis; through "birds, beasts, and fishes" on another; and through "demons and gods" (*kishin*) along the third. This schematized typology of Others was developed in conversations with Kuroda Hideo. The boundaries "separating" these realms of the continuum were themselves zones of gradation, represented, e.g., by the confusion of Ryūkyū (the kingdom of the Okinawan archipelago) and its homophone Ryūgū/Ryūkyū (the submarine palace of Ryūō, the Dragon King); or by the postmortem apotheosis of Hideyoshi, Ieyasu, and many other heroes, at their deaths. The "naturalness" or "reality" of demons, goblins, or changeling badgers and foxes was such that, as late as 1810, popular travellers' handbooks included advice on how to cope with them on the road. See "Ryokō yōjinshū," tr. C. Vaporis, in *Monumenta Nipponica*, 44, no. 4 (1989): 481. On the conflation of Ryūkyū (Okinawa) and Ryūgū (the Dragon Palace), see Yokoyama Manabu, *Ryūkyū shisetsu torai no kenkyū* (Yoshikawa Kōbunkan, 1987); on deification of hero/ancestors, Robert J. Smith, *Ancestor Worship in Japan* (Stanford, 1974), esp. 56–63.

Figure 11.1. "The first thing one noticed was how long its nose was! It was like a wartless conch shell, stuck onto its face as if by suction." Anon., screen painting, private collection.

the hundred-eighth sovereign since the Emperor Jinmu [mythic founder of the imperial line], around the Kōji era (1555–8), there came on a *Nanban* merchantman a creature one couldn't put a name to, that [appeared to have] human form at first [glance], but might as well be a long-nosed goblin, or a long-necked demon of the sort that disguise themselves as Buddhist lay-priests in order to trick people. Careful inquiry [revealed] that the creature was called a "Padre." The first thing one noticed was how long its nose was! It was like a wartless conch-shell, stuck onto [his face] by suction (Figure 11.1). How big its eyes were! They were like a pair of telescopes, but the irises were yellow. Its head was small; it had long claws on its hands and feet (Figure 11.2). It was over seven feet tall and was black in color, [but] its nose was red; its teeth were longer than a horse's teeth, and its hair was mouse-grey. Above its forehead it'd shaved a spot on its pate about the size of an overturned sake cup. Its speech was incomprehensible to the ear; its voice resem-

Figure 11.2. "It had long claws on its hands and feet." Drawing on the hirsute, taloned image of Other, Ishikawa Toyonobu (1711–85) depicts a Korean with hairy hand and clawed fingers. The British Museum.

bled the screech of an owl. Everyone ran to see it, mobbing the roads with abandon. They thought this phantasm more terrible than the more ferocious monster.

Well, indeed, might Japanese be puzzled by the arrival of the new manner of creature (Europeans, specifically Portuguese) that in 1543 landed on the island of Tanegashima, southwestern Japan, the first Europeans ever to visit Japan, or by the strangely frocked Francisco Xavier, a founder of the Society of Jesus and the first Jesuit to proselytize in Japan, who arrived in Kyushu from Goa six years later. Equally confusing, surely, were Xavier's colleagues Cosme de Torres (1551), Luis de Almeida (1552), and Allessandro Valignano (1566), their merchant and military companions, and the huge "black ships" that bore them.[6]

Yet if the Japanese were confused by these new men, their faces and bodies, their clothing, their language, and their "black ships" (and "black" slaves), imagine the Europeans' amazement when their Japanese hosts mistakenly (or so *they* thought) greeted them as a *Tenjikujin* – "men of Inde!"[7] What a sweet irony: At the very moment – broadly speaking – that westbound Europeans were "discovering" "men of Inde" at their first

[6] Kuroda Hideo examines why the "black ships" were black, and significations of black in sixteenth-century Japanese color symbology, in his *Kyōkai no chūsei, Shōchō no chūsei* (Tokyo University Press, 1986), ch. 6, "Kurofune no shinborizumu" (The symbolism of the black ships).

[7] *Tenjiku*, the Buddhist term for "the land [whence] the law of the Buddha was transmitted to China ("Morokoshi") over a span of three-hundred years." *Kojiki* (Record of ancient matters), entry of 13th year, 4th month, reign of Empress Suiko (605). *Vocabulario da Lingoa da Japam* (Nangasaqui [Nagasaki], 1603), 218, lists *Tengicu* as one of the *tres reinos (Sangocu)* comprising the Japanese cosmos, i.e., "China, Sião, Iapão." E.g., Fr. Cosme de Torres wrote to Xavier from Yamaguchi, 20 October 1551, that the Japanese, "nos disserão chensicus" (call us "Tenjiku"–i.e., "Indians"). *Cartas que os Padres e Irmãos da Companhia de Iesus* (1598), facsim., repr. (Yūshōdō, 1972), 18. This passage in the Portuguese translation is dropped in the Spanish text in *Cartos que los Padres y Hermanos de la Compania de Iesus...* (1575; Biblioteca Nacional, Madrid, ref. no. R-6654), 50. My thanks to Professor Gonoi Hiroshi for his aid in finding and understanding these passages in the Jesuit letters.

landfall in the New World, their eastbound compatriots were being construed as "men of Inde" at their farthest landfall, beyond the eastern rim of Asia. Xavier and his confrères at least "knew" where they were, and whom they saw – but they had the advantage of "knowing" where they were going: to Zipangu/Iapam, and of an awareness that none of their kind had preceded them. The Japanese who found these devils, salvages, or men of Inde clambering upon their shores were rather more like Miranda than Ferdinand: The landscape was – they thought – unchanged and 'twas only "such people" that made it brave and new. Little wonder, then, if Japanese had trouble mapping this brave new world.

But Stephen's first reading of Caliban offers the beginnings of a map from our own, and Xavier's, first bemusement at the "confusion," through the implicit ethnographies that inscribed these new-found aliens for Japanese readers of the text of encounter upon an already densely charted (if little visited) Japanese iconography of Other, a map "known" to encode "all the world," and all "such people [as were] in't." For though the Portuguese were hardly the first aliens the "Japanese" had met, they were the first "new" aliens encountered in nearly a millennium, nearly the first to come from beyond the familiar "human" realm of Japan-and-China, from the largely mythic *Tenjiku* where Buddhas and Bodhisattvas abode.[8]

We might follow Pirandello, and suggest that the Iberian arrivals were characters in search of an author for their text. Even more apt is Marshall Sahlins' provocative direction to "consider what happened to Captain Cook. For the people of Hawaii, Cook had been a myth before he was an event, since the myth was the frame by which the event was interpreted."[9] By contrast with Captain Cook and Hawaiian myth as represented by Sahlins, however, Japanese encounters with

[8] A monk often identified as an Indian (the *Tōdaiji zoku yōroku*, in *Zokuzoku gunsho ruijū*, 11:214f, identifies him as being from "Linyi" – probably part of what is now northern Vietnam) had a role in the ceremonies vivifying the Great Buddha in Tōdaiji (temple) in Nara in 752, but "m[e]n of Inde" were rarely on Japanese soil thereafter. A "Tenjikujin," i.e., an alien clearly not from China, Korea, or Ryukyu, most likely from southeast Asia, came as a trader to Japan in the late fourteenth century, residing in the area of what is now Osaka long enough to leave behind two sons. One of the sons, known by his Japanese name, Kusuha Sainin (1395–1486), distinguished himself in service of the great Nara temple Kōfukuji, making two trade voyages to Ming China, 1432 and 1453. Since Sainin's childhood name is recorded as *Musuru* (Japanese phonetic equivalent of Musul = Musulman?), it is likely that his "Inde"-ish father was a Muslim, suggesting Malacca as a likely origin. The definitive study of Sainin is Tanaka Takeo, "Kenminsen bōeki-ka, Kusuha Sainin to sono ichizoku" (Kusuha Sainin, trader to Ming, and his family), in *Nihon jinbutsu-shi taikei*, 2: *Chūsei*, ed. Satō Shin'ichi (Asakura Shoten, 1959): 193–225.

[9] Marshall Sahlins, *Islands of History* (Chicago, 1985; pb 1987), 73.

the Other in legend and tale more commonly occurred offshore, in the mode of Momotarō, the "Peach Boy," or Minamoto no Yorimitsu, hero of *Shuten dōji*. Both Momotarō and Yorimitsu went "out there," confronted the bestial/demonic Other, bested them, and returned with their treasure, their captives, and their magic.[10] In the "Xavierian encounter," by contrast, Other was not more-or-less safely "out there," but invasive, *here*, more closely analogous narratologically to the confrontation of Hakurakuten, the T'ang poet Po Chü-i, with the Japanese god Sumiyoshi, off the coast of northern Kyushu.[11] Hakurakuten, the archetype Invasive Other, was sent by the T'ang Chinese emperor to spy on Japan, only to be beaten at his own game, bested by Sumiyoshi in an offshore poetry contest, and driven off before ever landing in Japan by a divine wind (*kamikaze*) summoned by the god.[12]

It may be difficult to argue a "sense of radical difference" in this Xavierian encounter as great as that entailed in the Colombian encounter Todorov has tried to decode. Yet both the Jesuits and their European confrères, on the one hand, and their Japanese hosts on the other, each shared communally "certain images and ideas concerning other remote populations [which, surely] were projected upon these newly discovered beings,"[13] and even, indeed, on their ships, their beliefs, their behaviors. Each viewed new Others through lenses of culturally constructed iconographies built in, or just beyond the limits of, familiar universes, and tried at first to incorporate the new Other into its existing cosmology. In this, the Europeans may have had the upper hand, for they had already learnt of universes beyond the galaxy their mothers and fathers knew, of Colombo's Indies, of the "sal-

[10] For a basic version of the Momotarō tale, see Ichinose Naoyuki, *Nihon no gūwa*, 2 (Hōbunkan, 1960), 30–34; for *Shuten dōji*, see *Otogizōshi shū* (Nihon Koten Bungaku Taikei), vol. 38 (Iwanami Shoten, 1958), 361–384. *Otogizōshi shū* contains several other tales of the "conquest-of-Other" or "encounter-with-Other" type, but in each case, the encounter occurs "out there," offshore (or under the sea, in the case of Urashima Tarō).

[11] On Po Chü-i's status in Japan, see Pollack, *The Fracture of Meaning*; Robert H. Brower and Earl Miner, *Japanese Court Poetry* (Stanford, 1961), 180–181.

[12] For the *nō* play *Hakurakuten*, see *Yōkyokushū*, 2: 305–308 (*Nihon Koten Bungaku Taikei*, vol. 41 [Iwanami Shoten, 1963]). Sumiyoshi's invocation of the *kamikaze*, of course, serves as a prelude to divine winds that defeated the archetype of Invasive Other in Japanese historical consciousness, the two attempted Mongol invasions of 1274 and 1281. A popular puppet play of early 1719, the eve of an expected visit by a Korean mission, represents a thinly-masked Toyotomi Hideyoshi as reversing the scheme, making a pilgrimage to four Sumiyoshi shrines to pray for the success of his planned invasion of Korea. Chikamatsu Monzaemon, *Honchō sangokushi*, in *Chikamatsu zenshū*, 11 (Osaka, 1928): 733.

[13] Tzvetan Todorov, *The Conquest of America*, tr. Richard Howard (New York, 1985), 4–5.

vages" of Tierra del Fuego, and of a myriad of peoples in sub-Saharan Africa, (what we now call) India, Malacca, and all. Just as Gulliver knew he was going *somewhere*, and was thus prepared for "discovery," so too were the Portuguese "prepared," in a way the Japanese who greeted them were not (but soon enough would be).

What kind of cosmology, what "implicit iconography" (if not ethnography) of all the "goodly creatures" of the world, mapped the known, the expected, and the unexpected for Japanese in the preencounter age? Why were the first Jesuits "men of Inde" even before they were "southern barbarians" (*Nanban*); and if the Jesuits were "men of Inde," then why were their ships "black ships" (*kurofune*) rather than "Indiamen" (*tenjiku-fune*). Chinese ships, after all, were simply "Chinese ships" (*Karafune*), and Korean ships just Korean ships (*Komabune*). In the next few pages I hope to explore the Japanese cosmological/iconographic realm into which the Iberians sailed at midcentury, to suggest how they fit (or failed to fit) into it, and to speculate that their sojourn in, and expulsion from, Japan made for lasting changes in Japanese notions of ethnic Self,[14] and in their iconography of Other. The discussion is preliminary, speculative, and suggestive, rather than making any pretense to exhaustiveness or definitiveness.

THE IMPLICIT OTHER AND THE MANIFEST MEN OF INDE

In understanding the radical transformations that the arrival of these Iberian "men of Inde" wrought upon the deployment of iconographies of Other in Japanese elite and popular culture, we need to note two central characteristics of the stage onto which the Iberians walked.

It should be no surprise that Japanese iconographies had developed a highly articulated code of markers for Otherness, a (set of) code(s) formed over centuries of contact with the other peoples of continental and archipelagic northeast Asia.[15] As Japanese notions of Self and

[14] Neither "national" nor "ethnic" is entirely appropriate to represent the collectivity of "Japanese" at this historical moment, but the notion of ethnicity and the attendant constructs of boundary maintenance and identity vis-à-vis Other seems preferable in this context, as it is not burdened by nineteenth-century nation-state concepts of nationalism.

[15] It is important to note that this environment of Others included fellow inhabitants of what we now regard as the Japanese archipelago: unassimilated overland neighbors to the northeast and southwest who shared grosser genetic, cultural, and linguistic characteristics with "the Japanese"; and more-clearly "alien" Others, such as the ancestors of the Ainu and the Okinawans. As the boundaries of "Japan" and

Other changed, iconographies were reencrypted to accommodate them; yet the relationship was, as we have seen already in the arrival of the Portuguese, intersubjective and intertextual: Perceptions of both old and new Others were constrained by received codes of Other, while newly discovered Others provoked further articulation of those codes. Further, however, because Japan is an archipelago distant (120 miles at nearest landfall; 550 miles from the Chinese coast) from the continent, and because of the relative disinterest of Chinese and Koreans in journeying to Japan, there were long periods when foreign traffic to Japan was rare indeed. Even at times of relatively intense foreign contact, prior to the 1630s, more contact came from Japanese going abroad, than Others coming to Japan. Consequently, perhaps, iconographies of Other seem less contested than they might otherwise have been.

When the Portuguese stepped off their ships onto Japanese soil, they were dressed to role: dark skin (sunburnt from months at sea; naturally dark), curly hair, heavy beards and general hirsuteness, and other observable bodily characteristics of the Nanban were already heavily signed as markers of alienness and barbarianness.[16] Likewise, the ruffled collar of the elite of Iberia (and much of contemporary southern and western Europe) in the mid-sixteenth century conformed ideally to a rich Japanese iconography of Other that, at least since the eleventh century, had used frilled and ruffled collars, sleeves, and hems as explicit markers of the Other.[17]

But what interests us most in this encounter is the transformation in the iconographic venue of Other that, apparently, was wrought by the European irruption, and the century (ca. 1550–1640) of dense Euro-Japanese contact. It is difficult to be precise about dating, and about the transformation of content, but broadly speaking, Other, the clear-cut foreigner, with a few rare exceptions, is portrayed in pre-Nanban art only abroad – in China (often in essentially Chinese-style painting) or Tenjiku/India – and not in Japanese settings. The major exceptions

"the Japanese" remained less-than-fully determined, so, too, did these Others occasionally cross boundaries in the iconography.

[16] Murai Shōsuke, *Ajia no naka no chūsei Nihon* (Azekura Shobō, 1988), discusses the signed quality of skin color, hair texture, meat-eating (and imputed cannibalism) in medieval Japanese cosmology.

[17] I have seen no serious discussion of this element of Japanese iconography, an element I am currently attempting to systematize further. However, it is clear that the "ruffled Other" is received with Buddhist iconography from Korea and China, where frills appeared to distinguish the Indian and Central Asian Other from the Chinese Self. Thus, the Chinese signification of frill = Other apparently consumed the Other = Indian/Central Asian, in its translation from Chinese to Japanese iconography.

to this iconological generalization seem to be portrayals of kinds of Other-in-Japan as invaders,[18] objects of border subjugation, or tributaries,[19] on the one hand, and portraits of Chinese Buddhist missionaries to Japan, on the other. The latter, however, are generally portrayed in a manner so decontextualized that there is no "setting," per se.

After 1550, by contrast, Other becomes omnipresent, a permanent and pervasive feature of Japanese iconography. For nearly a century, Japanese artists and sculptors enthusiastically, prolifically, painted Nanban-jin, not only in a native European habitat the artist had never seen (Japanese art had a long tradition of depicting idealized Others in idealized foreign settings – to say nothing of Japanese in idealized domestic settings – that the artist, poet, or writer knew only through the art or writing of others), but in Japanese ports, inland towns, and buildings of every description. Japanese took to the "new-wave" Other in many ways, adopting "Nanban" clothing styles, masquerading as "Nanban-jin" in festivals and plays, and mimicking "Nanban" tastes in furniture, food, and clothing.

Nearly simultaneously, Other-masquing, but rarely seen (in any case difficult to document) in earlier theatrical performance (when the "scene" of action was Japan[20]) or festival masquerading, becomes equally a regular characteristic of both formal (staged) and informal (festival) performance. In the Fall of 1604, for example, on the seventh anniversary (by Japanese count) of the death of Toyotomi Hideyoshi, military hegemon who had all-but-unified Japan, and himself a great aficionado of "Nanban" dress-up play, the shrine to his deified spirit, Hōkoku Jinja in Kyoto, held a great memorial festival.[21] If the *Hōkoku sairei-zu byōbu*, a contemporary screen painting of the event, is to be believed, many of the seemingly ecstatic celebrants followed their late

[18] Particularly in *Mōko shūrai ekotoba* (Illustrated narrative of the Mongol invasions), late thirteenth century.

[19] *Shōtoku Taishi eden* (Illustrated biography of Prince Shōtoku, 1069[?]) shows the prince conquering "barbarians" to the northeast (age 10); receiving tribute missions from Korea (ages 12, 26); later versions depict him in other dealings with foreigners. See *Shōtoku Taishi eden* (Nara Kokuritsu Hakubutsukan, 1965).

[20] There are, by contrast, numerous fourteenth- and fifteenth-century *Nō* plays involving Japanese-performing-as-Chinese, but with few exceptions (e.g., *Tōsen* [China Boat], *Fuji* [Mt. Fuji]), they are set in a somewhat-mythic China (*Morokoshi* or *Tōdo*).

[21] Some of Hideyoshi's *nanban*-style clothing survives, e.g., a gold-colored velvet mantle, with gold and beaded embroidery, in the collection of the Nagoya Municipal Museum. The Portuguese Jesuit João Rodrigues reported that Hideyoshi's *nanban* tastes inspired such a fad for Portuguese styles that there were not enough tailors in Nagoya (the *other* Nagoya, in Kyushu) to keep up with the orders. Michael Cooper, *Rodrigues the Interpreter* (New York, 1974), 104.

Figure 11.3. Though chroniclers called them *Tōjin*, these revelers at the seventh anniversary of Hideyoshi's death are in Nanban dress, with *hats, *ruffles, *buttoned jackets, and *pantaloons; they can be identified as Japanese by their sandals, kimonos, and musical instruments, and their whitened faces. *Hōkoku sairei-zu byōbu*, Hōkoku Shrine.

lord's tastes, getting up in drag as Nanban-jin, or even in blackface, mimicking some of the African, Goan, and Javanese who had accompanied the Portuguese to Japan (Figure 11.3). Similarly, a screen painting depicting scenes of the construction of a fortified castle in the late sixteenth or early seventeenth century shows numerous participants dressed in *nanban* style, and the entire atmosphere curiously more that of a festival than a construction site.[22]

[22] *Chikujō-zu byōbu*, six-panel screen, color on paper, collection, Nagoya Municipal Museum.

Figure 11.4. At 1622 festivals for the seventh anniversary of Ieyasu's death, too, the chroniclers' *Tôjin* wore *Nanban* dress. *Tōshōsha engi*, Waka Tōshōgū.

There is little verbal testimony that entitles us to certainty that *our* identification of these "Other-masqued" and "Other-dressed" Japanese as reproducing or enacting *specifically* Nanban, as opposed to some other Other, is correct. Most references in contemporary observers' diaries merely speak of people "in drag" (J. *fūryū*), or of "various and several strange (or "alien") styles" (J. *iroiro samazama ifū no tei o idetate*),[23] but Gien, a high-ranking Buddhist priest of noble birth, notes "Plebeians arrayed themselves in fives and tens, dressed as pleased them. They wore accessories of gold and silver, and put on performances in all sorts of styles: one group arrayed as the four Deva Kings,

[23] "Gien Jugō nikki," 9, Keichō 9/8/15 (8 September 1604), in *Dainihon shiryō* (DNSR), 12th ser., 27: 512, "Hōkoku Daimyōjin rinji matsuri nikki," Keichō 9/8/15, in ibid., 12th ser., 27: 516.

another as Chinamen (*Tōjin*), still others as [the gods] Daikoku and Ebisu,[24] or aged ascetics from Mt. Kōya."[25] Tokugawa Ieyasu, successor to Hideyoshi's national hegemony, and founder of the Tokugawa shogunate only a year before this festival, promoted and observed the festival, hoping to subsume the divinity of his predecessor in his own regime and person, and anticipating his own posthumous deification.

Ieyasu died in 1616, and was deified as the Great Avatar Tōshō, enshrined in Tōshō shrines in Nikkō, in Edo, and at numerous other sites around the country. Only a few years later, in 1622, at festivals at the Wakayama Tōshō shrine, and several others around the country to mark the seventh anniversary of his death, masquers whose clothing appears to us today indistinguishable in aspect from the *Nanban* style of the Hōkoku *matsuri* masquers of 1604 are uniformly described as being dressed as "Chinamen" (J. *Tōjin*), a term that was to become an omnium gatherum for foreigners in Japanese discourse for the next two-and-a-half centuries[26] (Figure 11.4).

[24] Daikoku and Ebisu are two of the "seven gods of good fortune" (*shichi-fukujin*), deities identified specifically as alien, and often depicted as arriving by ship from across the seas. Ebisu, protector of mariners, fishermen, and merchants, is also a loose metaphor for the "northern barbarians," the "Ebisu," or "Emishi," whom the Japanese expelled from the northern half of Honshū in ancient times. Daikoku (Skt., Mahākālā), originally a war-god, and popularly revered as the god of the kitchen, is iconographically marked with a hat and other clothing strongly resembling elite Iberian dress of the sixteenth century.

[25] *Gien Jugō nikki*, 9, in *Dainihon shiryō*, 12.2: 512. It is significant that Gien places "Chinamen" (perhaps signifying "generic aliens"), "Deva Kings," "Daikoku and Ebisu," and "Kōya ascetics" on the same classificatory level: they are of equal ontological status. Mt. Kōya, a center of Buddhism and Shinto since the eighth century, was the base of numerous itinerant (i.e., Other-surrogate) ascetics.

[26] For illustration of the masquers at Wakayama, Tenkai Sōjō, text; Sumiyoshi Jokei, illust., *Waka Tōshōqū engi emaki*, ca. 1640 (MS, 5 scrolls, Coll. Waka Tōshōgū, Wakayama City). For the verbal tag *Tōjin*, "Waka Tōshōgū gosairei no shidaigaki," Genna 8/4/17 (27 May 1622), in *DNSR*, 12.51: (suppl.), 30–41, lists five "Chinaman" or "China-ship" (*Tōjin; Tōsen*) performances in the order of march for this festival, with over eighty performers, and one "black boy" (*kuronbō*) costume, but no *Nanban* performances. Accounts of the dancing in Kanazawa, a castle-town on the Japan Sea coast, from "the beginning of the Summer" (i.e., the 4th month in Japanese reckoning), culminated with "Tōjin dances in the inner shrine hall" (*DNSR*, 12.51: 79). The appearance of the "black boy"–as distinct from the Japanese hero Musashibō Benkei, who though "black-skinned," was gigantic, and never called *kuronbō*–which was a separate trope in Japanese iconography, and seems also to become prominent from the time of the *Nanban* incursions, is a related issue of great ongoing significance. The term *kuronbō* (*kuro* = black + [*n* = non-signifying euphoneme] + *bō* = diminutive/pejorative), first documented in the sixteenth century, can be glossed as "little black" and is still in common use as a pejorative. Helpful in understanding the qualities of skin color in Japan are Hiroshi Wagatsuma, "The Social Perception of Skin Color in Japan," in *Daedalus* (Spring 1967), reprinted in Irwin Scheiner, ed., *Modern Japan: An Interpretive Anthology* (Macmillan, 1974), 51–77, and for the signedness of black in medieval Japan, Kuroda Hideo, *Kyōkai no chūsei, Shōchō no Chūsei*, ch. 6.

A dozen years later, in 1635, in the initial celebration of the annual festival at the newly rededicated Hachiman Shrine in the provincial castle town of Tsu, the conflation of *Nanban* and *Tōjin* seen at Kyoto and Wakayama was repeated: All verbal texts, from the festival's inception to the present day, agree that the residents of the wealthy merchants' quarter of Wakebe-chō, just outside the castle walls, presented themselves in the guise of *Tōjin*. Nowadays, residents of the ward dance in iconographically orthodox *Tōjin* garb, accompanied by orthodox instruments, and parade as a stylized version of a seventeenth-century Korean ambassador's retinue, complete with correct pennants and regalia. They too believe that they have "always" been *Tōjin* and Koreans in the festival performance.[27] Yet pictorial records of the early festival, believed to date from the inaugural 1635 festival, show these Wakebe-chō *Tōjin* in unmistakable *Nanban* costume, wearing high-topped *boots, *billowing pantaloons, *button-front jackets, *flowing locks with a *reddish tinge, and thick, black *side-whiskers, beards, and moustaches.[28] They carry *straight-bladed swords, and one, most tellingly, shoulders an *arquebus; a bit later in the retinue, a little-boy Chinamen (in garb distinct from the *Nanban* style) plays a **charumera*, while farther back, another little-boy Chinaman brings up the rear[29] (Figures 11.5a and 11.5b).

[27] Field notes, 9–11 October 1990.

[28] For the sake of clarity and brevity, I have indicated with an asterisk those physical characteristics, items of clothing, and other paraphernalia signifying alien in the iconography, both representational and performative.

[29] *Hachiman-gū sairei emaki*, 2 scrolls, n.d. (1630s?), ink, color, and gilt on paper. Spencer Collection, New York Public Library. Spencer Collection no. 56. Tsu-shi Kyōiku Iinkai, ed., *Tsu-shi no bunkazai* (1989), front matter, gives a color reproduction showing a section of the Wakebe-chō *Nanban/Tōjin* masquerade; other details and bibliographic data published in Miyeko Murase, *Tales of Japan* (Oxford, 1986), 173–175; Shigeo Sorimachi, *Catalog of Japanese Illustrated Books and Manuscripts in the Spencer Collection of the New York Public Library*, rev., enl. ed. (The Kōbunsō, 1978), 26–27. When a facsimile of this scroll was displayed during the 1990 Tsu Hachiman Festival, several local participants remarked that the costumes seemed "all wrong"; that they "didn't look like *Tōjin* or "Korean" costumes"; etc. An ethnic Korean born in Japan, who has been active in identifying and studying "Korean-embassy masquerades," was perplexed that these "Koreans" looked like *Nanban*. (Field notes.) The *Tōjin* qual-

Figure 11.5. Though Portuguese were being expelled from Japan, the *Nanban*-garbed *Tōjin* costume remained briefly, until replaced by Korean and other alien motifs, as in the Tsu Hachiman Festival. (a) *Tsu Hachiman sairei emaki*. Spencer Collection, New York Public Library, Tilden, Lenox and Astor Foundations. (b) The Tsu Hachiman parade of 1990 "preserves" only the Korean/*Tōjin* costumery, with no "memory" of its *Nanban/Tōjin* antecedents.

a

b

It seems likely that this revaluation of overtly *Nanban* clothing as *Tōjin*, perhaps the reemergence of the *Tōjin* from the shadow of the *Nanban*, is but another side-effect of the rising fear of Christianity, and concomitant suspicion of Portuguese, that had led to edicts prohibiting evangelization as early as 1587. Hideyoshi's edict of 1587 was honored in the breach, but in 1612, Ieyasu had issued a more explicit proscription that in fact resulted in the expulsion of many missionaries and Japanese Christians; in 1619, over sixty Christians had been executed in Kyoto; and just four months after the festival for the seventh anniversary of Ieyasu's death, fifty-five Christians were executed in Nagasaki.[30] It was becoming dangerous to "play" at *Nanban*; it was safer to call this rose by another name, "Chinaman."

Indeed, in the rising tide of Christian persecution and xenophobia, it becomes increasingly difficult to find either visual or textual evidence of the *Nanban* in Japanese iconography. But as the "blurred genre" of the *Tōjin*-in-*Nanban* clothing in the festivals of 1604, 1622, and 1635 suggests, the desire both to masque as Other, and to represent Other visually, was more perdurant than the specifically *Nanban* style. The representation of Other was essential to the perpetuation of community, to the inscription of boundaries, and to the reconstitution of categories of Self and Other, in the aftermath of the *Nanban* interlude. As the *Nanban* were driven from Japan (ultimately in 1639), and Christianity virtually extirpated, or driven underground thereafter, the Other had to find new clothes. The reclothing of Other found convenient sources in a different, more familiar direction, also suggested by the "Chinaman" tags of 1622: Japanese masquers and artists alike turned back to the Other they had known all along, the Other of the continent and archipelago (primarily Korea and Ryūkyū), for themes and tropes of Alterity.

The initial Japanese ascription of Indianness to Iberians, accords with the analogous Iberian "error" in their "New World," or the Hawaiian inscription of Captain Cook in earlier texts of Alterity. In each case, the earlier text (Tenjiku; India; the Hawaiian god Lono) had been a text "read" vicariously, not directly: No Japanese had been to Tenjiku; Columbus had not seen "India"; Lono had not (likely) visited Hawaii in memory of those who greeted Cook. The nomination of the

ity of costume in all later depictions I have seen is thoroughly cleansed of any hint of *Nanban*ness, whether in Tsu, or elsewhere.

30 The increasingly severe suppression of Christianity (or rising tide of persecution, in most accounts sympathetic to the evangelical enterprise) is outlined in C. R. Boxer's classic, *The Christian Century in Japan, 1549–1650* (Berkeley, CA, 1951), and in Elison, *Deus Destroyed*.

Iberians as Indians, as Tenjiku/Chensicus, inscribed them in a sacred text, the land of the Buddha, and hence sacralized and exalted this Other. The ready renomination of Chensicus as *Nanban*, too, represents but their reinscription from sacred text (India) to profane, for the *Nanban* were one of the savages of the four directions (*shi'i*) in a Chinese cosmology that had been mapped onto Japan.[31]

The assimilation of a new, inadequately known form of Other, Iberians, first to a prior category of indirectly experienced Other is one thing. Their subsequent absorption to a category of well-known Other, *Tōjin*, evident in the naming – as opposed to costuming – of the masquers of the Hōkoku and Tōshō memorial festivals, is somewhat different, yet no less unprecedented. The envoy who bore the letter of James I of England to Japan reported in 1613, for example, that "the place [was] exceedingly peopled, [and they were] very Civill and courteous," save,

> onley that at our landing, and being here in Hakata [a major port in Kyushu], and so through the whole Countrey, whithersoever we came, the boyes, children, and worser sort of idle people, would gather about and follow along after us, crying Coré, Coré, Cocoré, Waré, that is to say, You Coreans with false hearts: wondering, hooping, hallowing, and making such a noise about us, that we could scarcely heare one an other speake, sometimes throwing stones at us (but that not in many Townes), yet the clamour and crying after us was every where alike, none reprooving them for it.[32]

We need to take note that tens of thousands of Korean ("Coré" = J. *Kōrai;* K. *Koryŏ*) had passed through Hakata as captives during Japanese invasions, 1592–98, and thousands, at least, still lived in the region, forming the core of potters' communities, acting as Confucian advisers, and the like; there is no reason to believe that "Coré" was only a vicarious text for the "boyes, children, and worser sort of idle people" there. Further, we should recall that the term *Kōrai* itself was a deliberately alienating archaism in Japanese discourse: The Kory state had fallen in 1392, some two hundred years earlier; its successor state, Chosŏn (J. Chōsen, 1392–1910), while recognized in official correspondence, was unrecognized in popular discourse.[33]

[31] China (and Japan) surrounded themselves with "northern fire-dogs" (*hokuteki;* Ch., *beidi*); "eastern flying squirrels" (*tōi;* Ch., *dong'i*); "southern snakes" (*nanban,* Ch., *nanman*); and western giants (*seijū,* Ch., *sirong*—note that in the Chinese version of this, the Japanese were *wo,* dwarves, to the east).

[32] The diary of John Saris, in Samuel Purchas, *Purchas, His Pilgrimes in Japan,* ed. Cyril Wild (Kobe, 1939), 148–149, quoted in Michael Cooper, ed., *They Came to Japan: An Anthology of European Reports on Japan, 1543–1640* (Berkeley, CA, 1965), 287–288.

[33] The varying names for Korea in early-modern Japanese discourse (and even today)

Eighty years after Saris, long after the Iberians had been expelled, Engelbert Kaempfer, German physician to the Dutch trading factory in Nagasaki, likewise reported that "In some towns and villages," during his two journeys to Edo,

> . . . the young boys, who are childish all-over the world, would run after us, call us names, and crack some malicious jests or other, levell'd at the Chinese, *whom they take us to be*. One of the most common, and not much different from a like sort of compliment, which is commonly made to Jews in Germany, is Toosin bay bay [*Tōjin baibai*], which in broken Chinese, signifies, Chinese, have ye nothing to truck?[34]

Catalyzed by Christophobia and Iberiophobia, Europeans were reinscribed as subcategories of less threatening Others, Koreans, and Chinese.

ALTER OTHERS: KOREANS, OKINAWANS, AND CHINESE IN THE JAPANESE TEXT

Japanese cosmologies were amply supplied with Others prior to the Iberian irruption of the mid-sixteenth century. I have alluded to a core Japanese Self, bounded to the east by limitless seas and to the west by China (*kara/morokoshi* = continental, and including Korea), with *Tenjiku* (the "chengicu" of Cosme de Torres's letter to Xavier), the land of the Buddhas, beyond it. Unlike Japan's Iberian encounter, however, most Japanese meetings with the Chinese and Indian Other had occurred "out there," in China and Tenjiku, not only in iconographic conceit, but in historic practice.[35] With some exceptions, of course, it

are charged with differing ethnic and political significations, a matter I intend to take up at a separate opportunity.

[34] Kaempfer, *The History of Japan*, tr. J. G. Scheuzer, 3 vols. (London, 1727; repr., Glasgow, 1906), 2: 357. The close parallels between Kaempfer's phrasing and Saris's suggests either that Kaempfer had read Saris (unlikely), or that there was a corpus of lore that circulated among the Japan hands of early-modern Europe, a European iconography of Other, in which this was a common trope. It reappears in the writings of other westerners in Japan in the nineteenth century, as well, e.g., Edward Barrington de Fonblanque, *Niphon and Pe-che-li; or Two Years in Japan* (London, 1863), 15; Robert Fortune, *Yedo and Peking: A Narrative of a Journey to the Capitals of Japan and China* (London, 1863), 96. There is little doubt that both de Fonblanque and Fortune had read Kaempfer.

[35] An early eighth-century monk was reputed to have tried to go to Tenjiku, only to be eaten by a tiger in Vietnam; other than him, I know of no Japanese claims to visiting Tenjiku before the seventeenth century. A seventeenth-century mariner gained notoriety as "Tenjiku Tokubei" for his fabulous claims to have visited *Tenjiku*, and came to personify the evil potentialities of the foreign in numerous popular plays of the eighteenth and nineteenth centuries.

was Japanese monks who made the pilgrimage to China, rather than the reverse; Japanese merchants who bore them there.

The Xavierian moment, the mid-sixteenth-century era of Iberian irruption into East Asia, and Japanese consciousness, coincided with a half-century of low ebb in Japan's relations with nearby East Asia. Civil war in Japan had unleashed "Japanese" piracy up and down the East Asian coast; piracy had provoked China to embargo direct trade with Japan, banning both Japanese voyages to China, and Chinese voyages to Japan. Relations with all East Asia reached nadir with Japan's invasion of Korea in 1592, and the ensuing seven-year war between Japan and a Sino-Korean alliance.

The devastation of Korea was mirrored by an enrichment of Japan. Not only were countless Korean cultural treasures taken as booty by Japan's generals; entire communities of potters and other craftsmen were uprooted and taken captive to Japan, where they established new centers of ceramic arts in Japan, or reinvigorated old communities. These tens of thousands of Koreans constitute the largest documented immigration to Japan before the twentieth century. Some of the communities they established remained ethnically distinct into modern times.[36] Yet these communities of eternal internal Others do not appear to have excited artists' brushes.

The decade after the war, when Korea and Japan had resolved their overt differences, Korea sent an embassy of nearly five hundred men to the Tokugawa capital of Edo (modern Tokyo), the first of seven such missions in the seventeenth century. Likewise, after a short, Granada/Panama-style Japanese invasion of Ryūkyū (Okinawa) in 1609, the Ryukyuan king was brought to Edo in 1610, and followed by six other Ryukyuan missions to Edo that century.[37] Just as the Europeans,[38] the Koreans and Ryukyuans, too, were objects of curiosity, confusion, and wonder.

Each embassy was a major popular cultural event, a once-in-a-lifetime tourist attraction for people along the route.[39] Along the In-

[36] E.g., the Korean potters' community of Naeshirokawa in Satsuma (southern Kyushu), which remained *identified as Koreans* for at least two-and-a-half centuries after originally being transplanted to Japan as captives in the 1590s. See *The Status System of and Social Organization of Satsuma: A Translation of the Shūmon Tefuda Aratame Jōmoku*, tr. Torao Haraguchi, *et al.* (Tokyo University Press, 1975), Art. 13 (original text, pp. 199–200; trans., pp. 88–89). Then (1852), like today, Japanese appear to have regarded even distant descendants of Korean immigrants as inherent (genetic?) aliens, whose "home country" (*hongoku*) they had never seen.

[37] See my *State and Diplomacy in Early Modern Japan* (Princeton, 1984), for a fuller account.

[38] Recall John Saris's account of his passage through Hakata.

[39] Embassies travelled by ship through the Inland Sea to Osaka, then up to the Yodo

land Sea, people rode out into the channel to get a closer look when the flotilla passed; at each port-town where they spent the night, hundreds would gather to gawk and stare. At Osaka in 1682, wrote a Korean diarist in the entourage, "A million onlookers swarmed like ants on the riverbanks . . . ; pontoon bridges spanned the water, and countless thousands lined up on them to watch us." And the spectators and gawkers were neither solely the lower classes, who could afford no loftier entertainment, nor exclusively those a few minutes' or hours' walk from the route, for whom the trip was no expense[40]:

> At the arrival of the Ryukyuan tribute mission [of 1832] . . . great numbers of spectators, both male and female, flocked to see, lining both sides of the river, and even floating boats out into the middle of the river, clogging the channel . . . when they went upriver by boat . . . to Fushimi . . . it's said the spectators lined the route all the way. What's more . . . Imperial Princes, members of the Regent's House, and senior courtiers were pleased to [watch], and it's even rumored that the Retired Emperor secretly made an Imperial Progress to watch.

A half-century of *Nanban* art had firmly established a canon of representing Other on Japanese soil, in Japanese settings from Kagoshima and Nagasaki to Kyoto. A half-century of *Nanban* fashion had generated new forms of Other in festival masquing, as we have seen in the festivals at the seventh anniversaries of the deaths of Hideyoshi and Ieyasu. The reappearance of Japan's other Others, ambassadorial entourages from Korea and the Ryukyuan kingdom, in Japan, beginning in the first decade of the seventeenth century, was quickly translated into visual representations of Other-in-Japan: As early as 1624, a (court?) painter (on commission from a Japanese feudal lord?) depicted the parade of a Korean embassy in a scroll painting (a format ideally suited to representing a parade), accompanied by a Japanese escort, marching to its audience with the shogun.[41]

River on galleys to Yodo. They entered Kyoto on foot, horseback, or palanquin, and travelled to Edo by road, passing through four of the five largest cities in the land (Osaka, Kyoto, Nagoya, and Edo). For a discussion of the tourist appeal of these events, see my "Carnival of the Aliens: Korean Embassies in Edo-Period Art and Popular Culture," in *Monumenta Nipponica*, 41, no. 4 (1986): 415–456.

40 *Ukiyo no arisama*, in *Nihon shomin seikatsu shiryō shūsei*, 11: 239.

41 *Kan'ei Chōsenjin raichô zukan*, color on paper, 32.1 × 984.2 cm., Central National Library of Korea. For a partial reproduction, *Tokubetsu tenkan: Chōsen tsūshinshi* (Tokyo National Museum, 1985), Plate 8. The customary dating of this scroll painting to 1624 must be regarded as tentative, for it is neither signed nor dated. Note that the Korean costumes depicted, while minimally consistent with the established iconography of Other outlined above, are clearly distinct from the *Nanban*/*Tōjin* costumes of either the *Nanban* art tradition, or the finery of the masquers at the seventh anniversary

The Koreans are readily distinguishable from their escorts: they wear *hats, *shoes, *trousers, and *collars; the hatless pages have *unshaven pates.[42] (There is no emphasis of the Koreans' beards, characteristic of later representations, both visual and performative, perhaps because the clean-shaven face had yet to dominate *Japanese* men's fashion. Many of the Japanese are represented sporting moustaches.) Yet, remarkably, these Koreans and their Japanese escorts were not represented as *being anywhere*: They march along an unrepresented road, past no "millions of onlookers," no "pontoon bridges," no countryside or cityscape. There are no visual clues to "locate" the Koreans in an identifiable context. They are signed Other; their escorts signed Self. Yet all context is omitted/obliterated, unlike the canons of *Nanban* art, as both Japanese Self and Korean Other march past no one, on no road, through nothingness.

But shortly the Korean and Okinawan Other who ventured to Japan would be explicitly located in *Japanese* scenes, Japanese cityscapes, dis-/re-placing the expelled and tabooed Iberian Other. This process, we have seen, began in the confusions of genre implicated in the Nanban-costumed Japanese of the Hōkoku Festival and the Wakayama and Tottori festivals in memory of Ieyasu, dubbed "Tōjin" (Chinamen) by the priest Gien, and in the written records of the program of march; in the epithet "Coré" hurled so often at Saris, and later "Toosin" (Tōjin) spat at Kaempfer.

By the 1640s, the time the last Iberians were expelled (1639), at the latest, Koreans and Okinawans, *plume-*hatted, *bearded, *frill-collared, *booted, *shod, *trousered, and all, were being incorporated into particular city- and landscapes in Japan. In 1640, Kanō Tan'yū, the premier painter in the shogun's entourage, executed the illustrations for Tenkai's history of the shrine to Tokugawa Ieyasu, *Tōshōsha engi*, in response to a shogunal command. Most of the verbal and pictorial text recounts the pre-life and life of Ieyasu; the final chapters expand on the great reverence he has received since his deification. Heavily-*tagged in the codes that had marked the invasive Iberian Other, East Asian Others who had formerly been kept safely Out There (iconographically) usurped their predecessors' place In Here, in overtly Japanese settings. Where the Nanban screen paintings had depicted Iberians sightseeing in the shrines and temples of Miyako (Kyoto), Tan'yū showed them entering the Tōshōsha (later Tōshōgū)

memorial festivals for Hideyoshi and Ieyasu. For an introduction to the modes of representing Koreans in Edo-period art, see my "Carnival of the Aliens."

[42] I have put an asterisk (*) by characteristics that are established iconographic marks of Other.

shrine in Nikkō, north of Edo, to worship the deified Tokugawa Ieyasu.[43] The place is indisputably *Japan*, the entrance to a quintessentially *Japanese* sacred space, a *torii* shrine gate; the pine trees are *Japanese* pines,[44] and the spectators are dressed in styles characteristic of particular *Japanese* social statuses and life-stages: The Koreans are clearly Other; they are clearly in *Japan*, as they had rarely been in pre-Nanban representation.

Similarly, the centerpiece of *Edo-zu byōbu*, an anonymous Edo cityscape screen painting, most likely produced for display before the shogun, is the march of a Korean parade through the streets of the shogunal capital.[45] Here, too, the Koreans are signed Other with *frilled collars and sleeves, *plumed hats, *beards, *shoe and *boots, and the like. They, more even than the parade of Korean "pilgrims" to the shrines at Nikkō, are inscribed in a richly signed Japanese scene, passing through the streets of Japan's most populous city, crossing the moat to enter the walled, ramparted shogunal castle, before clusters of gawking, staring, pointing Japanese – again in rank- and status-coded dress and hairstyles. The scene is richly evocative of the scenes of a Nanban-peopled Kyoto a half-century before, and entirely at variance with the nearly totally Other-less Japanese landscape that preceded the Iberian arrival a century earlier. Iberian style at the moment of encounter had been in fortuitous conformity with the iconographic text of Other that anticipated their arrival; the absence of Other on the Japanese domestic stage enabled them to enter an open role already costumed. By the time the Iberians left, the role was established in the text of the Japanese landscape; in the absence of Iberians, Koreans, Okinawans, and other Others were asked to stand in their stead.

This ironic interplay of tropes[46] in the assumption of roles and

[43] In my "Contesting the Centre: International Sources of Japanese National Identity," in *The International History Review*, 7, no. 3 (1985): 347–363, and in *State and Diplomacy*, 204, I argue that the "worship" of Ieyasu by foreigners (the Koreans were told it was a "sightseeing trip") was part of a program to universalize the sacral reach of Ieyasu-the-god, an element in the ideological agenda of the early Tokugawa state.

[44] There is a distinction in Japanese iconography between a Japanese pine and Chinese pine; though I have not seen it demonstrated rigorously, pines painted as these never occur in Japanese paintings of foreign settings.

[45] Pair of six-panel painted screens, collection National Ethnohistorical Museum, Sakura City. For full reproductions, see Suzuki Susumu, ed., *Edo-zu byōbu* (Heibonsha, 1971). Kuroda Hideo, *Ō no shintai; ō no shōzō* (Heibonsha, 1993), ch. 1, has recently shown that this screen was painted sometime in late 1634 or early 1635, to celebrate the early years of the reign of the third shogun, Iemitsu (r. 1624–1651); the Korean procession shown, therefore, depicts the mission of 1624, the first of three Iemitsu received.

[46] I adapt this phrase from James W. Fernandez, "Convivial Attitudes: The Ironic Interplay of Tropes in an International Kayak Festival in Northern Spain," in Edward

niches in Japanese iconography and folklore, by Iberians and their *kuronbō* entourage, who assumed (appeared in) the garb of *chensicus* and Tōjin, of demons and goblins (and of monkeys, dogs, and other animals[47]) in which guise they entered Japan after a millennium offshore; by Coré and Tōjin, who stepped into the onshore places of Iberians and Englishmen (and later Dutch and Germans, but almost invariably men, not women); and finally by Koreans, Okinawans, and later again the Dutch, bespeaks a profound continuity in the iconographies of Other in late-medieval and early-modern Japan. Yet also the inescapable contrast between the absence of Other from Japanese iconographic soil prior to 1550, and the pervasive presence of Other in the performative, literary, and artistic Japanese landscape after 1550 – even after the expulsion of the Iberian interloper – represents a profound transformation of the field on which Japanese dialogues of Self and Other were played out.

A further playing field, beyond the festival masque,[48] folding screen, and narrative scroll, for the iteration of Other On Our Shores, which again continued tropes rehearsed in the representation of the Nanban, was the adoption of Nanban-Tōjin/Korean-coded costume for a broad range of itinerant acrobats, jongleurs, monkey-trainers, and pedlars, some of whose activities remain a part of the encoding of Other on the Japanese scene even today. Other-as-acrobat likely predates the Iberians, at least, I am not certain that it does not, and the clothing of acrobats and jugglers in temporarily or spatially alien garb is as familiar as the Ringling Brothers' Circus. But clearly the representation of Iberian sailors, and more often, the *kuronbō* who accompanied them,

M. Bruner, ed., *Text, Play, and Story: The Construction and Reconstruction of Self and Society* (Prospect Heights, IL, 1984), 199–229.

47 This is not the place for a full discussion of the issues involved in the bestialization of Other in Japanese folklore, iconography, cosmology, and demonology. However, readers should note that the position I take here contests recent assertions by Emiko Ohnuki-Tierney, *Monkey as Mirror: Symbolic Transformations in Japanese History and Culture* (Princeton, 1987), of an unalloyedly "positive attitude toward foreigners" (p. 146), and an implicit separation of the alterities of bestial and of human Others. John W. Dower, too, implies that bestialization of Other was more characteristic of United States constructions of its Other, Japan, before and during the Pacific War, than of Japanese of the West, in *War Without Mercy: Race and Power in the Pacific War* (New York, 1987).

48 By the middle of the sixteenth century, organized, coordinated Other-masquing was almost a compulsory figure in urban–and many village – festivals. A half-dozen of the performances in the 1622 Wakayama festival mentioned above were tagged "Tōjin," and in a similar festival in Tottori; from the 1630s, "Korean" or "Tōjin" masques were a regular feature of festivals in Edo, Nagoya, Ōgaki, Tsu, and elsewhere. By the 1670s, mechanical-doll acrobats (*karakuri ningyō*) of Other were the predominating mode of entertainment on the giant cart-floats of the festival of Nagoya and other towns.

a

b

c

at work in the rigging of "Black Ships" as acrobats, sometimes nearly simian in aspect, performing tricks on the high-wire, was a favorite motif of the artists of the Nanban screens. It is no accident that the *ruff-collared, *puff-sleeved, *elongated crew members doing handstands on the bowsprit, hanging from the yards, and sliding down the stays of the ship riding at anchor are deeply, darkly *black, in Kanō Naizen's screen-painting of the Portuguese *kurofune* in Nagasaki harbor (Figure 11.6a). The "Nanban" acrobats in the ship's rigging in another Kanō-school screen are likewise nearly all *kuronbō*[49] (Figure 11.6b).

The sight of a slightly simian acrobatic Other swinging in the rigging of Other ships anchored off the quay was too succulent a metaphor to drop from the table simply because the Iberians had been expelled. Rather, ultimately, Koreans and Okinawans were made to climb halyards and hawsers in their stead. Thus, in a votive painting presented in 1695 to a Shinto shrine south of Osaka, Koreans are shown disporting themselves on the cabin roofs of each vessel in the six-ship flotilla, while in a cheap monochrome print – of much later provenance, to be sure – intended for mass sales, a dragon-headed Korean ship arriving in Tsushima is shown with *bearded, *hatted, *shod and *pantalooned crewmen swinging from line to line, mast to mast[50] (Figure 11.6c). In the eighteenth century, when it again became safe to depict Europeans, Dutch sailors too would be forced into acrobatics in the rigging, at least in the harbor of imagination in Japanese prints, if not above the wetter waters of Nagasaki Harbor itself.[51]

[49] Kanō Naizen screen, coll. Kobe Municipal Museum, reproduced in Michael Cooper, S.J., ed., *The Southern Barbarians: The First Europeans in Japan* (Tokyo and Palo Alto, CA, 1971), pl. 94; Kanō-school screen, coll. Suntory Museum; *ibid.*, pl. 1. These are typical, rather than exceptional representations.

[50] For a color reproduction of the votive painting, see my "Carnival of the Aliens: Korean Embassies in Japanese Art and Popular Culture," in *Monumenta Nipponica*, 40, no. 4 (1986): pl. 4; for *Chōsenjin tokai fune no zu*, anon., private collection, Japan. See Shin Kisu, *et al.*, *Chosen tsūshinshi ezu shūsei* (Kōdansha, 1985), pl. 56.

[51] *Oranda nyūsen zu*, anon. (Nagasaki: Ōhata Toyojiemon, n.d.), coll., Kobe Municipal

Figure 11.6. (a) Ruff-collared, pantalooned, black-skinned crewmen scamper (b) acrobatically in the rigging of a *Nanban* "black ship," circa 1600. Kanō Dōmi, screen painting. Museu Nacional de Arte Antigua, Portugal. (c) After the Iberians, with their black slaves, were banished from Japan, Koreans, Okinawans, Chinese, and Dutch took their place in representation, and were made to climb the halyards in their stead, as in this cheap monochrome print of 1811, showing a Korean ship arriving in a Japanese port. Anon., *Chōsenjion tokai fune no zu*, Seikyū Bunka Hall.

a

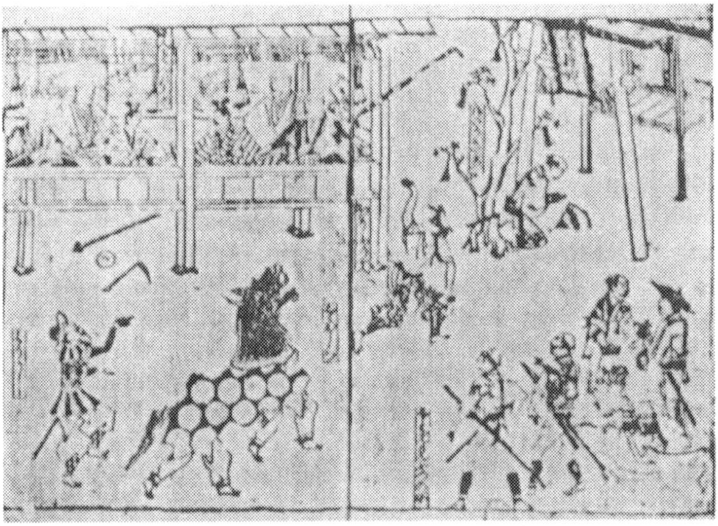

b

c

The image of the acrobatic Other received even stronger impetus from the shogun's request that the Korean court send a troupe of equestrian acrobats to his court in 1635[52] (Figure 11.7a). These equestrian troupes became a regular feature of every official Korean visit to Japan thereafter, and an inspiration to countless Japanese artists – to say nothing of Japanese acrobats.[53] (In fn 45 I refer to the importance of associating Other with Animal.) The trope of Acrobat Other (read: capable of remarkable feats; simian; horselike – recall the equine simile for Xavier's teeth) was reiterated by itinerant Japanese acrobats and pedlars, who adopted Other-dress, with *frilled sleeves and collars, *conical/comical hats, *shod feet, and all, who appeared on the streets of Japan from at least the middle of the seventeenth century, if the plates of a 1661 edition of the tale *Aigo no Waka*, are at all representative. There a *bearded, *hatted, *ruff-collared, *pantalooned juggler parades the streets of Kyoto, at the approach to the shrine of Sannō Gongen (the posthumously deified Aigo no Waka),

Museum. See *Kōbe Nanban Bijutsukan zuroku*, 5 vols. (Kōbe Nanban Bijutsukan, 1970), vol. 3: pl. 4. Several other such prints are also reproduced in this catalog.

[52] For details, see my *State and Diplomacy*, 82; 208.

[53] See, e.g., the 1683 print of Hishikawa Moronobu, a founder of the school of Japanese printmaking known as *ukiyo-e* (pictures of the floating world) in the Philadelphia Museum collection, reproduced as pl. 4 in David Waterhouse, *Early Japanese Prints in the Philadelphia Museum of Art* (Toronto, 1983), or the early eighteenth-century guidebook to Kyoto, *Hōei Karaku saiken-zu* (Kyoto, 1706), showing the Korean equestrians practicing in the grounds of a Kyoto temple.

Figure 11.7. The association of Other with curative powers – Chinese medicine, Korean ginseng, *Tenjiku* rhinoceros horn – made Other-masquing an irresistable choice for itinerant pedlars, some of whom also adopted the guise of acrobat-Other or juggler-Other. (a) The trope of the acrobatic Other was sustained, too, by troupes of Korean equestrians who traveled the Inland Sea and Pacific coast to and from Edo several times in the seventeenth and eighteenth centuries. Here they are shown practicing on the grounds of a Kyoto Buddhist temple. *Karaku saiken zu* (1703). (b) The trope of the acrobat Other was reiterated by itinerant acrobats like this troupe, illustrated in *Aigo no Waka* (1661), in false *beard, *ruffed collar, and *pantaloons, approaching a Sannō shrine in the streets of Kyoto. Two * pantalooned colleagues in horse costume evoke tro(u)pes of Korean equestrians. (c) A peddlar of "Chinaman-candy" (*Tōjin-ame*), clothed in a *Korean-style hat and *trousers, with *ruffs at his waist and ankles, and an obviously false *beard, decorates his sash with a *chili-pepper. He entertains children with a dance, while his *karakuri-ningyō* ("mechanical doll," a pun on *kara/Tō*, meaning "China"/"alien") with *Tōjin* *beard, *pantaloons, and *button-front coat, plays a **charumera*. *Itchō gafu*, 1770, from a painting by Hanabusa Itchô (1652–1724).

while his "horse" (two *pantalooned colleagues dressed as a horse) prances before him. Not only does the illustration reinforce the associations of the acrobatic Other inherent both in the depiction of *kuronbō, nanban,* Dutch, Chinese, and Koreans in the rigging of their ships, and in the visits of Korean equestrian acrobats to Japan. As significantly, the depiction of these acrobats in Altered states approaching the Sannō shrine reinforces notions of the universal reach of Japanese gods underscored elsewhere by (the appearance of) Other coming to worship Japanese gods, already observed in the Korean "pilgrimages" to Nikkō.[54]

Itinerant pedlars, too, particularly ones who dealt in products – like candy or medicines – often assimilated to acrobatics, Other-masqued dress, Other-marked musical instruments, to announce themselves and attract an audience for their patter (Figure 11.7b). The association of itinerant pedlars of certain products, such as "Chinaman-candy" (*Tōjin ame*), with Other, seen, for example, in Hanbusa Itchō's *Tōjin-ame* (Figure 11.7c), was so well established that a comic poet wrote, "It's the Chinaman, he shouted, pointing at the candyman." Itchō's Chinaman-candyman wears a blatantly false *beard, a *plumed, *conical hat, *frill-cuffed *pantaloons, and a *frilled girdle from which hangs a giant *chili-pepper[55]; on his trunk rests a **charumera* (from Port. *charamela*), a kind of oboe signed as Other, that was a regular part of the musical troupes accompanying Korean and Okinawan visits to Japan; also on his trunk dances a mechanical doll, a *karakuri ningyō*, in the shape of a **charumera*-playing monkey-in-Dutchman's clothing![56]

[54] *Aigo no Waka* (Kyoto: Yamamoto Kyūbei, 1661), repr. in *Sekkyōbushi shōhonshū*, 2 (Ōokayama Shoten, 1937): 383–387. The illustrations of the Yamamoto edition, the oldest printed edition extant, are not followed in the 1708 Ringyōya edition, in ibid., 338–391; in the current context, there is no illustration of a juggler of any sort in the 1708 edition. Aigo no Waka, the son of a courtier couple conceived through the intervention of the bodhisattva Kannon, was hounded to his death by wrongful slanders, and reborn as the avatar of Mt. Hiei, Sannō Gongen, who is worshipped more as a Shinto god than a bodhisattva. Korean/Tōjin masquing was a stock feature of the annual Edo festival to the god Sannō, as in many urban festivals, and one of the festival's main attractions for spectators. See my "Carnival of the Aliens."

[55] Called *Tō-garashi* (the *Tō* of *Tōjin*, "foreign pepper"), the chili-pepper was introduced from the Americas in the sixteenth century. Not merely "domesticated," but "indigenized" in Korean, and many regional Chinese cuisines, it remained, true to its new name, an "exotic" item in Japanese cuisine, tagged foreign, and used sparingly.

[56] Hanabusa Itchō (1652–1724) was a painter of sufficient note that his paintings were later reproduced as a three-volume collection of prints, models for the aspiring young artist. Itchō's original may not be extant, but it was later published as a print in the collection of Itchō's work, *Itchō gafu*, 3 vols. (1770), 2: 5–6. Note the gear-wheel half-visible behind the doll. For the satiric poem, *Haifū yanagidaru*, 44:10, in *Haifū yanagidaru zenshū, sakuin hen* (Sanseidō, 1984), 34. The *karakuri ningyō*, mechanical dolls

THE INVASIVE OTHER: FEAR OF FOREIGNERS AND THE CHANGING ICONOGRAPHIC FIELD

The sense of vulnerability to the foreign engendered by the Iberian irruption and its aftermath made it impossible to keep Other safely "out there," sapped the evocative power of the god Sumiyoshi, and the Divine Wind he invoked to repel Hakurakuten; the Divine Wind that had twice protected Japan from the Mongol onslaught. The Iberians stepped into an iconographic, cosmological, and cognitive text in Japan long in the writing, well-rehearsed in the reading, and ironically filled a space available in the text: There were many Others Out There, but few had come In Here; the Iberians filled that space, added to the text. After the Iberians were expelled – indeed the few remaining Europeans were virtually imprisoned in Nagasaki – the text continued to demand a presence of Other In Here, but denied the reader an Iberian image for the reading.

Readers, however, transposed other Others into the text, rewriting the Iberian part for Koreans, Chinese, Okinawans, and others, who had largely been formerly excluded from the domestic text, but were now essential to its reading. As the Iberians had so conveniently arrived in *costume at the first, now, too, their costume – and role – could be conceded to these other Others, keeping Others In Here, reminding readers of the Intrusive Other, sustaining fear of foreigners (along with fascination, excitement, titillation) long after the Other had been defanged of its horse-teeth, and sent packing away.

of remarkable complexity, that some neo-nativist Japanese have credited for Japan's expertise in robotics, incorporate a pun on the foreign (*kara*, meaning "alien"; "continental"), and *karakuri* < *karakuru* ("to manipulate; to trick"); characteristic of great urban festivals, most *karakuri ningyō* physically represent, as well as connoting, the foreign. For example, see Ise Monsui's study of the half-life-size *karakuri* dolls of the Nagoya festival, *Nagoya matsuri* (1910; repr. Murata Shoten, 1980).

PART III

Adjustments to encounter

CHAPTER 12

Essay on objects: Interpretations of distance made tangible

MARY W. HELMS

"Earlier, things had possessed a value not because of what they were but because of what they meant" (Umberto Eco, *Art and Beauty in the Middle Ages*, p. 64).

PLACES OF ORIGINS AND THE NATURE OF GOODS

During the fifteenth, sixteenth, and into the seventeenth century, the cosmogony and cosmography of Western Europe underwent a tremendous temporal-spatial expansion. The European worldview was forced to accommodate novel concepts of "distance" identified in time by a new recognition of classical antiquity and in space by the identification of heretofore unknown foreign lands.[1] This relatively sudden amplification of cosmological and intellectual space and time necessitated conscious intellectual adjustment if it were to be successfully contained. Not only were there new parameters to be accommodated but serious efforts were required to keep this burgeoning conceptual system under firm control, its underlying unity and harmony intact and its basic tenets reaffirmed, lest an overly rapid broadening of horizons should somehow get out of hand and threaten to fly apart, "all in peeces, all coherence gone," philosophically and ideologically (cosmologically) speaking.[2]

Various means were available to effect such control, to keep the pieces – or at least representative pieces – of these expanded cosmological realms literally in hand. One such technique is evidenced by an increased passion for the collecting of things, particularly by eco-

[1] Charles Trinkaus, "Renaissance and Discovery," in *First Images of America*, ed. Fredi Chiappelli (Berkeley, 1976), 3–4.

[2] John Donne, quoted in R. J. W. Evans, *Rudolf II and His World* (Oxford, 1973), 266.

nomic, political, and religious elites – wealthy merchants, princely heads of state, and high clergy alike. The compilations of objects accumulated by such personages are generally discussed in the literature either as collections of fine art or as aggregations of esoterica composed of the strange, the rare, and the mysterious as evidenced by the various types of wonder or curio cabinets (*wunderkammer*). In this essay I regard such collections and the collecting activity they represent as means to address – that is, to recognize, encompass, and control – the broadened dimensions of temporal and spatial distance that had to be accommodated especially at the highest levels of European political and ideological life where, concurrently, new heights and dimensions of political and religious prominence and centricity were developing too.

In pursuing this topic I hasten to emphasize that I do not intend to discuss the detailed content of specific collections. Rather I intend to suggest and discuss underlying political and ideological contexts within which various *types* of collections and of collecting activity can be recognized. I also imply a certain universality in such activities, for in the first half of this essay I will introduce the basic issues with reference to patterns of collecting and of cosmology characteristic of various non-Western cultures both because in that context they can be readily perceived and because I have become aware of such patterns by study of non-Western ethnography (see note 4). Since temporal and spatial distances of the non-West and the West eventually came to overlap in most profound fashion during and after the Age of Discovery, I will endeavor to illustrate salient points of non-Western collecting with examples that include Western materials. Similarly, in the second half of the essay I will draw attention to the inclusion of "foreign" things in collecting activities of Europeans, for it is at this juncture and in this type of activity that implicit assumptions about the place and significance of the Other for both the West and the non-West also appear.

The "skillfully crafted" and the "naturally endowed"

In considering "collectibles" with political and ideological import in the context of non-Western, non-industrial, "traditional" cultures (generally considered, for the moment, without regard for degree of sociopolitical complexity), it is necessary, first of all, to identify the definitive characteristics of certain broad categories of "things" that are considered appropriate for acquisition. To begin, such goods are best identified as *tangible* rather than as material things, for their significance and the qualities assigned to them and, by extension, to their collectors rests not in their physical characteristics per se but in the belief that such items are imbued with cosmological qualities and powers that they represent or encapsulate in their physical forms.[3] For this reason, such things are frequently termed "prestige" goods or "luxury" items in the ethnographic literature, meaning that they generally are regarded by the native population as public or "high profile" objects rather than as private or domestic things, as durables rather than as consumables, and are valued for ideological rather than strictly utilitarian or pragmatic (economic) reasons. Such goods also associate their collectors with personal qualities of honor or of high intellect – that is, with qualities taken as indicative of the "ideal" human being. Considered overall, it is a particular context of association with the extraordinary rather than with the mundane that marks such things as qualitatively distinctive: "woodcarvers, potters and smiths might produce for the palace on special days and recognize that their labour was of a different quality from normal."[4]

Such qualitatively distinguished goods may be further differentiated according to whether they are regarded as having been crafted by skilled artisans or as being in their natural, meaning uncrafted, state. The difference between skillfully crafted things and natural things is contextually significant primarily because such contrasts relate to the presence or absence of a particular type of personal human endeavor – that is, to the capacity for skilled crafting. At this point, however, an important caveat must be made quite explicit. Care must always be taken to identify the "crafted" or "non-crafted" condition of things in accordance with the dictates of the particular culture involved rather than in accordance with the opinion of an outside observer, for things that may be considered man-made by an outside observer (for example, manufactured Western goods) may be categorized as noncrafted or "natural" by a non-Western native society. To take one example, the Nilotic Pakot of Kenya regard both particular natural objects and imported Western ("americani") cloth with a

[3] In addition to physical things, certain types of behaviors, such as song, dance, and oratory, can be accorded such properties and qualities, too, but are not considered in this essay. Full discussion of these and other points in the first section of this essay is presented at length, with supporting ethnographic data and documentation, in Mary W. Helms, "Craft and and the Kingly Ideal," unpublished manuscript.

[4] Michael Rowlands, "Power and Moral Order in Precolonial West-Central Africa," in *Specialization, Exchange, and Complex Societies*, eds. Elizabeth Brumfiel and Timothy Earle (Cambridge, 1987), 61.

glossy finish as beautiful natural objects from afar that stand in contrast to crafted items made by the Pakot themselves.[5]

Similarly, we must accept under the rubric of "skilled" crafting whatever particular talents or manifestations are recognized as such by a given culture. Common to virtually all such identifications, however, is the belief that such skills go significantly beyond ordinary expressive talents and that such exceptional skills, by definition, are derived from and/or speak to the presence (manifestation) or cooperation of supernatural entities in the person, the tools, the skills, and the ideas and inspirations of the craftsperson him or herself.[6] Indeed, the very finest skilled craftsmen are frequently identified as creator gods, founding ancestors, or creative culture-heroes who, at the dawn of time, either created (crafted) the earth or the first humans or the first "civilized" society by means of a particular skilled art[7] or introduced such skills to human societies by offering instruction in the arts of metallurgy or weaving or ceramics or carving or lapidary work, and so on.[8] Consequently, the skilled artisans who continue these activities among living populations are regarded, often quite literally, as continuing the work of distinctive ancestral beings. Through their skills, they provide constant contact with a very personalized expression of cosmological origins by re-creating, over and over again, the original skilled activities of such ancestral creator-craftsmen. "During the ritual of artistic creation, painters say they feel the living presence of the god. . . ." "Man does now what the gods did originally."[9] In short, the work of skilled craftsmen relates the society for whom they labor directly with the time of original cultural creation, maintains an inalienable tie with that most exceptional era, and serves as a conduit by which ancestral spirits and ancestral "energies" may be made available for continued life and social benefit.

5 Harold K. Schneider, "The Interpretation of Pakot Visual Art," in *Art and Aesthetics in Primitive Societies*, ed. Carol Jopling (New York, 1971), 57–8.

6 For examples, see Anthony Forge, "The Abelam Artist," in *Social Organization: Essays Presented to Raymond Firth*, ed. Maurice Freedman (Chicago, 1967), 80, on the Abelam; Paula Ben-Amos, " 'A La Recherche du Temps Perdu': On Being an Ebony-Carver in Benin," in *Ethnic and Tourist Arts*, ed. Nelson H. H. Graburn (Berkeley, 1976), 321, regarding Benin carvers; Georges Balandier, *Daily Life in the Kingdom of the Kongo* (New York, 1968), 110–14, 224, regarding smiths in general.

7 Myths from many societies worldwide relate how the world was created by some form of artistic skill, perhaps by dancing (Laos) or by singing (Pawnee), or how in similar fashion people were originally molded from clay (Quiché Maya) or sculpted from wood and given life by drumming (Asmat) or forged as iron is forged (Fang).

8 See Urs Ramseyer, *The Art and Culture of Bali* (Oxford, 1977), 60, for an excellent example from Balinese myth.

9 Renaldo Maduro, "The Brahmin Painters of Nathdwara, Rajasthan," in Graburn, *Ethnic and Tourist Arts*, 232–4.

Because of this capacity to conjoin the contemporary world of the here-and-now with the distant world of the there-and-then, skilled craftsmen and the products of their talents are particularly favored by political and religious leaders who, in fact, may themselves seek to become (or be expected to become) skilled craftsmen themselves.[10] Failing such abilities, or in addition to them, political-ideological elites in traditional societies unfailingly seek to attract skilled craftsmen to their seats of power and to subsidize their work, sometimes even to take ultimate credit for the goods they craft, for such associations are an invaluable and necessary expression of the linkages between current lineage heads and ancestral lineage founders, between chiefs and ancestral gods, between kings and supreme deities. These ties with cosmological personages and with times of cultural origins, in turn, provide hopefully indisputable authenticity and legitimacy for political incumbents in the immediate present.

Skilled craftsmen are also recognized as such, and political elites seek their association as such, because in traditional society the work of skilled artisans (master craftsmen) is regarded, by definition, as also containing the quality of aesthetics. "Knowing how to make an object well *includes* knowing how to make it beautiful. . ."[11] Aesthetics in this context refers not just to what is pleasing but more directly to morality. Which is to say, that which is aesthetically beautiful is also that which is good or true.[12] Hence those persons who would be associated with, or representative of, the highest ideals or qualities of humanness must be associated with aesthetically acceptable things – that is, with skillfully crafted things. Consequently, in tribal societies, where social hierarchies do not exist, all adults may be expected to at least attempt to become proficient in one or more of the arts as a mark of true humanness ("every initiated Abelam man aspires to be an artist. . . ,"[13]) while in socially ranked societies members of the aristoc-

[10] The widespread identification of the king as builder represents the epitome of this association, but it is also seen in expectations that political leaders excel in some form of art. For good examples see Donald F. Tuzin, "Politics, Power and Divine Artistry in Ilahita," *Anthropological Quarterly* 51 (1978); Phyllis Rabineau, "Artists and Leaders: The Social Context of Creativity in a Tropical Forest Culture," in *The Cashinahua of Eastern Peru*, ed. Jane Dwyer, Haffenreffer Museum of Anthropology, Studies in Anthropology and Material Culture, Brown University, vol. 1 (Providence, RI, 1975).

[11] Daniel J. Crawley, "Aesthetic Value and Professionalism in African Art; Three Cases from the Katanga Chokwe," in *The Traditional Artist in African Societies*, ed. Warren L. d'Azevedo (Bloomington, 1973), 228 [emphasis in original].

[12] Ananda K. Coomaraswamy, *The Transformation of Nature in Art* (Cambridge, 1935), 16–17.

[13] Forge, "Abelam Artist," 78; for additional examples, see John C. Messenger, "The Role of the Carver in Anang Society," in d'Azevedo, *The Traditional Artist of African*

racy, as superior persons, work assiduously to subsidize, produce, collect, and display skillfully crafted and aesthetically pleasing tangible things.[14]

Yet not all valued objects need to be skillfully crafted. Certain types of things may be regarded as endowed with highly valued qualities even though they are maintained in a natural or uncrafted form. Fundamental to recognition of such "naturally endowed" things is the belief, widespread in the non-industrial world, that virtually all physical objects are encapsulations, to varying degree, of life-giving energies or powers that pervade the universe.[15] However, some types of things are believed to encapsulate this cosmological potency in greater quantities or concentrations than others and such items are thus particularly sought after for the powers they are believed to contain. Among North American native peoples, for example, who conceive of the natural world as vitalized by powerful spirit forces, many items of traditional dress and adornment were produced from potent natural items such as seeds, dried hooves, feathers, stones, and varieties of shell. "When seen in full ceremonial clothing covered with direct and extensional symbols of spiritual power, the American Indian was truly a *Gesamtkunstwerk* in honor of man's harmony with the sacred forces of nature."[16] Equally potent are curious objects that are deemed to be unusual or unnatural in some way – rare, monstrous, or perfect, for their distinctive characteristics are thought to constitute evidence of exceptional qualities and magical potencies.[17]

Such naturally endowed items also relate to concepts of primordial conditions and cosmological origins, though of a somewhat different sort or in a different context than those associated with skillfully crafted goods. The unique qualities of naturally endowed goods are not attributed to personalized creator-craftsmen, ancestral or living, but are associated instead with anonymous or impersonal primordial conditions or powers. Often both types of cosmogonal contexts are recognized in native myths and cosmologies; they are frequently ex-

Societies, 125–6; Nancy Williams, "Australian Aboriginal Art at Yirrkala: The Introduction and Development of Marketing," in Graburn, *Ethnic and Tourist Arts*, 270.

14 Examples may be found in any account of an aristocratic lord who lives and works in elegant surroundings featuring elaborate regalia, exceptional architecture and household furnishings, musical salutes, elaborate entertainments and the like.

15 See Irving Goldman, *The Mouth of Heaven* (New York, 1975), 22.

16 Evan M. Mauer, "Symbol and Identification in North American Indian Clothing," in *The Fabrics of Culture*, eds. Justine M. Cordwell and Ronald A. Schwarz (The Hague, 1979), 122–3. See also George R. Hamell, "Strawberries, Floating Islands, and Rabbit Captains: Mythical Realities and European Contact in the Northeast During the Sixteenth and Seventeenth Centuries," *Journal of Canadian Studies* 21:4 (1986–87), 72–94.

17 Mircea Eliade, *Patterns in Comparative Religion* (New York, 1958), 13.

pressed in terms of solar or celestially-related personalized ancestors, on the one hand, and impersonal chthonic powers on the other. For example, native residents of the island of Aoriki in the Eastern Solomon Islands believe that there are two separate orders of deities, one identified as "deities from humans" and the other as "deities of the land." The "deities from humans" derive from human spirits that are deified during great funeral celebrations. The "deities of the land" do not have personalities, but were present in the area before humans arrived. For the Aoriki, "the two classes of deities have no direct interaction. The only link between them is the humans who worship and depend upon both, but in different ways."[18]

Because both skillfully crafted and naturally endowed things provide direct, authentic, inalienable, and legitimating links with times, places, and conditions of cultural (political) creations and primordial human origins, respectively, they are avidly sought and accumulated by authority figures of traditional societies. Depending on the historical particulars, however, acquisition of such goods by elites of a given polity may fit one of several patterns, the parameters of which are largely determined by the location of skilled craftsmen or skillfully crafted goods. Since elements of both acquisitional patterns may be found in the collecting activities characteristic of Renaissance Europe during the Age of Discovery, diagnostic characteristics of both are briefly summarized.

Patterns of acquisition

Every society may be said to recognize two ideological centers – one at the heartland (center) of the polity (x^2 in Figure 12.1) and the other somewhere outside its social or political borders at a temporally/spatially distant locale associated with personalized ancestors or places of cultural origins and therefore also associated with skilled crafting/craftsmen and the production of skillfully crafted goods (x^1 or x^3). One type of outside center is associated with otherworldly locales typically situated cosmologically in the celestial realm above (or sometimes below) the earth and identified as the home of society's ancestors and original creator-beings (x^1). Since such domains are not physically or geographically reachable (though they may be attained by trance or other forms of spiritually induced "travel"), tangible crafted goods

[18] William H. Davenport, "Two Kinds of Value in the Eastern Solomon Islands," in *The Social Life of Things*, ed. Arjun Appadurai (Cambridge, 1986), 103–4; Georges Balandier, *Political Anthropology* (New York, 1970), ch. 5, 106.

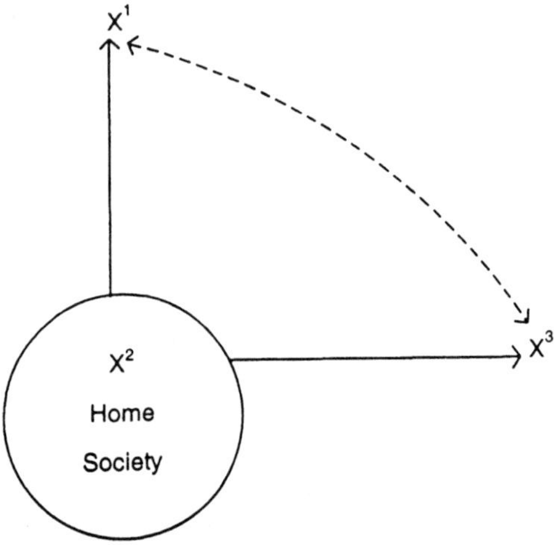

Figure 12.1. Locations of creative centers. X^1 – original creative ancestors (first potters or first carvers or first smiths, and so on), now frequently associated with celestial places of Origin. X^2 – living craftsmen of the home society whose skills recreate those of the original ancestors. X^3 – geographically distant craftsmen whose skills and products are similarly associated with the powers of places of Origins (for example, X^1).

that evidence the beauty and truth of ancestral links must be forged by skilled artisans living at the earthly political center (x^2), where they recreate the work of godly creator-craftsmen.

In such societies, where skillfully crafted valuables are produced at home, the types of articles collected from geographically distant places will generally be classified as naturally endowed things. Collections of such objects are frequently characterized by marked ecclecticism, as all sorts and manner of strange items, united only by the fact that they are all regarded as naturally exceptional or unique in some way, are acquired. Their avid collection is seen as enhancing the political-ideological potency of the political heartland by amassing things redolent of the anonymous primordial "wilderness" that stretches beyond the cultural boundaries whence vitalizing cosmological energies may be obtained and, equally important, controlled.

T.C. McCaskie has provided an intriguing and insightfully interpreted example of such collecting in the nineteenth century kingdom of Asante. McCaskie points out that the Asante were acutely aware that their culture, as it had progressed historically from hunting and gathering to agriculture, had been literally "hacked out of nature" and that this state of affairs required constant vigilance lest "an irruptive and anarchic" nature would reclaim its own from the fragilely maintained cultural space. In an attempt to prevent such cultural dissolution, nature had to be constantly controlled by "domesticating" objects perceived to belong to it. "As a direct consequence of this view, the embrace of accumulation aspired to the universal" to include all manner of things (among which gold dust and nuggets were most valued). Included in the acquisitional urge (it is interesting to note) were a vast array of European things:

> ... the incidental manufactures and artifacts of Europe, an enormous gallery of the haphazard, the trivial, the broken and the arcane. These were sedulously garnered irrespective of any primary considerations of utility or intentional function. Once acquired and hoarded, these (and other) objects might be safely ignored but never discarded; their assimilated presence was part of the most fundamental equation, the strengthening of culture (the realm of man) against nature (the realm of non-man).... [19]

To protect this great collection, a large stone house was built by the Asantehene Osei Tutu Kwame (1804–23), allegedly after learning of the British Museum. The perception of Europe as constituting part of nature (that is, as potent but untamed) rather than of culture in Asante eyes is also readily apparent.[20]

A different type of acquisitional pattern is found in societies where the outside center of personalized ancestral identification is not located vertically in a cosmological realm "up (or down) there" but is situated at a cosmologically important place located horizontally and geographically "out there" (x^3 in Figure 12.1). Such sacred outside centers, sometimes also places of pilgrimage and/or of other appropriate forms of diplomatic obeisance, are regarded as places of cultural origins and as the homes of original creator-ancestors in exactly the same sense as are celestially located places of origins. Since it is possible to contact such earthly outside centers by physical travels and/or to receive living representatives of the outside center at home, the

[19] T. C. McCaskie, "Accumulation, Wealth and Belief in Asante History," *Africa* 53 (1983), 28–9.

[20] See also Ivor Wilks, *Asante in the Nineteenth Century* (Cambridge, 1975), 200–1; C. A. Bayly, "The Origins of Swadeshi (Home Industry): Cloth and Indian Society, 1700–1930," in Appadurai, *The Social Life of Things*, 305, gives a somewhat comparable example from Mughal India regarding "the insatiable desire of India's rulers for novelties." "European writers tended to see the demand for novelties as a childish desire for trinkets. Actually, the profusion of novelties in a court was considered another work of great kingship. It bespoke vast and varied realms, connections with far-off kings; as God the ruler of the universe had created all manner of beasts and objects, so his earthly shadow must rule over a profusion of creations."

work of skilled artisans at home (who reproduce the skillfully crafted items that bespeak the ties relating the home polity to its ancestral point of origins) may be augmented by skillfully crafted items (relics, regalia) obtained directly from the outside center itself, where such goods are either still being produced by living creator-craftsmen or were formerly so produced in the past. Consequently, political elites at home may direct their collecting efforts not only toward subsidizing skilled artisans who copy these items but also toward acquisition of skillfully crafted things directly from the outside center or toward the enticement of skilled craftsmen themselves from that distant place. It is, of course, equally valid for political elites of the home society to accumulate strange and curious naturally endowed items from distant places, too, although the regions that yield these items will be different from the locale that provides skilled craftsmen and/or skillfully crafted aesthetic products.

Any situation in which political or religious elites obtain highly valued crafted items, including ceremonial dress or regalia, household furnishings, scholarly or sacred writings, or relics, from a distant place may exemplify this acquisitional pattern. A well-described case is that of the Nafana state of Banda, western Ghana, and its association with the Asante state, especially in the eighteenth century when Banda first accepted (and later commissioned) Asante art forms, textiles, and regalia, including the ancestral "stool of the state."[21] A particularly curious variation on this theme of acquisition of valued crafted goods from a geographically distant locale associated with creative ancestors-cum-craftsmen is offered by Harms[22] with reference to the central Zaire basin in the nineteenth century, when quantities of European goods, including weapons, alcohol, and especially cloth, could be acquired by chiefs and wealthy traders in exchange for local products (ivory, slaves). Imported cloth, a skillfully crafted "luxury" good, not only was worn by wealthy persons but very large quantities were also accumulated and saved to be buried with elites as a way of gaining honor and ancestral status in the afterlife. Harms provides cosmological context for this behavior, explaining that the Europeans (who arrived in the Zaire basin from the coast with much wealth) were widely believed to live beneath the sea, where they wove cloth in large quantities.[23]

[21] For fuller discussion see René A. Bravemann, "The Diffusion of Ashanti Political Art" in *African Art and Leadership*, ed. D. Fraser and H. M. Cole (Madison, 1972), 164–5, 170. Native peoples on the frontier of traditional Chinese states provide another obvious example.

[22] Robert W. Harms, *River of Wealth, River of Sorrow* (New Haven, 1981).

[23] Harms speculates that this theory may have been derived from observations that

White people were also associated with spirits of dead ancestors. This tied in with a widespread view of the slave trade which held that slaves went to America, died, and as spirits worked at producing sums of wealth unknown in the land of the living. Indeed, [it has been argued that] Mpoto, the name generally taken to mean "the country where white people come from," actually means "the land of the dead." A similar explanation was current in the 1880s among the Libuka, who said that when rich Africans died they went to Europe and became white. The cloth with which they were buried was their merchandise when they came back to trade.[24]

COLLECTING AND THE WEST

The patterns of collecting and the political and cosmological associations that they convey in traditional societies can be readily applied to Europe during the Renaissance and the Age of Discovery. However, in order to reaffirm that certain fundamental cosmological concepts vital to the basic argument also existed in traditional European thought, it seems appropriate to review various intellectual characteristics of preceding medieval centuries before considering Renaissance developments. For the sake of brevity, I will restrict this summary largely to material provided by Umberto Eco's *Art and Beauty in the Middle Ages*.[25]

Acquisition, aesthetics, and the medieval world

Eco's discussion emphasizes a number of salient points relevant to this discussion, beginning with the first sentence of his first chapter, which directly relates the issue of medieval artistry and aesthetics to classical antiquity – that is, to an earlier era of cultural origins.[26] He concludes his opening paragraph with the observation that "it has been said that, where aesthetics and artistic production are concerned, the Classical world turned its gaze on nature but the Medievals turned their gaze on the Classical world; that medieval culture was based, not on a phenomenology of reality, but on a phenomenology of a cultural tradition."[27] A few pages further the astonishing beauty of some of this artistic production is described, particularly as it was expressed in various expressions of skilled crafting prepared for, or

when a ship appeared over the horizon it could seem as if the ship were rising out of the water. Ibid., 210.

[24] Ibid.

[25] Umberto Eco, *Art and Beauty in the Middle Ages*, trans. H. Bredin (New Haven, 1986).

[26] "Most of the aesthetic issues that were discussed in the Middle Ages were inherited from Classical Antiquity," in ibid., 4.

[27] Ibid.

at least displayed in, church decorations, a major political and ideological setting for collections of stained glass, sculpture, paintings, fine carpets, and artifacts fashioned from precious metals and fabrics.[28] Indeed, in the opinion of the esteemed Suger, twelfth-century Abbot of St. Denis, "the House of God should be a repository of everything beautiful," toward which end Abbot Suger, like other prelates of his day, crammed the treasury of his church with jewelry, gems, and objets d'art.[29] Medieval rulers followed suit, for "the ruler's treasure-house was the seat of his power. He needed to amass the most delectable treasures hidden within the earth: silver, and above all gold and precious stones. Kings had to live surrounded by marvels, which were the tangible expression of their glory."[30]

Yet such treasures were not appreciated simply for the immediate pleasures and impressions they gave. According to Eco, there was also an awareness and appreciation of the materials used in works of art and a comprehension that a number of relations subsisted between such objects "and a cosmos which opened on to the transcendent. [Medieval taste] meant discerning in the concrete object an ontological reflection of, and participation in, the being and the power of God." "The Medievals inhabited a world filled with references, reminders and overtones of Divinity, manifestations of God in things."[31] Such objects, like all things of creation, in their essence reached into a world beyond the here-and-now and thus were not merely material but tangible manifestations of "God in His ineffable beauty" and "the divinely diffused unity of life."[32] More than anything else, the ubiquity of light and of color contained and evidenced this inherent divinity and universal creative energy, for light was "an active quality deriving from the substantial form of the sun," "the ubiquitous origin of all motion, which penetrated to the very bowels of the earth to form its minerals and sow the seeds of its life."[33]

With respect to the concept of aesthetics itself, Eco notes "the absence in medieval times of a distinction between beauty (*pulchrum, decorum*) and utility or goodness (*aptum, honestum*)"; that in practice, if not always in theory, the two values were mingled rather than distinguished and that there was a unity in the moral and aesthetic re-

[28] Ibid., 6.
[29] Eco, *Art and Beauty*, 13; see also Francis Henry Taylor, *The Taste of Angels* (Boston, 1948), 36–8.
[30] Georges Duby, *The Early Growth of the European Economy* (Ithaca, 1974), 52.
[31] Eco, *Art and Beauty*, 15, 53.
[32] Ibid., 18, 24.
[33] Ibid., ch. 4, 50.

sponses to things; that "the goodness of a substance, and its beauty, are the same thing" and that recognition of this meaning of beauty was not expressed as mere poetic sentiment but rested on metaphysical certainty and represented the presence of God made manifest in things.[34]

Beauty and goodness were expressed in things by the orderliness of their shapes, their forms, and their proportions.[35] Such aesthetic order could be obtained by crafting or be expressed in the positions things filled within their proper element, "as stars in the sky, birds in the air, fish in the sea, men on earth."[36] Such orderliness, such harmony indicative of God's own skillful creativity, stood in contrast to and was opposed by the chaos of the primeval and the primordial. Similarly, some objects did not contain beauty but appeared unorderly or out of proportion, aggregated rather than composed, out of place or without a place in the organized universe, and garnered attention because of these very anomalies or abnormalities.

Indeed, this contrast not only applied to particular objects but also characterized collections of things. That is to say, collections composed of skillfully crafted, beautiful things had to be themselves aesthetically structured, ordered, and integrated in composition in order to be morally appropriate, and efforts were expended to make them so. Duby, for example, comments on how "the best" craftsmen were brought to royal courts where "they were employed in transforming the multifarious objects arriving as gifts into a coherent collection."[37]

Other types of collections, however, seem noteworthy because they were not (could not be) so ordered and proportioned (coherent) but were characterized instead by an odd assortment of seemingly unrelated things – "absurd oddities" that were themselves significant because they were strange or curious or rare rather than because they were aesthetically compelling. Such collections, and the objects of which they were composed, may be taken to represent the category of the naturally endowed rather than of the skillfully crafted. For example, the famed and oft-cited collection of Jean duc de Berry included "the horn of a unicorn, St. Joseph's engagement ring, coconuts, whales' teeth, and shells from the Seven Seas. It comprised around

[34] Ibid., 15–16, 21–5. See also discussion in ch. 2.

[35] Ibid., 25–6, chs. 3 and 7.

[36] Ibid., 34, 39.

[37] Duby, *Early Growth*, 52; see also James Clifford, "Objects and Selves—An Afterword," in *Objects and Others*, ed. George Stocking, Jr. (Madison, 1985), 238–9, regarding the moral virtues of creating tasteful, orderly, carefully, and systematically selected "good" collections as opposed to the distasteful practice of obsessive or miserly possession.

3,000 items. Seven hundred were paintings, but it also contained an embalmed elephant, a hydra, a basilisk, an egg that an Abbot had found inside another egg, and manna which had fallen during a famine." Eco feels that we may be "justified in doubting the purity of medieval taste, their ability to distinguish between art and teratology, the beautiful and the curious."[38] It is more likely, however, that this seeming confusion was not conditioned by doubtful purity of taste but by the fact that two separate and distinct types of valued things were involved – those that were valuable because they were endowed with the ordered aesthetics indicative of a divinely created (crafted) beauty and those that were valuable because they were naturally endowed with the equally mysterious powers inherent in that which, being strange or curious, lacked order, remained uncrafted, and was still primordial.[39]

Classical antiquity and cultural origins

Although the aesthetic sensibilities of the Middle Ages were rooted in the matrix of the classical world, recognition of that world as the ancestral place and condition of European cultural origins as defined by a sense of temporal distance from the living European society did not fully emerge until the Renaissance. This expansion in perspective has been quite appropriately identified not just as an awakening to the distinctive characteristics of the Classical era that set it apart from – and thus allowed comparison with – Renaissance Europe[40] but more specifically as an awakening to Classical *antiquity*[41] – that is, to the realm of ancient Greece and Rome as the font and focal point of the cosmology that ordered Renaissance political-ideology. To be sure, Classical studies had always continued throughout the Middle Ages, and Rome, like Jerusalem, had long been regarded as the Christian *axis mundi*. During the medieval centuries, Rome, like Jerusalem, had

[38] Eco, *Art and Beauty*, 14; see also Taylor, *The Taste of Angels*, 50–1.

[39] Eco himself notes a dual approach in medieval symbolism that states the matter in terms somewhat different from, though not necessarily incompatible with, my approach. He recognizes two forms of aesthetic conception, the first being "*metaphysical symbolism*, related to the philosophical habit of discerning the hand of God in the beauty of the world" and the second "*universal allegory*; that is, perceiving the world as a divine work of art, of such a kind that everything in it possesses moral, allegorical, and analogical meanings in addition to its literal meaning." Eco, *Art and Beauty*, 56 [emphasis in original].

[40] John H. Rowe, "The Renaissance Foundations of Anthropology," *American Anthropologist* 67 (1965): 1–20.

[41] Roberto Weiss, *The Renaissance Discovery of Classical Antiquity*, 2nd. ed. (New York, 1988).

never lost its appeal as an awe-inspiring place of religious pilgrimage, as provider of precious relics, or as source of ideological legitimation for medieval kings. But

> what led to the collection of antique objects during the Middle Ages was not their antiquity but their appeal to the eye or their rare or unusual materials, or simply because they were different; or even in some cases because they were thought to be endowed with magical powers. The antiques preserved in the treasuries of cathedrals were kept there because their materials or their craftsmanship were considered precious, not because they were ancient. Even those few who had a genuine interest in Antiquity were drawn to it by an attraction tempered by utilitarian considerations. The Latin classics were considered above all as repositories of unusual information or moral teachings or as collections of fine phrases, suitable for quotation or insertion into one's own writings. They were certainly not seen as the expressions of a great civilization.[42]

Earlier efforts by a few outstanding scholars notwithstanding, the expansion of cosmological spacial/temporal parameters during the Renaissance sharpened and emphasized the sense of distance between the Renaissance present and Classical past, emphasized antiquity as origins, and identified the "greatness" of Classical civilization. Concurrently, more conscious efforts were necessitated, especially on the part of political and religious elites or would-be elites, to reemphasize contacts and connections with this authenticating Classical world that now was important because it was *old* as well as conspicuous[43] because evidencing ties to times and conditions of origins, to a source of "original civilization," was critical to the legitimation of their own political positions.

As would be expected, it was by way of the arts – that is, by way of skilled crafting – that this ancestral tie was publicly evidenced and celebrated. Aesthetics – the inherent integration of the good and the beautiful – became synonymous with Classical styles of artistic expression, and since association with aesthetics was expected to define the goodness and moral validity of those who presumed to govern,[44] it was essential that persons (families) holding high political positions (or ambitions) of church and state should seek avidly to

42 Weiss, *Renaissance Discovery*, 2; see also Niels von Holst, *Creators, Collectors and Connoisseurs* (New York, 1967), 42–3, regarding evil powers ascribed to ancient objects.

43 Weiss, *Renaissance Discovery*, 5.

44 Here, as in many other societies, association with aesthetics represented the supreme or ideal condition of humanness just as the ideal individual came to be associated with the accumulation of goods and properties. See C. B. Macpherson, *The Political Theory of Possessive Individualism* (Oxford, 1962); also Clifford, "Objects and Selves."

surround themselves with aesthetic things redolent of Classical antiquity. Consequently, subsidizing of skilled artisans who worked in the classical style was combined with serious, even frenetic, collecting of artifacts – especially objects that had been skillfully crafted – from ancient Greece and Rome. Ironically, such efforts did little to slow the destruction of the ruins of Rome itself as the city continued to be used, as it had been for centuries, as a seemingly inexhaustible stone quarry or fell prey to schemes for "modernization." Indeed, "the Renaissance passion for building on classical lines was the main cause of the destruction of what still remained of ancient Rome."[45] It was the *idea* of Rome as temporally distant *fons et origo* and the ability to relate oneself to that cosmological construct that was important, not the fallen stones of the place itself. Unless, of course, those stones could be moved to grace the grounds of one's own estate and authenticate one's own identification with the ennobling past.

During the fifteenth century, such collecting began on a large scale, "in the grand manner."[46] Painters and sculptors gathered as many pieces of Classical sculpture and carving as they could afford to serve as models to copy, adapt or paraphrase.[47] Similarly, throughout the newly emerging nation-states of Europe members of the nobility, princes and prelates alike, sought endlessly to acquire busts and statues, cameos, intaglios, engraved gems and coins (valued for the effigies they bore of famous rulers of ancient times), vases and cups of semi-precious stones, as well as books and ancient manuscripts. All these things and more were accumulated in great numbers[48] to grace gardens, courts, and palaces with objects that were both beautiful and ancient. Such collecting was expected, indeed required, if a person of rank were to be "authentic."[49]

Wunderkammer and the strange and curious

Magnificent as these great collections of classical art were, they often shared pride of place in showcase galleries with a very different type of collection which is of particular interest here because included among its wonders were objects from little known foreign lands and

[45] Weiss, *Renaissance Discovery*, 98–104.
[46] Taylor, *The Taste of Angels*, 59; Weiss, *Renaissance Discovery*, ch. 13.
[47] Weiss, *Renaissance Discovery*, 180, 182.
[48] Quantity as a concept in and of itself indicates the sense of wellbeing that is expected to result from good government and is associated with abundance.
[49] Weiss, *Renaissance Discovery*, pp. 199–200; see also Taylor, *The Taste of Angels*, bks. 2, 4; Holst, *Creators*, ch. 2.

newly discovered continents. Since the cosmological expansions of the Renaissance included spatial as well as temporal dimensions, it was just as necessary to accumulate objects from geographically distant and primordial places as it was to accumulate inalienable authenticating aesthetic creations from temporally distant places of origin.

The prototype of these collections, of course, was found in the various "cabinets of curiosities" or wonder-cabinets that, like their medieval counterparts and predecessors mentioned earlier, were composed of all manner of strange, curious, exotic "natural" wonders from both home and abroad; heterogeneous aggregations of objects whose interest and value lay in the fact that they were rare, unique, bizarre, or even monstrous because such apparent deviations from ordinary or normal forms or states of being were believed endowed with inchoate powers of the still untamed or primordial and impersonal universe of Nature.[50]

Remember that the traditional cosmology that still pertained during the Renaissance interpreted "the world of men and of nature [as] linked by 'hidden sources of knowledge'" – that is, as linked by magical properties and means that were regarded as proper subjects for legitimate investigation and contemplation.[51] In the paradigm used in this essay, the sources of this "hidden knowledge" lay in the impersonal or anonymous (sometimes referred to as "timeless") powers of the earth (as contrasted with the more personalized artistic and ancestral ties with a more clearly temporally-anchored Classical antiquity). Investigation of such mysteries included collecting those unusual things which, by their strangeness, both symbolized and manifested this power.

The ultimate goal of such accumulating was to assemble a "microcosm of the universe"[52] with intent to organize and classify this heterogenity, thereby to enhance understanding and appreciation of the unity and harmony in the invisible divine scheme of things.[53] Speaking of the collecting activities of Rudolf II, Holy Roman Emperor, King of Bohemia and Hungary, and inveterate accumulator, Evans notes

[50] See Steven Mullaney, "Strange Things, Gross Terms, Curious Customs: The Rehearsal of Cultures in the Late Renaissance," *Representations* 3 (1983): 40–67; Taylor, *The Taste of Angels*, bks. 3–5; Margaret T. Hodgen, *Early Anthropology in the Sixteenth and Seventeenth Centuries* (Philadelphia, 1964), ch. 4; Detlef Heikamp, *Mexico and the Medici* (Florence, 1972), 26.

[51] "Research is only now showing how widespread were mystical and occult preoccupations throughout late-Renaissance Europe . . . ," in Evans, *Rudolf II*, 3–4, 172, ch. 6; see also Taylor, *The Taste of Angels*, 123–4.

[52] Heikamp, *Mexico*, 7.

[53] Evans, *Rudolf II*, 4, 195, 119, 219, 245.

that "the assembling of many and various items reflected the essential variety in the world, which could nevertheless be converted into unity by a mind which brought them together and divined their internal relations one with another"; "[contemporaries] spoke of the Rudolfine *Kunst- und Wunderkammer*, cabinet of arts and curiosities, implying that whatever the physical dimensions of the collections, its underlying idea was to present much in a limited space, an encyclopedia of the visible world."[54] "The collecting mania of the period was thus not idle curiosity, but an attempt to organize diverse objects in a way which would reflect their original disposition, their place in the chain of creation."[55] This matter became all the more urgent as widening spatial/temporal horizons presented increasing evidence of the diversity of earthly things, things that might prove to have special attributes, perhaps for curing or enriching, or alternatively, for witchcraft or sorcery.[56]

This expanding world was broad. Rudolf's collection, for example, included not only a wide range of Classical items and other objets d'art *(Kunst)* but also all manner of exotic objects, including some from as far away as the distant reaches of the Spanish empire and the Orient; indeed, it sought to encompass, if possible, "all hidden secrets in the whole of nature."[57] Given such a goal, it is not surprising that collections could easily range into the thousands of items,[58] and could include such wonders as (among other things) an African charm made of teeth, a felt cloak from Arabia, shoes from many strange lands, an Indian stone ax, the twisted horn of a bull seal, an embalmed child or *Mumia*, a unicorn's tail, paper made of bark, an artful Chinese box, flies that "glow at night in Virginia instead of lights, since there is often no day there for over a month," the Queen of England's seal, crowns made of claws, a sea mouse, a mirror which "both reflects and multiplies objects," reed Pan pipes, and a long narrow Indian canoe (usually hung from the ceiling).[59] In like fashion, the catalogue "of the

[54] Ibid., 177. Rudolf, like other notables of his era and before, also collected living curiosities, filling his gardens, stables, and menageries with a profusion of strange plants and exotic animals from America, Africa, and Asia, for both zoology and botany bespoke cosmological mysteries, too. See Hodgen, *Early Anthropology*, 117; Hugh Honour, *The New Golden Land* (New York, 1975), 34–5; Heikamp, *Mexico*, 11, 14.

[55] Evans, *Rudolf II*, 247, 252.

[56] Taylor, *The Taste of Angels*, 124; Heikamp, *Mexico*, 11; Otto Kurz, "A Mexican Amulet against Kidney Stones," in *Science, Medicine and Society in the Renaissance*, ed. Allen G. Debus (London, 1972), 83.

[57] Evans, *Rudolf II*, 217; see also Heikamp, *Mexico*.

[58] Taylor, *The Taste of Angels*, 126.

[59] Mullaney, "Strange Things," 40.

chiefist Rarities of the Public Theatre and Anatomie-Hall of the University of Leyden" included "a Norway house built of beams without mortar or stone; shoes and sandals from Russia, Siam, and Egypt; the skin of a man dressed as parchment; a drinking cup made out of the skull of a Moor killed in the beleaguering of Haarlem; warlike arms used in China; Chinese gongs, paper, and books; Egyptian mummies and idols; a petrified toadstool; and 'a mallet or hammer that the savages in New Yorke kill with'."[60] And the same was true in the museum assembled by the great Aldrovandi to describe and illustrate external nature. Indeed, in all such collections man-made objects were positioned in the same categories with natural wonders, including rocks, fossil plants, shells, and fish. Taylor summed up the matter well:

> New forms or freaks ... were matters of collector's envy and speculation. Dwarfs, persons exhibiting deformities and abnormalities of any kind, strange animals, stones of unconventional shape, petrifications, ores and coral reefs - all these developed fascinations which soon imbued them with hidden meanings and significance. So the strange, the wonderful, the curious, the rare, were more and more welcomed by the credulous with each passing day. The discovery of whole new sections of the world, the acquaintance with new peoples and their customs, only served to strengthen their predilections for collecting tribal fetishes trimmed and decorated with shells and feathers.[61]

Speaking of the Emperor Charles V, Taylor also summarized the relevance of such collecting for those in authority: "No little part of his outward magnificence was dependent upon the objects accumulated from one generation to the next in his *Wunderkammer;* the more obscure and superstitious the objects, the more they were revered because of their association with the supreme and God-given power of the emperor."[62] And, we might note, vice versa.

Wonder-cabinets and the geographical other

Since the strange and curious objects collected in wonder-cabinets included numerous items from foreign lands, including the Americas,[63]

[60] Hodgen, *Early Anthropology,* 122; Honour, *New Golden,* p. 32–3; Taylor, *Taste,* p. 190, unnumbered footnote.
[61] Taylor, *The Taste of Angels,* 125.
[62] Ibid., 141.
[63] Heikamp, *Mexico;* Detlef Heikamp, "American Objects in Italian Collections of the Renaissance and Baroque: A Survey," in Chiappelli, *First Images of America,* 455–82; Donald Robertson, "Mexican Indian Art and the Atlantic Filter: Sixteenth to Eighteenth Centuries," in Chiappelli, 483–94; Honour, *New Golden Land,* 28–34.

the attitudes and intents associated with such collections also tell us something of the interpretations accorded strange peoples and foreign customs by Renaissance Europeans. Most obviously, such domains were not identified with that axis of the European cosmos that accorded political and ideological authenticity by way of association with the source of cultural origins or personalized ancestors. This cosmological dimension related contemporary European political-ideology and European nobility and rulership to the temporally distant classical world of the Mediterranean. The Americas and other relatively unknown spatially distant realms (Cathay, India, East Asia) with which, in some contexts, it tended to be lumped[64] were identified instead with a different dimension of cosmological origins – that associated with the impersonal, anonymous powers that imbued the shapes and forms and beings of the "natural" world.

This realm did not contain the Classical world of European founding fathers and culture-heroes. Thus *by definition* it could not be defined in the same cosmological terms as the Classical world. Since skilled crafting and beauty-cum-moral goodness (that is, qualities of aesthetics) were related to the Classical axis of European cultural origins, there could not be any such aesthetic attributes or qualities attributed to the phenomena of non-Western foreign lands and peoples no matter what their superficial physical appearance. Instead, as source of anomalous, power-filled naturally endowed things rather than of aesthetic, skillfully crafted things, the objects of the New World had to be identified as *lacking* aesthetic qualities – that is, as lacking form and proportion, lacking order, and lacking goodness – just as the inhabitants of the Americas were alleged to have most bestial habits and to lack God, law, and breeches.[65] As New World inhabitants were regarded as not truly "civilized," meaning they were not believed to possess the qualities of truly or completely human beings, so the other objects[66] of the New World, though highly valued and avidly sought, could not be regarded as truly crafted or as evidencing the quality of aesthetics. Instead, such objects, frequently identified as anomalous, barbarous, gross, dissimilar, alien, or rude,[67]

[64] For example, Suzanne Boorsh, "America in Festival Presentations," in Chiappelli, *First Images of America*, 503–15.

[65] Hayden White, "The Noble Savage Theme as Fetish," in Chiappelli, *First Images of Americap*, 124–6.

[66] Ibid., 126. As has often been noted, the depiction of natives as non-aesthetic and not truly human served to transform them into natural objects, too, such that they could be treated like pieces of wood or flocks of sheep, to be used and moved about as the Spaniards wished.

[67] Mullaney, "Strange Things," 43.

represented more chaotic primordial conditions of the (European) cosmos that needed to be controlled, coordinated, or collated before they could be properly understood and perhaps refashioned to better fit the European cultural milieu.

Regarded in such terms, it becomes more comprehensible why even the most stunning pieces of native American arts and crafts in, for example, metallurgy, lapidary, or featherwork were generally regarded as curiosities rather than admired for their aesthetic qualities.[68] Even such generous and tolerant viewers as Albrecht Dürer, Hernando Cortés, and Peter Martyr, who marveled at and found much to admire in such treasures, are on record as having been particularly appreciative of the formal technical ingenuity of the workmanship involved.[69] "The rarity of the materials, the strangeness of the object, the cunning of the craftsmen – it was these which impressed sixteenth-century Europeans when they looked at Amerindian artifacts."[70] Similarly, the fact that Europeans could not apply standards of beauty and goodness to such artistry by virtue of its positioning within European cosmology adds another dimension to our understanding of the widespread and systematic destruction of native ritual objects[71] and helps elucidate why immense stores of magnificently fashioned native goldwork crafted and displayed as chiefly ornamentation and regalia in Mesoamerica, Central America, and the Andes could be so summarily melted down by Europeans, surely one of the most radical expressions of collecting and of cultural and cosmological "refitting" or refashioning (as economically necessary bullion) on record.

CONCLUSION

Discussing the Renaissance fascination with the strange and the curious, as evidenced (among other things) by wonder-cabinets and their incredible *mélange* of the incredible, the exotic, and the anomalous, Mullaney presents the development of this and related phenomena[72] as "a process of cultural production synonymous with cultural performance"[73] directed not toward understanding foreign cultures

[68] Mullaney, "Strange Things," 43; Honour, *New Golden Land*, 28–32; Heikamp, *Mexico*.
[69] Harold Jantz, "Images of America in the German Renaissance," in Chiappelli, *First Images of America*, 93–4; Heikamp, "American Objects," 457–58; Honour, *New Golden Land*, 28–9.
[70] John H. Elliott, "Renaissance Europe and America: A Blunted Impact?" in Chiappelli, *First Images of Americap*, 21.
[71] Robertson, "Mexican Indian Art," 491–2.
[72] For example, the depiction of foreign peoples in royal fetes.
[73] Mullaney, "Strange Things," 43, 48.

by ethnology but toward interpreting them by way of a kind of ritual activity that expresses Europe's own interests. He refers to this ritual activity or performance as a *rehearsal* of cultures, using the term not in the more familiar theatrical sense of a practice run before a perfected public performance but in a context of jurisprudence in which an already accomplished or perfected activity or condition was reviewed or presented in its final form (rehearsed) before some figure or board of political authority which would judge its political suitability. As an example of cultural rehearsal in this context, Mullaney notes how, in the course of the colonization of Wales during the reign of Edward I, Edward "'rehearsed' Welsh culture as a necessary prolegomenon to full colonization," meaning that the unfamiliar Welsh laws and customs were reviewed and explained to him and his nobles, who then either abolished, permitted, or corrected them as they deemed appropriate. Considered more broadly, Mullaney notes, "we are concerned here with a cultural practice that allows, invites, and even demands a full and potentially self-consuming review of unfamiliar things."[74]

In considering the two complementary space/time dimensions of Renaissance cosmology, we find that both Classical antiquity and foreign lands and peoples were reviewed, meaning rehearsed, in this manner, and that objects from these realms that would identify them as places or conditions of European cultural or cosmological origins were, for this reason, selected and accumulated. The same practice continued in later centuries, and though the cosmological context was redefined in some respects, the same "rehearsal" of foreign conditions continued. In the interpretations accorded foreign lands and especially in the continued collecting of foreign esoterica, the self-reflective contemplation of these exotic things took a dual perspective: on the one hand the development of ethnological museums designed to educate and, on the other, the development of collections of "primitive art" designed to captivate.

In the case of education, the intent continued to be to organize and classify accumulations of exotic objects from foreign lands in order to identify, reconstruct and illustrate, in museum displays and other typological arrangements, fundamental "relations" between things. In the eighteenth, nineteenth, and twentieth centuries such relations came to be interpreted not in terms of a divine cosmic unity and harmony nor in terms of hidden sources of power but in terms of the

[74] Ibid., 49.

coherent order believed expressed in natural laws and principles of human cultural development ("progress") or of natural evolution.[75]

In the case of "primitive art," particularly as it developed in the late nineteenth and twentieth centuries, collecting continued to identify the non-Western world as inchoate and primordial, impersonal and anonymous, even magical in character. To take one example, that such "primitive" work was still relegated to the more "natural" and non-aesthetic dimension of Western cosmography was succinctly indicated by the Marquis de Nadaillac when he argued in an 1833 article that native American sculpture had "bizarre qualities" because the "ancient American races failed to comprehend the beautiful as we do, formed as we are by the immortal creators of great art in Greece."[76]

As Sally Price has emphasized,[77] *art primitif* continues to be regarded as strange, even repugnant, as primordial ("childlike" or "unconscious"), and as timeless rather than as beautiful, and its creators, being by definition also morally suspect,[78] still are frequently kept impersonal and anonymous ("dehumanized"). Indeed, Price notes, if the artist did not remain anonymous, the art would not be considered "primitive" in collectors' eyes.[79] The world-view of the West thus remains comfortably intact. On the one hand it continues secure in the belief that the "Aesthetic Order upon which our Culture reposes is solid and legitimate, and in harmony with the ideals of a moral Social and Political Order."[80] On the other hand, the continuing wish to remain ignorant of the humanity of the non-Western other indicates a cultural rehearsal that continues to view the non-West as a cabinet of curiosities.[81] It is only fitting to realize that some non-Western cultures, such as nineteenth-century Asante, which in their own inveterate collecting of the "naturally endowed" included objects from the Western world, have in that respect returned the compliment.

[75] William Ryan Chapman, "Arranging Ethnology: A. H. L. F. Pitt Rivers and the Typological Tradition," in Stocking, *Objects and Others*, 15–48; Curtis M. Hinsley, "From Shell-Heaps to Stelae: Early Anthropology at the Peabody Museum," in ibid., 58–9; Clifford, "Objects," in ibid., 238–9.

[76] Quoted in Elizabeth A. Williams, "Art and Artifact at the Trocadero: *Ars Americana* and the Primitivist Revolution," in Stocking, *Objects and Others*, 161.

[77] Sally Price, *Primitive Art in Civilized Places* (Chicago, 1989); see also Clifford, "Objects and Selves," 242–5.

[78] Price, *Primitive Art*, ch. 3.

[79] Ibid., ch. 4, 100.

[80] Ibid., 10, paraphrasing and interpreting remarks by the noted art historian, Kenneth Clark.

[81] Ibid., 103.

CHAPTER 13

*The indigenous ethnographer: The "*indio ladino*" as historian and cultural mediation*

ROLENA ADORNO

In Spanish colonial times, individuals of indigenous American background who were familiar with Spanish language and customs were commonly described as *ladino*. The seventeeth-century Castilian dictionary of Covarrubias defined the term as referring to any non-native speaker of Castilian who had some proficiency in the language, Moriscos and foreigners being cited as examples.[1] Implying as well the idea of cultural assimilation, the phrase *indio ladino*, applied to Amerindian natives, could refer to such diverse social types as the first natives who served the Spaniards as interpreters during the conquests, the ethnic lords who became the negotiators between their local communities and Spanish colonial officials, and persons of any rank or station who worked in the employ of Spanish masters. In addition, persons of mixed Spanish and Amerindian parentage (*mestizos*) as well as African slaves were also referred to by the adjective ladino (*"un mestizo muy ladino," "negro ladino"*) in order to signal their acquaintance with Spanish language and culture.

Obviously, ladino was not a term of self-identification; it was employed instead from the outside by those who considered themselves Castilian or Spanish and therefore equipped to discern and judge how successfully non-Castilians handled the Spanish language and adapted themselves to Spanish customs. The complex history of the meanings of the concept and the particularities of its use in Spanish America in the sixteenth and seventeenth centuries merit a discussion

[1] Sebastián de Covarrubias Horozco, *Tesoro de la lengua Castellana o Española* [1611], Martín de Riquer, ed. (Barcelona, 1943).

before we consider the cultural mediations practiced by those who were described by the term.

A. THE MANY MEANINGS OF THE TERM LADINO

In the long and multiple histories of the concept, we turn to its original use to refer to the common Romance vernacular of Spain excluding Catalonia as well as its simultaneous and subsequent meanings. Roger Wright has studied the relationship of the concepts *latín* and ladino in medieval Spain; his work provides the missing link between the generalized use of ladino to refer to the language of vernacular Romance and the language of the Sephardic Jewish community. Because of their importance, his conclusions bear reiteration:

> *Ladino* was the normal word used before 1080 by all Romance-speakers of any religious group in non-Catalan Spain to describe their own language, whether written or not, and it was only contrasted with other languages entirely such as Arabic, Greek or Hebrew.[2]

In 1080, the Council of Burgos decided to abandon the old Visigothic Christian liturgy, and adopted a new Christian liturgical Latin pronunciation. This led ultimately to the erection of a semantic and conceptual boundary between Latin and Romance vernacular; according to Wright, "*latín*" meaning Latin and "*ladino*" meaning Romance would have been spelled the same way until

> the general adoption of the Romance-based method of spelling in the early thirteenth century; so there must have been some confusion, when reading, over whether the written form *latinus* meant *latín*, "Latin," or *ladino*, "Spanish," and it may be for this reason that those circles that used the new Christian liturgical Latin pronunciation stopped using that written form with the meaning of "Romance," and kept to that of "Latin," and eventually preferred in speech to use a word other than *ladino* to refer to Romance vernacular. . . . Meanwhile, Spanish-speaking Jews continued as before to think of their own language as *ladino*, unaware, perhaps, of the distinctions newly brought into the Christian community.[3]

[2] Roger Wright, "Early Medieval Spanish, Latin, and Ladino," in *Litterae Judaeorum in Terra Hispanica*, I. Benabu and J. Yahalom, eds. (Jerusalem, in press), text following fn 5. I am grateful to Roger Wright for his permission to cite this important essay and his helpful comments on my interpretation of it.

[3] Ibid., text at fn 6.

Wright summarizes the final division between Latin and vernacular Romance in Spain and the fate of the concept *ladino* as follows:

By the time we reach the age of Alfonso el Sabio in the second half of the thirteenth century, Latin and Romance have become conceptually distinct languages throughout the Kingdom; the new *litterae* pronunciation plus the old traditional way of writing were considered together to be the one language Latin, and the old ordinary colloquial pronunciation of Castile, plus the newly-elaborated methods of writing Castilian Romance, were considered together to be the one language now officially called *castellano.* Dialectal divisions had become psychologically and politically salient during the thirteenth century, so the general "Romance" meaning of the word *ladino* no longer seemed so suitable.[4]

Although ladino as a noun was used to refer to the language of the Sephardim, its use in reference to Castilian, as Manuel Alvar demonstrates, did not disappear.[5] On the contrary, in the sixteenth and seventeenth centuries, the adjective ladino continued to carry one of its original meanings in reference to Latin – that of linguistic purity – now applied to proper pronunciation, usage, and cultivated speech in Castilian; this is the meaning captured in phrases like "ladino español" and "ladino castellano."[6] Inasmuch as the term implied skill in the use of Castilian on the part of those who possessed it, it was logically applied as well to any foreigner who spoke it; one could be described, for example, as "muy ladino" or "no muy ladino."[7] Such was the usage in which it spread to Spanish America to apply to nonnative speakers of Castilian.

Although the term referred specifically to language use, the descriptions presented by early chroniclers of the Indies suggest as well the meaning of acculturation to Spanish ways. If in the sixteenth century our modern concept of culture did not exist, the intimate connections between language and customs were well understood. Hence we find Oviedo's vivid description of the cacique Enriquillo of Hispaniola: "Among these modern and most recent lords of this island Hispaniola, there is one who is called Don Enrique, who is a baptized Christian and knows how to read and write and is very ladino and speaks the Castilian language very well."[8] Another sixteenth-century chron-

[4] Ibid., text following fn 7.

[5] Manuel Alvar, "Aceptaciones de *ladino* en español," in *Homenaje a Pedro Sainz Rodríguez, II. Estudios de lengua y literatura* (Madrid, 1986), 25–34.

[6] Manuel Alvar, "Aceptaciones de 'ladino' en español," in *Homenaje a Pedro Sainz Rodríguez, II. Estudios de lengua y literatura* (Madrid, 1986), 28.

[7] Ibid., 29.

[8] Gonzalo Fernández de Oviedo y Valdés, *Historia general de las Indias,* 4 vols. (Madrid, 1851–3), I., 140 [part 1, book 5, chapter 4]; my translation.

icler of the Indies, Fray Pedro de Aguado, used the phrase "ladino o españolado" to refer to Hispanicized Indians.[9] Language proficiency, literacy, Christianity and custom all converged around this concept.

But these are positive meanings. The connotations of the modifier ladino were multiple and diverse. For example, it connoted the qualities, at one extreme, of prudence and sagacity and, at the other, cunning and craftiness.[10] At the opposite pole of the positive values of linguistic expertise and practice of Christian customs, it could refer to the "big talker" and the charlatan.[11] The Andean native Felipe Guaman Poma, who felt the sting of its negative as well as its positive sign as applied to himself, remarked that those called *indios ladinos* were often scorned as "ladinejo" or "santico ladinejo" – that is, as zealous converts and busybodies, and as *bachilleres,* great and impertinent talkers and scoundrels.[12]

The examples provided by Guaman Poma suggest the conflictive nature of the sign ladino as used in America, where its application always implicitly carried – even at its neutral best – the notion of the outsider to full participation in Castilian society. At its worst, it painted its object as suspect or guilty of insubordination after submission[13]: One of the great themes of Spanish dominion in America is the number of times that rebellions and insurrections were spawned by mestizos, Indians, or African blacks who had been Hispanicized. This topic in Spain's history in America runs through the eighteenth century, yet one of the first historical examples suffices to make the point. Oviedo's account of the rebellion of the lord Enrique who was "muy ladino" is framed by the chronicler's chapter on native customs and his final comment about the results of Christian evangelization. The few remaining Indians could be saved, he asserted, if they were baptized and would keep the faith and not return to the customs of their fathers. "But what are we to say," he laments, "about those who, in spite of being Christian, have spent years as renegades in the mountains and foothills with Enrique and other Indian lords?"[14]

9 Alvar, "Aceptaciones de 'ladino' en español," 30.

10 Covarrubias Horozco, *Tesoro de la lengua Castellana o Española,* 747.

11 Alvar, "Aceptaciones de 'ladino' en español," 31.

12 Felipe Guaman Poma de Ayala, *El primer nueva corónica y buen gobierno* [1612–15], John V. Murra and Rolena Adorno, eds., Jorge L. Urioste, Quechua trans. (Mexico, 1980), 733, 738, 796, 838.

13 See Rolena Adorno, "Images of *Indios Ladinos* in Early Colonial Peru," in *Transatlantic Encounters: Europeans and Andeans in the Sixteenth Century,* Kenneth J. Andrien and Rolena Adorno, eds. (Berkeley, CA, 1991), 232–70, for a discussion of the range of social roles played by those identified as indios ladinos according to sixteenth- and seventeenth-century native and Spanish sources.

14 Oviedo, *Historia general de las Indias,* I., 139 [part 1, book 5, chapter 3].

B. THE INDIGENOUS ETHNOGRAPHERS

For Oviedo, this vexing question was unanswerable, and the issue he raised in the 1535 publication of the first part of his *Historia general de las Indias* – that is, the suspicion of culturally mixed and Hispanicized individuals, be they lords or commoners – would remain on the horizon for a long time. The well-known legislation passed in the latter part of the sixteenth century against mestizos signals the ever-greater concern about this issue.[15] This historical situation is central to understanding what was at stake for the writers of dynastic history considered here, and it helps us to frame our examination of their cultural mediations in writing. Our point of departure is that in one way or another they wrote from the position of cultural outsiders. The central issue in this discussion, therefore, is not the veracity of their histories, but rather their authority as writing subjects and the positions that they took to handle in writing the complexities of cultural plurality.[16]

Although ladino is the category of external description that orients this discussion, it should not be understood as the category of analysis.[17] Hence it is crucial to emphasize that none of the writers considered here would have found that they had much – if anything – in common with one another. It would be irresponsible to deny their subjectivity and uniqueness; to preserve them, it seems essential to emphasize that this discussion is not a collective analysis of their works but rather a glimpse at the similar roles of cultural mediation realized in them. Their narratives argue similar positions and it is to them that the following discussion is directed. These common threads do not reveal similarities among the writers as historical individuals but rather the similarities of the subject positions they took in their interactions with the institutions of church and state and their representatives. With these qualifications in mind, we turn to some of the common features that appear in the writings of these very different individuals who represented a variety of Amerindian traditions and a broad range of relationships to Spanish Christian culture.[18]

[15] See Richard Konetzke, "Los mestizos en la legislación colonial," *Revista de Estudios Políticos*, 112 (1960): 113–29.

[16] Created by the historical author, the literary persona or subject that exists for the reader may or may not take the same positions as the author; the subject is vulnerable to readers' interpretations, which the historical author cannot correct. I use the analytical category of the literary subject – the persona on the written page – because it is the only version of the historical author to which we have access.

[17] To do so would merely reproduce the stereotype I have sought to avoid by outlining the philological history of the term.

[18] J. Jorge Klor de Alva, in "Colonialism and Postcolonialism as (Latin) American Mi-

The post-conquest writers of native tradition to be considered here include persons of autochthonous background as well as individuals of mixed European and Amerindian parentage. In particular, the texts produced by those who wrote the history of their ethnic groups are revealing both for what they say and for what they suppress. The adjustments to the intermingling of diverse cultures in a colonial society is nowhere more problematic than in the works of history and ethnography that these heirs of native traditions wrote, with the expectation that their writings would reach audiences within and beyond their own communities. These writers had to be twice ethnographers, not only mapping their own systems of cultural practice and belief but also – and implicitly – mapping and responding to those of their culturally European readers.

The most sensitive topics were native religion and Christian evangelization. We shall examine the common elements of their narratives on these subjects and the purposes for which these special kinds of history and ethnography were written. The aim of exploring the elusive and sometimes contradictory qualities of these subject positions is to show, first, that they do not lend themselves to the simple or dichotomous characterizations of European versus Amerindian society and culture and, second, that they reveal instead the richer, more ambiguous strategies that characterize the roles of cultural mediation they inevitably played.

The time period covered by this cluster of historians runs from the middle of the sixteenth century to the middle of the seventeenth, from the coming of age of the first native and mestizo generations born after the conquest to the maturity of those whose great-grandparents had experienced the European invasion. For Mexico, the post-conquest writers of native tradition represent several of the basic ethnic divisions of the Central Valley of Mexico at the time of the Spaniards' arrival.[19] Most notable are Hernando Alvarado Tezozomoc (active 1598-early seventeenth century), Fernando de Alva Ixtlilxochitl (ca. 1578–1648), Domingo Francisco de San Antón Muñón Chimalpahin Quauhtlehuanitzin (born 1579), Diego Muñoz Camargo (ca. 1529–1599), and Juan Bautista de Pomar (active 1582).[20]

rages," *Colonial Latin American Review* 1, nos. 1–2 (1992): 7–8, 19, warns against falling into the trap of essentializing dichotomies and underscores the importance in sixteenth and seventeenth century Spanish American society of innovative interethnic alliances and cultural identities that were more ambiguous than fixed, more constructed and manipulated than given. I am grateful for his insights into the problems of cultural mestizaje.

[19] Charles Gibson, *The Aztecs Under Spanish Rule: A History of the Indians of the Valley of Mexico, 1519–1810* (Stanford, 1964), 9, 21.

[20] Chimalpahin descended from the Chalcas and wrote in Nahuatl detailed accounts of

Alvarado Tezozomoc was of Mexica (Aztec) descent; as the son of one of the *tlatoani* or lords of Tenochtitlán under the Spaniards and Francisca de Moctezuma, he was a grandson of Moctezuma II.[21] Tezozomoc left a major narrative account of the Mexica rise to power in the late fourteenth century up to the time of the Spanish conquest in his *Crónica mexicana* [1598]; he wrote his *Crónica Mexicayotl* in Nahuatl in 1609.[22] Alva Ixtlilxochitl was the son of a Castilian, Juan Navas Pérez de Peraleda, and Ana Cortés Ixtlilxochitl, who descended from the Acolhuaque, the lords of Texcoco; Don Fernando left abundant accounts of Acolhua history in his *Historia chichimeca* and various *relaciones*, all of which he wrote in Spanish. Diego Múñoz Camargo was the son of the Spanish conquistador Diego Muñoz and a native woman; he married a noblewoman of Tlaxcala.[23] His work presents the perspective of the Tlaxcalans, who inhabited the area northeast of the Central Valley of Mexico and were unconquered enemies of the Mexica. His *Historia de Tlaxcala* (late sixteenth century) covers the ancient migration of the group, its dynastic history, and its role as allies of the Spanish in the conquest of Mexico.[24] Juan Bautista de Pomar was also of mixed, European and Mexican parentage and his mother descended from the preconquest Acolhua rulers of Texcoco. Pomar's *Relación de Texcoco*, which Alva Ixtlilxochitl later read, was written in response to the 1577 questionnaire for geographic and census information for the *relaciones geográficas de Indias* and is considered a major source on native deities and other aspects of pre-Columbian and colonial culture.[25] Each of these authors, like their counterparts in Peru after the tenure of the Viceroy Francisco de Toledo (1569–1581), inter-

their history. I have not considered the Nahuatl writings of Chimalpahin here, but the reader is recommended to the recent studies of Susan Schroeder, "Chiampahin's View of Spanish Ecclesiastics in Colonial Mexico," in *Indian-Religious Relations in Early Colonial Spanish America*, Susan Ramírez, ed. (Syracuse, NY, 1989), 21–38, and *Chimalpahin and the kingdoms of Chalco* (Tucson, 1991).

[21] Angel María Garibay, *Historia de la literatura nahuatl, Primera parte (Etapa autónoma: de c. 1430 a 1521), Segunda parte: El trauma de la conquista (1521–1750)* [1953–4], 2 vols., 2nd ed. (Mexico, 1971), II., 299, and Benjamin Keen, *The Aztec Image in Western Thought* [1971] (New Brunswick, NJ, 1985), 132.

[22] Charles Gibson and John B. Glass, "A Census of Middle American Prose Manuscripts in the Native Historical Tradition," in *Guide to Ethnohistorical Sources, Part Four*, Howard F. Cline, Charles Gibson, and H.B. Nicholson, eds., *Handbook of Middle American Indians*, vol. 15 (Austin, 1975), 326.

[23] Keen, *The Aztec Image in Western Thought*, 127.

[24] Gibson and Glass, "A Census of Middle American Prose Manuscripts in the Native Historical Tradition," 350–51; Diego Muñoz Camargo, *Descripción de la ciudad y provincia de Tlaxcala* [late 16c], René Acuña, ed. (Mexico, 1981).

[25] Gibson and Glass, "A Census of Middle American Prose Manuscripts in the Native Historical Tradition," 355.

preted native history from the origins of the dynasties whose history they reconstructed to the period of Spanish domination. In every case, as we shall see later, the retrieval of the past was undertaken to influence the present.

Colonial Peru produced only a handful of texts in Spanish and Quechua that were written by bilingual native Quechua-speakers.[26] Missionary writers have been important in giving access to others, such as the dictated account of Titu Cussi Yupanqui.[27] There are three writings in the chronicle tradition: Juan de Santacruz Pachacuti Yamqui Salcamayhua, *Relación de antigüedades deste reyno del Pirú* (1613?); Felipe Guaman Poma de Ayala, *El primer nueva corónica y buen gobierno* (1612–1615); and El Inca Garcilaso de la Vega, *Primera y segunda partes de los Comentarios reales de los Incas* (1609, 1616).[28] Of these three accounts of Inca history, only El Inca Garcilaso, the son of the Spanish captain Sebastián Garcilaso de la Vega and the Inca *palla* (noblewoman) Isabel Chimpu Ocllo, reconstructed the dynastic history of the Incas from the Inca perspective. Guaman Poma identified himself primarily with the pre-Incaic dynasty of the Yarovilca of the Huánuco region of Chinchaysuyo, even though he claimed matrilineal descent from the Incas. Santacruz Pachacuti was also an outsider to the Cuzco royalty, being a *kuraka* (ethnic lord) of the Collahuas, midway between Cuzco and Lake Titicaca in Collasuyo, which was nevertheless an area associated with Cuzco from the origins of its state expansion.[29]

[26] Although the extent of colonial recordkeeping in Quechua has been debated and remains to be ascertained, the quantity of colonial documents so far examined suggests that there is nothing like the centuries-long notarial traditions that exist in the languages of the Nahuas and Mayas of colonial Mesoamerica.

[27] See Jesús Lara, *La literatura de los quechuas: ensayo y antología* [1969], 4th ed. (La Paz, 1985). Titu Cussi Yupanqui, who ruled the post-conquest Inca state at Vilcabamba from 1557 to 1571 dictated an account of Manco Inca's complaints against the Spanish in Cuzco (see John Hemming, *The Conquest of the Incas* [New York, 1970], 504–5). His Quechua testimony was transcribed by the Augustinian friar Marcos de García in 1570; only the Spanish translation survives (see Diego de Castro Titu Cussi Yupanqui, *Yntrucción del Ynga don Diego de Castro Titu Cussi Yupanqui. . .*, Luis Millones Santa Gadea, ed. [Lima, 1985]). Other Inca testimonial accounts of the Spanish conquest are found in Edmundo Guillén, *Versión Inca de la conquista* (Lima, 1974).

[28] Juan de Santacruz Pachacuti Yamqui Salcamayhua, *Relación de antigüedades deste reyno del Pirú* [1613?], Francisco Esteve Barba, ed., in *Biblioteca de Autores Españoles* 209 (Madrid, 1968), 281–319; Felipe Guaman Poma de Ayala, *El primer nueva corónica y buen gobierno* [1612–15] (1980); and El Inca Garcilaso de la Vega, *Comentarios Reales de los Incas, primera y segunda parte* [1609, 1616], in *Obras completas del Inca Garcilaso de la Vega* II–IV, Carmelo Sáenz de Santa María, ed., in *Biblioteca de Autores Españoles* 133–35 (Madrid, 1963–5).

[29] Franklin Pease, "El mestizaje religioso y Santa Cruz Pachacuti," *Revista Histórica* 28 (1965): 125, 131; and Jan Szeminski, "Un kuraka, un dios y una historia: *Relación de antigüedades deste reyno del Pirú* por don Joan de Santa Cruz Pacha Cuti Yamqui Salca Maygua," *Antropología y Historia 2* (1987):4.

El Inca Garcilaso elucidated Andean cultural concepts through the analysis of Quechua terms as part of his effort to make known Inca history and culture; Guaman Poma and Pachacuti Yamqui included significant Quechua language interpolations in their Spanish language texts. Like the colonial Mesoamerican writings of historical tradition, the authors of these works painted theirs in broad strokes, elaborating grand cosmological designs written from a strong sense of the need to redeem the present. Only one of them, Felipe Guaman Poma de Ayala, commented extensively on postconquest society from the 1570s onward; in this respect his *Nueva corónica y buen gobierno* stands out from its counterparts in both the viceroyalties of New Spain and Peru and makes explicit the culturally hybrid historian's need to relate traditional, historical prerogatives to contemporary colonial claims. That is, insofar as Guaman Poma's version of Andean history supports his claims about the Andean right to sovereignty in Peru, his testimony is particularly useful for elucidating the circumstances in which these historical ethnographies were written and the goals they sought to achieve.[30]

Despite the great differences among their various heritages, as writing subjects, these Mexican and Peruvian authors assumed similar subject positions: First, each presented himself as a lord or leader of his respective group, thereby claiming authority to speak on behalf of all. Second, each engaged actively in legal petitioning for the restoration of rights, privileges, and properties. Third, their works were aimed at enhancing the prestige of the dynastic traditions they represented. As a result, in articulating their viewpoints on native history, they inevitably emphasized certain components of their cultural traditions and suppressed or ignored others. In this regard, their efforts conformed to certain theoretical principles of cross-cultural interactions and exchange recognized today.[31] Fourth, they occasionally

[30] See Rolena Adorno, *Guaman Poma: Writing and Resistance in Colonial Peru* (Austin, 1986).

[31] Some of the anthropological concepts that Angel Rama applied to the processes of creation of literature and nationhood in post-Independence Latin America may also be applied to the writings studied here (Rama, *Transculturación narrativa en América Latina* [Mexico, 1982]). For example, Fernando Ortiz's notion of transculturation – that is, the elaboration of new cultural forms common to neither the donor nor the recipient culture, and the suppression or loss of certain traditional ones – is especially pertinent (Ortiz, *Contrapunteo cubano del tabaco y el azúcar* [1940] [Caracas, 1978]). Also relevant is George Foster's idea of a "stripping down process," by which the conquest culture refrains from presenting and imposing all its institutions and customs (Foster, *Culture and Conquest: America's Spanish Heritage* [New York, 1960]). My point here, however, is that all social participants – not merely the representatives of the dom-

appropriated to their ethnic heritage traditions not necessarily their own.[32] Whether they did so knowingly or not, the practice had the effect of universalizing the local and particular and extending its prestige to readerships whose knowledge of the native traditions under discussion could not be guaranteed.

The results of these various processes may be observed in the way these authors dealt with the following transcultural issues: For pre-Columbian times, they acknowledged the ancient existence of idolatry but they disassociated it from their own dynastic heritage; they considered pre-Columbian, oral and written historiographic traditions as important sources, although they showed deference to European histories; they claimed the highest achievements of autochthonous American civilization for their own ethnic traditions; they identified their own language as the most prestigious among native Amerindian language groups; they acknowledged ancient practices of human sacrifice but distanced it from their own heritage. For the post-conquest era, they claimed their forebears' incorporation as allies at the highest levels into the Spanish military campaigns of conquest, and they claimed their ancestors' swift conversion to Christianity and subsequent leadership in evangelizing the rest of the native population.

C. THE ARGUMENTATIVE POWER OF THE NARRATIVE ANECDOTE

To illustrate the problems of writing history from a culturally hybrid perspective, Fernando de Alva Ixtlilxochitl's *Sumaria relación de todas las cosas . . . en la Nueva España* provides a useful anecdote.[33] Don Fernando recalls that he had asked an old cacique to recount the origin of the ancient prince Ixtlilxochitl, the father of the king Nezahualcoytzin. The cacique replied that Ixtlilxochitl came into existence when a great eagle flew down from the sky and laid a great egg in a nest in a tree. After a certain period of time, the egg broke open; thus the child who was to become the great Ixtlilxochitl was literally "hatched

inant or official culture – exercise roles of agency and innovation in these processes. These chronicles are testimony of that fact.

[32] For example, El Inca Garcilaso identified Tiahuanacu as an Inca ruin; Alva Ixtlilxochitl made all Mexican kings descend from the source of the Texcoco dynasty, and Guaman Poma contradicted, not without reason (see José Varallanos, *Historia de Huánuco* [Buenos Aires, 1959]), the notion that the Incas were the source of civilization in the Andes by attributing the role to his Yarovilca ancestors.

[33] Fernando de Alva Ixtlilxochitl, *Obras Históricas*, Edmundo O'Gorman, ed., *Serie de historiadores y cronistas de Indias* 4, 2 vols. (Mexico, 1975), I, 288.

from an egg." Laughing, Don Fernando, whose ancestors on his mother's side were from the house of Texcoco, told the old gentleman that it was foolish to spin such yarns. But the old lord replied that, on the contrary, he would retell the story, and others like it, to anyone who asked, especially to the Spanish! Don Fernando concludes the tale by commenting that many old lords did not want to tell the truth about their history, seeing that every day they were asked about it, but never taken seriously by their interlocutors.

Recounting the remarks of the elder, Fernando de Alva Ixtlilxochitl revealed his own frustration with the problems of recovering native history, when the venerated authorities on whom the burden rested had lost hope that such could be achieved. Moreover, the old cacique's scornful reference to Spaniards suggests that cross-cultural historical inquiry created special problems of credibility and verification, at the root of which was mutual mistrust. The case that Don Fernando presents is repeated by many other writers of his time, not only Mexican but Andean as well. The mediations are complex because they involve first of all the web of interests of the writer, who must take into account the atmosphere of mutual mistrust that has to be overcome. Second are the historical and political debates in which his writing is engaged; third, the expectations and threshold of cultural tolerance of the readers whom he seeks to reach and persuade.

Although the writers considered here come from significantly different ethnic traditions, their discussions of pre-Columbian and post-conquest religion sound remarkably similar. Monotheism was the key issue on which the arguments that could identify the group with the colonial civil and religious order rested. From the Spanish perspective, proselytization and the Amerindian acceptance or rejection of Christianity was the fulcrum on which the justification for Castilian dominion in America turned. With the threat of Protestantism abroad in Europe and the continuing struggle against Islam in Europe, the triumph of Christianity meant national unity and empire, while its defeat meant certain social and cultural disintegration. Within this purview, writing historical and ethnographic accounts was a challenge of great consequence for the author who could be identified as ladino. In their writings, the principal ethnographic question concerned the beliefs of the natives, both about their own gods and in the presumably prophesied coming of Christianity. The crucial historical issue to be addressed was how the natives responded to Christian indoctrination.

In general, the Spanish ecclesiastical histories of the religious orders that recounted the triumphs of the faith in the Indies exploited the illustrative anecdote when they could not lay claim to numbers or quantifiable evidence about the success of conversion in the New World. In my view, this is an extremely important principle, in evidence throughout the writings on Spanish America in the sixteenth and seventeenth centuries.[34] Its immediate roots are in the medieval tradition of the morally edifying exemplum, employed not only in the writing of history but also in the religious oratory of the spoken sermon. This universal rhetorical figure was theoretically not a mere interpolation or diversion but rather a key device of argumentation and persuasion. The theoretical importance of the exemplary anecdote was no less central to the writings of the ladino authors than it was to the Castilian writers with whose works they interacted. Thus, we can better understand the weight and significance of the tale told if we rightly gauge its structure and placement as central – not accessory – to the author's broader goals.

The first and fundamental common theme that emerges among these writers asserts that the ancients, either the whole group or some privileged member of the dynasty, understood monotheism to be the essence of authentic spiritual experience. For example, in his *Historia de Tlaxcala,* Diego Muñoz Camargo attributed this knowledge to the ancient Tlascalans.[35] Juan Bautista de Pomar's *Relación de Texcoco* [1582] credited the king Nezahualcoyotzin, among the lords of Texcoco, as the one who most doubted the identity of the idols as gods.[36] Although Nezahualcoyotzin did not receive divine illumination and thus returned to his parents' tradition, he authored many *cantos* (lyrical compositions) which attested – according to Pomar – to his apprehension of the monotheistic nature of true divinity.[37] Fernando de Alva Ixtlilxochitl made a similar claim on behalf of the ancient Toltecs, who called this supreme god Tloque Nahauque.[38] He too attributed to Nezahualcoyotzin the special gift of the knowledge of the true God, as evidenced in the extant fragments of his *cantos.*[39] Each of these writers also asserted that the ancients had – in one

[34] I have used prominently here three anecdotes – from Alva Ixtlilxochitl, Pomar, and Muñoz Camargo – on the strength of this conviction; I developed arguments on this topic in my study of Guaman Poma's use of European rhetorical types and historiographic models (Adorno, *Guaman Poma,* 43–51, 69–70).

[35] Diego Muñoz Camargo, *Historia de Tlaxcala,* 2nd ed. [reprint of 1892 ed.] (Mexico, 1947), 141.

[36] Juan Bautista de Pomar, *Relación de Texcoco,* in *Nueva colección de documentos para la historia de México,* vol. III. (Mexico, 1941), 23.

[37] Ibid.

[38] Alva Ixtlilxochitl, *Obras Históricas,* I, 263.

[39] Ibid., 405.

form or another – knowledge of the existence of Satan, evil, and eternal punishment.[40]

Interestingly, the Peruvian writers of the same generation offered similar accounts. Whereas El Inca Garcilaso de la Vega attributed to the first Incas the knowledge of the universal and invisible god, called by the Andeans *Pachacamac,* Guaman Poma de Ayala asserted that the civilizations of pre-Incaic times possessed the *sombra* or shadow of the knowledge of monotheism and that the Incas – specifically, Mama Uaco Coya, the mother of Manco Capac Inca – subsequently invented idolatry.[41] Like the *rastro* or trace of the same knowledge that Muñoz Camargo assigned to the ancient Tlaxcalans, these claims were consistent with the standard Christian theological view that knowledge of the divine could be gained through the exclusive use of natural reason.[42] In all these Mexican and Peruvian cases, the authors insisted upon the ancients' original possession and subsequent loss of the knowledge of the creation and the Adamic age.[43]

Another characteristic tendency was for these authors to regularly bring together the events of ancient biblical and New World history. Alva Ixtlilxochitl, for example, coordinated ancient events in Mexico with the coming of Christ, suggesting that a possible ancient knowledge of the event was once recorded and then lost.[44] In Peru, Santacruz Pachacuti asserted that, upon the crucifixion of Christ, the *hapinuños* ("infernal spirits") disappeared, raising mournful laments.[45] It was Guaman Poma, however, who presented the most elaborate intersection of New World and biblical history, likening the standard version of biblical ages to corresponding eras of ancient Andean civilization, and interrupting his narration of the reigns of the Incas to interpolate the birth of Jesus Christ and to claim that, soon afterward, the apostle Saint Bartholomew came to the Andes to make the first Andean conversions to Christianity. He claimed that the historical cross of Carabuco stood as proof of that apostolic visit.[46] El Inca Garcilaso also credited St. Bartholomew with a pre-Columbian

[40] Muñoz Camargo, *Historia de Tlaxcala,* 142,163; Pomar, *Relación de Texcoco,* 24; Alva Ixtlilxochitl, *Obras Históricas,* I, 447.

[41] Garcilaso de la Vega, *Comentarios Reales de los Incas,* 2 vols., Angel Rosenblat, ed. (Buenos Aires, 1943), 43; Guaman Poma de Ayala, *El Primer nueva corónica y buen gobierno,* 50, 54, 58, 65, 81, 121.

[42] Muñoz Camargo, *Historia de Tlaxcala,* 142; Fray Luis de Granada, *Del symbolo de la fe, tercera parte,* in *Obras de Fray Luis de Granada* (Madrid, 1944), I, 400.

[43] Alva Ixtlilxochitl, *Obras Históricas,* I, 397; Guaman Poma de Ayala, *El primer nueva corónica y buen gobierno,* 50.

[44] Alva Ixtlilxochitl, *Obras Históricas,* I, 265.

[45] Santacruz Pachacuti, *Relación de antigüedades deste reyno del Pirú,* 132.

[46] Guaman Poma de Ayala, *El primer nueva corónica y buen gobierno,* 88–94.

visit to the Andes, although he attributed to the Spanish – quite possibly correctly – this syncretic interpretation of the identity of a particular statue.[47] Finally, we find that Santacruz Pachacuti associated the cross of Carabuco with the apostolic visit of Tonapa, who was really Saint Thomas.[48]

Within such narrations of spiritual origins and biblical/New World contacts, the post-1492 arrival of Christianity is portrayed as a natural narrative development and an implicit fulfillment of the divinely ordained preparation for the gospel. The Mexican writers claimed that the introduction of Christianity had occurred during the earliest days of the conquest of Mexico. Muñoz Camargo and Alva Ixtlilxochitl both asserted that the four lords of Tlascala requested and received baptism in the first twenty days during which Cortés and his company camped in Tlaxcala in 1519.[49] The baptism of Moctezuma was claimed by Alva Ixtlilxochitl; Guaman Poma insisted that sincere conversion accompanied the forced baptisms of Atahualpa and the last prince of Vilcabamba, Tupac Amaru, who died baptized "in a most Christian manner."[50] Santacruz Pachacuti also attested to the baptism of Atahualpa, telling how he had been christened "Don Francisco" at the same time as he was executed as a traitor.[51] Regardless of their historical veracity, these claims of early baptisms are crucial because of their dramatization of the peaceful and willing acceptance of Christianity by the native lords.

Specifically, these episodes reveal that their writers recognized the exemplary power of the spectacle of the native lord submitting to the spiritual – if not so easily to the temporal – authority of the foreign invaders. The last-hour conversions claimed for the reigning lords serve as prefiguration for the widespread evangelization process subsequently narrated. Miracles and martyrdoms are the outstanding episodes in these dramas, but they are not as significant as the prophecies about the return of vanished lords. Such accounts are com-

[47] El Inca Garcilaso also noted that a confraternity of *mestizos*, desirous of disassociating themselves from the colonists, claimed Saint Bartholomew as their patron, openly declaring that it mattered not to them whether the apostle's visit to Peru had been real or apocryphal (*Comentarios Reales de los Incas* [1943], I, 272).

[48] Santacruz Pachacuti, *Relación de antigüedades deste reyno del Pirú*, 134–5.

[49] Muñoz Camargo, *Historia de Tlaxcala*, 220; Alva Ixtlilxochitl, *Obras históricas de don Fernando de Alva Ixtlilxochitl*, Alfredo Chavero, ed., 2 vols. (Mexico, 1892), II, 371. Such an action seems unlikely; no sources mention the event until several decades after the Mexican conquest (Charles Gibson, *Tlascala in the Sixteenth Century* [New Haven, 1952], 30).

[50] Alva Ixtlilxochitl, *Obras históricas* [1892]), II., 388; Guaman Poma de Ayala, *El primer nueva corónica y buen gobierno*, 393, 454.

[51] Santacruz Pachacuti, *Relación de antigüedades deste reyno del Pirú*, 233.

mon to various post-conquest traditions among Mesoamerican as well as Andean peoples. These narratives provide a transitional argument between assertions about the ancient knowledge of the Judeo-Christian deity and contemporary claims about a Christian Indian society. At the same time, the arguments about the native lords' immediate acceptance of Christianity serve as the narrative fulfillment of the ancient prophecies.

Alvarado Tezozomoc's account, in his *Crónica mexicana* [1598], tells that Quetzalcoatl would return, bringing sons very different from the Mexica: stronger, braver, wearing different garb, speaking in a manner unintelligible to the Mexica, and coming to rule forever.[52] In his version of the ancient prophecy of the returning lords, the mestizo Muñoz Camargo emphasized the mixing of the races: "we have it understood from ancient times that people would come from where the sun rises, that they are to intermarry with us and we are to be all one."[53] Alva Ixtlilxochitl set forth the themes of dissension and punishment, telling that the astrologer Huematzin foretold that a lord would come to rule, with the good will of some and against that of others; that there would arise men of the same lineage who would pursue him with great wars until destroying themselves; that there would be a final destruction and that those who escaped it would suffer destruction sometime later. He concluded this bitter recital with the statement: "And it almost came to pass, with the will of God, just as it was foretold".[54] On the Peruvian side, Guaman Poma and El Inca Garcilaso attributed to Huayna Capac the foreknowledge of the coming invasion and conquest.[55]

Despite the differences in the ways these writers told the religious history of the ancients, they all followed the same basic scheme, including the claims about monotheism in ancient times, and the baptisms of native lords when the Spaniards arrived. Together with the prophecies that mediated between the two, these events constituted the central organizing principles around which these narrations of the histories of the Acolhuas, the Texcocans, the Tlaxcalans, the Incas, the Yarovilcas, and the Collahuas were articulated.

What are the factors that helped to produce these often repeated assertions? One is a matter of religious indoctrination. There is now

[52] Hernando Alvarado Tezozomoc, *Crónica Mexicana* [1598], Manuel Orozco y Berra, ed. (Mexico, 1944 [reprint of 1878 ed.]), 527.
[53] Muñoz Camargo, *Historia de Tlaxcala*, 197.
[54] Alva Ixtlilxochitl, *Obras Históricas* (1975), I, 271.
[55] Guaman Poma de Ayala, *El primer nueva corónica y buen gobierno*, 114, 380; Garcilaso de la Vega, *Comentarios Reales de los Incas* (1943), II, 250.

persuasive evidence that the ancient promise of returning lords was to a great extent a missionary elaboration of native myths of local importance.[56] For both Mexico and Peru, the pre-Hispanic existence of the prophecies of the coming of new lords or the return of old ones is dubious. Even if historical, the doubt remains as to how extensive or limited such traditions were. In any case, by the time even the earliest of these authors was writing, the prophecies had been incorporated into the major Spanish chronicles of the conquests of Peru and Mexico.

Apart from personal experience or historiographic antecedents that these authors chose to elaborate or follow in their own works, there were immediate and pragmatic reasons for reconstructing the religious history of their people as they did. In spite of claiming the Christian conversion of their ethnic groups, they acknowledged, sometimes inadvertently, the failure of religious evangelization as they described the persistence of traditional ritual practices.[57] Muñoz Camargo's solution to the problem of avoiding a subject that he could not ignore was to declare that the Franciscan missionaries had already written so thoroughly on the subject of traditional religion that there was no need for him to explore it in his own work.[58] He then went on to present a picture of exemplary religious piety on the part of the Tlaxcalans in order to demonstrate that the Christian faith was well-rooted and broadly extended among them.[59]

In general, the persistence of traditional ritual practices was a topic suppressed in these texts. Only in certain cases, such as Guaman Poma's, was native religion given voice, which is then drowned out by contradictory "evidence" of massive conversion. In discussing pre-

[56] See Susan Gillespie, *The Aztec Kings: The Construction of Rulership in Mexica History* (Tucson, 1989); Franklin Pease, "La conquista española y la percepción andina del otro," *Histórica* 13, no. 2 (1989):179–96; and Inga Clendinnen, " 'Fierce and Unnatural Cruelty': Cortés and the Conquest of Mexico," *Representations* 33 (1991):65–100. Gillespie (1989, 179–201) has argued persuasively that the primary sources of Aztec/Spanish history do not sustain the idea that the Aztecs believed that Cortés was either an ancient lord come back again or the deity Quetzalcoatl. She traces the process by which that interpretation grew to legendary proportions through the early missionary period despite limited evidence to support it; see also Clendinnen (1991: 69–70). Franklin Pease (1989: 181–191) shows how the stereotypical account of the conquest of Peru, which attributed to the Andeans the identification of the Spaniards as the returning god Viracocha and his helpers, was the work of Spanish chroniclers of the 1550s and later; this tale did not appear in the initial eyewitness Spanish accounts written in the 1530s; only later did it become a way of rationalizing the conquest.

[57] Guaman Poma de Ayala, *El primer nueva corónica y buen gobierno*, 1088; Muñoz Camargo, *Historia de Tlaxcala*, 149, 258; Alva Ixtlilxochitl, *Obras Históricas*, I, 287.

[58] Muñoz Camargo, *Historia de Tlaxcala*, 169.

[59] Ibid., 257.

sumably ancient religious practices, he acknowledged that he has seen them in the course of his work assisting in extirpation campaigns at the same time as he claimed that the people of the Andes had become Christian.[60]

By the time these Amerindian and mestizo writers were at work, the large-scale Christian conversions – both the dream and the limited reality realized particularly by the early Franciscan establishment in Mexico – had suffered serious setbacks.[61] If works published in Spain grandly celebrated the triumphs of the faith in the New World (Estéban Salazar and Alonso Fernández provide widely disseminated examples), the culturally hybrid writers of America were often simultaneously engaged in gathering information for treatises on the extirpation of idolatry. Consequently, their own works were polemical and defensive; the limited mention they made of the persistence of idolatrous practices, and the way they compensated for them with tales of conversion and native Christian martyrdom, register the degree to which they aspired to create a harmonious picture of Christianization, at the same time as they acknowledged the impossibility of sustaining such an optimistic interpretation.

These works reveal an awareness of the colonial authorities' attempts to suppress and destroy all sources of information on native religion, both the Amerindian codices and European-authored works on native ritual life. Such representations of Amerindian culture and religion, either in pre-Columbian codices or in colonial treatises, were not considered innocent repositories of culture but rather implements of dangerous cultural and social practices. Pomar, for example, said that it was because of the Inquisition's execution in 1539 of Don Carlos Ometochtzin, a lord of Texcoco and the son of Nezahualpilli (see *Proceso*), that the codices not already confiscated by Archbishop Francisco de Zumárraga's extirpation efforts were destroyed by the lords who still possessed them.[62] He declared that these lords destroyed their sacred property out of fear of being accused of idolatry if such artifacts were found in their possession.

This anecdote, with which Pomar began his *Relación de Texcoco*, may provide the best clue to the general Amerindian and mestizo writers' silence on the subject of traditional belief. Each of these authors was careful to distance himself as far as possible from the knowledge of these traditional survivals. Even Guaman Poma, who gave an exacting

[60] Guaman Poma de Ayala, *El primer nueva corónica y buen gobierno*, 282, 285, 298; and 403, 834–57.
[61] See Charles Gibson, *Tlaxcala in the Sixteenth Century*, 29.
[62] Juan Bautista de Pomar, *Relación de Texcoco*, 4.

catalogue of such practices, went to extremes to prove his own Christianity and put his knowledge of traditional ritual firmly in the context of his own work in assisting Cristóbal de Albornoz in the extirpation of idolatries.[63]

Regarding the suppression of works that dealt with native belief systems and customs, the case of the confiscation of Fray Bernardino de Sahagún's writings by the Franciscan order and the crown provides a pertinent example. Sahagún's efforts to preserve the knowledge of Nahua culture through its language were controversial because they proposed evangelization based on the knowledge of Christian doctrine and Scriptural passages in Nahuatl; at the same time they were considered dangerous, potentially perpetuating traditional native customs through the recording of ancient history. Thanks to the president of the Council of the Indies, Juan de Ovando, the Spanish crown since 1572 had promoted research into the history and ethnography of the New World. However, Ovando's death in 1575 and the implementation by the Spanish Inquisition in 1576–77 of the 1545 decision of the Council of Trent to prohibit Scripture in the vernacular, brought about the reversal of crown policies on Sahagún's *Historia* and on all writings on pre-Columbian civilizations.[64] Subsequently, in 1577, Sahagún's papers were ordered confiscated by royal decree.[65]

Not only were Sahagún's works to be gathered up, but the viceroy and the audiencia were to prohibit similar initiatives from being taken in the future: "And you will be advised not to permit anyone, for any reason, in any language, to write concerning the superstitions and ways of life these Indians had. Thus it is best for God our Lord's service and for our own."[66] At bottom is the perceived danger that the written word, particularly in an indigenous language, would perpetuate practices identified by the church with superstition, magic, and witchcraft.[67]

[63] Guaman Poma de Ayala, *El primer nueva corónica y buen gobierno*, 282, 285; see Adorno, "Las otras fuentes de Guaman Poma: sus lecturas Castellanas," *Histórica 2*, no. 2 (1978): 137–58, and Pierre Duviols, "Albornoz y el espacio ritual andino prehispánico," *Revista Andina* 1 (1984): 169–222.

[64] Arthur Anderson and Charles Dibble, *Florentine Codex: General History of the Things of New Spain. Introductions and Indices*, Monographs of the School of American Research 14, part 1 (Santa Fe, NM, 1982), 35–6.

[65] Manuel Ballesteros Gaibrois, *Vida y obra de Fray Bernardino de Sahagún* (León, 1973), 76. The royal decree is printed in the *Codice Franciscano. Siglo XVI* (Mexico, 1941), 249–250.

[66] The cédula of 22 April 1577 is here translated by Anderson and Dibble, *Florentine Codex*, 36–37.

[67] In the dedication of his work (the Florentine Codex) to Fray Rodrigo de Sequera and, more completely, in his prologue to Book Two, Sahagún summarized his problems

D. FICTIONALIZING THE FAILURE OF EVANGELIZATION

If the preservation of sacred objects and traditions was problematical for the native lords who participated in the destruction of their own cultural monuments, it was perhaps less obvious but no less dramatic for the bi- or polycultural authors of later generations whose works we are discussing here. To render their deliberate silences more audible, we turn to the writings of European authors who gave voice to what the indigenous and mestizo writers never could. Such works were didactic and literary; they did not describe native religion ethnographically (the reason, perhaps, why some of them were not suppressed)[68] but rather created fictional situations that nevertheless commented forcefully on the predicament of indoctrinated natives. Such reflections on the state of Amerindian Christianity and the outlook of its presumed adherents reveal the social and spiritual problems the missionary evangelizers actually faced. These fictional accounts allow us to focus more sharply the interpretations of native spiritual/religious history offered by writers as diverse as Muñoz Camargo, Guaman Poma, and El Inca Garcilaso de la Vega.

Pedro de Quiroga's *Coloquios de la verdad,* written around 1563 but not published until the twentieth century, provides a relevant example.[69] Another is Fray Fernando de Valverde's *poema sacro,* written and published almost a century later, entitled *Santuario de Nuestra Señora de Copacabana en el Perú* (Lima, 1641). Quiroga wrote the *Coloquios* when some of the authors discussed here were adolescents, or already adults; the *Santuario* appeared some years before the death of the last of them (Alva Ixtlilxochitl died in 1648).

Quiroga's work deals with Spanish/Indian relations in the first

with censorship and confiscation within the Franciscan order (Sahagún, *Historia General de las Cosas de Nueva España,* Angel M. Garibay, ed. [Mexico, 1979], 15, 73–5). He told about the elimination of his native scribes and collaborators, the subsequent confiscation and circulation of his writings among members of the Franciscan order in Mexico, and only belatedly the eventual return of his manuscripts to him, thanks to the support of Sequera, the new Franciscan commissary who encouraged him to resume his work.

68 See Adorno, "Literary Production and Suppression: Reading and Writing About Amerindians in Colonial Spanish America," *Dispositio* 11, nos. 28–29 (1986):1–25.

69 The autograph manuscript of the *Coloquios de la verdad* comes from the library of the Count-Duke of Olivares and is preserved in the library of the monastery of San Lorenzo el Real of El Escorial. Its author was a priest who had experienced the chaotic years of civil war following the conquest of Peru (Pedro de Quiroga, *Coloquios,* Julián Zarco Cuevas, ed. [Seville, 1922], 2–4). The location and circulation of the manuscript in the sixteenth century are unknown.

thirty years after the Peruvian conquest. One of the major characters in the dialogue is Tito, an Indian whose attempted suicide is thwarted by two Spanish passersby. After the two men remove him from the scaffold, Tito tells them his life story. His attempt to take his own life becomes more disturbing when his interlocutors [discover?] that Tito is a baptized Christian. Thus Quiroga presents, through the voice of a former Inca noble, a ringing condemnation of the failure of Spanish evangelization among the early generations of those who were called "indios ladinos."

Working first for a captain at Cajamarca and later for a soldier, Tito was unaccustomed to doing the manual labor he saw his own former vassals doing. Hence he became a thief, much loved by his Spanish master whose friends envied him so clever a servant. Only on taking up service with a Spanish merchant was he indoctrinated in the Christian faith. Tito tells of his swift but meaningless Christianization through several baptisms, and his subsequent, more thorough religious indoctrination which turned to bitter disillusionment when he visited Spain and saw the depravity of the Christians he had been taught to emulate. Finally, he narrates how he returned to Peru and his own people with the intention of preaching the gospel to them. Instead, they persuaded him to return to traditional beliefs and practices, to which he refers – unable to undo the lessons of Christianity – as sins.

This fictional self-description reveals the partial character of Christian indoctrination. In this way, Quiroga revealed the trauma of the acculturated native for whom it was impossible to go forward and impossible to go back. Such persons were caught in the position described aptly by the Nahuatl word *nepantla,* "in between." Used by a Mexican lord as recalled in an anecdote narrated by Fray Diego Durán in his *Historia de las Indias de Nueva España y islas de tierra firme, nepantla* was the "situation in which a person remains suspended in the middle between a lost or disfigured past and a present that has not been assimilated or understood."[70] The record of this drama, reenacted over and over again in early colonial Mexico and Peru, is almost entirely suppressed in the works of the authors we are discussing. Only Guaman Poma, in his extensive depictions of colonial society, described at length ladino apostates; this exceptional report is worth noting:

[70] Durán, *Historia de las Indias,* 2 vols. (Mexico, 1951), II, 268; Jorge Klor de Alva, "Spiritual Conflict and Accommodation in New Spain: Toward a Typology of Aztec Responses to Christianity," in *The Inca and Aztec States, 1400–1800: Anthropology and History,* George Collier, Renato Rosaldo, and John Wirth, eds. (New York, 1982), 353.

. . . the most Christian, although he may know how to read and write, carry a rosary and dress like a Spaniards, . . . – he seems a saint – on getting drunk, he speaks with demons and worships the *wagakuna* [Andean deities and sacred places] . . . speaking of his ancestors, performing their ceremonies.[71]

In the 1640's Fray Fernando de Valverde presented a tantalizing portrait of the defeated Inca in a poetic composition that celebrated the foundation of the faith and honored the Christain shrine at Copacabana. The Inca Yupanqui plays a small role in this pastoral/heroic poem; however, it is one deemed sufficiently important to represent his figure in the frontispiece engraving. There, he sets up a ringing and bewildered lament: How can it be that he, the Inca, finds himself defeated by subjection to a mere woman? He harangues: "Don't ask me to revere one who was so poor that she gave birth in a manger and so humble that she obeyed a husband who was a carpenter and who, on top of everything else, saw her son expire, nailed to a tree!".[72] Fictionally framed and assigned to a dynastic lord vanished for a century, the words echo very closely the kinds of statements reported about Indians in the extirpation instructions and other church documents.

For example, native Andean responses to the doctrines of Christianity, recorded by Juan Polo de Ondegardo in the 1560s and reprinted in the Third Church Council of Lima's 1585 *Confesionario,* ring remarkably true to the fictional (but not fictitious) utterances just cited. In Polo's "Instrucción contra las ceremonias y ritos," Chapter 6 is devoted to "the errors against the Catholic faith, into which some Indians tend to fall."[73] Among the natives, it was the indios ladinos who most commonly thwarted the progress of the faith by preaching to the Indians against the gospel and its ministers, not unlike the confused and frustrated experience of Quiroga's Tito. The "Instrucción" speaks as well about how Andeans (like Valverde's Inca Yupanqui) often could not fathom the idea of omnipotence of a deity presenting himself as a humble and lowly carpenter. When faced with the demand to abandon their gods, native Andeans frequently responded that they would gladly worship the Christians' god alongside their own, because the deities "had contrived with one another and were related like brothers."[74]

[71] Guaman Poma de Ayala, *El primer nueva corónica y buen gobierno,* 877.
[72] Valverde, *Santuario de Nuestra Señora de Copacabana en el Perú. Poema Sacro,* ff.236r-v.
[73] Polo de Ondegardo, "Instrucción contra las ceremonias y ritos que usan los indios, conforme al tiempo de su infidelidad," in *Revista Histórica* 1, no. 1 (1906): 202–3, [1585]: ff5–6.
[74] Ibid., 202, [1585]: f5.

Such admissions, however, were seldom to be found in the writings of those who would have heard such arguments against the Christian faith made by the native peoples whose histories they sought to dignify. Here, Muñoz Camargo provides an apparent exception, but he moved swiftly to neutralize the damage his narration might incur. He mentioned an offer made by the Tlaxcalan lords at the time of the conquest to negotiate such a compromise with the invaders, that is, to accept the new Christian religious while preserving their own.[75] However, he immediately undercut the episode with the account of the joyous conversion of the principal lords, who requested baptism and were determined to take up the new, Christian precepts.[76] In this regard, the tale Muñoz Camargo tells about one Don Gonzalo Tecpanecatl Tecuhtli is also pertinent.

Confessing one Holy Week, Don Gonzalo acknowledges the troublesome presence in his home of the ashes of the deity Camaxtli, much venerated by the Tlascalans. He brings the remains to the priest, Fray Diego de Olarte; Fray Diego burns the ashes and absolves the cacique. Shortly afterward, Don Gonzalo dies while flagellating himself – full of remorse and repentance for his sins – before the image of the Virgin Mary in the Hospital of the Annunciation on Holy Thursday. The burned ashes of the deity, which had been spread about with great scorn by Fray Diego, are now discovered to have blond hairs among them, "because the elders affirm that Camaxtli had been a white man and blond".[77]

This story provides a transition from the old gods to the new, however unresolvable the conflict between them. On one hand, the anecodte can be read as an overt summary of Muñoz Camargo's work: the sincerity of conversion of the old cacique, the success of efforts to root out native religion, as undertaken with the collaboration of the natives themselves, and the Christian fulfillment of the ancient prophecy. The remains of the old god are found to contain blond hairs, which denote the foreign culture and possibly its providential message. The fact that the narrative contains the scorn and "great exhortations" of "the good religious" Fray Diego, and ends with the spectacle of the scourged corpse of the old lord of Tepeticpac, suggests

[75] Muñoz Camargo, *Historia de Tlaxcala*, 218.
[76] Ibid., 220.
[77] Ibid., 258. The association of blond hair with the Spaniards is confirmed by native sources of the conquest, such as the Codex Aubin in which Pedro de Alvarado is called *tonatiuh* ("the Sun") because of his fair hair and skin (see Miguel León-Portilla, *The Broken Spears: The Aztec Account of the Conquest of Mexico*, Angel M. Garibay, Spanish trans., Lysander Kemp, English trans. [Boston, 1962], 71, 80).

an edifying interpretation of this episode. In this reading, and far from the image of the pathetic old Inca as presented by Fray Fernando de Valverde, Muñoz Camargo presents the tragic tale of a lord who practiced self-censure and self-castigation in an exemplary fashion, only to die without knowing that his devotion was, implicitly, not misplaced.

On the other hand, the tale could be read as the text of a different revelation: that the Spaniards (represented by the blond hairs) were diabolical and even though the old gods were destroyed, evil – a new evil – remained. Whichever reading Muñoz Carmargo might have preferred (and he certainly overtly favored the former), the literary subject Muñoz Camargo permits a tantalizing ambiguity of interpretation.

E. CULTURAL MEDIATION OR WRITING HISTORY FOR THE PRESENT

Like all writing of history, these narrations, so marginal in their time from the viewpoint of participation in elite literary culture, are not disinterested. In each case, the reevaluation of the past has a present-oriented objective. Unlike the Spanish histories their authors read, however, these works were not designed to inspire men to great deeds in the king's service or the exercise of virtue and valor in the name of Spanish imperial culture. These were not exemplary tales which the sons of Texcoco and Tlaxcala could emulate in the future, in line with the didactic goals of history of the day. They were, as Frank Salomon has written, "chronicles of the impossible"[78]; if the cultural ambiguity which they experienced were erased, the necessity of writing from or about that condition would disappear. Because of that cultural hybridity, they had more immediate and practical objectives which were related more to legal than historiographic prerogatives.

As legal petitions, these works brought together two traditions. On one hand, their initiatives were related to the appeals by which the Spanish conquistadores regularly sought recognition and reward. As descendents of the conquistadores and/or their native allies who had thus served the Spanish king, these writers employed and elaborated the format of the *relaciones de méritos y servicios* and the *probanzas* of services rendered to the crown.[79] As such, their insistence on religious

[78] Frank Salomon, "Chronicles of the Impossible: Notes on Three Peruvian Indigenous Historians," in *From Oral to Written Expression*, ed. R. Adorno (1982), 9–39.

[79] On the character of the *relaciones de méritos y servicios*, see Murdo MacLeod, "Self-Promotion: The *Relaciones de Méritos y Servicios* and their Historical and Political In-

monotheism in the ancient past and loyal Christianity in the present fulfilled the same role – although in much more elaborate narrative versions – as the declarations of faith found, in one formula or another, in the relaciones and probanzas of Spanish soldiers.

On the other hand, the culturally mestizo writers put forward several arguments that had much in common not with the conquistadores of America, but rather that other colonized population, the Moriscos of peninsular Spain.[80] Both traditions insisted on their obedience and service to the crown, their unjust suffering at the hands of the Christian overlords, their insistence upon the harmony of traditional cultural practices with the Christian faith, and the argument that all policies prejudicial to local native interests would have severe economic consequences for their foreign rulers. The Morisco testimonies set in clear relief those of the ladino historians. Encoding the practices of the ancient culture into formulas appropriate for advocating for rights and privileges in a new foreign regime, the historiographic and testimonial practices of the ladino Americans echo those of the pluricultural sons and daughters of Spain of prior and contemporary generations.

In sum, upon representing native Amerindian traditions in relation to the European, the ladino historians were ethnographers of their own cultural hybridization. As individuals of mixed background and loyalties, they understood that the boundary between identity and alterity was artificial and arbitrarily set in place by those who had something to gain by the exclusion. Indigenous histories of the post-conquest period could not afford to be so qualified. The function of such narrative efforts was not only to undertake the preservation of

terpretation," in *Proceedings of the Conference "The Book in the Americas"* (Providence, RI, in press), and Adorno, "History, Law, and the Eyewitness: Protocols of Authority in Bernal Díaz del Castillo's *True History of the Conquest of New Spain*," in *The Project of Prose in the Early Modern West*, Elizabeth Fowler and Roland Greene, eds. (Cambridge, in press).

80 I have studied elsewhere such similarities in the writings of Morisco and Amerindian advocates on behalf of their peoples in the late sixteenth and early seventeenth centuries. Although separated by some forty years and entirely different cultural identities and social circumstances, the respective interactions of Don Francisco Núnez Muley and Felipe Guaman Poma de Ayala with the Castilian state and its representatives abroad produced very similar protests (Adorno, "La *ciudad letrada* y los discursos coloniales," *Hispamérica* 16, no. 48 [1987]: 3–24). See K. Garrad, "The Original Memorial of Don Francisco Núñez Muley," *Atlante* 2, no. 1 (1954): 199–226, for the protest written by Francisco Núñez Muley and Luce López-Baralt, "Crónica de la destrucción de un mundo: la literatura aljamiado-morisca," *Bulletin Hispanique* 82 (1980): 15–68, for an illuminating overview of the *aljamiado-morisco* tradition of writings of sixteenth-century Spain.

the past but also to keep the present alive. In this respect, the old Texcocan lord who told the tale of the great egg, and his "muy ladino" interlocuter, the historian Alva Ixtlilxochitl who wrote down his story, may have enjoyed together, after all, the last laugh.

CHAPTER 14

What to wear? Observation and participation by Jesuit missionaries in late Ming society

WILLARD J. PETERSON

CLUTTERING our memories are images of men fully clothed in an apparently European style, some with armor, stepping up a tropical shore (weren't they hot?, I wonder now) to confront a small crowd of men and women clad only according to the minimum decency required at the time the picture was concocted. I suspect this is close to being an archetypal image, from a European perspective, of conquerors and about-to-be conquered as their meetings were rehearsed for several centuries in the so-called Age of Expansion, expansion by Europeans, that is. The roles are made obvious by who is naked and who is robed. (Robed is the appropriate word here because buried in the etymology of the English word "robe" is the idea of robes being the spoils of conquest.)

All of this becomes more complicated, both as an image and as history, when missionaries in their distinctive robes are added to the picture. Missionaries, of course, also sought to conquer in the sense of seeking and winning, in our case souls for Christ, as their compatriots sought other conquests, such as portable wealth. Their task was more difficult when they confronted not "naked natives" but men already wearing the robes, and even the swords, symbolic of dominance and exploitation in their own societies.

In Ming China there was a well-established pattern of using robes and other adornments (which in modern Chinese are summarized in the term *fu-shih*) to denote social status.[1] Although the Ming state was

[1] Basing himself on his analysis of the adornment practices of an Amazonian Kayapo tribe, Terence Turner suggested that what he called the "social skin" could be seen as a constructed medium between the individual and other individuals, between the social "self" and the pre-social, libidinous "self," and between "categories or classes

not wholly successful in enforcing sumptuary laws, including those prescribing the type of cloth and the cut for various groups,[2] the language used at the time is suggestive. The term "red silk belts" (*chin shen*), although not literal, was a standard way to refer to those who had held official appointments. "Blue lapels" (*ching chin*) were first-degree holders, the certified students (*sheng-yuan*). "Belts and lapels" (*shen chin*) was a rubric for officials and degree holders. Commoners were identified as "plain [cotton] clothes" (*pu yi*).[3] And so on. The system of accoutrements to denote official status was elaborately detailed, but in simple terms all Ming military and civil officials were required after 1393 to wear as their public dress a hemp or thin silk, round-collared robe, fastening on the right, with sleeves three feet wide. Those of the top four (of nine) ranks wore a crimson robe; ranks five to seven wore deep blue; the eighth and ninth ranks, and expectant officials, wore green. Each of the nine ranks also had its insigniae, a square silk brocade of certain dimensions and design, with birds adorning the civil officials' and beasts on the military's. Each rank also had distinctive shoes and hat and belt ornaments. Away from public business, officials were to wear the appropriate round-collared robe, their official belt (which was correlated with rank), and a black silk hat (*wu-sha mao*).[4] Ricci's general description is verified for us in many sources, and there can be no doubt that robes and roles were ostentatiously correlated in the upper ranks of Ming society.

As a missionary resident in late Ming China, Matteo Ricci (1552–1610) was in a position to observe the system of official clothing, and he wrote a summary description of it just prior to his death in Peking.

All the mandarins, whether high or low, whether of the military or civil branches, have the same hats of black material and with two flaps on either side of the hat that readily fall down, and these oblige one always to proceed erect and gently, with the gravity becoming an official. They all also have one type of robe, boots of the correct style of black suede, a large belt with various patterns only proper for officials, and two squares embroidered with varying figures, one on the chest and the other on the back. The girdle and these

of individuals" in relation to other such categories. In these terms, I am primarily concerned with the third aspect. Terence C. Turner, "The Social Skin," in *Not Work Alone: A Crosscultural View of Activities Superfluous to Survival*, ed. Jeremy Chafas and Roger Lewin (Beverly Hills. 1980), 112–40.

[2] See *Ming-shih* (Peking, 1974), 67:1649–50 (for proscriptions involving clothing for commoners), 1639 (for sixteenth-century examples of the court's inability to control what even officials wore).

[3] It is noteworthy that in twentieth-century English we have such terms as hard hats, blue collars, and white collars to denote social groups without being literal.

[4] *Ming-shih*, 67:1634–7.

squares have significant differences and enable one to distinguish higher and lower ranks, whether military or civil, by the embroidery of most artfully rendered beasts and birds, with flowers. The girdles differ according to the standing of the wearer, with fasteners of wood, horn, aloe, silver, gold, or jasper [probably referring to jade], which is the more prestigious.[5]

Ricci wrote descriptions not only of the clothing of the mandarins, as he called them using the new Portuguese word, but of the food and drink, marriage and funeral rituals, the etiquette used in greeting and in eating, prostitution, and homosexuality, institutions of government and religion, modes of transport, physiognomy, and so on, covering what his twentieth-century editor called an "anthropology of the Chinese."[6] Ricci even explained that unlike the Japanese the Chinese sit on chairs, sleep in beds, and eat at tables. Ricci's report was carried back to Europe by another Jesuit, Nicolas Trigault (1577–1628), who published a Latin version that was widely disseminated and reappeared in vulgar, and vulgarized, versions. Excerpts and summaries appeared in English in 1625 in the great compendium of travel accounts, *Purchas His Pilgrimes,* produced by Samuel Purchas in London. The gap between what the observer wrote and what his nearly contemporary reader might infer after the intervention of two translations can be illustrated by juxtaposing the paragraph labeled Aparell in the seventeenth-century English version of Trigault's Latin with my version of the relevant section of Ricci's Italian.

Author's translation	**17th century Apparell**
Like the women, men wear garments which reach the ground.	The men and women wear long garments.
The men's is one part of a toga, which is tied on the right side with *bindelle;* women tie in the middle.	The men double them on their breasts, and fasten them under both the arme-holes; the women on the midst of the breast.
Although both have long sleeves, like our Venetians, those worn by men are closed except to allow the hand to be extended; those of women are open.	They weare wide sleeves, but the women wider, the mens straighter, at the wrists.

[5] Pasquale D'Elia, ed., *Fonti Ricciane: Documenti originali concernenti Matteo Ricci e la storia delle prime relazioni tra l'Europa e la Cina, 1579–1615,* 3 vols. (Rome, 1942–9), 1:65–6 n. 108.

[6] Ibid., 88.

Author's translation	**17th century Apparell**
The hats of men are made with much work and decorated with fine work. The more costly are made of horsetail.	Their Caps are artificially wrought.
In the winter they are of felt, and now also of velvet.	
But what strikes us as quite strange are the shoes, which are so well worked with silk and flowers that not even our women wear ones of such elegance.	Their Shooes are much differing from ours; the men weare them of Silke with divers workes and flowers, exceeding the elegance of our Matrons.
Other than for taking a stroll outside, leather shoes are not the thing, except among common people.	Shooes of Leather none but the meaner sort weare; and scarcely admit they Leather soles, but of cloth.
The hats of the literati (*letterati*) are square; others are only able to wear round hats.	The Caps of their Learned are square, of others, round.
Everyone spends at least an hour in the morning combing and dressing his hair, which would seem to us a great burden.	Every one spend halfe an houre at least in combing and trimming his haire.
They customarily wrap their feet and legs with long strips of cloth, and therefore their leggings are always bulky.	They winde also long clouts about their feet and legs, and therefore weare their Breeches loose.
They do not wear shirts, but wash their bodies often.	They weare no Shirts, but a white Coat next the skinne, and washe often.
On the street a large umbrella to ward off sun and rain is carried by a servant. Poor people carry a small one in their own hand.[7]	They have a servant to carrie a Shadow or great Sumbrero over their heads against the raine and Sunne; the poore carrie one for themselves.[8]

[7] Ibid., 89 n. 138.

[8] Samuel Purchas, *Purchas His Pilgrimes* . . . (London, 1625), vol. 3, bk. 2, chap. 7, 394 ("taken out of Ricius and Trigautius").

Ricci's intentions were not anthropological, and he was not describing everyone in China. As in the passages on clothing, he was most concerned with the elite. Working men and women in late Ming did not wear long robes (*ch'ang pao*) reaching to the ground: They wore short coats (*tuan yi*) with trousers or leggings.[9] They did not wear fancy hats or fancy shoes and did not routinely enjoy the protection of an umbrella. Living in the capital, Ricci wrote about the set of men whom he had learned to emulate in his own dress. It had taken him at least a decade to perceive the type of robe, and role, that would enable him to "conquer" in China to the extent that he did in his lifetime.

In 1557, Portuguese merchants had been granted the privilege of maintaining permanent residence at what came to be called Macao. It became a small settlement on a peninsula in Hsiang-shan district, south of Canton, which they were officially allowed to visit twice a year for trade. Portuguese ships had reached the China coast by 1513, and a trade mission visited Peking in 1520.[10] Missionaries traveled with the merchants and like them were restricted in their opportunities by the Chinese authorities, although both groups hoped to pursue their goals in China. After two or three years of mission work in Japan, the Jesuit Francis Xavier (1506–1552) determined that converting China was the key to converting Japan. He proposed to travel with another Portuguese embassy to Peking as a papal envoy and there persuade the emperor to allow Christians to live, travel, and preach in the empire. Portuguese rivalries thwarted the plan in Malacca, and Xavier attempted to proceed on his own. He was taken as far as a small island southwest of what was to become Macao and, his plans aborted, died there in the winter of 1552.[11]

Over the next thirty years, more than fifty priests and lay brothers – mostly Jesuits and Franciscans, but also a few Augustinians and Dominicans – attempted vainly to establish residence in Ming territory for purposes other than trade.[12] After decades of frustration, a major change was initiated by Alessandro Valignano (1539–1606), who was appointed the Visitor for all Jesuit activities east of Africa. On his way from Goa to Japan he stopped by Macao in 1577–1578. Against the predilections of Jesuits who ministered to the Macao community, Va-

[9] See the example in Shen Ts'ung-wen, *Chung-kuo ku-tai fu-shih yen-chiu* (Hong Kong, 1981), 401–13.

[10] D'Elia, *Fonti Ricciane*, 1:149.

[11] Joseph Sebes, "The Precursors of Ricci," in *East Meets West: The Jesuits in China, 1582–1773*, ed. Charles E. Ronan and Bonnie B.C. Oh (Chicago, 1988), 23–7.

[12] Sebes, "Precursors," 27–30.

lignano decided missionaries for China should learn Chinese customs and the spoken and written language. In response to his order, Michele Ruggieri (1543–1607) was sent from Goa.[13]

Ruggieri arrived in Macao in the summer of 1579 and began an intensive course in Chinese. He progressed enough with his tutors to try putting the "Great Learning" into Latin,[14] and in 1580 he began to go with the merchants on their regular trips to Canton.[15] At this time Ruggieri reported that his study of Chinese was being criticized in Macao, even by fellow Jesuits. According to him, some asked,

> What is the sense of this Father occupying himself with this sort of thing when he could be of service in the other ministries of the Society? It is a waste of time for him to learn the Chinese language and to consecrate himself to a hopeless enterprise.[16]

Valignano protected him, and in 1582 ordered that instead of trying to make converts more like Portuguese, the strategy was to recognize Chinese Christians as Chinese. In response to a suggestion by Ruggieri, Valignano also had the Goa authorities dispatch two more Jesuits to study Chinese in Macao. They arrived in the summer of 1582.[17]

Just prior to this, Ruggieri went with the mayor of Macao to Chao-ch'ing, the seat of the provincial governor of Kwang-tung, to be told of the violation of Ming rules by a Spanish group led by a Jesuit from the Philippines. They had landed in southern Fukien and were brought to Canton as spies.[18] Supposedly Ruggieri made a favorable impression on the governor, who sent for him after his return to Macao with the "spies." Ruggieri accepted the invitation and took one of the newly arrived Jesuits, Francesco Pasio (1554–1612), with him to take up residence in a Buddhist temple.

Instead of the European garb and full beard in which he had presented himself to the governor earlier in the year, Ruggieri wore Bud-

[13] D'Elia, *Fonti Ricciane,* 1:147; George Harris, "The Mission of Matteo Ricci, S.J.: A Case Study of an Effort at Guided Culture Change in China in the Sixteenth Century," *Monumenta Serica* 25 (1966): 36–7; Sebes, "Precursors," 32–3.

[14] Kund Lundbaek, "The First Translation from a Confucian Classic in Europe," *China Mission Studies Bulletin* 1 (1979): 1–11.

[15] Sebes, "Precursors," 29, 34.

[16] Letter by Ruggieri in Pietro Tacchi Venturi, ed., *Opere storiche del P. Matteo Ricci, S.J.* (Macerata, Italy, 1911–3), as translated in George H. Dunne, *Generation of Giants, The Story of the Jesuits in China in the Last Decades of the Ming Dynasty* (London, 1962), 19. See also Harris, "The Mission of Matteo Ricci," 55.

[17] Dunne, *Generation of Giants,* 19; Sebes, "Precursors," 34; Harris, "The Mission of Matteo Ricci," 7.

[18] Sebes, "Precursors," 29–30; Dunne, *Generation of Giants,* 19–20.

dhist robes and had shaven his head and face. According to Ruggieri, the governor

> wanted us to dress in the fashion of their priests which is a little different from ours; now we have done so and, in brief, have become Chinese in order to win China for Christ.[19]

A few years earlier, at Valignano's direction, the Jesuit missionaries in Japan had adopted Zen Buddhist robes, and Ruggieri and Pasio were adopting them as part of the strategy to gain permission to reside in Chao-ch'ing.[20] However, they were ordered back to Macao almost immediately. Pasio then went on to Japan. When the invitation was renewed, perhaps by the prefect at Chao-ch'ing, Ruggieri went back in the summer of 1583. Still with Buddhist robes and a shaven head, this time he was accompanied by the other recently arrived Jesuit, Matteo Ricci.[21]

In a nice coincidence, Matteo Ricci (1552–1610) was born in Italy a few months before Francis Xavier died off the south coast of China.[22] After studying law in Rome for three years, he joined the Society of Jesus in 1571 as a novice and met Alessandro Valignano. Valignano, who left in 1574 for Goa and East Asia, helped draw Ricci to China.[23] In his studies under the Jesuits in Rome, he was exposed to Christopher Clavius (1537–1612), a leading academic mathematician who was instrumental in the formulation of the Gregorian calendar announced in 1582, and to Robert Bellarmine (1542–1621), the celebrated Jesuit theologian who arrived to teach in Rome in 1576 and whose views eventually won papal support.[24] To prepare for his mission in the East,

[19] As translated in Harris, "The Mission of Matteo Ricci," 83, from *Opere storiche,* 2:416. The final phrase is "siamo fatti Cini ut Christo Sinas lucrifaciamus."

[20] Harris, "The Mission of Matteo Ricci," 82, 84. See Sebes, "Precursors," 58, 72n, for testimony by a new Jesuit newly arrived in Japan that he was starting life anew.

[21] Harris, "The Mission of Matteo Ricci," 55–6; Sebes, "Precursors," 35–6.

[22] For brief biographical summaries, see the entry on Matteo Ricci by Wolfgang Franke in *Dictionary of Ming Biography,* ed. L. Carrington Goodrich with Chaoying Fang (New York, 1976), 2:1137–44; Harris, "The Mission of Matteo Ricci," 6–18. The central, indispensable source on Ricci in China is his own account, available in D'Elia, *Fonti Ricciane.* The fullest accounts of his life in English are: Vincent Cronin, *The Wise Man from the West* (London, 1955); Dunne, *Generation of Giants.* A richly detailed reconstruction of aspects of Ricci's experience is in Jonathan D. Spence, *The Memory Palace of Matteo Ricci* (New York, 1984). All of these include further bibliography relevant to Ricci.

[23] Sebes, "Precursors," 32.

[24] Ibid., 36; A.D. Wright, *The Counter-Reformation: Catholic Europe and the Non-Christian World* (London, 1982), 91; T.M Parker, "The Papacy, Catholic Reform, and Christian Missions," in *The New Cambridge Modern History,* ed. R.B. Wernham (Cambridge, 1968), 67. Even from China, Ricci remained in touch with Clavius.

Ricci went in 1577 to the university at Coimbra in Portugal, where what were to become the authoritative versions of Aristotelian natural philosophy were being developed for eventual publication in the 1590's.[25] Thus Ricci in his early twenties was exposed to the rapidly evolving idea of a Jesuit mission in Asia under Portuguese control, to the most up-to-date established concepts in mathematics and astronomy, to the new ideas in technical theology that were intended to win arguments with Protestants and, conceivably, pagans, and to the latest exposition of an elaborate, systematic account of natural phenomena that was to be the standard of most Catholic universities in the first half of the seventeenth century. It was a heady experience.

Matteo Ricci sailed from Lisbon in 1578 for Goa with twelve other Jesuits, among them Michele Ruggieri. There Ricci completed his theological studies, and he received ordination as a priest in 1580.[26] He then was sent to Macao, where he began to learn Chinese immediately after his arrival in the summer of 1582.[27] A year later, Ricci went with Ruggieri to Chao-ch'ing. Ruggieri had been granted permission to reside there, presumably with the support of the district magistrate, Wang P'an, a *chin-shih* from Shao-hsing, Chekiang. They had a residence and chapel built, continued to learn to speak Mandarin (*kuan-hua*) and to read. With their teachers' help, they put the Ten Commandments, prayers, and a catechism into Chinese. Ricci worked out a map of the world and the place names represented in Chinese characters. Ruggieri traveled north to Shao-hsing and also west into Kuang-hsi and up into Hunan; he was looking for contacts rather than converts so as to expand the mission beyond Chao-ch'ing.[28] In 1588, Ruggieri was ordered by Valignano to return to Rome to persuade the authorities to commission a papal embassy to the Ming emperor. This had been Xavier's hope as the most effective means to secure permission to proselytize in China, and Valignano wanted to try it again. Ricci remained in the Chao-ch'ing residence with another Jesuit, Antonio de Almeida, who also began to study the Chinese language.[29]

Already in 1585, Ricci claimed, "I can now converse with everyone

[25] See W.J. Peterson, "Western Natural Philosophy Published in Late Ming China," *Proceedings of the American Philosophical Society* 117, no. 4 (1973): 297; Sister Patricia Reif, "Textbooks in Natural Philosophy, 1600–1650," *Journal of the History of Ideas* 30 (1969): 23

[26] Harris, "The Mission of Matteo Ricci," 7, 151.

[27] D'Elia, *Fonti Ricciane*, 1:154 n. 207. Ricci was specific that he was learning what he called *mandarina*. See Harris, "The Mission of Matteo Ricci," 38–9.

[28] Harris, "The Mission of Matteo Ricci," 8–10, 40–1.

[29] Ibid., 10.

without an interpreter and can write and read fairly well."[30] In a letter in 1592 he recalled more modestly, "I diligently gave myself to the study of the language and in a year or two I could get along without an interpreter. I also studied the writing. This is more difficult, however, and although I have worked hard at it up to the present time, I am still unable to understand all books."[31] The previous year Ricci had been told by Valignano to translate the Four Books into Latin, which immersed him in the key classical Confucian texts. In 1594 he started again with a tutor, after being without one for at least seven years:

> Every day I have two lessons with my teacher and devote some time to composition. Taking courage to write by myself, I have begun a book presenting our faith according to natural reason. It is to be distributed throughout China when printed.[32]

Ricci was acquiring the skills that would enable him to reach the Jesuits' target audience, the elite, by using their language and "natural reason."

In the meantime, Ricci and Almeida had been expelled from Chao-ch'ing in 1589, but were allowed to take up residence in Shao-chou, several hundred *li* to the north in Kwang-tung. They still wore Buddhist-style robes and shaved heads. Local men seem to have regarded their chapel and residence as a Buddhist temple (*ssu*). They would arrange to have their own gatherings there, including banquets, as had been the practice at Chao-ch'ing. They were also attracted by the books, pictures, maps, and curious mechanical instruments, including clocks and astrolabes.[33] Ricci had realized at Chao-ch'ing that officials could come because it was not a private residence; it had a quasi-public status. When important people were gathered there, "the street was filled with their palanquins and the river bank in front of our door was filled with the large, handsome boats of the mandarins."[34]

One of the literati who called on them was Ch'ü Ju-k'uei, a certified student (*sheng-yuan*) from Soochow.[35] Ch'ü went to Ricci for information about silver and quicksilver (mercury), but it is not clear if his

[30] As translated in Ibid., 41, from a letter Ricci sent to the General of the Society of Jesus, which appears in Venturi, *Opere storiche*, 2:60.
[31] As translated in Harris, "The Mission of Matteo Ricci," 43, referring to Venturi, *Opere storiche*, 2:91.
[32] As translated in Harris, "The Mission of Matteo Ricci," 44, referring to Venturi, *Opere storiche*, 2:122.
[33] Harris, "The Mission of Matteo Ricci," 86–7.
[34] D'Elia, *Fonti Ricciane*, 1:259, 312n; slightly altered from the translation in Ibid., 86.
[35] D'Elia, *Fonti Ricciane*, 1:295 n. 1.

purpose was alchemical or metallurgical. (New processes involving mercury or quicksilver for increasing the yield of silver extracted from ore had been developed in the sixteenth century and were being used with great effect in Peru and Mexico.[36] Regardless of Ch'ü's intent, Ricci thought such requests concerned making real silver (*vero argento*) from quicksilver (*argento vivo*), and the missionaries could not help.[37] Nevertheless, Ch'ü continued to associate with Ricci over a two-year period. Apparently he was the one who suggested Ricci and Almeida ought not to be (Buddhist) monks (*seng*), but should let their hair grow and be called Confucians (*ju*).[38]

For such a change, Ricci had to receive permission from Valignano, who arrived in Macao from Japan in the autumn of 1592. Another year or more passed before Lazzaro Cattaneo, a newly arrived Jesuit, pressed the question with Valignano. As Ricci later explained, up to then the missionaries had been willing to be called by what they understood to be a generic term for priests, *ho-shang*, which they romanized as *osciani*. They wore their hair cut short, shaved their beards, did not marry, performed liturgies, and stayed in religious buildings, all of which were characteristic of religious persons in Christendom and also the usual practice of *ho-shang* in China. Ricci recognized a disadvantage to the Jesuits' appearing as *ho-shang* – that is, they suffered the same disparaging treatment inflicted by officials and literati on the *ho-shang*. Valignano agreed to recommend that the Jesuits in China be allowed to let the hair grow on their head and face and to wear silk robes for visiting with important men. He also recommended that Ricci leave Shao-chou, where he was already well known as a *ho-shang*.[39] Cattaneo then went to Shao-chou in 1594 to help Ricci. (Almeida had died of fever in Macao in 1591, as did his replacement.) According to Ricci, the priests at Shao-chou slowly began to implement the change. They still wore Buddhist-style robes, but they stopped shaving. Their local friends supposedly could now converse more politely with them than with *ho-shang*. "When they went to audiences with officials, they began to act according to the etiquette of *siuzai* [i.e., *hsiu-ts'ai*, or *sheng-yuan*, first degeee holders] and *letterati*

[36] Spence, *Memory Palace*, 185–8; Harris, "The Mission of Matteo Ricci," 44, 124.

[37] D'Elia, *Fonti Ricciane*, 1:240 n. 295.

[38] According to Li Chih-tsao in his discussion of the Nestorian inscription from T'ang times. Li Chih-tsao, "Tu Ching-chiao peishu hou," 13a, in *T'ien-hsüeh ch'u han* (reprint, Taipei, 1965), 1:85. Presumably Li was told this by Ricci. Cf. Harris, "The Mission of Matteo Ricci," 87; Paul Rule, *K'ung Tzu or Confucius?* (Sydney, 1986), 18.

[39] D'Elia, *Fonti Ricciane*, 1:335–7 n. 429. Partly translated in Harris, "The Mission of Matteo Ricci," 89.

[i.e., literati], which is more ponderous than that for priests [i.e., *ho-shang*], and the officials responded in the style with which they treated *siuzai*."[40] Ricci acknowledged that in Kwang-tung the Jesuit missionaries mostly continued to be called *ho-shang*, but elsewhere they became known as what he called *predicatori letterati*, literati preachers.[41]

Ricci had learned that wearing robes like those of a Buddhist priest did not make him "more Chinese," as Ruggieri had supposed, but marked him as an outsider relative to other social groups. Priests had been assigned distinctive clothing by imperial regulations set down at the beginning of the Ming dynasty. Reclusive monks were to wear a brown robe and a jade-colored outer vestment (*chia-sha*, or *kasaya*) with a blue strip; preachers wore a jade-colored robe and a pale red outer vestment with a green strip; and teaching priests wore a black robe and a pale red outer vestment with a black strip.[42] Enforcement could not have been strict, especially away from the capital, when we consider the ease with which Jesuits and others could go about wearing such robes. (I have not found a description of the robes worn by Ricci, Cattaneo, and others before 1594.) As well as wearing different robes, Ricci later pointed out that Buddhist priests (and, for a while, Catholic priests) shaved their heads and beards, "contrary to the customs of China."[43]

Of course, the Buddhist priests were "Chinese" in an ethnic sense, but their robes and hair cuts readily distinguished them as an "other" social group. In 1588, Li Chih took off the robes to which he was entitled as a former prefect, put on a Buddhist-style robe, and shaved his head "as much to dramatize his self-imposed exile from polite society as to symbolize his [supposed] conversion to Buddhism."[44] Technically, Li Chih was never a priest. In one of his several explanations he said he had shaved his head to make manifest his decision not to return "home"; another explanation was that he was ironically fulfilling the expectation of those who were saying he was deviating from his role by following "other strands" (*yi tuan*) of thought.[45] In other words, Li Chih for his own reasons had changed robes and hair style to demonstrate he was changing roles just a few years before

[40] D'Elia, *Fonti Ricciane*, 1:338 n. 430.

[41] Ibid., 1:338 n. 431. Citing only circumstantial evidence, D'Elia proposed that the Chinese counterpart for *predicatori letterati* was *tao-jen*.

[42] *Ming-shih*, 67:1656.

[43] D'Elia, *Fonti Ricciane*, 1:125 n. 187.

[44] K.C. Hsiao, "Li Chih," in *Dictionary of Ming Biography*, 1:810.

[45] Jung Chao-tsu, *Li Chih nien-p'u* (Peking, 1957), 64–5.

Matteo Ricci made the same move, but in the opposite direction, in 1594.[46]

The next spring, Ricci left Shao-chou and traveled north into Kiangsi. At Chi-shui, in Ch-an prefecture, he called on an official who had served in Shao-chou. For the first time in public, he wore his new clothes.[47] He described his robe in a letter written later in 1595:

> The formal robe, worn by literati (*letterate*) and notables, is of dark purple silk with long, wide sleeves; the hem, which touches my feet, has a border of bright blue silk half a palm in width and the sleeves and the lapel, which drops to the waist, are trimmed in the same way . . . The Chinese wear this costume on the occasion of visits to persons with whom they are not well-acquainted, formal banquets, and when calling on officials. Since persons receiving visitors dress, in accordance with their rank, in the same way, my prestige is greatly enhanced when I go visiting.[48]

His robe was of a color permitted to commoners, and did not have the round collar more usual for an official's robe. By the end of the year, when he had established a residence at Nan-ch'ang, Ricci was also being carried in a chair and accompanied by a retinue of servants.[49] Ricci was quite explicit that he would not present himself as an official representative of a foreign power, whether the Spanish king or the pope, but as a peer to learned Chinese with cultivated relations to officials.

Later in his detached, third-person account, Ricci explained to his readers in Europe about the etiquette of clothing for formal visits to the elite of Ming society, the men who wore robes.

> Officials and degree holders when making these visits wear the clothing proper to their office and rank, which is quite different from that of commoners. Those who have neither office nor rank but are [assuming the role of ?] important personages also have a garment appropriate for visiting, still quite different from the ordinary, in which they receive as well as make visits, as even we have in this kingdom.[50]

With no apparent irony Ricci tried to illustrate the social importance of this robe.

[46] It should be noted that Li Chih said he sometimes reverted to what he called his "former clothing" (*chiu-fu*). Ibid., 65.

[47] D'Elia, *Fonti Ricciane*, 1:346–7 n. 7.

[48] Slightly altered from translation in Harris, "The Mission of Matteo Ricci," 90, referring to Venturi, *Opere storiche*, 2:199–200. See the Rubens drawing, which appears as the frontispiece and opposite p. 176 in Dunne, *Generation of Giants*, and which may depict Trigault in such robes and hat.

[49] Harris, "The Mission of Matteo Ricci," 90–1.

[50] D'Elia, *Fonti Ricciane*, 1:74 n. 125.

If two men happen to meet, one with his visiting garment and the other not, they do not perform the courtesies without the other putting on his, which is always carried by a servant when one goes away from home. When this is not possible, he who has the courtesy clothing takes it off and is in his ordinary clothes, and only then they make the courtesies of which we spoke above.[51]

Wearing his new clothes, Ricci traveled down the Kan River to Nan-ch'ang, and then down the Yangtze to Nanking, which he reached at the end of May, 1595. He called on various contacts he had made in Chao-ch'ing and Shao-chou, but within a couple of weeks he was forced to leave, although he vowed he would rather be imprisoned than leave the Southern Capital.[52] Ricci retreated to Nan-ch'ang, where after some initial tribulations he was able to reside for three years. He cultivated provincial officals and imperial princes, but mostly he engaged in extensive social and intellectual exchanges with the local literati.[53] As a direct outcome of these involvements, in 1595 Ricci wrote an essay in Chinese entitled "Yun lun" ("On Friendship"), or as he referred to it, *Amicitia* or *Amicizia*.[54] It circulated in manuscript and then in printed versions, although Ricci himself complained he could not publish it as he could not secure the requisite permission from his superiors in the Society of Jesus.[55] Similarly, in response to the admiration expressed for his powers of memorization, which he was pleased to demonstrate at gatherings of literati, he completed another small treatise in 1596 in Chinese, "*Chi fa*" ("The Art of Memory") or as he referred to it, "*Trattato della memoria locale*" (A Treatise on Compartmentalized Memory).[56] He was able to buy a house in Nan-ch'ang, but instead of having a chapel, as at Chao-ch'ing and Shao-chou, Ricci had a room or hall for discussions, or what the literati would call discourses on learning (*chiang hsüeh*).[57] In addition to going out to visit, Ricci reported he was inundated by visitors in the autumn of 1597, when thousands of literati assembled in Nan-ch'ang for the

[51] Ibid.

[52] See translation in Dunne, *Generation of Giants*, 39, referring to Venturi, *Opere storiche*, 2:201.

[53] Dunne, *Generation of Giants*, 41.

[54] A Wan-li print of the treatise bears the title *Yu lun;* it later went under the title *Chiao yu lun*.

[55] Dunne, *Generation of Giants*, 44, referring to Venturi, *Opere storiche*, 2:248.

[56] D'Elia, *Fonti Ricciane*, 1:359–60, 362–3, 376–7 nn. 469, 475, 490; Dunne, *Generation of Giants*, 40; Spence, *Memory Palace*, 135–42.

[57] Two letters written by Ricci in the autumn of 1596, in Dunne, *Generation of Giants*, 46, referring to Venturi, *Opere storiche*, 2:215, 230. See also D'Elia, *Fonti Ricciane*, 2:46 n. 536.

Kiangsi provincial examination.[58] Thus two years after he put on robes to present himself as a literatus rather than as a cleric, Ricci was demonstrating in his conversations and writings, and in his conduct and environment, that he could act as one.

Recalling this transition, Ricci wrote, "Thus, it was better now to proceed confidently as though we were in fact men of China."[59] There is perhaps an intentional ambiguity in Ricci's sentence, which was written for his European audience, but in the late Ming context it is clear that Ricci was functioning not simply as a "man of China" but as an approximation of a special group, the literati. Although not a literatus (*shih*) in the sense of one skilled enough in the written language to produce passable examination-style essays, Ricci made himself acceptable as a peer of literati roughly to the degree as were Buddhist clergy, such as Te-ch'ing (1546–1623) and Neo-Confucians such as Wang Ken (1483–1541).[60] In 1595 he embarked on his new role as a literatus or even Confucian from the West (*hsi ju*). He wrote books. One he was drafting in these years, which was first printed in 1603 as the *True Meaning of the Lord of Heaven (T'ien chu shih yi)*, was structured as a dialogue between a Chinese literatus (*chung shih*) and a literatus from the West (*hsi shih*), referring to Ricci himself. That was the role, and robe, he had adopted.

Ricci was persuaded by his friends that it was not practicable to try to reach Peking as part of an embassy from a king or pope, but he still had Peking as his goal. He had raised the possibility that one of the princes at Nan-ch'ang might make arrangements for him,[61] but a real opportunity presented itself when Cattaneo arrived from Shao-chou with the news that Wang Hung-hui (1542–1601?) was coming to see him in a few days. Wang, a 1565 *chin-shih* from Kwang-tung, had passed through Shao-chou a few years earlier on his way home after retiring as Minister (*Shang-shu*) of the Nanking Ministry of Rites. In his conversations with Ricci, Wang raised the idea that Ricci might be able to contribute to the current discussions on the reform of the Ming calendar, which was under the supervision of the Ministry of Rites.[62] Now, in 1598, as Wang was traveling north in hopes of again receiving

[58] Dunne, *Generation of Giants*, referring to Venturi, *Opere storiche*, 2:242.

[59] D'Elia, *Fonti Ricciane*, 1:378 n. 491. Altered from translation in Harris, "The Mission of Matteo Ricci," 70.

[60] On Te-ch'ing, see Pei-yi Wu, *The Confucian's Progress: Autobiographical Writings in Traditional China* (Princeton, 1990), 142–59.

[61] D'Elia, *Fonti Ricciane*, 2:6–7 n. 503.

[62] The discussions were precipitated by a long memorial in 1596 proposing calendar reform. See Willard J. Peterson, "Calendar Reform Prior to the Arrival of Missionaries at the Ming Court," *Ming Studies* 21 (1986), 49–55.

an appointment to office, he stopped at Shao-chou to offer to take Ricci with him. Thus in June, Ricci and Cattaneo, accompanied by two Chinese Brothers (*Fratelli*), Chung Ming-jen and Yu Wen-hui, embarked from Nan-ch'ang in the entourage of Wang Hung-hui. Wang was going to Nanking and then on to Peking to take part in the birthday congratulations for the emperor in the eighth lunar month.[63]

Ricci's first trip to Peking did not go well. Wang went north from Nanking separately from Ricci's group. Once in the capital, Ricci found no way to present the gifts he had brought for the emperor, and his contacts all seemed wary of him. Ricci retreated south, first to Soochow, where Ch'ü Ju-k'uei cared for him while he was ill, and then in the spring of 1599 to Nanking. With Wang Hung-hui's encouragement, he managed to buy a house there, and pursued the activities that had made him an attractive figure in Nan-ch'ang: interviews with the curious and influential, displays of his clocks, prisms, musical instruments, maps, pictures, and other exotic items, and discussions of his ideas. In the spring of 1600 he set out again for Peking, accompanied by Chung Ming-jen, Yu Wen-hui (who was skilled in Western-style painting), and the Jesuit Diego de Pantoja (who knew how to tune, play, and teach the clavichord, which was being presented among the gifts intended for the emperor).[64] After various difficulties, attendant especially on the ambiguities over whether his was an embassy bearing tribute to the court, and, if not, how he and the gifts were to be handled, Ricci, by the beginning of 1601, was ensconced at the capital for the remainder of his life.

As a literatus in Peking, Ricci was an enormous success. There was a constant flow of visitors to the Jesuits' residence, many of which Ricci had to repay. As Ricci acknowledged, he was a beneficiary of the large numbers of literati and officials who came to Peking each year for examinations or government matters.

> Among the thousands who thus flock here from all fifteen provinces, there are many who either already know the Fathers in Peking or in other residences, or who have heard of us and our teachings, or have seen the books which we have published or which speak of us. As a consequence, we have to spend the entire day in the reception hall to receive visitors. . . . To all of them we speak of the things pertaining to our holy faith.[65]

[63] D'Elia, *Fonti Ricciane,* 2:8–10 nn. 504–6. See also Dunne, *Generation of Giants,* 50.

[64] Harris, "The Mission of Matteo Ricci," 14; Dunne, *Generation of Giants,* 53–60, 69–71. For a discussion of gifts, see Spence, *Memory Palace,* 194–5, and the lists in D'Elia, *Fonti Ricciane,* 2:123–4.

[65] Harris, "The Mission of Matteo Ricci," 2:353–4 n. 769, altered from translation in Dunne, *Generation of Giants,* 92.

Most callers were merely curious, but with some Ricci also was able to maintain serious intellectual relationships that lasted for years, and a few of those cases included their conversion to his "holy faith."

To be a literatus was not simply a matter of changing clothes. Ricci had committed himself to a mode of living that may or may not have been detrimental to the Christianizing mission that was the purpose of his being in China. The tactic of being more Chinese, initiated by Valignano, had no necessary stopping point. Learning to speak Chinese led to reading, which led to writing. Writing Chinese entailed using Chinese vocabulary to express non-Chinese concepts, and losing important distinctions in the translation. The boundary shifted. For example, after Ricci's death the written version of the Latin formula used at baptism began to be translated rather than just transliterated.[66] For his part, Ricci was confident he was drawing his hosts' ideas closer to his own. "I make every effort to turn our way the ideas of the leader of the literati sect, that is Confucius, by interpreting any ambiguities in his writing in our favor."[67] However, describing the Chinese literati's rather than reflecting on his own experience, Ricci observed, "This doctrine [of the literati] is not acquired by choice, but is imbibed with the study of literature, and neither degree holder nor official leaves off professing it."[68] To some extent, then, by learning to read and write in Chinese, Ricci and the other missionaries were indoctrinating themselves as they prepared to disseminate the Learning from Heaven (*T'ien hsüeh*) they had brought with them. This tension between what was Western and what was Chinese, between the imported and the indigenous, and how much compromise was permissible, was at the core of the debates among missionaries as well as among Catholics back in Europe over the policy of accommodation, over decisions of whether and how to translate key terms, and over the status of rituals that might continue to be performed by converts or adapted by missionaries.[69] From the way he conducted himself after 1595, it seems clear that Ricci had decided acting as a literatus did not jeopardize his Christian mission even as it diminished his foreignness.

From Ricci's perspective, he was talking and writing about and for "our holy faith." He used ancillary parts of his cultural baggage the

[66] Harris, "The Mission of Matteo Ricci," 146; D'Elia, *Fonti Ricciane*, 1:370.

[67] D'Elia, *Fonti Ricciane*, 2:296 n. 709. Also translated in Rule, *K'ung Tzu or Confucius?*, 1.

[68] D'Elia, *Fonti Ricciane*, 1:115 n. 176. Partly translated in Harris, "The Mission of Matteo Ricci," 112–13. "Questa legge pigliano loro non per elettione, ma con lo studio delle lettere la bevono, e nessuno graduato né magistrato lascia di professarla."

[69] Dunne, *Generation of Giants*, 227–30. The debates are considered in Rule, *K'ung Tzu or Confucius?*, 43–50, 70–149.

way he used curious non-religious objects, such as clocks and prisms, and curiosity about himself to attract and hold men long enough for God to "soften their hearts."[70] Ricci knew he was leading them to the Gospel, but it was not his starting point, either in his discussions or in his writings. The bulk of his literati audience probably never had access to the central doctrines of his holy faith. Leaving aside the relatively few who were baptized, most literati whose acquaintance with Ricci and his writings passed beyond satisfaction of their curiosity were confronted with a range of ideas that went by the broad but distinguishing label of the Learning from Heaven (*T'ien hsüeh*). While he was alive, and even after he died in 1610, Ricci and his writings were treated as a novel part of the literati intellectual milieu.

Much of Ricci's vocabulary and some of his ideas were shared by all literati, but part of the attraction was that some of the vocabulary and many of his ideas were new or strange or odd or, finally, foreign. There was a continuum. For example, Ricci introduced his collection of a hundred items on friendship with a perfectly apt allusion to *Analects* 16.8: He had traveled by sea from far to the west in order to show his respect for the cultural power (*wen te*) of the Son of Heaven of the great Ming.[71] Ricci demonstrated expectable willingness to be patronized when he explained the impetus for his compilation came at a banquet in Nan-ch'ang where a prince took his hand and asked to hear of the way of friendship in his Western country.[72] Once the manuscript was circulating, his readers could not have been surprised by such observations as that one should be circumspect in making friends and steadfast in keeping them, or that merchants in pursuit of profits could not truly be friends. The idea, and ideal, of friendship or fellowship (*yu*) had been discussed among literati, especially those involved in discourses learning, for several decades, so Ricci's contribution could be assimilated to that debate. His readers would notice that some of Ricci's examples named some hitherto unknown countries and persons as explicitly Western. (This was inevitable as Ricci drew the mostly aphoristic comments of ancient authors from an anthology of friends compiled by André de Resende, 1498–1573.[73]) Most

[70] Dunne, *Generation of Giants*, 91, referring to Venturi, *Opere storiche*, 2:376: "ammollira i loro cuori."

[71] Matteo Ricci, "Chiao yu lun," la, in *T'ien hsüeh ch'u han*, 299. The passage is also translated in Fang Hao, "Notes on Matteo Ricci's *De Amicitia*," *Monumenta Serica* 14 (1949–55), 574.

[72] Ricci, "Chiao yu lun," 1b, 300.

[73] Spence, *Memory Palace*, 142, 150. Spence infers that Ricci dredged the examples from what he remembered of de Resende's book. Cf. Pasquale D'Elia, "Further Notes on Matteo Ricci's *De Amicitia*," *Monumenta Serica* 15 (1956), 366.

literati would have paused at reading that friends come in pairs just as "The divinity on high (*shang ti*) gave humans two eyes, ears, hands and feet. . . ."[74] They would not have previously seen the classical term *shang ti* in such a sentence, and Ricci's book on friendship did not explain how he meant it. Similarly, his treatise on the art of memory, which describes techniques for mnemonic associations and for placing and finding images, particularly Chinese written words,[75] includes many unknown Western names in passing, and it begins with the propositions, "The spiritual soul bestowed on humans by the lord, maker of things (*tsao wu chu*), is the most intellective compared to the other ten thousand things."[76] Thus in his writings that he began to circulate in the mid-1590s and that have a strong humanistic rather than religious orientation, Ricci interjected new names as well as a new, central concept he hoped to disseminate in China, the Christian idea of a supreme deity.

The story of Ricci's changing clothes – from student clothes in Rome to a clerical habit of Christian Europe[77] to a Buddhist-type robe in Kwang-tung to the formal dress of one claiming proximate status to Confucian literati and officials of the Ming dynasty – is usually taken to illustrate the accommodative strategy adopted by Jesuit missionaries in China in the sixteenth century. On a more general level, it also seems to show that an "outsider" might move from being an observer to being more of a participant in his hosts' community, regardless of where he starts on some imaginary axis between the stranded victim of a shipwreck and the immigrant eager to be assimilated, with tourists, *conquistadores*, merchants, missionaries, and ethnographers arrayed between the poles. Adopting "others' " clothing may be an obvious indicator of such a move, but language acquisition, food acceptance, use of categories of thought, so-called bad habits, and other criteria also would serve as indicators of penetration of a boundary separating "them" from "us" even as the outsider might be seen to end up less like his "us" than before. Understanding and participating are interactive, as Ricci's case shows, but as one becomes an insider he must yield in detachment.

[74] Ricci, "Chiao yu lun," 6a, 309. In a note Ricci observed that in the seal style of writing, both words for friend, *p'eng* and *yu*, involve a pair of images.

[75] Spence, *Memory Palace*, is constructed on the basis of Ricci's second section, which explains how to use the technique. See Ricci, "Chi fa," 4b–5b, reprinted in *T'ien-chu chiao tung ch'uan wenhsien* (Taipei, 1965), 16–18.

[76] Ricci, "Chi fa," la, 9.

[77] The regulations of the Society of Jesus did not specify a particular costume, at least in the sixteenth century. "Jesuits wore whatever was available." Lynn Martin, *The Jesuit Mind: The Mentality of an Elite in Early Modern France* (Ithaca, 1988), 147.

Ricci's case should also teach us to be wary of such simple dichotomies as "European and foreign" and "Chinese and foreign." Ricci's reports sent back to Europe make clear that in late Ming society there were several status groups – all Chinese to be sure – and that to some extent one could join one or another grouping by adopting its "robe" and otherwise acting in accord with its particular "role." On nearly every page of his account Ricci implicitly revealed he had been adopting literati values and view points. Even today his readers are misled if they infer that "this culture of ours" (*ssu wen*), which characterized the literati, is identical with "Chinese culture."

CHAPTER 15

Demerits and deadly sins: Jesuit moral tracts in late Ming China

ANN WALTNER

Those of their country who came to the East were for the most part men of intelligence and uncommon capacity. Their only purpose was to preach religion, with no desire for honors or gain. The books they wrote contained much that Chinese people had never before encountered. For this reason, those who were given to novelties were greatly attracted to them.[1]

Thus the imperially sponsored history of the Ming dynasty, the *Ming-shih,* compiled in the latter part of the seventeenth century, described the missionary enterprise with bemusement and admiration.[2] The analysis of the compilers of the dynastic history, written nearly a century after Matteo Ricci (1552–1610) first set foot on Chinese soil, is prefigured by the famous comment made by the iconoclastic thinker Li Chih (1527–1602), a man himself rather given to novelties. Li, who had actually made the acquaintance of Ricci, wrote:

Now he is perfectly capable of speaking our language, writing our characters and conducting himself in accord with our etiquette and ceremonial (*i-li*). He is an altogether remarkable man . . . But I do not know why he has come here. I have now met with him three times, and I still do not know what he is doing here. I considered that he wanted to take his learning to transform our

[1] *Ming-shih* (Peking: Chung-hua shu-chü), *chüan* 326, 28:8461. My translation is modified from that of Albert Chan, "Late Ming Society and the Jesuit Missionaries," in Charles E. Ronan and Bonnie Oh, eds., *East Meets West: The Jesuits in China 1582–1773* (Chicago, 1988), 159.

[2] The first time I mention a Chinese text, I give its title in the original, followed by a translated title. I subsequently refer to it by its translated title. The letters "cs," which are frequently given after a man's dates, refer to the date he received the *chin-shih* degree, the highest degree offered by the civil-service examination system. I would like to thank Peter Ditmanson, Hsu Pi-ching, Wang Yuh-shiow, Lisa Irving, Allyson Poska and Jiang Yonglin for their help.

teachings of the Duke of Chou[3] and Confucius. But that would be too foolish – that surely can't be it![4]

Thus both the iconoclast and the officially sanctioned history agree: There is much to admire in these men from the West. But their enterprise, and they themselves, remain something of a mystery.

The Jesuits may have been unlike any foreigners the Chinese had ever encountered, but they were by no means China's first foreigners. Not only had China had extensive (and often catastrophic) contact with her neighbors to the north, but in the early fifteenth century, Chinese fleets under the command of Cheng Ho traveled as far as the east coast of Africa. Dynastic histories routinely contained sections about life in foreign lands. Nor were the Jesuits the first missionaries to come to China to preach a religion of salvation. Buddhist missionaries had come from India more than a millennium earlier, with considerably more success than their Jesuit counterparts. But the Jesuit encounter with late Ming literati did represent a new kind of encounter. It was an encounter between two great civilizations, which had developed more or less independently of one another. It provides an occasion to look at the question that animates this volume: In what ways might initial contacts between civilizations prompt the parties to the encounter to a reevaluation of the meaning of their own civilization as well as an interpretation of the other?

The Ming encounter between Jesuits and literati is amply documented.[5] In this chapter I will discuss a very small part of the story of the Jesuit enterprise in China, centering on the work of one man, the Spanish Jesuit Diego de Pantoja (1571–1618), and contemporary Chinese responses to that work. Pantoja wrote in European languages about China for a European audience, and in Chinese about European religion and science for a Chinese audience. Among his writing is a

[3] A culture hero from the days of high antiquity.

[4] Li Chih, *Hsü Fen-shu* (Peking, 1961), 36. My translation is modified from that of Jacques Gernet, *China and the Christian Impact: A Conflict of Cultures* (New York, 1985), 18–19.

[5] The literature on the Jesuit enterprise in China is voluminous. There is a splendid and growing literature on the Chinese response to the missionary efforts. In addition to works cited elsewhere in these notes, I would like to draw particular attention to two articles by Erik Zürcher, "The Lord of Heaven and the Demons: Strange Stories from a Late Ming Christian Manuscript," in Gert Naundorf, Karl-Heinz Pohl, and Hans-Hermann Schmidt, eds., *Religion und Philosophie in Ostasien: Festschrift für Hans Steininger* (Würzburg, 1985), 359–75, and "The Jesuit Mission in Fujian in Late Ming Times: Levels of Response," in E.B. Vermeer, ed., *Development and Decline of Fukien Province in the Seventeenth and Eighteenth Centuries* (Leiden, 1990), 417–57.

tract in Chinese on the seven deadly sins, the *Ch'i k'o* (Seven Victories). The *Seven Victories* was written with the assistance of Yang T'ing-yün (1557–1627, cs 1592), a noted literatus. During the early seventeenth century, a number of Chinese authors graced various editions of the text with prefaces and colophons. The *Seven Victories* provides us with some indication of how Pantoja sought to present Christian morality to the Chinese; the prefaces provide some measure of how the text and its author were received by their Chinese audience. I will suggest that the *Seven Victories* was assimilated by its audience to a genre of morality books current in late Ming China, and that some of the strongest proponents of the text perceived its utility as separable from its Christian context.

Diego de Pantoja was born in 1571 in Valdemoro, near Seville. He joined the Jesuit order in 1589. He arrived in Macao in 1597 and in Peking in 1601. Pantoja was one of the Jesuits commissioned in 1611 by the Board of Rites to translate Western astronomical texts into Chinese.[6] This commission was short-lived, but the practice of Jesuits working under the auspices of the Board of Rites is one that would cause continued controversy. The 1617 decree banishing Jesuits from China mentioned Pantoja by name. He fled to Macao, where he died within the year.[7]

Shortly after Pantoja's arrival in Peking, he wrote a long letter to Louis Guzman, the provincial at Toledo, which was subsequently published as *Relacion de la entrada de algunos padres de la companie de iesus en la China.* The text was first published in Valladolid in 1604, and subsequently appeared in numerous editions in French, Italian, German and Latin, as well as Spanish. By 1608, it had been published in ten editions in five languages.[8] Pantoja's letter, published a full

[6] See the discussion in *Ming-shih, chüan* 326, 8:8460.

[7] On Pantoja, see the article by George H. Dunne in the *Dictionary of Ming Biography*, ed. L. Carrington Goodrich and Chaoyang Fang (New York, 1976), 2:1116–17. See also the entry in Aloys Pfister, *Notices biographiques et bibliographiques de l'ancienne mission de Chine, 1552–1773*, vols. 59 and 60 in the series *Variétés Sinologiques* (Shanghai, 1932–34), 59:69–73. On the banishment of the Jesuits, see Edward Thomas Kelly, "The Anti-Christian Persecution of 1616–1617 in Nanking" (Ph.D. diss., Columbia University, 1971). The banishment of 1617 was short-lived.

[8] Jesuit letters were long and comprehensive documents, that could easily number hundreds of pages. Diego de Pantoja, *Relacion de la entrada de algunos padres de la compañia de Iesus en la China* (Valencia: Juan Chrysostomo Garris, 1606). A copy is held at the James Ford Bell Library at the University of Minnesota. Information about the edition published in Seville in 1605 is provided by a handwritten note in the volume, and is corroborated by Pfister. The Italian translation is entitled *Relatione dell'entrata d'alcuni padri della compagnie di giesu nella Chine* (Rome, 1607). A copy of this volume is also held at the Bell Library. Pfister lists the edition published in Valladolid in 1604, as well as French translations in Arras and Lyon (1607), and Rouen (1608). A Latin

decade before Trigault's recension of Ricci's journals, is an important early document in the history of the formation of European perceptions of China.

Pantoja finds much to admire in China, though his admiration is tinged with condescension. Chinese philosophers remind him of Plato and Seneca, though he writes the Chinese philosophers "write grand sentences, but are not as good as ours."[9] He is impressed by the education system, and discusses ways in which it differs from the European system.[10] He is alert to distinctions of class and gender. He comments on three social classes: "mandarines," "gente grave," and "gente baxa." He notes that there is a high degree of social mobility among the various social groupings, saying that many officials came from ordinary families.[11] He comments that although most of the women one encounters on the street are from the lower classes, they seem honest and well-mannered. He also notes that Chinese women and men of the lower classes dressed like European men. (Chinese men of the upper classes wore gowns. Presumably he is referring to the tunic and trousers worn by peasants.[12]) He further comments on the tiny feet of Chinese women, and tells his European audience that he has not been able to find a Chinese man who could explain to him why tiny feet were thought to be a necessary attribute of a beautiful woman. He adds that while some Chinese men told him that tiny feet made women beautiful, others told him that the advantage of footbinding is that it made it more difficult for women to leave the house.[13] It is a conversation one can scarcely imagine: a celibate foreigner interrogating Chinese men about tiny feet, a subject so erotically charged that it is hard to find non-pornographic discussions of it.

Pantoja is centrally interested in the religion of China, but his accounting of religion is somewhat perplexed. He refers to the Chinese as atheists (Atheos), and amplifies upon this by saying that they believe in no god, true or false. Nor do they believe in an afterlife, a paradise, or a hell.[14] Elsewhere he says that an aversion to matters of morality and salvation is the second great impediment to converting the Chinese. (The first great impediment is their disdain for things

translation was published in Mayence in 1607 and a German edition in Munich in 1608. See Pfister, *Notices Bibliographiques*, 59:73.

[9] Pantoja, *Relacion*, 132.

[10] Ibid., 125–9.

[11] Ibid., 136.

[12] Ibid., 161.

[13] Ibid.

[14] Ibid., 67–8.

foreign.[15]) But he describes in great detail a funeral, which clearly demonstrates Chinese belief in a spirit world.[16] He discusses Chinese "idols," but says that the people do not believe in them: They reverence them but do not adore them as they would a god.[17] He notes the omnipresence of fortune tellers, and wonders at the fact that in spite of their "good understanding," the Chinese are duped by charlatans.[18]

A particular form of charlatanry which attracts Pantoja's scorn is the search for immortality (or, failing that, long life). He says that "a thousand inventions" and many drugs are expended in the quest for long life. There are people who feign advanced age, in order to advertise the success of their longevity devices and immortality potions. (The paired quests for longevity and immortality are in fact a major aspect of popular Taoism in the late Ming.[19]) Pantoja notes that the Chinese believed the Jesuits to be very old, and refused to believe them when they insisted they were not. (Pantoja was himself thirty-one when he wrote this letter.) Indeed, the Jesuit practice of celibacy was interpreted as but a step in their attainment of long life. Other powers were ascribed to these strange men from the western seas. Pantoja tells us that people believed that the Jesuits were alchemists who could make silver.[20]

Pantoja had been in China about a year when he wrote this remarkable letter. Much of what he wrote was doubtless based on first-hand observation. Many of his observations ring true: Social mobility in Ming China was relatively high, and the practice of female seclusion among the upper classes would have meant that most of the women he encountered on the street were of the lower classes. But much else was probably filtered through the eyes of his Chinese literati friends. It could well be that his equivocal position on "idols" is derived from literati disdain for popular religion.

Some of his observations are simply false: Chinese conceptions of hells and the afterlife were in fact quite wonderfully elaborate.[21] His confusion about Chinese religion is honestly come by: Chinese religion

[15] Ibid., 66.
[16] Ibid., 113–18.
[17] Ibid., 117.
[18] Ibid., 118–19.
[19] See Ann Waltner, "T'an-yang-tzu and Wang Shih-chen: Visionary and Bureaucrat in the Late Ming," *Late Imperial China* 8, no. 1 (June, 1987): 105–133.
[20] Pantoja, *Relación*, 119–20.
[21] The literature on this is very rich. See, for example, Steven Teiser, " 'Having Once Died and Returned to Life': Representations of Hell in Medieval China," *Harvard Journal of Asiatic Studies* 48, no. 2 (1988): 433–464; Michael Loewe, *Ways to Paradise: The Chinese Quest for Immortality* (London, 1979).

was very different from Christianity. The religious scene in the late Ming was particularly complex. Monks like Chu-hung (1535–1615) and Han-shan Te-ch'ing (1566–1623) led a revival of interest in Buddhism.[22] The predominantly Taoist cult of the young woman T'an-yang-tzu (1577–1580) attracted many literati.[23] Lin Chao-en (1517–1598) preached the unity of the three teachings of Buddhism, Taoism, and Confucianism.[24] And Confucian philosophers themselves, especially the followers of Wang Yang-ming, showed a marked interest in mystical experience. Sectarian religions gained new vitality; indeed, the most important deity of sectarian religion, the Wu-sheng lao-mu, the Venerable Eternal Mother, appears for the first time during the late Ming.[25] The attempt to classify various Chinese practices, and to determine whether or not they constituted religion in Christian terms, was to be a major problem in Jesuit relations with the Chinese for years to come.[26]

Diego de Pantoja wrote several texts in Chinese. Aloys Pfister lists several other religious texts from his hand: *Jen-lei yüan-shih* (The Origins of the Human Race); *T'ien-shen mo-kuei shuo* (Treatise on Angels and Demons); *Shou-nan shih-wei* (Complete Story of the Passion of Christ) *P'ang-tsu i-ch'üan* (Pantoja's Explanations); *Shih-i hsü-pien* (Appendix to the *True Meaning*[27]) and *Pien-chieh* (Refutations).[28]

The "I-wen chih" (Bibliography Section) of the *Ming Dynastic History* lists Pantoja as the author of a text entitled *Hai-wai yü-t'u ch'üan-shuo* (A Complete Examination of the Geography of Lands Beyond the

22 On Chu-hung, see Yu Chun-fang, *The Renewal of Buddhism in China: Chu-hung and the Late Ming Synthesis* (New York, 1981). On Han-shan Te-ch'ing, see Hsu Sung-pen, *A Buddhist Leader in Ming China: The Life and Thought of Han-shan Te-ch'ing* (University Park, Penn., 1979).

23 Ann Waltner, "T'an-yang-tzu and Wang Shih-chen"; idem, "Learning from a Woman: Ming Literati Responses to T'an-yang-tzu," *International Journal of Social Education* 6, no. 1 (1991):42–59.

24 See Judith Berling, *The Syncretic Religion of Lin Chao-en* (New York, 1980).

25 On sectarian religion see Daniel Overmyer, *Folk Buddhist Religion* (Cambridge, Mass., 1976); Richared Shek, "Religion and Society in Late Ming: Sectarianism and Popular Thought in Sixteenth and Seventeenth Century China" (Ph.D. diss., University of California, Berkeley, 1980); idem, "Eternal Mother Religion: Its Role in Late Imperial Chinese History" (Paper presented at the Second International Conference on Sinology, Academia Sinica, Taipei, December, 1986).

26 The chief issues in the Rites Controversy centered around ancestor worship and the sacrifices to Confucius. If it could be demonstrated that these practices were signs of respect, then there was no impediment to a Chinese Christian participating in them. For a convenient summary of the Rites Controversy, see George Minamiki, *The Chinese Rites Controversy from its Beginning to Modern Times* (Chicago, 1985).

27 This is a reference to Matteo Ricci's *T'ien-chu shih-i* (The True Meaning of the Lord of Heaven).

28 Pfister, *Notices bibliographiques*, 72–3.

Seas).[29] There is some indication that Pantoja was involved with the production of the *Chih-fang wai-chi*, a crucial geography text introducing Western lands to Chinese audiences.[30] An early twentieth-century catalog lists Pantoja as the author of a work on astronomy, the *T'ien-wen lüeh* (Outline of Astronomy). Yang T'ing-yün, his collaborator on *Seven Victories*, also participated in the production of the *Outline of Astronomy*.[31] Thus Pantoja's writings span a range of Jesuit interests in late Ming China. Geography and astronomy were two of the aspects of Western learning that held the most appeal to Chinese literati in the late Ming and Pantoja was happy to oblige.

The first edition of *Seven Victories* was published three years after Pantoja arrived in China. He does not claim to have written it alone. The *Relacion* talks about the difficulties of learning Chinese (because of the lack of, as Pantoja puts it, "ordinary letters"), and in the preface to *Seven Victories* he talks about his own struggle to learn the language.[32] He was ably assisted in the production of the *Seven Victories* by Yang T'ing-yün.[33]

Prior to his conversion to Christianity, Yang T'ing-yün had been a noted lay Buddhist. Yang had been drawn to Christianity years before he could be baptized: The impediment was his concubine. A Jesuit biography of Yang reports on a conversation he had with the recently monogamous Li Chih-tsao: "The western fathers are really strange ... Can they not allow me to have just one concubine?" Li (whose own monogamy was precipitated by his conversion) explains to Yang that "the commandments of the west were promulgated by God and observed by the saints of former times. To observe them is virtue. Go against them and you will be punished." Yang is convinced, sets his concubine up in a separate residence and is baptized in 1611.[34]

Yang T'ing-yün's writings also indicate intimacy with the Confucian

[29] *Ming-shih, chüan* 99, 8:2405.

[30] The biography of Li Chih-tsao written by Paul Yap Teh-lu and J.C. Yang says that Pantoja began the *Chih-fang wai-chi* and Aleni finished it. *Eminent Chinese of the Ch'ing Period*, ed. Arthur W. Hummel (Washington, 1943–44; reprint, Taipei, 1964), 453.

[31] M. Courant, *Catalog des Livres Chinois, Coreéns, Japonais, etc.*, (Paris, 1912), 4904.

[32] Pantoja, *Relacion*, 134. Hsü Tsung-tse, *Ming Ch'ing chien Yeh-su-hui shih-chu t'i-yao* (Taipei, 1957), 55. *Ch'i k'o*, in Li Chih-tsao ed., *T'ien-hsüeh ch'u-han* (Taipei, 1965), 713.

[33] Jacques Gernet at one point says that the *Seven Victories* was written by Pantoja in collaboration with Hsü Kuang-ch'i (*China and the Christian Impact*, 142). At another point he says that the text is by Sabatino de Ursis (Ibid., 20). He gives no source for either attribution, and I have seen neither Hsü's nor Sabatino's name associated with the text elsewhere.

[34] *Yang Ch'i-yüan hsien-sheng shih-chi*, 4a–5a. Cited and translated in N. Standaert, *Yang Tingyun, Confucian and Christian in Late Ming China: His Life and Thought* (Leiden, 1988), 54.

classics, notably the *I-ching* (Book of Changes). The only mention Yang receives in the *Ming Dynastic History* is in the "Bibliography" section, as the author of a work on the *I-ching* (Book of Changes), entitled *I-hsien* (The Book of Changes Made Apparent).[35] He wrote several other texts on the *Book of Changes*.[36] Nor was *Seven Victories* his only Christian tract. He was apparently the author of a text entitled *Hsi-hsüeh shih-chieh chu-chieh* (An Explanation with Commentary of the Ten Commandments of Western Studies) which is no longer extant.[37] Yang T'ing-yün participated in the production of at least three moral texts in addition to the *Seven Victories*, which we shall discuss in detail below.

One of the main characteristics of Chinese religion and thought in the sixteenth and seventeenth century was the proliferation of morality books. The late sixteenth and early seventeenth century were times of great change in China: There was an increase in urbanization and in commercialization, and many contemporaries perceived traditional society to be in a state of crisis. Late Ming literati such as Yüan Huang (1533–1603) responded to the crisis by writing and circulating a genre of morality books known as *kung-kuo-ke*, ledgers of merit and demerit.[38] Other genres of what we might regard as moral tracts, such as family instructions and ritual handbooks, retained their popularity.

Yang T'ing-yün was deeply involved in the production of texts offering moral guidance. The first of the morality books Yang assisted with was the *Yang-shih shu-hsün* (Instructions from Yang's Family School), a book of family instructions compiled by his father, Yang Chao-fang. Yang T'ing-yün and his brother Yang T'ing-ts'e collated the work and Yang T'ing-yün extolled the work in a preface.[39]

A second text Yang published was the *Su-shih chia-yü* (Family Sayings of Mr. Su) compiled by Su Shih-chien, the father of the noted legal scholar Su Mao-hsiang (1567–1630, cs 1592). (The younger Su, it should be noted, received his *chin-shih* degree the same year as did

[35] *Ming-shih, chüan* 96, 8:2349.

[36] For example, the *Wan I wei-yen chai-ch'ao* (Excerpts of Subtle Words Examining the Book of Changes) and *I-tsung* (Summary of the Book of Changes). See the listings and brief descriptions in N. Standaert, *Yang Tingyun, Confucian and Christian in Late Ming China; His Life and Thought* (Leiden and New York, 1988), 17–18.

[37] Gernet, *China and the Christian Impact*, 255, n. 78, citing Fang Hao, *Chung-kuo t'ien-chu-chiao shih jen-wu chuan*, 2 vols. (Hong Kong, 1970). 1:138.

[38] Cynthia Brokaw, *The Ledgers of Merit and Demerit: Social Change and Moral Order in Late Imperial China* (Princeton, 1991); idem, "Yüan Huang (1533–1603) and the Ledgers of Merit and Demerit," *Harvard Journal of Asiatic Studies* 47, no. 1 (June 1987):137–95.

[39] A copy of this work exists at the Naikaku Bunko. Discussed in Standaert, *Yang Tingyun*, 43–5.

Yang T'ing-yün.[40]) The text is a collection of anecdotes about historical personages who behaved in exemplary fashion. Virtually all of the stories are set in the distant historical past, and many of the stories are quite well known. One is not told how one should act: One is merely shown how exemplary people of the past behaved. The reader makes his (or her) own conclusions. (Women were a part of the intended audience for Ming moral texts, and at least a third of this text deals with female behavior.[41]) The text is organized by relationships. It begins with the relationship between grandparent and grandchildren. Then we are given exemplary fathers, mothers, and stepmothers.[42] Then follows a section on serving one's father, followed by four sections that detail how one might serve one's mother or stepmother.[43]

Yang T'ing-yün also edited and published an edition of the *Chu-tzu chia-li* (Chu Hsi's Family Rituals). The version published by Yang was that edited by Ch'iu Chün (1420–1495) a century earlier. It is hard to overestimate the significance of this text.[44] The Ming dynastic history recognized the *Family Rituals* as one of the most authoritative references for the conduct of funerals for officials.[45] The *Family Rituals* was included in the *Hsing-li ta-ch'üan* (1415), a standard text studied by candidates for the civil service examinations.[46] And the *Family Rituals* had a special importance during the late Ming: Timothy Brook has argued that more editions of the *Family Rituals* were published during the Wan-li era (1573–1620) than at any time before or since,[47] and

[40] Having passed the *chin-shih* examination in the same year created a profound bond among men in traditional China.

[41] The text as preserved in the *Shuo-fu* (*hsü fu*, 29) is brief. I have not yet seen other editions.

[42] The text deals with two categories subsumed under the English word stepmother: *chi-mu*, a woman one's father marries after his marriage with one's mother has ended [by death, or, less frequently, by divorce] and *t'i mu*, a term used by the children of a concubine to refer to their father's principal wife.

[43] In addition to the *chi-mu* and *t'i-mu* we discussed (see n.42), this section discusses a *shu-mu* (a mother who is a concubine) and a *sheng-mu* (one's biological mother).

[44] See the translation of the *Chu-tzu chia-li* by Patricia Ebrey, *Chu Hsi's Family Rituals: A Twelfth-Century Chinese Manual for the Performance of Cappings, Weddings, Funerals and Ancestral Rites* (Princeton, 1991.) On the *Chu-tzu chia-li*, see Patricia Ebrey, "Education through Ritual: Efforts to Formulate Family Rituals through the Sung Period" in *Neo-Confucian Education: The Formative Stage*, ed. John Chaffee and W. Theodore de Bary (Berkeley and Los Angeles, 1989). See also Kao Ming, "Chu Hsi's Discipline of Propriety" in *Chu Hsi and Neo-Confucianism*, ed. Wing-tsit Chan (Honolulu, 1986), especially 312–36. See also the discussion in Timothy Brook, "Funerary Ritual and the Building of Lineages in Late Imperial China," *Harvard Journal of Asiatic Studies* 49, no. 2 (December, 1989):465–99. The edition of the text that I have used was published in eight *chüan* by the Tz'u-yang shu-yüan with a preface dated 1701.

[45] *Ming-shih*, *chüan* 60, 5:14900. Discussed by Brook, "Funerary Ritual," 475–6.

[46] Ibid., 476.

[47] Ibid., 477, citing, among other things, the *Ssu-k'u ch'üan-shu tsung-mu* 25/33a–38b.

Patricia Ebrey has suggested ways in which late Ming editors adapted the text to fit the predilections of their audiences.[48]

The structure of the *Family Rituals* differs markedly from the *Family Sayings of Mr. Su.* While the former text is anecdotal and provides models to emulate, the latter takes the view that proper moral behavior can be elicited through ritual. Yang's preface to the *Family Rituals* encourages people to follow the rites so that "gentlemen would not become ordinary people and ordinary people would not become strange beings."[49] Thus it is clear that Yang T'ing-yün is committed to the notion that human behavior can be reformed through textual exhortation. His work on the *Seven Victories* may be seen as a part of this larger project.

The Chinese predilection for morality texts did not go unremarked. In his *Relacion,* Pantoja notes several times how attached the Chinese literati are to their books. Indeed, at one point he says, "They resemble atheists. They have no gods they believe in, they only have their books."[50] Elsewhere he points out how Chinese learning concerns itself with moral tracts and government.[51] Pantoja's decision to write a moral tract seems to be a calculated one: He chooses to write in a genre he knows to be current in the late-Ming Chinese context. The European conceit of the seven deadly sins is admirably suited to a Chinese context. The *Seven Victories* appeared in time of social crisis, when Chinese literati themselves were addressing that crisis through the widespread production and distribution of morality books.

The *Seven Victories* is a ponderous text, numbering some 400 pages. Indeed, as we shall see, some of its Chinese critics deemed it verbose. It was first published in 1604 and republished in 1614, 1628, and 1643.[52] It is written in simple and straightforward classical Chinese. The edition included in Li Chih-tsao's (1565–1630) *T'ien-hsüeh ch'u-han* (An Introduction to the Rudiments of Christianity), a collection of early Chinese Christian texts first published in 1628, is graced with the rudiments of punctuation.[53] The various editions of the text seem

[48] Ebrey, *Chu Hsi's Family Rituals,* xxvi–xxviii.

[49] Cited and translated in Standaert, *Yang Tingyun,* 47.

[50] Pantoja, *Relacion,* 67–8.

[51] Ibid., 133.

[52] Pfister lists six editions: Peking 1614 (7 *chüan*); Peking 1643 (4 *chüan*); Peking 1798 (7 *chüan*); Se-king (I have not been able to decode the French romanization for this place name) 1843 (2 *chüan*); Shanghai 1849 (4 *chüan*); Tou-se-wei 1873 (4 *chüan*). Hsü Tsung-ts'e, *Ming Ch'ing chien Yeh-su-hui shih-chu t'i-yao,* 52, lists the 1604 and 1614 editions. Harvard University holds a 1798 edition which is a reprint of a 1643 edition published by Ching-tu Shih-t'ai-t'ang. I have consulted this edition, as well as the *T'ien-hsüeh ch'u-han.*

[53] *T'ien-hsüeh ch'u-han* (Taipei, 1965).

to have differed in format: The sins are arranged in at least two different orders.[54] The longest section is devoted to pride (81 pages in *An Introduction to the Rudiments of Christianity*), followed by sloth (71 pages), anger (62 pages), greed (58 pages), gluttony (56 pages), lust (52 pages) and envy, with a mere 37 pages. Some of the entries are anecdotes; others are exhortations. Each individual entry is brief – the chapter on pride, for example, has 127 separate entries. (See the Appendix at the end of the chapter for a listing of the subheadings.)

Before we move to a discussion of the text itself, a word about the title. The astute reader will have noted its cheerful bent: What is stressed about the seven sins is not that they are deadly but that they can be conquered. The word *k'o* in the title (which I have sometimes translated as the noun victory or mastery and sometimes as the verb to conquer or to master) alludes to a line from the *Analects* of Confucius. Yen Hui, Confucius' favorite disciple, asks the master what *jen* (humanity) is. Confucius replies that humanity (*jen*) consists of conquering the self (*k'o chi*) and returning to ritual (*fu li*).[55] The concept of *k'o chi*, of self-mastery, is central to the concept of self-cultivation, one of the chief activities of the Confucian gentleman. In selecting a term laden with Confucian overtones of self-mastery as the title of their text, the authors are seeking to place it in a particular context of Chinese texts dealing with the problem of self-mastery.

Indeed, that context is clearly alluded to in Pantoja's own preface to the *Seven Victories*. He begins by saying that the task of moral cultivation can be summed up in one phrase: Accumulate good and get rid of evil.[56] He continues: Evil comes from desires, which are not evil in and of themselves.[57] Desires were granted to humankind by God in order to protect our bodies and nourish our souls. But people became confused and used their desires for private ends. That is the origin of sin.[58]

Then Pantoja enters into a long discussion of the relationship of desire and sin: The desire for wealth creates the sin of greed, and so forth. He suggests that a person bent on virtue embark on it gradually. Mastering selfish desires is like tearing down a house: If you begin with the foundation, then the house will come crashing down around

[54] In the *T'ien-hsüeh ch'u-han*, the order is: pride, envy, greed, anger, gluttony, lust and sloth. In the 1798 edition it is pride, greed, lust, anger, gluttony, envy and sloth.
[55] *Lun-yü chu-shu*, Ssu-pu pei-yao ed., 12/1a. James Legge, *The Chinese Classics*, 5 vols. (Hong Kong, 1960), 1:250. The sentence is: *k'o chi fu li wei jen.*
[56] The preface is dated 1614. Hsü Tsung-ts'e (p.52) says that the 1604 edition contained a preface by Pantoja. Presumably this preface is a revision of the earlier one.
[57] This is perhaps a refutation of the Buddhist notion that desires are evil.
[58] *Ch'i k'o*, 709; Hsü, *Ming Ch'ing chien Yeh-su-hui shih-chu t'i-yao*, 52.

you and do great harm. But if you begin with the roof tiles, the project can be easily accomplished. Moral cultivation is like climbing a ladder: One must proceed cautiously, else one might fall. One need attack sins one by one.

Near the end of the preface, Pantoja writes, "I am a traveller from a far-away land, eighty thousand *li* from my home." He writes of his realization that the happiness of this world is but transitory and fleeting, and that true happiness is to be found in the afterlife. He speaks of the powerful experience of his Jesuit training, and his sorrow at the fact that there were places in the world that

> did not know that God is the true master of the universe, that were not aware there is a sure road to get to heaven. So I came with several friends east. [The trip] was like dying nine times in one life. We were at sea for three years before we reached China. And when we got here we were totally ignorant of Chinese speech and writing. I studied hard. It was like being an ignorant schoolboy again.

But after a while, Pantoja tells us he got the general drift of the language and noticed that Confucian sages were much occupied with the question of self-mastery. He continues, "Both they and I had the same intention. A thousand *li* became no distance at all."[59] Thus he perceives the sages of Confucianism to be kindred spirits. Kindred, yet their modern heirs are in need of enlightenment.

The text proper of the *Seven Victories* begins with a discussion of pride, the root of all evils. The text is rather predictable: Other sins attack the body (*hsing*); pride attacks the soul (*shen*).[60] The reader is warned that prideful thoughts accompany good deeds, as shadows follow sunlight. Mindfulness of the Christian God is the only way to avoid the sin of pride.[61] No matter how good a person is, if he does not use his goodness to honor the Christian God, he is evil.[62]

The particular danger pride poses to a good man is illustrated by an anecdote. Of old (time and space are left unspecified in this story) a nameless saint was crossing a river. The boat capsized and all of the passengers were on the point of death. The saint prayed to God, who sent an angel who led the hapless victims to shore. As the saint was contemplating the power of his virtue, his horse stumbled and fell. Then and only then he realized the sin of pride and repented. He

[59] *Ch'i k'o*, 713.
[60] Ibid., 1/4b, 724.
[61] Ibid., 1/5b-6a, 726–7.
[62] Ibid., 1/8a, 731.

prayed for mercy, and was once more saved.[63] The anecdote does not merely advocate humility: It teaches that virtue itself comes from God.

The *Seven Victories* attacks relatively few Chinese social customs. But the section entitled "The Correct Meaning of Marriage" represents a critique of Chinese marriage, especially concubinage. (There is an irony here: The text was, the reader will recall, first published in 1604; Yang T'ing-yün did not divest himself of his concubine until 1611.) The first entry tells us that monogamy was created by the Lord of Heaven when he created one wife, Eve, for Adam.[64] The final entry does concede that Western sages of old did on occasion have more than one wife, but Pantoja tells his reader the custom did not last for more than a few generations. The Old Testament polygamists were sages of particular virtue, and besides, we are told, they had been enjoined by God to spread holy teachings throughout the world.[65]

One line of argument against concubinage affirms the value of marriage and castigates concubinage for diminishing that value. The text tells us, paraphrasing a Han dynasty dictionary, the *Shuo-wen chieh-tzu*, "A wife (*ch'i*) is an equal (*ch'i*)."[66] Later on, the entry in the *Seven Victories* goes on to say, "A concubine is not your wife; she is your slave."[67]

But one can be a critic of polygamy and a misogynist at the same time. One entry begins, "Now women are easily angry and easily jealous. They are often suspicious and often in the wrong." The entry goes on to enumerate the difficulties that could result from living with two such creatures.[68]

The line of argument is a mixture of quotations from Western and Chinese modes of thought. This is especially clear in a section on homosexuality. The text reads:

> The sin of lust has many manifestations, but male homosexuality is the greatest. In my Western country, all sins have a name. Only this is the sin that dare not speak its name. As for this sin, those who commit it pollute their hearts, and those who speak of it pollute their mouths.

The text then explains why homosexuality is blasphemous in the eyes of God:

[63] Ibid., 1/10a, 735.
[64] Ibid., 6/22a, 1043.
[65] Ibid., 6/26a-b, 1051–2.
[66] *Shuo-wen chieh-tzu* (Peking, 1963), 12 *hsia*/2a, 259.
[67] *Ch'i-k'o*, 6/23b, 1046.
[68] Ibid., 6/23a, 1045.

The male is *ch'ien* and the female is *k'un*. This is the principle of generation (*sheng li*). A man and a woman, this is the way of humankind.

Ch'ien and *k'un* are trigrams from the *Book of Changes*. *Ch'ien* is associated with *yang*, *k'un* with *yin*. The dynamic of interaction between *yin* and *yang* is one of the primary generative forces of the cosmos. In traditional China, human sexuality was perceived as a microcosm of cosmic generation; homosexuality was an abomination because it could not be fit into the binary mode of *yin* and *yang*.

But Christian legend is invoked to reinforce the argument made by Chinese cosmology. The text then goes on to tell the story of the destruction of Sodom (The country of So-to-ma). Lot's (The wise man Lo-te) escape is chronicled. The text tells us that this episode transpired 3,000 years ago, and still the site of the destruction is barren. The text concludes, "We Westerners know from this story how deeply God abominates and how heavily he punishes the sin of homosexuality." The moral logic is clear: homosexuality is a sin because God abhors it.[69]

The text is very self-conscious in its refusal to use Buddhist analogies. Even to someone only moderately well-versed in Buddhist literature, several of the tales recounted by Pantoja recall Buddhist counterparts. For example, the text tells us that in "the West" there was an exceedingly handsome young man, who was disturbed by the amorous thoughts he aroused in women. He prayed to God to rid him of his curse. Shortly thereafter, he was struck with an illness, which blinded him in one eye, and (more to the point here) disfigured him. The text tells us "No one ever looked at him again. He was delighted by it."[70]

The Christian tale of the wise man's delight at his own disfigurement has echoes in the well-known story of Lien-hua nü, a Buddhist tale of a wise and beautiful woman who disfigures herself. She had formerly been a courtesan, and had spurned a man's advances because he had no money. He managed to obtain the requisite money, but she in the meanwhile had converted to Buddhism and taken up the life of an ascetic. He pursued her to her forest dwelling. She asked him what part of her body gave him pleasure. He responded that her

[69] See the discussion in John Boswell, *Christianity, Social Tolerance and Homosexuality: Gay People in Western Europe from the Beginning of the Christian Era to the Fourteenth Century* (Chicago, 1980), 92–8. The discussion in Genesis does not in fact specify what terrible sins the inhabitants of Sodom are indulging in. Boswell suggests that homosexuality was a late addition to the story, but certainly by the seventeenth century it had become commonplace.

[70] Ibid., 6/12a, 1623.

eyes did, so she gouged them out and gave them to him.[71] The familiar story (and while Pantoja might not have known it, Yang T'ing-yün surely would have) could have been cited to reinforce the message about the burdens imposed by the beauty of the human body. But it was not.

The Jesuits were at considerable pains to distinguish themselves from Buddhists, for reasons both theological and social. They had concluded that there was nothing in classical Confucianism which contradicted Christianity. Buddhism, on the other hand, was seen as a religion in competition with Christianity. And furthermore, sectarian Buddhism, with which Christianity was occasionally conflated, was largely a prohibited religion.[72] Thus a tendency toward theological consistency – Christian truth ought to be demonstrated by Christian anecdote – is reinforced by a clear need on the part of the Jesuits to demonstrate what they were and what they were not.

What did the seventeenth-century Chinese audience make of the *Seven Victories?* We are fortunate in having several prefaces to the text that allow us to address this question. In addition to Yang and Pantoja, Ts'ao Yü-pien (1558–1634, cs 1592),[73] Cheng I-wei (cs 1602, d 1634),[74] Hsiung Ming-yü (cs 1602),[75] and Ch'en Liang-ts'ai (cs 1595) all wrote prefaces to the work. A postface dated the summer of 1614 was written by Wang Ju-liang, and the edition published in 1643 has prefaces by Ts'ui Ch'ang (cs 1602) and P'eng Tuan-wu (cs 1602).[76] The

[71] *Taishô shunshû Daisôkyô*, vol. 25, no. 1451. "Ken-pen shuo i-chieh Pi-na-ya li-shih" *chüan* 32, 363. The conclusion to the story is that nuns should not live in secluded places.

[72] There is a substantial body of scholarship that discusses this point. See, for example, Gernet, *China and the Christian Impact.*

[73] Association for Asian Studies, Ming Biographical History Project Committee, *Dictionary of Ming Biography, 1368–1644*, ed. L. Carrington Goodrich, assoc. ed. Chaoying Fang, 2 vols. (New York, 1976). 2:1474. Ts'ao also wrote a preface to Sabatino de Ursis' *Ta Hsi shui-fa* (Water Management in the Great West), which is contained in Hsü Tsung-tse, *Ming Ch'ing chien Yeh-su-hui shih-chu t'i-yao*, 310. The *Ch'i-jen shih-p'ien* documents discussions Ts'ao had with Ricci (Standaert, *Yang Tingyun*, 84). The "I-wen chih" section of the *Ming shih* (chüan 99, 2489) lists a text by Ts'ao entitled *Liao-chieh t'ang-chi.* Modern indexes also list a text entitled *Ts'ao chen yü chi.* Hsü refers to the preface on 52.

[74] Cheng I-wei is the author of two collections, the *Ling-shan tsang-chi* and the *Hu-ni chi* (neither of which I have seen – they are listed in the *Ming jen chuan-chi tsu-liao suo-yin*, 783). The Harvard-Yenching library holds a Ming edition of a text by him, entitled *Ch'üan-pi ku-shih*, in four *chüan.* See his biography in the *Ming-shih, chüan* 251, 21:6494. See also the entry on him in the *Ming Shih-tsung* (Taipei, 1961), 59/2a-b, which preserves two poems by Cheng.

[75] See his biography in the *Ming shih, chüan* 257, 8:6629–31. See also the entry in the *Ming Shih-tsung* (59/2b-3a) which preserves a poem by him.

[76] The information on the prefaces is drawn from Hsü Tsung-ts'e, *Ming Ch'ing chien Yeh-su-hui shih-chu t'i-yao*, 54.

prefaces are useful as accounts of readers' responses to the text. But they also form an integral part of the text, as instructions to the reader. They provide metaphors and analogies with which to assimilate the *Seven Victories*, metaphors and analogies with which to construct implicit ethnographies.

Wang Ju-liang is the only member of the list of preface writers who does not seem to have received his *chin-shih* degree. Four of the men (Cheng, Hsiung, Ts'ui and P'eng) received their *chin-shih* degrees in the same year. The experience of having passed the examination in the same year created a profound and permanent bond among men in traditional China. Thus these preface writers are bound to one another in extra-textual ways. Possession of the *chin-shih* degree qualified one for a position in the bureaucracy, but it also signified that one had passed through a rigorous educational system that aimed at enforcing ideological orthodoxy. The men who are writing the prefaces to the *Seven Victories* are not marginal men, and the issues they find the text to address are central to the concerns of late Ming literati.

All of the preface writers (again, except for Wang Ju-liang) are prominent enough so that their biographies are recorded in Chinese local histories and other sources. These sources do not identify our preface writers as Christian, but in fact this is not particularly surprising.[77] Some of the prefaces clearly profess Christianity; others, as we shall see, do not. There is no particular reason to think that writing a preface to a Christian text means that a man is a Christian. Writing a preface to a text like the Buddhist *Heart Sutra* does not mean that a man has vowed to forsake all other texts: It merely means that he finds the text itself to be of compelling value. There is no reason to believe that the men who wrote the prefaces to Pantoja's text took a different stance.

The first preface contained in the edition of the *Seven Victories* published in the *Introduction to the Rudiments of Christianity* is by Cheng I-wei. Cheng seeks to place the text into the context of Neo-Confucian cultivation of the self. One of the main preoccupations of late Ming Neo-Confucianism (indeed, of Confucianism at any time) is the cultivation of the self and the mastering of emotions. Through a series of metaphors Cheng explores the relationship between the original tranquil nature of the self and the self that is stirred by passion. The original self is tranquil. Wind whips water into billows and waves,

[77] Ch'eng I-wei's biography is placed in the *Ming shih* as an appendix to that of Hsü Kuang-ch'i. Hsü's biography does discuss the fact that he studied with Matteo Ricci. Thus the dynastic history places the two men in the same category.

but does not damage the original form of the water. Water remains water; the self remains the self. The task of moral cultivation is to recover the original, tranquil self, before it has been whipped by the wind of passion.

Cheng makes scant reference to the fact that the author of the *Seven Victories* is a foreigner. He concludes with a reference to Fu-ch'ai (r. 495-473 B.C.), the ambitious and profligate king of the peripheral and semi-barbarous state of Wu. The story goes that Fu-ch'ai admired the hats of the people from the central kingdoms, and thus desired to pay tribute to them. He is reported to have said: "I've come because I like the hats! I've come because I like the hats!"[78]

Fu-ch'ai came because he liked the hats (and surely this implies that he coveted the rank and riches that ceremonial dress implied: he was profligate but not stupid). But Pantoja, Cheng tells us, came because he admired Chinese morality (*i*), and borrowed the words of the Chinese sages.

Pantoja comes, in this version of events, as a supplicant, not as a missionary. Cheng regards Pantoja as engaged in an enterprise similar to his own: the exploration of the nature of the true self, mastery of the emotions, and so on. Cheng has universalized the tract on the seven deadly sins and separated it from its Christian context. But, finally, Cheng's approbation is conditional. He concludes by telling his reader that although he is not certain that *Seven Victories* applies to the search for the tranquil self, he still finds it a good text and is happy to write the preface.[79]

A very different attitude is present in the second preface, by Hsiung Ming-yü. He begins:

> Extraordinary men have come from countries in the far west. The first was Ricci, followed by Pantoja and Sabatino de Ursis. They came together with ten or so disciples. They crossed ninety thousand *li*[80] of ocean to set their eyes on China – so great was their diligence! The maps, books, clever objects they brought and foreign objects and customs they recount are really quite remarkable.

[78] The source of the analogy is *Ku-liang pu-chu*, Ssu-pu pei-yao edition, vol. 289, 24/14b-15b. The Ku-liang is the only commentary to the *Ch'un-ch'iu* to recount Fu-ch'ai's obsession with the hats. The Chou dynasty lasted from approximately 1122-256 B.C. By the fifth century, the Chou king was in many ways no more powerful than the king of any other state. But other states continued to recognize him as the son of heaven.

[79] *Ch'i-k'o*, 689–96.

[80] A *li* is approximately a third of a mile.

Hsiung continues with a discussion of the marvels brought by these extraordinary men. But having first stressed the exoticism of the Jesuits, Hsiung continues in his essay to assimilate them. He says that in their diligent study of Chinese texts late in the night, they are no different from Confucians. He continues:

> [This text] introduces us to the words and actions of Western sages. It has the novelty of the *Huai-nan-tzu* or the *Lun-heng,* without the exaggerations of the *Lieh-tzu* or the *Chuang-tzu.*[81]

Thus in the eyes of Hsiung Ming-yü the foreign represents a kind of safe exoticism. Part of the authority of the text comes from the fact that its author travelled ninety thousand *li* to come to China: Part of what is remarkable about it is that it is more sensible to Huang than what he regards as some of the more fanciful texts in the Chinese tradition.

Ch'en Liang-ts'ai begins the third preface by recounting how as a young boy growing up near the coast he had occasion to encounter missionaries from the West. He says that when Pantoja gave him the *Seven Victories,* the Jesuit said:

> The talent and wisdom of you gentlemen from the East is quite excellent. In terms of scholarship, you are in no way deficient. It is just that your original natures have become confused.

Pantoja of course suggests that Christianity is the way to clarify one's original nature, and Ch'en seems persuaded. But that does not involve a renunciation of the tenets of Confucianism. When Ch'en describes his reaction to the *Seven Victories,* he says that the book in its essence approaches Confucianism: "Each word of the text goes through to the bone and penetrates to the heart." He suggests that a function of the text is to arouse Confucians. In Ch'en's view, Christianity offers the possibility of revivifying a complacent tradition.

Ch'en served in a variety of bureaucratic posts. After his death, he

[81] *Ch'i k'o,* 697–709. The *Huai Nan-tzu* was compiled by followers of Liu An (d. 122 B.C.) The *Lun-heng* was written by Wang Ch'ung (27–100?) and is a clear and critical attack on what Wang regarded as the irrational beliefs that infected the Confucianism of his day. The *Lieh-tzu* and the *Chuang-tzu* are both Taoist texts. The dates of the Lieh-tzu are contested, and range from the fifth century B.C. to the second century A.D. The *Chuang-tzu* dates from the fourth century B.C. Here Hsiung refers to the *Huai Nan-tzu* as *Hung-pao,* the *Lieh-tzu* as *Ch'eng-pu* and the *Chuang-tzu* as *Ch'i yüan.*

was worshipped at a shrine for local worthies.[82] Thus his enthusiasm for Christianity represented no barrier either to a conventional career or to his incorporation into officially sanctioned local religion.

The preface to *Seven Victories* by Yang T'ing-yün was written sometime between 1614 and 1617.[83] Yang too is impressed by the difficulty of Pantoja's journey to China. But he has no doubt as to how to interpret it: When the unicorn visits the phoenix it is an auspicious omen.

Yang concedes that the words of the men from the West are hard to understand, but says that the essence of their teaching can be expressed in two sentences: Honor God as the lord of all creation and love others as you would yourself, and further argues that neither precept is alien to Confucian thought.

The prefaces by P'eng Tuan-wu and Ts'ui Ch'ang are not included in the *T'ien-hsüeh ch'u-han,* but can be found in an edition first published in 1643, the year before the Manchu conquest of China, and reprinted in 1798. In these prefaces we can see expressed a heightened sense of crisis, and a clear hope that Christianity (or at least the moral advice in the *Seven Victories*) would save China from her peril.

The preface-writer who is most lyrical about the potential of Christian salvation is P'eng Tuan-wu. P'eng's father, P'eng Hao-ku, was a noted Taoist. Four tracts on alchemy by his hand (or edited by him) are preserved in Taoist canonical collections, and other works are preserved elsewhere.[84] P'eng Hao-ku had a modestly successful official

[82] *Ch'i-k'o,* 701–8. His biography may be found in *Chin-chiang hsien-chih* (Taipei, 1967), 10/67a. The listing of the local worthies is at 5/10b. Su Mao-hsiang, the son of Su Shih-chien whose *Su-shih chia-hsün* we discussed above, was worshipped at the same shrine.

[83] Standaert, *Yang Tingyun,* 71. Hsü says that the preface is included in the *T'ien-hsüeh ch'u-han,* but it is not included in the 1965 reprint edition. The text I have used is that in Hsü, *Ming Ch'ing chien Yeh-su-hui shih-chu t'i-yao,* 53–54. Much of the preface is translated in Standaert, *Yang Tingyun,* 120–1.

[84] He, along with Li P'an-lung, annotated the *Ju-yao ching* (A Mirror on the Induction of Pharmaceuticals), written by Ts'ui Hsi-fan in the tenth century. See Judith M. Boltz, *A Survey of Taoist Literature: Tenth to Seventeenth Centuries,* China Research Monograph no. 32, Institute for East Asian Studies, University of California (Berkeley, 1987), 234, 236. The commentary edition is contained in the *Tao-tsang chi-yao,* ed. P'eng Han-jan and Ho Lung-hsiang (n.p., n.d.; reprint, n.p., 1906), 244 vols., vol. 98 *Hsü chi,* vol. 5 Also contained in the *Tao-tsang chi-yao* (vol. 67, *Tou chi* 4:97a-113a) are the *Chin-pi ku-wen lung-hu shang-ching (The Ancient Text of Gold and Jade; The Supreme Classic of Dragon and Tiger)* which P'eng Hao-ku annotated and the *Chin-tan ssu-pai tzu chu (Annotations to the Four Hundred Words on Alchemy)* (vol. 129, *K'uei chi* 2:50a-61b.) which he compiled. The *Tao-tsang hsü-pien,* first collection, contains his annotations to a text entitled *Chin-tan ssu-pai tzu chu shih (Explanations of Annotations to the Four Hundred Words on Alchemy).* He also compiled a text entitled *P'eng-shih lei-pien tsa-shu (Mr. P'eng's Miscellaneous Encyclopedia)* (1591 edition held at Harvard

career. According to his biography in the local history of Hsia-i, his native place, after his death, the local people established a shrine and worshipped him.[85]

P'eng Tuan-wu served in a variety of posts, most notably in the administration of the salt monopoly. It was not an easy posting, and the difficulties he had there doubtless contributed to the sense of urgency we find in his preface.[86]

P'eng Tuan-wu, the alchemist's son, entitled his preface "The Seven Compilations of the Western Sage." He says that when Pantoja showed him the text,

> I treasured and read it. It was like holy water that bathed my heart, an essential drug whose efficacy I can confirm.

He goes on to allude to a story contained in the biography of Yüan Ts'an in the *Sung-shu*. Long ago, in a nameless country, there was a spring of madness. Everyone in the country but the king (who had his own water supply) drank from it and became mad. The king alone remained sane. His subjects thought he was mad, and forcibly administered moxibustion, acupuncture, and drugs in an effort to cure him. The medical regimen became too much for the king to bear, and so he finally drank from the spring. When he too became mad, everyone lived happily ever after.[87] The analogy is clear: Pantoja is the sole sane person. He seems mad merely because he is different. When times are out of joint, sanity and madness are confounded. Pantoja may be sane, but he is not omniscient. P'eng's preface continues:

> Pantoja came to transmit the learning of his country, that is to say, these seven remedies. Although Mr. P'ang (i.e. Pantoja) lives among Chinese, his understanding is only superficial, and can't see through to the visceral essence of the Chinese temperament.

Nonetheless, what Pantoja has written can enlighten and illuminate. P'eng ranks the text with a range of Chinese classics and compares it to the Forty-two Chapter Sutra, a Buddhist text generally attributed

University). In addition, he compiled a collection in twenty *ts'e* entitled *Tao yen nei-wai mi chüeh ch'uan shu* (A Complete Book of Esoteric Taoist Texts) (prefaces dated 1597 and 1599, held at the Harvard-Yenching library).

85 *Hsia-i hsien-chih*, 3 vols. (Chung-kuo fang-chih ts'ung-shu reprint of 1920 edition), 6/21a, 2:689.

86 See the biography of P'eng Tuan-wu in the *Hsia-i hsien-chih*, 6/22a-24a, 2:691–694. See the reference to his career in the *Dictionary of Ming Biography*, 2:1422.

87 *Sung-shu* (Peking, 1974), *chüan* 89 8:2231. The *Sung-shu* is the history of the Liu-Sung dynasty (420–479) compiled by Shen Yüeh (441–513).

to the first Indian monks to arrive in China.[88] He talks about the desperate straits China is in (this is, after all, 1643, the eve of the Manchu conquest), and says that all present-day scholars revere is *Hsin-hsüeh* (Study of the Mind). He charges that what they mean by mind is not the mind of heaven, but rather their own particular minds. They engage in all manner of reckless talk and they follow their desires.[89] (These tendencies in late Ming thought which P'eng is attacking were in fact blamed by early Ch'ing scholars for the fall of the Ming.)

P'eng Tuan-wu is making an argument for the utility of the *Seven Victories*. He argues that Pantoja's tract on the seven deadly sins will remedy a defect in Chinese philosophy. Moral cultivation as prescribed by Christianity will restore moral rigor to China. It is a remedy for a Chinese crisis.

Another preface writer working with a clear sense of crisis is Ts'ui Ch'ang.[90] The format of Ts'ui's commentary differs from that of the others: he writes a separate preface for each chapter. These internal prefaces form a set of instructions to the reader which set up a dynamic interplay with the discussion of the seven sins.

His preface to the section on lust reminds his Chinese readers of a story from the *Spring and Autumn Annals*, the story of the Lady Li (Li-chi). The Lady Li, a woman of the Jung tribe, beguiled the Chin ruler and compelled him to expel his sons by other women and install her son on the throne. His lust for her blinded him to her political ambition. The Lady Li is one of a category of state-toppling beauties: women who enchant the ruler so that he neglects his duties and the kingdom collapses.[91] As Ts'ui tells his readers: "When there is honey on the knife, you see only the honey. When you are chasing a rabbit on a dangerous road, you see only the rabbit, you do not see the danger."[92] There is irony here: The Lady Li is a foreigner. Indeed, Ts'ui cites only one example of the danger of lust: a foreign femme fatale. A foreign text will teach you to guard against lust, which will protect you from foreign women and foreign domination. And in 1643

[88] *A Dictionary of Chinese Buddhist Terms*, comp. W. E. Soothill and Lewis Hodous (London, 1937), 171, discusses the attribution of the text to Kasyapa Matanga and Gobharana, the first Buddhist monks to arrive in China from India, but says that in fact the text probably dates from the Chin dynasty. See also the discussion in Kenneth Chen, *Buddhism in China: A Historical Survey* (Princeton, 1964), 34–6.

[89] *Ch'i k'o*, 1978 edition, preface.

[90] See his biography in *Wu-hu hsien-chih* (Chung-kuo fang-chih ts'ung-shu edition), 2: 894.

[91] On the Lady Li, see Burton Watson, trans. *The Tso Chuan: Selections from China's Oldest Narrative History* (New York, 1989), 21–5. For the account of the Lady Li in the Kuo-yü, see the translation in Idem., *Early Chinese Literature* (New York, 1962), 69–73.

[92] *Ch'i k'o*, 1798 edition, preface to *chüan* 3.

the Manchu conquest was only one year off. The concerns of the preface writer are a far cry from those of Pantoja, yet he finds the text apt.

Thus the preface writers take a range of positions on this man from afar and his weighty text. The significance of the fact that the author is foreign seems to vary with the preface writer, as do their evaluations of the utility of the text. But they all seem to be struck, as is Pantoja himself, by the commonality of the enterprise they share with the Jesuit. The exigencies of moral cultivation transcend cultural difference.

That is one point of view. The *Seven Victories,* in addition to the approbation we have seen, attracted a certain amount of criticism. A certain Wang Chiao-shih attacks the text (along with the Ten Commandments) for being a work designed to lure "men of letters bent on improvement" to Christianity.[93] The same sentiment is echoed in an anti-Christian pamphlet, the *Tsui yen* (A Discussion of Crimes), contained in the collection *P'o-hsieh chi* (A Collection to Smash the Heterodox), published in 1639. The text laments that "With their *Seven Victories* and their ten prohibitions, they win over to them those men who are preoccupied with morally perfecting themselves."[94] What renders Chinese literati vulnerable to Christianity is the concern with self-mastery. Even critics of the text see the commonality of interest between the Jesuit and the literatus.

The method and reasoning of the *Seven Victories* is called into question by Huang Wen-tao, who wrote:

> What they call the seven [things] to be overcome are pride, avarice, envy, anger, greed, jealousy and sloth. Although all of this involves the cultivation of the self, they are only clumsy methods for controlling oneself. What Confucius told Yen-tzu had to do with a far more elevated concept: he considered the virtue of humanity (*jen*) as the basis, and ritual (*li*) as the substance. When one knows how to preserve humanity within oneself, whatever is contrary to humanity disappears of its own accord. When ritual is re-established, whatever is contrary to rituals eliminates itself of its own accord.[95]

Huang has no quarrel with what he sees as the ultimate goal of the text: the cultivation of the self. He simply finds Confucius' statement,

[93] Cited in Gernet, *China and the Christian Impact,* 47.

[94] *Tsui yen,* in *P'o-hsieh chi,* 3:27a. Cited in Gernet, *China and the Christian Impact,* 145.

[95] *P'i-hsieh chi* in *P'o-hsieh chi,* 5:20b. Cited and translated in Gernet, *China and the Christian Impact,* 145. I have changed the romanization to Wade-Giles for consistency, and made other minor modifications.

"humanity consists in mastering the self and returning to ritual," to be a more elegant and thoroughgoing approach to morality.

Hsü Ta-shou also finds the moralizing of the *Seven Victories* to be inelegant and verbose.

> In their book entitled *The Seven Victories*, overcoming one's pride is placed in a position of first importance. But the simple axiom from the "Little Rules of Seemliness," "One should not allow one's pride to grow," is quite enough to exhaust the subject. What is the point of becoming attached to the inelegant and obscure ideas of these people? What is the point of speechifying on and on forever?[96]

Huang and Hsü are both objecting to the *Seven Victories* because it is a vulgar popular tract. Hsü would have us believe that Chinese moral writing was all in the lapidary prose of the classics. But seventeenth-century editions of popular texts such as the *Book of Retribution* and *Response of the Lord on High* are quite verbose. It is entirely possible that Hsü would have found such texts to be verbose and inelegant as well.

Thus we have seen that the text had its proponents and its critics. What else can we learn about its audience? Who read the *Seven Victories?* Some degree of its assimilation as a Chinese text is shown by the fact that Chuang Ch'i-yüan made oblique reference to it in the palace examination in 1610. According to Benjamin Elman, neither Chuang nor his examiners seems to have found anything controversial in his essay.[97] I would like to suggest that this shows the remarkable rapidity with which the *Seven Victories* entered the repertoire of intellectual discourse in the late Ming.

The *Seven Victories* also appeared in the library catalogs of several literati. The library catalog of Ch'ien Ch'ien-i (1582–1664) contains a section on "Christian Books," which lists the *Seven Victories*.[98] The *Pa-ch'ien-chüan-lou shu-mu* (Catalog of the Library of Eight Thousand Volumes), a catalog completed in 1899 by the bibliophile Ting Ping, lists

[96] *Tso p'i* in *P'o-hsieh chi*, 4:33b. Cited and translated in Gernet, *China and the Christian Impact*, 162. The "Little Rules of Seemliness" is the "Ch'ü li", the first chapter of the *Li chi*.

[97] Benjamin A. Elman, *Classicism, Politics and Kinship: The Chang-chou school of New Text Criticism in Late Imperial China* (Berkeley and Los Angeles, 1990), 89–91.

[98] *Chiang-yün-lou shu-mu*, T'sung-shu chi-ch'eng ch'u pien ed., vol. 18, *chüan* 3, 68. One of Ch'ien Ch'ien-i's most prominent students, Ch'ü Shih-ssu (1590–1651) was a Christian, baptized under the name of Thomas. This might well account for Ch'ien's special interest in Christian tracts. See the biography of Ch'ü by J.C. Yang and T. Numata in *Eminent Chinese of the Ch'ing Period*, 199–201 and the biography of Ch'ien by L. Carrington Goodrich and J.C. Yang in the same volume, 148–50.

a Ming edition of the *Seven Victories*, with the author listed as "Pantoja of the Western Seas."[99]

The *Seven Victories* was included in the great book catalog of the Ch'ien-lung reign period, the *Ssu-k'u ch'üan-shu t'i yao*. (The Annotated Catalog of All the Books in the Four Treasuries.) Taking the dictum that knowledge is power quite literally, the Ch'ien-lung emperor in 1772 commissioned local and provincial officials to collect all manner of books and forward them to the capital. A catalog of the books so collected (including some 10,000 titles) was compiled. Books that were deemed by a board of editors to be particularly praiseworthy were copied into the collectanea, the *Ssu-k'u ch'uan shu*. Others were merely entered in the catalog.[100] The *Seven Victories* falls in the latter category. After a short summary of the table of contents, the brief entry in the catalog (six lines in a modern, typeset version) runs:

> Its words are derived from those of the Confucians and Mohists.[101] As far as individual topics go, it is not unreasonable. But for every topic, the text returns to the theme of revering the Lord of Heaven in order to find happiness. Thus its error lies in the essence of the religion, not in the words it uses.
>
> In the discussion of celibacy, the text cites an interlocutor who asks, if everyone were celibate and did not marry, would not the human race become extinct? The response is that if all humans were celibate, and the human race become extinct, the Lord of Heaven would surely look after things so there would be no need to worry. The text is muddled.
>
> The text also says that it is a condition of human life that there be birth and that there be death, and that things regularly begin and end, are completed and destroyed . . . The text unwittingly slips into Buddhism, so how can it be a refutation of Buddhism?[102]

The evaluation of the *Four Treasuries* editors, though hostile, was astute. The *Seven Victories* is a moral text that appeared in a time when China was awash in moral tracts. But it was, as the editors of the *Catalog of the Four Treasuries* pointed out, a moral tract with a difference. The conception of ethical causality was radically different than that of Chinese moral texts, or as the *Four Treasuries* editors put it, "for every topic, the text returns to the theme of revering the Lord of

[99] *Pa-ch'ien-chüan lou shu-mu*, 12/17b. The text is in a section entitled "Tsa chia"—miscellaneous authors.

[100] Kent Guy, *The Emperor's Four Treasuries: Scholars and the State in the late Ch'ien-lung Era* (Cambridge, Mass., 1987), 109–11.

[101] Mo-tzu was a philosopher who flourished 479-431 B.C. He differed on many points from the Confucian philosophers. Perhaps his most radical idea was the notion of "universal love": that one should love strangers as much as one loved one's kinsmen.

[102] Hsü Tsung-tse, *Ming Ching chien Yeh-su-hui shih-chu t'i-yao*, 52.

Heaven in order to find happiness." The *Seven Victories* portrays ethical choices as a battleground between the will of God and the devil. For example, we are told lust is the devil's favorite sin, because by tempting one person he can snare two.[103] This is not an argument against lust that those unconvinced by the power of the devil will find compelling. One strives to be good because God wills it. If one does not believe in the Christian God, one will not be compelled by his will.

The nature of ethical causality in Chinese philosophy is a complex question, and here I can only hazard a sketch. The dominant view of human nature in late Ming China stems from the classical Confucian writer Mencius, who argued that human nature was in its essence good. The logical demonstration that this is true is an anecdote. If a passerby sees that a child has fallen into a well, he will instinctively save the child, before any thought of reward or fame can enter his mind.[104] This fundamental human goodness is fragile, and the basic task of moral cultivation is to recover it. One strives to be good because it is one's fundamental nature to be so. It is a far cry from Christian notions of sin and salvation.

Pantoja's text resonated profoundly to the men who wrote about it. Especially in the later prefaces, there is a sense that the *Seven Victories* might be enlisted in the attempt to rouse China from its complacency, or its philosophers from their self-indulgence and reflexivity. It is a text that contains moral advice that is useful and sound, regardless of one's theological predilections. The writers of the prefaces are clearly putting the *Seven Victories* to their own uses. In the process of doing so, they have changed the text and its implications. They are engaged in a project of cultural appropriation, in a small but significant way.

Erik Zürcher has written recently of Chinese Christianity in late Ming dynasty Fukien province as a Chinese popular religion. One of the things that impressed the Fukien congregations about Christianity was its efficacy, especially its power to exorcize demons. To be sure, the Fukien congregations and the writers of the prefaces to the *Seven Victories* have different interests. But they may be approaching the men from the West with the same question, namely: What do they have to offer? The question has many answers: indeed, to some Ming Chinese, the answer was religious salvation. The men who wrote the prefaces to Pantoja's text found it to be a text that provided useful

103 *Ch'i-k'o*, 6/2b, 1004.

104 Legge, *The Chinese Classics*, 2:202. *Meng-tzu shu-chu*, Ssu-pu pei-yao edition, 3 *hsia*/4a.

moral guidance within a framework dominated by Chinese categories. They were not primarily concerned with who Pantoja was or why he came to China: They were interested in how they might use his teachings. They assimilated his book on deadly sins with the Chinese genre of ledgers of merits and demerits, and found it to be useful. There was no need, in the eyes of the preface writers, to discard moral advice because it was foreign. But the new moral advice caused no radical re-evaluation of self and other. It could be comfortably accommodated in the late Ming context. The radical re-evaluation of self and other in the face of foreign ideas would not come until the nineteenth century, when ethnographies and much else have become all too explicit.

APPENDIX

The structure of the *Seven Victories* (taken from the *T'ien-hsüeh ch'u-han* edition).

Pride
Introduction (9 entries)
Difficulties in conquering pride (6 entries)
Admonitions against pride in one's good fortune (3 entries)
Admonitions against pride in one's virtue (11 entries)
Admonitions against cherishing one's uniqueness (4 entries)
Admonitions against cherishing fame (16 entries)
Admonitions against feigning goodness to gain fame (5 entries)
Admonitions against heeding praise (12 entries)
Admonitions against cherishing high rank (20 entries)
Discussions of the virtue of humility (24 entries)
Guarding humility by knowing yourself (17 entries)

Envy
Introduction (12 entries)
Admonitions against bearing grudges (5 entries)
Admonitions against committing slander (11 entries)
Admonitions against listening to slander (7 entries)

Greed
General (48 entries)
Discussion of the virtue of dispensing one's goods (17 entries)

Anger
General (24 entries)
Loving your enemy (7 entries)

Overcoming difficulties through the virtue of forbearance (36 entries)
Acquiring virtue through adversity (17 entries)

Gluttony
General (34 entries)
Discussions of the virtue of moderation (22 entries)

Lust
General (30 entries)
The virtue of chastity (12 entries)
The correct meaning of marriage (9 entries)

Sloth
General (46 entries)
Discussions of the virtue of diligence (11 entries)

PART IV

Observers observed: Reflections on encounters in the age of Captain Cook

CHAPTER 16

The theatricality of observing and being observed: Eighteenth-century Europe "discovers" the ? century "Pacific"

GREG DENING

A SEASON FOR OBSERVING

LET me take you to the end of the eighteenth century, to the years 1767–1797 to be precise. These years are toward the end of the period in which European philosophes exhilaratingly and self-consciously knew themselves to be "enlightened." Identifying with those who, as Immanuel Kant described them, "dared to know" belonged to the naming process of discourse. We know the comfort it brings. The "Enlightenment" of one century is "structuralism," "neo-Marxism," "post-modernism" of another. Recognition of keywords, a sense of the metaphoric nature of styles of thought, a feeling that what one has just read is what one was about to say, knowing the truth in the caricatures of oppositional stands made by one's associates, knowing on the other hand how untrue the stereotypifications are of oneself – all the stuff by which paradigms are made and seen – had given for nearly a hundred years a tribal sense to the lovers of criticism, the "enlightened." They had been to the top of the mountain with Petrarch and opened Augustine's *Confessions* with him: There "Men went forth to behold the high mountains and the mighty surge of the sea, and the broad stretches of the rivers and the inexhaustible ocean, and the paths of the stars and so doing lose themselves in wonderment." "A new thought seized me," Petrarch had written, "transporting me from space into time." To have discovered that everything in nature, everything in human beings was set in time, that the abstractions of law, science and the market, even God himself, were in time was indeed enlightening. It made for a season of observing.

In that season for observing, the years 1767 (when Samuel Wallis "discovered" Tahiti) to 1797 (when the first successful missionary stations in the Pacific were established) were a short and intensive period in which the Pacific was *theatrum mundi*. It was a period in which the nations of Europe and the Americas saw themselves acting out their scientific, humanistic selves. Government-sponsored expeditions from England, France, and Spain followed one another, self-righteously conscious of their obligations to observe, describe and publish, to be humane and to contribute to the civilizing process of natives out of their superior arts and greater material wealth. It was a time of intensive theater of the civilized to the native, but of even more intense theater of the civilized to one another. The civilized jostled to see what the Pacific said to them of their relations of dominance. They vied in testing the extensions of their sovereignty and the effectiveness of their presence – through territorial possessions, protected lines of communication, exemplary empire. They shouted to natives, in that loud and slow way we use to communicate with those that do not share our language, the meaning of flags and cannons and property and trade, and lessons of civilized behavior. But they were always conscious that this theater was always a play within a play – about world systems of power, about reifications of empire, about encompassing the globe and hegemony. We historians for decades have poured scorn on the metaphor of the "expansion" of Europe. Yet the theater of the Pacific was about making that unreal metaphor real at home and abroad.

In that same season for observing during which the Pacific was *theatrum mundi*, England itself was something of a theater to the world. Anglophilia was strong among the enlightened, mostly because the English were deemed to have managed time so well, so expediently and so stylishly – in government, in law, in political economy, in religion, in moral philosophy. Joseph Addison had helped make it so as "The Spectator" in *The Spectator*. "I live in the World rather as a Spectator of Mankind, than as one of the Species." "I have acted all the Parts of my life as a Looker-On." Irony was the enlightened's trope, the spectator's worldliness. Irony requires a perspective, a line of vision that the looker-on has but that the participant does not. Of course, this can often be merely a matter of physical angles of vision in which one can be enlightened by seeing something from a different angle. But perspective is more composed than that. Perspective is the persuasion that vision is geometric and that our representations are the more real by that. Roland Barthes commented on the relationship between geometry and theater well before me.

> The theater is precisely that practice which calculates the place of things *as they are observed:* If I set the spectacle here, the spectator will see this; if I put it elsewhere, he will not, and I can avail myself of this masking effect and play on the illusions it provides. The stage is the line which stands across the path of the optic pencil, tracing at once the point at which it is brought to a stop and, as it were, the threshold of its ramification . . . Representation is not defined directly by imitation: even if one gets rid of the "real," of the "vraisemblable," of the "copy," there will still be representation for so long as a subject (author, reader, spectator, or voyeur) casts his gaze toward a horizon on which he cuts out the base of a triangle, his eye (or his mind) forming the apex.

The tricks of seeing the parts of the world "as if" from the point of the pyramid of one's mind's eye are many. They were largely elaborated in the Enlightenment.

The exhilaration at seeing the world from new perspectives was manifold. From a balloon, in a microscope, through a telescope, by the precision of a perfect calibrating machine, the world looked different and inspired description. Above all, the world looked different from a ship. "Navigation" was a subject in every school, even the most landlocked, as the measurability of the heavens made the earth measurable as well. But navigation was really the metaphor of the age as the world was encompassed. Our ethnographic present of 1767–1797 was supremely a moment of voyaging. *Voyage into Substance* (1984), Barbara Stafford has called it, to indicate the eyes of Europe's ships probing eclectically into anything new – into icebergs, waterspouts, Banksia trees, cannibals, *hula* dances . . . In many it was the actual voyaging more than the discovered substances that excited. It was the experiencing of otherness rather than otherness itself. That was its theater. The market for vicarious voyaging was immense. The mountain of texts describing that experiencing of otherness grew high. Paintings, engravings, journals, government reports, inside stories, pantomimes, ballets, poems – the ethnographic output was vast. And every single text of it had the reflective character of every ethnographic experience. It mirrored self in the vision of the other. It mirrored all those hegemonies that suborn self in suborning the other.[1]

[1] I am dependent for general remarks about the Enlightenment on Peter Gay, *The Enlightenment. An Interpretation* (New York, 1977) and Jean Gebser, *The Ever Present Origin* (Athens, OH, 1984), 13–14, on Petrarch. Immanuel Kant, "What is Enlightenment?" in Peter Gay, ed. *The Enlightenment. A Comprehensive Anthology* (New York, 1973), 383, offers his own definition of the Enlightenment. H.L. Wesseling, ed. *Expansion and Reaction*

The theater and theatricality of ethnography

Now that the word theater has been raised, I feel I have some excuse to become theatrical. Ethnography, I have told my students for years, is about the present participle, not life but living, not gender but gendering, not culture but culturing, not science but sciencing. Not even change but changing. Ethnography catches motion and process. When I began – oh! so long ago – to teach these students history by first teaching them ethnography, I would introduce them to Erving Goffman's *The Presentation of Self in Everyday Life* (1959) and Peter Berger's *Invitation to Sociology* (1963). They were both very disturbing books. They were both about what would be called these days "performance consciousness." Goffman's notion of the theater in person (*persona*, the classical stage masks) and role disturbed because it stressed the inventiveness of culturing and blurred the division between sincerity and insincerity. It became difficult after reading Goffman to know when and if one were only acting. Berger's thesis that sociology was a liberating form of social knowledge because it undermined the "bad faith" of believing society was imposed from outside was never altogether convincing, but it alerted students to the dialogic nature of social forms. Any ethnographic observer had to know that observation was always a reflection in the double sense of the word. The observer was mirrored in the observed: the observing consciously bridged known and unknown, familiar and different. That was true whether the ethnography was of a current experience of otherness or whether that otherness was past. Historians must read "present" for "self" and "past" for "other." Such self-consciousness in representation is commonly called "being theatrical." I am being theatrical. My chapter is about the theatricality of ethnography – implicit, explicit, both.

Theatricality is deep in every cultural action. Even if our sign worlds seem unconsciously performed, in hindsight, in our vernacular history-making, we will catch our performance consciousness and know how we manage the signs, make distinctions in the level of their meanings. That theatricality, present always, is intense when the moment being experienced is full of ambivalences. The "encounters in

(Leiden, 1978), 1–16, prompted the comment on the metaphor of expansion. Roland Barthes, Diderot, Brecht, Einstein, in Philip Rosen, ed. *Narrative, Apparatus, Ideology* (New York, 1986), 172–8, relates theatre and perspective. David Marshall, *The Figure of Theatre* (New York, 1986), 9, introduced me to "The Spectator" and provides a remarkable reader on English observers in the Enlightenment. Barbara Maria Stafford's *Voyage into Substance. Art, Science, Nature and the Illustrated Travel Account, 1760–1840* (Cambridge, MA, 1984) offers the most comprehensive survey and analysis of Enlightenment and post-Enlightenment observation.

place" of natives and strangers in the Pacific, 1767–1797, were full of such charades that were directed at producing effects in others. Government, law, property, justice, empire, civilization, God – were represented by the strangers in gesture, stylized action, and all the props of flags and weapons. The natives had their theater too. The intruding strangers were mimicked or mocked or explained away. The ambivalences of the occasion were danced or sung or told in story or painted or carved. My thesis for this ethnographic present of an ethnographic moment is that I must present its theater and its theatricality if I would represent what actually happened. Not what really happened. I do not care so much about what really happened. About what actually happened, I do.[2]

"PERSPECTIVING"

Victor Turner at the end of his life was seeking "the key to modernity" for much the same reason as I. He was inquiring about "The Anthropology of Performance," wanting to distinguish the theatricality of culture. Let me quote Victor Turner quoting Richard Palmer quoting the Swiss historian of perspective, Jean Gebser.

> Perspective spatializes the world; it orients the eye in relation to space in a new way ... it represents a rationalization of sight ... Perspective leads to the founding of mathematical geometry, which is the prerequisite for modern engineering and modern machinery ... for steadily increasing naturalism in European pictorial representation (but also for its purely schematic and logical extensions) ... Both are due to the growth and spread of methods which have provided symbols, repeatable in invariant form, for representation of visual awareness, and a grammar of perspective which made it possible to establish logical relations not only within the system of symbols but between that system and the forms and locations of the objects it symbolizes ... The combi-

[2] Kirsten Hastrup, "The Ethnographic Present: A Re-invention," *Cultural Anthropology* 5 (1990): 45–61, has some contemporary suggestions on how the ethnographic present might be constructively understood. Mary W. Helms, *Ulysses Sail. An Ethnographic Odyssey of Power, Knowledge and Geographical Data* (Princeton, 1988) has an engaging analysis of the politics of describing otherness. I have made my suggestions about the differences between the real and the actual elsewhere, Greg Dening, *History's Anthropology: The Death of William Gooch* (Washington, D.C., 1988) and "A Poetic for Histories: Transformations that Present the Past," in Aletta Biersack, ed. *Clio in Oceania* (Washington, 1991), 247–80. I have expanded on the double sided nature of theatricality between native and stranger in the Pacific in "Towards an Anthropology of Performance in Encounters in Place," in Donald H. Rubenstein, ed., *Pacific History* (Mangilao, Guam, 1992), 3–7, and there explain why I prefer D.J. Mulvaney's *Encounters in Place: Outsiders and Aboriginal Australians, 1606–1985* (St. Lucia, 1989) term "encounters in place" to "culture contact."

nation of the abstractedness of numbers as symbols that measure, with perspective, a way of relating those numbers as symbols to the visual world, leads to a sense of space as measured, as extending outward from a given point; ultimately the world is measurable – epitomized by Galileo's maxim, "to measure everything measurable and to make what is not measurable capable of being measured." The spatialization of vision has metaphysical and epistemological implications . . . The overemphasis on space and extension divides the world into observing subject and alien material objects . . . Words are seen as mere signs for the material objects in the world . . . Time itself is perceived in spatialized terms . . . It is regarded as measurable, as a linear succession of present moments . . . The perspectival model makes man the measure and the measurer of all things . . . Technologized rationality harmonizes with the protestant ethic – God places his blessing on the individualistic, competitive person (implicitly male) who exercises restraint and repressed desires in the interest of more "rational" goals: power and control . . . History, perceived as a straight line that ever circles back on itself, becomes the story of man's gradual self-improvement through the exercise of reason.[3]

The really wicked run to and fro

Mary W. Helms begins her "Ethnographic Odyssey of Power, Knowledge and Geographic Distance," *Ulysses Sail* (1988) with a citation from the Book of Daniel, 12:4: "Many shall run to and fro, and knowledge shall be increased." I thought it an apt citation for our discussions of Implicit Ethnography. "Implicit Ethnography" is something we have invented. It has no established meaning other than what we will come to. We will run to and fro through four hundred years of intercultural observation and a world encompassed. Our knowledge will increase as we discover the many meanings of "Implicit Ethnography." Noting, however, that the citation of Daniel 12: 4 by Helms was from the King James Version of the Bible, I wondered ethnographically how other versions might put it. Relics of bygone piety litter my library shelves, among them *The Jerusalem Bible* (1966), an authorized Roman Catholic English translation of French translations of ancient texts. There was something of a parable of the ethnographic process in that, I thought: All our historico-anthropological work will be transformations of transformations, observations of observing. Daniel 12:4 of *The Jerusalem Bible* reads: "Many will wander this way and that, and wickedness will go on increasing."

Ah! Wickedness and knowledge are often associated. We have a long mythological tradition that says that the knowledge of good and

[3] Victor Turner, *The Anthropology of Performance* (New York, 1988), 73.

evil was the beginning of our wickedness. And there are those who believe that ethnography is wicked, too. Ethnography, they say, is wicked because it promotes wimpish still-life portraits of twee cultural performances – of morris dancing and the like. It is unpolitical: It does not change the world. But others will say that ethnography is wicked not because it is unpolitical, but because it is too political. Ethnography is the voice of the powerful. Ethnography is a possession of the colonized. Let me say that it is not surprising that ethnography is seen as wicked from such polar opposite perspectives.

Ethnography rouses the "anti-theatrical prejudice" wherever it is found. Ethnography, by purporting to describe what actually happened rather than what really happened is very disturbing. Cliff Geertz in his essay on "thick description" told the story of the sahib querying the guru on an explanation of the world. "The world stands on an elephant, sahib." "And what does the elephant stand on?" "On a turtle, sahib." "And the turtle?" "On another turtle, sahib." "And that turtle?" "Sahib, there are turtles all the way down." To claim to see what really happened is to claim to be the last turtle on which everything else stands. We are familiar with many claims to be the last turtle – theology, philosophy, economics, psychology. What would it be now? Genetics, sociobiology?

It takes large blinkers, much socializing, a great deal of the politics of knowledge and a fear of theater to see oneself as the last turtle. Ethnography suggests that in representation there are no last turtles, because all reality like all culture is implicit, virtual. Representation is always a realization of the significance of totally particular expressions. In representation, reality, in Francis Bacon's term, is always negotiated. The anti-theatrical prejudice, confident that there are levels of meaning and that some one level of meaning has primacy over appearances of things, finds negotiation and process disturbing. Yet ethnography is nothing if it is not about the negotiations of meaning and the processes of invention out of what is given and determined, and what is created. Ethnography is not so much about culture as about culturing.[4]

THAT'S "CLAPTRAP," SOMEONE SAYS

Interesting that someone should say claptrap. "Claptrap" is a word that comes from the eighteenth-century theater. I flirt dangerously with it. It has a vulgar feel. The 1811 *Dictionary of the Vulgar Tongue*

[4] Clifford Geertz, *The Interpretation of Cultures* (New York, 1973).

and Dictionary of Buckish Slang, University Wit and Pickpocket Eloquence defined "clap" as "a venereal taint." "He went out by Had'em and came round by Clapham home; i.e. He went out wenching and got a clap!" Trapped the clap we might surmise. But claptrap is more innocent than that. The "clap" that is trapped is a hand-clap, applause. An actor trapped a clap when he or she evoked applause in the middle of a dramatic scene. By a gesture, a pose, a look, a pause, an actor drew the attention of the audience away from the part being acted to the acting of the part. Mimesis – the representation of reality – was broken or changed. The realism of a represented King Lear or Macbeth was transformed into the realism of brilliant performing. It was a disturbing transformation, however, often seen as self-indulgent on the part of the actor and a sign of the artificiality of theatricality. So nowadays we would be comfortable with *Roget's Thesaurus'* equivalences of "claptrap" with "blither, blather, blah-blah, flap-doodle, guff, pi-jaw, poppycock, humbug." Indeed in the incipient post-post-modernist age we are experiencing, claptrap, any form of representation that draws attention to its own representing, is decried as an insidious evil. From conference room floors and platforms, from new journals and monographs comes the call to return to the good old modernist days, when a fact was a fact was a fact. So I flirt doubly dangerously when I suggest that the only true science is claptrap. I am not so bumptious, however, that I do not add that there is art in being a true science.

Claptrap, in my more positive view of it, is the moment of theatricality in any representation, the space created by the performance consciousness of the representer in which the audience – or the reader or the viewer – participates in the creative process of representing. I like to think that the idea of such a space is not analytically new. It is as old as Aristotle. He called the space "catharsis," which – if I can follow the most recent commentator on *Aristotle's Poetics,* Stephen Halliwell – in Aristotle's meaning was not "purging" but "enlightening." Claptrap is the moment of enlightenment at which *muthos* (plot-structure) transforms the specificity of words, gestures and actions into something universal. By that, Aristotle rescued mimesis from Plato's denigration. Plato's narrow concept of mimesis as exact reproduction made him label every representation as something untrue to reality, as something less than reality, empty, fraudulent. Mimesis on the other hand for Aristotle was creative. It generated reality not merely repeated it. I warm to his insight. I understand what he was saying. There is a space in representing – in a poem, in a narrative, in a play... there is a space in culturing – in a ritual, in a role, in a social drama . . . there is a space in the ethnographic process - in describing, in depicting – in which the dialogic relation between the represented and the representing are seen to be a key to realism.

Others later than Aristotle, of course, have recognized the power of this space in the culturing and ethnographic process. James W. Fernandez has referred to "revelatory incidents"; Marshall Sahlins to the fact that "an event is not just a happening in the world; it is a relation between certain happenings and a given symbol system"; Edwin Ardener to "semantic density"; James Boon to "cultural operators." And Aristotle to "catharsis." And I to "claptrap." Don't let us worry about whether we are all saying the same thing. Let's say that we are attracted to the same phenomenon. The sense of artefactuality in representing does not necessarily detract from its realism. It is the key to realism. And realism is what ethnography and observing are about. The theatricality of observing and being observed is that guarantee of their being faction rather than fiction.[5]

ETHNOGRAPHY ON MY MIND

A lifetime would not be long enough to read all the products of the Euroamerican/Polynesian ethnographic experiences of the thirty

[5] Discovering the meaning of claptrap was such a pleasant surprise that it became connected in my mind's eye with what I had been reading of ethnography: James Clifford, *The Predicament of Culture* (Cambridge, MA, 1988); James Clifford and George Marcus, eds., *Writing Culture* (Berkeley, CA, 1984); Paul Rabinow, "Discourse and Power: On the Limits of Ethnographic Texts," *Dialectical Anthropology* 10 (1986): 1–14, and what I learned of the theatre: Jean Christophe Agnew, *Worlds Apart: The Market and the Theater in Anglo-American Thought, 1550–1750* (Cambridge, 1986); Peter Stallybrass and Allon White, *The Politics and Poetics of Transgression* (Ithaca, NY, 1986); Jonas Barish, *The Anti-Theatrical Prejudice*. (Berkeley, 1981), and mimesis: Stephen Halliwell, *Aristotle's Poetics* (Chapel Hill, NC, 1986); Karl F. Morrison, *The Mimetic Tradition of Reform in the West* (Princeton, 1982); Eric A. Havelock, *Preface to Plato* (Cambridge, MA, 1963); Erich Auerbach, *Mimesis: The Representation of Reality in Western Literature* (Princeton, 1968), and acting performance: Victor Turner, *From Ritual to Theatre* (New York, 1982), and *The Anthropology of Performance* (New York, 1988); Richard Schechner, *Between Theater and Anthropology* (Philadelphia, 1981); Martin Meisel, *Realization: Narrative, Pictorial and Theatrical Arts in Nineteenth Century England* (Princeton, 1983); Richard Handler and William Saxton, "Dyssimulation: Reflexivity, Narrative and the Quest for Aesthetics," *Cultural Anthropology* 3 (1988): 242–260; John Gassner and Ralph G. Allen, *Theatre and Drama in the Making* (Boston, 1964). James Fernandez, *Persuasions and Performances: The Play of Tropes in Culture* (Bloomington, IN, 1986); Marshall Sahlins, *Islands of History* (Chicago, 1985); James Boon, "Further Operations of Culture in Anthropology," in L. Schneider and C. Bonjean, eds., *The Idea of Culture in the Social Sciences* (Cambridge, 1973), 1–32; Edwin Ardener; Social Anthropology, Language and Reality, in D. Parkin, ed., *Semantic Anthropology* (London, 1982), 1–14, might be surprised to see their notions joined to claptrap. They must be patient and wait for an explanation.

years of the season of observing, and the archaeology of knowledge of the two hundred years that followed. We think we stand alongside this deposit and see its strata. In reality we stand on its surface and are part of it as much as observers of it. It is thirty years since I first read Cook, Bougainville, Forster, La Pérouse, Bligh, Vancouver and the rest of the Euroamerican intruders into the Pacific. The thirty years of my ethnographic experience of the Pacific matches the thirty years of ethnography of which I write. I need to give witness to the enjoyment of those years to reveal something of the archaeology of its knowledge.

Thirty years ago we had a sense that Pacific waters were still uncharted. We were brash. We thought that we had discovered something. We called it prehistory. We called it ethnohistory. We were careless with the words we used, not knowing the politics that were in them. We thought we might make their meaning out of what we did rather than bow to some claim of territoriality that others might make. We felt we had a lodestone in these uncharted waters. It was our history.

Anthropology scandalized us. We took British anthropology's rhetorical scorn for history personally, not knowing it for the politics of discipline that it was. We knew American cultural anthropology only in its most generalized form and thought A. L. Kroeber as distant from an historical past as Oswald Spengler and Arnold Toynbee. We reserved our deepest skepticism for Pacific ethnography. It was founded, we thought, on the false premise of an "ethnographic present." It was essentialist in character, taking "Polynesian" and "Melanesian" out of time as if 200 years of contact had made no difference. The ethnographers seemed to assume that there was nothing in between the "now" of their observation and the "then" of island cultures before contact. And when the ethnographers used Cook, Bougainville and the others as we did, we knew that *we* read our primary sources with much more of a sense of their conditioned, contexted nature than did the anthropologists. Anthropologists stopped at the library and published sources. They did not seem to have the zeal to track down the unlikely letter or log or to chase home the past into all the nooks and crannies of personal, social and institutional life. We had the heady experience of knowing that there was not a cultural trait or ritual or legend or collected artefact that did not have an historiography. We *knew* that anthropologists had no patience for all the lateral pursuits that were essential to history. Every new source found raised a question about its relation to the rest, the interpretive framework into which it must be put, the contextual knowledge that would make sense of it. And we had R.G. Collingwood and his archaeological history of Roman Britain to help us understand Easter Island, Marc Bloch and his study of feudalism to know what culture might really be. R.H. Tawney and Max Weber with their delicious ironies on the unseen reality behind religion informed our missionary studies. We stood on archaeological peaks with Sir Mortimer Wheeler and felt that we had been offered a kingdom. We even flew in a "Tiger Moth" with O.G.S. Crawford and saw *The Lost Villages of England* in shadows on wheat and barley and marveled at what new skills we would need to learn to write the history we wanted to write.

It was an exciting time to begin Pacific studies. Andrew Sharp had just written *Ancient Voyagers of the Pacific* (1957), a maverick challenge to the orthodoxy of how the Pacific was settled. But we did not think he had it right because he had not read the sources as carefully as we had. We could tap the European voyagers' natural interest in navigation and map the hundreds of deliberate and accidental canoe voyages they recorded. We were confident that we could "see" or at least catch an ethnographic glimpse of Polynesian navigation through explorers' eyes. Thor Heyerdahl had completed his Kon Tiki voyage. His *American Indians in the Pacific* (1952) was made for training jousts. We practiced skepticism on him and thought we were being critical. We enjoyed every small discovery of how unhistorical his thesis was. We saw Bernard Smith's *European Vision and the South Pacific* (1966) in manuscript and caught the idea that ethnography in image, like ethnography in words, was culture bound. The young Marshall Sahlins had just published *Social Stratification in Polynesia* (1958). We saw it as the latest and most sophisticated effort to cre ate time without history. His typology of social structures in relation to island environments gave a new abstraction to Pacific studies. It teased the historian in us to discover what function models had in historical explanation. Botanists, glottochronologists, geneticists buzzed about the "Polynesian Problem" – where did the Polynesians come from? We discovered that disciplines were about creating languages and being comfortable with different sets of blinkers. These were years of innocence in which we read E.D. Merrill on botany, Bengt Anell on fish-hooks, A.C Haddon and James Hornell on canoes, Peter H. Buck on material culture, Edwin G. Burrows on boundaries, E.S.C. Handy on religion, and Katherine Luomala on myths in the belief we were doing history. We felt immodestly superior to the "antiquarians" of the pacific – Elsdon Best, Percy Smith, F.W. Christian. Their vast knowledge only served madcap theories about Polynesian origins and movements. In out of the way places from Finland to New Zealand, from

Leningrad to Valparaiso, men and women had collected the products of their experience of the Pacific. We felt that there was not an archive or a library or a museum, a learned society or a colonial bureaucracy in all of Europe and the Americas in which the ethnographic experience of the Pacific was not texted in some way. That immense variety of texts – logs, diaries, letters, journals, government reports, lectures, books, notes, written-down oral traditions, notes of memories – encapsulated the experience of those who made the texts as well as something of the otherness of nature and cultures that was experienced. We felt that the peculiar joy of Pacific history was to catch the seers, the seen and the seeing.

In this most humbling experience of how much a plagiarism living and knowing is, I feel I have made one or two small rediscoveries pertinent to our interests. My work in the Pacific has been principally among those who have experienced otherness from both sides of the beaches of islands – the Polynesians experiencing the otherness of the Euroamericans, the Euroamericans experiencing the otherness of the Polynesians. "Polynesian"! "Euroamerican"! Believe me, I know the differences of culture, role, gender, personality, class, institution that both sets of quotation marks enclose. But the differences were great enough to say that they do not matter either in the Pacific or out of it at the level of abstraction I am going to talk at. "It was not like that in Yucatan in the 16th Century," "The French were different in the 17th Century" are dissenting sentiments that will not faze me or end our conversation. I am going to describe people and events totally particular in time, place and character and ask, nonetheless, that we all talk about them for the qualities that join them. My particular interest in the Polynesian/Euroamerican experience of each others' otherness has been in those who have "gone native," the ways in which both sides of a cultural boundary possess one another, the stridency with which cultural forms especially among those like missionaries and colonial administrators who want to change the other in some way are represented on the margins of culture, and the ways in which this experience is emplotted, narrated, or, in a word I have come to appreciate, "realized." Let me offer these four foci of the ethnographic moment for our common conversation.[6]

[6] Marshall Sahlins, *Social Stratification in Polynesia* (Seattle, 1958); E.D. Merrill, *The Botany of Cook's Voyages, in Chronica Botanica* 14 (1954): 161–384; Bengt Anell, *Contribution to the History of Fishing in the South Seas* (Uppsala, 1955); A.C. Haddon and James Hornell, *Canoes of Oceania* (Honolulu, 1936–8); P.H. Buck, *The Material Culture of the Cook Islands* (New Plymouth, 1927); Edwin G. Burrows, "Breed and Border in Polynesia," *American Anthropologist* 41 (1939): 1–21; E.S.C. Handy, *Polynesian Religion* (Honolulu,

The ethnographic moment

"Ethnographic Moment" has entered my discourse as if we had agreed on what it might mean. We have not. Let me say what I mean. Anthropology, of course, has long been concerned with an "ethnographic present." Indeed anthropology's current lack of confidence turns around all the deconstructions being made of the ethnographic present. The word "ethnography" has probably driven us all to the dictionary to discover that it means scientific description (*graphos*) of groups (*ethnos*) of human beings. My friend Rhys Isaac, who has made significant contributions to our notions of ethnographic history, recently waved (metaphorically!) a volume of the full Oxford English Dictionary under my nose and excitedly pointed to the OED's citations for "ethnography." One was from the *Penny Cyclopaedia* II, 97 (1834). It reads "the term ethnography (nation-description) is sometimes used by German writers in the sense that we have given anthropography." Indeed the *Penny Cyclopaedia of the Society for the Diffusion of Useful Knowledge* has a small dissertation on anthropography (man-description), ethnography (nation-description) and *volkerkunde* (people-knowledge) and their relations. [And a small essay on "Anthropology" – what was said to be Immanuel Kant's summertime escape from more gruelling wintertime philosophy – which takes me too far afield. And a nice little essay on "Antipodes" – where opposites meet toe-to-toe, which takes me back to juxtaposed othernesses.]

Rhys Isaac's real enjoyment came from the OED's citation of Thomas De Quincey (1857) *China, Works* 1871, xvi 233: "The Englishman of Chinese ethnography has not a house except in crevices in the rocks." It seems so appropriate that the OED should cite a usage – even that of a confessed opium user – that implied that "natives" have ethnographies too. That it should be so laughably wrong might give us pause about what is seen either way in ethnography or, better, ask what it could possibly mean. The two matters stressed in the dictionary-understanding of ethnography are on human beings seen as groups and on the scientific nature of the description. I make the didactic point out of this that (a) the object of ethnographic observation is human behavior in its systematic dimension. Identity in, communication by, consistency and interconnectedness of signs makes boundaries around groups and sets of behavior. It is the job of the

1927); Katherine Luomala, *Maui-of-a-Thousand-Tricks: His Oceanic and European Biographers* (Honolulu, 1949), are a small part of the joy of the Pacific as *theatrum mundi* to an anthro-archaeologico-historico-academic order.

ethnographer to catch these systems at work. (b) The description can never be divorced from the discourse of which it is a part. So inevitably ethnographies feed on one another. The Other is rarely met in a present divorced from all the meetings that have gone before.

ETHNOGRAPHIC PRESENTS

For a number of years, the ethnographic present of my historical studies has been reduced roughly to a decade, 1785–1795. Anthropologists claim authenticity for their ethnograpahies out of the shock of "being there." The pain and embarrassment of being in their ethnographic present marks their I-witnessing with sincerity and a never-to-be-repeated quality. And while they know now in 1994 how illusory is their sense of being engulfed in the cultures they observe, they nonetheless feel they experience the ambience of living differently, in its fullness, in the interconnectedness of a myriad cultural signs. The historian's ethnographic present is no less painful but it is much more linear and stretched out and much less total. The living, in an historian's ethnographic present, comes in sentences, one after the other. But both the anthropologist and the historian will invent the culture he or she observes. Both will make that invention out of texted, rather than actual, experience. For the anthropologist, the experience is mediated by memory-written-down in fieldnotes – by the informant already having invented the culture being mediated to the ethnographer – and all the systems of recording. Perhaps, the historian is better served than the anthropologist by the variability of the genres of texts of culture, and certainly he or she has more checks on the ways in which culture is mediated. The historian's ambition is to be exhaustive of all the texts available, knowing that in the end the return on all the lateral pursuits is a sense of balance and possibility. There is the authenticity in that of having done all that can be done, of having confronted all there is to be confronted. The anthropologists are forever left wondering in what way the mediating point of entry into another culture – their informants, their own experiences – is prejudiced by any number of selectivities – class, gender, personality, age, among them. The ambitions of historians and anthropologists about their ethnographic presents are the same. The Past and the Other should be re-presented as they were. But that representation is never a duplication, a copy, an instant replay. Neither the Past nor the Other need recognize themselves in ethnography. Both are transformed into something else. They are not made to relive. They are made texts in other people's living, in other times.

So my ethnographic present of 1785–1795 is made up of texts I can hardly number and in genres I could barely describe, given sense by readings over time that change and leach each other out. And when I confront the issue of writing the culture I describe, I have options and strategies without end.

My goal now is to describe "perspectiving," the process by which ways of seeing are made natural, culturally comfortable. Perspectiving, I have long decided, is a social process. All the socializing forces – of sanctions, of rites of passage, of language, of caricature and joking – are at work in making ways of seeing seem natural. We call ways of seeing academically, "disciplines." To see the world theologically, psychologically, medically, economically or in any mode in which ways of seeing are blinkered requires great discipline. That discipline is a powerful thing. It makes us see facts as if they are found and not the fictions we make. I thought one strategy in displaying the power of perspectiving would be to catch the passion and elation created by new perspectives in my ethnographic present. I had a chapter planned in my mind's eye on ballooning, on microscopes, on calibration. I understood the sweetness in the experience and the promise of the air-balloon, newly invented in 1785. The balloon gave access to patterns in the land below, to the aetherial elements above, to a world without noise. Look through a microscope and design in nature becomes exquisitely apparent. Know the aesthetics of a machine that could callibrate an instrument of astronomy to a thousandth of an inch. My ethnographic present is full of the excitement of seeing the world from a new perspective. And in the end, I thought I might take you to the top of the Monument in London and let you see the world from the perspective of *The Devil on Two Sticks* (1790). The devil, mediated by William Combe, made a good spectator. Combe's ironies were strong. There is a very satisfying perspective in a satirical laugh.

The exhilaration of seeing something differently – from a new perspective – lends a sort of self-righteousness to perspectiving. The passion for the beauty of the experience gives a dispassionate claim to its science, authenticates its disinterestedness, lends a moral quality of discipline. The world is more factual the more passionate the disinterestedness of the observer. Claptrap about such disinterestedness suddenly seems distasteful, immoral even. Dare one say it so anachronistically. Claptrap seems so postmodern.

My strategies are more conniving, I fear, than to persuade you that exhilaration at perspectiving was "the key to modernity," that perspectiving opens the door to my ethnographic present. I frankly don't believe that there is a deep epistemic divide between modernism and postmodernism. Perspectiving always involves claptrap, always has. My strategy for the rest of my paper is to persuade you to that.[7]

THE THEATER AS AN ETHNOGRAPHIC PRESENT

Jean-Christophe Agnew (1986) has argued in his *Worlds Apart: The Market and the Theater in Anglo-American Thought, 1550–1750* that if you would understand the civilizing process in capitalism you must understand the didactic relationship between the theater and the marketplace. England was made modern by learning to reify the abstractions of the economy in the theater. I want to add to that argument that the theater was a learning place for perspectiving as well and that what was learned in theater was that mimesis, or representation of reality, included a sense of its making, of claptrap. For those whose vested interests in hegemony required that mimesis in all its forms be reproduction of reality and not a representation of it, the liberating role of theater was very threatening and was the basis of their "anti-theatrical prejudice." I would like to understand this liberating process in perspectiving – ethnographically.

I am drawn to the theater by a pantomime at Christmas time, 1785, in which the Pacific was made *theatrum mundi*. The pantomime was called "Omai: Or a Voyage Round the World." Omai had been a Tahitian brought back by James Cook – "collected" would be a better word. He had excited London to no end ethnographically. He was the opportunity to play "The Spectator" to the Noble Savage. He titillated sexuality: the gentle folk could nudge one another at the awkwardness of his 'nobility'. In the end when he had come and gone, London knew that the Noble Savage was a joke. Omai was the pantomime of that joke.

Omai was the heir apparent to the Tahitian throne. He was in love with "Londina" the daughter of "Britannia." But a Spaniard, "Don Struttolando," was conniving to stop the marriage. (One has to say in passing that the Other that really interested Englishmen was not the savage at all, but the other Europeans.) The Don chases the lovers all over the world – they escape in a balloon at one point: it is the year of its invention! They flee to all the places "discovered" by Cook. In the end the lovers triumph at Tahiti, are married and crowned. (Their chief opponent at Tahiti is a sorceress called "Oberea." Oberea was

[7] I have described my understanding of the poetics of histories and the transformations of the past into an ethnographic present elsewhere: Greg Dening, *History's Anthropology*, and "A Poetic for Histories."

the Queen of Tahiti who the English imagined had handed over Tahiti to Samuel Wallis in 1767. She had been Joseph Banks' lover. The English as "spectators" of this meeting with the Noble Savage laughed her into absurdity and made her a sorceress instead.)

The pantomime ended with a magnificent procession of all the nations of the Pacific discovered by Cook. The costumes worn were designed by John Webber, the "illustrator" for Cook's third voyage. The artefacts they held were copied from "artificial curiosities" brought back. The procession paraded before a giant portrait of Cook being apotheozied by Fame and Britannia. All raised their voices in a paean of praise:

> The hero of Macedon ran o'er the world
> Yet nothing but death could he give;
> 'Twas George's command and the sail was unfurl'd
> And Cook taught mankind how to live.
> He *came* and he *saw*, not to *conquer* but save,
> The Caesar of Britain was he:
> Who scorn'd the conditions of making a slave
> While Britons themselves are so free.

Wouldn't you say the British in seeing the Native are seeing themselves? Wouldn't you feel that the Native is transformed into an object of humane engagement with the better self of the civilized? The critics of the London *Times* were ecstatic with the pantomime. Out of all the burlesque and fantasizing of the formal pantomime structure, they declared, this was a "school for the history of man." "It is a spectacle worthy of the contemplation of every rational being, from infant to the aged philosopher. A spectacle that holds forth the wisdoms and dispositions of Providence in the strongest view."[8]

THE PARADOX OF ACTING

When I puzzle at how such "catharsis" can occur, at how the audience could make such *muthos*, or plot-structure, out of such extravagant fantasy, I think it is because of the "perspectiving" of the theatrical experience. You must allow me to I-witness my ethnographic experience. Believe me that I could describe the brilliant staging of Omai by Philippe de Loutherbourg. He transported the audience visually

[8] See Greg Dening, "Possessing Tahiti," *Archaeology in Oceania* 21 (1986): 103–18, where the pantomime and its reviews are described in detail. Greg Dening, *Mr Bligh's Bad Language: Passion, Power and Theatre on the Bounty* (Cambridge, 1992), 262–303, puts the issue into a broader context of the 18th century theater.

into an ethnographic experience of native otherness by stunning them with the brilliance of his representation of the totally familiar. He liberated the audience for serious interpretation of the totally flippant by engaging their eyes in the illusions of reality.

Be patient with my own perspectiving. I must blinker you to see what I am saying. Let me bypass all that needs to be said of mimesis (and of Erich Auerbach) to make my point. Let me assume that I could persuade you to a history of late eighteenth-century theater which showed how audiences were educated to claptrap – by prologues, by soliloquies, by plays within a play, by attention drawn to the conventionalities of emotional expression, by all the *rites de passage* which end everyday life and begin the theatrical state of being an audience, by all the mechanisms of enclosing dramatic unity with a curtain, with a "stage door." I must even ask you to let me set aside a small paragraph on the theater as metaphor of the ethnographic experience. I am desperate to get to Denis Diderot.

It was Denis Diderot's famous contention that there was a "Paradox of Acting." Diderot's paradox was that the more a great actor appeared to be overwhelmed by the emotion of his role, the cooler he was and the more in command of himself. "It is extreme sensibility that makes actors mediocre. It is middling sensibility which makes a multitude of bad actors. And it is the lack of sensibility which qualifies actors to be sublime." I take "sensibility" for Diderot to mean such absorption in representation that there is no consciousness of the authorship of signs. Supreme realism requires an inner claptrap in the actor. "I require of [the actor] a cold and tranquil spectator. Great poets, great actors and perhaps in general all the great imitators of nature . . . are the least sensitive of beings . . . They are too engaged in observing, in recognizing or imitating, to be vitally affected witnesses. All [the actor's] talents consist not in feeling, as you imagine, but in rendering so scrupulously the external signs of feeling, that you are taken in." "Reflect a little as to what, in the language of the theater, is being true. Is it showing things as they are in nature? Certainly not. Were it so, the true would be commonplace. What then is the truth for stage purposes? It is the conformity of action, diction, face, voice, movement and gesture to an ideal type invented by the poet and frequently enhanced by the player."

I hear Aristotle in Diderot. I read Barthes in him. I see Picasso. Maybe Nietzsche, maybe Foucault. But not to burden these great men with these responsibilities, I see me. For sensibility, read perspectiving. The supreme realism in perspectiving was and is not in the facts revealed but in understanding the authorial role of producing those facts. That authorial understanding is implicit in the exhilaration of discovering perspectives in the late eighteenth century. I offer it as my implicit ethnography. In every modernist there was a latent postmodernist. If you ask me why the claptrap was so latent, then you must expect another paper on the power and hegemony of the "antitheatrical prejudice."[9]

"GOING NATIVE"

"Going Native," the impossible dream of anthropology, has held, of late, some fascination for the historian and the literary critic. True, one will hear the occasional sigh: "I am growing so tired of the Other," or, "I myself have never met the Other, only others." True, also, the Other of this latter day fascination has more to do with reflections of the Same that are seen in the Other. The Other is "Mirror for Man," we can safely say, given the gendered images of power to be found in reflections of the discovered and colonized Other. Of course, the Other is nearer home than the South Seas or the New World. The grotesque is recognizable as a trope of reflexivity now that we have read Mickail Bakhtin's history of laughter. The Other whether this is the monkey at the fair or the cannibal savage on display or the educated worker, or the chauvinist-appearing woman is reduced to a frightening or comic spectacle set against the antithetical normality of the spectator, as Peter Stallybrass and Allon White have noted. The theater of the grotesque, these two writers suggest, is not so much in the display of total strangeness as in the awkward mimicry of the truly civilized by these strangers. The Other is the Same, only worse, and inept, ugly or evil. The laughter in the theater of the grotesque is the laughter of relief at discovering that the Other is not Other after all.

That is why going native has always been such a scandalous act. In the Pacific, the beachcomber who escaped regulated ship-life, the missionary who made some distinction in the accidents and essentials of belief, the colonial administrator who accepted native political and social status as something more than make-believe, even the occasional explorer who wondered what he had "discovered" and whether his "discovery" was truly to the good of the native were a scandal to the civilized and became objects of prurient interest.

In the view of those at the center of empires, of course, distance

[9] Denis Diderot, *Paradox sur le Comédien* [1769] (Paris, 1958); Arthur Wilson, *Diderot* (New York, 1972), 621; Toby Cole and Helen Kirch Chinoy, eds., *Actors on Acting* (New Haven, 1949), 163–6.

made everybody a little "native." The changed accent and vocabulary, the social awkwardnesses, the unstylishness of dress and behavior marginalized the colonials as somewhat strange, as having given deference to something uncivilized. Colonials are always grotesque because they lie in the liminal space between being stylishly modern and nostalgically antique. Recognition of such grotesquerie is laughable and empowering but not threatening in itself. Going native stirs the blood a little more. Going native always began – always begins – with some deference to the realism of another cultural system. It catches in that deference something of the consistency and interconnectedness of things. It was – and is – a lonely act, better done out of sight of the mocking gaze of co-culturalists. Even a touch of cultural relativism, like a dab of post-modernism, is counted dangerous. The world is suddenly filled with threatened people, the moment one cuts the cultural tie subjunctively. Cast one rope of a cultural tie and someone is sure to shout: "The pier is sinking."

In the Pacific and for the beachcomber, this deference to the realism of another cultural system, as likely as not, began with a tattoo. *Tatau* is a Polynesian word. A tattoo was a badge of any eighteenth-century sailor's ethnographic experience in the Pacific. All Polynesian cultures within the great triangle of Hawaii, New Zealand, Easter Island practiced tattooing with differing degrees of intensity. Polynesians marked their bodies permanently in token of their membership in different cohorts, as history of major events and achievements in their lives, as cosmetic. Its permanent obviousness on a beachcomber was a mark of cultural estrangement to the "civilized," especially if he wore it on any part of his body which he could not clothe over, his face most especially. Inclusion and estrangment were the double marks of tattooing and going native.

Tattooing was theater as well as symbol. The Polynesians included the beachcombers in both the seriousness and the joke of tattooing. The pain of tattooing was a test for both native and "native" alike. But it was also clear that the Polynesians read the Euroamerican observers for their interest in nativeness. And while the "civilized" played out in high hyperbole and caricature their civilized discipline, the natives acted out their expected nativeness. They caught the Euroamerican attraction to the bizarre and displayed to them the grotesque of their nativeness – whether it was in their tattoos, or in their make-believe warrior behavior or in "cannibalism" or extravagant misuse of European artefacts. (They could, after all, see the Euroamericans collecting them.) The islanders expected those who wanted to share in the real exchange of going native to display nativeness just as grotesquely.

For the beachcombers these marks of nativeness were serious and joking too. Of the hundreds of beachcombers that we know, of the hundreds more exemplars of the civilized going native that we might cite, almost all crossed over cultures only temporarily, and all took on a mediating role – interpreting, controlling the extravagant behavior of both sides of the beach. For beachcombers the marking was serious. However permanently they were signed with nativeness they would return to their own ways and always be marked by some grotesque difference. The marks were a joke as well. The designs of their tattoos were always a mixture of Polynesian and Euroamerican commentary. The mutineers of the *Bounty* enjoyed the joke of tattooing themselves with the star emblem of the Knights of the Garter. One of them had *Honi Soit Qui Mal y Pense* tattooed on his thigh. One wonders what their sailors' yarns made of the half lubricious mythologies concerning the Garter and its connection with the Crown against which they were rebelling. And with what brazenness did they dare anybody to say 'shame' to their going native.

Tattoos might seem a somewhat trivial historical pursuit. But going native was a highly marketable experience, as Daniel Defoe discovered before our period, as Herman Melville after it, as anthropology discovered since. Having the story of being native guaranteed a publisher. Having the marks on one's body or the things collected gave the opportunity for theater. Having a vicarious native accessible to observation in familiar surroundings of academies, learned societies, courts, marketplaces and fairs, made for a special sort of ethnographical experience. There were, of course, *bona fide* natives brought back for observation, native beachcombers on Euroamerican beaches. In all of this, there was as much thrill in the air from 1767 to 1797 as if the antipodes or South Seas were a world of "wolf-children" or a world, as Michel Foucault suggested, filled with children born blind suddenly seeing for the first time. The narratives of going native and 'being native' emplotted the civilizing process.

Let me make one such narrative to show it to be so. Joseph (or Jean) Kabris (or Cabry or Cabri or Cabrit or Kobrite) was a French sailor from Bordeaux. He was captured by the British in the battle of Quiberon, 1795, taken as prisoner to the hulks at Portsmouth, then allowed to go in an English whaler to the South Seas. He deserted in the Marquesas and made his deferences by being profusely tattooed in Marquesan style (but leaving space on his belly for a tattooed clay pipe). He entered Marquesan society by becoming the secondary husband in a chiefly family with all the warrior obligations of that exchange. He "fished" for human sacrifices in that role. In 1804 the Russian expedition to the Pacific under Adam J. von Krusenstern was delighted to have the native culture of the Marquesas mediated for them by Kabris and another beachcomber, Edward Robarts, gone native for six or seven years. The Russians' whole ethnographic experience of the Marquesas was transformed by this mediation and by their reflections on what it meant. By accident (probably) the Russians took Kabris away with them and in the end landed him at Kamchatka. He acted out for them on the way there various rituals of Marquesan sacrificial and sorcery life. He made his way by land from Kamchatka to Moscow, Leningrad and Kronstadt. He had learned how marketable his 'native' skills had become. So he danced and charaded and showed his tattoos in court theaters and fairs from Moscow to Paris to Brittany.

One special skill of the Marquesans – their swimming prowess – earned him employment as swimming instructor to the marines at Kronstadt. He quickly learned that his theater needed a text. So he had pamphlets written narrating his life of being a native. He emplotted the pamphlets with stories of his royal marriages, of Pocahontas-like princesses, hints at savagery, denials of cannibalism, suggestions of international rivalries. He absorbed the stories of his companion native, Robarts, to his own and made of it all a very satisfying experience for those who expected to be horrified at savagery and reinforced in their own civilized ways. In the end, when the sprightliness of his performances was slowed and the competition of the even more grotesque too sharp, only the permanence of his tattoos remained. Entrepreneurs at Valenciennes where he died thought they might have had a more enduring monument to his nativeness if they tanned his hide. There were, in other places, pickled penises and shrunken heads that gave some drama to collecting natives. However, the city fathers of Valenciennes baulked at flaying his dead body, and buried him sandwiched between two paupers' corpses to stop anybody trying. If we are talking of the "ethnographic moment" in which the Euroamerican met the Other of the Pacific, it seems to me that it is not unlikely that the Other that was really met was of the likes of Joseph Kabris in the theater of his 'going native.'[10]

[10] Michel de Certeau's *The Writing of History* (New York, 1989), Mikhail Bakhtin's, *Rabelais and His World* (Bloomington, IN, 1984), and Peter Stallybrass and Allon White's *The Politics and Poetics of Transgression* would be essential reading for any notion of implicit ethnography of whatever period and whatever culture.

PRODUCING EFFECTS

"Effects" is a word of the theater and representation. We meet it nowadays in such phrases as "effects microphone," "special effects": the one catching and controlling the noise of crowds, the crunch of bodies, the crack of bat on ball to give a sense of presence and immediacy; the other exploiting the blinkered view of camera or stage to create the illusion of realism. There is more than a two-hundred-year history to its changing use in criticism, as thinkers from Diderot to Wagner puzzled with the problem of how the manipulation of signs could be conventional and real at the same time. But the problem is not just an aesthetic one. Everywhere – where a missionary friar whispers over bread and wine that they are body and blood, where a judge and executioner preside over capital punishment, where an observer provides an "illustration" for his ethnography, where a voyaging captain makes an example by a bombardment – everywhere where there are signs made there is room for the sign-maker and the sign-seer to reflect on the effects produced. No circumstance calls for reflection more than a cross-cultural one.

Let me begin where we all begin as historians, with our own experience. It is, I think, our own ambivalences about what happens in sign-making that makes some of us skeptical that as historians we can ever see the complexities that must be in sign-making in the past. When we "ethnocraft" our own experience – in a ritual, say – we discover how silent much of the sign-making is, how multivalent its meanings are, how multivalent our own actual experience. As historians we often despair at the silences of the past and the partiality of its sounds. Be of good cheer, I say. What we have we must make sense of. What we have is a partial past and the reflective present.

Let me make a little history first. In 1792 there were two sets of public executions designed to produce effects. One was in Portsmouth, England, where three *Bounty* mutineers were hanged for mutiny. The other was off Waikiki on the Hawaiian island of Oahu, where three Hawaiians were executed by George Vancouver as the supposed murderers of two Englishmen, Lieutenant Richard Hergest and Astronomer William Gooch of the supply vessel *Daedalus*.

It is tempting to say of the *Bounty* executioners what Thomas Paine wrote of Edmund Burke's *Revolution in France,* and I will quote Paine for what I also want to make of Burke's ideas on producing effects.

> I cannot consider Mr. Burke's book in any other light than [as] a dramatic performance; and he must have considered it in the same light himself, by

> the poetical liberties he has taken of omitting some facts, distorting others, and making the whole machinery bend to produce a strange effect . . . It suits his purpose to exhibit the consequences without their causes. It is one of the arts of the drama to do so. If the crimes of men were exhibited with their sufferings, the strange effect would sometimes be lost, and the audience would be inclined to approve where it was intended they should commiserate.

The whole drama of the *Bounty* courtmartial and executions was directed to representing the mutiny as an act against the sovereign power of the crown, having no causes or history and allowing no claptrap on the part of the court, its witnesses or its victims. The "poetical liberties" taken to see the events *legally* and not as they *actually* happened, required great discipline of language, of selective vision, of managed courtroom behavior. No representation of the processual, or the accidental, in human events could be allowed, no sense of the complexities in the exchanges of language and gesture, no sense of the indeterminacy and multivalency of the signals being made. Then the executions themselves were carefully rubricized by naval law and custom, carefully rhetoricized by the speeches of the condemned, the sermons of the ministers, the words of command, the order of the space of participants and audience, the explicit allegories in who did the hanging (the condemned men's peers), who did the comforting (those like the victims who had been condemned but freed by the king's mercy).

I, the historian, have some pale sense of the ambivalence of signs and sounds and smells. I can see signs that the audience is divided by its different preoccupations – by keeping the witnessing boats steady, by the scandal of officers at improprieties, by awareness of itself and its sniggers and dissent. I cannot hear the minds of all those on whom the effects were being produced, but I can suspect that the silence was of various sorts – of boredom, of cynicism, of anger, of stupidity, of reverence, of fear. I know that if my ethnographic history is only of rubric and rhetoric without hint of distraction and diversity, then, like Burke, I too can be accused of representing the staged effect. On the other hand, I know enough about ritual to understand that its meaning is not in its bits and pieces or even in itself. Its theatricality is in the way its parts are pulled together and understood in their relation to something else. That something else in the case of the *Bounty* executions was the fact that all who witnessed them were there – disapproving or approving – because of fear, or by force, or thinking they were properly there. They might have had as many explanations as they were numbered, but they suffered themselves to be present. There is an awful power in that. My ethnography must show it so.

Vancouver had a different problem. He wanted to produce in Hawaiians a sense of retributive justice. He wanted the Hawaiians to make giant leaps in the civilizing process and see that sovereign power reached over distances they could not imagine from an English kingship about whose abstractions and praxis they had no idea. He had all the cultural presumptions of *realpolitik* as well. The Hawaiians would connect all the universal signs of justice, of mercy, of terror – of the sublime – with actions for which they were personally, communally, politically responsible. If he played judge, jury and executioner to them, they would see his universal theater. If he did not, they would know his inaction for pusillanimity. He wanted instant empire.

What he got was something entirely different. But it hardly mattered. The truth was that his formal judgments and his capital punishments were a play within a play. His theater was as much for the Lords of the Admiralty, for his own crew, for the audience of a British Public that had expectancies of national honor. It was theater in the round, if you like. Ethnographically speaking we have difficulty in knowing which way the stage was facing.

The mockery of all Vancouver's signs is not ours now to describe except to make the point of it. He executed the wrong Hawaiians. The chiefs saw the executions as sacrifices to themselves, not to the King of England. There was nothing natural at all in his signs of sublimity. The otherness of the Hawaiians escaped him altogether, as his otherness escaped them.

That the theater of execution and death should be so ethnocentric would have both surprised and not surprised Edmund Burke. In his aesthetics, the Sublime was natural, universal and immediate. Would a crowd watching some staged execution in the theater and hearing of a public execution outside stay in the theater, he once asked. No, they would thrill to the quivering flesh of a hanging man and the much more thrilling question of "What if I were him?" But Burke was also conscious of how *realpolitik* might manage such natural signs and how different circumstances might change the poetics of their reading. He offered advice to governments on how to stage public executions to maximize their effect. I would say such advice was claptrap, a sign of the theatricality of sign-making.[11]

[11] I have described the theatre of the execution of the Bounty mutineers in *Mr Bligh's Bad Language* and that of Vancouver in *History's Anthropology*. Thomas Paine, *The Rights of Man* (New York, 1967), 297.

POSSESSING OTHERS

Nothing has undermined the confidence in anthropology in recent years so much as the sense that the apparent tolerance of ethnography as a science only masked intolerant power, that description of the Other never lost its instrumentality for the interests of self, that power never loses its ugliness even in its most alluring guises. It is true, I think, that the history of "implicit ethnography" in the Pacific is one of massive dispossession and transformation. From 1767 the Pacific was "collected" in word, picture, artefact and person and transformed into cultural objects of the Euroamerican possessors. Museums, archives, libraries, galleries became the European "way of seeing" itself. The Other of the Pacific became institutionalized by publication, by study, by display, so that otherness became a familiar thing of profit and institutional care, an object for decisions by writers, professors, directors. Knowledge of the Other, be it language, vocabulary or the understanding of cultural systems, became an instrument of change and management for missionaries, administrators, even for the casual representatives of empires. And there was never a way in which this knowledge was disembodied from the advantages of social status and the security and prestige it gave to the knowers. Haggle if you like over theories of imperialism and the profits and loss of empire, it is nevertheless difficult to point to any individual, no matter how high-flown the declared motivations, whose mediation between native and civilized did not work to his or her own advantage, or who did not try to make it so.

There were formal acts of possession as well, as England, France, Spain, the Netherlands, the United States claimed this or that group of islands. There were cultural sets of possession rituals, as sods were turned, trees carved, flags raised, crowns toasted and blessed, bottles buried, sand thrown. The new possessions were named, renamed with successive acts of possession or sometimes had their native names retained *ex gratia*. The whole of the Pacific was emplotted in this way by the calendar of saints, by patronage lines, by the accidents of the occasion of discovery. Its points and reefs and bays as well as its islands became an antiquarian directory of a myriad ethnographic moments. Most importantly, these now historicized places were mapped in all the complex dimensions of that word – set in relation to some center-point, related to some model of diplomacy, military strategy or economic system, abstracted from all the praxis of travelling, of wind and water, into some simplified model of a world encompassed so that men of power or men craving power could see crossroads, highways, toll-stations on the ocean. All this possessing, naming, mapping was done with little or no reference to those possessed, named or mapped. It was theater not to the native but to the competing civilized. The natives too made a theater of history at one another so that they could demand deference to their signs of possession.

The natives of the Pacific were possessed in the images made of them. There is a prejudice in this sort of history that the image corresponds to some formal image – the Noble Savage, say – which thinkers, tapping the "semantic density" or using the "cultural operators" of their own society, present. These I-witnesses of their own culture – Rousseau, say – present an otherness which is both critique and image of what should be. I do not say that is not so, but I would like to describe what I think to be more like the actual processes of ethnographic possession.

First it is not otherness that attracts the attention of a wider public. It is the experiencing of otherness, the ethnographer mediating the strangeness. Then there is recognition that the native is not other at all. There is relish of the irony that the native is not different, only worse, somehow deformed morally, aesthetically, physically. The other is self writ comically.

The mediating experience, of course, had to be dramatized, mythologized or, if we might borrow Aristotle's notion, "plot-structured." In the Pacific of our period, the encounter with the other was dramatized by the narratives of the voyagings and death of James Cook, the loss and search for La Pérouse, the hedonism in the mutiny on the *Bounty*, the debate over whether the English or French introduced venereal disease into Tahiti, the theoretical foolishness of the stay-at-home savants about the Great South Land and northwest passages. The vicarious thrill in making sense of such travelling was great. That it was done at government expense made it more homely. Political consciousness gave every reader critics' tools. Such narrations foregrounded the problem of mediating otherness. It demanded a scandalous sort of relativism.

Let me offer the example of Dr. John Hawkesworth. His editing of the Pacific voyages of Wallis, Byron, Carteret and Cook as much as any publication set up the ethnographic present of the Pacific to the public of the Enlightenment. Dr. Hawkesworth's greatest scandal was that he was full of claptrap. Dr. Samuel Johnson, Horace Walpole, and John Wesley were only a few of those who disapproved of his authorial intervention. His first problem was that he was paid 6,000 pounds to edit the logs and journals of simple seamen. That made his *Account of Voyages Undertaken* (1773) an event in itself fatally familiar to those thousands who knew how easy a task it was. He made it worse by deconstructing his authorial role. Was the *Voyages* his book? he asked himself and his reader. Who was the "I" of the author when there were so many "he's"? What did it mean to join together dozens of logs and journals? What was the real experience – the dull data of sailing or the moral issues of the encounter? Hawkesworth made it worse again by affecting a neutral role. He presented the native as the explorers had experienced them – in their sexuality, their nakedness, their violence – without adding the moral condemnation that they deserved. Worse even than that, he suggested that the shift of winds, the rise of water which saved Cook's *Endeavour* on the reefs of the Australian coast were natural and circumstantial, that Providence did not intervene to change the regularities of nature, even for Englishmen. Then he emplotted the Tahitians in the decadent behavior of Joseph Banks. His capers with native "queens" made differences absurd. What nobility was there in a queen's "pinked bum" or "tattooed breech"? The English possessed the Tahitians with smirks and nudges and winks. Truth is they did not see Tahitians at all. They saw grotesque Englishmen.

Or they saw natives suffused in the light of their own English humanism. That humanism was apotheosized in James Cook, not just in England but in continental Europe as well and the emerging United States. His spirit was an ethereal veil behind which the otherness of the native Pacific was staged. If the native was noble, it was because Cook was the disinterested observer of them, made them objects of science and receivers of the graces of the civilized. Natives were never so noble as in giving deference to the generous concern of the civilized. In the end, such self-disinterested possessiveness will justify any *realpolitik*. Otherness then is essentially ungrateful.[12]

DISCOVERING

It is difficult to get away from James Cook. He personified the ethnographic moment, 1767–1797. His three expeditions and nearly ten years of voyaging were full of the claptrap of discovering. He began on his first voyage of the *Endeavour* with an essentially private view

[12] J.L. Abbott, *John Hawkesworth, Eighteenth Century Man of Letters* (Madison, 1982), tells Hawkesworth's sad story. There is also Hawkesworth's own version, *An Account of the Voyages Undertaken by the Order of His Present Majesty for Making Discoveries in the Southern Hemisphere*, 3 vols. (London, 1773). A.S. Keller, O.J. Lissitzyn and F.J. Mann, *Creation of Rights of Sovereignty through Symbolic Acts, 1400–1800* (New York, 1938), is one of the few studies of rituals of possession I am familiar with.

of discovering. He was content to discover precisely where he was at any moment, to combine the art of science and navigating in perfect praxis, to relate his own space exactly to a world system. There was not much claptrap in that. He bound his men to his grind in its execution. But his voyage in the *Endeavour* was not over before he realized how much theater there was in discovering, how much of a performance he must give.

This sensitivity to the claptrap of Discovering came as much as anything from Cook's own ethnographic experience with "experimental gentlemen" in his own great cabin. On his first voyage it was Joseph Banks with his botanical and artistic assistants. Then, less congenially, he sailed with that most reflective ethnographer Johann Reinhold Forster and his young son Georg and then a succession of brilliant "illustrators." He learned from them their fussiness about "plain language," about the advantages of comparison, about the historicity and dialogic nature of knowledge, about the need for a referential framework in observation and of structure in presentation. There is a marvelous moment in early April 1769 when Cook has completed the (not very successful) observation of the transit of Venus at Tahiti, has circumnavigated the two islands of New Zealand, and is about to sail westward toward the east coast of Australia whose longitude he did not know and whose extension north and south no one had seen. He knows that if there is a Great South Land it is within the triangle from Cape Horn to Tahiti and New Zealand. He cannot go east and close the triangle. His ship will not last the violent conditions of those high latitudes. He already has the plan of his second voyage, its logistics made easy by a decision to come from the west by the Cape of Good Hope along the high latitudes with their constant westerly winds. It is a decision that will revolutionize Pacific voyaging. At that moment he has six months' supplies. He has the capacity of going home easily, duty done, or striking to the unknown, using every last ounce of food and inch of rope that the Admiralty begrudgingly had given him. He decides to go west and north.

The 2,000 mile voyage up an unknown coast, surveying every mile and making profiles of the shore, was a remarkable feat. Cook sees that as commander he always has the decision to make between adding to discovery or prudently avoiding dangers. Fame or foolishness is his constant dilemma. The viewers of his performance will always have the advantage of hindsight. But he knows that will not save him. The ambiguity of things is his constant companion. It clearly softens the perspective of his cultural perceptions. He is the first to confront the problem of the material simplicity and cultural complacency of the Aborigines of "New South Wales." He wonders if he really has got anything to give them. It is a touch of cultural relativism that will enrage his readers in Dr. Hawksworth's study.

If James Cook were to address us on the implicit ethnography of Discovering, I am sure he would tell us how different it was actually to the rhetoric that described it, how lateral to the glory of it were all the circumstances of the decisions that led to discovering. He was, I think, a very ethnographic man.

The 6,000 pound publishing fee paid to Dr. Hawksworth should alert us to the fact that the spectators to late eighteenth-century voyages of discovery were many. Very quickly the voyagers realized that "discovery" meant "discovering to" somebody as much as "discovery of" some place. The entrepreneurial spirit grew apace when the market-value of the discovering experience was realized. Elaborate controls – and elaborate schemes to escape those controls – were introduced to protect the monopolies on I-witness knowledge. Where the participants in discovering did not have the skill or the means to transform their experiences into saleable books, they had the opportunity to souvenir otherness and memorabilia-ize the events of discovering by collecting "artificial curiosities." The lowliest seaman, like the most ambitious experimental gentleman, jealously eyed the profitability of materializing his first-hand experience.

The library from these thirty years of discovering is large – John Hawkesworth, James Cook, Johann and Georg Forster, William Bligh, Louis Antoine de Bougainville, Charles de Brosses, William Broughton, Antoine de Bruny d'Entrecasteaux, Louis Claude de Freycinet, Jean-François de la Pérouse, Adam J. Von Krusenstern, Jacques Julien de Labillardière, Urey Lisiansky, Sydney Parkinson, Andrew Sparrman, George Vancouver, John Webber, James Wilson, to list only the best known. They share a common quality. They are preoccupied with the question of the language with which they engage the spectator of their experience. They see their language as plain, direct, unelaborated with metaphor, allegory or style. Sometimes they are archly modest about how ordinary they are, but mostly they are passionately defensive of the propriety of offering witness in bland monotone. There is, as well, more than a suggestion that such a language is appropriately manly. (Style is clearly seen as feminine: as is the native transformed into the object of humanism.)

La Pérouse spoke for them all. He had preempted the possibility that all his discovering be lost by sending home copies of his journal half-way through his voyage. (He had come across the first fleet of convicts at Botany Bay in their first terrible days of arrival.) He was an author speaking to his future editor from the grave. Above all, he instructed, that editor must not be a "man of letters." A man of letters will either "sacrifice the proper terms which the seaman and man of learning would prefer (and will look in vain), but which to him will appear barbarous, and for the turn of a phrase; or respecting all the nautical and astronomical detail, and endeavoring to make a pleasing romance, he will commit mistakes for want of the knowledge his education has not allowed him to acquire which may prove fatal to those who follow me." La Pérouse wanted an editor versed in mathematical science and who would respect the "rude but coarse style of a seaman." Naming all the elements of an environment which these explorers viewed for the first time, the experimental gentlemen of their expeditions had Linnaeus and Buffon for their models. The seamen had the example of their own sailors' language, brilliantly economic and precise. Their language made their observations factual, was the pledge of their objectivity.

These I-witnesses wore their sincerity privately. Their experience of otherness put them in a class apart from their readers and the stay-at-home philosophers. But in an age of 'The Spectator' who viewed the world ironically, sincerity was a tender virtue. Spectators were expected to be sincere as well. The Observer and the Spectator had to make a space apart, an unworldly space, where mutual respect was at play. Being scientific was as theatrical as a *rite de passage.* Listen to Johann Reinhold Forster setting the stage in the preface to his *Observations Made During a Voyage Round the World, on Physical Geography, Natural History and Ethnic Philosophy, Especially on 1. The Earth and Its Strata, 2. Water and the Ocean, 3. The Atmosphere, 4. The Changes of the Globe, 5. Organic Bodies, and 6. The Human Species.* He introduced himself as "John Reinhold Forster, LL.D., F.R.S., and S.A., And a member of Several Learned Academes in Europe." (There were pamphlets abroad at the time purportedly written by such characters as a "Professor of the Otaheite Language in Dublin and of All the Languages of the Undiscovered Islands of the South-Seas" and by a "Second Professor . . . of Every Other Unknown Language": The Spectators were casting a quizzical gaze.) Forster's *Observations* were in fact a striking transformation of the narrative forms of voyaging literature. Forster had evaded the monopoly on that form vested in James Cook by the publication of a *Journal of a Voyage* under the name of his eighteen-year-old son, Georg, who technically escaped the contractual obligations on everybody else. It was by no means a "sincere" act in any but his publisher's eyes. *Observations* however was a strikingly creative piece of science in its sculpted presentation. "The present performance," Forster began in his Preface: "Performance" in his day carried the "ordinary" meaning of a completed work executed by command or request, but it long had the special connotation of a presentation heightened in some way by having an audience. *"The present performance has undergone so many changes in its form since my return from my voyage that the public will excuse my delay in publishing it, and some of my friends will, I flatter myself, be able to judge what considerable improvements it has received both from their friendly strictures and my own meditation and reading."*

It was a dialogic performance. His *Observations* were not just a witnessing. They were transformed into a discourse, honed and sharpened by criticism and reflection. He was not observing but, if we might borrow the pregnant phrase from current reflections on ethnography and culture, "Writing Observations." *"The subject I have treated is so varied, that I have been obliged to have recourse in many points to the Sages of early age."* He lists these sages and tries to express how his ideas are both old and new. He has that eternal authorial problem of how to designate his own creative process, confident that the patterned whole is his, sensitive to the ways others see the same things analogically. His special interest, he declares, is not in a history of mankind: that has been done. His voyage around the world has given him an observation of graduated humanity *"from the most wretched savages, removed but in the first degree from absolute animality [*Tierra del Fuegians, Australian aborigines*] to the more polished and civilized inhabitants of the Friendly [*Tonga*] and Society Isles [*Tahiti*]. Facts are the basis of the whole structure; a few fair inferences enabled me to finish the whole."*

Forster draws his authenticity from his I-witness. These are his facts. But his observations are on the whole structure. He has a perspective: it makes sense of his multiple experiences: it is objective. But *"I cannot expect to have satisfied everybody."* His certainties are not unshakeable. But he must define the way in which they must be put. *"If proofs be brought that my opinions are not admissable, and if these arguments be communicated without rancour, I am open to conviction, and shall think myself much indebted to the man who will be kind enough to convince me of my mistake in a friendly manner: If, on the contrary, scurrility and abuse serve instead of argument, the Public will not, I hope, have a worse opinion of me for thinking such treatment beneath my resentment and unworthy of reply."* He is proposing the etiquette of scientific debate. His ideas are to be seen as divorced from his person. He has performed them. They lie somewhere between the self of his authorship and the public of his readers. To be scientific is to be good mannered, disengaged, but to have as well a passion for discovery. Diderot might have written on "The Paradox of Sciencing" as well as "The Paradox of Acting." In fact, the performance consciousness of the simple honest scientist and seaman – their theatricality – is perfect claptrap. It is acting, hiding and presenting acting at one and the same time.[13]

EXITING STAGE

Exiting stages has always been a moment of claptrap. David Garrick, the greatest of all English eighteenth-century actors, abhorred claptrap. He nonetheless always exited with a little trick of a bridled head and exaggerated alertness. It was a sort of signature on his roles but it also left a sense of anticipation that the ending of something was also a beginning. It is proper, I think, to exit stage on an issue of "implicit ethnography" full of alertness, anticipating not so much an end as a beginning. Nothing is clearer than that the ethnographic moment in all places and in all times begins not ends conversation.

[13] James Cook s reflections on "discovering" are to be found in J.C. Beaglehole, ed., *The Voyage of the Endeavour, 1768–1771* (Cambridge, 1968), 288–294, and (1967) *The Voyage of the Resolution and Discovery, 1776–1780* (Cambridge, 1967), 1372. Georg Forster, *A Voyage Round the World* (London, 1777); Johann Reinhold Forster, *Observations Made during a Voyage Round the World.* (London, 1778); William Bligh, *A Voyage to the South Sea for the Conveying of the Breadfruit Tree to the West Indies, including the Narrative of the Mutiny* (London, 1792); Louis Antoine de Bougainville, *A Voyage Round the World* (London, 1772); L.C. Desaules de Freycinet, *Voyage autour du monde* (Paris, 1827–9); Jean de la Pérouse, *A Voyage Round the World* (London, 1799); Otto von Kotzebue, *A Voyage of Discovery into the South Seas and Bering Straits* (London, 1821); A.J. Krusenstern, *Voyage Round the World* (London, 1813); M. Labillardière, *Voyage in Search of La Perouse* (London, 1800); G.H. von Langsdorf, *Voyages and Travels in Various Parts of the World* (London, 1813); Urey Lisiansky, *A Voyage Round the World* (London, 1814); James Wilson, *A Missionary Voyage to the Southern Pacific Ocean* (London, 1799); Anders Sparrman, *A Voyage to the Cape of Good Hope and Round the World* (London, 1785); George Vancouver, *A Voyage of Discovery to the North Pacific Ocean and Round the World* (London, 1984); Sydney Parkinson, *A Journal of a Voyage to the South Seas in HMS Endeavour* (London, 1773), are the most quoted discoverers. Patrick O. Reilly and Édouard Reitman, *Bibliographie de Tahiti et de la Polynésie francaise,* 2 vols. (Paris, 1967), offers more than 10,000 items comprehensively described, and is the indispensable tool for Enlightenment and post-Enlightenment ethnography (implicit and explicit) in the Pacific.

CHAPTER 17

North America in the era of Captain Cook: Three glimpses of Indian-European contact in the age of the American Revolution

PETER H. WOOD

WHAT Christopher Columbus started, James Cook completed. The impulse for global exploration set in motion by the voyages of the late medieval mystic from Genoa reached its culmination, nearly 300 years later, in the travels of a day laborer's son from Yorkshire. Columbus, of course, did not initiate the process of European outreach made possible by fifteenth-century changes in ship design, financial structures and national motivations. Nor did Cook conclude the process of probing and mapping at which he proved so enormously capable. But, as his contemporaries rightly judged, by the time of his death in 1779 Captain Cook had "fixed the bounds of the habitable world, as well as those of the navigable ocean."[1]

In an ear of impressive European explorers – Byron, Wallis, Bougainville, Vancouver – Cook's accomplishments stand out as emblematic of the age. In little more than a decade he covered more deep ocean than any previous captain, crossing the Antarctic Circle in the south and passing through the Bering Strait into the Arctic Ocean in the north. Though his circumnavigations touched all the continents, they had particular bearing for North America. He initiated his career as a naval cartographer in North American waters, helping to map the Gulf of St. Lawrence and providing safe access to General Wolfe's convoy ascending the river to capture Quebec in 1759. After the British victory he continued his observations of Nova Scotia and Newfound-

[1] Sir John Pringle, in appendix to James Cook, *A Voyage toward the South Pole* (London, 1777), 2:369–96.

land for several more years, returning again between 1763 and 1767 to extend his survey. A decade later, during the American Revolution, Cook was at a similar latitude, on the opposite side of the continent. Aboard the *Resolution*, he and his crew were exploring the Northwest Pacific Coast, solving the final great riddle of early North American geography. Before his death in Hawaii, he had proven at last that the fabled Northwest Passage (for which Cabot, Verrazano, Frobisher, Baffin, Hudson and others had searched so diligently) did not exist.

Cook, like Columbus, has become an emblematic figure both in the history of exploration and in the discourse of cultural contact.[2] Just as Columbus seems to represent the end of one era of exploring and/or the start of another,[3] Cook too represents a transition. "He was not semi-mystical, striving as some rarefied explorers have done after the meaning of existence or some absolute human affirmation," concludes his biographer, J.C. Beaglehole; "he was not searching for or fleeing from himself. . . . His was not the poetic mind, or the profoundly scientific mind. He was the genius of the matter of fact."[4]

It would be possible to use this European, who died at the hands of non-Europeans, to launch a wide-ranging discussion of "implicit ethnographies." But in the North American sphere, at least, such a discussion may be premature. We are still only beginning to come to terms with *explicit* ethnographies, relearning the sheer breadth and complexity of Native American cultures in the post-contact era and the extraordinary diversity of early interchanges with Westerners that took place over several centuries. Fortunately, the current resurgence of North American ethnohistory is rapidly giving us access to scores of separate cultures, each of which responded in distinctive ways to contacts with Europeans. From the distance, these contacts and their social and intellectual repercussions can seem formulaic and repetitive – epidemics and warfare, trade and intermarriage, religious conversion and rebellion. But in fact, upon closer inspection, they vary widely, and we are reminded how much we have oversimplified these exchanges in the past. It is the variety of interactions at any particular moment that I want to emphasize, by concentrating on the very decades when Cook undertook his momentous explorations.

At any one time in colonial North America, whether the 1590s, or

[2] See Marshall Sahlins, *Islands of History* (Chicago, 1985); Paul Carter, *The Road to Botany Bay: An Exploration of Landscape and History* (New York, 1988).

[3] The recurring debate as to whether Columbus is best seen as a medieval mystic or a Renaissance navigator is summarized well in "Full Circle," a review article by Simon Schama in the *Guardian Weekly*, 23 February 1992.

[4] J. C. Beaglehole, *The Life of Captain James Cook* (London, 1974), 698.

the 1680s, or (as here) the 1770s, the *explicit* contacts – that will later give rise to *implicit* ethnographies – cover an enormous range, both geographically and culturally. This is particularly striking in the eighteenth century, during the generation considered briefly here. For if, in Columbus's lifetime, a few "blindfolded" Europeans made contact with the "elephant" that they would name as America, by Captain Cook's era three centuries later whole "committees" of explorers, so to speak, had groped around virtually the entire outline of the behemoth. Bit by bit, they had gained an unprecedented overview of America's coastal geography and a limited awareness of the varied populations within its shores.

Awareness among Native Americans was changing gradually as well, and it is important to underscore at the outset the significant chronological dimension that emerges from careful study of any one area. Even as we use images such as "clash of cultures," suggesting the sudden collision of two opposing cymbals, we need to recall that most such encounters begin slowly and last a very long time. As the inheritors of a long tradition of "frontier" history, we are in danger yet again of conceiving North American intercultural contacts as brief, decisive, and one-sided confrontations rather than as protracted, cumulative and reciprocal associations – involving war and peace, weapons and diseases, sexuality and kinship, food and clothing, songs and stories, ideas and beliefs – that extended over many generations. To help us avoid this pitfall of traditional frontier history, a bevy of recent books, earning numerous prestigious awards, now show us how interdisciplinary scholars are exploring the chronological dimension in fresh ways in different parts of the continent.[5]

As we begin to understand chronological depth on the intercultural frontier more clearly, it is not surprising to learn that eighteenth-century Europeans in America often saw evidence and heard recollections regarding memorable encounters that had occurred in the sixteenth and seventeenth centuries. In 1733, for example, when James Oglethorpe initiated English colonization in Georgia, an elderly leader of the local Yamacraw Indians named Tomochichi pointed out an ancient burial mound near the projected townsite of Savannah. He ex-

[5] These first-rate studies include: Albert L. Hurtado, *Indian Survival on the California Frontier* (New Haven, 1988); James H. Merrell, *The Indians' New World: Catawbas and Their Neighbors from European Contact through the Era of Removal* (Chapel Hill, 1989); Joel W. Martin, *Sacred Revolt: The Muscogees' Struggle for a New World* (Boston, 1991); Richard White, *The Middle Ground: Indians, Empires, and Republics in the Great Lakes Region, 1650–1815* (New York, 1991); Daniel H. Usner, Jr., *Indians, Settlers, and Slaves in a Frontier Exchange Economy: The Lower Mississippi Valley Before 1783* (Chapel Hill, 1992).

plained to the English that the "Jamacraw King" buried there long ago had once "entertained a great white Man with a red Beard, who had entered the Port of Savannah Stream with a very large Vessel, and himself came up in his Barge to Jamacraw, and had expressed great Affection to the Indians, from which he hath had the Return of as much."[6] Oglethorpe and the English wanted to believe the bearded visitor had been Sir Walter Raleigh himself, but in fact it appears to have been Jean Ribault, a red-bearded French captain who had visited the coast in 1562 and whose story had been kept alive over six generations.[7]

By the 1760s, when a Dutch-born surveyor and geographer named William Gerhard De Brahm publicized the story told by Tomochichi in coastal Georgia, Indian interactions with non-Indians had come to span the entire North American continent. And yet, for several reasons, most of the encounters remain virtually invisible. Ask any U.S. citizen to tell you something about the years leading up to and including the American Revolution, and you are sure to hear mention – whether vague or detailed – of the founders and events in the national heritage. But ask about Indian relations throughout North America in that period, and you are likely to hear only silence.

Why should this be so? In part, no doubt, it is because when Americans consider the long colonial era, they still think primarily about Virginia and Massachusetts – first Jamestown and Plymouth, then Williamsburg and Boston. Moreover, for the era of the Revolution our collective memory becomes especially narrow (in geographical, as well as ethnic and gender terms), since we focus irresistibly and al-

[6] Louis De Vorsey, ed., *De Brahm's Report of the General Survey in the Southern District of North America* (Columbia, S.C., 1971), 153. De Brahm recounts the Yamacraws' first encounter with written language, as he heard it two centuries later: "The white Man with his red Beard, intending to present the King with a Piece of Curiosity he had on board his Vessel, for which he signified: some Indians might go down to receive it from his Lieutenant on board, to Whom he wrote a Note, which he desired the Indians would deliver to this Officer, who (pursuant to the Order in the Note) delivered what was demanded, and the Indians brought it up to Jamacraw, at which their King was greatly surprised, but more so, that this white Man could send his Thoughts to so great a Distance upon a white Leaf, which surpassing their Conception, they were ready to believe this white to be more than a Man, as the Indians have no other way to express times passed or to come than by rising and setting of the Sun, by New Moons, by Sprouting of the Trees, and the Number of their Ancestors."

[7] Peter H. Wood, "Circles in the Sand: Perspectives on the Southern Frontier at the Arrival of James Oglethorpe," in Phinizy Spalding and Harvey H. Jackson, eds., *Oglethorpe in Perspective: Georgia's Founder after Two Hundred Years* (Tuscaloosa, 1989), 9–11. Paul E. Hoffman, *A New Andalucia and a Way to the Orient: The American Southeast During the Sixteenth Century* (Baton Rouge, 1990), provides the Atlantic context for Ribault's visit, but despite its subtitle, the book is silent on the Native American dimension of such early encounters.

most exclusively upon the dramatic political and military events that unfolded near the Atlantic Coast. The silence, however, may also stem from the fact that modern America's central public images regarding Indian-European contact, shaped largely by Hollywood, are drawn inordinately from nineteenth-century warfare on the Great Plains. As a result, we still lack any real sense of the variegated contacts outside the Northeast before the nineteenth century.[8]

While numerous studies have probed regional contact in chronological depth, fewer have looked horizontally across the continent at a specific period. This chapter represents a brief sampling for such an approach – what archaeologists might call a "test probe." It will touch three distinctive native groups, chosen to emphasize the point of geographic scope and widely differing experiences at any given time. (Keep in mind, after all, that the very concept of "Indian" is a unifying misnomer imposed from the outside upon peoples who had built up separate identities over thousands of years.)

In order to call into question, or at the least to make apparent, our culture's inherited Atlantic perspective and East Coast orientation, let us take as our point of departure the confluence of the Missouri and Mississippi Rivers. If Frederick Jackson Turner could place himself at Cumberland Gap in order to envision the European "frontier" advancing from the east, then it is high time for a later generation to push further west. When we stand by the stream that long-term residents regarded as the Father of Waters and that poet Walt Whitman called the spinal column of the nation, we can view the continent from the heartland rather than from the periphery.

Here, as elsewhere, there is a chronological dimension to cultural contact.[9] Jean-Bernard Bossu, a captain in the French Marines, saw this clearly when he was sent to the Mississippi Valley in 1752 in anticipation of the pending conflict with the English. He found himself among the Quapaws, or "Downstream People," concentrated near the mouth of the Arkansas River. (Ever since their encounter with La Salle's party exploring the Mississippi River seventy years before, they had been known to the French as the Arkansas.) "I spoke to you in my last letter of an old Arkansas who said he had seen La Salle,"

[8] Raymond William Stedman, *Shadows of the Indian: Stereotypes in American Culture* (Norman, 1982), 155. "With the coming of the movies, the Indian was ensnared, then filmically embalmed, by a coincidence of history . . . the moviemakers . . . and most of the waiting audience knew the Indian wars of the West not only from the history books but also from their daily newspapers." See also, Kevin Brownlow, *The War, the West, and the Wilderness* (New York, 1979).

[9] Robert S. Weddle, *The French Thorn: Rival Explorers in the Spanish Sea, 1682–1762* (College Station, Texas, 1991).

Bosso wrote to a French nobleman. "This good Indian added that from that time on he has had a great deal of esteem for the French, who were the first white men he had ever seen. As chief," according to Bossu, "he had always urged his nation to have no European allies but the French."[10]

Captain Bossu had been assigned to Fort Chartres, the French administrative center of the Illinois Territory until 1762. But after the Treaty of Paris in 1763 gave land east of the Mississippi to England and turned over the Louisiana territory west of the river to Spain, the French traders at Chartres and nearby Kaskaskia moved across the river. On the west bank of the Mississippi, just below the mouth of the Missouri River and across from the ancient Indian mounds at Cahokia, they founded the town of St. Louis on land that would now be in the hands of the Spanish until it returned to France in 1800. Here they continued their traffic with Indians coming from all directions.[11] Moreover, they offered clandestine support to Indians inspired by the nativist message of Neolin, "the Delaware Prophet." These warriors – from the Potowatamie, Miami, Ojibwa, Huron, Shawnee, and Delaware – rallied around the Ottawa chief, Pontiac, in a drastic effort to expel the British from their newly acquired lands west of the Allegheny Mountains.[12]

Suppose we place ourselves in the new settlement of St. Louis in 1764 – where forty years later Meriwether Lewis will accept formal session of the region from France to the United States before setting out on his historic trip with William Clark, up the Missouri and down

[10] Seymour Feiler, ed., *Jean-Bernard Bossu's Travels in the Interior of North America, 1751–1762* (Norman, 1962), 60. Cf. W. David Baird, *The Quapaw Indians: A History of the Downstream People* (Norman, 1980), 35.

[11] Daniel H. Usner, Jr., "An American Indian Gateway: Some Thoughts on the Migration and Settlement of Eastern Indians around Early St. Louis," *Gateway Heritage* [Missouri] 11, no. 3 (Winter 1990–91):42–51. Usner writes (p. 44): "My investigation of the various Indian groups that settled in the riverine region of southeastern Missouri during the late eighteenth and early nineteenth centuries is part of a new surge of interest in a wide range of native American groups and experiences that defy convenient categories. By looking at the praying towns of New England and mission reserves of New France, the so-called settlement Indians or small nations of the colonial southeast, and at the migrant camps and makeshift villages of the nineteenth-century West, historians are learning about Indian forms of socioeconomic adaptation and cultural persistence that previously escaped our attention."

[12] For the context of this Native American war of independence, see Francis Jennings, *Empire of Fortune: Crowns, Colonies, and Tribes in the Seven Years War in America* (New York, 1988); Bill Gilbert, *God Gave Us This Country: Tekamthi and the First American Civil War* (New York, 1989); Gregory Evans Dowd, *A Spirited Resistance: The North American Indian Struggle for Unity, 1745–1815* (Baltimore, 1992); and White, *Middle Ground*.

the Columbia River to the Pacific.[13] From here, if we climb up in an imaginary arch far taller than the Saarinen Gateway that now spans the St. Louis waterfront, we can look off across the continent of North America in all directions. To underscore the sheer diversity of the cultural contacts unfolding before our eyes nearly three centuries after Columbus, let us face north and then peer beyond the horizon in several directions, moving clockwise to catch successive glimpses of three explicit ethnographic encounters in North America during the era of the Revolution.

If we turn first in the direction of two o'clock, we can look off toward the northeast, over the flames and smoke created by Pontiac's Rebellion, toward the St. Lawrence River. Beyond Lake Erie, Lake Ontario, and Quebec (where James Wolfe's British army defeated the French on the Plains of Abraham only five years before), we come to the Strait of Belle Isle between Labrador and Newfoundland and to the nearby shelters of Eastern Eskimos. It is appropriate to begin on the east coast of Canada, at the northernmost entrance to the Gulf of St. Lawrence, for it is here that the earliest confirmed settlement of Europeans in the New World occurred shortly after 1,000 A.D., when Vikings from southern Greenland attempted to establish a colony at L'Anse aux Meadows near the northern tip of Newfoundland.[14] And it is here that the young James Cook, after wartime service in the Gulf of St. Lawrence, showed himself "very willing to go out to Survey the Harbour & Coasts of Laborador."[15]

Cook sailed in the squadron of Hugh Palliser, the naval officer who was made Governor of Newfoundland and Labrador after Britain acquired from the French the rocky region with its lucrative fishing grounds. Palliser governed the new colonies from aboard his 50-gun flagship, the *Guernsey*, writing to superiors in 1766 that his fleet was trying to "prevent clandestine trade between the French and all our colonies" and to

> preserve peace and some degree of order amongst the fisheries, especially amongst the mixed multitudes now resorting to the new northern banks about the Straits of Belle Isle, composed of about 5000 of the very scum of the most disorderly people from the different colonies, . . . besides a number of

[13] James P. Ronda, *Lewis and Clark among the Indians* (Lincoln, 1984).
[14] Erik Wahlgren, *The Vikings in America* (London, 1986), ch. 7.
[15] Undated Admiralty note from 1763, quoted in Beaglehole, *The Life of Captain James Cook*, 65. According to Beaglehole, p. 69, "Cook was to carry out many accomplished pieces of surveying, in one part of the world or another, but nothing he ever did later exceeded in accomplishment his surveys of the southern and western sides of Newfoundland from 1763 to 1767."

wild, ungovernable people from the interior of Newfoundland, who are in every respect as savage and as barbarous as the most savage tribes of the American continent.

The whole number of vessels and men employed in these parts this year, amounts to about 3,500 vessels, and 15,000 men, one thousand of which number of vessels are French, with nearly 8000 men employed on board them, which adds to the confusion, and this upon a coast inhabited by the most savage people in the world – the Esquimeaux.[16]

Like many colonial governors before and after him, Palliser was more blunt and disparaging of native peoples in his letters home than in his public pronouncements to them. The previous year, at Chateau Bay on the Labrador side of the Straits of Belle Isle, he had met for peace talks with a contingent of Eskimos who arrived in their kayaks, led by a sachem, or "angikok," named Seguilla. Palliser's 350-man crew saluted them with three cheers from the yardarms, which caused predictable fright and confusion among the Eskimos. He then took them ashore and had them sit in a circle around him while his translator, Mr. Drachardt, read to them his prepared remarks. The Governor said he was glad to see them. "Our King," he related, "is exceeding angry" at news that "some Europeans coming to this Coast have treated some of you Ill & killed some of your people. . . . For he loves you & will not let any Body do you harm."

Palliser promised them extensive goods if they would trade with the English, and to demonstrate his good intentions he offered them a sturdy tent as a gift. In response, the Indians "brought Whalebone to the Governor" as a present, "but he declin'd it," pointing them instead to merchants in his party who had goods with them and were ready to trade for whalebone (the long strips from the upper jaws of certain whales that were valued in Europe to stiffen dress stays, corsets, and fans). It is unclear whether the governor was ignorant of ceremonial gift exchanges, or wished to retain the advantage he perceived in acting as the lone benefactor, or simply hoped to obtain more of the valuable whalebone through immediate trade.

What is clear is that the governor wished to allay deep Eskimo suspicions and divert a profitable trade to the English that had long gone to the French. He took several angikoks back to his ship in Chateau Bay and "gave them an Idea of the English Flag which till now they had an aversion to" and which the British therefore rarely displayed in their presence. Reconciled to the Union Jack, the angikoks

[16] Robert M. Hunt, *The Life of Sir Hugh Palliser, Bart.* (London, 1844), 88–9.

asked the commander to raise it aloft, "which was accordingly done & they sayd, this is a Sign of Friendship, when we see this Flag out at sea we will come out of the Harbours where we are & welcome you." The governor, meanwhile, continued to ask the angikoks repeatedly "If they would remain our good friends?" Seguilla replied by calling him "Captain Chateau" and shaking his hand in the European manner, then striking him on the chest and kissing him in the local fashion, while assuring him through the translator, "we will remain your good friends."[17]

Key to the governor's strategy for peace and trade with the Labrador Eskimos were the Moravian missionaries who served as his translators. These members of the Brethren were part of a "startlingly energetic burst of worldwide missionary activity" among this resurgent pietist sect. Beginning in the 1730s, this tide had carried a generation of intrepid Moravian proselytizers to such different places as the Danish West Indies and southern Greenland.[18] Several of the missionaries with Palliser had learned the Eskimo language in Greenland and were therefore able to communicate with the Labrador Eskimos, who shared the region with Indian groups who were their enemies.[19] The Moravian desire to expand their Eskimo missions and the English eagerness to open up trade with the whalehunters of Labrador coincided readily in the decades after 1763.

By 1771, Christian Drachardt and a dozen other men and women had founded their first mission at Nain on Hancock's Inlet, and two years later a Moravian mission ship began making annual visits that would continue for more than a century and a half. Additional missions and trading posts were established at Okkak in 1775 and Hopedale in 1781.[20] All three of these sites were far up the coast, for after

[17] "An Account of the Voyage of the Four Missionaries Sent by the Unitas Fratrum to the Esquimaux on the Coast of Labrador . . . 1765," in A. M. Lysaght, *Joseph Banks in Newfoundland and Labrador, 1766: His Diary, Manuscripts and Collections* (Berkeley, 1971), 199–201.

[18] Johann Jakob Bossard, ed., *C. G. A. Oldendorp's History of the Mission of the Evangelical Brethren on the Caribbean Islands of St. Thomas, St. Croix, and St. John* (Ann Arbor, 1987), xix. "From 1732 until 1768, some seventy-nine missionaries gave their lives in one way or another to help lay the foundation of the mission among the slaves of the Danish West Indies. If the sacrifice was considerable, so were the results, for in that same thirty-seven year period the Brethren baptized 4,560 slaves and brought them into the church."

[19] "The Eskimos of Labrador occupied coastal tundra and the neighboring islands, fiords, shores and strips of woodland; the Indians lived in the forest lands and on the inland mountains and tundra. But the boundaries between the two were uncertain, and bitter disputes resulted when either people attempted to hunt in areas claimed by the other." Lysaght, *Joseph Banks*, 167, n.111.

[20] Lysaght, *Joseph Banks*, 183.

1770 disease and violent conflict with Europeans had forced the remaining Labrador Eskimos to move northward. They were soon clustered around the three posts, professing Christianity and adopting new techniques of net fishing. This isolated population would remain stable for several generations, with the Moravians standing as "the most effective and visible buffer between Eskimos and the harsher representatives of European and European-American culture."[21]

If we now turn on our imaginary platform above the Mississippi, so that we are looking toward the southeast at "four o'clock," we face the domain of the Cherokee people in Southern Appalachia. In 1752, the same year Moravian missionaries first contacted the Labrador Eskimos, the American Bishop of the Moravian Church was scouting the interior of North Carolina, close to Cherokee hunting grounds, in search of land for a Moravian settlement. Within a few years, Bethabera and Salem had been established near the Yadkin River; these communities of German-speaking pacifists watched with trepidation the ebb and flow of volatile relations between the Cherokee nation and the rapidly encroaching English colonists.

The early incursions of de Soto and other Spaniards into the Southeast in the sixteenth century had devastated Florida Indians and certain coastal tribes that were repeatedly subjected to warfare and novel diseases.[22] But archaeological evidence suggests that less exposed piedmont and mountain communities did not experience these major disruptions until the end of the seventeenth century, when an expanding English presence in coastal Virginia and Carolina began to be felt in the interior.[23] According to John Lawson, traveling through the Carolina Piedmont after 1700, "The Small-Pox and Rum, have made such a Destruction amongst them that, on good Grounds, I do Believe, there is not the sixth Savage living within two hundred Miles of all our Settlements, as there were fifty Years ago."[24]

In the 1670s, when the English gained a foothold in South Carolina, the Cherokees probably numbered well over 30,000 people, one of the

[21] Wendell H. Oswalt, *Eskimos and Explorers* (Novato, CA, 1979), pp. 282–5. Quote on 285.

[22] Henry F. Dobyns, *Their Numbers Become Thinned: Native American Population Dynamics in Eastern North America* (Knoxville, 1983).

[23] H. Trawick Ward and R. P. Stephen Davis, Jr., "The Impact of Old World Diseases on the Native Inhabitants of the North Carolina Piedmont" (Paper presented at the Forty-Sixth Annual Meeting of the Southeastern Archaeological Conference, Tampa, 10 November 1989).

[24] John Lawson, *A New Voyage to Carolina* (1709; reprint Chapel Hill, 1967), 231–2. For a more extended discussion, see Peter H. Wood, "The Impact of Smallpox on the Native Population of the 18th Century South," *New York State Journal of Medicine* 87 (January, 1987):30–36.

largest Indian nations on the continent. But a virulent smallpox epidemic brought from Charleston in 1697 destroyed nearly half the tribal population, and in the 1730s the next generation of Cherokees again "received a most depopulating shock, by the small pox." According to British Indian agent James Adair, the Cherokee medicine men "who were consulted on so alarming a crisis, reported the sickness had been sent among them, on account of the adulterous intercourses of their young married people," and they set about prescribing moral and physical remedies, but all to no avail. When "the infection gained upon them" despite their most varied and intensive efforts, it prompted a crisis of belief among the healers themselves. They "broke their old consecrated physic-pots, and threw away all the other pretended holy things they had for physical use, imagining they had lost their divine power by being polluted; and shared the common fate of their country."[25]

In 1760, another smallpox epidemic and a war with the English made further inroads. When the Quaker naturalist William Bartram visited the region in the mid-1770s, he referred to "the present generation" as "the posterity and feeble remains of the once potent and renowned Cherokees."[26] On the eve of the American Revolution, therefore, their nation seems to have numbered no more than 8,500 persons, roughly one-quarter of its size a century earlier.[27] Moreover, these survivors had become deeply divided in their response to this continuing demographic and cultural crisis. The tension was developing largely along generational lines, as Moravians and other neighbors soon perceived. On March 6, 1774, for example, the Moravian Meeting in Bethabera recorded a visit from Joseph Müller and his wife, who "reported that there were Cherokee Indians in the Hollow; that the older Indians did not want war, but the younger ones did, so the older ones were seeking the protection of the white people."[28]

The following spring the tribal dispute over survival strategies in the face of mounting white land pressures could no longer be contained. In March 1775, this generational conflict erupted publicly at

[25] James Adair, *Adair's History of the American Indians* (1775; reprint Ann Arbor, 1966), 244–5.

[26] William Bartram, *Travels through North & South Carolina, Georgia, East & West Florida, the Cherokee Country . . .* (Philadelphia, 1791), 332.

[27] Peter H. Wood, "The Changing Population of the Colonial South: An Overview by Race and Region, 1685–1790," in Peter H. Wood, Gregory A. Waselkov, and M. Thomas Hatley, eds., *Powhatan's Mantle: Indians in the Colonial Southeast* (Lincoln, 1989), 35–103.

[28] Adelaide L. Fries, ed., *Records of the Moravians in North Carolina* (Raleigh, 1968), 2: 832.

Sycamore Shoals on the Watauga River, during a conference with Judge Richard Henderson and his associates who had come to "purchase" more Cherokee land. A young warrior named Dragging Canoe broke with tribal elders, something that rarely occurred in the consensus-oriented world of Indian diplomacy. Indeed, his own father, Attakullaculla, who had travelled to England as a young man a generation earlier, was among those he denounced for conceding too much to the whites. Before walking out of the meeting, Dragging Canoe disparaged his older kinsmen for selling Cherokee territory, and he warned the white purchasers, "You will find its settlement dark and bloody."[29]

When English Indian agent Henry Stuart met the young Cherokee dissident early in 1776, Dragging Canoe protested for his nation against "the encroachments of the Virginians and inhabitants of North Carolina; he said that they were almost surrounded by the White People, that they had but a small spot of ground left for them to stand upon and that it seemed to be the intention of the White People to destroy them from being a people."[30] In May, as the Continental Congress was convening in Philadelphia, Stuart was present at an Indian council in southern Appalachia, when a party of Mohawks, Ottawas, and Shawnees visited the town of Chota, to seek an alliance with the Cherokees. He informed his brother John Stuart that the visitors brought a large war belt with them. The "red people who were once masters of the whole country," exhorted the Shawnee spokesperson, now "hardly possessed ground enough to stand on." Hearing his own sentiments echoed so exactly, Dragging Canoe accepted the war belt.[31] Taking the majority of the Overhill Cherokees with him, Dragging Canoe withdrew to the west, near Chicamauga Creek on the Tennessee River, joining with militant Shawnees and others to create an armed resistance force that became known and feared among whites as the "Chicamaugas." To emphasize their desperate and unprecedented break with their older and more accommodating relatives, these militants took the name *Ani-Yunwiya*, "the Real People," and their spirited resistance movement lasted well over a decade.[32]

The situation of the Cherokee inhabitants of the Smoky Mountain

[29] Quoted in John P. Brown, *Old Frontiers* (Kingsport, 1938), 12.

[30] William L. Saunders, ed., *The Colonial Records of North Carolina, 1662–1776*, 10 vols. (Raleigh, 1886–1890), 10:764.

[31] Henry Stuart to John Stuart, Pensacola, 25 August 1776, *Documents of the American Revolution*, K. G. Davies, ed. (Shannon, Ireland, 1976), 12:203.

[32] James Paul Pate, "The Chicamauga: A Forgotten Segment of Indian Resistance on the Southern Frontier" (Ph.D. diss., Mississippi State University, 1969).

region in the 1770s, even when sketched in a few brief paragraphs, is vastly different from that of the Eskimos in Labrador. It illustrates notably different aspects of the confrontation between Europeans and Native North Americans in the late eighteenth century. Central to the story is the generational conflict between older accommodationists and younger militants; equally important is the background of warfare and epidemic disease that had sharply reduced the population and drastically torn the social fabric. In contrast to the English traders and missionaries in Labrador, seeking furs, fish, and Christian converts, the rapidly expanding white population in the Southern Piedmont desired land, and would go to great lengths to obtain it. Meanwhile, the majority of the Cherokees, in contrast to most of the eastern Eskimos, had reached a point where they were more than willing to consider suggestions for a pan-Indian alliance of resistance. As Gregory Dowd concludes succinctly: "By the late eighteenth century the idea of united Indian resistance to settler expansion had taken hold among the Eastern Woodlands peoples."[33]

A different story unfolds from our vantage point on the Mississippi River if we now turn 180 degrees and face northwest, toward "ten o'clock." Looking in that opposite direction, up the huge length of the Missouri River Valley and across the distant Rockies and the Northern Plateau, we come to what is now known as Vancouver Island, home of the Nootka Indians. Needless-to-say, in our 180-degree turn we have swept past the entire South and Southwest, including the broad Gulf Coast, the Lower Mississippi Valley, and the desert crossroads of the Upper Rio Grande. Cultural contact between Europeans and indigenous peoples had been going on in these important and diverse places for several centuries before the time of Captain Cook, and numerous fresh encounters continued in the years we are considering. It was in 1776, for example, that Father Francisco Garces visited the Havasupai people at Cataract Creek Canyon, near where it enters Grand Canyon, and that Fathers Dominguez and Escalante undertook their expedition among the Ute Indians while seeking unsuccessfully to find a way through the Great Basin to California.[34]

On the west coast of North America, continuous contact was only beginning during the years of the American Revolution, spurred in

[33] Dowd, *A Spirited Resistance*, 49.

[34] Elliott Coues, ed., *On the Trail of a Spanish Pioneer: The Diary and Itinerary of Francisco Garces (Missionary Priest) in His Travels Through Sonora, Arizona, and California, 1775–1776*, 2 vols. (New York, 1900); Herbert Eugene Bolton, ed., "Pageant in the Wilderness: The Story of the Escalante Expedition to the Interior Basin, 1776; Including the Diary and Itinerary of Father Escalante," *Utah Historical Quarterly* 18 (1950):1–265.

part by Vitus Bering's "discovery" of Alaska in 1741. The results of Bering's mission prompted, within decades, an aggressive descent upon the Alaskan coast by Russian *promyshlenniki*, adventurers seeking furs that could be sent back to Moscow or traded across the Siberian border into the empire of China.[35] This Russian encroachment, in turn, sparked a counter-effort by the Bourbon King of Spain.[36] Sea captains were dispatched further north to chart the waters and strengthen Spanish claims. In 1774, Juan Perez, accompanied by a priest named Juan Crespi, explored the shores of present-day British Columbia. According to Crespi's account they visited the Nootka Indians briefly, laying claim to their territory but never going ashore.[37]

But except for a few visits from Russian scouts in search of furs and Spanish captains sent out by the Viceroy of New Spain, this entire coastline remained unknown to Westerners, even as they speculated about its geography and its inhabitants.[38] English author Jonathan Swift, in his famous tale of *Gulliver's Travels* (1726), had even located the land of Brobdingnag somewhere along America's Northwest Coast, beyond the western entrance to the fabled Strait of Anian.[39] For centuries there had been rumors that such a strait provided an ice-free passageway, linking the North Atlantic and the North Pacific.[40] When Captain Cook set sail from Plymouth, England, on July 12, 1776,

[35] Basil Dmytryshyn, et al (eds. and trans.), *Russian Penetration of the North Pacific Ocean: A Documentary Record, 1700–1797* (Portland, Oregon, 1988); Hector Chevigny, *Russian America: The Great Alaskan Venture, 1741–1867* (Portland, 1979); Derek Pethick, *First Approaches to the Northwest Coast* (Seattle, 1979).

[36] Beginning in 1769, royal officials in Mexico City sent Franciscan padres, led by Junípero Serra, to establish a chain of missions along the California coast between San Diego Bay and San Francisco Bay. Presidios were organized at San Diego (1769), Monterey (1770), San Francisco (1776) and Santa Barbara (1782), and towns were founded at San José (1777) and Los Angeles (1781).

[37] Warren L. Cook, *Flood Tide of Empire: Spain and the Pacific Northwest, 1543–1819* (New Haven, 1973), ch. 3. Cf. Herbert Eugene Bolton, ed., *Fray Juan Crespi, . . . Missionary Explorer on the Pacific Coast, 1769–1774* (Berkeley, 1927), 348–350. The following year another Spanish navigator, Bruno de Hezeta (or Heceta), visited the vicinity again.

[38] See Glyndwr Williams, "Myth and Reality: James Cook and the Theoretical Geography of Northwest America," in Robin Fisher and Hugh Johnston, eds., *Captain James Cook and His Times* (Seattle, 1979), 58–80.

[39] For a fanciful eighteenth-century map illustrating the location of Lemuel Gulliver's Brobdingnag ("Discover'd A.D. 1703") somewhere north of the California coast explored by Sir Francis Drake, see David Conner and Lorraine Miller, *Master Mariner: Capt. James Cook and the Peoples of the Pacific* (Seattle, 1978), 21.

[40] The British government had made an offer of twenty thousand pounds for any English ship that could locate the passage, but no one had succeeded by the time Cook returned from his second Pacific voyage in 1775. Increasing British activity in the China tea trade was adding to London's interest in a shorter route to the Orient, and an associate of Cook's, Richard Pickersgill, was dispatched to Baffin Bay to look once more for the Atlantic entrance to the Northwest Passage.

he carried specific instructions to probe the Northwest Coast of America for the Strait of Anian.[41]

In that regard, from a European perspective Cook's final voyage represented what one might call a successful failure, or a disappointing success. After all, his ships *Resolution* and *Discovery*, despite their ambitious names suggestive of the American Space Shuttle Program, could only demonstrate a negative, proving the non-existence of any ice-free transcontinental passage. According to historian Ken Coates: "Whereas Cook's earlier expeditions brought Europe news of unknown lands, unique peoples, exotic fauna, and geographic wonders, the final voyage to Alaska was little more than a flawed exploratory thrust, enveloped in fog, mist and ice, and unmarked by the single bold stroke of magnificent discovery."[42] From the Nootka perspective, however, the expedition proved highly significant.

Not until the early spring of 1778, after twenty-one months on two oceans, did Cook's ships finally sight the Northwest Coast – just as Washington's rebel army, on the other side of the continent, was beginning to thaw out from its ordeal at Valley Forge. Standing out to sea to avoid treacherous weather on the Northwest Coast, Cook missed the mouth of the Columbia River. (Nearly three decades later, Lewis and Clark would reach the same place, encountering Chinook Indians who had already experienced the arrival of European traders by sea.) By the end of March, Cook had anchored in Nootka Sound to spend a month repairing his vessels before sailing northward up the Alaskan coast. This allowed time, in the words of the official instructions for the voyage, "to observe the Genius, Temper, Disposition, and Number of the Natives and inhabitants."[43]

As Robin Fisher has observed, Captain Cook, during his short but much studied visit among the Nootka people, was not "the white messenger of doom," bringing sudden darkness and "the evil star of European civilization," as some recent commentators have con-

[41] Only days before Cook's departure on his third voyage, Americans in Philadelphia had thrown down the gauntlet of independence. But Cook's search was considered of transcending scientific importance in the whole English-speaking community, as shown by the fact that he carried a letter from Benjamin Franklin urging American privateers to grant the expedition safe passage.

[42] Ken Coates, "James Cook and Russian America: Reflections on the Legacy of Cook's Third Voyage to the Pacific, 1776–1780," *Pacifica*, 2, no. 2 (November, 1990):90. "On closer examination, however, it is clear that Cook's third voyage was a remarkable feat of seamanship," Coates adds. "The expedition, moreover, held considerable significance in the early history of Russian America and deserves greater attention on that score."

[43] Quoted in Robin Fisher, "Cook and the Nootka," in Fisher and Johnston, *Captain James Cook*, 84.

tended.[44] Instead, Fisher argues, "Cook's visit to Nootka Sound produced reverberations in both cultures."[45] For the English, the stopover marked the beginning of a lucrative new trade in sea otter furs. For many months later, after Cook's death in Hawaii, his crew sold these North American furs for such enormous profits during a stopover in China that sea otter pelts soon came to be known as "soft gold." The rush to extend this trade after 1780 would prompt the Nootka Sound Controversy at the end of the decade, as Spain and England competed for control of the region.[46]

For the Nootka, these new contacts meant an extension of their already elaborate processes of trade and exchange, building on their keenly developed sense of individual possessions. In all his Pacific travels, Cook had never met another group that "had such high notions of everything The Country produced being their exclusive property." Even the grass turned out to be for sale when sailors went ashore to cut fodder for the ships' goats. According to Cook:

> The Moment our people began to cut they stoped them and told them they must Makook for it, that is first buy it. As soon as I heard of this I went to the place and found about a dozen men who all laid claim to some part of the grass which I purchased of them and as I thought liberty to cut where ever I pleased, but here again I was misstaken, for the liberal manner I had paid the first pretended pr[o] prietors brought more upon me and there was not a blade of grass that had not a separated owner, so that I very soon emptied my pockets with purchasing, and when they found I had nothing more to give they let us cut where ever we pleased.[47]

Cook had entered into the world of the "potlatch," where the salmon-eating northwestern coastal tribes had evolved an elaborate sense of reciprocal exchange and gift-giving designed originally as a way to assure renewal of the abundant resources of the sea. In such a society, "no man could become a man of position without giving away property."[48] Cook's own journal gives a first-hand account of these competitive cycles of giving, for as his ships were preparing to leave the captain offered a "small present" to one of the local leaders as a farewell gift, probably the man familiar to later traders as Maquinna. In return, the chief immediately "presented me with a Beaver skin Cloak he had on, that I knew he set a value upon. And as I was

[44] Ibid., 81.
[45] Ibid., 98.
[46] Thomas Vaughan, *Soft Gold: The Fur Trade and Cultural Exchange on the Northwest Coast of America* (Portland, 1982).
[47] Quoted in Conner and Miller, *Master Mariner*, 95.
[48] Lewis Hyde, *The Gift: Imagination and the Erotic Life of Property* (New York, 1983), 28.

desirous he should be no sufferer by his friendship and generosity to me, I made him a present of a New Broad Sword with a brass hilt which made him happy as a prince."[49]

Cook himself would be dead in less than a year, but Maquinna would go on to become a powerful and respected trader. From the start, Nootka Indians had proven themselves shrewd and assertive traders, refusing to accept the strings of beads that had proven popular among Indians of the California coast and elsewhere. Instead they sought metal goods that would be useful or decorative, and they accepted the European traders into their world of elaborate ritual and song. The Europeans, meanwhile, had found a western access point where they could acquire sea otter pelts and transport them across the Pacific to trade for Chinese porcelain and tea. For both the Nootka and the English in 1778, as Robin Fisher notes, "Cook's presence was the beginning, not the end of something."[50]

Obviously, the worlds of Maquinna at Nootka Sound, Dragging Canoe at Sycamore Shoals, and Seguilla at Chateau Bay are different indeed. Although they all lived in the same decades, a cursory sketch of their situations, such as this, suggests the wide differences that marked the experiences of different groups on the vast North American continent. While one contends with seaborne traders, another confronts hungry land speculators, and the third deals with dedicated Protestant missionaries. Each has a different cultural experience to draw upon, and each faces a thoroughly separate set of circumstances. We could usefully continue these flights in literally every direction, at almost any point in the colonial era, comparing and contrasting the situations of different Native American groups as they confront intruders from abroad.

Even the briefest thumbnail sketch illustrates that little is crudely predictable or predetermined about the actions and reactions of any single Indian group, just as little is inevitable about the course of each people's encounter with the West. European ideas of "Divine Providence," "Manifest Destiny," and "Historical Inevitability" must be understood as rationalizations of aggression devised by successive

[49] Quoted in Conner and Miller, *Master Mariner*, 99. Cf. John Meares, *Voyages Made in the Years 1788 and 1789 From China to the North West Coast of America* (Amsterdam, 1967), 114: "The manner in which these people give and receive presents is, we believe, peculiar to themselves. However costly the gift may be in their own eyes, they make wish to take away all idea of conferring any obligation on the receiver of it. We have seen two chiefs meet on a visit of ceremony provided with presents of the richest furs, which they flung before each other with an air that marked the most generous friendship. . . . "

[50] Fisher, "Cook and the Nootka," in Fisher and Johnston, *Captain James Cook*, 98.

generations of a conquering culture. At every step there are options open to all parties concerned, both in terms of measures taken and conclusions drawn. "In the long drama of Indian-White interaction," writes sociologist Stephen Cornell, "each actor has been forced to respond to the actions of the other or to the consequences of those actions, manifest in concrete social conditions and relationships."[51]

This drama of interdependency received its most vivid portrayal, perhaps, in the violent painting of Charles Deas entitled *The Death Struggle* (1845), in which a White and an Indian rider, locked in combat, hurtle over a steep precipice while still on horseback. According to one commentator, Deas "depicted their combat with unmistakable bias and yet came close to expressing the intertwined fates of red man and white since the invasion of North America."[52] However, to insist – through words or pictures – on the active ways in which Indians have conditioned their interactions with America's newcomers does not necessarily imply equally broad power or open options. As Cornell observes: "While mutual, this conditioning process has been uneven. Although in early years Native Americans on occasion exerted considerable influence over the actions of the invaders and the shape of events, over time they found themselves increasingly constrained, caught in an ever more elaborate mesh of circumstances and relationships beyond their control."[53]

Another generation is again pursuing the complicated and unpredictable reality of crosscultural encounters with renewed vigor. For current scholars of North American contact, as for earlier generations, the tensions continue to exist between a desire for sweeping observations and a fascination with specific conditions and people. Obviously, we must eventually examine the forest as well as the trees. But for the moment it remains important to forgo all-encompassing generalizations of contact and reexamine the precise circumstances of individual groups. Just as patient "case law" leads to sound legal doctrine, so too focused local and comparative work in North American ethnohistory should lead us to fresh conclusions that will stand the test of time.

[51] Stephen Cornell, *The Return of the Native: American Indian Political Resurgence* (New York, 1988), 7.

[52] Richard Drinnon, *Facing West: The Metaphysics of Indian-Hating and Empire Building* (New York, 1980), 120.

[53] Cornell, *The Return of the Native*, 7.

CHAPTER 18

An accidental Australian tourist: Or a feminist anthropologist at sea and on land

DIANE BELL

In fourteen hundred and ninety-two
Columbus sailed the ocean blue.

Captain Cook, chased a chook[1]
all around Australia.
He lost his pants, in the middle of France,
and found them in Tasmania.

THAT'S what we chanted as we skipped our intricate jump rhythms in the playground. In class we mapped the discovery of the New World and recorded the occasional and often accidental visits of explorers along the Australian coast.* We read the accounts of Portuguese, Dutch, and English explorers and traders. From these tales of the triumph of reason over superstition, we learnt that the world was round; the South Land was not a physical balance for northern land masses; native peoples could be compared, classified, even civilized and saved; and their knowledge, labor, and resources were to be turned to profit. With the voyage of James Cook in the *Endeavour*, the final piece of the cartographic puzzle was known to the West. And, as a bonus, the inhabitants of this land lived in a Rousseauian state of nature, in Cook's words "far happier than we."

[1] "Chook" is Australian slang for chicken, as in edible fowl. Here it evokes the image of the barnyard chase to lop off its head and the subsequent jerky, lifeless movements. Another reference to Cook is in Australian rhyming slang "have a Captain Cook," which translates as "have a look," and is often shortened to "a captains."

* A number of people have assisted me in locating sources, in suggesting leads, and in orienting this accidental tourist in their expert fields: I thank Barry Alpher, Genevieve Bell, Genée Marks, Tony Reid, Karen Turner, and John von Sturmer, but take responsibility for the use to which I have put their generous assistance.

Forty years later, I can only marvel at the Europe-centric vision of these accounts. As an anthropologist I want to know, what did the "natives" make of this stream of crusading, trading, invading strangers? What of regional trade and communications among the peoples of New Guinea, Timor and Torres Strait? What of the intellectual traditions and trade networks of the Hindu, Muslim, and Chinese worlds? I note the silences regarding women in the literature of the explorers, and my feminist sensibilities counsel me to bring to the threshold of consciousness the situated and gendered nature of the authorial voice. Where are women located in the explorers' schema, and what impact did these strange males from afar have on local gender relations? But my research interests lie on land and this search for meaning in the period between the childhood rhymes is taking me into relatively uncharted waters. I feel rather like the Dutch, who, following the new and faster route pioneered by Hendrick Brouwer in 1611, passed around the Cape of Good Hope, caught the westerly trade winds as far as the longitude of Java and, in taking their left turn too late, became accidental tourists on the west coast of Australia.

WHERE LAND AND SEA MEET: AN INTERACTIVE HISTORICAL ETHNOGRAPHY

I am persevering with some of the questions I have thought important for the period of colonization of the Australian continent, but I am posing them in the earlier period of sea exploration. In so doing, I'm interested to plumb the continuities and discontinuities, divergences and convergences, reverberations and dissonances between the period of sea exploration and the period of land colonization, to map the terrain on which the Enlightenment confidence in knowing the "other" was built. In reading the journal entries that have survived, I note omissions, confusions, and plagiarisms that generate questions about the interpretation of texts, and the editing of journals, and choice of the apt representative phrase. In contextualizing the sources I ask: What did Europeans know of the inhabitants of the South Land? What motivated their expeditions? What informed their observations? What can we know of their personality, training and interests? Through what sources do we gain access to their understandings? Who was the intended audience of their observations and musings? The observations of explorers tell us as much about the observers' preoccupations as the observed "facts." How far might we get if we were to subject the "texts" of the inhabitants of the South Land to a similar scrutiny? What did Aborigines know of other? What were their interpretative frames? How did they accommodate others in religious and economic practice? How was new information transmitted? Who was their audience? My questions help us tease out the implicit ethnographies of the explorer and the explored, of the native as other, and of the explorer as other. In so doing, I'm wanting to activate the passive partner of the interpretive dyad (observer-observed: explorer-explored), and to write a more interactive historical ethnography. I am bringing into dialogue bodies of literature and experience that are usually held discrete; I am attempting to build a different sort of ethnographic map of other, one of the classic other's other (Figure 18.1).

The anthropological criticism of the Western orientation of knowledge seeks the perspective of the other, but still leaves other as external, potentially exotic, and elsewhere. The feminist critique is of the situated knower and asks how does the male-male communication silence/exclude/mute women and how might she be reinscribed? Clearly, the anthropological obsession with other and the other of feminist discourses are not isomorphic. However, I intend to subject the existing "texts" to against-the-grain readings from both perspectives. With some novel navigation, the tensions engendered by attempting readings that are informed by anthropological notions of ethnocentrism and feminist critiques of the past as a patriarchal construct can invigorate my search. In Mary Daly's terms, finding one's way through the "maze/haze of deception [is] the journey of women becoming . . . springing into free space, which is an a-mazing process".[2] On my voyage of discovery, my trusty vessel will henceforth be known as "A-Mazing," and its log will become the record of its feminist anthropologist skipper.

Finding ways of explaining other to self has an intellectual history rarely shared by the other and is itself an act of domination and appropriation. In so saying I am not wishing to curtail enquiry to only those fields that may be perceived by the other as of immediate relevance, but I am arguing that the discourse of search for self in other privileges certain concepts/questions/constructs, which colonize many different others by universalizing and incorporating. This "reach into otherness" is a post-Enlightenment preoccupation,[3] and the impulse to search elsewhere for material from which to construct taxonomies of humanity is a peculiarly Western one and, we should

[2] Mary Daly, *Beyond God the Father* (Boston, 1978), 2.

[3] Kenelm Burridge, *Encountering Aborigines: A Case Study: Anthropology and the Australian Aboriginal* (New York, 1973), 6ff.

Cartography by Mui D. Le and Jim Kirschling at the University of Minnesota Cartography Laboratory.

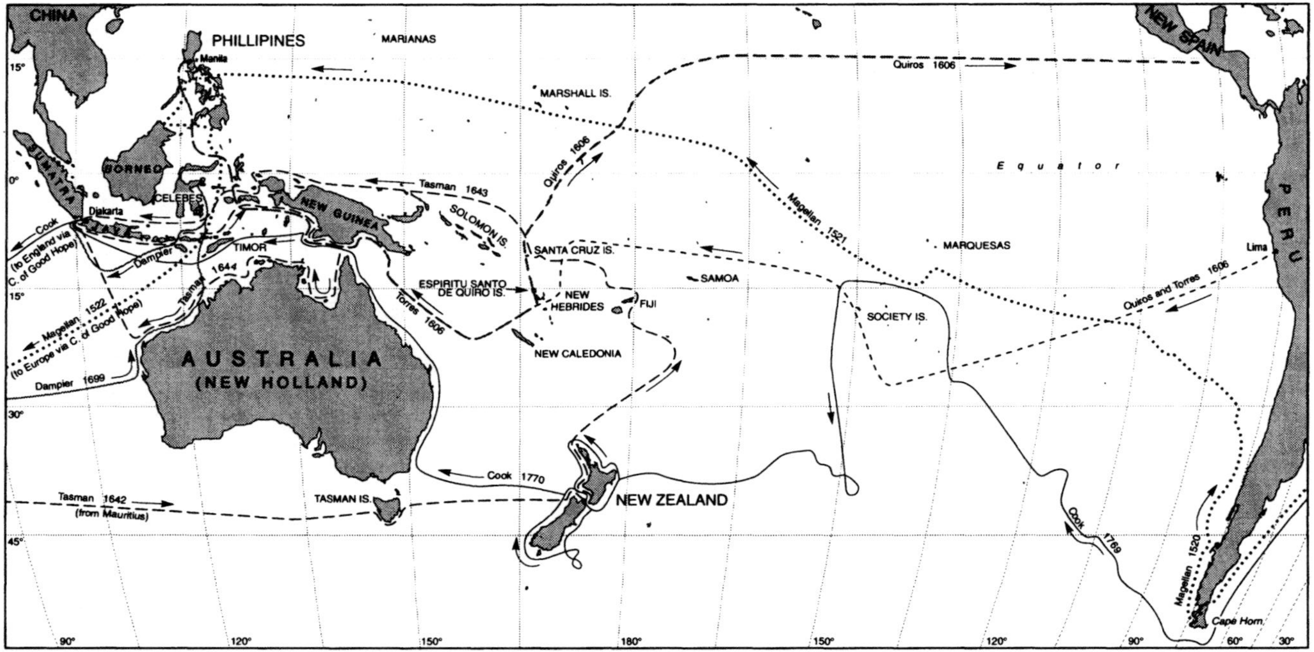

Source: John Bartholomew and K. R. Cramp, The Australian School Atlas (Melbourne, 1939).

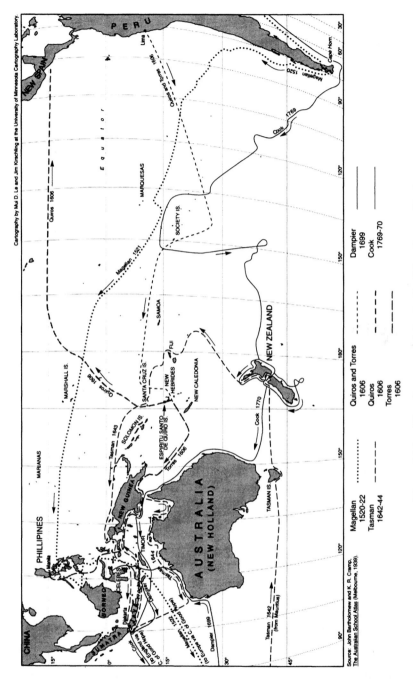

Magellan 1520-22	....	Quiros and Torres 1606	- - - - - -
Tasman 1642-44	— — — —	Quiros 1606	▬ ▬ ▬ ▬
		Torres 1606	—— —— ——
Dampier 1699	————	Cook 1769-70	————

Figure 18.1. The discovery of Australia: Magellan to Cook.

note, one in which Aborigines have figured prominently: never intrinsically known, ever the prototypical print on the first rung of the evolutionary ladder.

In thinking of ways I might explore Aborigines as self to the explorers as other, I mapped onto one spatial template the contacts as experienced by the "natives" and included not just Europeans in the Pacific, but a range of other local peoples. In so doing I am moving from organizing the explorers' observations according to nationality and chronology, to locating the experiences of outsiders from the perspective of the groups on which their visits impacted. The most intense and constant contacts were those with Yolngu of Eastern Arnhemland, the Wik group of the west coast of Cape York, the Tiwi of Melville and Bathurst Islands, and the peoples from the Kimberleys and down to Houtman Abrolhos. These groups had sufficient contact experience to begin to formulate ways of dealing with outsiders. Knowledge was uneven, but could be transmitted over long distances. Like Europe, there was communication between groups and knowledge spread ahead of physical contact: Some, no doubt, was withheld, some considered uninteresting, some distorted, much fragmented. What information was shared, with whom, and how, are matters on which I can only begin to speculate.

In filling out the map, I focused on actual contacts between Aborigines and outsiders in the texts of exploration and asked: Where? When? For what purpose? With what consequences? From this exercise it was apparent that the patterning of Aboriginal behaviors was anything but constant. Not only was the contact experience different around the Australian coast, but there were significant differences in the cultures of Aboriginal groups. For instance, life in the tropics where Macassans fished was radically different from life in the desert regions of Central Australia where Europeans did not venture until the mid-nineteenth century. The dry, hostile lands of the west coast where the Dutch made frequent landfall provided a very different niche from that of the east coast peoples contacted by Cook, with their reliable water supply, varied diet, and population density. The differences among Aboriginal groups are obscured when we look only at Aborigines as other to the explorers. We do not speak of seventeenth-century Europe as an undifferentiated cultural bloc occupied by one people, nor, for example, do we speak of the Dutch as if all Dutchmen will behave identically. Yet "natives," "blacks," "Indians" were differentiated on the basis of their material culture, not concepts of self, humanity, or race. Aborigines may have lived in relative isolation for millennia, but they were certainly not lacking in fascination with cer-

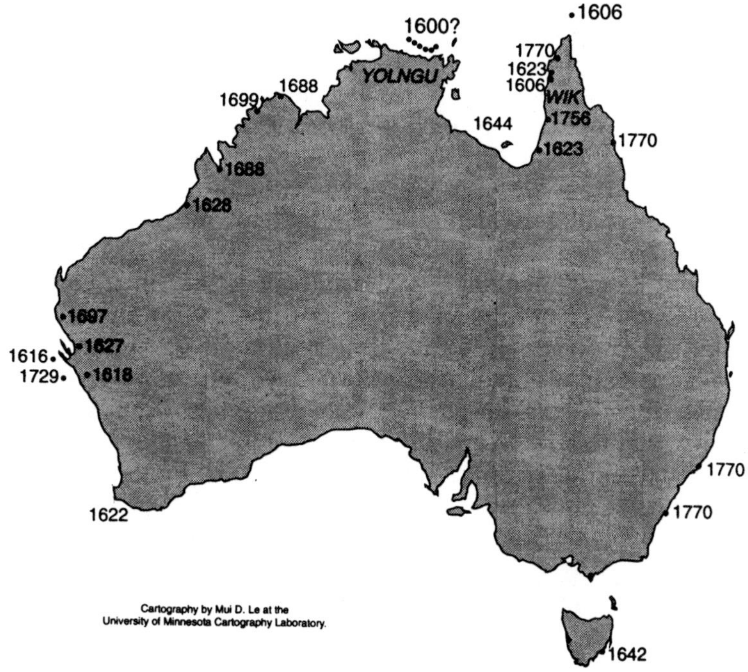

Figure 18.2. Landings and encounters.

tain sorts of new experiences. Aborigines were not the passive bystanders they appear to be in the "Discovery of Australia" genre of literature as they provide case material for the systematizing of sons of the Enlightenment. Aboriginal experiences of other did inform their subsequent behavior, but it was not in a comparative global classification: There were those who could be incorporated and those who should be excluded. While Europe expanded its horizons and encompassed all men, Aborigines built understandings of outsiders. They responded on the basis of these encounters, partial though they were (Figure 18.2).

In short, Aboriginal interpretative frames for the accommodation of outsiders were diametrically opposed to that of the expanding European consciousness. Theirs was not a land discovered by sea, mapped from the outside in, but one pioneered by the ancestral heroes who in the founding era, glossed the "Dreamtime," marked out the land. Their tracks, which criss-cross the continent, infusing it with meaning, linked people, resources, and land. In this schema, the dogma of

Dreaming binds all living beings and natural phenomenon into a huge interfunctional world and all is explicable by reference to the activities of the ancestors. Through mundane daily practice and through seasonal, cyclical, and idiosyncratic ceremonial practice, sacred and secular knowledge was transmitted from generation to generation. The landscape, itself a text to be read by those schooled in the ways of the ancestors, holds out the promise that everything has meaning, but prescribes that only those with the right to know may make claim on it and the resources that knowledge unlocks.

The belief in the power of the ancestral heroes to define life was a common feature of Aboriginal religion, but the content of the narratives and the practices varied radically. Within broad cultural blocs, Aboriginal territorial boundaries were known, but some were more permeable than others (the demarcation was more dramatic in the north than the desert). When in foreign territory, one makes no assumptions about one's rights, but must wait to be invited. Marriage was polygynous but the number and age difference of spouses varied across the continent. The mode of subsistence was hunting and gathering, but in the north the protein content was high, in the desert vegetables predominate, and in the south there is evidence of incipient farming. Access to sacred sites was restricted and serious violations could carry the death penalty. There were elaborate rules of religious etiquette in how one may approach a site, and at those sites where there was a scarce resource (water, ochre, certain foods), rigid rules concerning who could take what, with whom, and in what manner. Permission to visit was required, and ideally visits were supervised by local custodians. At the site, one took only what was needed, and took care to maintain the integrity of the site. As we shall see, all of these rules were broken by the European explorers on shore in search of water, wood, food, and information.

The culture of the group that experiences the encounters with outsiders becomes important, and there were significant differences amongst Aboriginal groups. What, if any, place in its practice is available for "strangers"? In face-to-face societies, with no written traditions, where kin organizes relationships, outsiders present a conceptual problem. How should one regard them? Are they from the spirit world? Another tribe? There are ways of dealing with these possibilities, but the strangers did not behave according to any known rules; their visits were too fleeting for incorporation. The seafaring parties (with notable exceptions) were all male, and such a configuration indicates that there is a hostile or sacred agenda. Single-sex groups, especially of men whose bodies were hidden from view, was a sign of danger. Yolngu have a category for outsiders, "*balanda*," from "Hollander" (presumably taken from the Malay/Indonesian "*belanda*" for Dutch or European in general), and its usage confers certain characteristics on outsiders. Many Aboriginal languages distinguish insiders (us) from outsiders (not us) through use of inclusive and exclusive pronouns. In certain desert ceremonies in which I have participated (as classificatory kin), there is a category of persons called "the strangers," who are actually members of non-adjacent land holding groups to those staging the ceremony. At a critical point in the ceremonial cycle, the strangers must have arrived. By the completion of the ceremony, they have been incorporated within the ritual taxonomy of those present. They have become neighbors. These are persons I am terming "inside others." Those who cannot be accommodated I will call "outside others."

Aborigines knew nothing of the preoccupations of Europe, of the emerging concepts of "man," or the contesting of "states of nature," but they knew much about how a person should behave on their land, and few of these seafaring outsiders behaved in a way that made it possible for them to be brought within the Aboriginal classification of "us" – that is, "the people." Because they remained outside Aboriginal sociality, reciprocity, ceremonial exchange, and kin obligations, the available responses were to ignore, monitor at a distance, intervene only when absolutely necessary to protect sites, treat as hostile, and retaliate when life or land was damaged. Here I would argue that the impact of dealings with others on Aboriginal societies has been underestimated because our narratives of the past and growing sense of global humanity are refracted through a prism of our own self realization. Within the Aboriginal schema, the new was brought within the realm of the known and within these traditional modes of incorporation it is difficult to identify introduced ideas.[4] To ask, "Is this traditional or new?" once an item, idea, or practice has been incorporated within the ritual domain and thus brought under the control of the Law makes no sense.

PROVISIONS FOR "A-MAZING": TEXTS AND CONTEXTS

My research for this journey represents a culling of what is available to a non-specialist and is itself a commentary on the problems of interdisciplinary research. In speculating regarding Aboriginal concepts

[4] See Diane Bell, *Daughters of the Dreaming* (Melbourne/Sydney, 1983), 90–4.

of other and contacts between Torres Strait and New Guinea, I am dealing with the traces of non-literate peoples. I am drawing on my fieldwork, personal communications, published ethnographies (and these raise questions of mediation, of reading historical texts into those written in the timeless "ethnographic present"), evidence from linguists, and prehistorians (and here note I am neither linguist nor prehistorian). Where possible I began with the journals of the explorers. I wanted to hear at firsthand the accounts of the encounters, but the documentary trail was thin and I have had to content myself with translations. Even the accounts that purported to be eye witness accounts had been amended and revised by various parties, including the original authors. I found it helpful to read the accounts within the cultural contexts that informed the missions, and even more interesting to see which parts of journal entries have achieved prominence, and which have been left to moulder in the primary sources. In the most frequently quoted section of William Dampier's best seller of 1697, *A New Voyage Around the World,* the inhabitant of Australia was "the miserablest," but other ethnographic details I gleaned from Dampier's 1699 *A Voyage to New Holland* raised questions concerning daily life and put the adjective into a context.[5] His portrait of west coast life still reads as tolerably good ethnography. I found the most accessible texts to be the edited journals and the overview volumes of exploration of individuals, nationalities, a geographical region, a century. These were organizational frames my mapping exercise was busily dismantling, and I found I was often wading through the moralizing and misreadings of twentieth-century historians.

In the years between Columbus and Cook, the philosophies driving European exploration and discovery of new lands were enriched by experience of indigenous cultures. The categorizations of the others of the Pacific, and the Americas, were framed by differing religious beliefs, commercial considerations, and recorded by sea captains with varying degrees of skill. They were interpreted within the social, moral, and political schema of Hobbes, Locke, and Rousseau. The traces left by the seafaring expeditions in journals, charts, museum collections, interpreted by generations of scholars tell of the spiritually charged missions of the Spanish of the fifteenth and sixteenth centuries, the more pragmatic Dutch traders of the sixteenth and seventeenth for whom human depravity, rather than redemption, was key. Dutch seamen were more interested in keeping ships intact than ex-

[5] William Dampier, *A New Voyage Round the World* (New York, 1968); *New Voyage to New Holland: The English Voyage of Discovery to the South Seas in 1699* (London, 1981).

ploring treacherous coasts. The English, brought into the Pacific by the 1577–80 circumnavigation of Francis Drake, confirmed the Dutch impressions of the west coast, and then in 1770 mapped the east coast. All eye witness accounts of encounters with inhabitants of the South Land are remarkably consistent, until Cook, and even there when one reads his accounts of his onshore encounters, his "noble savage" is not all that different from the "wretched" west coast peoples.

The information gathered addressed questions asked by those sponsoring the various expeditions, and it is helpful to scan the instructions with which the the Portuguese, Dutch, and English sailed. Pedro de Quiros, fired with religious ambition, dreamed of an Empire greater than Spain had ever known.[6] His instructions of January 1606 read: "Our position should be as fathers to children, but they must be watched as if they were known enemies . . . Our part is to be always in the right, with open and honest intentions."[7] On reaching the New Hebrides (Vanuatu), the peace ended in a pitched battle, and after three weeks, Quiros left. However, Quiros did not let observation cloud his mission, and his Petition spoke of "a decent people, clean, cheerful, and grateful," a description that was clearly at odds with his experience, but happily consonant with his beliefs.[8] Quiros thought he had reached the South Land and called it Australia del Espíritu Santo. His "discovery" of Australia may have been dismissed in the secular world, but as late as the 1890s, Cardinal Moran of Sydney was teaching that Quiros, a Catholic, discovered Australia.[9] Much has been written of Quiros' grand vision, but it is possible other Portuguese touched on the north coast in exploration in the Timor area. Unlike the Dutch, the Portuguese traveled from the Cape to Goa and from there to the Strait of Malacca.

The fleeting contacts of the Dutch, who being deep-sea sailors avoided the intricate coastal inlets where resources for Aboriginal hunter-gatherers were varied and plentiful, left the impression of a miserable, wretched, fly infested, arid land. Successive instructions issuing from the Dutch East India Company reflected the growing awareness and knowledge of the region, and evinced a more tolerant view of other than is manifest in the reports filed by their captains. The Company required detailed information, and a good example of

[6] J.C. Beaglehole, *The Exploration of the Pacific, 3d ed.* (Stanford, 1966), 81–2.
[7] *Ibid*, 85.
[8] D.J. Mulvaney, "The Australian Aborigines 1606–1929: opinion and fieldwork," *Historical Studies*, 8, pt 1, (1958), 132.
[9] See C. M. H. Clark, *A History of Australia: from the Earliest Times to the Age of Macquaire*, 6 vols. (Melbourne, 1962), I: 16.

the tone of instructions is contained in those of September 29, 1622, to the yachts *Harringh* and *Hasewint*.

You will moreover go ashore in various places and diligently examine the coast in order to ascertain whether or not it is inhabited, the nature of the land and the people, their towns and inhabited villages, the divisions of their kingdoms, their religion and policy, their wars, their rivers, the shape of their vessels, their fisheries, commodities and manufactures, but specially to inform yourselves what minerals, such as gold, silver, tin, iron, lead, and copper, what precious stones, pearls, vegetables, animals and fruits, these lands yield and produce.
... In landing anywhere you will use extreme caution, and never go ashore or into the interior unless well-armed, trusting no one, however innocent the natives may be in appearance, and with whatever kindness they may seem to receive you, being always ready to stand on the defensive, in order to prevent sudden traitorous surprises, the like of which sad to say, have too often been met with in similar cases. And if any natives should come near your ships, you will likewise take good care that they suffer no molestation from our men.
... In places where you meet with natives, you will either by adroit management or by other means endeavour to get hold of a number of full grown persons, or better still, of boys and girls, to the end that the latter may be brought up here and be turned to useful purpose in the said quarters when occasion shall serve.[10]

Only with Cook's voyage do we find emphasis on recording by experts.[11] Cook, at home with the shoals and shores, was assisted in his observation by experts in fields of interest to the sponsors of the voyage. He also carried with him a library and "Hints," a paper provided by the president of the Royal Society, the Earl of Morton, on "the humanitarian treatment of native peoples, the reading of prayers ... the systematic description of human beings and other phenomena animal, vegetable and mineral."[12] Cook's secret instructions, dated July 30, 1768, for the forward journey from Tahiti, show a shift in focus regarding the native, whose life now has intrinsic value.

You are likewise to observe the Genius, Temper, Disposition and Number of Natives, if there be any, and endeavour by all proper means to cultivate a Friendship and Alliance with them, making them presents of such Trifles as

[10] J. E. Heeres, *The Part Borne by the Dutch in the Discovery of Australia, 1606–1765* (Leiden, 1899), 20–1.
[11] See Bernard Smith, *European Vision and the South Pacific, 1768–1850: A Study in the History of Art and Ideas* (London, 1960), 6ff.
[12] James Cook, *The Journals of Captain James Cook on His Voyage of Discovery*, Vol. 1, *The Voyage of the Endeavour, 1768–1771*, ed. J.C. Beaglehole, Hakluyt Society (London, 1955–6), lxxvii.

they may Value, inviting them to Traffick, and Shewing them every kind of Civility and Regard; taking Care however not to suffer yourself to be surprized by them, but to be always on your guard against any accident.[13]

Australian pre-historian John Mulvaney has been one scholar prepared to speculate regarding the nature and extent of Aboriginal interaction with the outside world.[14] He points to the possibility of journeys of the seafaring islanders of Indonesia and New Guinea to the north, resulting in landfall on the northern Australian coast; of the Chinese explorers in Timor in the early fifteenth century and Portuguese a century later making accidental contact with Aborigines; and to the eighteenth-century evidence of "frequent and complex contacts between Cape York and Papua by way of the Torres Strait Islands."[15] If we take the area of South East Asia and then read into it European expansion, we see the Portuguese partly displaced the Muslims, the Dutch the Portuguese. Each wave disrupted and dislocated local trade routes, ports, and alliances.

Received wisdom holds that the limit of voyaging of the Chinese and Portuguese in the fifteenth and sixteenth centuries was Timor and Macassar and that the Muslim traders had reached New Guinea by the end of the sixteenth. Torres met "Moors" in New Guinea who were said to be colonizing the Papuans. Was this the limit of their expansion? All speculated about what was beyond their empires.[16] However, the knowledge available to present-day scholars is that which made it into official accounts. There is always the possibility of

[13] *Ibid*, cclxxxiii.

[14] J.D. Mulvaney, "The end of the beginning: 6,000 years ago to 1788," in *Australians to 1788*, ed. D.J. Mulvaney and J. Peter White (Broadway, 1987). Since writing this chapter I have read D.J. Mulvaney's *Encounters in Place: Outsiders and Aboriginal Australians 1606–1985* (St Lucia, 1989), and note that we are relying on the same range of sources and that we draw similar conclusions regarding the importance of rereading the texts in the light of Aboriginal knowledge and etiquette. However, Mulvaney's interest lies in making the case for listing sites on the Register of the National Estate. His mapping of the encounters reflects the precision of meticulous archaeological and historical research informed by ethnographic observation, but he pays no particular attention to gender.

[15] See Mulvaney, "The End," 94; 1989, op.cit., 15. The Portuguese had annexed nearby Timor and the Aru Islands in 1511, and there is some cartographic evidence of knowledge of the Australian coast, so it may be that some contact had been made in the early sixteenth century. Portuguese sources are yet to be fully investigated by Australianists. Like the Macassans, their visits are hard to trace and much of their knowledge was not shared with other European traders and voyagers. They may have been in Papua New Guinea by 1602, see Heeres, *The Part Borne*, iii; 3. Bugis fishermen or Malays in Timor might have told the Portuguese of Australia, see Clark, *History*, 11. See also the debate on the work of Arnold G. Wood, *The Discovery of Australia* (London, 1922).

[16] Clark, *History*, 5.

local, unnoted contacts and knowledge being passed through folk histories of Torres Strait Islanders, Papuans, to Malays, and Chinese without there being actual contacts.

MANY ENCOUNTERS: YOLNGU TO TIWI

I'm beginning my ethnographic mapping with the Yolngu of Arnhemland and the Tiwi of Melville and Bathurst Islands. Both are cultural areas that exhibit a capacity to absorb new ideas and to adopt things they find attractive. This suggests they have been dealing with outside others more routinely than say the Wik peoples of Cape York. I'd like to suggest the earliest sustained contacts between outsiders and mainland Aborigines were in the context of northern neighbors, predominantly Macassans, seeking to harvest trepang (bêche-de-mer, sea slug) and to collect tortoise shell. There is live debate about the degree of penetration (sic) of foreign influences, but historians,[17] linguists,[18] prehistorians,[19] and anthropologists[20] have found ample evidence of contacts with Macassan, Portuguese, and Dutch. The context and sequencing of the contact is important, and helps explain the legendary hostility of groups such as Tiwi to "visitors" and the accommodations of some Yolngu. In Berndt's recording of Aboriginal mythology, he claims that before Macassans there was contact with a race of peoples known as *Baijini* by the Yolngu.[21] Although Macknight challenges this evidence of an earlier people,[22] I shall record the possibility in the log of *A-Mazing*. In my experience, Aboriginal periodization in both mythic and historic reckoning is always worth further investigation.

Whether we will ever know more of *Baijini* is doubtful. What is important here is that Yolngu had a classification in their culture for others and their taxonomy admitted chronology. We know the market for trepang opened up in Canton in the sixteenth century and that by 1615 the Chinese had arrived in Macassar, which had been developing

[17] C. C. Macknight, "Macassans and Aborigines," *Oceania*, 42: 4, (1972), 283–321.

[18] See James Urry and Michael Walsh, "The lost 'Macassar language' of Northern Australia," *Aboriginal History*, 5, Pt. 2, (1981), 91–108.

[19] See Mulvaney, *Australian Aborigenes;* Mulvaney, "The End;" Mulvaney, *Encounters.*

[20] See Lloyd Warner, *A Black Civilization: A Social Study of an Australian Tribe*, (New York, 1937); R.M. and C.H. Berndt, *Arnhemland: Its History and its People*, (London, 1954); C. W. M. Hart and Arnold Pilling, *The Tiwi of North Australia*, (New York, 1960); Jane C. Goodale, *Tiwi Wives: A Study of the Women of Melville Island, North Australia*, (Seattle, 1971).

[21] R.M. Berndt, *Djanggawul: An Aboriginal Religious Cult in North-Eastern Arnhemland*, (New York, 1953), 28.

[22] Macknight, "Macassans," 313.

as a major trade center from the late sixteenth century onward.[23] Archaeologists have dated bronze hooks of Macassan style, found at a trepang site on the Arnhem coast, at 1,000 years.[24] That shred of evidence is at odds with all other known accounts of trepang visits, but may have some resonance in Aboriginal mythology and we will record it in the log of *A-Mazing*.

The impact of the Macassans abounds in Arnhemland art and ritual and the existence of an Aboriginal pidgin, heavily larded with Austronesian and used as a *lingua franca* not only with Macassans, but also with other Aborigines from different language groups in Northern Australia indicates the depth and importance of these others in the Aboriginal schema.[25] In reconstructing the nature of the contact and the organization of the industry, the most detailed eye witness accounts of harvesting this delicacy in Arnhemland waters date from the nineteenth century,[26] and given the realignments of local and European powers in the Malay archipelago and Indonesia over the preceding four centuries, we need to exercise caution in our use of them.

The existing ethnographic accounts paint a portrait of 20–60 praus with multilingual and multicultural crews of 30–40 sailing annually to northern waters. The Macassans brought their tools of trade with them: dugout canoes with outriggers for the harvest, demountable bamboo and rattan sheds, iron cauldrons for the boiling, smoking, and drying.[27] Aspects of the seafaring technology were adopted by Yolngu, and thefts of material objects led to fights. Iron, glass, tobacco, and cloth were traded with inland groups for items coastal peoples lacked.[28] During their seasonal visits, the trepangers are said to have cohabited with local women, which led to "jealous fights,"[29] a common gloss for any trouble that occurs in Aboriginal communities, but often a way of diverting the observer's gaze from the deeper and more complex aspects of disputes over ceremonial obligations and territorial aspirations. There are reports of young Aboriginal men traveling to

[23] Mulvaney, "The End," 99.
[24] Ibid.
[25] Following Urry and Walsh, "The Lost Macassar Language," 91-2, "Macassan" indicates people from southern Sulawesi and "Austronesian" denotes the family of languages spoken in Indonesia, Polynesia, Micronesia, parts of New Guinea, Formosa, mainland Southeast Asia and Madagascar. See also Warner, *Black Civilization*, 456.
[26] See Urry and Walsh, "The Lost Macassar language,"
[27] Mulvaney, "The End," 98–9; Mulvaney, *Encounters*, 22–8.
[28] D.J. Mulvaney, "The chain of connection," in *Tribes and Boundaries in Australia*, edited by Nicolas Peterson, Australian Institute of Aboriginal Studies, (Canberra, 1976); Josephine Flood, *Archaeology of the Dreamtime: The Story of Prehistoric Australia and Her People*, (Sydney, 1983), 237.
[29] Mulvaney, "The End," 101.

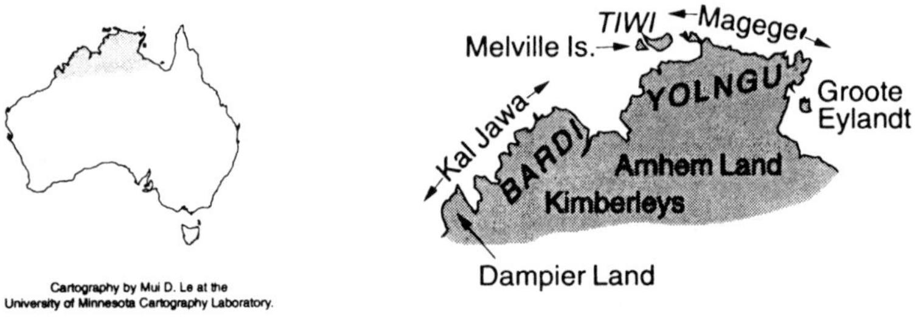

Figure 18.3. Arnhemland to Melville Islands.

Sulawesi with the trepangers, where they lived with the captain's family, and even more intriguing, reports of Muslim conversions. Earl writes of one person, from Goulburn Island, who "had been circumcised and refused to eat pork."[30] There are no reports of Aboriginal women traveling with the praus, but would we have been told if they had? Earl speaks of "one or two natives," and it is later writers who confer male gender, probably correctly, on the travelers.[31]

An interesting footnote on cross-cultural analyses of sexuality is provided by Walker and Zorc, whose linguistic analysis links certain homoerotic activities with the Macassan visits.[32] Citing several Yolngu-Matha phrases ("smooth penis," "smooth anus," "anus with semen") that draw on the Austronesian (in this case Southern Philippine) for "to masturbate" and the Makassarese for "smooth," Walker and Zorc state they are not expressly endorsing "the Macassans (including Bisayan slaves on board) as introducing the practices to Yolngu." They do suggest, however, that the linguistic evidence argues for a sharing of such activities with Macassans or other Austronesian speakers. The aspect of their interpretation I found most revealing was their conflation of marriage and sexuality. They point out that young women were "jealously guarded" from both the Macassans and younger Yolngu, who did not marry until they were older, wiser men. They assure us that now that young people may marry, the activities alluded to in the phrases, which were used as "affectionate or pejorative curses," are "no longer practiced."[33] Is the assumption that homosexu-

[30] George W. Earl, "An account of a visit to Kisser, one of the Serawatti group in the Indian archipelago," *Journal of the Royal Geographical Society*, 11 (1841), 116.

[31] *Ibid.*; Urry and Walsh, "The Lost Macassar language," 95.

[32] Alan Walker and David R. Zorc, "Austronesian loanwords in Yolngu-Matha of Northeast Arnhemland," *Aboriginal History*, 5, pt 2 (1981): 115.

[33] Ibid.

ality is a byproduct of gerontocratic marriage? Or that masturbation is an exclusively homosexual practice? Is the assumption that because young men may not marry, they do not engage in heterosexual activity? Or is the assumption that marriage between age mates eliminates homosexuality? In north and central Australia, ribald sexual joking characterizes many exchanges, especially in single-sex groups. Terms that are "joking" in these contexts may constitute grievous insults in another. From my own fieldwork I know that women have a catalogue of epithets that are graphic and unrelenting in nature. I shudder to think how they might be construed. As the field linguists were male, it is extremely unlikely they have undertaken any extensive work with women on their sex-specific exchanges.[34]

There are several features of the interactions with Macassans that merit note here. Their visits were regular, and the purpose was clear: Aspects of their technology were borrowed; there were sexual, affective, and commercial relations. Those young men who visited Sulawesi in the off-season must have brought back details of the home lives of the trepangers and given substance to the world beyond Arnhemland. The regular and sustained nature of these contacts brought other within the realm of the knowable. Thus the Macassans constitute a different sort of other from the explorer in search of souls or precious metals en route to the east. They were outside others. The Yolngu experience of other is multifaceted because they also had insider others – that is, persons from other Aboriginal groups with whom they might speak a *lingua franca* similar to that used with the trepangers, but from whom they could expect a different level of reciprocity, and upon whom they might impose their code of etiquette for site access, kin obligations, and marriage arrangements.

Here it is interesting to compare the experience of trepangers in the waters of Melville Island (Figure 18.3). It is true that these waters are not as rich in trepang as Yolngu sites, but the area was avoided because the Tiwi were known to have killed intruders. What then had been their formative experiences? Dutchman Pieter Pieterszoon, commanding the *Cleen Amsterdam* and *Wesel* in sailing along the coast of Melville Island in 1636, had sighted smoke, but no people. There were no doubt other passing visitors to the north, but the first recorded

[34] In Aboriginal society, men socialize with men and women with women. There are, of course, mixed gatherings but much of the daily activity is conducted within single sex groups. It is extremely difficult to try to do fieldwork with the opposite sex on matters that are sex-specific – for example, certain religious practices that are secret and/or considered dangerous to the opposite sex. See Bell, *Daughters*.

contact was with the Dutch expedition of Maarten van Delft in 1705 in *Vossenbosch, de Waijer,* and *Nova-Hollandia.*[35] He was instructed to bring back one of the inhabitants for study, but unlike the seventeenth-century instructions cited, the required person was "Indian" (not "native") and was a "man" (not "boys and girls").

> . . . you should come upon unknown Indians, of whom you might without violence or risk, and of their own free will, bring two or three hither, such men might possibly prove of great use in subsequent voyages, but this point we leave to your own judgement and discretion, as you shall find circumstances to shape themselves.[36]

The contact appears to have been favorable. Hart and Pilling recall, "They met natives several times and even allowed them aboard their ships." Subsequent encounters with the Portuguese on Timor, who until around 1800 raided the islands for slaves, may explain the later hostility, but the legacy of the intrusion of these outside others is discernible. The value of iron knives, axes, and matchlock guns was appreciated. But the young men who were the raiders of these goods from the Portuguese were also the ones who made the best slaves. Hart and Pilling ask: What might have been the impact of the removal of a disproportionate number of young men?[37] Could it have contributed to the rate of polygynous marriage and age difference at first marriage? Are the politics of "wife trading" linked to slave raiding?

Hart and Pilling offer a portrait of Tiwi society with male as ego, and their questions may be rephrased with some effect to making women visible as actors. Did the possibilities that Portuguese men provided for Tiwi women (as partners who bore gifts and were exotic) provoke and threaten Tiwi men, who responded by increasing restrictions on the movements of younger women? There are several readings of the "fact" that Tiwi women were out of sight of strangers.[38] The "control" of women evoked by the existence of polygynous gerontocratic marriage is more rhetorical than real. A man with many wives, especially an aging male, cannot keep track of all his wives, and as long as their affairs do not become public, as long as he can assert paternity for any children conceived, as long as the relationships are not incestuous, the matter will not be subject for public com-

[35] Heeres, *The Part Borne,* iii, 67, 88.
[36] Hart and Pilling, *The Tiwi,* 97–100.
[37] Ibid., 100.
[38] See Diane Bell, "Choose Your Mission Wisely: Christian Colonials and Aboriginal Marital Arrangements on the Northern Frontier," in *Aboriginal Australians and Christianity,* edited by Tony Swain and Deborah Bird Rose (Adelaide, 1988), 341–6.

ment. Furthermore, the notion of a "gaggle of wives" being set against each other for the favors of an elderly male is mostly illusion. The co-wives are often sisters who share bonds of family, ceremonial obligations, childcare, and are more likely to conspire to deceive the husband than to be kept in fear of his favors being bestowed elsewhere.[39] A degree of male bias and fantasy, not to mention homophobia, underwrites both observations and interpretations relating to sexual encounters and sexuality. The watch on *A-Mazing* is alert to these undercurrents.

From my fieldwork among Central Australian Aboriginal women, who recalled their first contacts with white men at the turn of the century, it was not the sexual liaisons with white men per se that caused fights. Rather, fights arose because Aboriginal men were gaining nothing and the women were negotiating their own deals. The women were accustomed to bestowing their sexuality where they pleased, and did not consider marriage to be the limits of sexual enjoyment.[40] However, if another Aboriginal man were the partner and it became known, then there would be a fight. Much is made in the literature about "wife lending," but again these practices were ones in which women engaged as a means of having sex with partners other than their husbands and without the likelihood of retaliation, as much as it is a case of men trafficking in women. The possibility of sexual partners outside the cultural constraints and rhetorical strategies of Aboriginal society constituted a challenge for the men that provoked attempts to tighten control over women. When women chose not to return to their husbands violence ensued. How real these "choices" were is moot, but by no means were all black woman/white man relationships forced and violent; some endured, and established dynasties in rural areas.

Moving a little further afield, the evidence for contacts becomes more tenuous, and *A-Mazing* may never emerge from this labyrinth, but I'm going to include it because it brings into play another perspective on sea-faring expeditions and contact with foreigners; reminds us that activity in the Indian Ocean was underwritten by diverse notions of race and other; underscores the geographic proximity of Australia to Southeast Asia and the technical capabilities of civilizations other than that of European kingdoms to put to sea; and furthers the decentering of Europeans as the discoverers of the South

[39] See Diane Bell, "Desert Politics: Choices in the 'marriage market,'" in *Women and Colonization: Anthropological Approaches*, edited by Mona Etienne and Eleanor Leacock, (New York, 1980), 250–262.
[40] Bell, *Daughters*, 99–101.

Land. Could there have been contact with the north of Australia from Southern China during the Ming dynasty (1368–1644)? The treasure ships and the diplomatic missions of the eunuch, Cheng Ho, would have introduced Aborigines to a most exotic other.[41]

It is doubtful whether records of traders in the islands would have been kept. Trade was not a valorized activity and was not monitored by the central government. It is from other sources that we may learn of trade to the south. Records of the activities of the Dutch East India Company in Taiwan between 1662 and 1690 supply abundant information,[42] but what of earlier trade? Did Indonesian seamen service the Chinese market for trepang before the Dutch arrived? Chinese vessels had reached Timor in the fifteenth century, a full century before the Portuguese: What did they learn of the land to the south? The Chinese had the skills to sail through the Indian Ocean, and in the first decade of the fifteenth century brought Malacca within the tribute system.[43] A soapstone figurine found in Darwin in 1879 is dated as of this period.[44] During Yung-lo's reign, various expeditions into the Indian Ocean gave substance to the notion of "showing that no one was left outside" and ensuring that there would be "no outer-separation" by bringing all into the "family of civilized peoples."[45] Did they reach Australia? How would they have accommodated the inhabitants? Could they have remained consistent with the Chinese view that foreign countries were equal and should be treated with impartiality, or would the native population have been designated as "savages"?

ISLANDS AND MAINLAND: CAPE YORK AND THE GULF OF CARPENTARIA

Before moving into the mainstream of the age of discovery, with the 1606 European activities on the Northern extremity of the mainland,

[41] See Gungwu Wang, "Early Ming Relations with Southeast Asia: A Background Essay," in *The Chinese World Order*, John K. Fairbank, ed. (Cambridge,MA., 1968), 53–4. One consequence of Cheng Ho's expeditions begun in 1405 was that a large number of countries were brought within the tributary system. Given the extent of their voyaging over these two decades, it is possible they learned of Australia. The movements of Cheng Ho himself are well documented and there is no suggestion that he visited Australia or Timor. Voyaging was curtailed in 1433 by a revolution in the Chinese court and the new regime frowned on trade, See Clark, *History*, 19.

[42] See John E. Wills Jr, "Ch'ing Relations with the Dutch, 1662–1690," in Fairbank, ed., *The Chinese World*, 225–6.

[43] Wang, "Early Ming," 56.

[44] Graeme Alpin and S.G. Foster, *Australians: Events and Places*, (Broadway, 1987), 169–173.

[45] Wang, *"Early Ming,"* 54, 60–61.

my adventurous barque *A-Mazing* has another, but different, regional route to pursue. What of the local traffic between Australia and Papua? What information was transmitted via the Torres Strait Island peoples who did have a seafaring tradition? There is evidence of cultural exchanges, but the time depth is hard to establish. Cape York shell ornaments were in demand in Papua, while Cape York peoples adopted dugout canoes with outriggers.[46] There are no journals, no carbon-dated sites, only selected traces in the material culture, language, and certain shared physical characteristics of the peoples. However, a glance at the map shows the intricate interlocking of the islands, and the crew of *A-Mazing* could potter here happily recording folk histories and daily life.

Mulvaney's presentation of the visits of the trepangers' fleets suggests the relatively short period it took for elements of the culture of the Macassans to be adopted by Yolngu. We do not need to argue for millennia for Papuan influences to "permeate Aboriginal culture from across Torres Strait."[47] I would certainly endorse the general principle that outside items, ideas, and practices can be quickly absorbed, and in several generations may be indistinguishable from other aspects of the Dreamtime. The power to incorporate is strong, but sorely tested when flooded by ideas and objects over which Aborigines can exercise little control of quantity. Aboriginal modes of accommodation bring the new within the ambit of existing narratives, and the assimilation process is rapid. There is ample documentation of ceremonial cults sweeping through an area in a matter of years, and after a few decades becoming part of the ritual repertoire.[48]

Whatever the degree of contact, it is ethnocentric in the extreme not to factor in some knowledge of these peoples. What is interesting about these contacts with others is that the outsiders were not from unknown locations: they could be brought within the ambit of the Law by incorporation; their homes might conceivably be visited; some reciprocity was possible. Mulvaney provides a rendition of the narrative of "Siveri the seagull and Nyunggu the Torres Strait pigeon," which appears to legitimate interrelationships, introduced objects, and practices within the region.[49] The Papuan-like cult heroes voyage from the mainland to the islands and beyond. This experience of other is what I'm glossing an insider's other. The experience of outsider other by the Wik people of the westerly coast of Cape York initially was of

[46] Mulvaney, "The End," 95.
[47] *Ibid.*, 98–9.
[48] Mulvaney, "The Chain of Connection," 91.
[49] Mulvaney, "The End," 95–8.

fleeting visitors, but all the reports mention violent resistance of the Wik to the stranger presence and document the cost in lives lost. The ferocity of reception of outsiders and the perceptions of the countryside as impoverished discouraged land exploration. There is a significant gap in the documentation of visits from the mid-seventeenth century to the late eighteenth, and a vast range of Dutch sources yet to be explored. So, rather than read the silence as "no contact," we will speculate that with further research the gaps will be filled.

The first recorded encounter on the mainland comes with the visit of Dutchman, Willem Jansz(oon). In November 1605 he sailed in the *Duifken* (Dove) from Bantam in search of the riches of "Papuas." In March 1606 he made landfall on the west coast of Cape York Peninsula at "Fly Bay," a name that summarizes many later encounters with the continent. Jansz went as far south as Cape Keer-weer (turn again), latitude 13° 45'. He had found no water and no provisions. In reconstructing his onshore encounter, we have to rely on reports of contemporaries in Batavia and subsequent explorers.[50] Tasman's instructions of 1644 referred to what had been ascertained:

> [The] unknown South and West coast of Nova Guinea . . . from 5 to 13¾ degrees of Southern Latitude . . . vast regions for the greater part uncultivated, and certain parts inhabited by savage, cruel, black barbarians who slew some of our crew.[51]

From a contemporary commentary of a British East India Company agent stationed in Bantam, Java, comes a slightly expanded interpretation. Captain Saris writes, "on sending their men on shoare to intreate trade, they were nine of them killed by the Heathens, which are man-eaters: so they were constrained to returne, finding no good to be done there."[52]

It is difficult to know if this occurred on the Australian mainland. The coast of New Guinea and Australia were thought to be continuous, and the area described falls within the latitudes cited. We can be certain, however, of the location of Wik killing a member of his party. Carstenz's journal relates that "we sailed past a large river (which the men of the *Duifken* went up in a boat in 1606, and where one of them

[50] Heeres, *The Part Borne*, v; See also Luise Hercus and Peter Sutton, eds., *This is What Happened: Historical Narratives by Aborigines*, Australian Institute of Aboriginal Studies (Canberra, 1986), 87–92.

[51] Ibid., 6.

[52] Quoted in Mulvaney, *Australian Aborigines*, 131–2; see also Hercus and Sutton, *This is What Happened*, 88.

was killed by the arrows of the blacks)." This was the Wenlock River near the present-day town of Weipa.[53]

Of Jansz's killing of peoples to the north of the Wik, Carstenz recorded:

> In our landings between 13° and 11° we have but two times seen black men or savages, who received us much more hostilely than those more to the southward; they are also acquainted with muskets, of which they would seem to have experienced the fatal effect when in 1606 the men of the Duyffken made a landing here.[54]

In another observation, Carstenz notes that in the tool kit of an Aborigine killed by one of his men was found a piece of metal and which he surmises "he probably got from the men of the Duyfken."[55] This willingness to allow that different contact experiences inform subsequent behavior is a striking feature of the explorers' journals I have read thus far and is oft times passed over by later homogenizing historians.

In September 1606, within two months of Jansz, Luiz Vaz de Torres, having become separated from Quiros in Vanuatu, explored the New Guinea coast and navigated *Almiranta* through the Strait that now bear his name. Torres, although attacked by the natives, noted they were:

> very corpulent and naked: their arms were lances, arrows, and clubs of stone ill fashioned . . . we caught in all this land twenty persons of different nations, that with them we might be able to give a better account . . . They give much notice of other people, although as yet they do not make themselves well understood.[56]

I have not been able to locate the original of Torres's observations, and again would sound a caution regarding the location of the attacks. I am assuming it was not on the mainland.

Jansz and Torres alike met with hostilities, but the experience was construed differently in their portraits of indigenous peoples. Mulvaney suggests the Dutch were contemptuous of these debased heathens in whom they saw no prospects of commercial gain, whereas Torres and popularizer Quiros were more benign and glimpsed the possibility of conversions.[57] For the Aborigines, the first encounter had

[53] Heeres, *The Part Borne*, 42.
[54] See Mulvaney, *Encounters*, 8; Hercus and Sutton, *This is What Happened*, 89.
[55] Ibid., 42–43.
[56] Mulvaney, *Australian Aborigines*, 132.
[57] Ibid.

been bloody on both sides. It would be helpful to know whether the Aborigines' killing of one of Jansz's party occurred before or after Jansz fired on them, but the chronological sequence is not reconstructable from the documents. Whatever, the outcome for the Wik was that the intruders left, and that was a desired outcome. Also these outside others had left the Wik some pieces of metal, and by the time that Carstenz visited, they had become part of the hunter-gatherer technology.

In less than one generation, the Dutch were back on Cape York shores. Jan Carstenz in 1623 was sent to retrace *Duyfken* in the *Pera* and *Arnhem*, but found nothing that was commercially viable.[58] There is a certain irony here, for the aluminum-rich bauxite of the red cliffs of weathered laterite near Weipa has made this region an important site for current generations of Europeans, and the resource rich coastal plains sustained life for countless generations of Wik.[59] Carstenz continued past Keer-weer to a salt river inlet where on April 24, 1623, he nailed a wooden tablet to a tree, and at latitude 17° 8' south turned around and sailed the *Pera* home. Meanwhile, the *Arnhem* under Willem Joosten Colster (Coolsteendt) continued across the Gulf of Carpentaria to the northeastern fringes of Arnhemland coast and Groote Eylandt. There is no record of any onshore activity by Colster, but the entries of Carstenz's "authentic journal" offer a wealth of information. Leading eight of the seventeen attempts to land, Carstenz encountered Aborigines on nine occasions, and his observations reveal a life style and technology consistent with contemporary ethnographic accounts[60] (Figure 18.4).

From the daily log it is evident that Carstenz's party killed Aborigines, but in his summarized report he mentions only the killings of his men. This indicates the relative importance he placed on loss of life. One of the distinguishing features of the journal is that he makes mention of women, and tells us "the natives drag their wives and children [over rivers] by means of dry sticks and boughs of trees."[61] The choice of verb (drag) is ambiguous, and it is difficult to know whether the implication is that the men must work hard to get the boughs across the rivers, or that the women are being dragged along. The tone of Beaglehole's presentation in *The Exploration of the Pacific* favors the latter.[62] Whichever reading is correct, it is significant that

[58] J.C. Beaglehole, *The Exploration of the Pacific*, 3d ed. (Stanford, 1966), 118.
[59] See Mulvaney, *Encounters*, 11–2.
[60] Heeres, *The Part Borne*, 21–42; Mulvaney, *Encounters*, 11.
[61] Heeres, *The Part Borne*, 45 (on deaths); 41 (on women).
[62] Beaglehole, *Exploration*, 110.

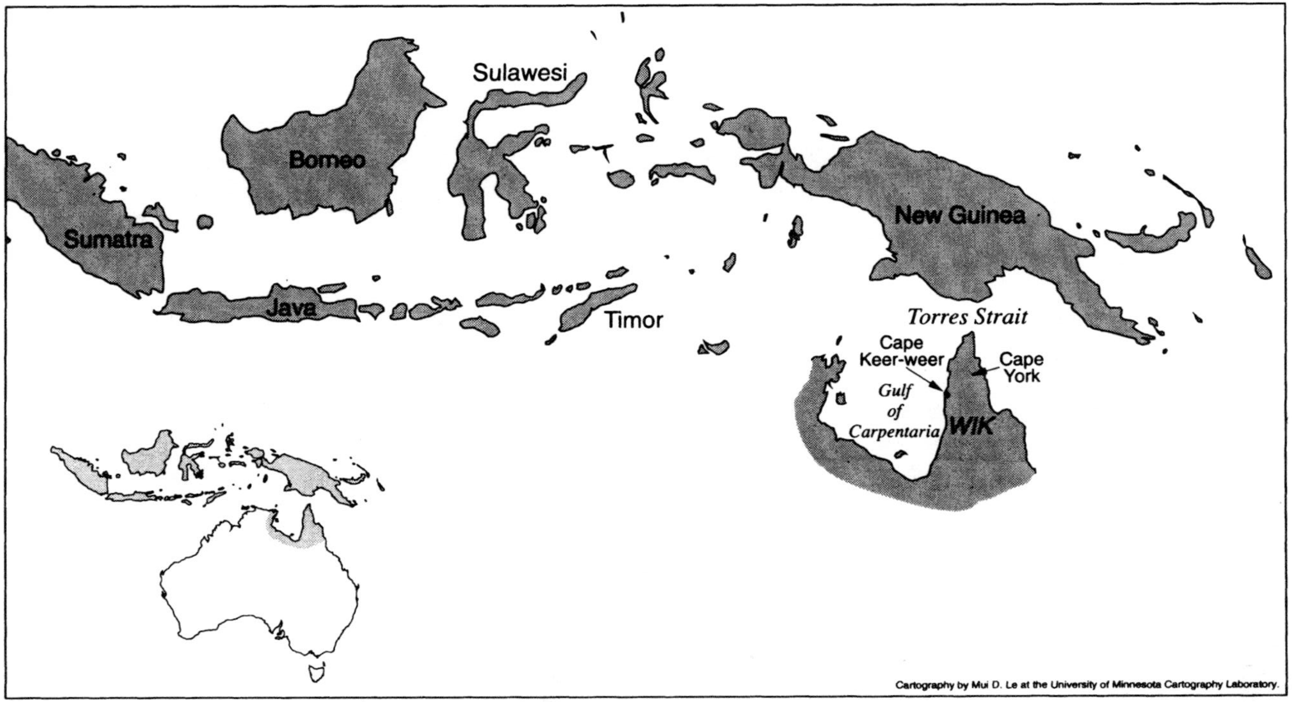

Figure 18.4. Cape York and the Gulf of Carpentaria.

he saw women. They are invisible in some later accounts, and that may be because they were reluctant to approach, were being restrained, or were not recorded. We can infer from Carstenz that he was observing a group in the process of moving, maybe to a new camp site, to visit, or to hunt, but the group was mixed, and the men were assisting the women. It was probably an extended family group moving to exploit the resources as the land dried inland as the wet season was ending.

There is potential confusion in Carstenz's journal in that he bestows the name "Keer-weer" on a point that is clearly on the New Guinea coast (7° south), but is easily mistaken for the Keer-weer Cape of Jansz on Cape York at 13° 45'. The distinction is significant because when the contacts with the natives of Papua are separated from those of Cape York, we find that all references to huts, pigs, penis gourds, and nasal perforations with bone are to New Guinea encounters.[63] The confusion is one that Beaglehole does little to resolve, and thus when he generalizes from Carstenz's observations of the natives, it is a mixture. As we shall see, the Cape York Aborigines showed no interest in the trinkets Carstenz offered, but Beaglehole writes of "poor abject creatures caring mainly for bits of iron and strings of beads."[64]

By April 15, at 14° 56', Carstenz is further south than the violent encounters with Jansz, and is probably observing Yir-Yorond, whom he tries to entice with strings of beads and iron. On the 18th the skipper of the *Pera* lands and is quickly surrounded by a large number of local people.

> . . . some of them armed and others unarmed, had made up to them; these blacks showed no fear and were so bold as to touch the muskets of our men and try to take the same off our shoulders, while they wanted to have whatever they could make use of; our men accordingly diverted their attention by showing them iron and beads and espying vantage, seized one of the blacks by a string which he wore around his neck, and carried him off to the pinnace; the blacks who remained on the beach, set up dreadful howls and made violent gestures, but the others who kept concealed in the wood remained there. The natives are coal black, with lean bodies and stark naked, having twisted baskets or nets about their heads; in hair and figure they are like the blacks of Coromandel coast, but they seem to be less cunning, bold and evil-natured than the blacks of the extremity of Nova Guinea . . . Your Worships will in time be able to get information from the black man we have got hold of.[65]

[63] Heeres, *The Part Borne*, 28–29.
[64] Beaglehole, *Exploration*, 119.
[65] Heeres, *The Part Borne*, 36.

On April 19, while his men are onshore cutting wood, thereby taking resources without permission of the landowners and possibly desecrating sites, they are surprised by a large group, "upwards of 200" who try to overcome them.[66] Perhaps the numbers of the attacking party is inflated by fear, but the increase in numbers from the day before shows that news of the incident of the 18th has spread and is informing the act of aggression. For such a large gathering of men to be possible, there must have been ceremonial business going on in the area; or an extremely quick bringing in of allies. A group of 200 adult men implies a group of some 500–600 women and children in toto, and that is a larger group than would normally be in one location. Even if we halve Carstenz's numbers, it is still a most impressive stand. The local people clearly considered these outsiders to be hostile. His men fired two shots, "upon which the blacks fled, one of their number having been hit and having fallen." We are not told of the fate of the one who fell. Carstenz's men pursue those who flee and come across camp sites at which there are "great quantities of divers human bones," from which they conclude that these peoples are cannibals. We do not know the degree of expertise the observer had on this matter: The identification may be incorrect, or the men may have stumbled on a burial site. Suspecting natives encountered of being cannibals is a recurrent theme in explorers' journals and is always reiterated in the histories of the voyage.

On the 24th he notes that "10 pieces of eight will be given to the boatman for blacks they shall get hold of" and he hopes this will make his men more diligent and careful. On April 25, while searching for water on shore, they find seven small huts made of dry hay, also "7 or 8 blacks" who "refused to hold parley." They continue south, almost certainly now in Yir-Yorond territory, and on May 3, at latitude 15° 20' Carstenz wrote:

> . . . we have not seen one fruit bearing tree, nor anything men can make use of; there are no mountains nor even hills, so that it may safely be concluded that the land contains no metals, nor yields precious woods, such as sandalwood, aloes or columbia; In our judgement this is the most arid and barren region that could be found anywhere on earth; the inhabitants too, are the most wretched and poorest creatures that I have ever seen in my age or time.

His interactions with the mainland peoples on his journey back up the Cape show that the deadly aspect of encounters with outsiders is

[66] The following account of Carstenz's voyage is drawn from Heeres, *The Part Borne*, 37–40.

apparent to the locals. By May 5, on their northward journey along the Cape, Carstenz goes ashore and is promptly attacked, but the blacks flee. He sees their cache of weapons but leaves them untouched. As an enticement, he leaves iron and beads but, they appear quite indifferent to such things, nor, in his opinion, do they appear to have knowledge of the gun for they "held up their shields with great boldness and threw them at the muskets." At latitude 13° 29' he is within Wik territory, and if he is correct that they are ignorant of guns, then there is a knowledge boundary between Wik and the peoples of 11°–13°. This is quite possible, but there are other possibilities. The previous shootings may not have been associated with the musket, but rather the noise, or the puff of smoke. Alternatively, they may "know" of guns, but not know how to overpower them. On some occasions people appear to be attempting to shout them down, on others to be mimicking the sound, but here they are trying to disarm the intruders.

On May 7 the skipper goes ashore but is surprised by some 100 men, who flee when a shot is fired. "They are quite black and stark naked, some having their faces painted red and others white, with feathers stuck through the lower part of the nose." Again, this is an extremely large gathering and indicates that the Aborigines were treating the outsiders as hostile and intent on expelling them. The red paint could be of the ritual avengers and the white of death, but it does suggest the people have a considered stance toward the outsiders and are summoning all their powers, natural and supernatural, to expel them. The next day Carstenz's men succeed in capturing an Aboriginal man by first showing bits of iron and strings of beads to those present. Then when close up, and one loses his weapon, the skipper seizes the man around the waist, while the quartermaster puts a noose around his neck. In attempting to rescue their countryman, one of the blacks is shot and the others flee.

In summarizing their interactions with the local people between 13° and 17° 8', Carstenz considers that for his part they have behaved with kindness, but everywhere the Aborigines received them as enemies. Between 11° and 13° he reports seeing few, but they were more hostile. Here we might speculate that the people further north had had more experience of outsiders and were ready to resist any encroachment on their territory. Again, the encounters have left Aborigines dead, and this time two of their number have been kidnapped. Nothing more can be learnt of their fate from published sources. As a memento of this historic meeting of Europeans, Aborigines obtained some trinkets. How these items were interpreted by the Aborigines of the Cape York is difficult to know, but Aboriginal encounters with Carstenz are logged as important on board *A-Mazing*, and for further ideas of the meanings attached to these encounters we can turn to narratives of contemporary Wik speakers, who tell proudly of how they repulsed the Dutch.[67]

The 1644 voyage of Abel Tasman mapped the Gulf of Carpentaria, but he tells us little of the inhabitants.[68] Tasman, according to Beaglehole, was the typical Dutch East Indies sailor, "hating shoals and a lee shore much worse than the devil, good at dead reckoning; a little at loss, it is possible, when emphasis was laid on the gentle treatment of native peoples; certainly no great love for setting foot on strange land and acquiring anthropological information."[69] Tasman's journal of this voyage has not survived, and information comes from a report van Diemen sent to Holland.[70] Tasman was rebuked for not having walked over the land in every direction to ascertain what it might yield and for finding only "naked, beach-roving wretches, destitute even of rice . . . miserably poor, and in many places of very bad disposition."[71]

Over a century later, in 1756, Jean Etienne Gonzal surveyed the east and west coasts of the Gulf of Carpentaria. His contacts with the natives were "frequent but cautious."[72] On April 29, Gonzal sighted huts, but the people took flight when they approached. On May 25, at latitude 12° 26' they were hailed by Aborigines, who signaled them ashore.

> . . . our men went ashore at daybreak [May 26], and on landing found several persons, who however all took flight directly . . . shortly after returned to them, when they found them armed with assagays . . . They were accompanied by a number of females who had their privities covered with a kind of small mats.[73]

They assisted the party to find water and led them to a pleasant valley where there were more women and children, huts and a soak (water welled up out of a hand dug pit). On returning to the beach, they found the natives with their praus and were then joined by

> nineteen natives came up to them, all of them with bodies daubed over with red; when said natives were by our men treated to some arrack with sugar,

[67] See Hercus and Sutton, *This is What Happened*, 93–107.
[68] Ibid., p. 72.
[69] Cook, *Journals*, lviii.
[70] Clark, *History*, 34.
[71] Beaglehole, *Exploration*, 158.
[72] Heeres, *The Part Borne*, vii.
[73] This account is drawn from Heeres, *The Part Borne*, 94–97.

they began to make merry and even struck up a kind of chant, at the conclusion of which they retired to the wood again.

The drinking scene is repeated two days later with the express purpose of capturing one or two: "While they were making merry, our men seized hold of two of them." The others fought back with their assagays but wounded only one. The crew, however, fired a volley, and wounded one person. The others fled. The captive resisted, biting and tearing to get loose. Fifty natives appeared but also dispersed when fired upon. The captive was carried off. On May 30, two praus approach but soon return to shore. (At least one of the captives reached Batavia, where he learned to speak a Malay language and provided evidence for local "scientists" of a continent inhabited by sub-humans.[74]

Further south at 13° they are again signaled ashore by men in a canoe, and once on shore are met by "eleven men and five females again came running up to them, armed with assagays . . . who directly tried to take our men's hats off their heads." On being thwarted in that task they throw their weapons and, all except one lad who is taken captive, flee when shots are fired. These people are said to have "some knowledge of gold," when lumps of the same were shown to them. Further south, Gonzal finds the more tractable natives, and at latitude 13° 3' south cuts across to the west coast of the Gulf and leaves Wik and Yir-Yorond territory.[75]

What are we to make of these exchanges? They are of a totally different nature from those of the seventeenth century and yet we have little evidence of visits for the intervening period. Clearly there has been contact, and one could infer some sexual liaisons and certainly some material goods. The initial approaches being made by mixed sex parties suggests that the people had been in contact with all male parties before and knew that they were not necessarily ritual avengers and that perhaps they carried gifts. People further north had possibly been raided from Timor. From the Dutch records we can learn a great deal of the way in which Wik and other Cape York groups learnt of outside others, and begin to build a portrait of their other. Unlike the Arnhemland *balanda* for other, for Wik speakers a white person is simply a "whitefellar" and an English speaker is Wik-kiith. It is through the pronoun system that Wik distinguish "we" (us)

[74] At least one captive reached Batavia, where he learned to speak a Malay language and provided evidence to local "scientists" of a continent inhabited by sub-humans. See Mulvaney, *Encounters*, 15–6.

[75] Heeres, *The Part Borne*, 97.

from "them." "Not us" are outside people who don't partake of our culture, and Wik were fierce about outsiders and initially quick to muster to repel them. Is the change in approach in mid-eighteenth century due to alcohol? The unscrupulous use of alcohol and the traumatic effect it continues to have on Aboriginal societies constitutes an entry in the log of *A-Mazing*.

Contemporary Aboriginal narratives, which, while clearly drawing on a range of encounters with outside others, offer a fascinating rendition of the events at Cape Keer-weer. One account from the Wallamby family, on whose land the Dutch "settled," recalls that initially both sides were happy with the meeting:

> A crowd of people saw their boat sail in and went to talk with them. They said they wanted to put up a city. Well, the Keerweer people said that was all right. They allowed them to sink a well and put up huts. The Europeans gave them tobacco. They gave them flour – they threw that away.[76]

The scene of happy co-residence is shattered when the Europeans begin to force the Aborigines to hunt for them and to take Aboriginal women. In the process of teaching the Aborigines to use a musket, the Dutch point at one Aborigine and others move to protect their fellow countryman. In the ensuing melee, Dutch and Aborigines are killed, but eventually the Dutch flee and name the site Cape Keer-weer. Aboriginal honor is satisfied.

The fullest account comes from Jack Spear Karntin, a Wik-Ngatharra speaker, born in 1905. It also has the Dutch building houses, and identifies "problems with women" and guns as precipitating deadly conflict, but unlike the other account, it makes specific reference to published material on the Dutch at Cape Keer-weer, and clearly elaborates on more recent encounters with Europeans by his actual kin.[77] It is a tale of triumph, and today sustains local Aborigines in their fraught dealings with Anglos.

WRECKS AND THE WRETCHED: THE WEST AUSTRALIAN COAST

The trepangers also made contacts with peoples in the Kimberley region and called the area "Kia Jawa." Some evidence suggests that these contacts were earlier than the regime of annual visits to Yolngu.[78] There is little recorded of Macassan activity in the area. The

[76] Hercus and Sutton, *This is What Happened*, 86.
[77] Ibid., 99–107.
[78] Urry and Walsh, "The Lost 'Macassar' Language," 101.

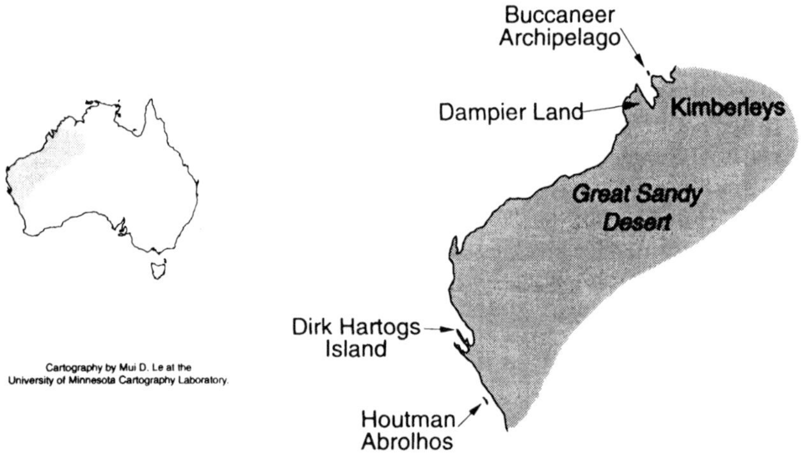

Figure 18.5. The West Australian Coast: Abrolhos to the Kimberleys.

visits appear to have been less regular than along the Arnhem coast. The best information comes from Port Keats (Northern Territory), where stands of tamarind trees flourish and language diversity suggests that outsiders have stimulated linguistic, social, and cultural exchanges[79] (Figure 18.5).

It was the Dutch who documented much of the west coast, and they found little joy in their discoveries. When in 1611 Brouwer pioneered the faster passage to the East Indies, the Dutch began to wreck ships with remarkable regularity on the Western Australian coast, and to do so on a quite restricted section. The first of the Dutch accidental tourists was in 1616 – Dirk Hartog(zoon) of Amsterdam in *Eendracht* (Concord). On 26 October he made landfall at Shark Bay, and nailed to a tree his pewter plate on which was recorded the details of his visit. There are no other known records of the journey. He spent three days on shore but found that the various islands were uninhabited.[80] Eendrachtsland was mapped by successive Dutch visits.

Possibly there were more, but the following gives a sense of the intensity of action: in May 1618, Claeszoon van Hillegom in the *Zeewolf*[81]; in July 1618, Jacobszoon in the *Mauritius;* Frederik Houtman

[79] Ibid., 101–2.
[80] Heeres, *The Part Borne*, 8.
[81] Alan Frost, "Toward Australia: The Coming of the Europeans 1400 to 1788," in *Australians to 1788*, D.J. Mulvaney and J. Peter White, eds. (Broadway, 1987), 377–8.

and Jacob Dedel in *Dordrecht* and *Amsterdam* in 1619 observed "no smoke or signs of inhabitants there"[82]; Landt van de Leewin 1622[83]; in July 1623, Klaas Hermansz(oon) in *Leyden*. In 1628, Gerrit Frederikszoon de Witt in the *Vyanen* was driven ashore at about 21° and "forced to throw overboard 8 or 10 lats of pepper and a quantity of copper." Grateful to get away safely, they sailed 50 miles along the coast. "It was a barren and dangerous coast, green fertile fields, and exceedingly black, barbarian inhabitants."[84] Thus, in the space of eight years, peoples of the west coast had experienced what must have seemed to be quite an extraordinary other. Unlike the Wik experiences, there are no murders reported nor any captures. The local people appear to have kept out of sight. Possibly they saw ships approach, strike reefs, jettison cargo, limp on, or fight and massacre each other. When they came ashore, they searched in vain for water. These incompetent others went away. The items washed ashore were from another world: Some were useful, some not.

Then, when in June 1629 the *Batavia*, under the command of François Pelsaert, struck south of Hartog's point, on Houtman Abrolhos reef, the locals were witness to further strange behavior of outside others.[85] For one thing, these very accidental tourists were unusual in that there were women and children on board. In an effort to save lives, 180 were transported to a larger island, 40 to a smaller one, and 70 were still on board when the ship was abandoned.[86] Pelsaert sailed north but found no safe landing place. On June 14, while looking for water, the leitmotif of traffic on these shores, four Aboriginal men were seen to be creeping up on all fours. The visitors surprised them, and they ran away. The next day Pelsaert's men found a camp site, ashes, and crab shells. They were grateful for the water and food they were able to glean on shore, and stayed overnight. On the 16th they saw some eight natives, each of whom was carrying a stick in hand, but who ran off. On September 17, 1629, Pelsaert, hoping to retrieve some of the jettisoned goods, returned to the Western Australia coast and found that there had been massacre and mayhem among the Batavia survivors in his absence.[87] One extraordinary piece of behavior of Pelsaert was the marooning of two convicts/delin-

[82] Heeres, *The Part Borne*, 16.
[83] Frost, "Toward Australia," 380.
[84] Heeres, *The Part Borne*, 54; Beaglehole, *Exploration*, 121.
[85] Beaglehole, *Exploration*, 123–6; Heeres, *The Part Borne*, 55–8.
[86] Beaglehole, *Exploration*, 125.
[87] Heeres, *The Part Borne*, 57–8.

quents, Wouter Loos and Jan Pelzroende, on land in hope that if they one day be rescued alive, they will tell of these parts. This was at 26° 28'.[88]

In the Abrolhos region, on November 15, while looking for water, Pelsaert's men set fire to the brush and unexpectedly found two pits filled with water. Their subsequent behavior was a grossly improper use of resources, an invasion of territory, and probably destroyed the efficiency of the native well.

> ... since they had only a small hole at the top, that would admit a man's arm, but below we found a large cistern or water-tank under the earth; after which with mattocks and sledge-hammers we widened the hole so as to be able to take out the water conveniently.[89]

For the time being the Dutch observations were more of the same: flies, anthills, no good water, inhabitants ran off in terror on seeing white man.[90] For the Aborigines, the observations were just beginning.

More words were devoted to the description of the kangaroo than to the people, and subsequent commentary has found intense interest in the anthills. Pelsaert tells us that they saw anthills that "from afar somewhat resembled huts for the abode of men." Beaglehole renders the observation thus: [They] "were able to observe nothing but anthills so large that they were taken for the habitations of the 'Indians'." Such romanticizing has several sub-texts: it demeans the Dutch and exoticizes the other. The fascination with haycocks and anthills runs as a counterpoint to the search for water. Dampier in 1699 also mentions "several Things like Haycocks . . . which at a distance we thought were Houses." Masefield, in a footnote to his editing of Dampier's journals, offers the insight that "Flinders suggests that these are the ant-hills of the kind seen by Pelsart (sic) in 1629." None of the secondary texts I have read thus far pursue details regarding the people: natives/blacks/Indians are not as interesting as cross-referencing anthills.[91]

Seven years later, in 1636, Dutch Commander Gerrit Thomaszoon Pool was sent to seek further knowledge of lands westward of Arnhem, and his instructions were to bring back the two Dutch delinquents. In his dealings with the natives, he was counseled by

[88] Beaglehole, *Exploration*, 127.
[89] Heeres, *The Part Borne*, 58.
[90] *Ibid.*; Clark, *History of Australia*, 26.
[91] Heeres, *The Part Borne*, 61; Beaglehole, *Exploration*, 124; Dampier, *A New Voyage New Holland*, 121; William Dampier, *Dampier's Voyages*, John Masefield, ed., 2 vols. (London, 1906), 2: 439.

Anthonio van Diemen to overlook "slight misdemeanors" so as not to "inspire them with aversion to our nation. Whoever endeavors to discover unknown lands and tribes, had need to be patient and long-suffering, noways quick to fly out, but always bent on ingratiating yourself."[92] I have found no reference to any onshore activity by Pool and his men.

The next recorded visit is from Abel Janszoon Tasman with Frans Jacobszoon Visscher in *Limmen, Zeeneeuw,* and *Brak* on his 1644 voyage.[93] Part of his impossibly wide instructions were to find the two men marooned by Pelsaert, and to find the remains of the *Batavia*.[94] There is no detailed account of what he and Visscher achieved on this trip. Tasman was clear that Eendrachstland and Carpentaria were parts of the same land, but he found nothing that could be turned to profit.

After the death of van Diemen, Governor General of the Dutch East India Company, in 1645, Dutch activity lessened, and it was only the search for the 1694 wreck of the *De Ridderschap van Holland* that brought the Dutch back into the waters. Willem de Vlamingh ventured on land in the search, and his 1697 visit included "at least 16 cautious land sorties" between the latitudes of 28° and 32° south.[95] In the course of six weeks, in the summer months, his onshore parties of up to eighty-six men failed to meet a single Aborigine, but they did find Hartog's plate, still standing. He took it down, and left his own with Hartog's message transcribed and a record of his visit. In 1801 the French found this evidence of Dutch activity, half buried in sand, and brought it to Paris. De Vlamingh had anchored off Rottnest Island, near Perth, in January 1697 but had failed to "discover" the harbor. As the Dutch signed off from Australian waters, the orthodoxy was that the natives were unfriendly, wretched, and poor.

The first sustained contact with west coast peoples was recorded under conditions quite different from the carefully instructed Dutch. On January 4, 1688, English buccaneer William Dampier, in the *Cygnet,* making his own rather accidental voyage around the world, sighted land. Dampier's exploits, recounted in *A New Voyage Round the World,* led to a new commission to explore New Holland and New Guinea. On this ill-fated second journey, in the woefully inadequate *Roebuck,* Dampier's instructions were to "bring home specimens, including any natives who came voluntarily," to keep a journal, in part as a means of producing documentary evidence of any mutinous ac-

92 Heeres, *The Part Borne,* 65–66.
93 Ibid., 48.
94 Beaglehole, *Exploration,* 158.
95 Mulvaney, *Australian Aborigines,* 133.

tions. On the first visit he spent some twelve days on or near shore, and his observations provide much greater detail than Cook's later visit to the east coast.[96] Dampier's second visit, in 1699, produced more careful ethnography, but *A Voyage to New Holland* (1981) is rarely quoted. Dampier is known as the man who identified the wretched of the earth in an arid, fly-infested land. No joy there.

The Royal Society, formed when Dampier was a boy, had published a set of directions for travelers to distant places, and Dampier's work demonstrates that he was following their urgings to record in fine detail.[97] His first book was dedicated to one President of the Royal Society, and his second voyage gained much from his interaction with the Society. Beaglehole tells us Dampier had a "taste for examination and adequate description of natural phenomena, whether plants, beasts, tides, winds or ways of strange tribes and peoples." He reworked his originals for publication, but the carefully crafted narrative style is all his own, Masefield assures us. Banks, on the other hand, thinks it possible that he wrote them once home – he was after all "on a ship of pirates."[98] The tone of Banks is peevish. Dampier's voyages herald the dawning of the scientific era of exploration and speculation on other peoples. Unlike information generated in the context of trade missions, his became public, and was savored: Dampier's sense of narrative sat well with his attention to detail.[99]

On his first visit, Dampier made landfall at latitude 16° 50' at Buccaneer's Archipelago, and for the next twelve days he observed and interacted with local people on the mainland and adjacent islands. His observations of the Bardi are far more detailed than any other and range over both physical and social features. He tells us of the soil, water, and animals, then the people, their homes, and something of the social organization, but Dampier's sweeping generalization is the focus of most commentaries: "The inhabitants of this country are the miserablest People in the World. The Hodmadoda of Monomatapa, though a nasty People yet for Wealth are Gentlemen to these . . . setting aside their Humane Shape, they differ but little from Brutes." The rest of the passage deals with the problem of the flies, so troublesome that "they cannot see far, unless they hold up their Heads." His de-

[96] Christopher Lloyd, *William Dampier* (Hamden, 1968) 77–8; Dampier, *A New Voyage Round the World*, 311–16.

[97] See Percy Adams, Introduction to *A New Voyage Round the World by William Dampier*, (Toronto, 1968), xi; Smith, *European Vision*, 8.

[98] Adams, "Introduction," ix; Beaglehole, *Exploration*, 166; Dampier, *Dampier's Voyages*, 2; 14; Sir Joseph Banks, *Journal of the Right Hon. Joseph Banks During Captain Cook's First Voyage*, Joseph D. Hooker, ed. (London, 1896), 297.

[99] See also Clark, *History of Australia*, 40.

scription of their physical features includes reference to their blackness, pubic covering, and missing front teeth in all, men and women, young and old and "neither have they any beards."[100] When one looks at the illustrations and descriptions of visits to other Pacific locations, it is apparent why Aborigines fare so badly on a comparative scale that takes a European aesthetic as a guide to skills and intelligence.[101] Our journal entry for *A-Mazing* notes that his depiction of the lives of the inhabitants as miserable suffers when read out of context in the twentieth century. It also helps legitimate subsequent theft of Aboriginal lands: They weren't really using it anyway! The details of the lives of the peoples Dampier met were not without purpose or logic, and he constantly assumed their behavior to be rational. What did strike him was that there was such a minimal level of material comfort and such a simple technology.

Dampier provides notes on their diet, food-getting techniques, and beliefs. "They live by fishing and gathering shell fish . . . I did not perceive that they worship any thing." He finds they have no weapons to defend themselves save wooden lances, and swords and metals were unknown. Fitting his observations into a comparative frame, Dampier assumed they were like the Indians of America, who used stone, and that they made fire with friction like the "Indians of Bon-Airy." Their speech, he noted, was "somewhat thro' the throat." The first group they saw on shore ran away, and in spite of searching for the next three days, they found nothing but old fires, no water, only old wells. They left a good many "toys" and departed the mainland.[102]

Dampier's first summarizing of his contact is interesting in that he clearly acknowledges the encounters are a two-way affair.

> At our first coming, before we were acquainted with them, or they with us, a Company of them who liv'd on the Main, came just against our ship, and standing on a pretty high Bank, threatened us with their Swords and Lances, by shaking them at us: At last the Captain ordered the Drum to be beaten, which was done of a sudden and with much vigor, purposely to scare the poor Creatures . . . when they ran away in haste, they would cry Gurry, Gurry, speaking deep in the throat.[103]

This is the only aspect of Dampier's 1688 encounter with Aborigines that his biographer, Christopher Lloyd, chooses to repeat.[104] He ren-

[100] Dampier, *New Voyage Round the World*, 312–313.
[101] Smith, *European Vision*.
[102] Dampier, *New Voyage Round the World*, 313–316.
[103] Ibid. 315–6.
[104] Lloyd, *William Dampier*, 57.

ders it thus: "They could make no contact with the aborigines (sic), who merely 'grinned like monkeys' and cried 'Gurry, gurry,' 'speaking deep in their throats.' " The reference to speech style is culled from Dampier's comments on the peoples of the island and not the mainland. The impact of the conflation is to entrench the savage as inarticulate. There is no attention to the content, motivation, or context of the interactions. The comments constitute a twentieth-century perpetuation of the construction of the native of this useless land.

On the off-shore islands, the visitors have more sustained contact. Dampier puts it down to the fact that they realize there is no escape from the island and that he clearly has them in his power. On one occasion they take on board several who are swimming (for they have no canoes) and feed them rice, turtle, and manatee. The food was "greedily devoured," but the Aborigines take "no notice of the ship" and when set ashore, flee.[105] The island people, Dampier notes, grew accustomed to their presence quickly, but the mainlanders always ran away. On another occasion he describes how there are forty men, women, and children, who initially responded as if they were threatened, but soon "the Men began to be familiar" and, in the hope of getting some of their number to carry water, the crew gave the men some odd pieces of clothing. However, the Aborigines show no intention of being pressed into service, and merely

> stood like Statues, without motion, but grinn'd like so many Monkeys, staring one upon another . . . So we were forced to carry our water ourselves, and they very fairly put the Cloaths off again, and laid them down, as if Cloaths were only to work in. I did not perceive that they had any great liking to them at first, neither did they seem to admire anything that we had.

I would not read the passage as suggesting that the Aborigines encountered were "monkey like," rather that Dampier was offering a wry acknowledgment of their resistance.

To me, Dampier's most interesting comments concern of marital arrangements and the response of Aboriginal women who glimpse his men. He writes: "Whether they cohabit one Man to one Woman, or promiscuously, I know not; but they do live in companies, 20 or 30 Men, Women, and Children together," and

> . . . they were much disordered at our Landing, especially the Women and Children: for we went directly to their Camp. The lustiest of the Women snatching up their Infants ran away howling, and the little Children ran after squeaking and bawling; but the Men stood still. Some of the Women, and

[105] Dampier, *New Voyage Round the World*, 315.

such People as could not go from us, lay still by a Fire making a doleful noise, as if we had been coming to devour them: but when they saw we did not intend to harm them, they were pretty quiet, and the rest that had fled from us at our first coming, returned again.[106]

From these references to male/female relations and interactions, we can guess that Dampier had come upon a rather large extended family, that old people were being cared for, and that there were young mothers caring for infants. The women were camped in their own section, a very common feature of Aboriginal social organization. For Dampier to have been able to answer his own question regarding marriage arrangements, he would have needed to engage in conversation, and he makes it plain no verbal communication was established. Of course, the issue of promiscuity only arises if one's cultural concept of sexuality is conditioned by the ideal of monogamous relationships. In a polygynous society, in Dampier's logic, the men would have to be promiscuous, and that term is not as routinely applied to male behavior as to women. He may have meant that there was no organized marriage system, but only unregulated couplings. In that he would have been foreshadowing later anthropological theorizing regarding evolution from promiscuity to matriliny, to patriliny.[107]

In *A Voyage to New Holland,* again there is Dampier's attention to detail and comparative framing of observations. On August 30, 1699, they make their first observation: "many great Smokes near the Shore," and steer toward it. The next day, with a party armed with muskets and cutlasses for defense, and shovels and pickaxes to dig wells, they go ashore. They catch sight of three tall black naked men, and once on shore and having secured their boat so as to avoid seizure, they pursue the men, who are joined by eight or nine others, but as they approach, the men flee.

Dampier's party search unsuccessfully for water nor do they find any houses or people. (Later, Dampier observes brush shelters and recognizes the sense of setting them against the sea-breeze.) They return to the shore where they dig for water. This taking of resources without permission, or any possibility of reciprocity, is tantamount to a declaration of hostilities. And the Aborigines have positioned themselves on a hill whence they are menacing, threatening and making "a great noise." One of the Aborigines comes forward, and Dampier goes "within 50 yards, making Signs of Peace and Friendship," but

[106] Ibid., 314.
[107] See Burridge, *Encountering Aborigines,* 104.

the man runs away. Dampier repeats his efforts without success. Finally, that afternoon, Dampier with two of his men set out with the explicit aim of catching an informant who might indicate where they get their fresh water. The episode ends in tragedy.

There were 10 or 12 of the Natives a little way off, who seeing us three going away from the rest of our Men, followed us at a distance. I thought they would follow us: But there being for a while a Sand-bank between us and them, that they could not see us, we made a halt, and hid our selves in a bending of the Sand-bank. They knew we must be thereabouts, and being three or four times our Number, thought to seize us. So they dispers'd themselves, some going to the Seashore, and others beating about the Sandhills. We knew by what Rencounter we had had with them in the Morning that we could easily out-run them; So a nimble young Man that was with me, seeing some of them near, ran towards them; and they for some time, ran away before him. But he soon over-taking them, they faced about and fought him. He had a Cutlass, and they had wooden Lances; with which, being many of them, they were too hard for him. When he first ran towards them I chas'd two or more that were by the Shore; But fearing how it might be with my young Man, I turn'd back quickly, and went to the top of a Sandhill, whence I saw him near me, closely engag'd with them. Upon seeing me, one of them threw a Lance at me, that narrowly miss'd me. I discharg'd my Gun to scare them but avoided shooting any of them; till finding the young Man in great danger from them, and my self in some; and that tho' the Gun had little frightd them at first, yet they soon learnt to despise it, tossing up their Hands, and crying Pooh, Pooh, Pooh; and coming on afresh with a great Noise. I thought it high time to charge again, and shoot one of them, which I did. The rest seeing him fall, made a stand again, and my young Man took the Opportunity to disengage himself, and come off to me; return'd back with my Men, designing to attempt the natives no farther, being very sorry for what had happened already. They took their wounded Companion; and my young Man, who had been struck through the Cheek by one of their Lances, was afraid it had been poison'd. But I did not think that likely.[108]

Beaglehole renders this episode as "unhappy encounter with a band of hostile natives" and repeats the note on their physical appearance.[109] Lloyd gives the full text – this is the stuff of adventure – but glosses the encounter "an attempt to catch one of these strange creatures."[110] Nowhere is there conveyed the sense that Dampier had deliberately intimidated the locals or that the Aborigines were protecting their territory. What distinguishes Dampier from the secondary

[108] Dampier, *A Voyage*, 120–122.

[109] J.C. Beaglehole, ed., *The Journals of Captain James Cook on His Voyages of Discovery. The Voyage of the Endeavour, 1768–71* (Cambridge, 1968), 173.

[110] Lloyd, *William Dampier*, 85.

sources is that he credits Aborigines with motives and strategies and has respect for them as men, if not an equal regard for their lives. This account is one where we have a sense of Aboriginal strategies, and may begin to infer their mode of classifying the outsider. First, there was curiosity, then on seeing that resources were to be plundered, anger and noise to dissuade. Throughout, the outsiders were monitored. The Aborigines attempt to draw out the men and then fight. It should have been a successful move: They had the numbers but not the technology.

Dampier also gives us an insight into differences among the people he meets. He remarks that there was one who by his "Appearance and Carriage . . . seem'd to be Chief of them, and a kind of Prince or Captain among them."

> He was a young brisk Man, not very tall, nor so personable as some of the rest, tho' more active and couragious: He was painted (which none of the rest were at all) with a Circle of white Paste of Pigment (a sort of Lime, as we thought) about his Eyes, and a white streak down his Nose from his Forehead to the tip of it. And his Breast and some part of his Arms were also made white with the same Paint; not for Beauty or Ornament, one would think, but as some wild Indian Warriors are said to do. He seem'd thereby to design the looking more Terrible; this his Painting adding very much to his natural Deformity; for they all of them have the most unpleasant Looks and the worst Features of any People that ever I saw, tho' I have seen a great variety of Savages.[111]

Given that this individual was young, and it is the elderly sages who are respected (though there are no absolute chiefs in the sense Dampier is suggesting), it is unlikely that he stood in any leadership role. However, Dampier's portrait of the "young brisk Man," if to be believed, tells us something more of how the outsiders were being classified. They were to be met male to male. It is possible that the young man was going through some ceremonial business, and hence the body paint. Of this episode, Lloyd writes: "As before a few shy aborigines were seen in the distance: tall black men painted with white circles all over their bodies and just as ugly as he remembered them."[112] Unless I'm missing something, this is an inaccurate rendering. Lloyd gives no dates or page numbers to Dampier's journal, but he does say it is in the area now called Dampier Land, and Dampier's account here puts us at latitude 18° 21′, which correlates, so it is the same incident.

[111] Dampier, *A Voyage*, 122.
[112] Lloyd, *William Dampier*, 84–5.

Dampier supposes these are the same peoples he saw on his previous trip, as it was "not above 40 or 50 Leagues of the N.E. of this," and they have similar physical features, are plagued by flies, but he had not had the "Opportunity to see whether these, as the former, wanted two of their Fore-Teeth."[113] This gap in his observations is surprising given the nature of the engagement and, if accurate, indicates that the Aborigines were successful in keeping the outsiders at a distance on this occasion. He also comments on the differences in diet, the former he had seen fishing, whereas on this trip they observe a great number of fires and remains of meals of shell fish. This may be a reflection of seasonal variation.

In terms of "discoveries," Dampier added little to what Tasman had established. There was little further European interest in the coast. In 1705, Maarten van Delft explored the northern coastal waters and declared Australia an archipelago because inhabitants of continents did not exhibit the defects visible in Aborigines.[114] In 1712, *Zuytdorp,* a Dutch East Indies ship, was wrecked north of Murchinson River, and in 1729, *Zeewijk* was wrecked on Houtman Abrolhos. The survivors charted and explored the coast, but there are no known records of interactions with the local peoples. *A-Mazing* leaves these waters, noting the irony of mineral rich Western Australia being dismissed so categorically, and wondering if the term used for whitefellars in the Kimberleys, "*kartiya,*" could be from "Dampier." It is not something over which linguists have puzzled, and to this tourist it is of more interest than anthill identification (Figure 18.6).

GIANT OTHERS: SIGNS ON THE SOUTHERN COASTS

The Dutch mapped the south coast from Perth around the Great Australian Bight, but I have found no observations of onshore encounters. In 1622, *Leewin* sailed along the south coast, and in 1627, with Pieter Nuyts on board, the *Guldenn Zeepaard* sailed along the south coast. The chart on this expedition remained the best for the next 175 years. Not until 1802 did the sea explorers push further east, and by that time there were land explorations under way.

The first voyage of Abel Tasman in 1642 established the southern extent of the South Land. His instructions required him to find out what the natives had, especially with reference to precious metals, but

[113] Dampier, *A Voyage,* 122.
[114] Mulvaney, *Australian Aborigines,* 134.

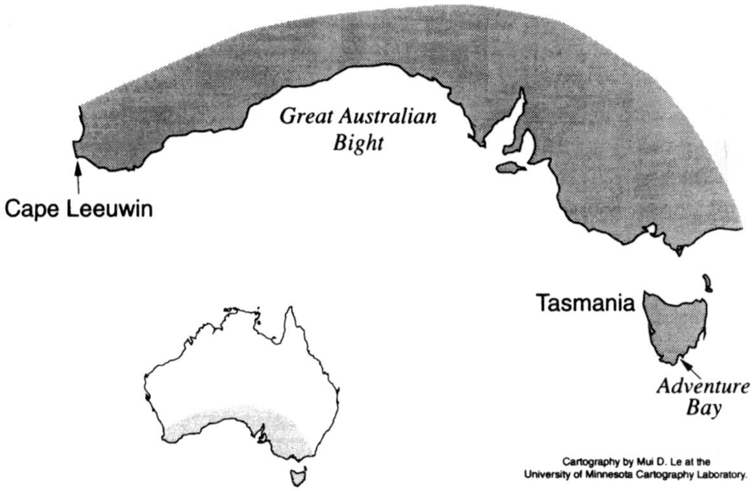

Figure 18.6. The south coast.

to do so in a way that did not alert them to the value placed on gold and the like over pewter, lead, and copper. In late November (when the sea was relatively warm for those latitudes), Tasman sailed around south of Tasmania, into Adventure Bay, made landfall at Blackman Bay, and explored in the immediate vicinity. One shred of evidence of Aboriginal occupation of Tasmania that is always cited but with different emphases concerns marks on tree trunks. Tasman saw two great trees with notches five feet apart and assumed that these must be very tall people who climb for birds' nests, or that they had some device to aid them. The commentaries on Tasman's "discoveries" make note of the "supposedly giant inhabitants." Smith offers Tasman's speculation, which he renders as "There can be no doubt there must be men here of extraordinary stature," as fact in his discussion of the comparative proportions of native people.[115] It is quoted out of context, and I have not found any commentary that bothers to pursue the matter ethnographically. The Tasmania Aborigines were not particularly tall: Perhaps the trunks were marked for bark for shelters.

As a memorial for those who followed and for the locals, Tasman planted a flag.[116] One wonders what the local people thought of the cloth. I would suspect it became part of the ceremonial store-house

[115] Beaglehole, *Journals of Cook*, 147; Wood, *Discovery of Australia*, 147; Oliver E. Allen, *The Pacific Navigators* (New York, 1980), 57; Smith, *European Vision*, 20.
[116] Clark, *History of Australia*, 32–3.

of rare objects and had a narrative ascribed to it. On his return, Tasman was censured for not learning more of the "lands and peoples discovered."[117] It appeared that the strategy of "leave them alone and they go away" was successful for the Tasmania peoples. In the log of *A-Mazing* we note that the early nineteenth century genocidal war waged on Tasmanian Aborigines demonstrated that seafaring outsiders were benign compared with land colonizers.

THE NOBLE SAVAGE: EAST COAST ENLIGHTENMENT

After the accounts and voyaging of Dampier, there was a hiatus in sea exploration in the Pacific but an upsurge in Europe in scientific interest in documenting and classifying the peoples and their customs. With Captain James Cook's first voyage, the Enlightenment put to sea. Cook sailed in the *Endeavour*, on a voyage sponsored by the Royal Society, to observe the transit of Venus across the sun from Tahiti. This was achieved in June 1769. In Tahiti, Joseph Banks took on board Tupia, who had extensive geographical knowledge, and Tupia was able to make himself understood in New Zealand but not in Australia.[118] On board the *A-Mazing* we note that there are limits to the ability of other to communicate with other: Or, put another way, not all others are the same.

After Tahiti came the second stage of the journey. Cook opened his "Secret Instructions" and sailed on to New Zealand (Tasman in 1642 being the last recorded visit) and then westward to Australia. On April 19, 1770, Cook sighted land at latitude 38°. Cook, at home with the rugged coasts of England and Newfoundland, carefully mapped the east coast, stopping at Botany Bay, but passing the entrance to Port Jackson, and having struck the Great Barrier Reef, spent two months repairing his boat near what is now Cooktown. He then sailed through the Torres Strait, and home.

Cook had ample opportunities to observe and record. The men of the Royal Society were not disappointed. Of his encounter with Aborigines, Cook wrote: "These people may be said to be in the pure state of Nature, and may appear to some to be the most wretched upon Earth: but in reality they are far happier than .. we Europeans." There is a remarkably similar passage in the journal of Joseph Banks who writes: "Thus live these, I had almost said happy people, content

[117] Beaglehole, *Exploration*, 156.
[118] Cook, *Journals*, 1: 117, 169, 305.

with little, nay almost nothing, far removed from the anxieties. . . ."[119] As we shall see, their experience was somewhat at odds with these opinions: There were many acquisitive acts and evidence of stress. However, their quest, although secular, has overtones of that of Quiros. The "native" that they encounter has an intrinsic self, one of nobility. That abiding sense of human dignity and a deep spirituality are qualities that I cherish in Aboriginal friends. The wretchedness of the extrinsics of their lives is at times so overpowering that the nobility is masked, but Cook looked inward at Aboriginal "primitivistic thought."[120] Unlike Banks, Cook did not extol the virtues of Tahitian "primitivism" with its luxuriant extrinsics, so I think we can say he saw a new other.

Cook's journals have appeared in many forms and have had various editors. He was not an educated man, and his entries concerning social and natural phenomena are reworked in the style of Banks.[121] On subsequent trips, Cook is less näive and less in wonder. As far as journals are concerned, Cook's is more straightforward than Banks's, whose erudition gets in the way of clear description, whose class prejudices constantly intrude, and who is prepared to generalize on the basis of very slim evidence. One of the great advantages of dealing with Cook is that there are journals of each of his three voyages to the Pacific and many commentaries. By being able to read his rendering of other onshore encounters, one can begin to develop a feel for his notion of what is significant and why the Australian entry reads as it does. For instance, in other locations, he makes mention of the indigenous women and the way in which his crew fraternizes. But in Australia, with one exception, it appears the exchanges were male/male. It may have been that he could not find a way of describing the women, according to his canons of feminine beauty and charm, that would not have undercut his general depiction of the happy state of nature, or it may have been that Banks was little interested in taking account of women. He mentions them as members of families.[122] In the log of the *A-Mazing* we note that it was, after all, an Enlightenment tenet that woman was other to the rational male.

Traveling along the coast, on Sunday, April 22, he sighted smoke, then several people "very dark or black in Colour but whether this was the real colour of their skins or the C[l]othes they might have on I know not." Banks is very interested in skin color, and later in

[119] Ibid., 136; Banks, *Journal*, 315.
[120] Smith, *European Vision*, 126.
[121] Cook, *Journals*, cxii.
[122] Banks, *Journal*, 281–324, 307; Cook, *Journals*, 395.

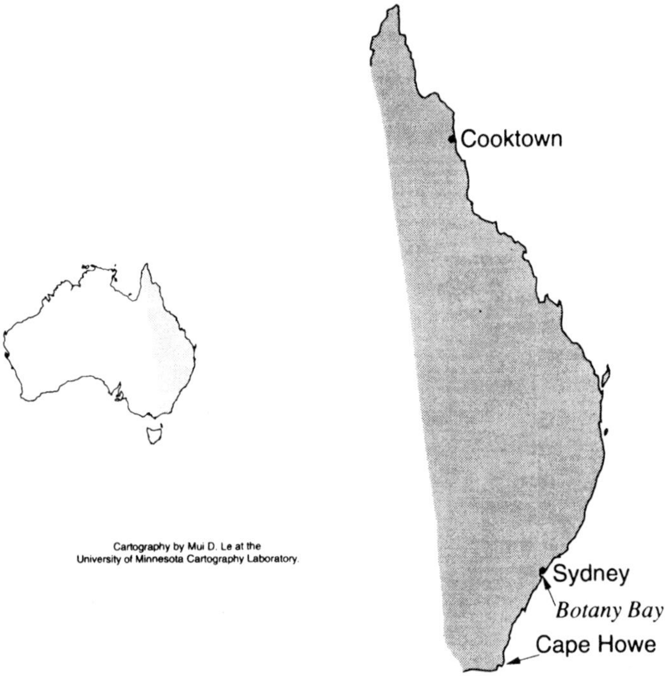

Figure 18.7. The east coast.

their exploits, engages in a little experiment by spitting on his finger and rubbing the skin to determine the real color. As they sail north, Cook names Pigeon House Rock but cannot find a good shelter on this part of the east coast (Figure 18.7). This is an area I know well, and the coast line is rich in resources – inlets, fresh water and brackish creeks, long sand dunes, and inland lakes where birds, fish, and vegetation abound. Walking along the beach, one can see middens exposed by erosion of tides and winds. It is an area where one would expect to find many groups, and it appears Cook saw just such activity. On Saturday the 28th they saw "several people on Shore four of whome were carrying a small boat or Canoe which we imagined they were going to put into the water in order to come off to us but in this we were mistaken."[123] However, when Cook with Solander, Banks, and Tupia try to land, they find the surf to be too high. they see three or four canoes hauled up on the beach.

[123] Cook, *Journals*, 301, 304, 308–309.

The first contact was made on April 29, at Botany Bay, where they sighted huts, men, women, and children, and were determined to land.

. . . as we approached the shore they all made off except two Men who seemed resolved to oppose our landing. As soon as I saw this I ordered the boats to lay upon their oars in order to speake to them but this was to little purpose for neither us nor Tupia could understand one word they said. We then threw them some nails beeds and came ashore which they took up and seem'd not ill pleased in so much that I thout that they beckon'd to us to come ashore; but in this we were mistaken, for as soon as we put in the boat in they again came to oppose us upon which I fired a musket between the two which had no other effect than to make them took up a stone and threw at us which caused my fireing a second Musquet load with small shott, and altho some of the shott struck the man yet it had no other effect than to make him lay hold of a Shield or target to defend himself. Emmidiately after this we landed which we had no sooner done than they throwed two darts at us, this obliged me to fire a third shott soon after which they both made off, but not in such haste but we might have taken one, but Mr Banks being of the opinion that the darts were poisoned, made me cautious how I advance into the woods.[124]

Despite the expertise on board, the treatment of the natives is that of countless explorers before: If challenged, fire a shot and fire to wound or kill. On shore they find huts and children. They leave more beads, which the next day are still on the ground, and take "a quantity of darts" they find lying about the huts. The theft of a person's weapons is a grave act and would have angered the owners whose labor was invested in the objects. Cook's party dig for water and cut wood, both acts offensive to the local land owners. On the 30th the Aborigines are beginning to muster to deal with these rude outsiders, and Cook notes "10 or 12 natives" in the morning and "16 or 18 of them" in the afternoon who came close and "made a stand." In Cook's view "all these armed men wanted was for us to be gone."

During their stay at Botany Bay, one of the crew died of consumption and was buried onshore near a watering spot. This certainly is not consonant with Aboriginal burial practices, which vary across the continent, but usually entail destruction of all the belongings of the deceased, a setting aside of their ceremonial knowledge for a period, and a shifting of camp sites. The area around water holes is kept clear of undergrowth, and people usually make camp at a distance from the actual water source. These are excellent strategies for preventing

[124] Ibid., 305.

the spread of diseases, and one wonders if any of the consumptive's clothes came in contact with the peoples of Botany Bay.

Cook's party continue exploring the area, and have many missed and muddled encounters. On May 3 they come across a camp with fires, mussels roasting and oysters laying near. They sample the food and leave in return more beads.[125] The next day one of Cook's men meets a very old man and woman and two small children. He gives them a bird he has shot, but they do not touch it. Cook comments that "they were quite naked, even the woman had nothing to cover her nuditie." For the most part they are watched by armed men, who keep their distance; sometimes they throw their spears, sometimes run off. In summary, Cook writes of the inhabitants of Botany Bay that they are dark brown, with black lank hair, their diet appears to be fish, they wear no clothes, sometimes they paint their bodies and faces. "However, we could know little of their customs as we never were able to form any connections with them" and all the gifts are left untouched by their huts.

After leaving Botany Bay on May 7, they sail north, and on May 12 and 15 sight more smoke. On June 8, Cook notes news of natives putting off, and then on June 11 they strike the Great Barrier Reef, and after heaving the boat off, they go into Endeavour River near Cooktown, where the next six weeks are spent on repairs and many land sorties. The Aborigines here are more forthright. On July 19 the ship is visited by "10 or 11 of the natives," while some six or seven more, mostly women, are on the other side of the river.

> . . . those that came on board were very desirous of having some of our turtle and took the liberty to haul two to the gangway to put over the side, being disappointed in this they grew a little troublesome and were for throwing everything over board they could lay their hands upon.[126]

Cook offers them bread, which they reject. In an editorial note, Price comments, "they no doubt thought that they owned both the country and the turtle."[127] The subsequent behavior suggests that the refusal is not going to be taken lightly, and as soon as Cook goes ashore, one of the Aboriginal party sets fire to a handful of dry grass, and marking out a circuit, quickly has the outsiders in trouble. One of Cook's young pigs is scorched to death. The Aborigines then go to where Cook's men are washing, and again "with the greatest obstinacy" set fire to

[125] This paragraph is drawn from Cook, *Journals*, 305, 309–12.
[126] Ibid., 361.
[127] A. Grenfell Price, ed., *The Explorations of Captain Cook in the Pacific as Told by Selections of his own Journals, 1768–1779* (New York, 1971), 73.

the grass. Cook is "obliged" to fire his musket, and believes some of the shot found its target. Cook, Banks, and several others seek out the Aborigines, who soon appear and throw their "darts." Cook seizes the first "six or seven darts they met with," and alarmed, the Aborigines make off. He pursues them, engages in some unintelligible exchanges, they lay down their darts, and he returns theirs, "which reconciled everything." Cook then says they are introduced "by name" to four strangers who are with them.[128] Without any transcriptions of the names, it is difficult to know what might have been communicated. What is evident is that Cook knows the group members well enough to identify "strangers," and the locals want to introduce them. From Banks we learn that this "tribe" comprised twenty-one people – twelve men, seven women, and a boy and a girl.[129] But he tells us they never stole, always asked, except in the case of the turtles, a conclusion clearly at odds with his characterization of their being content with what they have.[130]

The next encounter, on July 23, by a lone member of his crew who gets separated from the others and comes upon four Aborigines broiling a fowl and the hind leg of a kangaroo, offers an insight to the Aboriginal interest in the strangers:

> . . . he had the prescience of mind not to run away (being unarm'd) least they should pursue him, but went and sit down by them and after he had sit a little while and they had felt his hands and other parts of his body they suffer'd him to go away without offereing the least insult, and perceiving that he did not go right for the ship they directed him which way to go.[131]

One of the mysteries the European outsider presented for Aborigines was that their clothes hid their bodies and Aborigines could not be sure with what form of life they were dealing. They were much relieved to discover similar anatomical features in white men. In one encounter with Governor Phillip's men a decade later, Aboriginal men requested that one of the outsiders drop his trousers in order for them to be clear regarding his sex. After leaving the Endeavour River, Cook limps on, and on August 22, 1770, Cook lands, goes to the highest point on the island and formally takes possession of Eastern Australia for the British Crown. They see a number of people before and after they land. They are armed, one with a bow, "the first we have seen on this coast," and a bundle of arrows. He sails on through the Straits

[128] Cook, *Journals*, 361–2,
[129] Banks, *Journal*, 308.
[130] Ibid., 309, 315.
[131] Cook, *Journals*, 363.

and observes women gathering shell fish and men wearing large pearl shell breastplates.[132]

As they leave the east coast, Cook reflects on his observations. He mentions the several interviews he managed to have with the men, but comments, "whether through Jealousy or disrigard they never brought any of their women along with them to the Ship but always left them on the opposite side of the River where we had frequent opportunities of viewing them through our glass." Cook lists the words they elicited at Endeavour River (twenty-one of the thirty-eight are body parts).[133] It is apparent in the journals of Cook and Banks, indeed of all the explorers we have thus far met, that communication was mainly non-verbal. Banks admits the limitations – "we had connections with them at one place" – but goes on to sketch the essential east coast "Indian."[134] Cook, now at a safe distance from the daily harassments and clearly writing for an audience, summarizes:

> . . . this eastern side is not that barren and Miserable Country that Dampier and others have described the western side to be. We are to consider that we see this Country in the pure state of nature, the Industry of Man has had nothing to do with any part of it and yet we find all such things as nature hath bestow'd upon it in a flourishing state . . . From what I have said of the Natives of New-Holland they may appear to some to be the most wretched people on Earth, but in reality they are far happier than we Europeans; being wholly unacquainted not only with the superfluous but the necessary Conveniences so much sought after in Europe, they are happy in not knowing the use of them.[135]

The west coast was arid, the east coast flourishing. Dampier's natives were black, Cook's dark brown. The discussion of skin color is code for another part of the construction of the Australian native. Banks and Cook wonder if these are the same people. Banks believes Dampier was either wrong in stating they were black (would a pirate do the "spit test"?) or that they were a different race of people.[136] Dampier's natives were naked and hence primitive, Cook's natives were naked and hence in a state of nature. By being closer to nature, the Aborigines could also be seen as closer to animals and not part of the world of communications or power politics. The depiction denies the range of personalities, aptitudes, and preferences that the locals had demonstrated. Aborigines exemplified "hard primitivism" along

[132] Ibid., 387–8.
[133] Ibid., 395; see also 389–90, 392–399.
[134] Banks, *Journal*, 08.
[135] Cook, *Journals*, 399.
[136] Banks, *Journal*, 297; see also Burridge, *Encountering Aborigines*, 95.

with the Fuegians and Maoris. On board *A-Mazing* we reflect: Are the natives closer to nature, as women are closer to nature?

With Cook, my accidental tourism is terminated. Bougainville had touched on the Great Barrier Reef in June 1768, but not made it inside the breakers.[137] La Pérouse was too late, and Australia became a British outpost. Yet the log of *A-Mazing* is going to record an entry from Baudin's expedition of 1801–1804, because it illustrates that competing notions of other persist, particularly when the other is "woman." Of his first encounter with an Aboriginal woman, medical naturalist M.F. Péron recorded that she was "... horribly ugly and disgusting. She was uncommonly lean and scraggy, and her breasts hung down almost to her thighs. The most extreme dirtiness added to her natural deformity." Péron's encounters with men, further undermined the attributes of man in his savage state. Péron tested the much vaunted physical strength of the savage with his own invention, a "dynamometer," and found Europeans to be stronger than the exemplars of the savage state.[138] Women were not even on the scale for testing. Their appearance classified them. Subsequent observers' perception of older Aboriginal women as physically unattractive has also inhibited consideration of their cultural worth. Like the belief in the wretchedness of the other, this dismissal of women, because they were not perceived as attractive, persists. Hart and Pilling write of older Tiwi women as "ancient hags."[139] Yet it is these women who are the repositories of knowledge, who in their own domain – the single women's camp, an area taboo to men – discuss important ritual concerns.[140]

The Hobbesian native had little to offer those who sought commercial advantage: "The life of the native [was] solitary, poore, nasty, brutish and short"; Dampier's observations fed Locke's *Two Treatises on Government* and *Human Understanding;* Cook had seen the pure state of nature. In the texts of exploration there are competing notions of what it is to be human. Notions of wretched primitiveness were not expunged by Cook. In much of the rhetoric of the development lobbies in Australia today, I think we can hear echoes of the question asked by the Dutch: What good are they? In the comparative framing of the Enlightenment, Aborigines became the hard primitive to the soft primitivism of the Tahitian. In terms of physical beauty by the aesthetic standards of Europe, Aborigines compared poorly with other Indians:

[137] John Dunmore, *French Explorers in the Pacific: The Eighteenth Century,* 2 vols. (Oxford, 1965), 1: 222.
[138] See Mulvaney, *Australian Aborigines,* 139.
[139] Hart and Pilling, *The Tiwi,* 14.
[140] See Bell, *Daughters,* 16–17.

There was no rich jewelry, only crude body marks; no garlands of fresh flowers; no seductively sweet princesses, no negotiating chiefs, no elaborate Maori meeting places. This state of nature was one of charm and nobility if one sought inward qualities and looked to the land, but it was one of miserable wretchedness if one sought material profit and focused on externalities. This is a dichotomy that persists.

THE VIEW FROM THE LAND

As *A-Mazing* has skipped around the coast, by now fairly strung with beads and trinkets, the news of the outsiders and some of their possessions have been traveling too, greatly facilitated by ceremonial exchanges. Axe heads, ochres, and ideas moved across the continent with remarkable speed.[141] We know certain objects were traded across vast distances. For my purposes here, the most interesting ones are the pearl shells from the northwest of Australia and baler shells from Cape York.[142] On the map we can see that two of the peoples most encountered are also critically located on extensive trade routes (Figure 18.8).

It is now time to look back through the log of *A-Mazing* to see what we have learned. We have been faithful to the eye witness accounts in terms of location, dates, and the like, but we have undertaken many maneuvers: We've gone with the current; drifted with the tide, and tried to sound the depths of the encounters. I have proposed that "insider" and "outsider" others presented different sorts of problems for Aborigines in different parts of Australia. We have speculated about the impact of these clothed creatures, mostly in all-male parties, whose mode of transport seemed quite inadequate, who regularly jettisoned strange items, who desecrated sacred sites, who had weapons that wounded and killed, who would kidnap while conversing, who could not communicate verbally, who were incompetent in a land rich in resources, who mostly went away, but who had to be watched. On the other side of the encounter we have a similarly strange catalogue of characteristics: cannibals, giants, naked, black, brown, miserable, noble, fly-ridden, and totally lacking in gratitude. We have found good empiricists before the advent of the Royal Society's "Hints" pamphlet and some dubious use of sources by the interpreters of the era of exploration. Aborigines, we noted, resisted, strategized, and

[141] See Mulvaney, "The Chain of Connection," Flood, *The Archaeology of the Dreamtime*, 235.
[142] Ibid., 237.

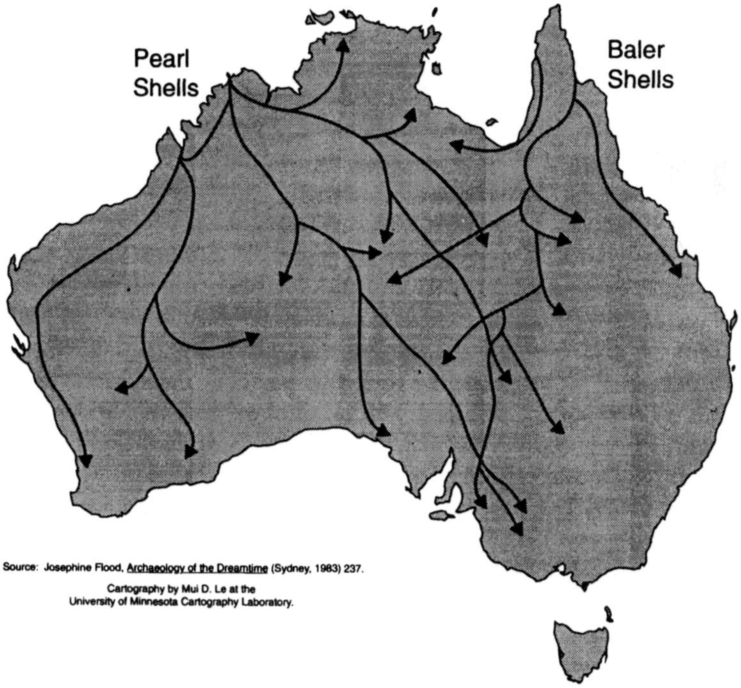

Figure 18.8. Trade routes.

sometimes were successful in maintaining the integrity of their lands. The texturing of the encounters has been enriched, but bringing bodies of literature and experience that are customarily held discrete into dialogue has been tricky.

In reconstructing the charts of the Observers, we had texts that purported to be accurate guides. But the log of *A-Mazing* has recorded some serious misidentifications: The knowledge is not secure, nationality informs observer and biographer. The journey has not been one straight from ignorance to knowledge. Have we in any way been able to bring the Observed into active voice? We know something of the patterning of responses, and of regional differences. But unlike Marshall Sahlins[143] in the islands, the history of Aboriginal Australia is locked into the land and we do not yet have the codes that could enrich our historical and ethnographic portraits. The records do not

[143] Marshall Sahlins, *Islands of History* (Chicago, 1985).

yet speak, and I have needed to tease meaning from the sources in other ways.

The modes of knowing one's world that I have here co-explored are most often used to explain post-settlement relations through concepts such as "colonization" and "race relations," but rarely applied to the pre-settlement period. The interactive ethnographic historical appreciation I am pioneering here is not currently in vogue in Australia. In the last two decades, historians and anthropologists dealing with this era have shifted focus on the grand vision of Europe opening the Pacific, discovering and interpreting the natives, to accounts of Australian society and culture that stress the continuity of occupation of the continent, and that, for the period after 1788, seek points of articulation between Aboriginal and colonial society. They have drawn attention to the highly political nature of the "factual" accounts of settlement. Juxtapose, if you will, two "facts." Captain Cook discovered Australia in 1770. Aborigines have occupied the continent for at least 40,000 years. The first fact is securely woven into a seamless web of supporting facts – Aborigines were nomadic, few in number and without recognizable systems of law, religion, or property relations. It has proved difficult to dislodge. Given the facts, there was no need to negotiate treaties, or to compensate for lands lost: Humanitarians exercised their concern in formulating policies to protect these "stone age" peoples.

However, as carbon dating extends the chronology of Aboriginal occupation back through the millennia, as research reveals the changing, adaptive nature of Aboriginal cultures, as we come to appreciate the delicate, yet resilient system of rights and responsibilities in land, the doctrine of *terra nullius*,[144] upon which the British relied in colonizing New South Wales, is revealed as a convenient legal fiction. But having acknowledged that the rights of the original inhabitants were trameled, what are we to make of the situation. New understandings nestle in a moral and political climate in which the meaning of being

[144] In the last two decades, the doctrine of *terra nullius*, that the land was empty and uninhabited, has come under scrutiny in academic, legal, and political arenas. A consequence of deeming the land uninhabited was that there was no perceived need to negotiate treaties. The land was neither conquered nor colonized, it was simply settled. This gives rise to a series of questions: Can one retrospectively reinterpret the law? Who is responsible to make good the dispossession? Should there be compensation or restoration? (see the Mabo Case, High Court of Australia, June 3, 1992). Cook's secret instructions, "You are also with the Consent of the Natives to take possession Of Convenient Situations . . . or if you find the country uninhabited. . ." indicate that there were principles to guide British in the South Land, and Cook's diaries show that he met people. Yet he took possession without negotiation with the inhabitants in their "state of nature." See Price, *Explorations of Captain Cook*, 19.

Aboriginal is contested (who speaks for whom?), in which policies of self-determination are instituted (who decides for whom?), in which Aborigines are charged with impeding economic growth (who benefits from what?). Competing images encode values, have histories, and constitute highly charged symbols, the clashing of which punctuates Australian society with staccato regularity.

When we turn to shifting notions of woman in Australian society, we find a similar set of forces at work, and when we ask about Aboriginal women, we find the sexism and racism of the imagining of a young nation are compounded. One strategy in unpicking the fabric of gendered and ethnocentric imaginings of Aborigines and women is to make explicit the epistemological stance of the observer/interpreter/author/narrator and thereby to provide a context for the texts. A more radical, albeit more dangerous strategy, would be to make explicit the stance of the observed/narrated/interpreted, and it is here that the parallel between "native" and "woman" diverge: Each constitutes a different sort of "other." The richness of the terrain a feminist anthropologist may survey has a sociopolitical history yet to be fully explored by those intent on rewriting the history of the occupation on the Australian continent. But my tourism is concluding, my luggage is bulging, the suitcases marked "ethnocentrism" and "feminist critiques" are full, *A-Mazing* is in dry dock, and I'm going back to the twentieth century.

CHAPTER 19

Circumscribing circumcision/uncircumcision: An essay amidst the history of difficult description

JAMES A. BOON

. . . What is this prepuce? Whence, why, where, and whither?

–P. C. Remondino, *History of Circumcision*

FORESKINS are facts – cultural facts – whether removed or retained. Absent *versus* present, prepuces have divided many religions, politics, and ritual persuasions. Plentiful too are styles of describing – often more thinly than thickly – practices of circumcision: travelogues, sermons, universal histories, doctrinal exegeses, encyclopedias, enthographies, medical treatises, and so on. (Un)circumcision involves signs separating an "us" from a "them" entangled in various discourses of identity and distancing.[1]

This essay engages a shifting semiotics of un(circumcision) in culture-crossings from the sixteenth century and before, through the Enlightenment, and since. I eventually dwell on two texts: an early-modern reading of circumcision among other ritual varieties and rarities (Montaigne's 1580s travel narrative); an encyclopedia diagnosis judging circumcision by presumably absolute standards (P. C. Remondino's 1891 universal *History*). Despite my dramatic leap from Montaigne to Remondino (whose "history" converts Montaigne's account to its own scheme), I seek not simply to reiterate a now-comfortable dichotomy between Medieval-Renaissance hermeneutics versus Enlight-

[1] I thank conference participants for patience responses, especially S. Schwartz, G. Dening, D. Merwick, M. Penn, D. Bell, D. Lipsett, S. Gudeman, R. Price, and A. Reid. At the 1990 American Historical Association Meetings, a brief version received helpful comments from D. Segal, H. Liebersohn, and N. Davis. Talks with S. Gilman and J. Geller have been crucial. D. Boyarin's (1992) lecture on Midrashic commentary, circumcision, and desire alerted me to key distinctions in reading-practice. Thanks also to J. Boyarin and students and colleagues at Princeton for responses.

enment analysis that extends to modernist practices of knowledge. Rather, I refer interpretations of history's "epistemologies" to disquieting evidence of ambiguous ritual difference inscribed in contrasting genres – travelogues, ethnographies, and universal histories, among others. This paper stresses Muslim/Hindu, Judeo-Christian, and surgical/antisurgical positions in discourses of circumcision/uncircumcision, in order to *refract* any easy periodication of times present or past. My connected fragments from ethnography, histories of ideas, intertextual travel, and panoramic ethnology afford neither sequential story, proper argument, nor symptomatic analysis. Rather, juxtaposing the fragments invites insights analogous to those offered me one day when I, an ethnographer, was led from the scene of Hindu-Balinese uncircumcision to a contrary place (see my later section, this Essay's Ethnographic Beginnings.[2]

DIVERSE BEGINNINGS FOR HISTORIES OF DIFFICULT DESCRIPTION

Intellectual historians might begin with Foucault's controversial notions of a "classical episteme" that led to diagnostic explanation (supplanting hermeneutic interpretation) promoted as the Enlightenment.[3] Foucault contests styles of power-knowledge consolidated during the seventeenth-eighteenth centuries that implemented institutions of control characterized by the impersonal gaze – sanitized inspection of distanced, de-voiced, dissectible "objects" made-visible.[4] Panoptic prison-technologies presumably became underpinnings to a "discourse of modernism," associated with clinical-minded regimes whose business was to colonize bodies, extract labor, and suppress resistance.[5]

Alternatively, historians of ideas might begin with the temporal eclipse of Renaissance heterodoxy by the combined forces of the Reformation and Ramism.[6] We know that early modern neo-Platonists

[2] A fuller project could add such fragments as a fourteenth century "Stanzaic Life of Christ," whose typological format foregrounds the circumcision, or the paradoxical ethnography of "circum-incision" in Malekula (see John Layard, *Stone Men of Malekula (Vao)* [London, 1943]). Any fragment of description, a beginning, may resemble a lexical prefix (Vorsilbe), if Freud and this essay pertain to each other.

[3] Michel Foucault, *The Order of Things* (New York, 1970).

[4] Michel Foucault, *Discipline and Punish: The Birth of the Prison*, trans. A. Sheridan (New York, 1977); and *The Foucault Reader*, ed. Paul Rabinow (New York, 1984).

[5] Timothy Reiss, *The Discourse of Modernism* (Ithaca, 1982).

[6] I allude to the late Frances Yates and Michel Foucault, plus literatures these disparate scholars have inspired. Insights from Yates and Foucault are applied to ethnography and the history of anthropological ideas in James A. Boon, *Other Tribes, Other Scribes: Symbolic Anthropology in the Comparative Study of Cultures, Histories, Religions, and Texts*

cultivated arts of permissive "Phantasy" devoted to eros and pneumatic magical sciences. After the late sixteenth century, their devices were purged by "rational" censoring procedures that rewrote history accordingly. In his synoptic study of *Eros and Magic in the Renaissance,* I.P. Couliano reviews a "Reformation" common to Protestantism and Catholicism hostile to neo-Platonists resemblances and analogies of microcosm and macrocosm (what Foucault deemed the "preclassical episteme"):

> If the Catholic Church did not abandon its cult of images and the celibacy of its priests, there are other fields in which the Reformation, both Protestant and Catholic, arrived at the same results. We have only to think of the persecution of witches or the fight against astrology and magic. . .
>
> The idea of the infinitude of the universe is not the only one which, extolled in the Renaissance, strikes terror in succeeding eras. . . . As soon as God withdraws into his complete transcendence, every human attempt to examine his design runs into a ghastly silence. . . .
>
> To read in the "book of Nature" had been the fundamental experience in the Renaissance. The Reformation was tireless in seeking ways to close that book. Why? Because the Reformation thought of Nature not as a factor for rapprochement but as the *main thing responsible for the alienation of God from mankind.*
>
> By dint of searching, the Reformation at last found the great culprit guilty of all the evils of individual and social existence: sinning Nature.[7]

Either style (Foucault's or Couliano's) of representing past ideas or epistemes itself relies on diverse styles and genres of "document." One such genre is the travelogue: a kind of writing-as-if one had "been there," but briefly, *en passant.* Another is ethnography, or its equivalent: a kind of writing-as-if one had "been there" longer, dwellingly. Both these genres contrast in turn with universal history, a kind of writing-as-if one had been everywhere, anonymously and omnisciently. Of course, any genre's rhetoric is written to be *read* accordingly: travelogue, as if the reading-voyage could be fleet; ethnography, as if the reading-stay could be participant; universal history, as if reading could occur neutrally, a-positionally. Each rhetoric indeed implies

(New York, 1977), chs. 2, 5; *Affinities and Extremes: Crisscrossing the Bittersweet History of East Indies History, Hindu-Balinese Culture, and Indo-European Allure* (Chicago, 1990), chs. 1–2, 4, 5–7; and *The Anthropological Romance of Bali: Dynamic Perspectives in Marriage and Caste, Politics and Religion* (New York, 1977), 237. Incongruous approaches to bodies (and souls) are often advisable (e.g., Peter Brown, *The Body and Society: Men, Women and Sexual Renunciation in Early Christianity* [New York, 1988]). See also Walter J. Ong, *Ramus: Method and the Decay of Dialogue* (Cambridge: 1983).

[7] I. P. Couliano, *Eros and Magic in the Renaissance* (Chicago, 1987), 202, 208.

paces of negotiating distance, or intimacy when "voyeuring," observing, translating, understanding, knowing. . . ; pick your betrayal.[8]

Some critical theorists have recently promoted travel-tropes as a superior brand of *theoria*. Scholars as disparate as Edward Said and James Clifford aspire to motility; they decry general "presenting" of a *them;* they challenge disciplines to evade stable categories, overturn positivist documentation, rattle "ethnographic authority."[9]

My responses to declarations "against fixity" are mixed, in part because of histories of describing certain rituals. Circumcision, for example, has been travel-told since the sixteenth century, and before. Accounts often transgress distinctions between "travelogue" and "ethnography"; indeed, upon encountering circumcision, the latter genre may prefer to resemble the former: to hurry on past, to avoid dwelling, to resist even as-if participation and/or collaboration in another's rite. This sudden haste can *look* like high critical motility or resistance to participant authority; but it may *be* just the opposite: reactionary. I am reminded of certain sixteenth-century European discoverers who narrated commonplace fears that they would wind up involuntary "Muslims" even in the East Indies.[10]

Although wary of recent "anti-authoritativeness" (often authorized as "postmodernist"), I still appreciate continuities between current critical fashion and centuries-long blurrings of travel-writing, ethnography, history, and literature. Thomas More's *Utopia*, for example – handed down since 1518 through tricky translations of its punning Latin – was an early modern exercise in verisimilitudinous travel-telling, framed as ethnography of un-us in a purposefully excessive present tense. Along with Lucian's *True Story* (More translated Lucian), *Utopia* is a prominent forerunner of the now-defamed "ethnographic present" (so decidedly ahistorical). The captivating format spans nearly two millennia (Lucian, to Hythloday, to Malinowski); it

[8] On "being there" as a seriocomic metaphor of and for ethnography, see Clifford Geertz, *Works and Lives* (Stanford, 1987); and Boon, *Other Tribes, Other Scribes*, 5.

[9] Relevant works include James Clifford, *The Predicament of Culture* (Cambridge, 1988) and his recent pieces on travel-practice using Edward Said, *Traveling Theory*, as one point of departure. My device of "beginnings" owes something to Said's *Beginnings* (Baltimore, 1975) and more to Kenneth Burke's *The Rhetoric of Religion: Studies in Logology* (Berkeley, 1970). A burgeoning literature on travel-writing, ethnography, history, fiction, and cultural studies includes Mary Campbell, *The Witness and the Other World: Exotic European Travel Writing, 400–1600* (Ithaca, 1988); Eric J. Leed, *The Mind of the Traveler: From Gilgamesh to Global Tourism* (New York, 1991); Marc Manganaro, ed., *Modernist Anthropology: From Fieldwork to Text* (Princeton, 1990); and Ivan Brady, ed., *Anthropological Poetics* (Savage, MD, 1991).

[10] See Tomé Pires, *The Suma Oriental*, trans. Armando Cortesão (London, 1944), Series II, 15: 258.

could be paraphrased something like: "I voyaged there, and am here to tell you that in Utopia (or some other no-place or someplace) *they* do thus and so." Another example of pre-postmodern travel-troping is Lévi-Strauss's *Tristes tropiques*, which critiqued a wide range of discovery accounts and voyage narratives – including his own – that converted the New World into "evidence for" the Old.[11] Substituting figural regret for the ineffable, plenitudinous tropics, his prose recaptures a spectrum of the politics of description: tribalisms, caste, colonialism, democracy, even reformist Islam likened to France. Differences thus engaged by Lévi-Strauss became mutually chromatic, along with the "self" engaging them.[12]

TOWARD A CHROMATICISM OF UN/CIRCUMCISIONS

Ambiguous difficulties also reverberate in rhetorics and rituals of circumcision/uncircumcision – practiced, reported, inscribed, interpreted, advocated, condemned, tolerated, puzzled over. Over time our ritual *topos* has been "diacritical" to diverse peoples and personages.[13] It marks off Muslim Indonesian from Hindu-Balinese Indonesian, but

[11] See Thomas More, *Utopia*, trans. and ed. Robert M. Adams (New York, 1975; originally published 1518). Also, Claude Lévi-Strauss, *Tristes tropiques* (Paris, 1955).

[12] Lévi-Strauss explores ambiguities of comparative knowing in tones of resignation, not nostalgia; on *figures* of his corpus, see James A. Boon, *From Symbolism to Structuralism: Lévi-Strauss in a Literary Tradition* (New York, 1972); "Between the Wars Bali: Rereading the Relics," in George Stocking, ed., *History of Anthropology*, 4 (Madison, 1986); "Lévi-Strauss, Wagner, Romanticism: A Reading-Back," in George Stocking, ed., *History of Anthropology*, 6 (Madison, 1989); and Boon, *Other Tribes, Other Scribes*, ch. 7. A fine guide to ethnographic writing in *histoire* is Michel de Certeau, *The Practice of Everyday Life*, trans. S. F. Rendall (Berkeley, 1984) and *Heterologies: Discourse on the Other*, trans. B. Massumi (Minneapolis, 1986). Lucianic aspects of anthropology appear in Boon, *Other Tribes, Other Scribes*, 264, 268, 279, and *Affinities and Extremes*, chs. 3–4. "Cross-cultural texts" derived from Menippean dialogue-style include More's *Utopia*, such anti-colonialist satires as Multatuli's *Max Havelaar*, and the contrasting *oeuvres* of both Bakhtin and Northrop Frye.

[13] This note substitutes for any scholarly apparatus remotely adequate to the tortuous history of interpreting, explaining, cataloging, justifying, condemning, or otherwise representing types of circumcision, or activities ever categorized with "it." Let Maurice Bloch's *From Blessing to Violence* (Cambridge, 1987) token circumcision and statecraft, beyond Madagascar; let Suzette Heald's ("The Making of Men: The Relevance of Vernacular Psychology to the Interpretation of a Gisu Ritual," *Africa*, 52:1 [1982]: 15–35) Gisu ethnography token sensitive accounts by such scholars as V. Turner; let Karen E. Paige ("The Ritual of Circumcision," *Human Nature* [May 1978]: 40–48) token "medicalized" arguments against circumcision. There are abundant exposés against female incision, infibulation, and clitoridectomy in African and Islamic areas and elsewhere, often lumped with circumcision as "mutilations." A discourse of sexual preference (in and out of the gay community) for foreskins or their absence can become intolerant of ethnography's differences.

not from "Hindu Javanese" or Tengger Indonesian.[14] Generally, it can differentiate any Muslim from any Hindu man, and many Muslim from non-Muslim women, if the term "circumcision" be admitted for infibulation or other genital alteration of females.[15] Un/circumcision has divided Paulien precepts from Christ, Christian from Jew, unmedicalized laggard from medicalized modern; and now demedicalized post-modern from still-surgicalized establishmentarian (to echo slogans of recent disputes). "Controls" so-named may be stretched to include women's labia or clitoris along with men's foreskins or *plusque*-foreskin – among other bits of bodies; contrasts separate neighboring groups who "circumcise" neither women nor men or just men. Ethnographic surveys have often categorized together "Circumcision, Incision and Subincision" from European, Mid-Eastern, Indonesian, Australian, Melanesian, Mesoamerican, and Native American spheres.[16] The topic elides with castration, eunuchism and "infibulation, muzzling, and other curious customs"; any constant content across cases for example, blood remains disputed.[17]

[14] Robert Hefner, *Hindu Javanese* (Princeton, 1987).

[15] Because this chapter began, ethnographically, with Muslim (versus Bali-Hindu) experience (see below), I note Islamic "encyclopedic" designations of male circumcision and female excision (*khafd*) by the term "*khitan*" (see *Encyclopedia of Islam* [1957], 4: 913–914; 5: 20–22); this entry also cites practices of *ghusl*, necessary if "the two circumcised parts have been in touch with one another" (p. 20). Clearly, any description of anyone's ritual practices relies on contestable categories. It bears repeating that my essay addresses empathy toward alter (*autre*), rather than *own*, circumcisions or uncircumcisions. Inscribing experience from the vantage of "own circumcision" involves difficulties of memory and forgetting – depending on relative age, but only in part. The recent movie based on S. Perel's *Europa, Europa* displays as-if unforgettability of "own" infant-circumcision in the most tragic times of National Socialist anti-Semitism (see Terence Rafferty, "Divided Self," *The New Yorker*, July 1, 1991, 81–83 [review of "*Europa, Europa*," Agnieszka Holland, dir., based on *Europa, Europa*, by Salomon Perel, Paris, 1990]). A striking "fiction" written as a memoir of "own" will-to-be-circumcised from childhood-into-manhood is P. A. Toer's Indonesian short story, "*Sunat*"; I cite for readers' convenience, D. Lombard's fine translation: "Comme tous mes autres camarades, je n'avais qu'un désurm celui d'être un bon musulman. . . . 'Ne bouge surtout pas!' me conseilla l'un des assistants. . . . Je regardais mon sang épais et noirâtre qui coulait comme un filet et se mêlait lentement au cendres de l'assiette. . . . Tous mes espoirs de devinir un vraie musulman s'évanouirent. . . , car je me rendais bien compte que mes parents étaient pauvres et que nous ne possédions pas ce qu'il fallait pour faire un pélerinage." See P. A. Toer, "La Circoncision" (*Sunat*), in *Histoires courtes d'Indonesie*, trans. Denys Lombard (Paris, 1968). See also Daniel Boyarin, "This We Know to Be the Carnal Israel: Circumcision and the Erotic Life of God and Israel," *Critical Inquiry*, 18, no. 3 (1992): 474–505. Readers interested in Derrida are "deferred" to fn 10.

[16] For example, see W.H.R. Rivers, *Psychology and Ethnology* (New York, 1926).

[17] P. C. Remondino, *History of Circumcision, From the Earliest Times to the Present* (Philadelphia, 1891). Howard Eilberg-Schwartz's *The Savage in Judaism: An Anthropology of Israelite Religion and Ancient Judaism* (Bloomington, 1990), chs. 6–7, ties together "blood," descent, pruning, or "the fruitful cut," seeking to make Israelite circumci-

An unwieldy array of functions, features, causes, and effects has been attributed to circumcision and associated rites: age-grade bonding and generation dividing; social exchange and rivalry; spilling blood, inflicting ordeals, remaindering prepuces, occasioning stoicism,. . . ; making boys into men, ordinary men into prophets, a people into chosen or condemned, men into women ("symbolic wounds"), phalluses into vaginas, human penises into marsupial-like ones (Australia) or rhinoceros-like ones (Borneo); to enhance or diminish virility, fertility, sacrality, holiness, or other kind of potency, either to augment or to limit population growth, and thereby curing or causing disease.[18] Variable indicators and claimed consequences of un/circumcision "itself," of course, render associated practices and ideas no less concrete to any (un)circumcisee or (un)circumcisor. (This includes infant circumcision, without suction, to be discussed later.) *The copiousness of*

sion (male, infant) thematically coherent. I question whether a given complex of usages can "add up," given anomalies implicit in diacritical rites. On ritual dispersal with respect to the anthropology of performance, *Annales* historiography, New Historicism, and a semiotics of resistance, see Boon, *Affinities and Extremes*.

[18] Australian subincision remains a classic ethnographic topic; a characteristic survey is Rivers, *Psychology and Ethnology*. A vast list of studies of "Circumcision *and* or *versus* X" includes D. E. Brown, J. Edwards, and R. Moore, *The Penis Inserts of Southeast Asia*, Occasional Paper No. 15 (Berkeley, 1988), a survey of Southeast Asian penis inserts (contrasted with circumcision); John R. Bowen's fine history of Gayo (Sumatra), heirlooms and circumcision in social dialectics (*Sumatran Politics and Poetics: Gayo History, 1900–1989* [New Haven, 1991], 232–233); circumcision and "warrior asceticism" (Max Weber, *Ancient Judaism*, trans. H. Gerth [New York, 1967], 92); circumcision and transvestism (Ernest Crawley, *The Mystic Rose*, ed. T. Besterman [New York, 1927] 1: 319). Needless to add, circumcision *and* writing (a style of incision) is an expansive figural and practical copula. *Now*, however, I do need to add Derrida. Since writing these notes two years ago, Bennington and Derrida's *Derrida* has appeared, first in French, then English. What can one add to Derrida's circumcision that he has not? In this essay's comparative sense of *autre* un/circumcisions (e.g., Buginese), I can only introduce Derrida's latest as an utter antithesis: "own circumcision" inscribed as a new center of *marges*. In Derrida's *sur* Augustinian "circumfessional" footnotes, he entwines an as-if subtext (his present-absence of prepuce) to his obsessive *ecriture*. Oh, the commentary that is bound to ensue from these positions! Bennington: " . . . Let me say that J. D. surprises me less than he thinks or pretends to think when he exhibits his circumcision here, for a long time now he has been talking of nothing else. . . . " (Geoffrey Bennington and Jacques Derrida, *Jacques Derrida* [Chicago, 1983], 327). Derrida: " . . . For years I have been going round in circles, trying to take as a witness not to see myself being seen but to re-member myself around a single event, I have been accumulating in the attic my 'sublime,' documents, iconography, notes, learned ones and native ones, dream narratives or philosophical dissertations, applied transcription of encyclopedic, sociological, historical, psychoanalytical treatises that I'll never do anything with, about circumcision in the world, the Jewish and the Arab and the others, and excision, with a view to my circumcision alone, the circumcision of me, the unique one, that I know perfectly well took place, one time, they told me and I see it but I always suspect myself of having cultivated, because I am circumcised, *ergo*, cultivated, a fantastical affabulation" (*ibid*., 59). No, indeed, there'll never be another Derrida.

significations still devolving on circumcision and uncircumcision is the subject of this essay.

Historically, (un)circumcision enters sectarian discourses in multifarious guises. Examples include Java's fourteenth century Indicized courtly rites (cremating, noncircumcising) eventually becoming Islamized (circumcising, noncremating); Abrahamic/Pauline Judeo-Christian liturgies as practiced or described up to and including Renaissance-Reformation ritual and iconography. Judeo-Christian-Islamic distinctions have revolved around options of infant/child/adolescent/adult circumcision (plus some non-circumcision for Christians and some female "circumcision" for Muslims); yet not, to my knowledge, either regularized corpse or pre-natal circumcision – both now perfectly conceivable. A key Scriptural tradition in this regard is Genesis 17: 24–27:

Abraham was ninety-nine years old when he circumcised the flesh of his foreskin. Ishmael was thirteen years old when he was circumcised in the flesh of his foreskin. Both Abraham and Ishmael were circumcised on the same day, and all the men of his household, born in the house or bought with money from foreigners, were circumcised with him.[19]

All of Genesis 15–26 deserves continual rereading, through "Isaac [a prototype first infant circumcisee] and his wife Rebecca laughing together" (Gen. 25: 8). Resonances with Judeo-Christian themes of sacrifice occupied Hubert and Mauss's fundamental essay on the ethnography and history of covenants:

The victim takes his place. It alone penetrates into the perilous domain of sacrifice, it dies there, and indeed it is there in order to die. The sacrificer remains protected; the gods take the victim instead of him. *The victim redeems him.* Moses had not circumcised his son, and Yahweh came to 'wrestle' with

[19] It remains hopelessly inviting to become versed in relevant Bible criticism; in Midrashic, Patristic, Kabbalistic, Gnostic, Talmudic, etc., commentary; in various Islamic traditions, e.g.: "La tradition musulmane rapporte que Ibrahim mene Ismail et non pas Isaac au sacrifice; il y a cependant des divergences entre auteurs musulmans a ce sujet" (Abdellah Hammoudi, *La Victime et ses masques* [Paris, 1988], 95). Equally vital is a "world history of ritual differences," what A. N. Hocart (*Social Origins* [London, 1954]) called "sacraments" everywhere, particularly Oceanic Fiji, Buddhist Ceylon, and Vedic-through-Hindu India (see also R. R. Marett, *Sacraments of Simple Folk* [Oxford, 1933]). Regarding contrasts that became Catholic *versus* Protestant in the sixteenth century, I recall Augustine's lingering trope of his pen's phallic tongue and its chaste, circumcised lips (see Eugene Vane, "Augustine's Confessions and the Poetics of the Law," *Modern Language Notes*, 93 [1978]: 618–634), plus exegetical sublimations of Saints' lives. One can contrast Luther (if only to remain ecumenical); comments on Genesis (and circumcision) occur in *Works* (3: 75–118, 133–135); on Luther's late anti-Semitism (and views of circumcision), see Mark U. Edwards, Jr., *Luther's Last Battles: Politics and Polemics, 1531–1543* (Ithaca, 1983), chs. 5–6.

him in a hostelry. Moses was on the point of death when his wife savagely cut off the child's foreskin and, casting it at Yahweh's feet, said to him: 'Thou art for me a husband of blood.' The destruction of the foreskin satisfied the god; he did not destroy Moses, who was redeemed. There is no sacrifice into which some idea of redemption does not enter.[20]

European history has yielded nonstop commentary about (un)circumcision plus appropriate "substitutes" (in the semiotic sense) of sacraments for rites of atonement, circumcision, forgiveness, manna, and sacrifice. To recall such difficulties, I might cite Peter Brown's *The Body and Society:*

Paul's apostolic mission had left the Christian communities with one decisive *lacuna*. He had imposed strict moral codes on all pagan converts; but he had bitterly resisted any attempt to encourage pagans to adopt the clear badges of a separate identity provided to those who converted to Judaism. They were to bear no physical mark on their bodies – no circumcision. They were to engage in no careful discrimination of clean and unclean foods – that would have involved a clear choice of dining companions and even separate marketing facilities (no *kashrut*). They were to observe no clear distinctions between profane and holy days – no Sabbaths and new moons. Many other Christians felt that they could not afford to be so off-hand with the venerable Law of Moses. In the cities of the Diaspora, Judaism continued to appeal to pagans precisely because it was an ancient religion as punctilious as their own. Jews observed the solemn rhythms of high festival. They held to codes of purity. They gave men and women an opportunity to approach, in a disciplined and thoughtful manner, the "things that lie between nature and culture, half-wild, half-civilised . . .[21]

[20] Robert Hubert and Marcel Mauss's Durkheimian study is paramount: *Sacrifice: Its Nature and Function*, trans. W. Hall (Chicago, 1964). Howard Eilberg-Schwartz argues, correctly I think, that "circumcision and sacrifice have overlapping functions" (*The Savage in Judaism*); but his study overlooks Hubert and Mauss, key works by Hocart, and, surprisingly, Max Weber (*Ancient Judaism*)–which forefront "sacrifice" (plus covenant and "sacrament"). These and others (even Herbert Spencer, *The Principles of Sociology* [New York, 1896], 1: 418–419) eroded–whether or not intentionally–any presumed boundary between "world religions" and "primitive" ones. Insights into what Eilberg-Schwartz thematizes as "the savage" *in* Judaism have been acknowledged in such works on comparative sacrifice (including Christianity, Islam, Hinduism, etc.). His challenge to colleagues to interpret Israelite religion less exclusivistically sometimes seems to suggest that "the savage" has been a constant idea of "other" against which "the chosen" or "the civilized" or "reason" has congratulated itself. If the history of "othering" were so stably polarized, it would have proved far easier to ameliorate (see my *Other Tribes, Other Scribes*, ch. 2; "Anthropology, Ethnology, and Religion," in *Encyclopedia of Religion*, ed. M. Eliade [New York, 1987]; and *Affinities and Extremes*). A fine ethnography of, and meditation on, sacrifice in Islam and the masquerades in its margins is Abdellah Hammoudi, *La Victime et ses masques* (Paris, 1988).

[21] Peter Brown, *The Body and Society: Men, Women and Sexual Renunciation in Early Christianity* (New York, 1988), 59.

It is eerily coincidental that Brown's splendid summary, covering dire conflicts throughout Judeo-Christian history, ends by applying to "us" a phrase from Greg Dening's *Islands and Beaches*, which book meditates upon that remotest "othered" left in the wake of Europe's expansion: the Marquesas in Oceania.

THIS ESSAY'S ETHNOGRAPHIC BEGINNINGS

Here we may call again on the custom of circumcision which – a kind of "Leitfossil" – has repeatedly rendered us important services.

–Freud, *Moses and Monotheism*[22]

It was a dank and sultry afternoon (Indonesian, *sore*) in 1972; obliviously engaged in fieldwork on Balinese ancestral rites, caste distinctions, marriage practices, and local politics, I was accosted by an affable Buginese acquaintance who urged me to witness tomorrow's circumcision ceremony (*sunat*) in his Islamic compound. My ethnographic encounter was briefly described in a book about Hindu-Bali; here are some extracts:

At 6:15 a.m. the surgeon arrived, and the initiates were ushered into a room lighted by the dawning sun, with a plastic-covered operating table, a shelf of instruments, medicine and cleansing agents, a tape recorder playing Arabic songs, and a lone calendar on the otherwise blank whitewashed walls. . . .

Each boy was held down by three or four men, including the conspicuously proud father. From eight to ten men mulled about, plus one vagrant tot in an orange dress who kept running up to inspect the initiates. The other women

[22] The few puffs of Freud in these pages suggest my reluctance to address his work squarely; in contrast, see the courageous studies of Sander Gilman, "The Indelibility of Circumcision," *Koroth*, 9:11–12 (1991), and Jay Geller, "The Unmanning of the Wandering Jew," *American Imago*, 49, no. 2 (1992): 227–262. Their work, plus nuanced attitudes of Janet Malcolm, *In the Freud Archives* (New York, 1984), comparative insights of Gannanath Obeyesekere's *The Work of Culture* (Chicago, 1990), and earlier work of Philip Rieff, "The Authority of the Past: Sickness and Society in Freud's Thought," *Social Research*, 21, no. 4 (1954) and *Freud: The Mind of the Moralist*, 3rd ed. (Chicago, 1979), help me want to commemorate Freud's aftermath in suitable writing (see fn 21). Regarding Freud's intertextual life, difficult ambiguities continue augmenting (as Freud perhaps foretold), the more successors presume to know. I recommend peculiar revisionist readings of Freud (e.g., Paul Vitz, *Sigmund Freud's Christian Unconscious* [New York, 1988]), as tactical antidotes against standardized scholarship that unduly "ameliorates" his example (e.g., Peter Gay, *Freud: A Life for Our Time* [New York, 1988]). Ever-spiraling intricacies of interpreting Freud interpreting (Freud interpreting) have moved far (progressed? regressed?) since Ernest Jones's biography (*The Life and Work of Sigmund Freud* [New York, 1953–1957]) attributed filial piety to the very subject who made patricide a household word! Oddly, Freud's lifeway still keeps winding up monumentalized, ennobled, indeed "enlightened." (Will a similar fate fall to Derrida? Jones, by the way, made nothing much of Freud's own circumcision.)

and girls watched from behind a partition. The first boy suffered most acutely; although the foreskin was stretched and clamped and partly anesthetized, the cuts provoked uncontrolled screams. 'Too much blood with this one,' the operator murmured in Indonesian. With much comforting, laughter, and prattle by all around, he quickly finished cutting, applied an antiseptic and bandage, and attached a protective brace to keep the boy's formal *sarong* from irritating the wound. The second initiate fared better, the last was exemplary. The latter's father, swelling with pride, related his son's stoic endurance and unflinching control even during the anesthesia injection to the boy's similar courage at the dentist's office. Finally, all three were perched in their mosque attire on linen-covered pillows to await the communal feast later in the day.[23]

The fuller description, stressing festive tonalities, was praised in a professional review; this led me to wonder about past representations of circumcision from Indonesia and – as anthropologists then were a bit overreaching – from everywhere else throughout all recorded time for any gender and any body part modern clinicians call "genital."[24]

My vignette of Buginese *sunat* in uncircumcising Hindu-Bali differed routinely from two precedents in Indonesian studies. Clifford Geertz's remarkable *Religion of Java* presented Javanese circumcision as shared across contrasting cultural identities: syncretist-peasant (*abangan*), reformist-Muslim (*santri*), and courtly-bureaucratic-propped-up-by-colonialist-regime (*prijaji*).[25] Because my project addressed rites outside Islam, I could only present foreskin removal as a diacritical dividing Buginese and Balinese, despite their cooperation and even intermarriage. Dutch surveys of Indonesian circumcision practices (*besnijdenis*)[26] used them to gauge intensity of Islamic identity (for example, of Buginese dispersed from their home territory of Sulawesi). Nothing *diagnostic* – or in Foucault's terms "symptomatological" – entered my evocation of a rite so "right" to Buginese sensibilities and so antipathetic next door:

There simply could be nothing less Balinese: a painful initiation rite in an imageless, flowerless, smokeless, holy-waterless cell. . . . Balinese informants could not even bring themselves to discuss circumcision per se; at the thought of it they were disgusted to the same degree Buginese are disdainful of Balinese for not practicing it. Conversely, in death rites it is Muslims who abhor

[23] Boon, *The Anthropological Romance of Bali*, 210ff.

[24] The review is David Moyer: "Review of J. Boon," *American Anthropologist* (1981); I thank Ivan Brady for authoring and encouraging comparative readings in complexities of rituals, poetics, politics, and history's cultures.

[25] See Clifford Geertz, *The Religion of Java* (New York, 1966).

[26] B.J.O. Schrieke, "Allerlei over de besnijdenis," *Tijdschrift voor Indische Taal-, Land- en Volkenkunde*, 60 (1921): 373–578, and 61 (1922): 1–94.

Balinese corpse preparation and later cremation and Balinese who disdain the Muslim community for refusing such responsibilities.[27]

My anthropological task in those days required siding with neither, even sympathizing with both.

Since that fieldwork in 1972, during routine chores of teaching and slide-showing, it has proved increasingly difficult to convey the convivial ambiance of four Buginese boys (average age seven years) being de-foreskinned. Students and colleagues in today's moralistic climate dispute any overall "well-wishingness" of these fete. Assumptions of coercive dimensions prevail among listeners – whether, I assume, circumcised or uncircumcised, feminist or masculinist, Marxist or not, hermeneuts or positivists, politically correct or less-than. Across such differences that doubtless divide my audience (and sometimes divide me), a shared reaction sets in: suspicions of trauma are voiced, charges of damage levied, the plight of victims identified with. *They* (my listeners) choose, when pressed, not to be any more understanding about *another's circumcision* than did my uncircumcising and flamboyantly cremating Balinese friends, when pressed. I, on the other hand, having "been there" – *chez* gregarious Buginese – emphathized with a diacritical rite offensive to many "Westerners" (again, whether circumcised or not) and, when pressed, to many Balinese.

I have since pursued some semiotics of circumcision in comparative discourse between Europe and Indonesia (both Islamic and "Indianized"), starting with the sixteenth century. I tracked Huguenot notions of circumcision as a similitude of sodomy associated with the Papacy and whatever people it contaminated.[28] I explored images of "anti-circumcision" (Hindu-Tantric icons of bedizened foreskins) from Pigafetta's 1520s account of Indonesian rituals.[29] That study tried to convey why this elusive evidence thwarted historicist evaluation in its own day and still should in ours.

The search for precedents – anywhere, anytime, regardless of the commentator's own condition – of non-judgmental depiction of diacritic un/circumcision has led to Montaigne. May I confess that it almost feels like coming home?[30]

[27] Boon, *The Antropological Romance of Bali*, 212.

[28] See my *Other Tribes, Other Scribes*, 162–168.

[29] See my *Affinities and Extremes*, 54–60.

[30] Whether "home" to Montaigne or to subjects he describes, I cannot tell; some form of recognition, doubtless uncanny, occurs. I also confess that when reading toward "the sixteenth century," this anthropologist often feels as if "it might as well be Bali." How, I wonder, would Montaigne have inscribed East Indies' practices (including Hindu-Bali, versus others), had he voyaged (painfully) thither to witness chords of differences.

MONTAIGNE'S PRE-ENLIGHTENMENT EMPATHIES FOR MANY AN "US"

It is the undiligent reader who loses my subject, not I.

–Montaigne, *Essays*

Among the steadier texts circumcribing un/circumcisions I have discovered from the sixteenth century (and before or since) are sections of Montaigne's *Travel Journal*.[31] This long-lost, indirectly transmitted narrative illustrates dimensions of Montaigne's writing stressed by D.L. Schaefer: double-voiced, heterodox, and ironic with different audiences in mind, although ostensibly of orthodox persuasion.[32]

Passing mention of circumcision-as-diacritical is made by Montaigne, writing in the first person in French. (Switching later to Italian, he tries "to speak this other language a little, especially since I am in this region where I seem to hear the most perfect Tuscan speech, particularly among those natives who have not corrupted and altered it with that of their neighbors."[33]) He reports a "memorable incident" involving one Giuseppe: Forced to be circumcised and become a Turk, then ostensibly redeemed to Christianity through sacraments, he remained, however, "implicitly" Islamic, winding up a strategic go-between, a kind of jack-of-all-sects. That much, at least, one gathers from Montaigne's text – compiled of hearsay from Giuseppe's relatives, just across the street – all about disguises among foes, friends, neighbors, and even mothers and sons (in Italy!); I abbreviate:

An inhabitant of this place, a soldier named Giuseppe, who is still alive and commands one of the galleys of the Genoese as a convict, and several of whose near relations I saw, was captured by the Turks in a battle at sea. To regain

[31] Michel de Montaigne, *Travel Journal*, trans. by Donald Frame, Foreword by Guy Davenport (San Francisco, 1983).

[32] Schaefer adds that Montaigne even dissimulated in his private family records (see David L. Schaefer, *The Political Philosophy of Montaigne* [Ithaca, 1989]). And the travelogue, not intended for publication, was only discovered in the eighteenth century; and evidence of it keeps emerging. It cannot necessarily be taken as true, nor as false; that is the problem or point. Related difficulties pertain to any effort to pull Montaigne into a present; Water's 1903 translation (see Michel de Montaigne, *The Journal of Montaigne's Travels in 1580 and 1581*, trans. by W. G. Waters [London, 1903]), for example, deleted descriptions of his bodily suffering, thus censoring a key early-modern travel motive.

For a powerful evocation of both sixteenth- and twentieth-century censorships (of Rabelais), see Natalie Zemon Davis, "Rabelais Among the Censors (1940s, 1540s)," *Representations*, 32 (1990): 1–32; it would take such stereoscopic (reflexive) historical reading to begin doing justice to possible allegiances in Montaigne's travels.

[33] Montaigne, *Travel Journal*, 126.

his liberty he became a Turk (and there are many of this condition, and especially in the mountains near this place, still alive) was circumcised, and married in their territory. Coming to pillage this cost, he . . . [was] caught by the people, who had risen up. He had the presence of mind to say that he had come to surrender deliberately, that he was a Christian. He was set at liberty a few days later, came . . . to the house opposite the one I am lodging in; he entered and encountered his mother. She asked him roughly who he was and what he wanted; for he still had on his sailor's clothes, and it was strange to see him there.[34]

A recognition scene ensues, followed by a maternal embrace after a decade's separation. The mother dies soon after; the shock had proved unbearable, as her doctors foretold. Then:

Our Giuseppe was feted by one and all, was received into the Church to abjure his error, and received the Sacrament from the bishop of Lucca, with several other ceremonies. It was just humbug: he was a Turk at heart.[35]

Montaigne's own narrative of the tale of deceit then enters Giuseppe's relatives' narrative present-tense:

To return to the Turks he steals away from here, goes to Venice, and mixes with them again. Resuming his travels, here he falls into our hands again; and because he is a man of unusual strength and a soldier well versed in naval matters, the Genoese still keep him and use him, well bound and fettered.[36]

And that's how Giuseppe became an Italian Turk, an unreconverted slave in Genoa's employ.

This picaresque story reads like circumcision's anticipation of *Candide:* our hero/culprit negotiating a borderland ("Venice") between Catholicism and Islam. Might Montaigne's *Travel*-text – as discourse – be read or experienced as something like a sublimated equivalent to such cross-cultural, multilanguage, inter-sectarian carryings-on?

Be that as it may, this roving tale of present/absent foreskin stands in sharp contrast to the *Journal's* ultralocated account of "the most ancient religious ceremony there is among men," the circumcision of the Jews, witnessed in the early 1580s on January 30, in Rome, as detailed by his secretary, on a page of manuscript authenticated by its proximity to a parenthetical passage inserted in the margins in Montaigne's own hand.[37] Before citing this ethnographic episode, let

[34] Ibid., 124.
[35] Ibid.
[36] Ibid.
[37] Ibid.

me underscore the copiousness of religions, landscapes, cuisines, and bodies Montaigne's narrative registers as he sallies away from his since-celebrated home-base, his tower. Even Rome's Jews – deemed timeless in their circumcising – reveal contrasts contributing an array of festive display, including that "renegade rabbi who preaches to the Jews on Saturday after dinner in the Church of the Trinity," with sixty other Jews in compulsory attendance.[38]

If Rome's Hebrew enclave harbors variety, how much more mottled is Switzerland's landscape of Reformation:

> We saw a great many men of learning. . . . Monsieur de Montaigne judged that they were not in agreement over their religion, from the answers he received: some calling themselves Zwinglians, other Calvinists, other Martinists; and indeed he was informed that many still fostered the Roman religion in their heart. The form of giving the sacrament is generally into the mouth; however, anyone who wants may put out his hand for it, and the ministers do not dare touch this *chord* in these *differences* in religion.[39]

Such chords of differences form, along with Montaigne's physical ills and profound misery, the very fabric of his travel-text. In Germany, for example (one I shall recall later):

> We went to see the Church of the Holy Cross . . . They make a great celebration there about a miracle that occurred nearly a hundred years ago. A woman would not swallow the body of Our Lord. Having taken it out of her mouth and put it, wrapped in wax, into a box, she confessed; and they found the whole thing changed into flesh. For this they cite plenty of attestations, and this miracle is written down in many places in Latin and in German. They show under crystal that wax, and then a little morsel having the redness of flesh. This church is roofed with copper, like the house of the Fuggers. . . [40]

Montaigne's account seems everywhere evenhanded and ecumenical despite such recent events as the Saint Bartholomew's Day massacre:

> The town was originally entirely Zwinglian. Later, when the Catholics were recalled, the Lutherans took the place of the Zwinglians; at present there are more Catholics in positions of authority, although they are greatly outnumbered. Monsieur de Montaigne also visited the Jesuits here and found some very learned ones.[41]

Catholics too display pungent contrasts: "Whereas we join our hands in prayer to God at the elevation of the host, [in Switzerland] they

[38] Ibid., 92.
[39] Ibid., 14 (emphases added).
[40] Ibid., 38–39.
[41] Ibid., 39.

stretch them apart wide open, and hold them thus raised until the priest exhibits the pax."[42] Such chords of difference appear even among poultry: "[In Germany] there is also an aviary twenty paces square . . . all full of birds. Here we saw some Polish pigeons, which they call Indian. . . ; they are large, and have a beak like a partridge."[43]

Could an author more conscientiously inscribe cultures as intersections of sectarian/cultural/linguistic/avial contrasts, collisions, and accommodations? (Montaigne even compares differences of words to differences of birds.) To commemorate the 1530 embrace between Charles V and Ferdinand of Hungary and Bohemia, his travelogue notes the Italian/German polyglossia of language and liturgy around Trent.[44] Ever open-minded himself, Montaigne applauds even the otherwise unecumenical Pope Gregory XIII for endowing colleges for Greeks, English, Scots, French, Germans, and Poles. Montaigne's extra-Catholic, indeed extra-Christian, catholicity extends to his most "personal" topic: those killingly painful kidney stones. He gladly contacts, among other experts and amateurs of bodily ailments, "an old patriarch of Antioch, an Arab, very well versed in five or six languages of that part of the world, and having no knowledge of Greek or any other of our tongues, with whom I had become quite intimate, [who] made me a present of a certain mixture of help my stone, and prescribed the use of it for me in writing."[45] Montaigne includes the prescription "in order that, if I should lose his writing, I may find it here."[46] The Arab's remedy (doubtless devised through "interpretation" more than "diagnosis") requires a drug to be taken "in a dose the size of two peas," five times, "leaving out every other day."

Montaigne's entire *Journal* – including that most pragmatic note of a recipe for health, recorded against loss – just keeps sounding the chords of religious, sectarian, and liturgical *differences*. A travelogue of our own reading-voyage through his text might circumscribe his descriptions as implicit emulations of myriad, musical fountains at the Villa d'Este:

> Here I examined everything most particularly. . . . The gushing of an infinity of jets of water checked and launched by a single spring that can be worked from far off. . . . The music of the organ . . . effected by means of the water, which falls with great violence into a round arched cave and agitates the air that is there and forces it, in order to get out, to go through the pipes of the

[42] Ibid., 17.
[43] Ibid., 37.
[44] Ibid., 44.
[45] Ibid., 87.
[46] Ibid.

organ and supply it with wind . . . other springs they set in motion an owl, which, appearing at the top of the rock, makes this harmony cease instantly, for the birds are frightened by his presence . . . elsewhere noise as of cannon shots. . . .

There are ponds or reservoirs. . . . The mouths, being thus turned inward and facing one another, cast and scatter the water . . . produce a continual rain falling into the pond. The sun . . . engenders a rainbow so natural and vivid that it lacks nothing of the one we see in the sky. This I had not seen elsewhere.[47]

If there is a discourse resembling this prism – one effecting across cultures similitudes of aqueous variations – Montaigne's *Journal* may embody it. Ebullient descriptions emerge despite his unspeakable spasms of agony produced by urinary malfunctions in an age of horseback travel. And midway through his travel-text occurs our sustained narrative of circumcision. The account begins thusly:

He had already seen their synagogue at another time, one Saturday morning, and their prayers, in which they sing without order, as in the Calvinist churches, certain lessons from the Bible in Hebrew . . . their doctors each in turn give a lesson on the Bible passage for that day, doing it in Italian. . . . [48]

Parallels offered and the scene set, the rite begins:

It is done in . . . the lightest room of the boy's house. They give the boys a godfather and a godmother, as we do; the father names the child. They circumcise them on the eighth day from their birth. The child is wrapped in our style; the godfather unwraps him below, and then those present and the man who is to do the operation all begin to sing. . . . they hold that he who has circumcised up to a certain number . . . when he is dead has this privilege, that the parts of his mouth are never eaten by worms.[49]

After details about the instruments, he describes the operation:

He takes his member and with one hand pulls back toward himself the skin that is over it . . . keeps the cutting edge from injuring the glans and the flesh . . . with a knife he cuts off this skin, which they immediately bury in some earth . . . there in basin . . . for this mystery. After that the minister with his bare nails plucks up also some other particle of skin . . . and tears it off. . . . [50]

[47] Ibid., 99.

[48] Ibid., 80. I truncate Montaigne's ethnography, just as I did my own (of Bugis) above. When obliged to excise description, ethnographers inevitably exaggerate a sense of climax or catharsis. On early modern "popular culture" of carnival-celebrations on the eve of Jewish circumcisions, see Elliott Horowitz, "The Eve of the Circumcision: A Chapter in the History of Jewish Nightlife," *Journal of Social History*, 23:1 (1989): 45–69.

[49] Ibid.

[50] Ibid.

The description culminates:

It seems there is much effort and pain in this; however, they find no danger in it and the wound is always cured in four or five days. The boy's outcry is like that of ours when they are baptized.... They hastily offer some wine to the minister, who puts a little in his mouth and then goes and sucks the glans of this child, all bloody, and spits out the blood he has drawn from it, and immediately takes as much wine again, up to three times... red powder, which they say is dragon's blood, with which he salts and covers the whole wound.... A glass full of wine... which he blesses by some prayers... takes a drop of it with his finger to the boy's mouth to be sucked;... this glass... to the mother and the women... to drink what wine is left.... Another person takes a silver instrument, round as a tennis ball... (pierced with little holes, like our cassolettes), and carries it to the nose, first of the minister, and then of the child, and then of the godfather: they suppose that these are odors to confirm and enlighten minds for devotion. He meanwhile still has his mouth all bloody.[51]

This intricately observed passage – here telegraphed – deserves revisiting by readers. Montaigne's paragraphs evenly convey not just foreskin removal but the since-notorious scene of "suction." The enacted image of a mouth placed round a wounded glans penis enters this travel-text's company of other sacramental extremes – such as that waxy bit of Christ's flesh, uningested, glimpsed in the reliquary mentioned earlier. Subsequent centuries' officials and the states pressuring them would prove unwilling to accommodate this "theatricality" of circumcision rites. In France, for example, suction was ultimately forbidden by the Hebrew Consistory and then by national law in 1854 (see later discussion).

But that was a long time – and an Enlightenment – away from Montaigne and his mode of displaying circumcision in a world of dramatic ritual usages. We must beware, I think, of Enlightenment-engendered notions of proper orality *versus* genitality that later ratified "rational" repressions of olfactory and tactile meanings. Presumably unanchronistic interpreters ought not project such assumptions back to the bodies (and souls) surrounding that "mouth all bloody" of 1580. Yes, aspiringly unethnocentric readers might question subsequent "diagnostics" if only because "enlightened" investigators – whether against circumcision or for it–have clinically promoted them. Never was this more the case than in the late nineteenth century, part of the "post preclassical episteme" still prevalent today.

[51] Ibid., 80–83.

SYMPTOMATOLOGICAL CONTRAST: DR. REMONDINO'S DIAGNOSTICS

The fate of foreskins is vividly analyzed according to assumptions of so-called modernity – an era envisioning absolute fixity – in P.C. Remondino's *History of Circumcision* (1891), No. 11 in the Physician's and Students' Ready Reference Series. Absolutely *not* a travelogue, this captivating work by a doctor and health officer from San Diego County consolidates conjectural prehistory, universal history, Lamarckian and/or Darwinian evolution, and theology in a declared, general "war against prepuces."[52] (It would, of course, be just as "modern" to be universally, diagnostically *for* foreskins.)

Remondino – rigorous laboratory worker, autodidact, humane professional and popularizer, and enthusiastic dabbler in world history – clinches his case against the outlaw prepuce with a pitch to the financial industry:

> . . . a prepuce was a dangerous appendage at any time, and life-insurance companies should class the wearer of a prepuce under the head of hazardous risks, for a circumcised laborer in a powder-mill or a circumcised brakemen [sic] or locomotive engineer runs actually less risk than an uncircumcised tailor or watchmaker. . . . It would be interesting to know, from the statistics of some of these companies, how much more the Hebrew is, as a premium-payer, of value to the company than his uncircumcised brother. Were they to offer some inducement, in the shape of lower rates, to the circumcised, as they should do, they would not only benefit the companies by insuring a longer number of years, on which the insured would pay premiums, but they would be instrumental in decreasing the death-rate and extending longevity.[53]

The book graphically depicts ill-effects of prepuces sure to make all but the most medical-minded reader wince: syphilis, phthisis, phimosis, cancer, gangrene of the penis, sysuria, enuresis, and retention of urine, among other maladies visited upon retainers of foreskins. Their presence/absence is made symptomatic of virtually every clinical effect. One could call Remondino's "episteme" ultradiagnostic.[54]

[52] See Remondino's *History of Circumcision*.

[53] Ibid., 290.

[54] With Remondino and Montaigne, plus other authors mentioned, I scrupulously avoid explaining any position on (un)circumcisions by the author's own "identity" (or the mother's). That question is conceivably as complex for Remondino as for Montaigne! Remondino's "enlightened" text, by the way, demonstrates thoroughgoing hyperbole. If I were not already sympathetic to certain own and others' circumcisions (as well as uncircumcisions – e.g., Hindu-Balinese), I may have become so upon reading Remondino, whether in 1891 or 1991 (time of writing).

Blended with the study's persuasive etiologies are metaphorical flights of fancy:

There is a weird and ghostly but interesting tale connected with the Moslem conquest of Spain, of how Roderick, the last of the Gothic kings, when in trouble and worry, repaired to an old castle, in the secret recesses of which was a magic table whereon would pass in grim procession the different events of the future of Spain; as he gazed on the enchanted table he there saw his own ruin and his country's and nation's subjugation.[55]

Having implied that circumcised Moslems surpassed Gothic rivals, the argument turns allegorical, practically "Frazerian":

Anatomy is generally called a dry study, but, like the enchanted brazen table in the ancient Gothic castle, it tells a no less weird or interesting tale of the past. Its revelations lighten up a long vista, through the thousands of years through which the human species has evolved from its earliest appearance on earth, gradually working up through the different evolutionary processes to what is today supposed to be the acme of perfection as seen in the Indo-European and Semitic races of man. Anatomy points to the rudiment – still lingering, now and then . . . in some one man. . . – of that climbing muscle which shows man in the past . . . nervously escaping up the trunk of a tree in his flight from . . . carnivorous animals. . . . The now useless ear-muscles . . . also tell us of a movable, flapping ear capable of being turned in any direction to catch the sound of approaching danger, . . . the ear being then used for some more useful purpose than having its tympanum tortured by Wagnerian discordant sounds.[56]

Evocations of pre-Wagnerian pragmatic ears (along with pre-bourgeois survivals of olfactory skills I here delete) preface a panoramic vision of human progress – Hegelian? Darwinian? Lamarckian? – from the circumcised priesthood of ancient Egypt to eventual eradication of our species' vestigial flaw:

Nature – always careful that nothing should interfere with the procreative functions – had provided him with a sheath or prepuce, wherein he carried his procreative organ safely out of harm's way, in wild steeple-chases through thorny briars and bramble-brakes. . . . This leathery pouch also protected him from the many leeches, small aquatic lizards . . . from the bites of ants or other vermin when, tired, he rested on his haunches on some mossy bank or sand-hill.[57]

55 See Remondino, *History of Circumcision*, 7.
56 Ibid., 8.
57 Ibid., 9.

Disputing Renan, Remondino hails forerunners of practices that accelerate Nature's own advancement toward a heartier humanity:

> Man has now no use for any of these necessaries of a long-past age – an age so remote that the speculations of Ernest Renan regarding the differences between the Semitic race of Shem and the idolatrous descendants of Ham . . . seem more as if he were discussing an event of yesterday. . . – and we find them disappearing, disuse gradually producing an obliteration of this tissue . . . The other conditions have nothing that interferes with their disappearance; whereas the prepuce, by its mechanical construction and the expanding portions which it incloses, tends at times rather to its exaggerated development than to its disappearance.[58]

The introduction advises that medical history confirms the budget required from civilization to advance evolution beyond the rudiment foreskin. Concluding, anachronistic similes revisit the primitive phallus gone unprotected: "In those days, but for the . . . preputial envelope. . . , the glans penis of primitive man would have often looked like the head of the proverbial duel-disfigured German university student, or the Bacchus-worshipping nose of a jolly British Boniface."[59]

Remondino's style of treatise is "enlightened" in a profounder sense than "secularized"; it demonstrates a thorough faith in progress: the amelioration of humankind through human agency. Medical analysis is readily reconciled with select Scriptures and the Old Testament easily accommodated to scientific evolutionism and etiologies of social diseases:

> We may well exclaim, as we behold this appendage to man, – now of no use in health and of the most doubtful assistance to the very organ it was intended to protect, when that organ, through its iniquitous tastes, has got itself into trouble, and, Job-like, is lying repentant and sick in its many wrappings of lint, with perhaps its companions in crime imprisoned in a suspensory bandage, – what is this prepuce? Whence, why, where, and whither? At times, Nature, as if impatient of the slow march of gradual evolution, and exasperated as this persistent and useless as well as dangerous relic of a far-distant prehistoric age, takes things in her own hands and induces a sloughing to take place, which rids it of its annoyance. In the far-off land of Ur, among the mountainous regions of Kurdistan, something over six thousand years ago, the fathers of the Hebrew race, inspired by a wisdom that could be nothing less than of divine origin, forestalled the process of evolution by establishing the rite of circumcision.[60]

[58] Ibid., 10.
[59] Ibid., 206.
[60] Ibid., 10.

This theme leads on to a powerful chronology of the persecution of Jews, with annotations:

I. 167 B.C. Antiochus forbids Hebrew mothers to circumcise sons, under penalty of death. . .
II. 218 A.D.: Heliogabalus is himself circumcised. . .
IV. Constantine: Death for Hebrews who circumcise slaves.
V. Justinian: Hebrews may not raise children as same.
VI. 7th cent: Unbaptised banished; renunciation of circumcision and Sabbath required.

His list ends with persecutions by Saracens and finally the fifteenth-century Spanish Inquisition. The legacy of repression points up a phenomenal vitality of circumcision: "Its resistance and apparent indestructibility would seem to stamp it as of divine origin."[61]

Suggestions of supernatural teleology behind circumcision's history would contravene "Enlightenment" standards only if they are equated with "secular." Again, that is not the usage I am following. There may, however, be vestiges of "pre-Enlightenment" in Remondino's idea of a process built into world destiny – the sloughing off of fore-skins – susceptible of acceleration by human arts in tune with a divine plan. This idea resembles neo-Platonist alchemy, which aimed to accelerate the world's growth into perfect-elements, to hasten the Book of Nature's too-gradual transformation of substances back-into gold's equivalent, to achieve the redemption of all matter: subterranean, aqueous, and hypereal.[62] But neo-Platonism (part of Foucault's "pre-classical episteme") was thoroughly organic; matter later deemed "inorganic (for example, metals) was assumed to be living (perhaps "ert" rather than inert). Recalling the "beginnings" (Foucault/Couliano) invoked at this essay's outset, I might generalize: It was only after concern for microcosmic-macrocosmic affinities yielded to convictions of a "dead" nature (that aftermath to "sinning"?) – advanced as a "Reform" against "magical erotic" arts – that the so-called "discourse of modernism" became consolidated around universalized diagnosis and analytic knowledge.[63] Or, phrasing matters in the ideological idiom of twentieth-century partisans[64]: Remondino's 1891 treatise promoted among surgeons and their clients what became the most common operation ever routinized in the era of triumphant medicalized technologies. (My own view would be more Montaignesque.)

[61] Ibid., 67.
[62] Mircea Eliade, *The Forge and the Crucible*, 2d ed. (Chicago, 1978).
[63] Timothy Reiss, *The Discourse of Modernism* (Ithaca, 1982).
[64] See, for example, Joseph Lewis, *In the Name of Humanity* (New York, 1967).

Remondino's coverage of cases relies largely on encyclopedic "histories" themselves coined in Enlightenment discourse, or on examples culled from seventeenth-nineteenth century derivatives. A notable exception is Montaigne. How, then, does Remondino's 1891 *History* – which I am using to epitomize one "Enlightenment" style of universalizing (un)circumcision – incorporate the little sixteenth-century evidence it inspects?

To begin at the beginning: Remondino's decorative frontispiece ("From an old sixteenth-century Italian print in the author's collection, representing the scene of the Holy Circumcision"). Remondino ignores iconographic traditions that began emphasizing Christ's circumcision, such as Hendrik Goltzius's "Life of the Virgin" series (1593–94), which includes the circumcision, plus the Visitation, Holy Family, and Adoration. The sixteenth century, of course, experimented with different solutions to dilemmas of whether to represent Biblical episodes through historicism or typification.[65] Goltzius's devices of display include not just "anachronistic" garb and setting common in Renaissance illustrations of such scenes, but eyeglasses on Christ's circumcisor. Remondino's frontispiece, in contrast, shows possibly "historicized" costume with the furnishings and architecture of early modern Europe. Yet contradictory devices in the iconographic history of illusioning or emblematizing the past are not addressed in his *History*. Rather, Remondino's frontispiece serves as a visible sign to label the book's object of analysis circumcision – captioned as "Hebraic Circumcision," although the source-reference declares the illustration "Holy Circumcision." So tagged, the visual device levels distinctions between Hebrew and Christological, reducing contradictory rites-represented to decorative diagnosis. The frontispiece, then, becomes an inadvertent emblem of what makes Remondino's study "Enlightened," even when depicting sixteenth-century depictions.

Other references to earlier times fill Remondino's chapter on "Miracles and the Holy Prepuce," a survey of eighth to eighteenth century

[65] I note lively debates in art history about emblematizing, illusioning, typifying, and describing. For arguments against iconology, see Svetlana Alpers's *The Art of Describing: Dutch Art in the Seventeenth Century* (Chicago, 1983) and the controversies it has fueled. To compensate for my inadequate sally into sixteenth-century visual styles, I might mention a persuasive icon of circumcision this gazer once touristically perused. It dates from 1505–10 and can be visited in Brussels (just where, I forget): the "Retable dit de 'Saluces'" showing "La Vie de la Vierge et l'enfance du Christ," with the moment of cutting carved into the wood in high relief, a spatter of red pigment applied. The circumcision scene in an adjoining "retable domestique" dating from 1480, does not depict the act of cutting. My ethnographic curiosity wonders about responses of devotees confronting these icons (see below).

sanctuaries reputed to house bits of Christ's foreskin, of curative power to devotees. "In the internecine wars of the sixteenth century," he writes, "the abbey [of Charroux, founded by Charlemagne in 783] fell into the hands of the godless and heretical Huguenots and the holy relic disappeared."[66] But little "history" is made of disputes between Catholics and Protestants, of the Reformation's rejection of thaumaturgical ideals, or of germane sectarian positions. The universalizing style skips from the Huguenots to the abbey's demolishment in 1856, when an unearthed piece of desiccated flesh was declared Christ's lost prepuce. Remondino's discourse converts events themselves into visual-decorative diagnostics. The implied "authority" of his description doubts the magical-efficacy of relics from any century, while profession faith in the health-efficacy of circumcision of any century. (What *is* Enlightenment?)

This brings us again to Montaigne, or rather his travelogue's fate in *The History of Circumcision,* which summarizes in a "reasonable" fashion the focal scene I emphasized here. Remondino (or perhaps a translation he employed) deletes much that seems specific to Montaigne's description. Detailed "chords of difference," separated from the comparative narrative that gives them resonance, transmogrify into a standardized sequence of averaged examples. Montaigne's stipulation that odors induce a devotional attitude in rabbi, godfather, and circumcisee alike, and his capstone repeated reference to the mouthful of preputial blood are sloughed off. Remondino cuts instead to an 1886 account (taken from the *Cyclopedia of Biblical, Theological, and Ecclesiastical Literature*) of circumcision in our modern synagogues, thereby eliding Montaigne's *Journal* entry with later ritual usages whose primary oral dimension is verbal or aural. After briefly alluding to knife, wound, and bandages, the *Cyclopedia* reports the sublime, resonant words and responses of congregation, circumciser, and father. Regrettably, I here abbreviate sacred words that are doubtless moving in their own way, albeit different from what Montaigne witnessed:

> Blessed is he that cometh to be circumcised and enter into the covenant... Thy father and mother shall rejoice... Blessed art Thou, O Lord our God, King of the Universe!... As he hath entered into the law, the canopy, and the good and virtuous deeds...[67]

Remondino next reviews later prohibitions of "Mezizah, the fourth or Objectionable Act of Suction," and approves history's progress toward proper measures of beneficial prepuce eradication:

[66] See Remondino, *History of Circumcision,* 72.
[67] Ibid., 149.

By virtue of this decree a regulation was passed by the Consistories on the 12th of July, 1854, ordering that thereafter circumcision should only be performed in a rational manner, and by a properly qualified person. Suction was likewise abolished, and the wound directed to be sponged with wine and water. This decree and the resulting regulations have been of the greatest benefit to the French Israelites, and some attention to the matter would not be amiss in the United States.[68]

In Remondino, all circumcision that can be surveyed – anywhere, anytime – is enlisted in the ranks of an ironed-out species of practice – reduced to medical benefits and thus ratified by rationality. And he extends this diagnosis to Montaigne's travel-telling of a dramatically different ritual from a possibly different episteme across significantly different times.

CONCLUSION: ETHNOGRAPHIES ENTRE-EPISTEMES, OR GNOSIS/DIAGNOSIS

In the Foucauldian scheme, an "Enlightenment" approach to normalized knowledge gathered force through the seventeenth century, became standard in part during the eighteenth century, perhaps culminated in the late nineteenth century, and endures today in the "analytic gaze."[69] With respect to the topic (un)circumcision, such Enlightenment views may be phrased as follows: Circumcision is seen not as something one does (or has done), or does not do, to be like oneself and different from another – relationally, diacritically, significantly; rather, circumcision of any variety is seen as something one does, or does not do, to be better, or worse, on a presumably absolute, knowable, measurable, and diagnosible scale.

Such an attitude establishes the possibility of a pro-circumcision vision of the prepuce as something that Reason (deified?) may help Nature (personified?) outgrow, relegate to a past, leave behind, slough off. But the opposite vision is simultaneously facilitated, whereby totalizing "rationalizers" could declare the prepuce universally justified, of absolute advantage intact. The imagined overall outcome in either

[68] Ibid., 157.

[69] Following Kant's question as to the nature of "Enlightenment," ought not a critical spirit turn *critique* on itself as well? I ask any theory of "Enlightenment" only that it be self-doubting rather than credulously congratulatory (see my *Other Tribes, Other Scribes*, ch. 2). In studies of ritual, one enlightenment-style assumption equates sexuality with genitality. (Some high critical theory still reduces historical and cultural "bodies" to genitality, despite critics' professed goal of resisting symptomatically "bourgeois" constriction, discontent, and repression.) Has not ethnography taught us that even so-called "genital" rites are polysensory?

diagnostic is neutralized sanitation: undialectical health "itself." The discourse associated with this future manufactures universality from the findings of incidental travel-writing or locally specific ethnographies. Ritual accidentals of dramatic, liturgical, and sectarian difference wind up synthesized in a conformist progress – whether toward proper circumcision (as in Remondino) or, tragically, toward intolerant uncircumcision in a history of prejudices too notorious to need reviewing here.

This brings us back to hermeneutics – whether in early modern discourse or in subsequent, dispersed murmurs beneath those Enlightenment analytics that supplanted interpretation. I here intend "early modern" less as an historicist construction than a figural non-"now" posed as an *alterite* to modernity or its postmodern extension. The "sixteenth century" has become a time many scholars consider partly prior to universalist codes of diagnostic othering. The 1500s (including Montaigne's 1580s), moreover, may have consolidated "travel writing" as a mode of description – when reading-the-world promised to reveal copious rarities and varieties and, through them, verities. Travel writing, and perhaps ethnography, ever since can only wish it were so, or recognize ironically that it cannot be so, or, more radically, could not have been so, even then. (That insight, possibly, was one tonality of Lévi-Strauss's *Tristes tropiques*.)

Regardless, counter-diagnostic description recalls aspects of Montaigne's . . . "episteme." Here, circumcision, for example, is something one does (or has done), or does not do, to be like oneself and different from another – relationally, sectarianly, culturally. Here (un) circumcision *means* variably, intricately, and ambivalently; none of its realizations *ameliorates* analytically, symptomatically, or uniformly. Un(circumcision), moreover, has been and remains a *topos* of exaggerated contrasts – there and here, then and now. Such rituals-cum-rhetoric effect chords of differences across a medley of senses – not just visual and verbal, but tactile, sartorial-material, aural, and olfactory, too.[70] Here is one textual example:

> Then Noah built an altar to the Lord. He took ritually clean beasts and birds of every kind, and offered whole-offerings on the altar. When the Lord smelt the soothing odor, he said within himself, 'Never again will I curse the ground because of man, however evil his inclinations may be from his youth upwards (Gen. 8: 20–21).

Even smelling enters covenants – whether signified by rainbows, foreskins, or other "sacrifices" that oscillate among and as hybrid sectar-

[70] See my *Affinities and Extremes*, ch. 3.

ian contrasts. Such semiotics call into question the predominance of any single sensory channel (for example, the visual) and set in doubt the isolability of "genitality," among other categories progressively fixed ever since the Enlightenment.[71]

For all that, a persistent characteristic seems to recur among circumscriptions of circumcision/uncircumcision, including the present one: an unsettled tonality marked by either reticence or overkill. (The latter rhetoric pervades some current sexual-politics against ritual "mutilation" – the general category universally applied and deployed.) In recent and venerable sources alike – whether pro-, con-, analytically neutral or interpretively empathetic – words about (un)circumcision tend to be hypertrophied – either oddly laconic and allusive or overwrought and effusive. Our ritual *topos* keeps calling forth the textual marks and prose registers of obsession.

Even as I mention this trait, ever so measuredly, my essay (joining many studies it cites) runs the risk of appearing obsessive, if not obsessed – likely guilty of saying too little or too much. (I have tried here to be true to this tonality – so real across different genres describing circumcision-or-not.) The peril of seeming so seems to me worthy because diacritical rites – once given in and over times and their cultures – can never be escaped or erased. Finally, to utopian critics, including some "post-modern" ones, who foresee a general solution regarding whether or not to circumcise or uncircumcise, I can only conclude with a final, celebrated reminder from Freud:

> In this case, too, the *unheimlich* is what was once *heimisch*, home-like, familiar; the prefix 'un' is the token of repression.[72]

[71] Ibid., 20.

[72] Sigmund Freud, "The 'Uncanny'," in *The Standard Edition of the Complete Psychological Works*, 20 (London, 1966; originally published 1919). Needless to add, "symptomatological" *analyses* of circumcision – whether pro or con – continue to our own era, even after Freud possibly canceled Jewish (-Egyptian) circumcision as a basic ingredient in Europe's tragic history of "othering" (see Freud, "Moses and Monotheism," in *The Standard Edition of the Complete Psychological Works*, 23 [London, 1964; originally published 1938], 3-137). Did Freud attempt the end of (or the last) patricide? For further questions, see Jay Geller, "A Paleontological View of Freud's Study of Religion: Unearthing the *Leitfossil* Circumcision," *Modern Judaism*, 13 (1993): 49–70. One significance of "Moses and Monotheism" – among copious possibilities – may be to annul the West's entire dialectic of sacrament/antisacrament. Brooding on Freud, I seeks ways to write *comparatively* of (un)circumcision that emulate his style's inscriptions of an *unheimlich*. Any scholar accentuating Freud's cancellation of circumcision could keep interpretations ecumenical by simultaneously reinstating it. He or she might, for example, cite Henry Adams, who (nearly) begins his 1918 *Education* (an autobiography in the "third person") with a paragraph that imagines himself having been Jerusalem-born and circumcised under the name "Israel Cohen" (see Adams, *The Education of Henry Adams* [Boston, 1961; originally published 1918], 3). Indeed,

AFTERWORD: FORESKINS AND ACADEMIC DISCOURSE

To illustrate the (symptomatic) tonality just signaled, I offer anecdotes of discussions overheard. Un/circumcision crops up in strange scholarly places, including a recent conference on "Iconography at the Crossroads" in central New Jersey. The papers roamed widely: rethinking Warburg and Panofsky's art history; decoding cryptic meanings of crucifixes in light of gender and class; addressing the accent on "body" that befell Christian art in Leo Steinberg's *The Sexuality of Christ in Renaissance Art and in Modern Oblivion.*[73] One paper on Florence – by a wonderful social historian of Renaissance ceremonies and ideologies – explored possible affects among devotees when confronting painted and sculpted icons. He considered naked infants versus bedraped Christs; the cross-dressing of crucifixes by female worshippers; male ambivalence vis-à-vis Christ's genitalia; the Church's anxieties that monks or laymen would suffer erections when viewing naked figures; the somatic-interpretive theme of Christ's unavoidable erection during crucifixion (like male martyrs at the moment of hanging, *à la Billy Budd*); the vogue for idealized and/or prurient crucifixion scenes of sensualized bodily suffering.

During the session's lively question period, an inordinately prominent art historian declared something like the following: Of three known icons (two crucifixions and one deposition) where – exceptionally – Christ's genitals were visible (in the deposition, through a veil gauzily), none demonstrated an erection and none, he added almost as an afterthought, was circumcised. The coffee-break intervened before anyone could query how positive he could be that the foreskin depicted was altogether intact. Ordinarily this art historian is wary of claiming definitive visual evidence even for highly conspicuous motifs. (Any ethnographer present among these iconographers might have noted folks growing all abuzz and atitter.) Was the bold comment prompted to demonstrate bravado in addressing such details? Regardless, there's that telltale, ambivalent, "hyptertrophied" tonality wherever un/circumcision looms.[74]

Adams could well have begun his *Education:* "Adams Jewish? . . . Were Adams Jewish. . . ," if only to anticipate Freud's beginning *re* Moses, as Egyptian (see "Moses and Monotheism"). Indeed, little seemed beyond historian Henry Adams's imagination–including Tahiti, even though he had "been there" (see my *Affinities and Extremes,* Prelude).

[73] See my *Affinities and Extremes,* ch. 3.

[74] This observation about uncircumcised crucifix genitals calls to mind Gilman's suggestion that Christian icons showing Christ uncut may serve to deny his Jewish

Nor was that the end of it. During the break I approached the podium to greet the social historian (a friend), only to be forestalled by a conferee upbraiding him for alluding to castration as making a victim "woman-like," for associating male homosexual receiver-roles with feminine "passivity"; and worse. She actually proclaimed his paper misogynist. Our scholar – whose feminist credentials are impeccable – replied that he had only paraphrased Renaissance Florentine views; she then decried *him* for not decrying *them* every step of the way. He kept the "conversation" going (doubtless to get his Florentines, along with himself, relatively off the hook) by adducing a case of what he called "even worse misogyny" – Islam. During Islamic circumcision rites, he assured his accuser, dominant male Muslims reduce passive males to utter subjugation. This assertion – well beyond either interlocutor's realm of expertise – received for him her first nod of approbation. *Pace*.

What has transpired during this revealing exchange? At a moment of internecine hostility among Europeanists (feminist *versus* misogynist), an "even worse" *other* is invoked, against which both sides can join forces. Islam – as usual, poorly "covered," and perhaps most so when circumcising – had leapt to mind as a transparent case of politics pure and simple: the unfettered dominance of senior males over novice boys or youths and women alike. Now, routinely my historian friend is alert to subtexts, ethnographic nuance, ambiguity, role reversals, switched signs and circuits. He stresses every imaginable veil between ceremonies interpreted and final interpretive certainty; in the case of Renaissance pageantry, he insists on subtlety even where others see misogyny. Yet having read a recent fieldwork account of circumcision in Morocco (as he later told me, although unfamiliar with the work on female "circumcision" elsewhere), he concluded that this case entailed unproblematic patriarchy (of male over male).[75] The

identity (see Sander Gilman, *Sexuality: An Illustrated History* [New York, 1989], 41). (Gilman's work explores attitudes underlying such prejudices as anti-Semitism, homophobia, etc.) However, any iconography's implications are convoluted. Other attributes in early modern representations are as "archaeologically" inaccurate as the foreskin; and Christ's circumcision could be stressed in Church-sponsored devices (see Simon Schama, *The Embarrassment of Riches* [New York, 1987), 588; and Leo Steinberg, *The Sexuality of Christ in Renaissance Art and in Modern Oblivion* [New York, 1983]). Even the *denial* of circumcision, then, is no constant "symptom;" significance varies across schemes making differences particular.

75 To illustrate more nuanced descriptions of Islamic variations on (male) circumcision, including the role of women, I cite Shurreef on "Moosulmans" in India in 1832: "It is customary with some women, (for others have no faith in it,) never to have a child circumcised *alone*, but always along with another to make an even number; . . . they get some poor woman's son to be circumcised with theirs. [Or] they substitute an

point here is that his cozy view surfaced when under attack by an assailant, to parry a tired kind of critique of his own work.

This scholar, peerless in my judgment, deals imaginatively and sympathetically with issues of both worship and repressions (for example, homoerotics/homophobia) in Christianity. Yet under pressure, he abruptly invoked "Islamic circumcision," seeming to imply that matters of ritual and power *elsewhere* might be explained in "symptomatological" analysis.

Will we never outgrow (or regress from) Enlightenment diagnostics? Is there no Montaignesque "space" left for real ambiguities of what Greg Dening calls theatricality – ungoverned by anyone's uniform gaze, whether uncircumcising *and* not?

earthen *budhna* (or pot having a spout); in the mouth of which, they insert a *pan ka beera* (or betel-parcel) . . . and, after circumcising the boy, they cut off the *pan ka beera* (or betel-parcel); which is to represent a second circumcision. . . . They guard the boy against the contact of dogs, cats, and other defilements–such as women who are *unwell;* for it is supposed, that to see them or receive their shadow is unlucky. . . ." (see Jaffur Shurreef, *Qanoon-e-Islam, or the Customs of the Moosulmans of India,* trans. G. A. Herklots [London, 1832], 43–46). This glimpse of intricate circumcision in Islamic India helps me remember that I glimpsed in Indonesia: a chromatic possibility along the scale (*gamme*) of difference separating circumcising-burying Muslim-buginese and uncircumcising-cremating Hindu-Balinese. Universal standards promoted by states tend to suppress chromaticisms of ritual practices (see my "Between-the-Wars Bali: Rereading the Relics," in George Stocking, ed., *History of Anthropology* [Madison, 1986]).

Annotated bibliography

THE following bibliography is intended only as an introduction to the vast literature on cultural encounters and cross-cultural description used by the authors. Brief annotations have been added to most items by the editor or the authors in order to guide the reader who wishes to pursue particular topics or areas. In many instances, only one or two works by an author have been cited as examples of a more extensive *opera*. Readers should also refer to the footnotes in each chapter for additional works and suggestions for further reading.

Adorno, Rolena. *Guaman Poma: Writing and Resistance in Colonial Peru.* Austin: University of Texas Press, 1986. An indio-ladino's appropriation of European written cultural traditions.

——"Images of *Indio-Ladinos* in Early Colonial Peru." In *Transatlantic Encounters: Europeans and Andeans in the Sixteenth Century.* Kenneth J. Adrien and Rolena Adorno, eds. Berkeley and Los Angeles: University of California Press, 1991. An examination of the roles of the indio-ladino in colonial society, based on Guaman Poma and other colonial Peruvian sources.

Adorno, Rolena. ed. *From Oral to Written Expression: Native Andean Chronicles of the Early Colonial Period.* Latin American Series, 4. Syracuse, New York: Maxwell School of Citizenship and Public Affairs, Sycracuse University, 1982. Includes essays on post-conquest Peruvian indigenous histories (Regina Harrison, Frank Salomon) and the Huarchirí traditions (George L. Urioste) based on analysis on Quechua/Spanish interactions.

Agnew, Jean Christophe. *Worlds Apart: The Market and the Theater in Anglo-American Thought, 1550–1750.* Cambridge: Cambridge University Press, 1986. A study of the function of the theater in the civilizing process and an implicit ethnography of the reifications of capitalist society.

Almeida Rodrigues, Graça, *et. al., Dimensões da Alteridade nas culturas de lingua portuguesa.* Actas. 1 Simpósio interdisciplinar de estudos portugueses. 2 vols. Lisbon, 1985. Extensive collection of studies from various disciplines on the problems of cultural perception and encounter in the Lusophone world.

Alva Ixtlilxochitl, Fernando de. *Obras Históricas.* Edmundo O'Gorman, ed. Serie de historiadores y cronistas de Indias 4, 2 vols. Mexico: Instituto de Investigaciones Históricas, Universidad Nacional Autónoma de México, 1975. A major edition and preliminary study of the many works of an heir of the lords of Texcoco whose writings are a major source on early Nahua society under Spanish rule.

Argensola, Leonardo de. *Discovery and Conquest of the Molucco and Phillipine Islands.* London, 1708. An important early primary source.

Asad, Talal. *Anthropology and the Colonial Encounter.* New York, 1973. General and case studies on the relationship between anthropological observation and the maintenance or fostering of colonialism.

Ashtor, E. *The Levant Trade in the Later Middle Ages.* Princeton, 1983. A comprehensive history of the commercial trade between Europe and the Near East.

Axtell, James. *After Columbus. Essays in the Ethnohistory of Colonial North America.* New York: Oxford University Press, 1988. Contains essays dealing with conversion, trade, and other forms of European-American Indian contact. Notable is the essay, "Through a Glass Darkly: Early Indian Views of Europeans."

Aznar Vallejo, E. *La integración de las Islas Canarias en la Corona de Castilla (1478–1526). Aspectos administrativos, sociales y económicos.* San Cristóbal de La Laguna: Universidad, 1983. A broad gauge study of the conquest of the Canary islands based on primary sources and a wide reading of secondary literature.

Barish, John. *The Anti-theatrical Prejudice.* Berkeley: University of California Press, 1981. A sobering description of how dangerously any theatricality has been seen to be by those, who by reason of politics, religion or philosophy, believe that reality is totally given to them, rather than made by them.

Bayley, Susan. *Saints, Goddesses, and Kings: Muslims and Christians in South Indian Society, 1700–1900.* Cambridge: Cambridge University Press, 1989. An excellent survey of integration of Muslims and Christians in Hindu society in South India.

Bennett, J.W. *The Rediscovery of Sir John Mandeville.* New York, 1954.

Boon, James A. *Other Tribes, Other Scribes: Symbolic Anthropology in the Comparative Study of Cultures, Histories, Religions, and Texts.* New York: Cambridge University Press, 1982.

——*Affinities and Extremes: Crisscrossing the Bittersweet History of East Indies History, Hindu-Balinese Culture and Indo-European Allure.* Chicago: University of Chicago Press, 1990. Boon discusses "how the cultural backgrounds and personal experiences of Western scholars have affected their descriptions, comparisons and interpretations of other culture, particularly cultures of Indonesia." R. Provencher, *Choice* 28, p.816.

Bosman, W. *A New and Accurate Description of the Coast of Guinea.* London: Cass, 1967. The most influential of many Portuguese and Dutch accounts of West Africa that contributed to the theory of primitive religion as "fetish."

Bouchon, Geneviève. "Les Musulmans du Kerala a l'epoque de la decouverte Portugaise." *Mare Luso-Indicum* II (1972): 3–59. A good survey of the Muslim community in Kerala and its early relations with the Portuguese.

——*Regent of the Sea: Cannannore's Response to Portuguese Expansion, 1507–1528.* New York: Oxford University Press, 1988. A detailed account of the early contacts between the Portuguese and a kingdom on the Malabar coast of India.

Boxer, Charles R. *The Dutch Seaborne Empire, 1600–1800.* London: Hutchinson, 1965. The best single-volume history of Dutch maritime activity and the social relations between the Dutch and other peoples.

Boyle, J. A. "The Il-Khans Persia and the Princes of Europe." *Central Asiatic Journal* 20 (1976) 25–40. Examines the correspondence from the Il-Khans to the rulers of the Christian West during the thirteenth and fourteenth centuries.

Brown, Peter. *The Body and Society: Men, Women, and Sexual Renunciation in Early Christianity.* New York: Columbia University Press, 1988. A study of the way in which early Christianity developed its doctrine on the issues of sexuality and gender.

Bucher, Bernadette. *Icon and Conquest. A Structural Analysis of the Illustrations of deBry's "Great Voyages."* Trans. of *Le sauvage aux seins pendants* (1977). Chicago: University of Chicago Press, 1981. Discusses the implicit ethnography contained in the iconography of the Indians in European representations and the way in which European religion and cosmography determined the ways in which Indians were portrayed.

Campbell, Mary. *The Witness and the Other World: Exotic European Travel Writing, 400–1600*. Ithaca: Cornell University Press, 1988. A history of European travel literature exploring the evolution of the genre as it dealt with medieval contact with non-Europeans.

Castanheda, Fernão Lopes de. *História do descobrimento e conquista da India pelos Portugueses*. Porto: Lello, 1979. One of the key sources on the creation of Portugal's empire in the Indian Ocean.

Chauduri, K.N. *Trade and Civilization in the Indian Ocean*. Cambridge: Cambridge University Press, 1985. "A discursive study of the cultural and economic roles of long-distance trade . . . between the eastern Mediterranean and the China Sea from the rise of Islam in the mid-seventh century to the beginning of European imperialism in the 1750's." *AHR* review by Brian Harrison 91:1, p.449.

Cherfas, Jeremy, and Lewin, Roger. *Not Work Alone: A Cross-Cultural view of activities superfluous to survival*. Beverly Hills: Sage, 1980. A collection of cross-cultural articles that discuss the role and development of play, dress, gambling and profanity.

Chevigny, Hector. *Russian America: The Great Alaskan Venture, 1741–1867*. (New York: Viking, 1965) 1979. A synthesis of Russia's attempt at the settlement of the North American frontier.

Clifford, James and George E. Marcus. *Writing Culture. The Poetics and Politics of Ethnography*. Berkeley: University of California Press, 1986. Collection of essays on the nature of ethnographic writing and the epistemological, political, and ethical problems involved in observing and writing about other cultures.

Cline, S.L. and León-Portilla, Miguel eds. *The Testaments of Culhuacan*, UCLA Latin American Center Nahuatl Studies Series, 1. Los Angeles: UCLA Latin American Center Publications, 1984. An extremely useful collection of Nahuatl wills from the later sixteenth century translated into English.

Collier, George A., Rosaldo, Renato I., and Wirth, John D. (eds.) *The Inca and Aztec States (1400–1800): Anthropology and History*. New York: Academic Press, 1982. Essays on indigenous culture and consciousness include spiritual accommodation of New Spain (J. Jorge Klor de Alva), Nahua views of self and history (James Lockhart), and Nahuatl literacy (Frances Karttunen).

Conner, D. and Miller, L. *Master Mariner: Captan James Cook and the Peoples of the Pacific.* Seattle: Universaty of Washington Press, 1978. This narrative account of Cook's third voyage focuses on his encounters with native peoples. Extensively illustrated with the sketches of Cook's official artist, John Webber.

Cook, James. *The Journal of Captain James Cook on His Voyage of Discovery.* Edited by J.C. Beaglehole. London: Hakluyt Society, 1955–56. The fundamental source of Cook's explorations.

Cooper, Michael. ed. *They Came to Japan: An Anthology of European Reports on Japan, 1543–1640.* California: University of California Press, 1965. An anthology of descriptions of Japan by early modern traders, travelers, and missionaries.

Dalgado, Sebestião Rodolpho. *Influencia do vocabulario português em linguas asiaticas (abrangendo cerca de cinquenta idiomas).* Coimbra: Imprensa da Universidade, 1913. Still the best single source on the influence of Portuguese on Asian languages.

D'Elia, Pasquale. ed. *Fonti Ricciane: Documenti originali concernenti Matteo Ricci e la storia delle prime relazioni tra l'Europa e la Cina, 1579–1615.* Roma: La Libreria dello Stato, 1942. Collection of the documents concerning Matteo Ricci and the relations between Europe and China.

Dening, Greg. *Islands and Beaches: Discourse on a Silent Land: Marquesas, 1774–1880.* Honolulu: University Press of Hawaii, 1980. An investigation of the interaction between Marquesans and outsiders that combines analyses of anthropological method and the history of the Islanders.

Dudley, Edward, and Novak, Maximilian E. eds. *The Wild Man Within: An Image in Western Thought from the Renaissance to Romanticism.* Pittsburgh: University of Pittsburgh Press, 1972. An early and influential work of "cultural studies" that has stood the test of time.

Dunn, Ross E. *The Adventures of Ibn Battuta.* Berkeley: University of California Press, 1986. Dunn discusses Ibn Battuta's travels and how being a Muslim allowed him to travel through the diverse Muslim cultures.

Eco, Umberto. *Art and Beauty in the Middle Ages.* Trans. H. Bredin. New Haven: Yale University Press, 1986. Principles of aesthetics in medieval Europe and their historical development from the sixth to the fifteenth centuries.

Eilberg-Schwartz, Howard. *The Savage in Judaism: An Anthropology of Israelite Religion and Ancient Judaism.* Bloomington: Indiana University Press, 1990. An anthropological examination of the role of the body and bodily functions in ancient Jewish thought.

Elison, George. *Deus Destroyed: The Image of Christianity in Early-Modern Japan.* Cambridge, MA: Harvard, 1973. An assessment of the failed Christianization of Tokugawa Japan from the Japanese perspective.

Elliott, J.H. *Spain and its World, 1500–1700: Selected Essays.* New Haven and London: Yale, 1989. A collection of essays discussing Spain's rise to world dominance, particularly good on the political and cultural aspects of Spain and its empire.

Evans, R.J.W. *Rudolf II and his World.* Oxford: The Clarendon Press, 1973. The life and times of Rudolf II, Holy Roman Emperor and King of Bohemia and Hungary, including Rudolf's activities as a collector of artistic treasures and the cosmologial concepts that lay behind such acquisition.

Fagan, B.F. *The Clash of Cultures.* New York: W. H. Freeman, 1984. A brief overview of a number of cultural encounters that emphasizes parallels and negative impacts.

Fernández-Armesto, F. *Before Columbus: Exploration and Colonisation from the Mediterranean to the Atlantic, 1229–1492.* London: Macmillan, 1987. Examines early Iberian expansion into the Mediterranean and the Atlantic, focusing on the role of trade and the Catalan expansion as the precursor to later voyages.

Foucault, Michel. *The Order of Things.* New York: Vintage Press, 1970. This book, which brought Foucault to prominence, examines the origins of modern scientific thought by using biology, economics, and linguistics to reveal the underlying structures of thought and expression.

Garibay, Angel María. *Historia de la literatura nahuatl, Primera parte (Etapa autónoma: de c. 1430 a 1521, Segunda parte: El trauma de la conquista (1521–1750).* 2nd edition. 2 vols. Mexico: Porrúa, 1971. The still indispensable survey of Nahuatl and Spanish language texts of the early colonial period; classification based on European genres and Nahua traditions.

Geertz, Clifford. *The Interpretation of Cultures.* New York: Basic Books, 1972. Two classic essays on "Thick Description" and the "Balinese Cockfight" have been seminal in the development of ethnographic history.

Gernet, Jacques. *China and the Christian Impact.* Cambridge: Cambridge University Press, 1985. Translated from *Chine et christianisme* (1982). A major attempt to see the Christian missionary effort of the seventeenth century from Chinese viewpoints and to examine basic differences between Chinese and Western *mentalités.*

Gibson, Charles. *Tlaxcala in the Sixteenth Century.* New Haven: Yale University Press, 1952. An early ethnohistorical study of the major pre-Columbian rival of Aztec Tenochtitlan. Gibson was a precursor in showing the continuance of many aspects of Nahua society after the conquest.

——*The Aztecs under Spanish Rule: A History of the Indians of the Valley of Mexico, 1519–1810.* Stanford: Stanford University Press, 1964. Based almost entirely on Spanish language sources, it explores the changes in Aztec culture from the conquest until independence. A classic of Mesoamerican ethnohistory.

Goodale, Jane C. *Tiwi Wives: A Study of the Women of Melville Island, North Australia.* Seattle: University of Washington Press, 1971. An anthropological study of women in traditional Aboriginal culture.

Greenblatt, Stephen. *New World Encounters.* Berkeley: University of California Press, 1993. Historians and literary critics concentrate on the nature of early European-Native American contacts and their presentation in this volume of essays, most of which appeared in *Representations* in 1989 and 1991.

——*Marvelous Possessions: The Wonder of the New World.* Chicago: University of Chicago Press, 1991. This book seeks to show how Europeans represented others, especially the peoples of the New World, and also took possession of their lands. Greenblatt sees in the European combination of wonder at the marvelous and "possesive madness" keys to an understanding of the colonial project.

Halliwell, Stephen. *Aristotle's Poetics.* Chapel Hill: University of North Carolina Press, 1986. Aristotle's mysterious and depleted text is shown in brilliant light, enough to be taken as a key element in any philosophy of representation.

Hammond, D. and Jablow, A. *The Myth of Africa.* New York: The Library of Social Science, 1977. British views of African culture, as found in travelogues, fiction, and official reports.

Hay, Denys. *Europe: The Emergence of an Idea.* Edinburgh: University Press, 1957. Shows how much can be drawn out of a history of a single word.

Heikamp, Detlef. *Mexico and the Medici.* Florence: Editrice Edam, 1972. A study of pre-Columbian Mexican objects in Florentine Renaissance collections and of the context in which they were accumulated as documents of erotic art.

Helms, Mary W. *Ulysses' Sail: An Ethnographic Odyssey of Power, Knowledge, and Geographical Distance.* Princeton: Princeton University Press, 1988. Long-distance contacts among elites of traditional, non-industrial societies examined in political and ideological contexts.

Hercus, Luise, and Sutton, Peter. eds. *This Is What Happened: Historical Narratives by Aborigines* Canberra: Australian Institute of Aboriginal Studies, 1986. Collection of Aboriginal oral traditions and stories relating to early contact with non-Aboriginals.

Hilton, A. *The Kingdom of Kongo.* New York: Oxford University Press, 1985. A revisionist history of Kongo-Portuguese relations and the impact of Christianity. Particularly interesting because of its use of Kongo cosmology as a means of understanding contact.

Hodgen, Margaret T. *Early Anthropology in the Sixteenth and Seventeenth Century.* Philadelphia: University of Pennsylvania Press, 1964. An intellectual history of Europe's changing ideas about other peoples and cultures which demonstrates the Classical and Renaissance influences on the development of Early Modern thought.

Hulme, Peter. *Colonial Encounters: Europe and the Native Caribbean, 1492–1797.* London and New York: Routledge, 1986. A multidisciplinary textual analysis of five narratives of the colonial contact in the Caribbean and of the discourse of colonization.

Hulme, Peter and Ludmilla Jordanova, eds. *The Enlightenment and its Shadows.* London: Routledge, 1990. Collection of essays on the intellectual impact and significance of the Enlightenment as a self-conscious movement, and including some post-structuralist attacks on its basic premises.

Isaac, Rhys. *The Transformation of Virginia, 1740–1790.* Chapel Hill: University of North Carolina Press, 1982. A transformation of a traditional historical field into a creative presentation of Virginian landscape and the social dramas that emplotted it, with reflections on what ethnographic history might be and how it might be done.

Jackson, Kenneth David. *Sing without Shame: Oral Traditions in Indo-Portuguese Creole Verse with Transcription and Analysis of a Nineteenth-Century Manuscript of Ceylon Portuguese.* Philadelphia: John Benjamins, 1990. Provides a good background on the kind of work being done today on oral traditions and song.

Jones, E.L. *The European Miracle: Environments, Economies and Geopolitics in the History of Europe and Asia.* 2nd ed. Cambridge: Cambridge University Press, 1987. A comparative account of Asian and European development that focuses on the conjuncture of political structures, economies, and environmental factors as the impetus for economic development.

Karttunen, Frances and Lockhart, James. *Nahuatl in the Middle Years: Language Contact Phenomena in Texts of the Colonial Period.* University of California Publications in Linguistics, 85. Berkeley and Los Angeles: University of California Press, 1976. An analysis of the cultural and linguistic changes in Nahuatl during the colonial period.

Kiernan, V.G. *The Lords of Human Kind: Black Man, Yellow Man, and White Man in an Age of Empire.* London: Weidenfield and Nicolson, 1969. A perceptive summary of the development of European ideas and perceptions of the people of the world during the nineteenth century Age of Imperialism.

Kimble. G.H.T. *Geography in the Middle Ages.* London, 1937, reprint New York, 1968. An excellent summary of the evolution of geographical ideas in both the Christian and the Muslim worlds during the Middle Ages.

Lach, Donald F. *Asia in the Making of Europe.* 3 vols., volume I, *The Century of Discovery.* Chicago: University of Chicago Press, 1965. An excellent compilation of European knowledge about Asia drawing mostly on published sources. It concentrates on the impact of that knowledge in the formation of Western culture.

Ladero Quesada, Miguel Angel. *Granada después de la conquista. Repobladores y mudéjares.* Diputación Provincial de Granada, 1988. A fundamental series of studies based on primary research that discusses the process by which Granada was colonized after its conquest. Includes articles on Jews and Mudejars and transcriptions of over 200 pages of documents.

Lewis, A.R. *Nomads and Crusaders, 1000–1368.* Bloomington, Indiana University Press, 1988. A comparative analysis of five European and Middle Eastern civilizations that seeks to explain the eventual domination of Western Europe.

Lockhart, James. *The Nahuas after the Conquest.* Stanford: Stanford University Press, 1991. A major study on Nahua society based on Nahuatl sources and including Nahua uses of written culture.

Lundbaek, Knud. "The First Translation from a Confucian Classic in Europe." *China Mission Studies Bulletin* 1 (1979), 1–11.

MacCormack, Sabine. *Religion in the Andes: Vision and Imagination in Early Colonial Peru.* Princeton: Princeton University Press, 1991. An examination of Andean religion and its confrontation with Christianity in which emphasis is placed on the missionaries' changing perception of Indian belief from an erroneous faith to evidence of cultural and rational deficiency.

MacGaffey, W. *Religion and Society in Central Africa.* Chicago: Chicago University Press, 1986. Social, economic, and cosmological dimension of Kongo religion, with comparative discussions.

Marrero Rodriguez, M. *La esclavitud en Tenerife a raíz de la conquista.* San Cristóbal de La Laguna: Instituto de Estudios Canarios, 1986.

Mason, Peter. *Deconstructing America. Representations of the Other.* London: Routledge, 1990. Drawing inspiration from Diderot and Derrida, this deconstructionist series of essays on alterity focuses on the "monstruous races," as a measure of European conceptions of "otherness." It draws on both anthropological and semiological approaches.

Mercado, Tomás de. *La economia en la andalucia del descubrimiento.* Biblioteca de la Cultura andaluza, 1985. A new edition of selections from *Summa de tratos y contratos* (1569), a classic description of trade in the Spanish empire.

Morales Padron, F. *Canarias: Crónicas de su conquista.* Las Palmas de Gran Canaria: Ayuntamiento, 1978.

Morgan, David. *Medieval Persia, 1040–1797.* London: Longman, 1988. A concise narrative of the political history of Persia.

——*Medieval Historical Writings in the Christian and Islamic Worlds.* London, 1982.

Moscoso, Francisco. *Tribu y clases en el Caribe antiguo.* San Pedro de Macoris, Universidad Central de Este, 1986. A Marxist reading of the pre-Columbian economy of the Caribbean.

Muldoon, James. *Popes, Lawyers and Infidels: The Church and the Non-Christian World, 1250–1550.* Liverpool, 1979. Helps demonstrate the importance of the medieval expansion of Europe to understanding 1492.

Mulvaney, D.J. *Encounters in Place: Outsiders and Aboriginal Australians, 1606–1985.* St. Lucia: University of Queensland Press, 1989. "Traces modern contacts between Aboriginal groups and explorers, travellers, traders, and settlers and relates how these episodes affected aboriginal culture." From the Foreword to the book by Pat Galvin, Australian Heritage Commission.

——, White, J. Peter. *Australians to 1788:* Broadway: Syme and Weldon Associates, 1987.

Pagden A. *The Fall of Natural Man: The American Indian and the Origins of Comparative Ethnology.* Cambridge: Cambridge University Press, 1982. An attempt to review the development of the study of other cultures in Europe as a result of the contact with the Americas, with attention to both intellectual and moral issues.

——*European Encounters with The New World: From Renaissance to Romanticism.* New Haven: Yale University Press, 1993. Interconnected essays on the development of European thought on other cultures with an emphasis on the eighteenth century. Includes discussion of the complexity of seeing ourselves in the observation of "others."

Pastor Bodmer, Beatriz. *The Armature of Conquest: Spanish Accounts of the Discovery of America, 1492–1589.* Stanford: Stanford University Press, 1992. A literary analysis of the narrative forms and content of the conquest that gives particular attention to the discourse of mythification and the use of those myths for political and ideological purposes.

Pearson, Michael. *Merchants and Rulers in Gujarat: The response to the Portuguese in the Sixteenth Century.* Berkeley: University of California Press, 1976. A good source on the attitudes of Asian kings on trade and merchants.

——*The Portuguese in India.* Cambridge: Cambridge University Press, 1987. The best single-volume account of the subject. Shows how little attention the Portuguese attracted in Indian life and records.

Peterson, W.J. "Western Natural Philosophy Published in Late Ming China." *Proceedings of the American Philosophical Society.* 117.4 (1973).

Phillips, J.R.S. *The Medieval Expansion of Europe.* Oxford and New York: Oxford University Press, 1988. A precise summary of medieval contacts between Europe and the rest of the world that analyzes the medieval European mentality of cultural contact and the relationship between the medieval expansion and that of the fifteenth century.

Phillips, William. *Historia de la esclavitud en España.* Madrid: Playor, 1990. Overview of slavery in Spain and the Spanish world.

Pietz, W. "The Problem of the Fetish, I." *Res* 9 (1983):5–17.

——"The Problem of the Fetish, II: The Origin of the Fetish." *Res* 13 (1987):23–45.

——"The Problem of the Fetish, IIIa: Bosman's Guinea and the enlightenment theory of fetishism." *Res* 16(1988):105–123. A comprehensive history of the idea of "fetishism" beginning with the early Church Fathers and showing how the picture of African religion developed by the Portuguese and Dutch as a result of their commercial experience on the West African coast contributed to the formation of one of the salient concepts of nineteenth-century European social scientific thought.

Price, Sally. *Primitive Art in Civilized Places.* Chicago: University of Chicago Press, 1989. Examination of concepts and attitudes of the contemporary Western world (particularly France and the United States) toward non-Western art and artists.

Quaisar, Ahsan Jan. *The Indian Response to European Technology and Culture, A.D. 1498–1707.* Delhi: Oxford University Press, 1982. An excellent introductory survey.

Rafael, Vicente. *Contracting Colonialism. Translation and Christian Conversion in Tagalog Society Under Early Spanish Rule.* Ithaca: Cornell University Press, 1988. A linguistic and cultural analysis of the Tagalog response to the Spanish colonization and conversion of the Phillippines.

Reid, Anthony. *Asia in the Age of Commerce I: The Lands Below the Winds.* New Haven: Yale, 1988. A Braudelian study of the social customs and organization of the people of Southeast Asia in the early modern era. A second volume is to follow.

——. ed., *Southeast Asia in the Early Modern Era. Trade, Power, and Belief.* Ithaca: Cornell University Press, 1993. Various specialists examine a range of topics from commerce, urbanization, state formation, and religion in the period of increasing contact with Europe.

Richard, J. "The Mongols and the Franks." *Journal of Asian History* 3 (1969): 45–57. A brief narrative of the thirteenth-century contacts between the Mongols and the Christian West.

Ronan, Charles E. and Oh, Bonnie B.C. eds. *East meets West: The Jesuits in China, 1582–1773.* Chicago: Loyola University Press, 1988. Collection of essays on various aspects of the Jesuit contact in the context of the Catholic Reformation.

Sahagún, Bernadino de. *Florentine Codex: General History of the Things of New Spain.* Trans. by Arthur J. O. Anderson and Charles E. Dibble. Salt Lake City and Santa Fe: University of Utah Press and School of American Research, Santa Fe, 1950–82. The essential source on Nahua culture before the conquest, composed by a Franciscan friar in the years immediately after the fall of Tenochtitlan.

Sahlins, Marshall. *Historical Metaphors and Mythical Realities.* Ann Arbor: University of Michigan Press, 1981. Sahlins has an anthropological genius for depicting structures as they are actually expressed and a historian's energy to discover the texts by which structures are imbedded.

——. *Islands of History.* Honolulu: University of Hawaii Press, 1980. A collection of essays centered on the Pacific, some of which discuss the relationship between structural analyses and history. An important example of the use of ethnohistorical approaches in understanding cultural contacts.

Said, Edward. *Orientalism.* London, New York: Random House, 1978. A controversial analysis of the history of the discourse of Orientalism and its effect on Western relations with the East.

Salomon, Frank, and Urioste, George. *The Huarochirí Manuscript: A Testament of Ancient and Colonial Andean Religion.* Austin: University of Texas Press, 1991. A major analysis and English translation of the Huarchirí manuscript and of the native responses to Christian indoctrination.

Sansom, George *The Western World and Japan: A Study in the Interaction of European and Asiatic Cultures.* New York: Knopf, 1950. "A thoughtful treatment of the nature and extent of European cultural influences in Japan before 1894." Review *AHR* 55 (1950): p.906.

Sauer, Carl Ortwin. *The Early Spanish Main.* Berkeley: Unversity of California Press, 1966. A study of the conquest and colonization of the Caribbean. A wonderful reminder of a lifetime's study demonstrating how history cannot be written without sensitivity towards questions of the environment.

Slessarev, V. *Prester John, the Letter and the Legend.* Minneapolis: University of Minnesota Press, 1959. A fine historical introduction to the legend of Prester John, a concept that proved to be highly influential in European expansion into Asia and the Americas.

Smith, Bernard. *European Vision in the Pacific, 1769–1850.* Oxford: Clarendon Press, 1960. A classic study of the interrelation of cultural forms and ethnographic expression in the Pacific.

Spence, Jonathan. *The Memory Palace of Matteo Ricci.* New York: Vintage, 1983. Explores the cultural connections between Europe and China using the famous missionary as a cultural intermediary.

Spicer, Edward H. *Cycles of Conquest: The Impact of Spain, Mexico, and the United States on the Indians of the Southwest, 1533–1960.* Tucson: University of Arizona Press, 1962. An extensive look at the Spanish contact with Amerindians and the variety of responses that the contact elicited.

Stafford, Barbara Maria. *Voyage into Substance: Art, Sciences and the Illustrated Travel Account, 1760–1840.* Cambridge, MA.: The MIT Press, 1984. A "total history" of Europe's encounter with environmental otherness in the late eighteenth century, marvellously illustrated.

Stallybrass, Peter and Allon White. *The Politics and Poetics of Transgression.* Ithaca: Cornell University Press, 1986. An implicit ethnography of the grotesque and the civilizing process.

Stocking, George, Jr., ed. *Objects and Others.* Madison: University of Wisconsin Press, 1985. A series of essays on the collecting of exotic foreign objects and exploring the development of ethnographic museums and museology from the late ninteenth century to the present day.

Sued Badillo, Jalil. *Los Caribes: realidad o fábula?* Río Piedras: Antillana, 1978. A critique of the dominant anthropological picture as enshrined in the *Handbook of South American Indians.*

Taylor, Francis Henry. *The Taste of Angels.* Boston: Little, Brown and Co., 1948. A history of art patronage and art collecting in European society from the Classical era to the Napoleonic Wars.

Turner, Victor. *The Anthropology of Performance.* New York: Performing Arts Journal Publications, 1988. Seminal reflections of a master ethnographer, posthumously published, on the theatricality of culture.

Vaughan, Thomas. *Soft Gold: The Fur Trade and Cultural Exchange on the Northwest Coast of America.* Portland: Oregon Historical Society, 1982.

Wachtel, Nathan. *The Vision of the Vanquished: The Spanish Conquest of Peru through Indian Eyes, 1530–70.* Trans. by Ben and Siân Reynolds, New York: Harper and Row, 1977. A pioneering study on Peruvian and Mexican peoples' interpretation of and resistance to foreign conquest in the early Spanish colonial period.

Weiss, Roberto. *The Renaissance Discovery of Classical Antiquity.* 2nd edition. New York: Basil Blackwell, 1988. The development of Renaissance interest in the antiquities of the Classical world including the building of collections of ancient objects and areas of study – epigraphy, numismatics – that developed therefrom.

White, Hayden. *Tropics of Discourse.* Baltimore: Johns Hopkins University Press, 1978. Essays on the intersection of literary criticism and history that argue for the creative nature of history and why it should therefore be approached as a literary form.

White, Richard. *The Middle Ground: Indians, Empires, and Republics in the Great Lakes Region, 1650–1815.* Cambridge: Cambridge University Press, 1992. Excellent monograph that deals with the long-term adjustment of Indian peoples of the Great Lakes to the presence of the French and English, with emphasis on the variety of Indian strategies.

Index

Printed in the United States
118659LV00002B/124-162/A

9 780521 458801